FLORA'S
PLANT NAMES

∾

FLORA'S

PLANT NAMES

❦

TIMBER PRESS
Portland, Oregon

This edition published in 2003 by Timber Press, Inc.
133 S.W. Second Avenue, Suite 450
Portland, Oregon 97204, USA

ISBN 0-88192-605-1

Produced by Global Book Publishing Pty Ltd
Unit 1/181 High Street, Willoughby, NSW 2068, Australia
Ph +61 2 9967 3100 Fax +61 2 9967 5891
Email rightsmanager@globalpub.com.au

Suggestions: The editors would be pleased to hear from plant nurseries,
general gardeners, and specialty groups about any plants they feel
should be added to future editions of *Flora's Plant Names*. Email
editor@globalpub.com.au

Printed in Canada by
Transcontinental Printing

Publisher	Gordon Cheers
Associate publisher	Margaret Olds
Art director	Stan Lamond
Consultant	Tony Rodd
Editors	Loretta Barnard
	Dannielle Doggett
	Fiona Doig
	Kate Etherington
Typesetting and assembly	Dee Rogers

Contents

Why Have a Dictionary of Common Names?

Common names for plants are often very evocative—describing their appearance, native habitat, and medicinal uses, or including the name of the person who discovered the plant—but they are not reliable ways to identify plants for many reasons. The common name for a specific plant may vary from country to country, or from region to region within a country, and may also be different from language to language. Therefore, some plants have more than one common name, and one common name may refer to a number of different plants. For example, in the British Isles, the plant called the bluebell in Scotland is not the same as the bluebell of England. The only unambiguous and reliable name for any plant is its Latin-based name.

Binomial nomenclature

Devised over 250 years ago, the system of binomial nomenclature (two-word names) for plants was first used consistently by the famous Swedish biologist Carolus Linnaeus. Each plant features a Latin-based genus and species name, with some species further divided into subspecies (subsp.), varieties (var.), forms (f.), and cultivars (with names presented in single inverted commas).

Botanical names of plants are usually printed in italics; sometimes they are simply presented in a typeface different from that of the rest of the text. If there is no chance of confusion, the name of the genus is abbreviated to the initial letter the second and subsequent times the name is used in a specific entry. The name of the genus will always begin with a capital letter, and the species name is always in lower case, even when it is derived from the name of a place or person.

The naming of plants is governed by *The International Code of Botanical Nomenclature,* the aim of which is to provide a stable method of naming plants that rejects the use of names which may cause error and ambiguity. Under the code, each plant has only one correct botanical name— when a plant is found to have more than one botanical name (as it had been identified by numerous people working independently), the earliest name published in print is taken as the accepted name.

How to use this book

This dictionary of common names lists in alphabetical order over 20,000 common names used in different places around the world, followed by the genera and species that are known by that name. For example, by looking up bluebell, gardeners will discover that *Campanula rotundifolia* and *Hyacinthoides non-scripta* are both known by that common name. Gardeners can then make a more informed choice when they visit their local nursery or garden center.

A

aalwyn, krans *Aloe mitriformis*
Aaron's beard *Hypericum calycinum*
Aaron's rod *Verbascum thapsus*
a'balai, latanier *Coccothrinax barbadensis*
abata cola *Cola acuminata*
abele *Populus alba*
abelia, glossy *Abelia × grandiflora*
abelia, golden *Abelia × grandiflora* 'Frances Mason'
abelia, Schumann's *Abelia schumannii*
abelia-leaf *Abeliophyllum distichum*
abiu *Pouteria cainito*
abscess root *Polemonium reptans*
absinthe *Artemisia absinthium*
abutilon, garden *Abutilon × hybridum*
abutilon, Indian *Abutilon indicum*
abutilon, trailing *Abutilon megapotamicum*
Abyssinian banana *Ensete ventricosum*
Abyssinian primrose *Primula verticillata*
Abyssinian sword lily *Gladiolus callianthus*
acacia, Berlandier's *Acacia berlandieri*
acacia, bullhorn *Acacia cornigera*
acacia, candle *Acacia hebeclada*
acacia, false *Robinia pseudoacacia*
acacia, mop-headed *Robinia pseudoacacia* 'Umbraculifera'
acacia, plains *Acacia berlandieri*
acacia, rose *Robinia hispida*
acacia, silky *Acacia rehmanniana*
acacia, steel *Acacia macracantha*
acacia, three-horned *Acacia senegal*
açaí *Euterpe oleracea*
acajou *Anacardium occidentale*
acanthus *Acanthus mollis*

acanthus, mangrove *Acanthus ilicifolius*
acanthus, spiny *Acanthus spinosus*
acerola *Malpighia glabra*
achiote *Bixa orellana*
achira *Canna edulis*
acidanthera *Gladiolus callianthus*
aciphyll, mountain *Aciphylla simplicifolia*
aciphyll, snow *Aciphylla glacialis*
aconite *Aconitum*
aconite, winter *Eranthis*
acorn banksia *Banksia hookeriana, B. prionotes*
acroclinium *Rhodanthe chlorocephala* subsp. *rosea, R. c.* subsp. *splendida*
acronychia, beach *Acronychia imperforata*
actinidia, bower *Actinidia arguta*
acuma *Syagrus flexuosa*
Adaminaby snow gum *Eucalyptus lacrimans*
Adam's needle *Yucca filamentosa*
Adam's needle-and-thread *Yucca filamentosa*
adathoda *Justicia adhatoda*
adder's fern *Polypodium vulgare*
adder's tongue *Erythronium americanum, Ophioglossum lusitanicum*
adder's tongue, yellow *Erythronium americanum*
adhatoda *Justicia adhatoda*
Adriatic bellflower *Campanula elatines*
aeonium, Canary Island *Aeonium canariense*
aerial yam *Dioscorea bulbifera*
aeroplane propeller *see* airplane propeller
Afghan cherry *Prunus jacquemontii*
Afghan lilac *Syringa protolaciniata*
Afghan yellow rose *Rosa primula*
African blue sage *Salvia aurita*

African box thorn *Lycium ferocissimum*
African boxwood *Myrsine africana*
African cherry *Prunus africana*
African corn flag *Chasmanthe floribunda*
African corn lily *Ixia*
African daisy *Arctotis stoechadifolia, Dimorphotheca, Osteospermum*
African daisy, blue-eyed *Arctotis venusta*
African fern pine *Afrocarpus gracilior*
African fountain grass *Pennisetum setaceum*
African harebell *Dierama*
African hemp *Sparmannia africana*
African holly *Solanum giganteum*
African iris *Dietes*
African juniper *Juniperus procera*
African lily *Agapanthus, A. africanus*
African linden *Sparmannia africana*
African locust *Parkia filicoidea*
African lovegrass *Eragrostis curvula*
African mangosteen *Garcinia livingstonei*
African marigold *Tagetes erecta*
African milk barrel *Euphorbia horrida*
African milk tree *Euphorbia trigona*
African milkbush *Synadenium grantii*
African oil palm *Elaeis guineensis*
African olive *Olea europaea* subsp. *africana*
African scurf-pea *Psoralea pinnata*
African squill *Ledebouria*
African sumac *Rhus lancea*
African thatching rush *Elegia*
African tree wisteria *Bolusanthus speciosus*
African tulip tree *Spathodea campanulata*
African violet *Saintpaulia, S. ionantha*
African walnut *Schotia brachypetala*
African wild date *Phoenix reclinata*
Afrikaner, marsh *Gladiolus tristis*

Afrikaner, summer marsh *Gladiolus tristis* var. *aestivalis*
agapanthus *Agapanthus, A. praecox* subsp. *orientalis*
agapanthus, Drakensberg *Agapanthus inapertus*
agapanthus, drooping *Agapanthus inapertus*
agapanthus, miniature *Agapanthus praecox* 'Baby Blue'
agapanthus, pink *Tulbaghia simmleri*
agaric, fly *Amanita muscaria*
agave *Agave*
agave cactus *Leuchtenbergia principis*
agave, octopus *Agave vilmoriniana*
ageratum *Ageratum houstonianum*
agrimony *Agrimonia, A. eupatoria*
agrimony, hemp *Agrimonia eupatoria*
aguaje *Mauritia flexuosa*
aibika *Abelmoschus manihot*
air plant *Bryophyllum pinnatum, Tillandsia*
air potato *Dioscorea bulbifera*
airplane propeller *Crassula perfoliata* var. *falcata*
airplant, powdery strap *Catopsis berteroniana*
ajam, mata *Clerodendrum buchananii, C. speciosissimum*
ajamente *Asclepias subulata*
ajowan *Trachyspermum ammi*
akakura *Metrosideros carmineus*
akapuka *Griselinia lucida*
akeake *Olearia avicenniifolia*
akeake, Chatham Island *Olearia traversii*
akepuka *Griselinia lucida*
akiraho *Olearia paniculata*
Alabama azalea *Rhododendron alabamense*
Alabama fothergilla *Fothergilla major*
Alabama snow-wreath *Neviusia alabamensis*

alabaster plant *Dudleya virens*
alamillo *Populus fremontii*
Alamo beardtongue *Penstemon
alamosensis*
Alaska blue willow *Salix purpurea*
Alaska cedar *Chamaecyparis
nootkatensis*
Alaska spruce *Picea sitchensis*
Alaskan holly fern *Polystichum* ×
setigerum, P. andersoni
Alaskan maidenhair *Adiantum
pedatum* var. *aleuticum*
Alaskan paper birch *Betula kenaica*
alaterne *Rhamnus alaternus*
alaternus *Rhamnus alaternus*
Albany banksia *Banksia verticillata*
Albany blackbutt *Eucalyptus staeri*
Albany bottlebrush *Callistemon
glaucus*
Albany daisy *Actinodium
cunninghamii*
Albany kangaroo-paw *Anigozanthos
preissii*
Albany pitcher plant *Cephalotus
follicularis*
Albany woollybush *Adenanthos
cunninghamii, A. sericeus*
Alberta white spruce, dwarf *Picea
glauca* var. *albertiana* 'Conica'
albizia, paperbark *Albizia
tanganyicensis*
Alcock's spruce *Picea alcoquiana*
Aldenham crab *Malus
'Aldenhamensis'*
alder *Alnus*
alder, berry-bearing *Frangula alnus*
alder, black *Alnus glutinosa, Ilex
verticillata*
alder, blush *Sloanea australis*
alder buckthorn *Rhamnus frangula*
alder, Caucasian *Alnus subcordata*
alder, common *Alder glutinosa*
alder, European *Alnus glutinosa*

alder, evergreen *Alnus acuminata*
alder, gray *Alnus incana*
alder, green *Alnus viridis*
alder hazel *Alnus serrulata*
alder, Italian *Alnus cordata*
alder, Japanese *Alnus firma,
A. japonica*
alder, Manchurian *Alnus hirsuta*
alder, Mexican *Alnus acuminata,
A. jorullensis*
alder, mountain *Alnus tenuifolia*
alder, Nepal *Alnus nepalensis*
alder, Oregon *Alnus rubra*
alder, oriental *Alnus orientalis*
alder red *Alnus rubra*
alder, seaside *Alnus maritima*
alder, sitka *Alnus sinuata*
alder, smooth *Alnus serrulata*
alder, speckled *Alnus rugosa*
alder, Syrian *Alnus orientalis*
alder, thinleaf *Alnus tenuifolia*
alder, white *Alnus rhombifolia,
Clethra acuminata*
alderleaf serviceberry *Amelanchier
alnifolia*
alecost *Tanacetum balsamita*
Aleppo pine *Pinus halapensis*
alerce *Fitzroya cupressoides, Tetraclinis
articulata*
Alexanders *Smyrnium olusatrum*
Alexandra palm *Archontophoenix
alexandrae*
Alexandrian laurel *Calophyllum
inophyllum, Danäe racemosa*
alfacinha *Lactuca watsoniana*
alfalfa *Medicago sativa*
alga, red *Chondrus, Gelidium*
algaroba *Prosopis pallida*
Algerian fir *Abies numidica*
Algerian iris *Iris unguicularis*
Algerian ivy *Hedera canariensis,
H. c.* var. *algeriensis*
Algerian oak *Quercus canariensis*

aliso *Platanus racemosa*
alkali sacaton *Sporobolus airoides*
alkanet *Alkanna tinctoria, Anchusa*
alkanet, dyer's bugloss *Alkanna tinctoria*
alkekengi *Physalis alkekengi*
all, heal *Prunella vulgaris*
allamanda *Allamanda, A. cathartica*
allamanda, bush *Allamanda schottii*
allamanda, climbing *Allamanda cathartica*
allamanda, golden *Allamanda cathartica, A. hendersonii*
allamanda, pink *Allamanda blanchetii*
allamanda, purple *Allamanda blanchetii*
allamanda, shrubby *Allamanda schottii*
Allegheny chinkapin *Castanea pumila*
Allegheny menziesia *Menziesia pilosa*
Allegheny monkey flower *Mimulus ringens*
Allegheny moss *Robinia kelseyi*
Allegheny pachysandra *Pachysandra procumbens*
Allegheny plum *Prunus alleghaniensis*
Allegheny serviceberry *Amelanchier laevis*
Allegheny spurge *Pachysandra procumbens*
Allegheny vine *Adlumia fungosa*
alligator flag *Thalia*
alligator flag, powdery *Thalia dealbata*
alligator juniper *Juniperus deppeana, J. deppeana* var. *pachyphlaea*
alligator pear *Persea americana*
alligator weed *Alternanthera philoxeroides*
allium, giant *Allium giganteum*
allseed, four-leaf *Polycarpon tetraphyllum*
allspice *Calycanthus fertilis, Pimenta dioica, Solenostemon amboinicus*

allspice, California *Calycanthus occidentalis*
allspice, Japanese *Chimonanthus praecox*
almond *Prunus dulcis*
almond, desert *Prunus fasciculata*
almond, dwarf flowering *Prunus triloba*
almond, dwarf Russian *Prunus tenella*
almond, flowering *Prunus × amygdalo-persica*
almond geranium *Pelargonium quercifolium*
almond, Indian *Terminalia catappa*
almond, South African wild *Brabejum stellatifolium*
almond-cherry *Prunus glandulosa*
almond-leafed groundsel *Senecio amygdalifolius*
almond-leafed pear *Pyrus amygdaliformis*
almond-leafed willow *Salix triandra*
aloe *Aloe*
aloe, American *Agave americana*
aloe, basuto kraal *Aloe striatula*
aloe, bitter *Aloe ferox*
aloe, cannon *Aloe claviflora*
aloe, Cape *Aloe ferox*
aloe, climbing *Aloe ciliaris*
aloe, cobweb *Haworthia arachnoidea*
aloe, coral *Aloe striata*
aloe, fan *Aloe plicatilis*
aloe, gold-tooth *Aloe mitriformis*
aloe, jeweled *Aloe distans*
aloe, krantz *Aloe arborescens*
aloe, lace *Aloe aristata*
aloe, partridge breast *Aloe variegata*
aloe, soap *Aloe maculata*
aloe, tiger *Aloe variegata*
aloe, tilt-head *Aloe speciosa*
aloe, tree *Aloe bainesii*
aloe vera *Aloe vera*
aloe, zebra *Aloe maculata*

aloewood *Aquilaria malaccensis*
alpenrose *Rhododendron ferrugineum*
alpenrose, hairy *Rhododendron hirsutum*
alpine ash *Eucalyptus delegatensis*
alpine aster *Aster alpinus*
alpine avens *Geum montanum*
alpine baeckea *Baeckea gunniana*
alpine ballart *Exocarpos nanus*
alpine balsam *Erinus alpinus*
alpine bearberry *Arctostaphylos alpina*
alpine beard-heath *Leucopogon montanus*
alpine bistort *Persicaria vivipara*
alpine bladderwort *Utricularia alpina*
alpine bluebell *Wahlenbergia gloriosa*
alpine boronia *Boronia algida*
alpine bottlebrush *Callistemon pityoides*
alpine burr *Acaena montana*
alpine buttercup *Ranunculus alpestris, R. graniticola*
alpine buttercup, Gunn's *Ranunculus gunnianus*
alpine calamint *Acinos alpinus*
alpine campion *Lychnis alpina*
alpine catchfly *Lychnis alpina*
alpine celery *Aciphylla glacialis*
alpine celery pine *Phyllocladus alpinus*
alpine celerytop pine *Phyllocladus alpinus*
alpine cherry, Japanese *Prunus nipponica*
alpine chrysanthemum *Leucanthemopsis alpina*
alpine cider gum *Eucalyptus gunnii*
alpine columbine *Aquilegia alpina*
alpine currant *Ribes alpinum*
alpine everlasting *Xerochrysum subundulatum*
alpine eyebright *Euphrasia collina* subsp. *glacialis*

alpine fir *Abies lasiocarpa*
alpine geranium *Erodium reichardii*
alpine grevillea *Grevillea australis*
alpine heath *Erica carnea*
alpine knapweed *Centaurea montana*
alpine kunzea *Kunzea muelleri*
alpine lady's mantle *Alchemilla alpina*
alpine laurel *Kalmia microphylla*
alpine leek orchid *Prasophyllum alpinum*
alpine mint bush *Prostanthera cuneata*
alpine mouse-ear *Cerastium alpinum*
alpine orites *Orites lancifolia*
alpine pasque flower *Pulsatilla alpina*
alpine pepper tree *Pseudowintera colorata*
alpine pepperbush *Tasmannia xerophila*
alpine poppy *Papaver alpinum*
alpine riceflower *Pimelea alpina*
alpine rose *Rhododendron ferrugineum*
alpine snowbell *Soldanella alpina*
alpine starbush *Asterolasia trymalioides*
alpine strawberry *Fragaria vesca*
alpine sundew *Drosera arcturi*
alpine sunray *Leucochrysum albicans* subsp. *alpinum*
alpine totara *Podocarpus nivalis*
alpine water fern *Blechnum penna-marina*
alpine wattle *Acacia alpina*
alpine yucca *Yucca baileyi*
Alstonville tibouchina *Tibouchina lepidota* 'Alstonville'
alstroemeria, climbing *Bomarea caldasii*
alstroemeria, parrot *Alstroemeria pulchella*
altai rose *Rosa pimpinellifolia* var. *altaica*

altai thorn *Crataegus altaica*
alternanthera, bedding *Alternanthera bettzichiana*
althea, shrub *Hibiscus syriacus*
alum root *Heuchera*
aluminum plant *Pilea cadierei*
aluminum plant, dwarf *Pilea cadierei* 'Minima'
alyssum, bedding *Lobularia maritima*
alyssum, flax-leafed *Alyssum linifolium*
alyssum, sweet *Lobularia maritima*
alyssum, yellow *Aurinia saxatilis*
alyxia, beach *Alyxia spicata*
alyxia, prickly *Alyxia ruscifolia*
amaranth *Amaranthus*
amaranth, cereal grain *Amaranthus hypochondriacus*
amaranth, globe *Gomphrena globosa*
amaranth, green *Amaranthus viridis*
amaranth, purple *Amaranthus cruentus*
amaranth, red *Amaranthus cruentus*
amaranth, spiny *Amaranthus spinosus*
amaranthus, two-toothed *Achyranthes bidentata*
amarga, palma *Sabal mauritiiformis*
amaryllis, blue *Worsleya rayneri*
amaryllis, butterfly *Hippeastrum papilio*
Amatungula *Carissa bispinosa, C. macrocarpa*
Amazon lily *Eucharis, E. × grandiflora*
Amazon vine *Stigmaphyllon ciliatum*
Amazon waterlily *Victoria amazonica*
ambal *Phyllanthus emblica*
amberbell *Erythronium americanum*
amelanchier *Aronia arbutifolia*
American aloe *Agave americana*
American alpine speedwell *Veronica wormskjoldii*
American angelica tree *Aralia spinosa*
American arborvitae *Thuja occidentalis*

American aspen *Populus tremuloides*
American barrenwort *Vancouveria hexandra*
American beauty berry *Callicarpa americana*
American beauty bush *Callicarpa americana*
American beech *Fagus grandifolia*
American bird cherry *Prunus virginiana*
American bistort *Persicaria bistortoides*
American bittersweet *Celastrus scandens*
American black poplar *Populus deltoides*
American black spruce *Picea mariana*
American blackcurrant *Ribes americanum*
American bladdernut *Staphylea trifolia*
American cherry, dwarf *Prunus pumila*
American chestnut *Castanea dentata*
American coral tree *Erythrina berteroana*
American cotton palm *Washingtonia filifera*
American cottonwood *Populus deltoides*
American cowslip *Dodecatheon, D. meadia*
American crabapple *Malus coronaria*
American cranberry *Vaccinium macrocarpon*
American cranberry bush *Viburnum trilobum*
American dewberry *Rubus canadensis*
American dittany *Cunila origanoides*
American dogwood *Cornus sericea*
American dwarf birch *Betula pumila*
American elder *Sambucus canadensis*
American elderberry *Sambucus canadensis*

American elm *Ulmus americana*
American filbert *Corylus americana*
American fringe tree *Chionanthus virginicus*
American germander *Teucrium canadense*
American ginseng *Panax quinquefolius*
American glasswort *Salicornia virginica*
American hackberry *Celtis occidentalis*
American hazelnut *Corylus americana*
American highbush cranberry *Viburnum trilobum*
American holly *Ilex opaca*
American hop-hornbeam *Ostrya virginiana*
American hornbeam *Carpinus caroliniana*
American horsemint *Monarda punctata*
American hybrid lilac *Syringa × hyacinthiflora*
American larch *Larix laricina*
American leatherwood *Cyrilla, C. racemiflora*
American linden *Tilia americana*
American lotus *Nelumbo lutea*
American maidenhair *Adiantum pedatum*
American maidenhair fern *Adiantum pedatum*
American mandrake *Podophyllum peltatum*
American mangrove *Rhizophora mangle*
American mountain ash *Sorbus americana*
American mountain mint *Pycnanthemum*
American oil palm *Elaeis oleifera*
American pennyroyal *Hedeoma pulegioides*

American persimmon *Diospyros virginiana*
American pistachio *Pistacia texana*
American pitcher plant *Sarracenia*
American plane *Platanus occidentalis*
American plum *Prunus americana*
American pussy willow *Salix discolor*
American red birch *Betula fontinalis*
American red elder *Sambucus pubens*
American red plum *Prunus americana*
American red spruce *Picea rubens*
American rock fern *Polypodium virginianum*
American rubber plant *Peperomia obtusifolia*
American sea rocket *Cakile edentula*
American sloe *Prunus umbellata*
American smoke tree *Cotinus obovatus*
American spikenard *Aralia racemosa*
American sweet chestnut *Castanea dentata*
American sweet crab *Malus coronaria*
American sweet crabapple *Malus coronaria*
American sweet gum *Liquidambar styraciflua*
American trout lily *Erythronium americanum*
American turkey oak *Quercus laevis*
American turk's cap lily *Lilium superbum*
American walnut *Juglans nigra*
American white oak *Quercus alba*
American wild columbine *Aquilegia canadensis*
American wisteria *Wisteria frutescens*
American yellowwood *Cladrastris lutea*
amethyst flower *Browallia*
amethyst sea holly *Eryngium amethystinum*
ammoniac *Dorema ammoniacum*

amulla *Eremophila debilis*
Amur chokecherry *Prunus maackii*
Amur cork tree *Phellodendron amurense*
Amur grape *Vitis amurensis*
Amur linden *Tilia amurensis*
Amur maackia *Maackia amurensis*
Amur maple *Acer tataricum, A. t.* subsp. *ginnala*
Amur privet *Ligustrum amurense*
Amur silvergrass *Miscanthus sacchariflorus*
anaba *Ficus palmeri*
anaboom *Acacia albida*
anchor bush *Colletia paradoxa*
anchor plant *Colletia*
anchor vine *Palmeria scandens*
ancient pine *Pinus longaeva*
Andean sage *Salvia discolor*
Andean silver sage *Salvia discolor*
Andean wax palm *Ceroxylon alpinum*
Anderson's holly fern *Polystichum andersoni*
Anderson's sword fern *Polystichum andersoni*
Andes, old man of the *Espostoa lanata, Oreocereus celsianus*
andromeda, marsh *Andromeda polifolia*
anemone *Anemone*
anemone buttercup *Ranunculus anemoneus*
anemone, buttercup *Anemone ranunculoides*
anemone clematis *Clematis montana*
anemone clematis, pink *Clematis montana* 'Rubens'
anemone, florist's *Anemone coronaria*
anemone, grapeleaf *Anemone tomentosa*
anemone, Japanese *Anemone hupehensis* var. *japonica, A.* × *hybrida*

anemone of Greece *Anemone pavonina*
anenome, rue *Anemonella thalictroides*
anemone, snowdrop *Anemone sylvestris*
anemone, tree *Carpenteria californica*
anemone, windflower *Anemone coronaria*
anemone, wood *Anemone nemorosa*
angel orchid *Coelogyne cristata*
angel wing jasmine *Jasminum nitidum*
angel wings *Caladium bicolor*
angelica *Angelica archangelica*
angelica, Chinese *Angelica polymorpha* subsp. *sinensis*
angelica tree *Aralia elata, Dendropanax arboreus*
angelica tree, American *Aralia spinosa*
angelica tree, Chinese *Aralia chinensis*
angelica tree, Japanese *Aralia elata*
angel's eyes *Veronica chamaedrys*
angel's fishing rod *Dierama*
angel's hair *Artemisia schmidtiana*
angel's tears *Narcissus triandrus, Soleirolia soleirolii*
angel's trumpet *Brugmansia* × *candida, B. suaveolens, Datura inoxia*
angel-wing begonia *Begonia coccinea*
angled flat pea *Platylobium obtusangulum*
angled lobelia *Lobelia alata*
angled loofah *Luffa acutangula*
angle-vein fern *Polypodium triseriale*
Anglo-jap yew *Taxus* × *media*
angophora *Angophora costata*
angostura *Galipea officinalis*
angular Solomon's seal *Polygonatum odoratum*
anise *Pimpinella anisum*

anise, Chinese *Illicium verum*
anise hyssop *Agastache anethiodora,*
    A. foeniculum
anise, Japanese *Illicium anisatum*
anise magnolia *Magnolia salicifolia*
anise, purple *Illicium floridanum*
anise shrub *Illicium anisatum*
anise, star *Illicium verum*
anise tree *Illicium*
anise tree, Florida *Illicium floridanum*
aniseed *Pimpinella anisum*
aniseed tree *Anetholea anisata*
anise-scented sage *Salvia guaranitica*
annatto *Bixa orellana*
annual beardgrass *Polypogon*
    monspeliensis
annual bluebell *Wahlenbergia*
    gracilenta
annual bluegrass *Poa annua*
annual cat's tail *Rostraria cristata*
annual chalkwort *Gypsophila australis*
annual mallow *Lavatera trimestris*
annual meadow grass *Poa annua*
annual pearlwort *Sagina apetala*
annual phlox *Phlox drummondii*
annual pigface *Portulaca grandiflora*
annual ryegrass *Lolium multiflorum*
annual sage *Salvia viridis*
annual toadflax *Linaria maroccana*
annual veld grass *Ehrharta erecta,*
    E. longiflora
anona blanca *Annona diversifolia*
ant bush *Senna clavigera*
ant orchid *Chiloglottis formicifera*
Antarctic beech *Nothofagus*
    antarctica, N. moorei
Antarctic sedge *Carex trifida*
antelope brush *Purshia tridentata*
antelope bush *Purshia, P. tridentata*
antelope orchid *Dendrobium*
    antennatum
ant-house plant *Myrmecodia*
    beccariana

anthurium *Anthurium*
anthurium, queen *Anthurium*
    warocqueanum
Antwerp hollyhock *Alcea ficifolia*
anu *Tropaeolum tuberosum*
aotus *Aotus ericoides*
Apache beggarticks *Bidens ferulifolia*
Apache pine *Pinus engelmannii*
Apache plume *Fallugia paradoxa*
apoon, desert *Dasylirion wheeleri*
apostle plant *Neomarica northiana*
apothecaries' rose *Rosa gallica*
    'Officinalis'
apple *Malus, Malus pumila*
apple, Argyle *Eucalyptus cinerea*
apple berry *Billardiera scandens*
apple, bitter *Citrullus colocynthis*
apple, black *Pouteria australis*
apple blossom cassia *Cassia grandis*
apple blossom tree *Cassia javanica*
apple box *Eucalyptus bridgesiana*
apple, broad-leafed *Angophora*
    subvelutina
apple, cocky *Planchonia careya*
apple, common thorn *Datura*
    stramonium
apple, coolabah *Angophora*
    melanoxylon
apple, coolibah *Angophora*
    melanoxylon
apple, crow's *Owenia venosa*
apple, custard *Annona* Atemoya
    Group, *A. cherimola, A. squamosa*
apple, devil's *Mandragora offinarum,*
    Podophyllum peltatum
apple, downy thorn *Datura inoxia*
apple dumpling *Billardiera scandens*
apple, dwarf *Angophora hispida*
apple, eating *Malus pumila*
apple, elephant *Dillenia indica*
apple geranium *Pelargonium*
    odoratissimum
apple gum *Angophora*

apple, hog *Podophyllum peltatum*
apple, Indian *Datura inoxia,
Podophyllum peltatum*
apple, Java *Syzygium samarangense*
apple, Jew's *Solanum melongena*
apple, kangaroo *Solanum aviculare*
apple, kei *Dovyalis caffra*
apple leaf *Lonchocarpus capassa*
apple, Malay *Syzygium malaccense*
apple mallee *Eucalyptus buprestium*
apple, May *Passiflora incarnata,
Podophyllum, P. peltatum*
apple mint *Mentha × rotundifolia,
M. suaveolens*
apple mint, variegated *Mentha
suaveolens* 'Variegata'
apple myrtle *Angophora*
apple, narrow-leafed *Angophora
bakeri*
apple of Peru *Nicandra physalodes*
apple of Sodom *Solanum hermannii,
S. linnaeanum*
apple, orchard *Malus pumila*
apple, pond *Annona glabra*
apple, red *Acmena ingens*
apple, rose *Syzygium jambos,
S. moorei*
apple rose *Rosa pomifera*
apple, rough-barked *Angophora
floribunda*
apple serviceberry *Amelanchier ×
grandiflora*
apple, small-leafed *Angophora bakeri*
apple, star *Chrysophyllum cainito*
apple, water *Syzygium aqueum*
apple, winter *Eremophila debilis*
appleberry, pale *Billardiera versicolor*
appleberry, purple *Billardiera
longiflora*
applemint, large *Mentha
alopecuroides*
apple-topped gum *Eucalyptus
angophoroides*

apricot *Prunus armeniaca*
apricot, black *Prunus × dasycarpa*
apricot, Briançon *Prunus brigantina*
apricot, desert *Prunus fremontii*
apricot, Japanese *Prunus mume*
apricot, Manchurian *Prunus
mandshurica*
apricot plum *Prunus simonii*
apricot, Siberian *Prunus sibirica*
aprons, fairy *Utricularia dichotoma*
Arabian coffee *Coffea arabica*
Arabian euphorbia *Euphorbia ammak*
Arabian grass *Schismus barbatus*
Arabian jasmine *Jasminum sambac*
Arabian jasmine, double *Jasminum
sambac* 'Grand Duke of Tuscany'
Arabian tea *Catha edulis*
arabis *Arabis caucasica*
Arab's turban *Crassula hemisphaerica*
aralia *Polyscias, Schefflera elegantissima*
aralia, balfour *Polyscias scutellaria*
'Balfourii'
aralia, castor *Kalopanax septemlobus*
aralia, false *Schefflera elegantissima*
aralia, fern-leaf *Polyscias filicifolia*
aralia, geranium *Polyscias guilfoylei*
aralia, Japanese *Fatsia japonica*
aralia, Ming *Polyscias fruticosa*
aralia, tree *Kalopanax septemlobus*
arar *Tetraclinis articulata*
araucaria, Ming *Polyscias fruticosa*
araucaria, rock *Araucaria scopulorum*
araucaria, Rule *Araucaria rulei*
arborvitae *Thuja*
arborvitae, American *Thuja
occidentalis*
arborvitae, Chinese *Platycladus
orientalis*
arborvitae, eastern *Thuja occidentalis*
arborvitae, false *Thujopsis dolabrata*
arborvitae, giant *Thuja plicata*
arborvitae, golden *Thuja occidentalis*
'Lutea'

arborvitae, Japanese *Thuja standishii*
arborvitae, Korean *Thuja koraiensis*
arbutus, trailing *Epigaea repens*
archangel *Angelica archangelica*
archangel, yellow *Lamium galeobdolon*
Arctic bearberry *Arctostaphylos alpina*
Arctic birch *Betula nana*
Arctic bramble *Rubus arcticus*
Arctic creeping willow *Salix reptans*
Arctic gray willow *Salix glauca*
Arctic polemonium *Polemonium boreale*
Arctic poppy *Papaver nudicaule*
Arctic willow *Salix arctica, S. lanata, S. purpurea*
ardisia, coral *Ardisia crenata*
aren *Arenga pinnata*
argan *Argania spinosa*
Argentine flame tree *Tabebuia impetiginosa*
Argentine mesquite *Prosopis alba*
Argentine tecoma *Tecoma garrocha*
Argentine trumpet vine *Clytostoma callistegioides*
Argyle apple *Eucalyptus cinerea*
Arizona ash *Fraxinus velutina*
Arizona barrel cactus *Ferocactus wislizeni*
Arizona cypress *Cupressus arizonica*
Arizona cypress, golden *Cupressus glabra* 'Limelight'
Arizona cypress, smooth *Cupressus glabra*
Arizona mountain laurel *Sophora arizonica*
Arizona necklace *Sophora arizonica*
Arizona plane *Platanus wrightii*
Arizona queen of the night *Peniocereus greggii*
Arizona walnut *Juglans major*
Arizona water-willow *Justicia candicans*

Arizona white oak *Quercus arizonica*
Arizona willow *Salix irrorata*
arjun *Terminalia arjuna*
Arkansas oak *Quercus arkansana*
Armand pine *Pinus armandii*
Armenian cranesbill *Geranium psilostemon*
Armenian knapweed *Centaurea macrocephala*
Armenian oak *Quercus pontica*
arnica *Arnica montana*
arnica, broad-leafed *Arnica latifolia*
arnica, mountain *Arnica latifolia*
Arnold crabapple *Malus × arnoldiana*
Arnold hawthorn *Crataegus arnoldiana*
arolla pine *Pinus cembra*
arorangi *Olearia macrodonta*
Arran service tree *Sorbus pseudofennica*
arrow arum *Peltandra*
arrow bamboo *Pseudosasa japonica*
arrowgrass, spurred *Triglochin calcitrapum*
arrowhead *Sagittaria, S. sagittifolia*
arrowhead vine *Syngonium podophyllum*
arrowleaf balsamroot *Balsamorhiza sagittata*
arrowroot *Maranta arundinacea*
arrowroot, Florida *Zamia integrifolia*
arrowroot, Guyana *Dioscorea alata*
arrowroot, Japanese *Pueraria lobata*
arrowroot, Polynesian *Tacca leontopetaloides*
arrowroot, Queensland *Canna indica*
arrowwood *Viburnum dentatum*
arrowwood, Indian *Philadelphus lewisii*
arrowwood, southern *Viburnum dentatum*
arroyo lupine *Lupinus succentulus*
arroyo willow *Salix lasiolepis*
artichoke, Chinese *Stachys affinis*

artichoke, globe *Cynara scolymus*
artichoke, Jerusalem *Helianthus tuberosus*
artillery fern *Pilea microphylla*
artillery plant *Pilea microphylla*
arugula *Eruca sativa*
arum *Arum*
arum, arrow *Peltandra*
arum, black *Arum palaestinum*
arum, dragon *Dracunculus vulgaris*
arum, green arrow *Peltandra virginica*
arum, hairy *Dracunculus muscivorus*
arum lily *Zantedeschia, Z. aethiopica*
arum, pink *Zantedeschia rehmannii*
arum, scrub *Typhonium brownii*
arum, snake *Amorphophallus rivieri*
arum, titan *Amorphophallus titanum*
arum, yellow *Zantedeschia elliottiana*
asarabacca *Asarum, A. europaeum*
ascending sunray *Rhodanthe diffusa*
ash *Fraxinus*
ash, alpine *Eucalyptus delegatensis*
ash, American mountain *Sorbus americana*
ash, Arizona *Fraxinus velutina*
ash, bastard crow's *Pentaceras australe*
ash, Bennett's *Flindersia bennettiana*
ash, Biltmore *Fraxinus biltmoreana*
ash, black *Fraxinus nigra*
ash, blue *Fraxinus quadrangulata*
ash, Blue Mountains *Eucalyptus oreades*
ash, blueberry *Elaeocarpus reticulatis*
ash, bumpy *Flindersia schottiana*
ash, Carolina *Fraxinus caroliniana*
ash, claret *Fraxinus angustifolia* 'Raywood'
ash, cliff mallee *Eucalyptus cunninghamii*
ash, crow's *Flindersia australis*
ash, desert *Fraxinus angustifolia* subsp. *syriaca, F. velutina*
ash, dogleg *Fraxinus greggii*

ash, dwarf Chinese mountain *Sorbus reducta*
ash, European *Fraxinus excelsior*
ash, European mountain *Sorbus aucuparia*
ash, evergreen *Fraxinus uhdei*
ash, flat-spine prickly *Zanthoxylum simulans*
ash, flowering *Fraxinus ornus*
ash, golden *Fraxinus excelsior* 'Aurea'
ash, golden European *Fraxinus excelsior* 'Aurea'
ash, green *Fraxinus pennsylvanica*
ash, ground *Aegopodium podagraria*
ash, Himalayan manna *Fraxinus floribunda*
ash, Jillaga *Eucalyptus stenostoma*
ash, Korean mountain *Sorbus alnifolia*
ash, leopard *Flindersia collina*
ash, Manchurian *Fraxinus mandshurica*
ash, manna *Fraxinus ornus*
ash, Mexican *Fraxinus greggii*
ash, Moreton Bay *Corymbia tessellaris*
ash, mountain *Eucalyptus regnans, Sorbus, S. aucuparia*
ash, narrow-leafed *Fraxinus angustifolia*
ash, northern prickly *Zanthoxylum americanum*
ash, oak-leafed mountain *Sorbus* × *thuringiaca*
ash, Oregon *Fraxinus latifolia*
ash, Pigeon House *Eucalyptus triflora*
ash, prickly *Zanthoxylum americanum, Z. simulans*
ash, pumpkin *Fraxinus tomentosa*
ash, red *Alphitonia excelsa, Fraxinus pennsylvanica*
ash, shamel *Fraxinus uhdei*
ash, showy mountain *Sorbus decora*
ash, silvertop *Eucalyptus sieberi*
ash, single-leaf *Fraxinus anomala*

ash, swamp *Fraxinus caroliniana, F. nigra*
ash, Swedish mountain *Sorbus intermedia*
ash, Utah *Fraxinus anomala*
ash, velvet *Fraxinus velutina*
ash weed *Aegopodium podagraria*
ash, white *Eucalyptus fraxinoides, Fraxinus americana*
ash, yellow *Emmenosperma alphitonioides*
ash, yellow-top *Eucalyptus luehmanniana*
Ashanti blood *Mussaenda erythrophylla*
Ashburton pea *Swainsona maccullochiana*
Ashby's banksia *Banksia ashbyi*
Ashe magnolia *Magnolia ashei*
ashy hakea *Hakea cinerea*
Asian beach-lily *Crinum asiaticum*
Asian bell *Radermachera sinica*
Asian bellflower *Radermarchera sinica*
Asian black birch *Betula dahurica*
Asian ginseng *Panax ginseng*
Asian mint *Persicaria odorata*
Asian pigeonwings *Clitoria ternatea*
Asiatic poison lily *Crinum asiaticum*
asoka *Saraca indica*
asparagus *Asparagus officinalis*
asparagus, Bath *Ornithogalum pyrenaicum*
asparagus bean *Vigna unguiculata* subsp. *sesquipedalis*
asparagus, Chinese *Asparagus cochinchinensis*
asparagus fern *Asparagus densiflorus, A. setaceus*
asparagus fern, Meyer *Asparagus densiflorus* 'Meyeri'
asparagus pea *Tetragonolobus purpureus*
asparagus, Sprenger *Asparagus densiflorus* 'Sprenger'

aspen *Populus tremula*
aspen, American *Populus tremuloides*
aspen, bigtooth *Populus grandidentata*
aspen, Chinese *Populus adenopoda*
Aspen daisy *Erigeron speciosus macranthus*
aspen, European *Populus tremula*
aspen, Japanese *Populus sieboldii*
aspen, quaking *Populus tremula, P. tremuloides*
aspen, silver *Acronychia wilcoxiana*
aspen, Swedish *Populus tremula*
aspen, trembling *Populus tremuloides*
asphodel, yellow *Asphodeline lutea*
aspidistra *Aspidistra elatior*
Assai palm *Euterpe oleracea*
assegai tree *Curtisia dentata*
Assyrian plum *Cordia myxa*
aster *Aster*
aster, alpine *Aster alpinus*
aster, beach *Erigeron glaucus*
aster, China *Callistephus chinensis*
aster, Engelmann *Aster engelmannii*
aster, golden *Heterotheca villosa*
aster, heath *Aster ericoides*
aster, Mexican *Cosmos bipinnatus*
aster, midsummer *Erigeron speciosus*
aster, New England *Aster novae-angliae*
aster, New York *Aster novi-belgii*
aster, perennial *Aster novi-belgii*
aster, prairie *Machaeranthera tanacetifolia*
aster, purple *Aster tataricus*
aster, Stokes' *Stokesia laevis*
aster, tansyleaf *Machaeranthera tanacetifolia*
aster, white *Aster engelmannii*
aster, wild *Aster subulatus, Felicia filifolia*
asthma weed *Euphorbia hirta*
astilbe *Astilbe*

astilbe, hybrid *Astilbe* × *arendsii*
atamasco lily *Zephyranthes atamasco*
atemoya *Annona* Atemoya Group
athel tree *Tamarix aphylla*
Atherton oak *Athertonia diversifolia*
Atherton palm *Laccospadix australasica*
Atlantic cedar *Cedrus atlantica*
Atlantic cedar, blue *Cedrus atlantica* 'Glauca'
Atlantic cedar, golden *Cedrus atlantica* 'Aurea'
Atlantic ivy *Hedera hibernica*
Atlantic white cedar *Chamaecyparis thyoides*
Atlantic wild indigo *Baptisia lactea*
Atlas cedar *Cedrus atlantica*
Atlas cedar, golden *Cedrus atlantica* 'Aurea'
Atlas fescue *Festuca mairei*
Atlas mastic *Pistacia atlantica*
au lako *Bambusa lako*
aubergine *Solanum melongena*
aubrietia *Aubrietia, Aubrieta deltoidea*
aucuba, Japanese *Aucuba japonica*
August lily *Hosta plantaginea*
austral brooklime *Gratiola peruviana*
austral ladies' tresses *Spiranthes sinensis* subsp. *australis*
austral leek-orchid *Prasophyllum australe*
Australian anchor plant *Discaria pubescens*
Australian bamboo *Bambusa arnhemica*
Australian banyan *Ficus macrophylla*
Australian baobab *Adansonia gibbosa*
Australian beech *Nothofagus moorei*
Australian bindweed *Convolvulus erubescens*
Australian blackthorn *Bursaria spinosa*
Australian bluebell *Wahlenbergia ceracea, W. communis*

Australian bluebell creeper *Sollya heterophylla*
Australian boxthorn *Bursaria spinosa, Lycium australe*
Australian bracken *Pteris tremula*
Australian brake *Pteridium esculentum*
Australian brush cherry *Syzygium paniculatum*
Australian buttercup *Ranunculus lappaceus*
Australian carrot *Daucus glochidiatus*
Australian celtis *Celtis paniculata*
Australian cherry *Exocarpos cupressiformis*
Australian clematis *Clematis aristata*
Australian cliff brake *Pellaea falcata*
Australian cypress-pine *Callitris*
Australian daphne *Philotheca myoporoides, Pittosporum undulatum*
Australian dodder *Cuscuta australis*
Australian dogwood *Jacksonia scoparia*
Australian edelweiss *Ewartia nubigena*
Australian elm *Aphananthe philippinensis*
Australian fan palm *Livistona australis*
Australian finger lime *Citrus australasica*
Australian flame tree *Brachychiton acerifolius*
Australian frangipani *Hymenosporum flavum*
Australian fuchsia *Correa*
Australian golden wattle *Acacia pycnantha*
Australian gypsy-wort *Lycopus australis*
Australian hollyhock *Lavatera plebeia*
Australian indigo *Indigofera australis*
Australian iris *Patersonia*
Australian ivy palm *Schefflera actinophylla*

Australian laurel *Auranticarpa rhombifolia*
Australian lime *Citrus australis*
Australian maidenhair *Adiantum formosum*
Australian mistletoe *Amyema*
Australian native broom *Viminaria juncea*
Australian native rose *Boronia serrulata*
Australian native rosella *Hibiscus heterophyllus*
Australian native violet *Viola hederacea*
Australian nutmeg *Myristica insipida*
Australian olive *Olea paniculata*
Australian pillwort *Pilularia novae-hollandiae*
Australian pine *Casuarina equisetifolia*
Australian red cedar *Toona ciliata*
Australian rhododendron *Rhododendron lochiae*
Australian rosella *Hibiscus heterophyllus*
Australian rosemary *Westringia fruticosa*
Australian samphire *Sarcocornia quinqueflora*
Australian sarsaparilla *Smilax glyciphylla*
Australian senna *Senna aciphylla*
Australian shield fern *Polystichum australiense*
Australian stonecrop *Crassula sieberiana*
Australian tea tree *Leptospermum laevigatum*
Australian teak *Flindersia australis*
Australian tree fern *Cyathea cooperi*
Australian tree violet *Hymenanthera dentata*
Australian trefoil *Lotus australis*
Australian violet *Viola hederacea*

Australian waterlily *Nymphaea gigantea*
Australian wild cotton *Gossypium australe*
Australian willow *Geijera parviflora*
Australian wintercress *Barbarea grayi*
Australian wisteria *Millettia megasperma*
Austrian black pine *Pinus nigra*
Austrian briar *Rosa foetida*
Austrian copper briar *Rosa foetida* 'Bicolor'
Austrian pine *Pinus nigra*
Austrian sage *Salvia austriaca*
Austrian yellow rose *Rosa foetida*
autograph tree *Clusia major*
autumn bird orchid *Chiloglottis reflexa*
autumn cassia *Senna corymbosa*
autumn crocus *Colchicum, Sternbergia*
autumn daffodil *Sternbergia*
autumn elaeagnus *Elaeagnus umbellata*
autumn fern *Dryopteris erythrosora*
autumn moor grass *Sesleria autumnalis*
autumn olive *Elaeagnus umbellata*
autumn sage *Salvia greggii*
autumn snowflake *Leucojum autumnale*
autumn squash *Curcurbita maxima*
avens *Geum*
avens, alpine *Geum montanum*
avens, Chilean *Geum chiloense*
avens, creeping *Geum reptans*
avens, scarlet *Geum chiloense* 'Mrs Bradshaw'
avens, mountain *Dryas octopetala*
avens, purple *Geum triflorum*
avens, water *Geum rivale*
avens, wood *Geum urbanum*
avens, yellow *Geum aleppicum*

avocado *Persea americana*
awapuhi *Zingiber zerumbet*
awl-leafed wattle *Acacia subulata*
axe-breaker *Geijera paniculata*
azalea *Rhododendron*
azalea, Alabama *Rhododendron alabamense*
azalea, balsam *Rhododendron indicum* 'Balsaminiflorum'
azalea, Chinese evergreen *Rhododendron simsii*
azalea, coast *Rhododendron atlanticum*
azalea, Cumberland *Rhododendron cumberlandense*
azalea, deciduous *Rhododendron molle*
azalea, five-leaf *Rhododendron quinquefolium*
azalea, flame *Rhododendron calendulaceum, R. flammeum*
azalea, Florida *Rhododendron austrinum*
azalea, Florida pinxter *Rhododendron canescens*
azalea, golden spire *Azara integrifolia*
azalea, Ilam *Rhododendron* Ilam Hybrids
azalea, Indian *Rhododendron indicum, R. simsii*
azalea, Japanese evergreen *Rhododendron indicum*
azalea, Kaempfer *Rhododendron kaempferi*
azalea, Korean *Rhododendron yedoense*
azalea, kurume *Rhododendron* × *obtusum*
azalea, Kyushu *Rhododendron kiusianum*
azalea, Piedmont *Rhododendron canescens*
azalea, pink-shell *Rhododendron vaseyi*

azalea, pinxter *Rhododendron periclymenoides*
azalea, pinxterbloom *Rhododendron periclymenoides*
azalea, plum-leaf *Rhododendron pruniflorum*
azalea, Pontic *Rhododendron luteum*
azalea, roseshell *Rhododendron prinophyllum*
azalea, royal *Rhododendron schlippenbachii*
azalea, swamp *Rhododendron viscosum*
azalea, sweet *Rhododendron canescens*
azalea, Taiwan *Rhododendron oldhamii*
azalea, tall evergreen *Rhododendron* × *mucronatum*
azalea, thyme-leaf *Rhododendron serpyllifolium*
azalea, western *Rhododendron occidentale*
azalea, Yodogawa *Rhododendron yedoense*
azarole *Crataegus azarolus*
azolla *Azolla filiculoides*
azolla, ferny *Azolla pinnata*
azolla, Pacific *Azolla filiculoides* var. *rubra*
Azores bay *Laurus azorica*
Azores bellflower *Campanula vidalii*
Azores blueberry *Vaccinium cylindraceum*
Azores heath *Daboecia azorica*
Azores holly *Ilex perado* subsp. *azorica*
Azores jasmine *Jasminum azoricum*
Aztec lily *Sprekelia formosissima*
Aztec marigold *Tagetes erecta*
azul, Navajita *Bouteloua gracilis*
azure ceanothus *Ceanothus coeruleus*
azure monkshood *Aconitum carmichaelii*

B

babaco *Carica* × *heilbornii*,
C. *pentagona*
baboon flower *Babiana*, *B. stricta*
baboon flower, red-eyed *Babiana*
rubrocyanea
babul *Acacia nilotica*
baby blue-eyes *Nemophila menziesii*
baby greenhood *Pterostylis parviflora*
baby rose *Rosa* (Dwarf China)
'Cécile Brunner'
baby rubber plant *Peperomia*
obtusifolia
baby toes *Fenestraria aurantiaca*
baby wood rose *Argyreia nervosa*
Babylon weeping willow *Salix*
babylonica
baby's breath *Gypsophila*,
G. paniculata
baby's tears *Soleirolia soleirolii*
baby's toes *Fenestraria rhopalophylla*
bachelor's buttons *Cenia turbinata*,
Centaurea cyanus, *Gomphrena*
canescens, G. *globosa*
bachelor's buttons, yellow
Ranunculus acris 'Flore Pleno'
backbone, devil's *Pedilanthus*
tithymaloides
badger's bane *Aconitum*,
A. lycoctonum
badja gum, big *Eucalyptus badjensis*
baeckea, alpine *Baeckea gunniana*
baeckea, mountain *Baeckea utilis*
baeckea, rosy *Euryomyrtus*
ramosissima
baeckea, swamp *Baeckea linifolia*
baeckea, tall *Baeckea virgata*
baeckea, weeping *Baeckea stenophylla*
Baeuerlen's gum *Eucalyptus*
baeuerlenii

bag flower *Clerodendrum thomsoniae*
bagras *Eucalyptus deglupta*
Bahama grass *Cynodon dactylon*
Bahamian thatch *Coccothrinax*
inaguensis
bahia grass *Paspalum notatum*
bai zhu *Atractylodes macrocephala*
baileya, desert *Baileya multiradiata*
Bailey's cypress-pine *Callitris baileyi*
Bailey's stringybark *Eucalyptus*
baileyana
Baja bush snapdragon *Galvezia*
juncea
Baja elephant tree *Pachycormus*
discolor
Baja fig *Ficus palmeri*
Baja rock fig *Ficus palmeri*
Baker's manzanita *Arctostaphylos*
bakeri
balai, latanier *Coccothrinax*
barbadensis
balata *Manilkara bidentata*
balau *Shorea*
bald cypress *Taxodium distichum*
bald cypress, Mexican *Taxodium*
mucronatum
baldmoney *Meum athamanticum*
Balearic box *Buxus balearica*
Balearic boxwood *Buxus balearica*
balfour aralia *Polyscias scutellaria*
'Balfourii'
balisier *Heliconia caribaea*
Balkan clary *Salvia nemorosa*
Balkan crabapple *Malus florentina*
Balkan primrose *Ramonda myconi*
ball cactus, golden *Parodia*
leninghausii
ball cactus, silver *Parodia scopa*
ball honey-myrtle *Melaleuca nodosa*
ball moss *Tillandsia recurvata*
ball nut *Floydia praealta*
ball tree, orange *Buddleja globosa*
ballart, broom *Exocarpos sparteus*

ballart, cherry *Exocarpos cupressiformis*
ballart, leafless *Exocarpos aphyllus*
ballart, pale-fruited *Exocarpos strictus*
balloon cotton bush *Gomphocarpus fruticosus, G. physocarpus*
balloon flower *Platycodon grandiflorus*
balloon pea *Sutherlandia, S. frutescens*
balloon vine *Cardiospermum, C. grandiflorum*
balloon vine, small *Cardiospermum halicacabum*
balm *Melissa*
balm, bee *Melissa officinalis, Monarda, M. didyma*
balm, Canary *Cedronella canariensis*
balm, lemon *Melissa officinalis*
balm of Gilead *Cedronella canariensis, Commiphora gileadensis, Populus × jackii* 'Gileadensis'
balsam *Impatiens, I. balsamina*
balsam, alpine *Erinus*
balsam azalea *Rhododendron indicum* 'Balsaminiflorum'
balsam, busy Lizzie *Impatiens walleriana*
balsam fir *Abies balsamea*
balsam fir, dwarf *Abies balsamea*
balsam, garden *Impatiens balsamina*
balsam, Himalayan *Impatiens glandulifera*
balsam pear *Momordica charantia*
balsam, Peruvian *Myroxylon balsamum* var. *pereirae*
balsam poplar *Populus balsamifera*
balsam root *Balsamorhiza sagittata*
balsam, tolu *Myroxylon balsamum*
balsam tree *Clusia alba*
balsam willow *Salix pyrifolia*
balsamroot, arrowleaf *Balsamorhiza sagittata*
bamboo *Bambusa*
bamboo, arrow *Pseudosasa japonica*

bamboo, Australian *Bambusa arnhemica*
bamboo, beechy *Bambusa beecheyana*
bamboo, black *Phyllostachys nigra*
bamboo, Buddha's belly *Bambusa ventricosa*
bamboo, Chinese edible *Phyllostachys dulcis*
bamboo, Chinese goddess *Bambusa multiplex* var. *riviereorum*
bamboo, common *Bambusa vulgaris*
bamboo, crookstem *Phyllostachys aureosulcata*
bamboo, dwarf fern-leafed *Pleioblastus pygmaeus*
bamboo, dwarf sacred *Nandina domestica* 'Nana'
bamboo, dwarf white-stripe *Pleioblastus variegates*
bamboo, edible *Phyllostachys edulis*
bamboo, elegant *Phyllostachys vivax*
bamboo, fern-leaf *Bambusa multiplex* 'Fernleaf'
bamboo, fishpole *Phyllostachys aurea*
bamboo, fountain *Fargesia nitida*
bamboo, giant *Bambusa balcooa*
bamboo, giant timber *Phyllostachys bambusoides*
bamboo, golden *Phyllostachys aurea*
bamboo grass *Eragrostis australasica, Stipa ramosissima*
bamboo grass, slender *Austrostipa verticillata*
bamboo, heavenly *Nandina domestica*
bamboo, hedge *Bambusa multiplex*
bamboo, Japanese timber *Phyllostachys bambusoides*
bamboo lily *Lilium japonicum*
bamboo, madake *Phyllostachys bambusoides*
bamboo, marble sheath *Chimonobambusa marmorea*

bamboo, Mexican *Fallopia japonica*
bamboo, narihira *Semiarundinaria fastuosa*
bamboo, Oldham *Bambusa oldhamii*
bamboo orchid *Arundina, Thunia alba*
bamboo, painted *Bambusa vulgaris* 'Vittata'
bamboo palm *Chamaedorea costaricana*
bamboo, pygmy *Pleioblastus pygmaeus*
bamboo, Queensland *Bambusa moreheadiana*
bamboo, sacred *Nandina domestica*
bamboo speargrass *Austrostipa ramosissima*
bamboo, square *Chimonobambusa quadrangularis*
bamboo, sweet *Dendrocalamus asper*
bamboo, sweetshoot *Phyllostachys dulcis*
bamboo, Timor black *Bambusa lako*
bamboo, tropical black *Bambusa lako*
bamboo, tropical blue *Chimonobambusa falcata*
bamboo, umbrella *Fargesia murielae*
bamboo, vivax *Phyllostachys vivax*
bamboo, yellow *Phyllostachys aurea*
bamboo, yellow groove *Phyllostachys aureosulcata*
bamboo, yellow-stemmed *Bambusa vulgaris, B. v.* 'Striata'
bamboo, yellow-striped *Bambusa multiplex* 'Yellowstripe'
bamboo, zigzag *Phyllostachys flexuosa*
bamboo-leafed oak *Quercus bambusifolia*
banana *Musa acuminata, M. × paradisiaca*
banana, Abyssinian *Ensete ventricosum*
banana fig *Ficus pleurocarpa*

banana, flowering *Musa ornata*
banana, maroon-stemmed *Musa banksii*
banana, Natal wild *Strelitzia nicolai*
banana passionflower *Passiflora mollissima*
banana passionfruit *Passiflora mollissima*
banana pepper *Capsicum annuum* Longum Group
banana red *Musa acuminata* 'Red'
banana, scarlet *Musa coccinea*
banana shrub *Michelia figo*
banana, sugar *Musa acuminata* 'Ladyfinger'
banana, velvet *Musa velutina*
banana, wild *Musa balbisiana*
banana yucca *Yucca baccata*
banana, zebra *Musa acuminata* 'Zebrina'
Bancroft's wattle *Acacia bancroftii*
band plant *Vinca major*
banded nardoo *Marsilea mutica*
bandicoot grass *Monachather paradoxa*
bands, parson's *Eriochilus cucullatus*
bane, badger's *Aconitum, A. lycoctonum*
bane, leopard's *Doronicum, D. orientale*
baneberry, red *Actaea rubra*
baneberry, white *Actaea pachypoda, A. alba*
bangalay *Eucalyptus botryoides*
bangalow palm *Archontophoenix cunninghamiana*
banjo fig *Ficus lyrata*
Banks' rose, double white *Rosa banksiae* 'Alboplena'
Banks' grevillea *Grevillea banksii*
banksia, acorn *Banksia hookeriana, B. prionotes*
banksia, Albany *Banksia verticillata*

banksia, Ashby's *Banksia ashbyi*
banksia, Baxter's *Banksia baxteri*
banksia, bird's nest *Banksia baxteri*
banksia, bull *Banksia grandis*
banksia, Burdett's *Banksia burdettii*
banksia, coast *Banksia attenuata,*
   B. integrifolia
banksia, creeping *Banksia repens*
banksia, firewood *Banksia menziesii*
banksia, fox *Banksia sphaerocarpa*
banksia, granite *Banksia verticillata*
banksia, hairpin *Banksia spinulosa*
banksia, heath *Banksia ericifolia*
banksia, heath-leafed *Banksia*
   ericifolia
banksia, hill *Banksia spinulosa* var.
   collina
banksia, holly-leaf *Banksia ilicifolia*
banksia, large-leafed *Banksia robur*
banksia, mountain *Banksia canei*
banksia, nodding *Banksia nutans*
banksia, old man *Banksia serrata*
banksia, possum *Banksia baueri*
banksia, red swamp *Banksia*
   occidentalis
banksia rose *Rosa banksiae*
banksia, saw *Banksia serrata*
banksia, scarlet *Banksia coccinea*
banksia, sceptre *Banksia sceptrum*
banksia, showy *Banksia speciosa*
banksia, silver *Banksia marginata*
banksia, slender *Banksia attenuata*
banksia, southern plains *Banksia*
   media
banksia, swamp *Banksia littoralis,*
   B. robur
banksia, teddy bear *Banksia baueri*
banksia, tropical *Banksia dentata*
banksia, wallum *Banksia aemula*
banksia, woolly *Banksia baueri*
banner bean *Lablab purpureus*
banner grass, silver *Miscanthus*
   sacchariflorus

banner, golden *Thermopsis*
   rhombifolia
banyalla *Pittosporum bicolor*
banyan *Ficus benghalensis*
banyan, Australian *Ficus macrophylla*
banyan, Chinese *Ficus microcarpa*
banyan fig *Ficus benghalensis,*
   F. microcarpa
banyan, Indian *Ficus benghalensis*
baobab *Adansonia digitata*
baobab, Australian *Adansonia gibbosa*
bar room plant *Aspidistra elatior*
bara bet *Calamus viminalis*
barb grass, coast *Parapholis incurva*
Barbados cherry *Malpighia glabra*
Barbados fig *Opuntia ficus-indica*
Barbados gooseberry *Pereskia aculeata*
Barbados holly *Malpighia coccigera*
Barbados lily *Hippeastrum puniceum*
Barbados nut *Jatropha curcas*
Barbados pride *Caesalpinia*
   pulcherrima
Barbassu palm *Attalea cohune*
barbed-wire cactus *Acanthocereus*
   pentagonus
barbed-wire grass *Cymbopogon*
   refractus
barbed-wire plant *Tylecodon reticulata*
barbel palm *Acanthophoenix crinita,*
   A. rubra
barberry *Berberis, B. vulgaris*
barberry, California *Mahonia dictyota*
barberry, Darwin's *Berberis darwinii*
barberry, hybrid purple *Berberis* ×
   ottawensis 'Superba'
barberry, Japanese *Berberis thunbergii*
barberry, Korean *Berberis koreana*
barberry, purple *Berberis thunbergii*
   'Atropurpurea'
barberry, Sargent *Berberis sargentiana*
barberry, Wilson *Berberis wilsoniae*
barberry, wintergreen *Berberis*
   julianae

barber's pole oxalis *Oxalis versicolor*
Barberton daisy *Gerbera jamesonii*
bare twig-rush *Baumea juncea*
bark, Bermuda olivewood *Cassine laneana*
bark, bitter *Alstonia constricta*
bark, cosmetic *Murraya paniculata*
bark, dita *Alstonia scholaris*
bark, Georgia *Pinckneya pubens*
bark, scaly *Eucalyptus squamosa*
bark, Winter's *Drimys winteri*
barleria, gray *Barleria albostellata*
barley *Hordeum*
barley, foxtail *Hordeum jubatum*
barley grass *Hordeum leporinum*
barley grass, northern *Hordeum glaucum*
barley grass, sea *Hordeum marinum*
barley, Mediterranean *Hordeum hystrix*
barley, six row *Hordeum vulgare*
barley, squirreltail *Hordeum jubatum*
barnyard grass *Echinochloa crus-galli*
barrel cactus *Echinopsis oxygona, Ferocactus*
barrel cactus, Arizona *Ferocactus wislizeni*
barrel cactus, California *Ferocactus cylindraceus*
barrel cactus, golden *Echinocactus grusonii*
barrel medic *Medicago truncatula*
Barren Mountain mallee *Eucalyptus approximans*
barren strawberry *Potentilla sterilis, Waldsteinia fragarioides*
Barrens claw flower *Calothamnus validus*
barrenwort *Epimedium*
barrenwort, American *Vancouveria hexandra*
barreta *Fraxinus greggii*
Barrier Range wattle *Acacia beckleri*
Bartram's oak *Quercus × heterophylla*

baseball plant *Euphorbia obesa*
basil *Ocimum, O. basilicum*
basil, bush *Ocimum basilicum*
basil, camphor *Ocimum kilimandscharicum*
basil, Chinese *Perilla frutescens*
basil, hoary *Ocimum canum*
basil, holy *Ocimum tenuiflorum*
basil, Indian *Ocimum gratissimum*
basil, sacred *Ocimum tenuiflorum*
basil, small-leafed *Ocimum basilicum* 'Minimum'
basil, South American *Ocimum selloi*
basil, sweet *Ocimum basilicum*
basil, Thai *Ocimum basilicum* 'Anise'
basil thyme *Acinos arvensis*
basket flower *Adenanthos obovatus*
basket grass *Lomandra longifolia, Oplismenus*
basket grass, broad-leafed *Oplismenus aemulus*
basket grass, narrow-leafed *Oplismenus imbecillis*
basket grass, variegated *Oplismenus africanus* 'Variegatus'
basket oak *Quercus prinus*
basket of gold *Aurinia saxatilis*
basket plant *Aeschynanthus*
basket willow *Salix purpurea*
basswood *Tilia, T. americana*
basswood, European *Tilia × europaea*
basswood, highland *Tilia truncata*
basswood, white *Tilia heterophylla*
bast, Cuban *Hibiscus elatus*
bastard box *Polygala chamaebuxus*
bastard cabbage tree *Schefflera umbellifera*
bastard crow's ash *Pentaceras australe*
bastard eurabbie *Eucalyptus pseudoglobulus*
bastard indigo *Amorpha fruticosa*
bastard ipecacuanha *Asclepias curassavica*

bastard mulga *Acacia stowardii*
bastard olive *Buddleja saligna*
bastard rocket *Reseda odorata*
bastard sage *Eriogonum wrightii*
bastard tallowwood *Eucalyptus planchoniana*
bastard white mahogany *Eucalyptus psammitica*
bastard yellowwood *Afrocarpus falcatus*
Bastard's fumitory *Fumaria bastardii*
Basuto kraal aloe *Aloe striatula*
bat fern *Histiopteris incisa*
bat flower *Tacca chantrieri, T. integrifolia*
bat flower, white *Tacca integrifolia*
bat plant *Tacca integrifolia*
bat's wing coral tree *Erythrina vespertilio*
bat's wing fern *Histiopteris incisa*
bath asparagus *Ornithogalum pyrenaicum*
Bathurst burr *Xanthium spinosum*
batoko plum *Flacourtia indica*
bats-in-the-belfrey *Campanula trachelium*
baubles *Berzelia galpinii*
bauera, Grampians *Bauera sessiliflora*
Bauer's grevillea *Grevillea baueri*
bauhinia, bell *Bauhinia tomentose*
bauhinia, climbing *Bauhinia glauca*
bauhinia, Natal *Bauhinia natalensis*
bauhinia, railway fence *Bauhinia pauletia*
bauhinia, yellow bell *Bauhinia tomentosa*
bauno *Mangifera caesia*
Baxter's banksia *Banksia baxteri*
bay, Azores *Laurus azorica*
bay laurel *Laurus nobilis*
bay, loblolly *Gordonia lasianthus*
bay rum tree *Pimenta racemosa*

bay, sweet *Laurus nobilis, Magnolia virginiana*
bay tree *Laurus nobilis*
bay willow *Salix pentandra*
bayberry *Myrica pensylvanica*
bay-leafed caper tree *Capparis flexuosa*
bayonet plant *Aciphylla, A. squarrosa*
bayonet, Spanish *Yucca aloifolia, Y. baccata, Y. glauca*
bayur, maple-leafed *Pterospermum acerifolium*
bayur tree *Pterospermum acerifolium*
beach acronychia *Acronychia imperforata*
beach alyxia *Alyxia spicata*
beach aster *Erigeron glaucus*
beach bean *Canavalia rosea*
beach bird's-eye *Alectryon coriaceus*
beach clerodendrum *Clerodendrum inerme*
beach daisy *Arctotheca populifolia*
beach evening primrose *Oenothera drummondii*
beach heather *Hudsonia tomentosa*
beach hibiscus *Hibiscus tiliaceus*
beach lily *Crinum pedunculatum*
beach morning glory *Ipomoea pes-caprae*
beach pennywort *Hydrocotyle bonariensis*
beach pine *Pinus contorta*
beach plum *Prunus maritima*
beach rose *Rosa rugosa*
beach sage *Salvia aurea*
beach salvia *Salvia aurea*
beach sand verbena *Abronia umbellata*
beach screw-pine *Pandanus tectorius*
beach she-oak *Casuarina equisetifolia*
beach spinifex *Spinifex hirsutus*
beach strawberry *Fragaria chiloensis*
beach vitex *Vitex rotundifolia*

beach wormwood *Artemisia stelleriana*
bead fern *Onoclea sensibilis*
bead plant *Nertera granadensis*
bead tree *Melia azedarach*
bead tree, golden *Duranta erecta*
bead tree, Indian *Elaeocarpus sphaericus*
bead tree, red *Adenanthera pavonina*
bead vine *Crassula rupestris*
beak, kaka *Clianthus puniceus*
beak, parrot's *Lotus berthelotii*
beak, pelican's *Lotus berthelotii*
beaked filbert *Corylus cornuta*
beaked willow *Salix bebbiana*
beaked yucca *Yucca rostrata*
beaks, brown *Lyperanthus suaveolens*
bean *Phaseolus*
bean, banner *Lablab purpureus*
bean, beach *Canavalia rosea*
bean, Bengal *Mucuna deeringiana*
bean, black *Castanospermum australe, Kennedia nigricans, Lablab purpureus*
bean, blackeye *Vigna unguiculata*
bean, bog *Menyanthes trifoliata*
bean, broad *Vicia faba*
bean, buck *Menyanthes trifoliata*
bean, calabar *Physostigma venenosum*
bean, caper *Zygophyllum*
bean, Cherokee *Erythrina herbacea*
bean, coastal jack *Canavalia rosea*
bean, coral *Erythrina herbacea*
bean, desert *Phaseolus acutifolius*
bean, dune *Vigna marina*
bean, Dutch case-knife *Phaseolus coccineus*
bean, eastern coral *Erythrina herbacea*
bean, Egyptian *Lablab purpureus*
bean, four-angled *Psophocarpus tetragonobolus*
bean, French *Phaseolus vulgaris*

bean, garbanzo *Cicer arietinum*
bean, green *Phaseolus vulgaris*
bean, hog's *Hyoscyamus niger*
bean, horse *Vicia faba*
bean, Hottentot *Schotia brachypetala*
bean, hyacinth *Lablab purpureus*
bean, ice-cream *Inga edulis*
bean, Indian *Lablab purpureus*
bean, Indian coral *Erythrina variegata*
bean, Java glory *Clerodendrum speciosissimum*
bean, kidney *Phaseolus vulgaris*
bean, lablab *Lablab purpureus*
bean, Leichhardt *Cassia brewsteri*
bean, lima *Phaseolus lunatus*
bean, Manchurian *Glycine max*
bean, mescal *Sophora secundiflora*
bean, mung *Vigna radiata*
bean, phasey *Macroptilium lathyroides*
bean plant, castor *Ricinus communis*
bean, precatory *Abrus precatorius*
bean, Queensland black *Castanospermum australe*
bean, red *Dysoxylum mollissimum, Geissois benthamiana*
bean, scarlet runner *Phaseolus coccineus*
bean, snail *Vigna caracalla*
bean, soja *Glycine max*
bean, soya *Glycine max*
bean, string *Phaseolus vulgaris*
bean, tepary *Phaseolus acutifolius* var. *latifolius*
bean, Texas *Phaseolus acutifolius*
bean, tonka *Dipteryx odorata*
bean tree *Catalpa bignonioides, Schotia latifolia*
bean tree, bell *Markhamia zanzibarica*
bean tree, elephant hedge *Schotia latifolia*
bean tree, Indian *Catalpa bignonioides*

bean, white *Ailanthus triphysa*

bean, wild tepary *Phaseolus acutifolius*

bean, yam *Pachyrhizus erosus,*
P. tuberosus

bean, yard-long *Vigna unguiculata*
subsp. *sesquipedalis*

beans, paternoster *Abrus precatorius*

bear oak *Quercus ilicifolia*

bearberry *Arctostaphylos uva-ursi*

bearberry, alpine *Arctostaphylos alpina*

bearberry, Arctic *Arctostaphylos alpina*

bearberry, black *Arctostaphylos alpina*

bearberry cotoneaster *Cotoneaster*
dammeri

bearberry willow *Salix uva-ursi*

bearclover, southern *Chamaebatia*
australis

beard, Aaron's *Hypericum calycinum*

beard, goat's *Aruncus dioicus,*
Tragopogon

beard, Jupiter's *Anthyllis barba-jovis,*
Centranthus ruber

beard, lion's *Geum triflorum*

beard, old man's *Clematis, Tillandsia*
usneoides

beard tongue *Penstemon*

bearded bellflower *Campanula*
barbata

bearded iris *Iris × germanica*

bearded iris, dwarf *Iris pumila*

bearded oat *Avena barbata*

bearded protea *Protea magnifica*

beardgrass, perennial *Polypogon*
littoralis

beard-heath *Leucopogon*

beard-heath, blunt *Leucopogon*
muticus

beard-heath, heart-leafed *Leucopogon*
amplexicaulis

beard-heath, lance-leaf *Leucopogon*
lanceolatus

beard-heath, long-flowered
Leucopogon juniperinus

beard-heath, mountain *Leucopogon*
suaveolens

beard-heath, subalpine *Leucopogon*
maccraei

beardless bog-rush *Schoenus imberbis*

beardlip *Penstemon barbatus*

beard-orchid, copper *Calochilus*
campestris

beard-orchid, purplish *Calochilus*
robertsonii

beard-orchid, red *Calochilus*
paludosus

beardtongue, Alamo *Penstemon*
alamosensis

beardtongue, foxglove *Penstemon*
digitalis

beardtongue, large *Penstemon*
grandiflorus

beardtongue, southwestern
Penstemon laevis

beardtongue, stiff *Penstemon*
strictus

beargrass *Nolina bigelovii,*
N. microcarpa, Xerophyllum tenax

beargrass, Parry's *Nolina parryi*

bear's breeches *Acanthus, A. mollis*

bear's ear *Cymbonotus lawsonianus,*
Primula auricula

bear's foot *Alchemilla, Helleborus*
foetidus

bear's foot fern *Humata tyermannii*

bear's paw *Cotyledon tomentosa*

bear's paw fern *Aglaomorpha*
meyeniana

bearskin grass *Festuca eskia*

bearwort *Meum*

Beatrice watsonia *Watsonia pillansii*

beautiful fir *Abies amabilis*

beauty berry *Callicarpa*

beauty berry, American *Callicarpa*
americana

beauty berry, bigleaf *Callicarpa*
macrophylla

beauty berry, Chinese *Callicarpa rubella*
beauty berry, Japanese *Callicarpa japonica*
beauty berry, purple *Callicarpa dichotoma*
beauty, bower of *Pandorea jasminoides*
beauty bush *Callicarpa, Kolkwitzia amabilis*
beauty bush, American *Callicarpa americana*
beauty bush, Chinese *Callicarpa rubella*
beauty bush, Japanese *Callicarpa japonica*
beauty bush, purple *Callicarpa dichotoma*
beauty buttons *Leptorhynchos tetrachaetus*
beauty, flaming *Carphalea kirondron*
beauty leaf *Calophyllum inophyllum*
beauty, spring *Claytonia, C. virginica*
beauty-heads, pale *Calocephalus sonderi*
beaver tail cactus *Opuntia basilaris*
bechtel crab *Malus ioensis* 'Plena'
bedding alternanthera *Alternanthera bettzichiana*
bedding alyssum *Lobularia maritima*
bedding begonia *Begonia* Semperflorens-cultorum Group
bedding forget-me-not *Myosotis sylvatica*
bedding geranium *Pelargonium* Zonal Hybrids
bedding lobelia *Lobelia erinus*
bedding pansy *Viola cornuta*
bedstraw *Galium, Galium aparine*
bedstraw, lady's *Galium verum*
bedstraw, yellow *Galium verum*
bee balm *Melissa officinalis, Monarda, M. didyma*

bee sage *Salvia apiana*
beech, American *Fagus grandifolia*
beech, Antarctic *Nothofagus antarctica, N. moorei*
beech, Australian *Nothofagus moorei*
beech, black *Nothofagus solanderi*
beech, blue *Carpinus caroliniana*
beech, broad-leafed *Faurea speciosa*
beech, brown *Cryptocarya rigida, Pennantia cunninghamii*
beech, Chilean *Nothofagus obliqua*
beech, Chinese *Fagus engleriana*
beech, common *Fagus sylvatica*
beech, copper *Fagus sylvatica* 'Purpurea'
beech, cut-leaf *Fagus sylvatica* 'Rohanii'
beech, dwarf Chilean *Nothofagus pumilio*
beech, European *Fagus sylvatica*
beech, Gunn's *Nothofagus gunnii*
beech, hard *Nothofagus truncata*
beech, Indian *Pongamia pinnata*
beech, Japanese *Fagus crenata*
beech, Japanese blue *Fagus japonica*
beech, mountain *Nothofagus solandri*
beech, myrtle *Nothofagus cunninghamii*
beech, New Zealand *Nothofagus solanderi*
beech, New Zealand red *Nothofagus fusca*
beech, New Zealand silver *Nothofagus menziesii*
beech orchid *Dendrobium falcorostrum*
beech, oriental *Fagus orientalis*
beech, purple *Fagus sylvatica* 'Purpurea'
beech, Queensland red *Dillenia alata*
beech, red *Dillenia alata, Nothofagus fusca*

beech, roble *Nothofagus obliqua*
beech, southern *Nothofagus*
beech, tanglefoot *Nothofagus gunnii*
beech, Tasmanian *Nothofagus cunninghamii*
beech, tortuous *Fagus sylvatica* 'Tortuosa'
beech, Transvaal *Faurea saligna*
beech, weeping *Fagus sylvatica* 'Pendula'
beech, white *Gmelina leichardtii*
beechy bamboo *Bambusa beecheyana*
beef plant *Iresine herbstii*
beefsteak begonia *Begonia* × *erythrophylla*
beefsteak geranium *Begonia* Rex-cultorum Group
beefsteak heliconia *Heliconia mariae*
beefsteak plant *Iresine herbstii, Perilla frutescens*
beefwood *Grevillea striata*
beefwood, scrub *Grevillea baileyana, Stenocarpus salignus*
beehive cactus *Escobaria vivipara*
beehive ginger *Zingiber spectabile*
beet *Beta, B. vulgaris*
beet, silver *Beta vulgaris*
beet, wild *Beta vulgaris* subsp. *maritima*
beetle grass, brown *Diplachne fusca*
beetle grass, small-flowered *Diplachne parviflora*
beetroot *Beta vulgaris* subsp. *vulgaris*
beggar's tick *Bidens*
beggar's ticks, bipinnate *Bidens bipinnata*
beggar's ticks, greater *Bidens subalternans*
beggarticks, Apache *Bidens ferulifolia*
begonia *Begonia*
begonia, angel-wing *Begonia coccinea*
begonia, bedding *Begonia* Semperflorens-cultorum Group

begonia, beefsteak *Begonia* × *erythrophylla*
begonia, Christmas *Begonia* × *cheimantha* 'Gloire de Lorraine'
begonia, Evans' *Begonia grandis*
begonia, eyelash *Begonia bowerae*
begonia, fuchsia *Begonia fuchsioides*
begonia, grapeleaf *Begonia dregei*
begonia, hardy *Begonia grandis*
begonia, hollyhock *Begonia gracilis*
begonia, Iron Cross *Begonia masoniana*
begonia, kidney *Begonia* × *erythrophylla*
begonia, king *Begonia rex*
begonia, leopard *Begonia manicata* 'Aureo-maculata'
begonia, Lorraine *Begonia* × *cheimantha* 'Gloire de Lorraine'
begonia, maple-leafed *Begonia dregei*
begonia, painted-leaf *Begonia rex*
begonia, piggyback *Begonia hispida* var. *cucullifera*
begonia, shrimp *Begonia radicans*
begonia, small-leafed *Begonia fuchsioides*
begonia, strawberry *Saxifraga stolonifera*
begonia, Swedish *Plectranthus australis*
begonia, tree *Begonia coccinea*
begonia, watermelon *Pellionia daveauana, Peperomia argyreia*
begonias, rex *Begonia* Rex-cultorum Hybrids
belah *Casuarina cristata, C. pauper*
Belgian evergreen *Dracaena sanderiana*
bell, Asian *Radermachera sinica*
bell bauhinia *Bauhinia tomentose*
bell bean tree *Markhamia zanzibarica*

bell gardenia *Rothmannia globosa*
bell heather *Erica cinerea*
bell pepper *Capsicum annuum*
bell, stink *Fritillaria agrestis*
bell, straw *Uvularia perfoliata*
bell vine, purple *Rhodochiton atrosanguineus*
bell, willow *Campanula persicifolia*
bella sombra tree *Phytolacca dioica*
belladonna *Atropa belladonna*
belladonna lily *Amaryllis belladonna*
belle de nuit *Ipomoea alba*
bellflower *Campanula*
bellflower, Adriatic *Campanula elatines*
bellflower, Asian *Radermarchera sinica*
bellflower, Azores *Campanula vidalii*
bellflower, bearded *Campanula barbata*
bellflower, bonnet *Codonopsis*
bellflower, Brazilian *Abutilon megapotamicum*
bellflower, Canary *Canarina canariensis*
bellflower, Canary Island *Canarina canariensis*
bellflower, Carpathian *Campanula carpatica*
bellflower, Chilean *Lapageria rosea, Nolana*
bellflower, chimney *Campanula pyramidalis*
bellflower, Chinese *Platycodon grandiflorus*
bellflower, clustered *Campanula glomerata*
bellflower, Dalmatian *Campanula portenschlagiana*
bellflower, giant *Campanula latifolia, C. l.* var. *macrantha*
bellflower, great *Campanula latifolia*

bellflower, Italian *Campanula isophylla*
bellflower, milky *Campanula lactiflora*
bellflower, nettle-leaf *Campanula trachelium*
bellflower, ring *Symphyandra*
bellflower, Serbian *Campanula poscharskyana*
bellflower, trailing *Cyananthus*
bellflower, tussock *Campanula carpatica*
bellflower, willow *Campanula persicifolia*
bellflower, window *Campanula fenestrellata*
bell-flowered gardenia *Rothmannia globosa*
bellfruit tree *Codonocarpus attenuatus*
bell-fruited mallee *Eucalyptus preissiana*
Bellinger River fig *Ficus watkinsiana*
bellis daisy *Bellis perennis*
bellota *Sterculia apetala*
bells, Canterbury *Campanula medium*
bells, cathedral *Cobaea scandens*
bells, Christmas *Blandfordia, B. grandiflora, B. nobilis, Sandersonia aurantiaca*
bells, coral *Heuchera*
bells, Coventry *Campanula trachelium*
bells, fairy *Disporum, Melasphaerula*
bells, fringe *Shortia soldanelloides*
bells, golden *Forsythia* × *intermedia, F. viridissima*
bells, grassy *Edraianthus*
bells, jungle *Fieldia australis*
bells, mission *Fritillaria biflora*
bells, Oconee *Shortia galacifolia*
bells of Ireland *Moluccella laevis*

bells, pink *Tetratheca ciliata,*
  T. ericifolia
bells, Qualup *Pimelea physodes*
bells, Roanoke *Mertensia virginica*
bells, rock *Aquilegia canadensis*
bells, scented *Rothmannia manganjae*
bells, September *Rothmannia globosa*
bells, sweet *Leucothoe racemosa*
bells, yellow *Tecoma stans*
bellwort *Uvularia, U. grandiflora*
bellwort, large-flowered *Uvularia*
  grandiflora
bellwort, perfoliate *Uvularia*
  perfoliata
bellwort, sessile *Uvularia sessilifolia*
bellyache bush *Jatropha gossypifolia*
Belmore kentia palm *Howea*
  belmoreana
Belmore palm *Howea belmoreana*
belvedere *Bassia scoparia*
Bendemeer white gum *Eucalyptus*
  elliptica
Bendigo wax flower *Philotheca*
  verrucosa
Bengal bean *Mucuna deeringiana*
Bengal clock vine *Thunbergia*
  grandiflora
Benjamin fig *Ficus benjamina*
Benjamin tree *Ficus benjamina*
benne *Sesamum orientale*
bennet, herb *Geum urbanum*
Bennett's ash *Flindersia bennettiana*
ben-oil tree *Moringa oleifera*
bent, browntop *Agrostis capillaris*
bent, creeping *Agrostis stolonifera*
bent grass *Agrostis*
bent grass, reed *Deyeuxia quadriseta*
bent, redtop *Agrostis gigantea*
bent trillium *Trillium flexipes*
bent, water *Agrostis viridis*
Bentham's cornel *Cornus capitata*
bent-leaf wattle *Acacia flexifolia*
benzoin *Styrax benzoin*

berberis, chalk-leaf *Mahonia dictyota*
bergaalwyn *Aloe marlothii*
bergamot *Monarda, M. didyma*
bergamot, lemon *Monarda citriodora*
bergamot orange *Citrus* × *bergamia*
bergenia, hairy *Bergenia ciliata*
bergkankerbossie *Sutherlandia*
  montana
bergvy *Ficus glumosa*
Berlandier's acacia *Acacia berlandieri*
Berlin poplar *Populus* × *berolinensis*
Bermuda buttercup *Oxalis pes-caprae*
Bermuda cedar *Juniperus bermudiana*
Bermuda grass *Cynodon dactylon*
Bermuda grass, Magennis *Cynodon* ×
  magennisii
Bermuda lily *Lilium longiflorum*
Bermuda olivewood bark *Cassine*
  laneana
Bermuda palmetto *Sabal bermudana*
berrigan *Pittosporum phylliraeoides*
berry, apple *Billardiera scandens*
berry, beauty *Callicarpa*
berry bladder fern *Cystopteris*
  bulbifera
berry, buffalo *Shepherdia argentea,*
  S. canadensis
berry, bush-tick *Chrysanthemoides*
  monilifera
berry, cheese *Cyathodes glauca*
berry, Christmas *Chironia baccifera,*
  Heteromeles arbutifolia
berry, coral *Ilex verticillata*
berry, crake *Empetrum nigrum*
berry, curlew *Empetrum nigrum*
berry, emu *Eremophila duttonii,*
  Podocarpus drouynianus
berry, golden *Physalis peruviana*
berry, Japanese beauty *Callicarpa*
  japonica
berry, kooboo *Cassine sphaerophylla*
berry, lime *Triphasia trifolia*
berry, male *Lyonia ligustrina*

berry, miracle *Synsepalum dulcificum*
berry, oso *Oemleria cerasiformis*
berry, partridge *Mitchella repens*
berry, pigeon *Duranta erecta*
berry, pink mountain *Leucopogon parviflorus*
berry saltbush *Einadia hastata*
berry, sapphire *Symplocos paniculata*
berry, silver buffalo *Shepherdia argentea*
berry, tassel *Antidesma venosum*
berry, turquoise *Drymophila cyanocarpa*
berry, water *Syzygium cordatum*
berry, wombat *Eustrephus latifolius*
berry-bearing alder *Frangula alnus*
besom heath *Erica scoparia*
be-still tree *Thevetia thevetioides*
betel *Piper betle*
betel palm *Areca catechu*
Bethlehem, star of *Campanula isophylla, Ornithogalum*
bethroot *Trillium erectum*
betle pepper *Piper betle*
betony *Stachys, S. officinalis*
betony, big *Stachys macrantha*
betony, water *Scrophularia auriculata*
betony, wood *Stachys officinalis*
betony, woolly *Stachys byzantina*
Betsy, sweet *Trillium cuneatum*
betung, pring *Dendrocalamus asper*
Beyer's ironbark *Eucalyptus beyeriana*
bhatavari *Asparagus racemosus*
Bhutan cypress *Cupressus cashmeriana, C. torulosa*
Bhutan pine *Pinus wallichiana*
bicacaro *Canarina canariensis*
bicolor sage *Salvia semiatrata*
bicolored ice plant *Drosanthemum bicolor*
bicolored lotus *Lotus formosissimus*
biddy biddy *Acaena, A. novae-zelandiae*

biddy bush *Cassinia arcuata*
bidgee-widgee *Acaena novae-zelandiae*
big badja gum *Eucalyptus badjensis*
big betony *Stachys macrantha*
big blue flax-lily *Dianella prunina*
big blue lobelia *Lobelia siphilitica*
big merrybells *Uvularia grandiflora*
big mountain palm *Hedyscepe canterburyana*
big sagebrush *Seriphidium tridentatum*
big shellbark hickory *Carya laciniosa*
big stinging nettle *Urtica dioica*
big tree *Sequoiadendron giganteum*
bigberry manzanita *Arctostaphylos glauca*
bigbud hickory *Carya tomentosa*
big-cone pine *Pinus coulteri*
bigflower *Prunella grandiflora*
big-horn euphorbia *Euphorbia grandicornis*
bigleaf beauty berry *Callicarpa macrophylla*
bigleaf groundsel *Telanthophora grandifolia*
bigleaf hydrangea *Hydrangea macrophylla*
bigleaf linden *Tilia platyphyllos*
bigleaf magnolia *Magnolia macrophylla*
bigleaf snowbell *Styrax grandifolia*
bigleaf storax *Styrax obassia*
bignay *Antidesma bunius*
bignonia, pink *Clytostoma callistegioides*
bigtooth aspen *Populus grandidentata*
bigtooth maple *Acer grandidentatum*
big-toothed euphorbia *Euphorbia grandidens*
big-tree plum *Prunus mexicana*
bilberry *Vaccinium myrtillus*
bilberry, bog *Vaccinium uliginosum*
bilberry cactus *Myrtillocactus geometrizans*

bilberry, dwarf *Vaccinium caespitosum*
bilimbi *Averrhoa bilimbi*
bill, parrot's *Clianthus puniceus*
billwort *Ammi majus*
billy buttons *Calocephalus, Craspedia, Pycnosorus*
billy buttons, yellow *Calocephalus platycephalus*
Biltmore ash *Fraxinus biltmoreana*
bimble box *Eucalyptus populnea*
bimli *Hibiscus cannabinus*
bindi-eye *Calotis cuneifolia, Soliva sessilis*
bindii *Soliva sessilis*
bindweed *Convolvulus arvensis*
bindweed, Australian *Convolvulus erubescens*
bindweed, blushing *Convolvulus erubescens*
bindweed, pink *Convolvulus erubescens*
bindweed, sea *Calystegia soldanella*
bine *Humulus lupulus*
binjai *Mangifera caesia*
binung *Christella dentata*
biota *Platycladus orientalis*
bipinnate beggar's ticks *Bidens bipinnata*
birch *Betula*
birch, Alaskan paper *Betula kenaica*
birch, American dwarf *Betula pumila*
birch, American red *Betula fontinalis*
birch, Arctic *Betula nana*
birch, Asian black *Betula dahurica*
birch, black *Betula lenta*
birch, blue *Betula × caerulea*
birch, brown *Scolopia braunii*
birch, canoe *Betula papyrifera*
birch, cherry *Betula lenta*
birch, Chinese red *Betula albosinensis*
birch, cut-leaf *Betula pendula* 'Dalecarlica'
birch, downy *Betula pubescens*

birch, dwarf *Betula nana*
birch, Erman's *Betula ermanii*
birch, European silver *Betula pendula*
birch, European white *Betula pendula*
birch, gold *Betula ermanii*
birch, gray *Betula populifolia*
birch, Himalayan *Betula utilis*
birch, Japanese cherry *Betula grossa*
birch, Kenai *Betula kenaica*
birch leaf pelargonium *Pelargonium betulinum*
birch, Manchurian *Betula mandschurica*
birch, monarch *Betula maximovicziana*
birch, paper *Betula papyrifera*
birch, resin *Betula glandulosa*
birch, river *Betula nigra*
birch, Russian rock *Betula ermanii*
birch, silver *Betula pendula*
birch, sweet *Betula lenta*
birch, Transcaucasian *Betula medwedewii*
birch, tropical *Betula nigra*
birch, water *Betula fontinalis, B. occidentalis*
birch, weeping *Betula pendula* 'Youngii'
birch, western *Betula occidentalis*
birch, white *Betula pendula, B. papyrifera, Schizomeria ovata*
birch, yellow *Betula alleghaniensis, B. lutea*
birch, Young's weeping *Betula pendula* 'Youngii'
birch-bark cherry *Prunus serrula*
birch-leaf *Pyrus betulifolia*
birch-leaf geranium *Pelargonium betulinum*
birch-leaf pear *Pyrus betulifolia*
birch-leaf spiraea *Spiraea betulifolia*
bird cherry *Prunus padus*

bird cherry, American *Prunus virginiana*
bird cherry, European *Prunus padus*
bird cherry, Himalayan *Prunus cornuta*
bird cherry, Mexican *Prunus salicifolia*
bird flower *Crotalaria agatiflora*
bird of paradise *Strelitzia reginae*
bird of paradise, false *Heliconia*
bird of paradise, giant *Strelitzia nicolai*
bird of paradise, leafless *Strelitzia juncea*
bird of paradise shrub *Caesalpinia gilliesii*
bird orchid *Chiloglottis*
bird rape *Brassica rapa*
bird vine, canary *Tropaeolum*
birdcatcher tree *Pisonia brunoniana, P. umbelliffera*
birdlime tree *Cordia dichotoma, Pisonia grandis, P. umbellifera*
bird's eye *Apodytes dimidiata, Gilia tricolor, Veronica chamaedrys*
bird's eye, beach *Alectryon coriaceus*
bird's eye, hairy *Alectryon tomentosus*
bird's eye primrose *Primula farinosa*
bird's foot, seaside *Lotus formosissimus*
bird's foot trefoil *Lotus corniculatus, L. uliginosus*
bird's foot viola *Viola pedata*
bird's foot violet *Viola pedata*
bird's mouth orchid *Orthoceras strictum*
bird's nest banksia *Banksia baxteri*
bird's nest bromeliad *Nidularium fulgens*
bird's nest fern *Asplenium australasicum, A. nidus*
bird's nest fern, climbing *Microsorum punctatum*

bird's tongue flower *Strelitzia reginae*
bird's-foot trefoil, hairy *Lotus suaveolens*
bird's-foot trefoil, slender *Lotus angustissimus*
birdwood grass *Cenchrus setiger*
birthwort *Aristolochia clematitis, Trillium erectum*
birthwort, frail *Aristolochia debilis*
bishop pine *Pinus muricata*
bishop's cap *Astrophytum myriostigma, Mitella*
bishop's hat *Epimedium*
bishop's miter *Astrophytum myriostigma, Epimedium*
bishop's weed *Aegopodium podagraria, Ammi majus*
bishop's weed, false *Ammi majus*
bishop's wort *Stachys officinalis*
bishopwood *Bischofia javanica*
bisnaga *Ammi visnaga*
bistort *Persicaria bistorta*
bistort, alpine *Persicaria vivipara*
bistort, American *Persicaria bistortoides*
bit, sheep's *Jasione laevis*
bitou bush *Chrysanthemoides monilifera, C. m.* subsp. *rotundata*
bitter aloe *Aloe ferox*
bitter apple *Citrullus colocynthis*
bitter bark *Alstonia constricta*
bitter cassava *Manihot esculenta*
bitter cherry, Oregon *Prunus emarginata*
bitter cress *Cardamine*
bitter gourd *Momordica charantia*
bitter melon *Citrullus lanatus*
bitter, mishmii *Coptis chinensis*
bitter orange *Citrus aurantium, Poncirus trifoliata*
bitter pea, blunt-leaf *Daviesia mimosoides*
bitter pea, gorse *Daviesia ulicifolia*

bitter pea, hop *Daviesia latifolia*
bitter pea, narrow-leaf *Daviesia mimosoides*
bitter quandong *Santalum murrayanum*
bitter rattan *Calamus viminalis*
bitter root *Lewisia rediviva*
bitter saltbush *Atriplex stipitata*
bitter sneezeweed *Helenium amarum*
bitter vine *Piptocalyx moorei*
bitterbush, coast *Adriana klotzschii*
bitterbush, eastern *Adriana glabrata*
bitterbush, mallee *Adriana hookeri*
bittercress, common *Cardamine hirsuta*
bittercress, slender *Cardamine tenuifolia*
bittercress, wood *Cardamine flexuosa*
bitternut hickory *Carya cordiformis*
bitter-pea, sandplain *Daviesia acicularis*
bitter-pea, slender *Daviesia leptophylla*
bittersweet, American *Celastrus scandens*
bittersweet, oriental *Celastrus orbicularis*
bitterwood *Quassia amara*
black alder *Alnus glutinosa, Ilex verticillata*
black apple *Pouteria australis*
black apricot *Prunus × dasycarpa*
black arum *Arum palaestinum*
black ash *Fraxinus nigra*
black bamboo *Phyllostachys nigra*
black bamboo, Timor *Bambusa lako*
black bamboo, tropical *Bambusa lako*
black bean *Castanospermum australe, Kennedia nigricans, Lablab purpureus*
black bean, Queensland *Castanospermum australe*

black bean tree *Castanospermum australe*
black bearberry *Arctostaphylos alpina*
black beech *Nothofagus solanderi*
black birch *Betula lenta*
black birch, Asian *Betula dahurica*
black bluebush *Maireana pyramidata*
black bog-rush *Schoenus melanostachys*
black box *Eucalyptus largiflorens*
black calabash *Amphitecna latifolia*
black caraway *Pimpinella saxifraga*
black cherry *Prunus serotina*
black cherry plum *Prunus cerasifera* 'Nigra'
black chokeberry *Aronia melanocarpa*
black columbine *Aquilegia atrata*
black coral pea *Kennedia nigricans*
black cosmos *Cosmos atrosanguineus*
black cottonbush *Maireana decalvans*
black cottonwood *Populus heterophylla, P. trichocarpa*
black crowberry *Empetrum nigrum*
black crumbweed *Chenopodium melanocarpum*
black cumin *Nigella sativa*
black cutch *Acacia catechu*
black cypress-pine *Callitris endlicheri*
black dalea *Dalea frutescens*
black elder *Sambucus nigra*
black false hellebore *Veratrum nigrum*
black fritillary *Fritillaria biflora*
black gram *Vigna mungo*
black gum *Eucalyptus aggregata, Nyssa sylvatica*
black haw *Bumelia lanuginosa, Viburnum prunifolium*
black haw, southern *Viburnum rufidulum*
black hawthorn *Crataegus douglasii*
black hellebore *Veratrum nigrum*
black henbane *Hyoscyamus niger*
black hickory *Carya texana*

black highbush blueberry *Vaccinium atrococcum*

black horehound *Ballota nigra*

black huckleberry *Gaylussacia baccata, Vaccinium atrococcum*

black ironbox *Eucalyptus raveretiana*

black ironwood *Olea capensis*

black Jessie *Pithecellobium unguis-cati*

black juniper, Himalayan *Juniperus indica*

black kangaroo paw *Macropidia fulginosa*

black locust *Robinia pseudoacacia*

black lovage *Smyrnium olusatrum*

black mangrove *Bruguiera gymnorhiza*

black medic *Medicago lupulina*

black mondo grass *Ophiopogon planiscapus* 'Nigrescens'

black monkey thorn *Acacia burkei*

black mulberry *Morus nigra*

black mustard *Brassica nigra*

black oak *Quercus velutina*

black oliveberry *Elaeocarpus holopetalus*

black or white pepper *Piper nigrum*

black palm, Queensland *Normanbya normanbyi*

black penda *Xanthostemon chrysanthus*

black peppermint, narrow-leafed *Eucalyptus nicholii*

black peppermint, Tasmanian *Eucalyptus amygdalina*

black persimmon *Diospyros digyna*

black pigweed *Trianthema portulacastrum*

black pine *Pinus nigra*

black pine, Austrian *Pinus nigra*

black pine, New Zealand *Podocarpus taxifolia*

black plum *Diospyros australis*

black poplar *Populus nigra*

black poplar, American *Populus deltoides*

black protea *Protea lepidocarpodendron*

black raspberry *Rubus occidentalis*

black rolypoly *Sclerolaena muricata* var. *semiglabra*

black roseau *Bactris major*

black sage *Salvia mellifera*

black sally *Eucalyptus stellulata*

black salsify *Scorzonera hispanica*

black sapote *Diospyros digyna*

black sarana *Fritillaria camschatcensis*

black sassafras *Atherosperma moschatum*

black seed *Nigella sativa*

black she-oak *Allocasuarina littoralis*

black spruce, American *Picea mariana*

black stem maidenhair *Adiantum formosum*

black tea-tree *Melaleuca bracteata, M. lanceolata*

black titi *Cyrilla racemiflora*

black toothbrushes *Grevillea hookeriana*

black tree fern *Cyathea medullaris*

black tupelo *Nyssa sylvatica*

black velvet *Colubrina arborescens*

black walnut *Endiandra globosa, Juglans nigra*

black walnut, Hinds' *Juglans hindsii*

black wattle *Acacia decurrens, Callicoma serratifolia*

black wattle, Queensland *Acacia leiocalyx*

black wattle, western *Acacia hakeoides*

black widow *Geranium phaeum*

black willow *Salix nigra*

blackberry *Rubus*

blackberry, kittatinny *Rubus bellobatus*

blackberry lily *Belamcanda chinensis*
blackberry nightshade *Solanum americanum, S. nigrum*
blackberry rose *Rosa rubus*
blackbrush *Coleogyne ramosissima*
blackbutt *Eucalyptus pilularis*
blackbutt, large-fruited *Eucalyptus pyrocarpa*
blackbutt, New England *Eucalyptus andrewsii, E. campanulata*
blackbutt, Western Australian *Eucalyptus patens*
blackcap *Rubus occidentalis*
blackcurrant *Ribes nigrum*
blackcurrant, American *Ribes americanum*
blackcurrant, Chilean *Ribes gayanum*
Blackdown bottlebrush *Callistemon pearsonii*
Blackdown fan palm *Livistona fulva*
blackeye bean *Vigna unguiculata*
black-eyed Susan *Rudbeckia, R. fulgida, R. hirta, Tetratheca, Thunbergia alata*
black-eyed Susan vine *Thunbergia alata*
blackfoot daisy *Melampodium leucanthum*
black-fruit saw-sedge *Gahnia melanocarpa*
blackhaw viburnum *Viburnum prunifolium*
blackhaw viburnum, rusty *Viburnum rufidulum*
blackjack oak *Quercus marilandica*
blackleaf podocarp *Podocarpus neriifolius*
blackroot *Veronicastrum virginicum*
blackseed panic *Panicum bisulcatum*
black-spine prickly pear *Opuntia macrocentra*
black-stem water fern *Blechnum nudum*

blackthorn *Prunus spinosa*
blackthorn, Australian *Bursaria spinosa*
blackwood *Acacia melanoxylon*
bladder campion *Silene uniflora, S. vulgaris*
bladder cherry *Physalis alkekengi*
bladder fern, berry *Cystopteris bulbifera*
bladder ketmia *Hibiscus trionum*
bladder pea, Cape *Sutherlandia frutescens*
bladder saltbush *Atriplex vesicaria*
bladder senna *Colutea arborescens*
bladdernut *Diospyros whyteana, Staphylea*
bladdernut, American *Staphylea trifolia*
bladdernut, Caucasian *Staphylea colchica*
bladdernut, Chinese *Staphylea holocarpa*
bladdernut, eastern *Staphylea trifolia*
bladdernut, European *Staphylea pinnata*
bladdernut, Japanese *Staphylea bumalda*
bladderwort *Utricularia*
bladderwort, alpine *Utricularia alpina*
bladderwort, floating *Utricularia inflata*
bladderwrack *Sargassum fusiforme*
blady grass *Imperata cylindrica*
blaeberry *Vaccinium myrtillus*
Blakely's red gum *Eucalyptus blakelyi*
blanca, anona *Annona diversifolia*
blanche, pomme *Psoralea esculenta*
blanket fern *Pleurosorus rutifolius*
blanket flower *Gaillardia, G. pulchella*
blanket, Indian *Gaillardia pulchella*

blanket leaf *Bedfordia arborescens*
blanketgrass *Melinis repens*
blazing star *Liatris, L. aspera,*
L. spicata, Tritonia crocata
blazing star, rough *Liatris aspera*
bleeding heart *Dicentra, D. spectabilis*
bleeding heart tree *Omalanthus*
populifolius
bleeding heart vine *Clerodendrum*
thomsoniae
bleeding heart, wild *Dicentra formosa*
blessed thistle *Silybum marianum*
Blireana plum *Prunus* × *blireana*
blonde Lilian *Erythronium albidum*
blood, Ashanti *Mussaenda*
erythrophylla
blood flower *Asclepias curassavica*
blood flower, Mexican *Distictis*
buccinatoria
blood lily *Haemanthus coccineus,*
Scadoxus, S. multiflorus
blood orange *Citrus aurantium*
'Blood'
blood trumpet, Mexican *Distictis*
buccinatoria
blood vine *Austrosteenisia blackii*
blood-in-the-bark *Baloghia inophylla*
bloodleaf *Iresine, I. lindenii,*
I. herbstii
blood-red heath *Erica cruenta*
blood-red tassel flower *Calliandra*
haematocephala
blood-red tea-tree *Leptospermum*
spectabile
blood-red trumpet vine *Distictis*
buccinatoria
bloodroot *Haemodorum corymbosum,*
Sanguinaria, S. canadensis
bloodroot, strapleaf *Haemodorum*
planifolium
bloodwing dogwood *Cornus sanguinea*
bloodwood, brown *Corymbia*
trachyphloia

bloodwood, brush *Baloghia inophylla*
bloodwood, long-fruited *Corymbia*
dolichocarpa
bloodwood, pale *Corymbia terminalis*
bloodwood, pink *Corymbia*
intermedia
bloodwood, red *Corymbia gummifera*
bloodwood, swamp *Corymbia*
ptychocarpa
bloodwood, western *Corymbia*
terminalis
bloodwood, white *Corymbia*
trachyphloia
bloodwood, yellow *Corymbia eximia*
bloodwort, burnet *Sanguisorba*
officinalis
bloody cranesbill *Geranium*
sanguineum
bloody dock *Rumex sanguineus*
blotchy mint bush *Prostanthera*
walteri
bloubos *Diospyros lycioides*
blowball *Taraxacum officinale*
blown grass *Agrostis aemula,*
A. avenacea
blown grass, coast *Agrostis billardieri*
blue African lily *Agapanthus africanus*
blue amaryllis *Worsleya rayneri*
blue ash *Fraxinus quadrangulata*
blue Atlantic cedar *Cedrus atlantica*
'Glauca'
blue Atlas cedar *Cedrus atlantica*
'Glauca'
blue ball sage *Salvia clevelandii*
blue bedder penstemon *Penstemon*
heterophyllus
blue beech *Carpinus caroliniana*
blue birch *Betula* × *caerulea*
blue blossom ceanothus *Ceanothus*
thyrsiflorus
blue boronia *Boronia caerulescens*
blue bottle-daisy *Lagenifera stipitata*
blue box *Eucalyptus baueriana*

blue brush *Ceanothus thyrsiflorus*
blue bugle *Ajuga genevensis*
blue burr daisy *Calotis cuneifolia*
blue butterfly bush *Clerodendrum ugandense*
blue candle *Myrtillocactus geometrizans*
blue cardinal flower *Lobelia siphilitica*
blue chalksticks *Senecio serpens*
blue cherry *Syzygium oleosum*
blue columbine *Aquilegia caerulea*
blue convolvulus *Convolvulus sabatius*
blue couch, Queensland *Digitaria didactyla*
blue cowslip *Pulmonaria angustifolia*
blue crocus *Tecophilaea*
blue crowfoot *Erodium crinitum*
blue crown passionflower *Passiflora caerulea*
blue cupidone *Catananche caerulea*
blue curls *Trichostema lanatum*
blue cycad, Eastern Cape *Encephalartos horridus*
blue daisy *Felicia amelloides*
blue dampiera *Dampiera stricta*
blue dawn flower *Ipomoea indica*
blue devil, prostrate *Eryngium vesiculosum*
blue dogbane *Amsonia tabernaemontana*
blue Douglas fir *Pseudotsuga menziesii* var. *glauca*
blue dracaena *Cordyline indivisa*
blue echeveria *Echeveria secunda*
blue false indigo *Baptisia australis*
blue false-flag *Neomarica caerulea*
blue fern *Phlebodium aureum* 'Mandaianum'
blue fescue *Festuca glauca*
blue fescue, large *Festuca amethystina*
blue fir *Abies concolor*

blue flax, perennial *Linum perenne*
blue flax-lily *Dianella caerulea, D. revoluta, D. tasmanica*
blue flax-lily, big *Dianella prunina*
blue gem hebe *Hebe* × *franciscana* 'Blue Gem'
blue ginger *Dichorisandra thyrsiflora*
blue grama *Bouteloua gracilis*
blue grass lily *Caesia parviflora* var. *vittata*
blue guarri *Euclea crispa*
blue gum *Eucalyptus globulus*
blue gum, mountain *Eucalyptus deanei*
blue gum, Queensland *Eucalyptus tereticornis*
blue gum, round-leaf *Eucalyptus deanei*
blue gum, South Australian *Eucalyptus leucoxylon*
blue gum, Sydney *Eucalyptus saligna*
blue gum, Tasmanian *Eucalyptus globulus*
blue hair grass, large *Koeleria glauca*
blue haze tree *Jacaranda mimosifolia*
blue hesper palm *Brahea armata*
blue hibiscus *Alyogyne huegelii, Hibiscus syriacus*
blue holly *Ilex* × *meserveae*
blue holly, hybrid *Ilex* × *meserveae*
blue lace flower *Trachymene coerulea*
blue latan palm *Latania loddigesii*
blue leschenaultia *Leschenaultia biloba*
blue lillypilly *Syzygium oleosum*
blue lungwort *Pulmonaria angustifolia*
blue lupine *Lupinus perennis*
blue mallee *Eucalyptus gamophylla, E. polybractea*
blue marble tree *Elaeocarpus grandis*
blue marguerite *Felicia amelloides*
blue mint bush *Prostanthera caerulea*
blue mist shrub *Caryopteris* × *clandonensis*

blue moor grass *Sesleria caerulea*
blue morning glory *Ipomoea indica*
Blue Mountains ash *Eucalyptus oreades*
blue mountain grass *Sesleria caerulea*
Blue Mountains mallee *Eucalyptus stricta*
Blue Mountains stringybark *Eucalyptus blaxlandii*
blue oak *Quercus douglasii*
blue oat grass *Helictotrichon sempervirens*
blue orchid *Vanda* Rothschildiana (grex)
blue passionflower *Passiflora caerulea*
blue pea *Clitoria ternatea, Psoralea pinnata*
blue pea bush *Psoralea pinnata*
blue petrea *Petrea arborea*
blue phlox *Phlox divaricata*
blue pigroot *Sisyrinchium iridifolium*
blue pimpernel *Anagallis arvensis, A. monellii*
blue pincushion *Brunonia australis*
blue pine *Pinus wallichiana*
blue plantain lily *Hosta ventricosa*
blue plum, Lord Howe *Chionanthus quadristamineus*
blue plumbago *Plumbago auriculata*
blue poppy *Meconopsis betonicifolia*
blue potato bush *Solanum rantonnetii*
blue quandong *Elaeocarpus grandis*
blue rod *Morgania floribunda, Stemodia florulenta*
blue sage *Eranthemum pulchellum, Salvia pachyphylla*
blue sage, African *Salvia aurita*
blue sage, California *Salvia clevelandii*
blue sage, Great Basin *Salvia dorrii*
blue sansevieria *Sansevieria ehrenbergii*
blue sedge *Carex riparia*
blue smokebush *Conospermum tenuifolium*

blue snow grass *Poa sieberiana* var. *cyanophylla*
blue Spanish fir *Abies pinsapo* 'Glauca'
blue spiderwort *Commelina cyanea*
blue spiraea *Caryopteris incana, C.* × *clandonensis*
blue spruce *Picea pungens* 'Glauca'
blue spruce, Colorado *Picea pungens*
blue spruce, Koster *Picea pungens* 'Koster'
blue spur flower *Plectranthus ecklonii*
blue squill *Scilla natalensis, S. siberica*
blue star *Amsonia tabernaemontana*
blue succory *Catananche caerulea*
blue sugarbush *Protea neriifolia*
blue taro *Xanthosoma violaceum*
blue thorn *Acacia erubescens*
blue tinsel-lily *Calectasia cyanea*
blue tongue *Melastoma affine*
blue trumpet *Brunoniella australis*
blue trumpet, dwarf *Brunoniella pumilio*
blue trumpet vine *Thunbergia grandiflora*
blue vervain *Verbena hastata*
blue violet, marsh *Viola cucullata*
blue waterlily, Cape *Nymphaea caerulea*
blue wattle, Buchan *Acacia caerulescens*
blue weed *Echium vulgare*
blue wheatgrass *Elymus magellanicus*
blue wild rye *Elymus canadensis, E. glaucus*
blue willow, Alaska *Salix purpurea*
blue woodruff *Asperula orientalis*
blue yam *Brunoniella australis*
blue yucca *Yucca baccata, Y. rigida*
blue-and-white daisy bush *Osteospermum ecklonis*
bluebeard *Caryopteris incana*
bluebell *Campanula rotundifolia, Hyacinthoides non-scripta*

bluebell, Australian *Wahlenbergia communis*
bluebell, California *Phacelia campanularia*
bluebell creeper *Sollya heterophylla*
bluebell creeper, Australian *Sollya heterophylla*
bluebell, desert *Phacelia campanularia*
bluebell, English *Hyacinthoides non-scripta*
bluebell, granite *Wahlenbergia graniticola*
bluebell, New Zealand *Wahlenbergia albomarginata*
bluebell, river *Wahlenbergia fluminalis*
bluebell, royal *Wahlenbergia gloriosa*
bluebell, Spanish *Hyacinthoides hispanica*
bluebell, tall *Wahlenbergia stricta*
bluebell, Texas *Eustoma*
bluebell, white *Hyacinthoides hispanica* 'Alba'
bluebells *Mertensia virginica*
bluebells, Siberian *Mertensia sibirica*
bluebells, Virginia *Mertensia virginica*
blueberry *Vaccinium, V. corymbosum*
blueberry ash *Elaeocarpus reticulatus*
blueberry, Azores *Vaccinium cylindraceum*
blueberry, black highbush *Vaccinium atrococcum*
blueberry, box *Vaccinium ovatum*
blueberry, creeping *Vaccinium crassifolium*
blueberry elder *Sambucus caerulea*
blueberry, highbush *Vaccinium corymbosum*
blueberry lily *Dianella caerulea*
blueberry, lowbush *Vaccinium angustifolium, V. a.* var. *laevifolium*

blueberry, rabbit-eye *Vaccinium ashei*
bluebird vine *Petrea*
blueblossom *Ceanothus thyrsiflorus*
bluebonnet, Texas *Lupinus texensis*
bluebonnets *Lupinus perennis*
bluebottle *Centaurea cyanus*
bluebush *Acacia caesiella, Cratystylis conocephala, Diospyros lycioides, Halgania lavandulacea, Maireana brevifolia*
bluebush, black *Maireana pyramidata*
bluebush, gray *Maireana radiata*
bluebush pea *Crotalaria eremaea*
bluebush, pearl *Maireana sedifolia*
bluebush, swamp *Maireana microcarpa*
bluebush, three-wing *Maireana triptera*
bluebush wattle *Acacia clunies-rossiae*
bluebuttons *Knautia arvensis, Vinca major*
blue-eyed Africa daisy *Arctotis stoechadifolia, A. venusta*
blue-eyed grass *Sisyrinchium angustifolium, S. graminoides, S. idahoense*
blue-eyed grass, California *Sisyrinchium idahoense*
blue-eyed Mary *Collinsia parviflora, Omphalodes verna*
bluegrass *Poa*
bluegrass, annual *Poa annua*
bluegrass, forest *Poa chaixii*
bluegrass, Kentucky *Poa pratensis*
bluegrass, pitted *Bothriochloa decipiens*
bluegrass, silky *Dichanthium sericeum*
bluejack oak *Quercus incana*
blue-leaf tussock grass *Poa sieberiana* var. *cyanophylla*
blue-leafed ironbark *Eucalyptus nubila*

blue-leafed mallee *Eucalyptus gamophylla*
blue-leafed stringybark *Eucalyptus agglomerata*
blue-lily, nodding *Stypandra glauca*
blue-lily, tufted *Thelionema caespitosum*
blue-pod lupine *Lupinus polyphyllus*
bluet, mountain *Centaurea montana*
bluets, creeping *Hedyotis michauxii*
bluewings *Torenia fournieri*
blunt beard-heath *Leucopogon muticus*
blunt greenhood *Pterostylis obtusa, P. curta*
blunt pondweed *Potamogeton ochreatus*
blunt spurge *Phyllanthus gasstroemii, P. gunnii*
blunt wattle *Acacia obtusata*
blunt-leaf bitter pea *Daviesia mimosoides*
blunt-leaf heath *Epacris obtusifolia*
blunt-leafed coondoo *Pouteria myrsinoides*
blush alder *Sloanea australis*
blush daisy bush *Olearia myrsinoides*
blush, maiden's *Sloanea australis*
blushing bindweed *Convolvulus erubescens*
blushing bride *Serruria florida, Tillandsia ionantha*
blushing philodendron *Philodendron erubescens*
bo *Ficus religiosa*
bo tree *Ficus religiosa*
boab *Adansonia gibbosa*
boat lily *Tradescantia spathacea*
bobo, mangle *Bontia daphnoides*
bodhi, *Ficus religiosa*
boer-bean, weeping *Schotia brachypetala*
bodhi tree, false *Ficus rumphii*
bog bean *Menyanthes trifoliata*

bog bilberry *Vaccinium uliginosum*
bog celmisia *Celmisia tomentella*
bog clubmoss *Lycopodiella serpentina*
bog hyacinth *Monochoria cyanea*
bog laurel *Kalmia polifolia*
bog laurel, eastern *Kalmia polifolia*
bog lily *Monochoria cyanea*
bog myrtle *Myrica gale*
bog onion *Owenia cepiodora*
bog pimpernel *Anagallis tenella*
bog pine *Halocarpus bidwillii*
bog rosemary *Andromeda, A. glaucophylla, A. polifolia*
bog sage *Salvia uliginosa*
bog sedge *Schoenus pauciflorus*
bog whortleberry *Vaccinium uliginosum*
Bogan flea *Calotis hispidula*
bogang *Clerodendrum buchananii*
Bogong gum *Eucalyptus chapmaniana*
bog-rush *Schoenus pauciflorus*
bog-rush, beardless *Schoenus imberbis*
bog-rush, black *Schoenus melanostachys*
bog-rush, common *Schoenus apogon*
bog-rush, fluke *Schoenus apogon*
bog-rush, hairy *Schoenus villosus*
bog-rush, heath *Schoenus ericetorum*
bog-rush, zigzag *Schoenus brevifolius*
bois-chene *Catalpa longissima*
bok choi *Brassica rapa* Chinensis Group
Bolivia, pride of *Tipuana tipu*
bolleana poplar *Populus alba* 'Pyramidalis'
bolly gum *Litsea reticulata*
bolly gum, green *Neolitsea australiensis*
bolly gum, white *Neolitsea dealbata*
Bolus pincushion *Leucospermum bolusii*
bolwarra *Eupomatia laurina*
bolwarra, small *Eupomatia bennettii*

bones, dragon *Euphorbia lactea*
boneseed *Chrysanthemoides
monilifera, C. m.* subsp. *monilifera*
boneset *Eupatorium perfoliatum*
bonewood *Medicosma cunninghamii*
Bonin Island juniper *Juniperus
procumbens*
bonnet bellflower *Codonopsis*
bonnet, Granny's *Angelonia
angustifoliam, Aquilegia, A. vulgaris*
bonnets, frog *Sarracenia oreophila*
boobialla *Myoporum acuminatum,
M. insulare*
boobialla, coastal *Myoporum
boninense* subsp. *australe,
M. insulare*
boobialla, creeping *Eremophila
debilis, Myoporum parvifolium*
boobialla, weeping *Myoporum
floribundum*
boobialla, western *Myoporum
montanum*
boojum tree *Idria columnaris*
bookleaf mallee *Eucalyptus kruseana*
boomerang wattle *Acacia amoena*
boonaree *Alectryon oleifolius*
boonaree, scrub *Alectryon diversifolius*
bootlace, cocky's *Lomandra effusa*
bootlace oak *Hakea lorea*
bootlace plant *Pimelea axiflora*
bootlace tree *Hakea lorea*
booyong, white *Argyrodendron
trifoliolatum*
bopple nut *Macadamia tetraphylla*
bopple nut, red *Hicksbeachia
pinnatifolia*
borage *Borago, B. officinalis*
borage, Russian *Trachystemon
orientalis*
border forsythia *Forsythia* ×
intermedia
border phlox *Phlox paniculata*
bordered panic *Entolasia marginata*

boree *Acacia pendula*
boree, weeping *Acacia vestita*
boronia, blue *Boronia caerulescens*
boronia, brown *Boronia megastigma*
boronia, hairy *Boronia pilosa*
boronia, kalgan *Boronia heterophylla*
boronia, ledum *Boronia ledifolia*
boronia, pale pink *Boronia
floribunda*
boronia, pinnate *Boronia pinnata*
boronia, red *Boronia heterophylla*
boronia, rock *Boronia bipinnata*
boronia, small-leafed *Boronia
microphylla*
boronia, soft *Boronia mollis*
boronia, sticky *Boronia anemonifolia*
boronia, stiff *Boronia rigens*
boronia, swamp *Boronia parviflora*
boronia, Sydney *Boronia ledifolia*
boronia, tall *Boronia molloyae*
borracho, sapote *Pouteria
campechiana*
bosistoa, ferny-leafed *Bosistoa
pentacocca*
bosistoa, five-leafed *Bosistoa floydii*
bosistoa, three-leafed *Bosistoa
transversa*
Bosisto's box *Eucalyptus bosistoana*
boskanniedood *Commiphora woodii*
Bosnian pine *Pinus heldreichii,
P. h.* var. *leucodermis*
bossiaea, leafy *Bossiaea foliosa*
bossiaea, showy *Bossiaea cinerea*
bossiaea, spiny *Bossiaea obcordata*
Boston fern *Nephrolepis exaltata*
Boston ivy *Parthenocissus tricuspidata*
Bot River protea *Protea compacta*
bottle gourd *Lagenaria siceraria*
bottle palm *Hyophorbe lagenicaulis*
bottle plant *Hatiora salicornioides*
bottle tree *Adansonia gibbosa*
bottle tree, broad-leaf *Brachychiton
australis*

bottle tree, Chinese *Firmiana simplex*
bottle tree, northern *Brachychiton australis*
bottle tree, Queensland *Brachychiton rupestris*
bottle tree, scrub *Brachychiton discolor*
bottle tree, South American *Ceiba insignis*
bottlebrush *Callistemon, Greyia*
bottlebrush, Albany *Callistemon glaucus*
bottlebrush, alpine *Callistemon pityoides*
bottlebrush, Blackdown *Callistemon pearsonii*
bottlebrush buckeye *Aesculus parviflora*
bottlebrush, Captain Cook *Callistemon viminalis* 'Captain Cook'
bottlebrush, cliff *Callistemon comboynensis, C. formosus*
bottlebrush, Flinders Range *Callistemon teretifolius*
bottlebrush, goldfields *Melaleuca coccinea*
bottlebrush, gold-tipped *Callistemon polandii*
bottlebrush grass *Hystrix patula*
bottlebrush, green *Callistemon flavovirens, C. viridiflorus*
bottlebrush, harkness *Callistemon viminalis* 'Harkness'
bottlebrush, lemon *Callistemon pallidus*
bottlebrush, lesser *Callistemon phoeniceus*
bottlebrush, lilac *Callistemon* 'Lilacinus'
bottlebrush, mountain *Callistemon pityoides*
bottlebrush, narrow-leafed *Callistemon linearis*

bottlebrush, Natal *Greyia sutherlandii*
bottlebrush, needle-leafed *Callistemon teretifolius*
bottlebrush, one-sided *Calothamnus quadrifidus*
bottlebrush orchid *Dendrobium smillieae*
bottlebrush, pine-leafed *Callistemon pinifolius*
bottlebrush, prickly *Callistemon brachyandrus*
bottlebrush, river *Callistemon sieberi*
bottlebrush, sand *Beaufortia squarrosa*
bottlebrush, scarlet *Callistemon citrinus, C. macropunctatus, C. rugulosus*
bottlebrush, Shiress's *Callistemon shiressii*
bottlebrush, stiff *Callistemon rigidus*
bottlebrush, swamp *Beaufortia sparsa, Callistemon sieberi*
bottlebrush, Tasmanian *Callistemon viridiflorus*
bottlebrush, thin-leafed *Callistemon acuminatus*
bottlebrush, Tinaroo *Callistemon recurvus*
bottlebrush, Transvaal *Greyia radlkoferi*
bottlebrush, wallum *Callistemon pachyphyllus*
bottlebrush, weeping *Callistemon viminalis, Melaleuca tamariscina*
bottlebrush, white *Callistemon salignus*
bottlebrush, willow *Callistemon salignus*
bottle-daisy, blue *Lagenifera stipitata*
bottle-tree spurge *Euphorbia stevenii*
bottlewashers *Enneapogon avenaceus*
bottom oak *Quercus* × *runcinata*
bougainvillea *Bougainvillea*

bougainvillea, purple *Bougainvillea glabra*

bougainvillea, variegated *Bougainvillea glabra* 'Variegata'

boulevard cypress *Chamaecyparis pisifera* 'Boulevard'

bouncing bet *Saponaria officinalis*

bouquet, bridal *Porana paniculata*

bouvardia, red *Bouvardia ternifolia*

bouvardia, scarlet *Bouvardia glaberrima*

bouvardia, scented *Bouvardia longiflora*

bouvardia, white *Bouvardia longiflora*

bower actinidia *Actinidia arguta*

bower creeper *Pandorea jasminoides*

bower, glory *Clerodendrum, C. philippinum*

bower of beauty *Pandora jasminoides*

bower plant *Pandorea jasminoides*

bower vine *Actinidia arguta, Pandorea jasminoides*

bower, virgin's *Clematis*

bower wattle, narrow-leaf *Acacia cognata*

bow-flower, tiny *Millotia perpusilla*

Bowles' golden grass *Milium effusum* 'Aureum'

Bowles' mint *Mentha* × *villosa*

bowman's root *Gillenia trifoliata, Veronicastrum virginicum*

bowstring hemp *Sansevieria, S. hyacinthoides*

bowstring hemp, Ceylon *Sansevieria zeylanica*

box *Buxus*

box, apple *Eucalyptus bridgesiana*

box, Balearic *Buxus balearica*

box, bastard *Polygala chamaebuxus*

box, bimble *Eucalyptus populnea*

box, black *Eucalyptus largiflorens*

box, blue *Eucalyptus baueriana*

box blueberry *Vaccinium ovatum*

box, Bosisto's *Eucalyptus bosistoana*

box, Brisbane *Lophostemon confertus*

box, brush *Lophostemon confertus*

box, Cape *Buxus macowanii*

box, Chinese *Buxus microphylla, B. sinica*

box, Christmas *Sarcococca*

box, coast gray *Eucalyptus bosistoana, E. moluccana*

box, Craven gray *Eucalyptus largeana*

box elder *Acer negundo*

box elder maple *Acer negundo*

box elder, variegated *Acer negundo* 'Variegatum'

box, English *Buxus sempervirens*

box, European *Buxus sempervirens*

box, fuzzy *Eucalyptus conica*

box hard-leaf *Phylica buxifolia*

box, Himalayan *Buxus wallichiana*

box, honey *Eucalyptus melliodora*

box honeysuckle *Lonicera nitida*

box huckleberry *Gaylussacia brachycera*

box, Japanese *Buxus microphylla, B. m.* var. *japonica*

box, kanuka *Tristaniopsis laurina*

box, Korean *Buxus microphylla*

box, mallee *Eucalyptus porosa*

box mistletoe *Amyema miquelii*

box, Moonbi apple *Eucalyptus malacoxylon*

box, Paddys River *Eucalyptus macarthurii*

box, peppermint *Eucalyptus odorata*

box, pink-flowering yellow *Eucalyptus melliodora* 'Pink'

box, poplar *Eucalyptus populnea*

box, prickly *Bursaria spinosa*

box red *Eucalyptus polyanthemos*

box, Rudder's *Eucalyptus rudderi*

box, sea *Alyxia buxifolia*

box, steel *Eucalyptus rummeryi*
box, swamp *Lophostemon suaveolens*
box, sweet *Sarcococca*
box thorn *Lycium*
box thorn, African *Lycium ferocissimum*
box thorn, Australian *Bursaria spinosa*
box thorn, Chinese *Lycium chinense*
box, Thozet's *Eucalyptus thozetiana*
box, variegated *Buxus sempervirens* 'Argentea', *B. s.* 'Marginata', *B. s.* 'Variegata'
box, Victorian *Pittosporum undulatum*
box, white *Eucalyptus albens*
box, white-topped *Eucalyptus quadrangulata*
box, yellow *Eucalyptus melliodora*
box-elder maple *Acer negundo*
box-leaf wattle *Acacia buxifolia*
box-leafed holly *Ilex crenata*
box-leafed honeysuckle *Lonicera nitida*
box-leafed wax flower *Philotheca buxifolia*
boxwood, African *Myrsine africana*
boxwood, Balearic *Buxus balearica*
boxwood, Korean *Buxus sinica*
boxwood, Oregon *Paxistima myrtifolia*
boxwood, plum *Amorphospermum whitei*
bracelet honey-myrtle *Melaleuca armillaris*
bracken *Pteridium, P. aquilinum*
bracken, Australian *Pteridium esculentum*
bracken, soft *Calochlaena dubia*
bracket fungus *Ganoderma lucidum, Poria cocos*
Bradford pear *Pyrus calleryana* 'Bradford'

Bradshaw's lomatium *Lomatium bradshawii*
brain cactus *Stenocactus multicostatus*
brake *Pteridium, Pteris*
brake, Australian *Pteris tremula*
brake, Australian cliff *Pellaea falcata*
brake, cliff *Pellaea*
brake, Cretan *Pteris cretica*
brake fern *Pteris cretica*
brake, jungle *Pteris umbrosa*
brake, painted *Pteris tricolor*
brake, purple rock *Pellaea atropurpurea*
brake, shaking *Pteris tremula*
brake, silver *Pteris argyraea*
brake, sword *Pteris ensiformis*
brake, tender *Pteris tremula*
brake, toothed *Pteris dentata*
bramble *Rubus, R. ulmifolius*
bramble, Arctic *Rubus arcticus*
bramble, crimson *Rubus arcticus*
bramble, Molucca *Rubus moluccana*
bramble wattle *Acacia victoriae*
branched comb fern *Schizaea dichotoma*
branching grass-flag *Libertia paniculata*
branching rush *Juncus prismatocarpus*
Brandegee hesper palm *Brahea brandegeei*
brandy bottle *Nuphar lutea*
brass buttons *Cotula coronopifolia*
brassica, hairy *Hirschfeldia incana*
Braun's sword fern *Polystichum braunii*
Brazil *Oreopanax xalapensis*
Brazil cherry *Eugenia brasiliensis*
Brazil nut *Bertholletia excelsa*
Brazil wood *Caesalpinia echinata*
Brazilian bell flower *Abutilon megapotamicum*
Brazilian cherry *Eugenia brasiliensis, E. uniflora*

Brazilian cocoa *Paullinia*
Brazilian coral tree *Erythrina speciosa*
Brazilian fireweed *Erechtites valerianifolia*
Brazilian flame vine *Pyrostegia venusta*
Brazilian ginger *Dichorisandra thyrsiflora*
Brazilian ironwood *Caesalpinia ferrea*
Brazilian jasmine *Mandevilla sanderi*
Brazilian milk tree *Mimusops elengi*
Brazilian nightshade *Solanum seaforthianum*
Brazilian oak *Posoqueria latifolia*
Brazilian pepper tree *Schinus terebinthifolia*
Brazilian plume *Justicia carnea*
Brazilian potato tree *Solanum wrightii*
Brazilian red cloak *Megaskepasma erythrochlamys*
Brazilian rosewood *Dahlbergia nigra*
Brazilian sand palm *Allagoptera arenaria*
Brazilian skyflower *Duranta stenostachya*
Brazilian tree fern *Blechnum brasiliense*
Brazilian water milfoil *Myriophyllum aquaticum*
bread, cuckoo *Oxalis acetosella*
bread, guarana *Paullinia cupana*
bread, St John's *Ceratonia siliqua*
bread wheat *Triticum aestivum*
breadfruit *Artocarpus altilis*
breadfruit, Mexican *Monstera deliciosa*
breadroot *Balsamorhiza sagittata*
breadroot, Indian *Psoralea esculenta*
breath, baby's *Gypsophila, G. paniculata*
breath of heaven *Coleonema album, C. pulchellum*
breath of heaven, pink *Coleonema pulchellum*
breath of heaven, white *Coleonema album*
breeches, bear's *Acanthus, A. mollis*
breeches, Dutchman's *Dicentra cucullaria*
Breede River yellowwood *Podocarpus elongatus*
Brewer's saltbush *Atriplex lentiformis* subsp. *breweri*
Brewer's spruce *Picea breweriana*
Brewer's weeping spruce *Picea breweriana*
Briançon apricot *Prunus brigantina*
briar, Austrian *Rosa foetida*
briar, common *Rosa canina*
briar rose *Rosa rubiginosa*
briar, Scotch *Rosa spinosissima*
briar, sweet *Rosa rubiginosa*
Bribie Island pine *Callitris columellaris*
bridal bouquet *Porana paniculata*
bridal heath *Erica bauera*
bridal veil *Gibasis pellucida*
bridal veil orchid *Dockrillia teretifolia*
bridal wreath *Francoa, Spiraea, S. 'Arguta', S. × vanhouttei*
bridal wreath spiraea *Spiraea prunifolia, S. × vanhouttei*
bride, blushing *Serruria florida*
bride's bush, forest *Pavetta lanceolata*
bridewort *Spiraea salicifolia*
brigalow *Acacia harpophylla*
bright eyes *Euryops pectinatus*
brilliant hopbush *Dodonaea microzyga*
brilliant sunray *Rhodanthe polygalifolia*
brinjal *Solanum melongena*
Brisbane box *Lophostemon confertus*
bristlecone fir *Abies bracteata*
bristlecone pine *Pinus aristata*

bristlecone pine, Great Basin *Pinus longaeva*

bristlecone pine, Rocky Mountain *Pinus aristata*

bristly cloak fern *Cheilanthes distans*

bristly knotweed *Persicaria strigosa*

bristly locust *Robinia fertilis*

bristly tree fern *Dicksonia youngiae*

brittle bush *Encelia farinosa*

brittle gum *Eucalyptus mannifera, E. praecox*

brittle gum, white *Eucalyptus mannifera*

brittle maidenhair *Adiantum concinnum*

brittle maidenhair fern *Adiantum tenerum*

brittle prickly pear *Opuntia fragilis*

brittle thatch palm *Thrinax morrisii*

brittle willow *Salix fragilis*

brittlewood *Claoxylon australe, Nuxia congesta*

brittlewood, Queensland *Claoxylon tenerifolium*

broad bean *Vicia faba*

broad buckler fern *Dryopteris dilatata*

broad rush *Juncus planifolius*

broadleaf *Griselinia littoralis*

broad-leaf bottle tree *Brachychiton australis*

broad-leaf cumbungi *Typha orientalis*

broad-leaf dock *Rumex obtusifolius*

broad-leaf drumsticks *Isopogon anemonifolius*

broad-leaf lilac *Syringa oblata*

broad-leaf millotia *Millotia myosotidifolia*

broad-leaf palm lily *Cordyline petiolaris*

broad-leaf parakeelya *Calandrinia balonensis*

broad-leaf star-hair *Astrotricha latifolia*

broad-leafed apple *Angophora subvelutina*

broad-leafed arnica *Arnica latifolia*

broad-leafed basket grass *Oplismenus aemulus*

broad-leafed beech *Faurea speciosa*

broad-leafed cherry *Exocarpos latifolius*

broad-leafed cockspur thorn *Crataegus prunifolia*

broad-leafed geebung *Persoonia levis*

broad-leafed hakea *Hakea dactyloides*

broad-leafed hickory *Acacia falciformis*

broad-leafed leopard tree *Flindersia collina*

broad-leafed lillypilly *Acmena hemilampra*

broad-leafed lime *Tilia platyphyllos*

broad-leafed linden *Tilia platyphyllos*

broad-leafed marsh orchid *Dactylorhiza majalis*

broad-leafed meadow grass *Poa chaixii*

broad-leafed meryta *Meryta latifolia*

broad-leafed mistletoe *Dendrophthoe vitellina*

broad-leafed paperbark *Melaleuca quinquenervia, M. viridiflora*

broad-leafed peppermint *Eucalyptus dives*

broad-leafed privet *Ligustrum lucidum*

broad-leafed red ironbark *Eucalyptus fibrosa*

broad-leafed sally *Eucalyptus aquatica, E. camphora*

broad-leafed scribbly gum *Eucalyptus haemastoma*

broad-leafed stringybark *Eucalyptus caliginosa*

broad-leafed white mahogany *Eucalyptus umbra*

broad-spined rose *Rosa sericea* var. *pteracantha*
broccoli *Brassica oleracea* Botrytis Group
broccoli, Chinese *Brassica oleracea* Alboglabra Group
broccoli, Romanesco *Brassica oleracea* 'Romanesco'
brodiaea, golden *Triteleia ixioides*
brodiaea, harvest *Brodiaea coronaria*
brome, foxtail *Bromus rubens*
brome grass *Bromus*
brome, Madrid *Bromus madritensis*
brome, native *Bromus arenarius*
brome, red *Bromus rubens*
brome, ripgut *Bromus diandrus*
brome, sand *Bromus arenarius*
brome, seaside *Bromus arenarius*
brome, silky *Bromus molliformis*
brome, smooth *Bromus racemosus*
brome, soft *Bromus hordeaceus, B. molliformis*
bromeliad, bird's nest *Nidularium fulgens*
Brompton stock *Matthiola incana*
Bronvaux medlar + *Crataegomespilus dardarii*
bronze fennel *Foeniculum vulgare* 'Purpurascens'
bronze paper tree *Commiphora harveyi*
brooch flower *Berlandiera lyrata*
brook wake robin *Trillium rivale*
Brooker's gum *Eucalyptus brookeriana*
brooklime *Veronica beccabunga*
brooklime, matted *Gratiola nana*
brooklime, stalked *Gratiola pedunculata*
brookweed, common *Samolus valerandi*
brookweed, creeping *Samolus repens*
broom *Cytisus*

broom, Australian native *Viminaria juncea*
broom ballart *Exocarpos sparteus*
broom, butcher's *Ruscus aculeatus*
broom, Cape purple *Polygala virgata*
broom, chaparral *Baccharis pilularis*
broom cluster fig *Ficus sur*
broom, common *Cytisus scoparius*
broom convolvulus *Convolvulus scoparius*
broom, desert *Baccharis pilularis*
broom, giant-flowered *Carmichaelia williamsii*
broom, hedgehog *Erinacea anthyllis*
broom hickory, hognut *Carya glabra*
broom honey-myrtle *Melaleuca uncinata*
broom, Madeira *Genista tenera*
broom milkwort *Comesperma sphaerocarpum*
broom millet *Sorghum vulgare* Technicum Group
broom, Montpelier *Genista monspessulana*
broom, Moroccan *Cytisus battandieri*
broom, Mount Etna *Genista aetnensis*
broom, New Zealand pink *Carmichaelia carmichaeliae*
broom, New Zealand pink tree *Carmichaelia glabrescens*
broom, New Zealand scented *Carmichaelia odorata*
broom, Portuguese *Chamaecytisus albus, Cytisus multiflorus*
broom, prostrate *Cytisus decumbens*
broom, purple *Cytisus purpureus*
broom, scented *Carmichaelia odorata*
broom, Scotch *Cytisus scoparius*
broom, silver *Argyrocytisus battandieri, Retama monosperma*
broom, silver-leafed *Genista linifolia*
broom, Spanish *Genista hispanica, Spartium junceum*

broom, spiny *Calicotome spinosa*
broom spurge *Amperea xiphoclada*
broom tea-tree *Leptospermum scoparium*
broom, Tenerife *Cytisus supranubius*
broom, Warminster *Cytisus* × *praecox*
broom, weeping *Carmichaelia stevensonii*
broom, white *Retama monosperma, R. raetam*
broom, white Spanish *Cytisus multiflorus*
broom, winged *Genista sagittalis*
broom, woolly-podded *Cytisus grandiflorus*
broombush, desert *Templetonia egena*
broom-corn millet *Panicum miliaceum*
broom-heath, prickly *Monotoca scoparia*
broom-heath, tree *Monotoca elliptica*
broomrape *Orobanche minor*
broomsedge *Andropogon virginicus*
browallia, orange *Streptosolen jamesonii*
brown barrel, cut tail *Eucalyptus fastigata*
brown beaks *Lyperanthus suaveolens*
brown bearded sugarbush *Protea speciosa*
brown beech *Cryptocarya rigida, Pennantia cunninghamii*
brown beetle grass *Diplachne fusca*
brown birch *Scolopia braunii*
brown bloodwood *Corymbia trachyphloia*
brown boronia *Boronia megastigma*
brown flowered hedgehog cactus *Sclerocactus uncinatus*
brown jack *Cryptocarya microneura*
brown kurrajong *Commersonia bartramia*
brown mustard *Brassica juncea*

brown myrtle *Choricarpia leptopetala*
brown pearwood *Amorphospermum antilogum*
brown pine *Podocarpus elatus*
brown salvia *Salvia aurea*
brown silky oak *Darlingia darliniana, Grevillea baileyana*
brown stringybark *Eucalyptus baxteri, E. capitellata*
brown tamarind *Castanospora alphandii*
brown top *Agrostis capillaris*
brown wattle *Acacia brunioides*
brown-back wallaby grass *Austrodanthonia duttoniana*
brown-eyed Susan *Rudbeckia triloba*
Brown's love grass *Eragrostis brownii*
browntop bent *Agrostis capillaris*
browntop, silky *Eulalia aurea*
bruisewort *Bellis*
Brunning's golden Monterey cypress *Cupressus macrocarpa* 'Brunneana'
brush bloodwood *Baloghia inophylla*
brush, blue *Ceanothus thyrsiflorus*
brush box *Lophostemon confertus*
brush cherry *Syzygium australe*
brush cherry, Australian *Syzygium paniculatum*
brush cherry, magenta *Syzygium paniculatum*
brush, coyote *Baccharis pilularis*
brush, deer *Ceanothus integerrimus*
brush ironbark wattle *Acacia aulacocarpa*
brush kurrajong *Commersonia fraseri*
brush mahogany *Geissois benthamii*
brush, monkey's *Combretum aubletii*
brush muttonwood *Rapanea howittiana*
brush pepperbush *Tasmannia insipida*
brush poison tree *Excoecaria dallachyana*

brush, tobacco *Ceanothus velutinus*
brush turpentine *Choricarpia leptopetala, Rhodamnia rubescens*
brush wilga *Geijera salicifolia*
Brussels sprouts *Brassica oleracea* Gemmifera Group
bruyère *Erica arborea*
buccaneer palm *Pseudophoenix sargentii, P. vinifera*
Buchan blue wattle *Acacia caerulescens*
Buchan weed *Hirschfeldia incana*
Buchanan's sage *Salvia buchananii*
buchu *Agathosma crenulata*
buchu, oval-leaf *Agathosma ovata*
buchu, round-leaf *Agathosma betulina*
bucida, oxhorn *Bucida buceras*
buck bean *Menyanthes trifoliata*
buck spinifex *Triodia mitchellii*
buckbrush *Andrachne phyllanthoides, Ceanothus cuneatus, Symphoricarpos orbiculatus*
buckbush *Salsola kali*
buckeye *Aesculus*
buckeye, bottlebrush *Aesculus parviflora*
buckeye, California *Aesculus californica*
buckeye, Ohio *Aesculus glabra, A. ohioensis*
buckeye, Parry's *Aesculus parryi*
buckeye, red *Aesculus pavia*
buckeye, sweet *Aesculus flava*
buckeye, yellow *Aesculus flava*
buckler fern *Dryopteris*
buckler fern, narrow *Dryopteris carthusiana*
buckler-leafed sorrel *Rumex scutatus*
buck's-horn plantain *Plantago coronopus*
buckthorn *Rhamnus, R. catharticus*
buckthorn bumelia *Bumelia lycioides*

buckthorn cholla *Cylindropuntia acanthocarpa*
buckthorn, alder *Rhamnus frangula*
buckthorn, Chinese sea *Hippophae sinensis*
buckthorn, common *Rhamnus cathartica*
buckthorn, Dahurian *Rhamnus dahurica*
buckthorn, false *Bumelia lanuginosa*
buckthorn, Italian *Rhamnus alaternus*
buckthorn, sea *Hippophae rhamnoides*
buckthorn, southern *Bumelia lycioides*
buckwheat *Fagopyrum esculentum*
buckwheat, California *Eriogonum fasciculatum*
buckwheat, Santa Cruz Island *Eriogonum arborescens*
buckwheat, shrubby wild *Eriogonum wrightii*
buckwheat tree *Cliftonia monophylla*
buckwheat, wild *Eriogonum*
buckwheat, Wright's *Eriogonum wrightii*
buckwheat, yellow *Eriogonum flavum*
budda *Eremophila mitchellii*
Buddha's belly bamboo *Bambusa ventricosa*
Buddha's coconut *Pterygota alata*
buddleja, fountain *Buddleja alternifolia*
buddleja, winter *Buddleja salviifolia*
buffalo berry *Shepherdia argentea, S. canadensis*
buffalo berry, roundleaf *Shepherdia rotundifolia*
buffalo berry, silver *Shepherdia argentea*
buffalo currant *Ribes odoratum*
buffalo grass *Buchloe, B. dactyloides, Stenotaphrum secundatum*

buffalo rose *Callirhoe involucrata*
buffalo thorn *Ziziphus mucronata*
buffel grass *Cenchrus ciliaris*
buffel grass, sandhill *Cenchrus pennisetiformis*
bugbane *Cimicifuga*
bugle *Ajuga*
bugle, blue *Ajuga genevensis*
bugle, European *Ajuga reptans*
bugle grass *Sarracenia oreophila*
bugle lily *Watsonia*
bugle, limestone *Ajuga pyramidalis*
bugle, pyramid *Ajuga pyramidalis*
bugle, red *Blancoa canescens*
bugle, upright *Ajuga genevensis*
bugler, royal red *Aeschynanthus pulcher*
bugler, scarlet *Penstemon centranthifolius*
bugleweed, Virginian *Lycopus virginicus*
bugloss *Anchusa, Echium*
bugloss, dyer's *Alkanna tinctoria*
bugloss, purple viper's *Echium plantagineum*
bugloss, Siberian *Brunnera macrophylla*
bugloss, viper's *Echium vulgare*
bulbine lily *Bulbine bulbosa*
bulbine lily, rock *Bulbine glauca*
bulbous oat grass *Arrhenatherum elatius* var. *bulbosum*
bulbous rush *Juncus bulbosus*
bull banksia *Banksia grandis*
bull bay *Magnolia grandiflora*
bull bay magnolia *Magnolia grandiflora*
bull mallee *Eucalyptus behriana*
bull nut *Trapa natans*
bull oak *Allocasuarina luehmannii*
bullace *Vitis rotundifolia*
bulldogs *Diuris longifolia*
bull-head *Tribulus eichlerianus*

bullhorn acacia *Acacia cornigera*
bullock's heart *Annona reticulata*
bullock's heart ivy *Hedera colchica*
bulo nipis *Schizostachyum brachycladum*
bulrush *Schoenoplectus lacustris, Typha*
bumbil *Capparis mitchellii*
bumelia, buckthorn *Bumelia lycioides*
bumelia, gum *Bumelia lanuginosa*
bumpy ash *Flindersia schottiana*
bunch wiregrass *Aristida behriana*
bunchberry *Cornus canadensis*
bunch-flowered narcissus *Narcissus tazetta*
bunching onion *Allium cepa* Aggregatum Group
bundy *Eucalyptus goniocalyx*
bundy, large-flowered *Eucalyptus nortonii*
bunny rabbits *Linaria maroccana*
bunya bunya *Araucaria bidwillii*
bunya bunya pine *Araucaria bidwillii*
bunya pine *Araucaria bidwillii*
Burdekin plum *Pleiogynium timorense*
Burdett's banksia *Banksia burdettii*
Burdett's gum *Eucalyptus burdettiana*
burdock *Arctium lappa*
burdock, great *Arctium lappa*
burgan *Kunzea ericoides*
buri palm *Corypha utan, Polyandrococos caudescens*
Burkwood daphne *Daphne* × *burkwoodii*
Burkwood viburnum *Viburnum* × *burkwoodii*
Burma, pride of *Amherstia nobilis*
Burmese rosewood *Pterocarpus indicus*
burnet *Sanguisorba*
burnet bloodwort *Sanguisorba officinalis*

burnet, Canadian *Sanguisorba
canadensis*
burnet, fodder *Sanguisorba minor*
burnet, garden *Sanguisorba minor*
burnet, great *Sanguisorba canadensis,
S. officinalis*
burnet rose *Rosa spinosissima*
burnet, salad *Sanguisorba minor*
burnet saxifrage *Pimpinella
saxifraga*
burnet saxifrage, greater *Pimpinella
major*
burnet, sheep's *Sanguisorba minor*
burning bush *Bassia scoparia,
Combretum microphyllum,
Dictamnus albus, Euonymus alatus,
E. atropurpureus*
burning bush, dwarf *Euonymus nanus*
burning bush, Turkestan *Euonymus
nanus*
burning bush, western *Euonymus
occidentalis*
burr, alpine *Acaena montana*
burr, Bathurst *Xanthium spinosum*
burr, cannonball *Dissocarpus
paradoxus*
burr cucumber *Cucumis anguria*
burr, galvanised *Sclerolaena birchii*
burr, goathead *Sclerolaena bicornis*
burr marigold *Bidens*
burr medic *Medicago polymorpha*
burr medic, spotted *Medicago
arabica*
burr, Narrawa *Solanum cinereum*
burr, needle *Amaranthus spinosus*
burr, New Zealand *Acaena*
burr, Noogoora *Xanthium occidentale*
burr oak *Quercus macrocarpa*
burr, Paraguay *Acanthospermum
australe*
burr rose *Rosa roxburghii*
burr, sheep's *Acaena, A. agnipila,
A. echinata, A. ovina*

burr stickseed *Omphalolappula
concava*
Burra Range grevillea *Grevillea
decora*
burrawang *Macrozamia, Macrozamia
communis*
burrawang, giant *Macrozamia moorei*
burr-daisy *Calotis*
burr-daisy, cut-leaf *Calotis
anthemoides*
burr-daisy, purple *Calotis cuneifolia*
burr-daisy, rough *Calotis scabiosifolia*
burr-daisy, tangled *Calotis erinacea*
burr-daisy, tufted *Calotis scapigera*
burr-daisy, yellow *Calotis
cymbacantha, C. lappulacea*
burrgrass, hillside *Cenchrus
caliculatus*
burrgrass, small *Tragus australianus*
burrgrass, spiny *Cenchrus incertus,
C. longispinus*
burr-marigold *Bidens tripartita*
burro's tail *Sedum morganianum*
Burrow's wattle *Acacia burrowii*
burrweed, button *Soliva anthemifolia*
burrweed, carpet *Soliva stolonifera*
bush allamanda *Allamanda schottii*
bush basil *Ocimum basilicum*
bush, bellyache *Jatropha gossypifolia*
bush, bitou *Chrysanthemoides
monilifera, C. m.* subsp. *rotundata*
bush, blue *Acacia caesiella, Diospyros
lycioides, Halgania lavandulacea*
bush, burning *Bassia scoparia,
Combretum microphyllum,
Dictamnus albus, Euonymus alatus,
E. atropurpureus*
bush, butterfly *Buddleja alternifolia,
B. davidii, Bauhinia variegata,
Petalostylis labicheoides*
bush, camel *Teucrium sessiliflorum*
bush, caper *Capparis spinosa*
bush caper berry *Capparis arborea*

bush, cardinal *Weigela*
bush, catkin *Garrya elliptica*
bush, Chinese snowball *Viburnum macrocephalum* 'Sterile'
bush chinkapin *Castanea alnifolia*
bush clock vine *Thunbergia erecta*
bush clover, Thunberg *Lespedeza thunbergii*
bush, cranberry *Viburnum trilobum*
bush, creosote *Larrea tridentata*
bush, elephant *Portulacaria afra*
bush fig *Ficus sur*
bush germander *Teucrium fruticans*
bush grape *Vitis rupestris*
bush, groundsel *Baccharis halimifolia*
bush, hobble *Viburnum lantanoides*
bush, honeybell *Freylinia lanceolata*
bush honeysuckle *Diervilla lonicera, D. rivularis, D. sessilifolia*
bush honeysuckle, Georgia *Diervilla rivularis*
bush honeysuckle, southern *Diervilla sessilifolia*
bush, hummingbird *Hamelia erecta, H. patens, Justicia candicans*
bush, kapok *Cochlospermum fraseri, Eriocephalus*
bush, kerosene *Ozothamnus hookeri, O. ledifolius, Richea scoparia*
bush lawyer *Calamus muelleri*
bush lemon *Citrus jambhiri*
bush, lily-of-the-valley *Pieris japonica*
bush lupine, silver *Lupinus albifrons*
bush, medicine *Pogonolobus reticulatus*
bush, minnie *Menziesia pilosa*
bush monkey flower *Mimulus aurantiacus*
bush, oil *Geijera linearifolia*
bush, pearl *Exchordia, E. racemosa*
bush, propeller *Dodonaea heteromorpha*

bush, punty *Senna artemisioides*
bush, puzzle *Ehretia rigida*
bush, quail *Atriplex lentiformis*
bush, robin redbreast *Melaleuca lateritia*
bush sage, Mexican *Salvia leucantha*
bush, Scotia *Eremophila scoparia*
bush scrub, creosote *Prosopis pubescens*
bush, sheep *Geijera linearifolia*
bush, sickle *Dichrostachys cinerea*
bush, silktassel *Garrya elliptica, G. flavescens*
bush, silver *Ptilotus obovatus*
bush, skunk *Garrya fremontii*
bush, snow *Breynia disticha* 'Roseo-picta', *Leucophyta brownii*
bush, spearwood *Pandorea pandorana*
bush, spice *Calycanthus occidentalis, Lindera benzoin, Triunia youngiana*
bush, star *Asterolasia correifolia*
bush, strawberry *Euonymus americanus*
bush, sugar *Protea repens, Rhus ovata*
bush sundrops *Calylophus serrulatus*
bush, tar *Eremophila glabra*
bush tomato *Solanum ellipticum*
bush, turkey *Calytrix exstipulata, Eremophila deserti*
bush violet *Barleria obtusa, Browallia speciosa*
bush, wallaby *Beyeria lasiocarpa*
bush, water *Bossiaea aquifolium, Myoporum montanum*
bush, wedding *Ricinocarpos pinifolius, R. tuberculatus*
bush, white butterfly *Bauhinia variegata* 'Candida'
bush, wire-netting *Corokia cotoneaster*
bush, yellow-berry *Maytenus cunninghamii*

bushman's poison *Acokanthera oppositifolia*
bushman's poison bulb *Boophone disticha*
bushmen's clothes pegs *Grevillea glauca*
bush-pea *Pultenaea*
bush-pea, gray *Pultenaea cunninghamii*
bush-pea, large-leafed *Pultenaea daphnoides*
bush-pea, loose-flower *Pultenaea laxiflora*
bush-pea, matted *Pultenaea pedunculata*
bush-pea, rough *Pultenaea scabra*
bush-pea, spreading *Pultenaea microphylla*
bush-pea, tall *Pultenaea altissima*
bush-pea, twiggy *Pultenaea largiflorens*
Bush's oak *Quercus × bushii*
bush-tick berry *Chrysanthemoides monilifera*
bushwillow, large-fruited *Combretum zeyheri*
bushwillow, river *Combretum erythrophyllum*
bushwillow, velvet *Combretum molle*
bushy clubmoss *Lycopodium deuterodensum*
bushy starwort *Aster subulatus*
bushy yate *Eucalyptus conferruminata, E. lehmannii*
busy Lizzie *Impatiens*
butcher's broom *Ruscus aculeatus*
butia palm *Butia, B. capitata*
butter daisy *Melampodium paludosum*
butterbur *Petasites, P. hybridus*
butterbur, white *Petasites albus*
butterbush *Eremophila duttonii, Pittosporum phyllyreoides*
buttercup *Ranunculus*

buttercup, alpine *Ranunculus alpestris*
buttercup anemone *Anemone ranunculoides*
buttercup, anemone *Ranunculus anemoneus*
buttercup, Bermuda *Oxalis pes-caprae*
buttercup, celery *Ranunculus sceleratus*
buttercup, common *Ranunculus ficaria*
buttercup, creeping *Ranunculus repens*
buttercup, double meadow *Ranunculus acris* 'Flore Pleno'
buttercup, dwarf *Ranunculus millanii*
buttercup, felted *Ranunculus muelleri*
buttercup, ferny *Ranunculus pumilio*
buttercup, Goldilocks' *Ranunculus auricomus*
buttercup, granite *Ranunculus graniticola*
buttercup, Gunn's alpine *Ranunculus gunnianus*
buttercup, hairy *Ranunculus plebeius*
buttercup, meadow *Ranunculus acris*
buttercup, Mount Cook *Ranunculus lyallii*
buttercup, Persian *Ranunculus asiaticus*
buttercup, poison *Ranunculus sceleratus*
buttercup, river *Ranunculus inundatus*
buttercup, snow *Ranunculus niphophilus*
buttercup, velvety *Ranunculus velutinus*
buttercup, white water *Ranunculus aquatilis*
buttercup winter-hazel *Corylopsis pauciflora*
butterfly amaryllis *Hippeastrum papilio*
butterfly bush *Buddleja alternifolia, B. davidii, Bauhinia variegata, Petalostylis labicheoides*

butterfly bush, blue *Clerodendrum ugandense*

butterfly bush, white *Bauhinia variegata* 'Candida'

butterfly flag *Diplarrhena morea*

butterfly flower *Bauhinia monandra, Schizanthus, S.* × *wisetonensis*

butterfly iris *Dietes bicolor, D. grandiflora, D. iridioides*

butterfly lily *Hedychium coronarium*

butterfly orchid *Psychopsis papilio*

butterfly palm *Dypsis lutescens*

butterfly pea *Clitoria ternatea*

butterfly plant *Gaura lindheimeri*

butterfly weed *Asclepias curassavica, A. tuberosa*

butterfly weed, yellow *Solidago confinis*

butterfruit *Diospyros blancoi*

butterknife bush *Cunonia capensis*

butternut *Cucurbita moschata, Juglans cinerea*

butternut, Chinese *Juglans cathayensis*

butternut pumpkin *Cucurbita moschata* 'Butternut'

butternut walnut *Juglans cinerea*

butterwort *Pinguicula, P. vulgaris*

button ball *Platanus occidentalis*

button burrweed *Soliva anthemifolia*

button everlasting *Helichrysum scorpioides*

button fern *Pellaea rotundifolia*

button grass *Dactyloctenium radulans, Gymnoschoenus sphaerocephalus*

button mangrove *Conocarpus erecta*

button orchid *Dischidia nummularia*

button sedge *Gymnoschoenus sphaerocephalus*

button snake root *Eryngium yuccifolium, Liatris spicata, L. pycnostachya*

button, mescal *Lophophora williamsii*

buttonbush *Cephalanthus occidentalis*

buttons, bachelor's *Cenia turbinata, Centaurea cyanus, Gomphrena canescens, G. globosa*

buttons, beauty *Leptorhynchos tetrachaetus*

buttons, billy *Calocephalus, Craspedia, Pycnosorus*

buttons, brass *Cotula coronopifolia*

buttons, golden *Tanacetum vulgare*

buttons on a string *Crassula rupestris*

buttons, scaly *Leptorhynchos squamatus*

buttons, water *Cotula coronopifolia*

buttons, woolly *Leptorhynchos panaetioides*

buttons, yellow *Chrysocephalum apiculatum, C. semipapposum*

buttonweed *Cotula coronopifolia*

buttonwood *Platanus occidentalis*

Buxton gum *Eucalyptus crenulata*

Byfield fern *Bowenia serrulata*

C

caballera de palo *Oreopanax capitatus*
cabbage *Brassica oleracea* Capitata
Group
cabbage, Chinese *Brassica pekinensis*
cabbage gum *Eucalyptus amplifolia*
cabbage, Macquarie Island
Stilbocarpa polaris
cabbage palm *Livistona australis,
Sabal palmetto*
cabbage palm, Central Australian
Livistona mariae
cabbage palm, fan-leafed *Corypha
utan*
cabbage palm, weeping *Livistona
decipiens*
cabbage, Peking *Brassica rapa*
Pekinensis Group
cabbage, St Patrick's *Saxifraga
spathularis, Sempervivum tectorum*
cabbage, skunk *Lysichiton*
cabbage tree, bastard *Schefflera
umbellifera*
cabbage tree, forest *Cussonia
sphaerocephala, Schefflera
umbellifera*
cabbage tree, highveld *Cussonia
paniculata*
cabbage tree, lowveld *Cussonia
spicata*
cabbage tree, mountain *Cordyline
indivisa*
cabbage tree, New Zealand *Cordyline
australis*
cabbage tree palm *Livistona australis*
cabbage tree, South African *Cussonia
spicata*
cabbage, warrigal *Tetragonia
tetragonioides*
cabbage, wild *Brassica oleracea*

cabbage, yellow skunk *Lysichiton
americanus*
cacalia sage *Salvia cacaliifolia*
cacao *Theobroma cacao*
cacao, madre de *Gliricidia sepium*
cacao, tiger *Theobroma bicolor*
cacao-shade, Nicaraguan *Gliricidia
sepium*
cacheo *Pseudophoenix vinifera*
cactus, agave *Leuchtenbergia principis*
cactus, Arizona barrel *Ferocactus
wislizeni*
cactus, barbed-wire *Acanthocereus
pentagonus*
cactus, barrel *Echinopsis oxygona,
Ferocactus*
cactus, beaver tail *Opuntia basilaris*
cactus, beehive *Escobaria vivipara*
cactus, bilberry *Myrtillocactus
geometrizans*
cactus, brain *Stenocactus multicostatus*
cactus, brown flowered hedgehog
Sclerocactus uncinatus
cactus, California barrel *Ferocactus
cylindraceus*
cactus, candelabra *Euphorbia lactea*
cactus, candelabrum *Cylindropuntia
imbricata*
cactus, candy barrel *Ferocactus
wislizeni*
cactus, caterpillar *Stenocereus eruca*
cactus, cat's claw *Sclerocactus
uncinatus*
cactus, Christmas *Schlumbergera* ×
buckleyi, S. truncata
cactus, cochineal *Opuntia
cochenillifera*
cactus, compass *Ferocactus
cylindraceus*
cactus, cotton ball *Espostoa lanata*
cactus, crab *Schlumbergera truncata*
cactus dahlia *Dahlia* Hybrid
Cultivars, Cactus Group

cactus, dumpling *Lophophora williamsii*
cactus, dwarf Turk's cap *Melocactus matanzanus*
cactus, Easter *Hatiora gaertneri, H. rosea*
cactus, Easter lily *Echinopsis*
cactus, fire barrel *Ferocactus gracilis*
cactus, foxtail *Escobaria vivipara*
cactus, Garambulla *Myrtillocactus geometrizans*
cactus geranium *Pelargonium echinatum*
cactus, goat horn *Astrophytum capricorne*
cactus, golden ball *Echinocactus grusonii, Parodia leninghausii*
cactus, golden barrel *Echinocactus grusonii*
cactus, harrisia *Harrisia martinii*
cactus, hatchet *Pelecyphora aselliformis*
cactus, hat-rack *Euphorbia lactea*
cactus, hedgehog *Echinocereus*
cactus, lace *Mammillaria elongata*
cactus, lady finger *Echinocereus pentalophus*
cactus, leafy *Pereskia bahiensis*
cactus, melon *Melocactus*
cactus, Mexican fence post *Pachycereus marginatus*
cactus mistletoe *Korthalsella disticha*
cactus, moon *Harrisia* 'Jusbertii', *H. martinii, Selenicereus*
cactus, night-blooming *Hylocereus undatus, Selenicereus*
cactus, night-flowering *Epiphyllum oxypetalum*
cactus, old lady *Mammillaria hahniana*
cactus, old man *Cephalocereus senilis, Pilosocereus leucocephalus*
cactus, old woman *Mammillaria hahniana*

cactus, organ pipe *Stenocereus thurberi*
cactus, paper-spined *Tephrocactus articulatus*
cactus pea *Bossiaea walkeri*
cactus, peanut *Echinopsis chamaecereus*
cactus, pincushion *Mammillaria*
cactus, pine-cone *Pelecyphora strobiliformis*
cactus, powderpuff *Mammillaria bocasana*
cactus, prickly pear *Opuntia humifusa*
cactus, prism *Leuchtenbergia principis*
cactus, rat's-tail *Aporocactus flagelliformis*
cactus, red orchid *Disocactus ackermannii*
cactus, saguaro *Carnegiea gigantea*
cactus, sea urchin *Astrophytum asterias, Echinopsis*
cactus, silver ball *Parodia scopa*
cactus, silver torch *Cleistocactus straussii*
cactus, spiny star *Escobaria vivipara*
cactus, sprawling *Bergerocactus emoryi*
cactus, strawberry *Mammillaria prolifera*
cactus, strawberry hedgehog *Echinocereus engelmannii*
cactus, sweet potato *Peniocereus greggii*
cactus, toothpick *Stetsonia coryne*
cactus, top *Strombocactus disciformis*
cactus, torch *Cereus hildmannianus* subsp. *uruguayanus*
cactus, woodlouse *Pelecyphora aselliformis*
cadaga *Corymbia torelliana*
cadagi *Corymbia torelliana*
caffre lime *Citrus hystrix*
cajeput *Melaleuca leucadendra*

calabar bean *Physostigma venenosum*
calabash, black *Amphitecna latifolia*
calabash tree *Crescentia cujete*
caladenia, musky *Caladenia gracilis*
caladenia, white *Caladenia alba*
calambac *Aquilaria malaccensis*
calamint *Acinos, Calamintha,*
C. sylvatica
calamint, alpine *Acinos alpinus*
calamint, large-flowered *Calamintha*
grandiflora
calamint, lesser *Calamintha nepeta*
calamondin *Citrus × microcarpa*
calamondin orange *Citrus ×*
microcarpa
calamus *Acorus calamus*
calamus, sweet *Acorus calamus*
calceolaria *Calceolaria ×*
herbeohybrida
calendula *Calendula officinalis*
Caley's grevillea *Grevillea caleyi*
Caley's ironbark *Eucalyptus caleyi*
calico bush *Kalmia latifolia*
calico flower *Aristolochia grandiflora,*
A. littoralis
calico plant *Alternanthera bettzichiana*
California allspice *Calycanthus*
occidentalis
California barberry *Mahonia dictyota*
California barrel cactus *Ferocactus*
cylindraceus
California black oak *Quercus*
kelloggii
California blue sage *Salvia clevelandii*
California bluebell *Phacelia*
campanularia
California blue-eyed grass
Sisyrinchium idahoense
California buckeye *Aesculus*
californica
California buckwheat *Eriogonum*
fasciculatum
California fescue *Festuca californica*

California fuchsia *Zauschneria*
californica
California gold fern *Pityrogramma*
triangularis
California goldenrod *Solidago*
californica
California goldenrod, southern
Solidago confinis
California gray rush *Juncus patens*
California holly *Heteromeles*
arbutifolia
California holly grape *Mahonia*
pinnata
California juniper *Juniperus*
californica
California laurel *Umbellularia*
californica
California lilac *Ceanothus,*
C. thyrsiflorus
California live oak *Quercus agrifolia*
California maidenhair *Adiantum*
jordanii
California nutmeg *Torreya californica*
California nutmeg yew *Torreya*
californica
California pitcher plant *Darlingtonia*
californica
California plane *Platanus racemosa*
California poison oak *Toxicodendron*
diversilobum
California polypody *Polypodium*
californicum
California poppy *Eschscholzia,*
E. californica, Platystemon
California poppy, tufted *Eschscholzia*
caespitosa
California, pride of *Lathyrus splendens*
California privet *Ligustrum*
ovalifolium
California privet, golden *Ligustrum*
ovalifolium 'Aureum'
California red fir *Abies magnifica*
California redbud *Cercis occidentalis*

California redwood *Sequoia sempervirens*
California rock fern *Polypodium californicum*
California sagebrush *Artemisia californica*
California scrub oak *Quercus dumosa*
California shield fern *Polystichum californicum*
California sycamore *Platanus racemosa*
California tree mallow *Lavatera assurgentiflora*
California tree poppy *Romneya coulteri*
California walnut *Juglans californica*
California wax myrtle *Myrica californica*
California white oak *Quercus lobata*
California white sage *Salvia apiana*
California wild grape *Vitis californica*
Calistoga ceanothus *Ceanothus divergens*
calla, golden *Zantedeschia elliottiana*
calla lily *Zantedeschia, Z. aethiopica*
calla, yellow *Zantedeschia elliottiana*
Callery pear *Pyrus calleryana*
calliopsis *Coreopsis lanceolata*
calomba *Jateorhiza palmata*
calotrope *Calotropis procera*
caltrop *Tribulus terrestris*
caltrop, spineless *Tribulus micrococcus*
caltrops, water *Trapa natans*
camas *Camassia*
camas, death *Zigadenus*
camash *Camassia quamash*
Cambridge oak *Quercus warburgii*
Camden woollybutt *Eucalyptus macarthurii*
camel bush *Teucrium sessiliflorum*
camel melon *Citrullus lanatus*
camel thorn *Acacia erioloba, A. giraffae*
camellia *Camellia*

camellia golden *Camellia nitidissima*
camellia, Hong Kong *Camellia hongkongensis*
camellia, oil *Camellia oleifera*
camellia, silky *Stewartia malacodendron*
camellia, snow *Camellia rusticana*
Camfield's hopbush *Dodonaea camfieldii*
camosh *Camassia quamash*
Campbell's magnolia *Magnolia campbellii*
camphor basil *Ocimum kilimandscharicum*
camphor laurel *Cinnamomum camphora*
camphor thyme *Thymus camphoratus*
camphor tree *Cinnamomum camphora*
campion *Lychnis, Silene*
campion, alpine *Lychnis alpina*
campion, bladder *Silene uniflora, S. vulgaris*
campion, Mexican *Silene laciniata*
campion, moss *Silene acaulis*
campion, red *Lychnis coronaria, Silene dioica*
campion, rose *Lychnis coronaria*
campion, sea *Silene uniflora*
camwood, Natal *Baphia racemosa*
Canada columbine *Aquilegia canadensis*
Canada pumpkin *Cucurbita moschata*
Canada wild rye *Elymus canadensis*
Canadian burnet *Sanguisorba canadensis*
Canadian dogwood *Cornus nuttallii*
Canadian fleabane *Conyza canadensis*
Canadian hemlock *Tsuga canadensis*
Canadian maple *Acer rubrum*
Canadian plum *Prunus nigra*

Canadian pondweed *Elodea canadensis*

Canadian poplar *Populus* × *canadensis*

Canadian yew *Taxus canadensis*

canaigre *Rumex hymenosepalus*

Canary balm *Cedronella canariensis*

Canary bellflower *Canarina canariensis*

canary bird vine *Tropaeolum peregrinum*

canary creeper *Tropaeolum peregrinum*

Canary grass *Phalaris, P. canariensis*

Canary grass, lesser *Phalaris minor*

Canary grass, reed *Phalaris arundinacea*

Canary Island aeonium *Aeonium canariense*

Canary Island date palm *Phoenix canariensis*

Canary Island holly *Ilex perado*

Canary Island ivy *Hedera canariensis*

Canary Island jasmine *Jasminum odoratissimum*

Canary Island juniper *Juniperus cedrus*

Canary Island lavender *Lavandula canariensis, L. pinnata*

Canary Island pine *Pinus canariensis*

Canary Island sage *Salvia canariensis*

Canary Island smokebush *Bystropogon origanifolius*

Canary Island viburnum *Viburnum rigidum*

Canary Island wormwood *Artemisia canariensis*

Canary Islands woodrush *Luzula canariensis*

canary laurel *Laurus azorica*

Canary oak *Quercus canariensis*

candelabra cactus *Euphorbia lactea*

candelabra flower *Brunsvigia orientalis*

candelabra tree *Araucaria angustifolia*

candelabra tree, Transvaal *Euphorbia cooperi*

candelabrum cactus *Cylindropuntia imbricata*

candellila *Euphorbia antisyphilitica*

candia tulip *Tulipa saxatilis*

candle acacia *Acacia hebeclada*

candle, blue *Myrtillocactus geometrizans*

candle, desert *Eremurus*

candle heath *Richea continentis*

candle orchid *Arpophyllum*

candle, Our Lord's *Yucca whipplei*

candle plant *Senecio articulatus*

candle, Roman *Yucca gloriosa*

candle tree *Parmentiera cereifera*

candle yucca *Yucca gloriosa*

candlebark *Eucalyptus viminalis*

candlebark gum *Eucalyptus rubida*

candleberry *Myrica pensylvanica*

candlenut tree *Aleurites moluccana*

candlenut tree, Queensland *Aleurites rockinghamensis*

candles *Stackhousia monogyna*

candles, golden *Pachystachys lutea*

candy barrel cactus *Ferocactus wislizeni*

candy carrot *Athamanta turbith*

candy palm *Syagrus comosa*

candy-cane oxalis *Oxalis versicolor*

candy-stick tulip *Tulipa clusiana*

candytuft *Iberis, I. amara*

candytuft, garden *Iberis umbellata*

candytuft, Gibraltar *Iberis gibraltarica*

candytuft, mauve *Harmsiodoxa puberula*

candytuft, perennial *Iberis sempervirens*

cane, chair-bottom *Calamus viminalis*

cane cholla *Cylindropuntia spinosior*

cane, dumb *Dieffenbachia*

cane, lawyer *Calamus*
cane palm, golden *Dypsis lutescens*
cane, rattan *Calamus rotang*
cane reed *Arundinaria gigantea*
cane, southern lawyer *Calamus muelleri*
cane spinifex *Zygochloa paradoxa*
cane, sugar *Saccharum officinarum*
canegrass *Eragrostis australasica*
canegrass, sandhill *Zygochloa paradoxa*
canegrass, swamp *Eragrostis australasica*
canistel *Pouteria campechiana*
canna *Canna*
canna, garden *Canna* × *generalis*
canna lily *Canna*
canna, water *Thalia dealbata*
cannon aloe *Aloe claviflora*
cannonball burr *Dissocarpus paradoxus*
cannonball tree *Couroupita guianensis*
canoe birch *Betula papyrifera*
cantaloupe *Cucumis melo* Cantalupenis Group
Canterbury bells *Campanula medium*
Canterbury bells, wild *Phacelia campanularia*
canthium, coast *Canthium coprosmoides*
canthium, large-leafed *Canthium lamprophyllum*
Canton ginger *Zingiber officinale*
canyon grape *Vitis arizonica*
canyon live oak *Quercus chrysolepis*
cap, bishop's *Astrophytum myriostigma, Mitella*
cap, friar's *Aconitum napellus*
cap, granny's *Angelonia angustifolia, A. salicariifolia*
cap, huntsman's *Sarracenia purpurea*
cap, jockey's *Tigridia pavonia*
cap, sailor's *Dodecatheon hendersonii*

cap, Turk's *Lilium martagon, Malvaviscus arboreus*
Cape aloe *Aloe ferox*
Cape bladder pea *Sutherlandia frutescens*
Cape blue waterlily *Nymphaea caerulea*
Cape box *Buxus macowanii*
Cape cherry *Cassine sphaerophylla*
Cape chestnut *Calodendrum capense*
Cape cowslip *Lachenalia*
Cape daisy *Arctotis fastuosa, Dimorphotheca pluvialis*
Cape dandelion *Arctotheca calendula*
Cape everlasting *Phaenocoma prolifera, Syncarpha vestita*
Cape fern *Cyathea capensis*
Cape fig *Ficus sur*
Cape figwort *Phygelius capensis*
Cape fuchsia *Phygelius capensis*
Cape gooseberry *Physalis peruviana*
Cape grape *Rhoicissus capensis*
Cape holly *Ilex mitis*
Cape honeysuckle *Tecoma capensis*
Cape hyacinth *Galtonia candicans*
Cape ivy *Delairea odorata, Senecio macroglossus*
Cape jasmine *Gardenia augusta, Rothmannia globosa*
Cape laburnum *Crotalaria capensis*
Cape leadwort *Plumbago auriculata*
Cape Leeuwin wattle *Paraserianthes lophantha*
Cape lilac *Virgilia oroboides*
Cape marigold *Dimorphotheca pluvialis*
Cape myrtle *Myrsine africana*
Cape phillyrea *Cassine capensis*
Cape pincushion *Scabiosa africana*
Cape pittosporum *Pittosporum viridiflorum*
Cape pondweed *Aponogeton distachyos*

Cape primrose *Streptocarpus*
Cape purple broom *Polygala virgata*
Cape statice *Limonium peregrinum*
Cape stock *Heliophila*
Cape strangler fig *Ficus sur*
Cape sundew *Drosera capensis*
Cape teak *Strychnos decussata*
Cape tree fern *Cyathea dregei*
Cape tulip *Homeria*
Cape waterlily *Nymphaea caerulea*
Cape yellowwood *Podocarpus elongatus*
Cape York fan palm *Livistona muelleri*
Cape York red gum *Eucalyptus brassiana*
caper bean *Zygophyllum*
caper berry, bush *Capparis arborea*
caper bush *Capparis spinosa*
caper spurge *Euphorbia lathyris*
caper tree, bay-leafed *Capparis flexuosa*
caper tree, Jamaica *Capparis cynophallophora*
capeweed *Arctotheca calendula, Phyla nodiflora*
capivi *Geijera paniculata*
Cappadocian maple *Acer cappadocicum*
capsicum *Capsicum annuum, C. a.* Grossum Group
Captain Cook bottlebrush *Callistemon viminalis* 'Captain Cook'
capulin *Prunus salicifolia, P. serotina*
carabeen, red *Geissois benthamiana*
carambola *Averrhoa carambola*
caramel grevillea *Grevillea polybotrya*
caranda *Copernicia alba*
caranda palm *Copernicia alba*
carandai palm *Trithrinax brasiliensis*
caranday *Copernicia alba*
caranday palm *Copernicia alba*

caraway *Carum carvi*
caraway, black *Pimpinella saxifraga*
caraway, cushion *Oreomyrrhis pulvinifica*
caraway, native *Oreomyrrhis eriopoda*
caraway thyme *Thymus herba-barona*
carbeen *Corymbia tessellaris*
cardamom *Elettaria cardamomum*
cardamom, tavoy *Amomum xanthioides*
cardboard palm *Zamia furfuracea*
cardinal bush *Weigela*
cardinal creeper *Ipomoea horsfalliae*
cardinal flower *Ipomoea × multifida, Lobelia cardinalis, Sinningia cardinalis*
cardinal flower, blue *Lobelia siphilitica*
cardinal flower, red *Lobelia fulgens*
cardinal, prickly *Erythrina zeyheri*
cardinal sage *Salvia fulgens*
cardinal spear *Erythrina herbacea*
cardinal's guard *Pachystachys coccinea*
cardinal's hat *Malvaviscus penduliflorus*
cardon *Pachycereus pringlei*
cardón gigante *Pachycereus pringlei*
cardoon *Cynara cardunculus*
Caribbean pine *Pinus caribaea*
Caribbean royal palm *Roystonea oleracea*
caricature plant *Graptophyllum pictum*
Carmel ceanothus *Ceanothus griseus*
Carmel creeper *Ceanothus griseus* var. *horizontalis*
carnation *Dianthus, D. caryophyllus*
carnation, perpetual-flowering *Dianthus × allwoodii*
carnauba *Copernicia prunifera*
carnival bush *Ochna serrulata*
carob *Ceratonia siliqua*
caroba-guazu *Aralia warmingiana*

Carolina allspice *Calycanthus floridus*
Carolina ash *Fraxinus caroliniana*
Carolina hemlock *Tsuga caroliniana*
Carolina jasmine *Gelsemium sempervirens*
Carolina jessamine *Gelsemium sempervirens*
Carolina laurel-cherry *Prunus caroliniana*
Carolina lupin *Thermopsis villosa*
Carolina poplar *Populus × canadensis*
Carolina silverbell *Halesia carolina*
Carolina tea *Ilex vomitoria*
Carpathian bellflower *Campanula carpatica*
Carpentaria palm *Carpentaria acuminata*
carpet burrweed *Soliva stolonifera*
carpet cypress, Siberian *Microbiota decussata*
carpet grass *Axonopus compressus*
carpet grass, narrow-leafed *Axonopus affinis*
carpet plant *Episcia cupreata*
carpetweed *Malephora crocea, Phyla nodiflora*
Carrington Falls grevillea *Grevillea rivularis*
carrion flower *Orbea variegata, Stapelia, S. gigantea*
carrizo *Phragmites australis*
carrot *Daucus carota*
carrot, candy *Athamanta turbith*
carrot weed *Daucus glochidiatus*
carrot, wild *Daucus carota*
carrot wood *Canarium australasicum*
carrot-burrs *Daucus glochidiatus*
Carthusian pink *Dianthus carthusianorum*
casacara sagrada *Rhamnus purshiana*
cascade onion *Allium cratericola*
cascade palm *Chamaedorea atrovirens*

cascarilla, green *Croton verreauxii*
cascarilla, native *Croton verreauxii*
cashew *Anacardium occidentale*
cashew nut, oriental *Semecarpus anacardium*
Caspian locust *Gleditsia caspica*
Caspian willow *Salix acutifolia*
cassava *Manihot esculenta*
cassava, bitter *Manihot esculenta*
cassava, variegated *Manihot esculenta* 'Variegata'
cassia *Cinnamomum aromaticum*
cassia, appleblossom *Cassia grandis*
cassia, autumn *Senna corymbosa*
cassia, eared *Senna petersiana*
cassia, feathery *Senna artemisioides*
cassia, pink *Cassia javanica*
cassia, ringworm *Senna alata*
cassia, scrambling *Senna acclinis*
cassia, silver *Senna artemisioides, S. phyllodinea*
cassia, silver leaf *Senna phyllodinea*
cassia, winged *Cassia alata*
cassinia, shiny *Cassinia longifolia*
cassinia, sticky *Cassinia uncata*
cast-iron plant *Aspidistra elatior*
castor aralia *Kalopanax septemlobus*
castor bean plant *Ricinus communis*
castor oil plant *Ricinus communis*
castor oil plant, purple *Ricinus communis* 'Cambodgensis'
cat *Parmentiera aculeata*
cat thyme *Teucrium marum*
Catalina cherry *Prunus lyonii*
Catalina ironwood *Lyonothamnus floribundus*
Catalina mountain lilac *Ceanothus arboreus*
Catalina nightshade *Solanum wallacei*
catalpa, northern *Catalpa speciosa*
catalpa, southern *Catalpa bignonioides*

catalpa, western *Catalpa speciosa*
catalpa, yellow *Catalpa ovata*
Catawba rhododendron
    Rhododendron catawbiense
catberry *Nemopanthus mucronatus*
catcher, moth *Araujia sericifera*
catchfly *Lychnis, Silene*
catchfly, alpine *Lychnis alpina*
catchfly, French *Silene gallica*
catchfly, German *Lychnis viscaria*
catchfly, Mediterranean *Silene
    nocturna*
catchfly, nodding *Silene pendula*
catchfly, sweet William *Silene
    armeria*
catclaw mimosa *Mimosa pigra*
catechu *Acacia catechu*
caterpillar cactus *Stenocereus eruca*
caterpillar fern *Goniophlebium
    subauriculatum, Polypodium
    formosanum*
caterpillar fungus *Cordyceps sinensis*
cat-head *Tribulus terrestris*
cathedral bells *Cobaea scandens*
cathedral windows *Calathea
    makoyana*
Catherine wheel *Leucospermum
    catherinae*
Catherine's pincushion
    Leucospermum catherinae
catjang pea *Cajanus cajan*
catkin bush *Garrya elliptica*
catkin grevillea *Grevillea synapheae*
catkin wattle *Acacia dallachiana*
catmint *Nepeta, N. cataria*
catmint, Himalayan *Nepeta clarkei*
catmint, hybrid *Nepeta × faassenii*
catmint, wild *Nepeta cataria*
catnip *Nepeta, N. cataria*
cat's claw *Gloriosa superba*
cat's claw cactus *Sclerocactus uncinatus*
cat's claw creeper *Macfadyena
    unguis-cati*

cat's ears *Antennaria, Calochortus,
    Hypochaeris radicata*
cat's ears, smooth *Hypochaeris glabra*
cat's moustache *Orthosiphon aristatus*
cat's paw *Anigozanthos humilis,
    Ptilotus spathulatus*
cat's whiskers *Orthosiphon aristatus,
    O. stamineus*
cat's whiskers, white *Clerodendrum
    glabrum*
catsfoot *Antennaria dioica*
cat-tail *Typha*
cat-tail, red-hot *Acalypha hispida*
cat-tails, red *Acalypha reptans*
cattle bush *Trichodesma zeylanicum*
Caucasian alder *Alnus subcordata*
Caucasian bladdernut *Staphylea
    colchica*
Caucasian fir *Abies nordmanniana*
Caucasian linden *Tilia caucasica*
Caucasian nettle tree *Celtis caucasica*
Caucasian oak *Quercus macranthera*
Caucasian peony *Paeonia
    mlokosewitschii*
Caucasian spruce *Picea orientalis*
Caucasian spurge *Andrachne
    colchica*
Caucasian wingnut *Pterocarya
    fraxinifolia*
Caucasian zelkova *Zelkova
    carpinifolia*
caucho *Castilloa elastica*
cauliflower *Brassica oleracea* Botrytis
    Group
cauliflower bush *Cassinia longifolia*
caustic bush *Sarcostemma australe*
caustic creeper *Chamaesyce
    drummondii*
caustic vine *Sarcostemma australe,
    S. brunonianum*
caustic weed *Chamaesyce drummondii*
caustic weed, red *Chamaesyce
    prostrata*

cavan *Acacia cavenia*

cayenne pepper *Capsicum annuum* Longum Group

ceanothus *Ceanothus*

ceanothus, azure *Ceanothus coeruleus*

ceanothus, blue blossom *Ceanothus thyrsiflorus*

ceanothus, Calistoga *Ceanothus divergens*

ceanothus, Carmel *Ceanothus griseus*

ceanothus, coast *Ceanothus ramulosus*

ceanothus, cropleaf *Ceanothus dentatus*

ceanothus, green bark *Ceanothus spinosus*

ceanothus, hoary-leafed *Ceanothus crassifolius*

ceanothus, holly-leaf *Ceanothus purpureus*

ceanothus, inland *Ceanothus ovatus*

ceanothus, maritime *Ceanothus maritimus*

ceanothus, Monterey *Ceanothus rigidus*

ceanothus, San Diego *Ceanothus cyaneus*

ceanothus, Santa Barbara *Ceanothus impressus*

ceanothus, tree *Ceanothus arboreus*

ceanothus, wart leaf *Ceanothus papillosus*

ceanothus, wavy-leaf *Ceanothus foliosus*

cedar, Alaska *Chamaecyparis nootkatensis*

cedar, Atlantic *Cedrus atlantica*

cedar, Atlantic white *Chamaecyparis thyoides*

cedar, Atlas *Cedrus atlantica*

cedar, Australian red *Toona ciliata*

cedar, Bermuda *Juniperus bermudiana*

cedar, blue Atlas *Cedrus atlantica* 'Glauca'

cedar, Chilean incense *Austrocedrus chilensis*

cedar, Chinese *Cunninghamia lanceolata*

cedar, cigar-box *Cedrela mexicana, C. odorata*

cedar, Clanwilliam *Widdringtonia cedarbergensis*

cedar, coast white *Chamaecyparis thyoides*

cedar, Cyprus *Cedrus brevifolia*

cedar, deerhorn *Thujopsis dolabrata*

cedar, deodar *Cedrus deodara*

cedar, eastern red *Juniperus virginiana*

cedar elm *Ulmus crassifolia*

cedar, golden Atlas *Cedrus atlantica* 'Aurea'

cedar hiba *Thujopsis dolabrata*

cedar, incense *Anthocarapa nitidula, Calocedrus decurrens*

cedar, Japanese *Cryptomeria japonica*

cedar, Java *Bischofia javanica*

cedar, Mackay *Paraserianthes toona*

cedar, Mlanje *Widdringtonia nodiflora*

cedar, mountain *Widdringtonia nodiflora*

cedar of Goa *Cupressus lusitanica*

cedar of Lebanon *Cedrus libani*

cedar, Oregon *Chamaecyparis lawsoniana*

cedar, pencil *Juniperus virginiana, Polyscias murrayi*

cedar, pink *Acrocarpus fraxinifolius*

cedar, Port Orford *Chamaecyparis lawsoniana*

cedar, red *Juniperus virginiana, Thuja plicata*

cedar sage *Salvia roemeriana*

cedar, salt *Tamarix chinensis*

cedar, stinking *Torreya taxifolia*

cedar, tamarisk salt *Tamarix*

cedar, true *Cedrus*
cedar, Turkish *Cedrus libani* subsp.
  stenocoma
cedar wattle *Acacia elata*
cedar, western red *Thuja plicata*
cedar, white *Melia azedarach, Thuja*
  occidentalis
cedar, willowmore *Widdringtonia*
  schwarzii
cedron *Simaba cedron*
celandine *Chelidonium majus*
celandine, greater *Chelidonium majus*
celandine, lesser *Ranunculus ficaria*
celandine poppy *Stylophorum*
  diphyllum
celandine poppy, Chinese
  Stylophorum lasiocarpum
celandine, tree *Bocconia frutescens,*
  Macleaya cordata
Celebes weeping fig *Ficus celebensis*
celeriac *Apium, A. graveolens* var.
  rapaceum
celery *Apium graveolens* var. *dulce*
celery, alpine *Aciphylla glacialis*
celery buttercup *Ranunculus*
  sceleratus
celery, leaf *Apium graveolens* var.
  secalinum
celery, mountain *Aciphylla glacialis*
celery pine *Phyllocladus,*
  P. trichomanoides
celery, sea *Apium prostratum*
celery, slender *Ciclospermum*
  leptophyllum
celery, water *Oenanthe javanica*
celery, wild *Apium graveolens*
celery wood *Polyscias elegans*
celery-top pine *Phyllocladus*
  aspleniifolius
celery-top pine, New Zealand
  Phyllocladus trichomanoides
celmisia, bog *Celmisia tomentella*
celosia *Celosia argentea*

celtis, Australian *Celtis paniculata*
celtuce *Lactuca sativa* var. *augustana*
cenizo, Monterey *Leucophyllum*
  langmaniae
centaury *Centaurium tenuiflorum*
centaury, common *Centaurium*
  erythraea
centaury, spike *Centaurium spicatum*
centipede pea *Bossiaea scolopendria*
centipede plant *Homalocladium*
  platycladium
Central Australian cabbage palm
  Livistona mariae
Central Australian ghost gum
  Corymbia aparrerinja
century plant *Agave, A. americana*
cerastium, starry *Cerastium arvense*
cereal grain amaranth *Amaranthus*
  hypochondriacus
cereal rye *Secale cereale*
cereus, golden *Bergerocactus emoryi*
cereus, golden spined *Bergerocactus*
  emoryi
cereus, golden torch *Echinopsis*
  spachiana
cerro hawthorn *Crataegus rivularis*
cestrum, green *Cestrum parqui*
cestrum, orange *Cestrum*
  aurantiacum
cestrum, purple *Cestrum* × *cultum*
cestrum, red *Cestrum* 'Newellii'
Ceylon bowstring hemp *Sansevieria*
  zeylanica
Ceylon ebony *Diospyros ebenum*
Ceylon gooseberry *Dovyalis*
  hebecarpa
Ceylon spinach *Basella rubra*
chaco *Sechium*
chaff flower *Achyranthes, A. aspera*
chaff-rush, curly *Lepidobolus*
  drapetocoleus
chaffy saw-sedge *Gahnia filum*
chain fern *Woodwardia*

chain fern, European *Woodwardia radicans*

chain fern, giant *Woodwardia fimbriata*

chain fruit *Alyxia ruscifolia*

chain, love's *Antigonon leptopus*

chain of hearts vine *Ceropegia linearis* subsp. *woodii*

chain of love *Antigonon leptopus*

chain orchid *Dendrochilum*

chain tree, golden *Laburnum anagyroides, L.* × *watereri*

chair-bottom cane *Calamus viminalis*

Chaka's wood *Strychnos decussata*

chalice vine *Solandra maxima*

chalk lettuce *Dudleya pulverulenta*

chalk maple *Acer saccharum* subsp. *leucoderme*

chalk-leaf berberis *Mahonia dictyota*

chalksticks, blue *Senecio serpens*

chamaedorea, climbing *Chamaedorea elatior*

chamburo *Carica pubescens*

chamise *Adenostoma fasciculatum*

chamizo *Atriplex canescens*

chamomile *Chamaemelum nobile*

chamomile, dyer's *Anthemis tinctoria*

chamomile, false *Boltonia*

chamomile, German *Matricaria recutita*

chamomile, lawn *Chamaemelum nobile* 'Treneague'

chamomile, native *Gnephosis eriocarpa*

chamomile, Roman *Chamaemelum nobile*

chamomile, stinking *Anthemis cotula*

chamomile sunray *Rhodanthe anthemoides*

chamomile, wild *Matricaria recutita*

chamomile, yellow *Anthemis tinctoria*

champaca *Michelia champaca*

champaca, white *Michelia* × *alba*

champagne fruit *Carica pentagona*

chandelier plant *Kalanchoe delagoensis*

Channel Island sage *Lepechinia fragrans*

chaparral broom *Baccharis pilularis*

chaparral clematis *Clematis lasiantha*

chaparral currant *Ribes malvaceum*

chaparral sage *Salvia leucophylla*

chaparral yucca *Yucca whipplei*

Chapman oak *Quercus chapmanii*

chard, Swiss *Beta vulgaris*

charity *Polemonium caeruleum*

Charlie, creeping *Pilea nummulariifolia, Plectranthus australis*

charlock *Sinapis arvensis*

charlock, jointed *Raphanus raphanistrum*

chaste tree *Vitex agnus-castus*

chat *Catha edulis*

Chatham Island akeake *Olearia traversii*

Chatham Island forget-me-not *Myosotidium hortensia*

chaulmoogra *Hydnocarpus kurzii*

chayote *Sechium edule*

Cheal's weeping cherry *Prunus* (Sato-zakura Group) 'Kiku-shidare Sakura'

checkerberry *Gaultheria procumbens*

checkerbloom *Sidalcea malviflora*

cheddar pink *Dianthus gratianopolitanus*

cheese berry *Cyathodes glauca*

cheese tree *Glochidion ferdinandi*

cheese tree, umbrella *Glochidion sumatranum*

cheeses *Malva sylvestris*

cheesewood, white *Alstonia scholaris*

chef's-cap correa *Correa baeuerlenii*

chempedak *Artocarpus integer*

chenault coralberry *Symphoricarpos* × *chenaultii*

chenille honey-myrtle *Melaleuca huegelii*
chenille plant *Acalypha hispida, Echeveria pulvinata*
chenille prickly pear *Opuntia aciculata*
chequen *Luma chequen*
chequer tree *Sorbus torminalis*
chequerboard juniper *Juniperus deppeana*
chequered lily *Fritillaria meleagris*
cherimoya *Annona cherimola*
Cherokee bean *Erythrina herbacea*
Cherokee rose *Rosa laevigata*
cherry *Prunus*
cherry, African *Prunus africana*
cherry, American bird *Prunus virginiana*
cherry, Australian *Exocarpos cupressiformis*
cherry ballart *Exocarpos cupressiformis*
cherry, Barbados *Malpighia glabra*
cherry birch *Betula lenta*
cherry, birch-bark *Prunus serrula*
cherry, bird *Prunus padus*
cherry, black *Prunus serotina*
cherry, bladder *Physalis alkekengi*
cherry, blue *Syzygium oleosum*
cherry, Brazilian *Eugenia brasiliensis, E. uniflora*
cherry, broad-leafed *Exocarpos latifolius*
cherry, brush *Syzygium australe*
cherry, Cape *Cassine sphaerophylla*
cherry, Catalina *Prunus lyonii*
cherry, Cheal's weeping *Prunus* (Sato-zakura Group) 'Kiku-shidare Sakura'
cherry, choke *Prunus virginiana*
cherry, clove *Prunus apetala*
cherry, cornelian *Cornus mas*
cherry, cyclamen *Prunus cyclamina*
cherry, downy *Prunus tomentosa*

cherry, duke *Prunus × gondouinii*
cherry, dwarf American *Prunus pumila*
cherry, dwarf flowering *Prunus glandulosa*
cherry, European bird *Prunus padus*
cherry, finger *Rhodomyrtus macrocarpa*
cherry, Florida *Eugenia uniflora*
cherry, Fuji *Prunus incisa*
cherry, gray-leaf *Prunus canescens*
cherry, ground *Physalis, Prunus fruticosa*
cherry guava *Psidium cattleianum*
cherry, Herbert River *Antidesma dallachyana*
cherry, Himalayan *Prunus rufa*
cherry, hoary *Prunus canescens*
cherry, Japanese alpine *Prunus nipponica*
cherry, Japanese bird *Prunus grayana*
cherry, Japanese cornelian *Cornus officinalis*
cherry, Japanese flowering *Prunus* Sato-zakura Group
cherry, Jerusalem *Solanum pseudocapsicum*
cherry, magenta *Syzygium paniculatum*
cherry, mahaleb *Prunus mahaleb*
cherry, Manchu *Prunus tomentosa*
cherry, Manchurian *Prunus maackii*
cherry, Mexican bird *Prunus salicifolia*
cherry, miyama *Prunus maximowiczii*
cherry, Nanking *Prunus tomentosa*
cherry orchid *Mediocalcar*
cherry, oriental *Prunus serrulata*
cherry, oriental bush *Prunus japonica*
cherry, Oshima *Prunus speciosa*
cherry palm *Pseudophoenix*
cherry palm, Florida *Pseudophoenix sargentii*
cherry peppers *Capsicum annuum* Cerasiforme Group

cherry pie *Heliotropium arborescens*
cherry, pin *Prunus pensylvanica*
cherry plum *Prunus cerasifera*
cherry prinsepia *Prinsepia sinensis*
cherry, purple *Syzygium crebrinerve*
cherry, purple ground *Physalis philadelphica*
cherry, purple-leafed sand *Prunus × cistena*
cherry, red *Prunus pensylvanica*
cherry, Rocky Mountain *Prunus besseyi*
cherry, rum *Prunus serotina*
cherry sage *Salvia microphylla*
cherry, Saint Lucie *Prunus mahaleb*
cherry, sand *Prunus besseyi, P. pumila*
cherry, Sargent *Prunus sargentii*
cherry, slender *Exocarpos sparteus*
cherry, sour *Prunus cerasus, Syzygium corynanthum*
cherry, Spanish *Mimusops elengi*
cherry, spring *Prunus × subhirtella*
cherry, steppe *Prunus fruticosa*
cherry, Surinam *Eugenia uniflora*
cherry, sweet *Prunus avium*
cherry, Syrian mountain *Prunus prostrata*
cherry, Taiwan *Prunus campanulata*
cherry, tassel *Prunus litigiosa*
cherry, Tibetan *Prunus mugus, P. serrula*
cherry, Tokyo *Prunus × yedoensis*
cherry tomato *Lycopersicum esculentum* var. *cerasiforme, L. pimpinellifolium*
cherry tree, Japanese *Prunus pseudocerasus*
cherry, Turkish willow *Prunus incana*
cherry, weeping *Prunus subhirtella* 'Pendula'
cherry, weeping Yoshino *Prunus × yedoensis* 'Shidare-Yoshino'
cherry, wild *Prunus avium*

cherry, winter *Physalis alkekengi, Solanum capsicastrum*
cherry, Yoshino *Prunus × yedoensis*
cherry-bark elm *Ulmus villosa*
cherry-laurel *Prunus laurocerasus*
cherrystone juniper *Juniperus monosperma*
chervil *Anthriscus cerefolium*
chervil, white *Cryptotaenia canadensis*
Cheshunt pine *Diselma archeri*
chestnut *Castanea sativa*
chestnut, American *Castanea dentata*
chestnut, American sweet *Castanea dentata*
chestnut, Cape *Calodendrum capense*
chestnut, Chinese *Castanea mollissima*
chestnut, Chinese horse *Aesculus chinensis*
chestnut, common horse *Aesculus hippocastanum*
chestnut, European horse *Aesculus hippocastanum*
chestnut, golden *Chrysolepis chrysophylla*
chestnut, horse *Aesculus, A. hippocastanum*
chestnut, Indian horse *Aesculus indica*
chestnut, Japanese *Castanea crenata*
chestnut, Japanese horse *Aesculus turbinata*
chestnut, lowveld *Sterculia murex*
chestnut, Moreton Bay *Castanospermum australe*
chestnut oak *Quercus montana*
chestnut oak, Japanese *Quercus acutissima*
chestnut oak, swamp *Quercus michauxii, Q. prinus*
chestnut oak, yellow *Quercus muehlenbergii*
chestnut rose *Rosa roxburghii*

chestnut, Spanish *Castanea sativa*
chestnut, sweet *Castanea sativa*
chestnut, water *Eleocharis dulcis,*
Trapa, T. natans
chestnut-leafed oak *Quercus*
castaneifolia
chiang mao *Schefflera heptaphylla*
Chiapas sage *Salvia chiapensis*
Chiapas white pine *Pinus chiapensis*
chickasaw plum *Prunus angustifolia*
chicken grape *Vitis vulpina*
chickens, hen and *Chlorophytum*
comosum
chickpea *Cicer arietinum*
chickweed *Stellaria, S. media*
chickweed, field *Cerastium arvense*
chickweed, large-flowered *Cerastium*
arvense
chickweed, lesser *Stellaria pallida*
chickweed, meadow *Cerastium*
arvense
chickweed, mouse-ear *Cerastium*
fontanum, C. glomeratum
chickweed, prairie *Cerastium arvense*
chickweed, water *Callitriche stagnalis*
chicory *Cichorium intybus*
chicot *Gymnocladus dioica*
chigo-zasa *Pleioblastus variegatus*
Chihuahua spruce *Picea chihuahuana*
chiku, mousou *Phyllostachys edulis*
Chile lantern tree *Crinodendron*
hookerianum
Chile nut *Gevuina avellana*
Chile, roble de *Eucryphia cordifolia*
Chilean avens *Geum chiloense*
Chilean beech, dwarf *Nothofagus*
pumilio
Chilean bellflower *Lapageria rosea,*
Nolana
Chilean blackcurrant *Ribes gayanum*
Chilean cranberry *Ugni molinae*
Chilean crocus *Tecophilaea,*
T. cyanocrocus

Chilean firebush *Embothrium*
coccineum
Chilean glory flower *Eccremocarpus*
scaber
Chilean goldenweed *Haplopappus*
foliosus
Chilean guava *Ugni molinae*
Chilean hazel *Gevuina avellana*
Chilean incense cedar *Austrocedrus*
chilensis
Chilean jasmine *Mandevilla laxa*
Chilean lily, miniature *Rhodophiala*
bifida
Chilean maidenhair *Adiantum*
excisum
Chilean potato vine *Solanum crispum*
Chilean rhubarb *Gunnera chilensis*
Chilean strawberry *Fragaria chiloensis*
Chilean whitlow wort *Paronychia*
brasiliana
Chilean wine palm *Jubaea chilensis*
chilgoza pine *Pinus gerardiana*
chilli *Capsicum annuum, C. frutescens*
chilli, dwarf Thai *Capsicum annuum*
'Thai Hot Small'
chilli, jalapeno *Capsicum annuum*
'Jalapeno'
chilli, Japanese *Capsicum frutescens*
'Yatsufusa'
chilli, joker's hat *Capsicum baccatum*
'Bi-Bell'
chilli, rocoto *Capsicum pubescens*
chillies, ornamental *Capsicum*
annuum Conoides Group
chimney bellflower *Campanula*
pyramidalis
China aster *Callistephus chinensis*
China fir *Cunninghamia lanceolata*
China flower *Adenandra uniflora*
China pear *Pyrus pyrifolia, P. p.* var.
culta
China, pride of *Koelreuteria*
bipinnata

China rose *Hibiscus rosa-sinensis,*
Rosa chinensis

China, rose of *Hibiscus rosa-sinensis*

China, rose tree of *Prunus triloba*

China tree *Koelreuteria paniculata*

China tree, wild *Sapindus*
drummondii

chincherinchee *Ornithogalum*
thyrsoides

chincherinchee, giant *Ornithogalum*
saundersiae

Chinchilla wattle *Acacia chinchillensis*

Chinese angelica *Angelica polymorpha*
subsp. *sinensis*

Chinese angelica tree *Aralia chinensis*

Chinese anise *Illicium verum*

Chinese arborvitae *Platycladus*
orientalis

Chinese artichoke *Stachys affinis*

Chinese asparagus *Asparagus*
cochinchinensis

Chinese aspen *Populus adenopoda*

Chinese banyan *Ficus microcarpa*

Chinese basil *Perilla frutescens*

Chinese beauty bush *Callicarpa*
rubella

Chinese beech *Fagus engleriana*

Chinese bellflower *Platycodon*
grandiflorus

Chinese bladdernut *Staphylea*
holocarpa

Chinese bottle tree *Firmiana*
simplex

Chinese box *Buxus microphylla,*
B. sinica

Chinese box thorn *Lycium chinense*

Chinese broccoli *Brassica oleracea*
Alboglabra Group

Chinese butternut *Juglans cathayensis*

Chinese cabbage *Brassica rapa*
Pekinensis Group

Chinese cedar *Cunninghamia*
lanceolata

Chinese celandine poppy
Stylophorum lasiocarpum

Chinese chestnut *Castanea mollissima*

Chinese chives *Allium tuberosum*

Chinese cinnamon *Cinnamomum*
aromaticum

Chinese cork oak *Quercus variabilis*

Chinese crab *Malus spectabilis*

Chinese date *Ziziphus jujuba*

Chinese delphinium *Delphinium*
grandiflorum

Chinese dogwood *Cornus kousa*

Chinese Douglas fir *Pseudotsuga*
sinensis

Chinese dwarf mountain ash *Sorbus*
reducta

Chinese edible bamboo *Phyllostachys*
dulcis

Chinese elm *Ulmus parvifolia,*
U. pumila

Chinese evergreen azalea
Rhododendron simsii

Chinese fan palm *Livistona chinensis,*
Trachycarpus fortunei

Chinese firethorn *Pyracantha*
atalantioides

Chinese fishtail palm *Caryota*
ochlandra

Chinese flame tree *Koelreuteria*
bipinnata

Chinese flowering crabapple *Malus*
spectabilis

Chinese flowering dogwood *Cornus*
kousa var. *chinensis*

Chinese flowering quince
Chaenomeles speciosa

Chinese forget-me-not *Cynoglossum*
amabile

Chinese foxglove *Rehmannia,*
R. elata

Chinese fringe tree *Chionanthus*
retusus

Chinese gall *Rhus chinensis*

Chinese goddess bamboo *Bambusa multiplex* var. *riviereorum*

Chinese gooseberry *Actinidia chinensis, A. deliciosa*

Chinese ground orchid *Bletilla striata*

Chinese hackberry *Celtis sinensis*

Chinese hat plant *Holmskioldia sanguinea*

Chinese hawthorn *Crataegus pinnatifida, Photinia serratifolia*

Chinese hazel *Corylus chinensis*

Chinese hemlock *Tsuga chinensis*

Chinese heptacodium *Heptacodium miconioides*

Chinese hibiscus *Hibiscus rosa-sinensis*

Chinese hickory *Carya cathayensis*

Chinese holly *Ilex cornuta*

Chinese horse chestnut *Aesculus chinensis*

Chinese houses *Collinsia bicolor*

Chinese jade *Portulacaria afra*

Chinese jasmine *Jasminum polyanthum*

Chinese jujube *Ziziphus jujuba*

Chinese juniper *Juniperus chinensis*

Chinese katsura tree *Cercidiphyllum japonicum* var. *sinense*

Chinese lacquer tree *Toxicendron vernicifluum*

Chinese lantern *Abutilon, A. megapotamicum, A. pictum, A. × hybridum, Nymania capensis, Physalis alkekengi*

Chinese lantern, desert *Abutilon leucopetalum, A. otocarpum*

Chinese lantern heath *Erica blenna*

Chinese lantern lily *Sandersonia aurantiaca*

Chinese larch *Larix potannii*

Chinese laurel *Antidesma bunius*

Chinese licorice *Glycyrrhiza uralensis*

Chinese lilac *Syringa × chinensis*

Chinese liquidambar *Liquidambar formosana*

Chinese lobelia *Lobelia chinensis*

Chinese locust *Gleditsia sinensis*

Chinese matrimony vine *Lycium chinense*

Chinese mourning cypress *Cupressus funebris*

Chinese mustard *Brassica juncea*

Chinese necklace poplar *Populus lasiocarpa*

Chinese nettle tree *Celtis sinensis*

Chinese new year flower *Enkianthus quinqueflorus*

Chinese paperbark maple *Acer griseum*

Chinese parasol tree *Firmiana simplex*

Chinese parsley *Coriandrum sativum*

Chinese pennisetum *Pennisetum alopecuroides*

Chinese peony *Paeonia lactiflora*

Chinese pistachio *Pistacia chinensis*

Chinese plumbago *Ceratostigma willmottianum*

Chinese plum-yew *Cephalotaxus sinensis*

Chinese potato *Dioscorea batatas*

Chinese preserving melon *Benincasa hispida*

Chinese privet *Ligustrum sinense*

Chinese quince *Pseudocydonia sinensis*

Chinese red birch *Betula albosinensis*

Chinese red pine *Pinus massoniana, P. tabuliformis*

Chinese redbud *Cercis chinensis*

Chinese St John's wort *Hypericum monogynum*

Chinese scholar tree *Sophora japonica*

Chinese sea buckthorn *Hippophae sinensis*

Chinese shrub *Cassinia arcuata*

Chinese snowball *Viburnum macrocephalum* 'Sterile'
Chinese snowball bush *Viburnum macrocephalum* 'Sterile'
Chinese snowball tree *Viburnum macrocephalum* 'Sterile'
Chinese soapberry *Sapindus mukorossi*
Chinese soap-pod tree *Gleditsia sinensis*
Chinese spinach *Amaranthus tricolor*
Chinese star jasmine *Trachelospermum jasminoides*
Chinese stewartia *Stewartia sinensis*
Chinese strawberry tree *Myrica rubra*
Chinese swamp cypress *Glyptostrobus pensilis*
Chinese sweet gum *Liquidambar acalycina, L. formosana*
Chinese sweetspire *Itea chinensis*
Chinese tallow tree *Sapium sebiferum*
Chinese tamarisk *Tamarix chinensis*
Chinese toon *Toona sinensis*
Chinese tree lilac *Syringa pekinensis*
Chinese trumpet creeper *Campsis grandiflora*
Chinese trumpet vine *Campsis grandiflora*
Chinese tulip tree *Liriodendron chinense*
Chinese tupelo *Nyssa sinensis*
Chinese Virginia creeper *Parthenocissus henryana*
Chinese walking-stick *Chimonobambusa tumidissinoda*
Chinese walnut *Juglans cathayensis*
Chinese wampee *Clausena lansium*
Chinese wayfaring tree *Viburnum veitchii*
Chinese weeping cypress *Cupressus funebris*
Chinese white pine *Pinus armandii*
Chinese windmill palm *Trachycarpus fortunei*
Chinese winter-hazel *Corylopsis sinensis*
Chinese wisteria *Wisteria sinensis*
Chinese wisteria, white *Wisteria sinensis* 'Alba'
Chinese witch hazel *Hamamelis mollis*
Chinese wormwood *Artemisia verlotiorum*
Chinese yam *Dioscorea batatas, D. esculenta, D. opposita*
Chinese yellow wood *Cladrastis sinensis*
Chinese yew *Taxus chinensis*
Chinese zelkova *Zelkova schneideriana, Z. sinica*
chinkapin, Allegheny *Castanea pumila*
chinkapin, bush *Castanea alnifolia*
chinkapin, Ozark *Castanea ozarkensis*
chinoti *Citrus aurantium* 'Myrtifolia'
chinquapin *Castanea pumila, Chrysolepis chrysophylla*
chinquapin oak *Quercus muehlenbergii*
chinquapin oak, dwarf *Quercus prinoides*
chinquapin, water *Nelumbo lutea*
chir pine *Pinus roxburghii*
chiretta *Swertia chirata*
chittamwood *Cotinus obovatus*
chittick *Lambertia inermis*
chives *Allium schoenoprasum*
chives, Chinese *Allium tuberosum*
chives, garlic *Allium tuberosum*
chloris, evergreen *Eustachys distichophylla*
chocho *Sechium edule*
chocolate cosmos *Cosmos atrosanguineus*
chocolate flower *Berlandiera lyrata*
chocolate foxglove *Digitalis parviflora*

chocolate, Indian *Geum rivale*
chocolate pudding tree *Diospyros digyna*
chocolate vine *Akebia*
chocolate-lily *Dichopogon strictus*
chocolate-lily, nodding *Dichopogon fimbriatus*
chocolate-scented plant *Cosmos atrosanguineus*
choi, pak *Brassica rapa* Chinensis Group
choke cherry, Georgia *Prunus cuthbertii*
chokeberry *Aronia*
chokeberry, black *Aronia melanocarpa*
chokeberry, red *Aronia arbutifolia*
chokecherry *Prunus virginiana*
chokecherry, Amur *Prunus maackii*
choko *Sechium edule*
cholla *Cylindropuntia imbricata*
cholla, buckthorn *Cylindropuntia acanthocarpa*
cholla, cane *Cylindropuntia spinosior*
cholla, club *Grusonia clavata*
cholla, coastal *Cylindropuntia prolifera*
cholla, cursed *Grusonia emoryi*
cholla, dagger *Grusonia clavata*
cholla, devil *Grusonia emoryi*
cholla, jumping *Cylindropuntia bigelovii, C. prolifera*
cholla, paper-spined *Tephrocactus articulatus*
cholla, sheathed *Cylindropuntia tunicata*
cholla, smooth chain-fruit *Cylindropuntia fulgida*
cholla, teddy bear *Cylindropuntia bigelovii*
chorogi *Stachys affinis*
Christmas bell, Natal *Sandersonia aurantiaca*
Christmas bell, Tasmanian *Blandfordia punicea*
Christmas bells *Blandfordia, B. grandiflora, B. nobilis, Sandersonia aurantiaca*
Christmas berry *Chironia baccifera, Heteromeles arbutifolia*
Christmas box *Sarcococca*
Christmas bush, New South Wales *Ceratopetalum gummiferum*
Christmas bush, Victorian *Prostanthera lasianthos*
Christmas cactus *Schlumbergera × buckleyi, S. truncata*
Christmas fern *Polystichum acrostichoides*
Christmas orchid *Calanthe triplicata*
Christmas palm *Veitchia merrillii*
Christmas pride *Ruellia macrantha*
Christmas protea *Protea aristata*
Christmas rose *Helleborus niger*
Christmas tree, Kalahari *Dichrostachys cinerea*
Christmas tree, New Zealand *Metrosideros excelsa*
Christmas tree, Western Australian *Nuytsia floribunda*
christophine *Sechium edule*
Christ's tears *Coix lacryma-jobi*
Christ's thorn *Paliurus spina-christi*
chrysanthemum, alpine *Leucanthemopsis alpina*
chrysanthemum, florists' *Chrysanthemum × grandiflorum*
chrysanthemum, garland *Xanthophthalmum coronarium*
chrysanthemum, Pacific gold and silver *Ajania pacifica*
chu, woo *Lactuca sativa* var. *augustana*
chufa *Cyperus esculentus*
chulta *Dillenia indica*
chuparosa *Anisacanthus thurberi*
chuparosa honeysuckle *Justicia californica*

churnwood *Citronella moorei*
chusan palm *Trachycarpus fortunei*
cicely, sweet *Myrrhis odorata*
cicendia, square *Cicendia quadrangularis*
cider gum *Eucalyptus gunnii*
cider gum, alpine *Eucalyptus gunnii*
cigar flower *Cuphea ignea*
cigar, Havana *Calathea lutea*
cigar-box cedar *Cedrela mexicana, C. odorata*
cigarette plant *Cuphea ignea*
cilantro *Coriandrum sativum*
cinchona *Cinchona officinalis*
cineraria *Pericallis, P.* × *hybrida*
cineraria, florist's *Pericallis* × *hybrida*
cinnamon *Cinnamomum zeylanicum*
cinnamon, Chinese *Cinnamomum aromaticum*
cinnamon clethra *Clethra acuminata*
cinnamon rose *Rosa cinnamomea*
cinnamon vine *Dioscorea batatas*
cinnamon, white *Canella winteriana*
cinquefoil *Potentilla*
cinquefoil, Himalayan *Potentilla atrosanguinea*
cinquefoil, red *Potentilla atrosanguinea*
cinquefoil, shrubby *Potentilla fruticosa*
cinquefoil, spring *Potentilla neumanniana, P. tabernaemontani*
cinquefoil, sticky *Potentilla glandulosa*
cinquefoil, sulfur *Potentilla recta*
cinquefoil, white *Potentilla alba*
cirio *Idria columnaris*
cistus, gum *Cistus ladanifer*
citron *Citrus medica*
clammy locust *Robinia viscosa*
Clanwilliam cedar *Widdringtonia cedarbergensis*
Clanwilliam euryops *Euryops speciosissimus*

claret ash *Fraxinus angustifolia* 'Raywood'
claret cup *Echinocereus triglochidiatus*
clarkia *Clarkia elegans*
clary *Salvia sclarea*
clary, Balkan *Salvia nemorosa*
clary, meadow *Salvia pratensis*
clary sage *Salvia sclarea*
clasped pondweed *Potamogeton perfoliatus*
clasping leaf pondweed *Potamogeton perfoliatus*
claw, cat's *Gloriosa superba*
claw, devil's *Harpagophytum procumbens, Ibicella*
claw feather-flower *Verticordia grandiflora*
claw flower *Calothamnus*
claw flower, Barrens *Calothamnus validus*
claw, lobster's *Clianthus puniceus*
claw, tiger's *Erythrina variegata*
clay sunray *Rhodanthe stuartiana*
clay-bush wattle *Acacia glaucoptera*
clear eye *Salvia sclarea*
cleavers *Galium aparine*
clematis, anemone *Clematis montana*
clematis, Australian *Clematis aristata*
clematis, chaparral *Clematis lasiantha*
clematis, orange peel *Clematis tibetana* subsp. *vernayi*
clematis, pipestem *Clematis lasiantha*
clematis, small-leafed *Clematis microphylla*
clementine *Citrus reticulata*
clerodendrum, beach *Clerodendrum inerme*
clerodendrum, hairy *Clerodendrum tomentosum*
clerodendrum, smooth *Clerodendrum floribundum*
clethra, cinnamon *Clethra acuminata*
clethra, Japanese *Clethra barbinervis*

clethra, summersweet *Clethra alnifolia*

Cleveland sage *Salvia clevelandii*

cliff bottlebrush *Callistemon comboynensis, C. formosus*

cliff brake *Pellaea*

cliff brake, Australian *Pellaea falcata*

cliff brake, green *Pellaea viridis*

cliff date *Phoenix rupicola*

cliff date palm *Phoenix rupicola*

cliff green *Paxistima canbyi*

cliff mallee ash *Eucalyptus cunninghamii*

cliff net bush *Calothamnus rupestris*

cliff rose *Cowania mexicana, C. plicata*

cliff spurge *Euphorbia misera*

cliffbush *Jamesia americana*

climber, elephant *Argyreia nervosa*

climbing allamanda *Allamanda cathartica*

climbing aloe *Aloe ciliaris*

climbing alstroemeria *Bomarea*

climbing bauhinia *Bauhinia glauca*

climbing bell, yellow *Littonia modesta*

climbing bird's nest fern *Microsorum punctatum*

climbing chamaedorea *Chamaedorea elatior*

climbing fan-flower *Scaevola enantophylla*

climbing fern *Lygodium*

climbing fern, Japanese *Lygodium japonicum*

climbing fumitory *Fumaria capreolata*

climbing geranium *Pelargonium peltatum*

climbing hempweed *Mikania scandens*

climbing hydrangea *Hydrangea petiolaris*

climbing lignum *Muehlenbeckia adpressa*

climbing lily *Gloriosa superba*

climbing maidenhair *Lygodium microphyllum*

climbing nightshade *Solanum jasminoides*

climbing oleander *Strophanthus gratus*

climbing orchid *Erythrorchis cassythoides*

climbing panax *Cephalaralia cephalobotrys*

climbing penstemon *Keckiella ternata*

climbing purple-star *Rhyncharrhena linearis*

climbing saltbush *Einadia nutans*

climbing swamp fern *Stenochlaena palustris*

climbing trigger plant *Stylidium scandens*

climbing twinleaf *Zygophyllum eremaeum*

climbing ylang-ylang *Artabotrys hexapetalus*

cloak fern *Cheilanthes*

cloak fern, woolly *Cheilanthes lasiophylla*

clock vine *Thunbergia grandiflora*

clock vine, bush *Thunbergia erecta*

clock vine, orange *Thunbergia gregorii*

clothes pegs, bushmen's *Grevillea glauca*

cloud grass *Agrostis nebulosa*

cloud podocarp *Podocarpus nubigenus*

cloud tree, white *Melaleuca decora*

cloudberry *Rubus chamaemorus*

clove *Syzygium aromaticum*

clove cherry *Prunus apetala*

clove currant *Ribes odoratum*

clover *Trifolium*

clover, clustered *Trifolium glomeratum*

clover, Cooper *Trigonella suavissima*

clover, elk *Aralia californica*

clover, Greek *Trigonella foenum-graecum*
clover, hare's foot *Trifolium arvense*
clover, hop *Trifolium campestre*
clover, Hungarian *Trifolium pannonicum*
clover, knotted *Trifolium striatum*
clover, narrow-leafed *Trifolium angustifolium*
clover, one-flowered *Trifolium uniflorum*
clover, purple owl *Castilleja exserta*
clover, red *Trifolium pratense*
clover, subterranean *Trifolium subterraneum*
clover, Thunberg bush *Lespedeza thunbergii*
clover tree *Goodia lotifolia*
clover tree, golden-tip *Goodia lotifolia*
clover, violet prairie *Dalea purpurea*
clover, water *Marsilea, M. mutica*
clover, white *Trifolium repens*
clover, woolly *Trifolium tomentosum*
clown fig *Ficus aspera*
club cholla *Grusonia clavata*
club, devil's *Oplopanax horridus*
club, golden *Orontium aquaticum*
club gourd *Trichosanthes cucumerina*
club, Korean devil's *Oplopanax elatus*
club-fruit lily *Corynotheca lateriflora, C. licrota*
club-leafed phebalium *Phebalium obcordatum*
clubmoss *Lycopodium, Lycopodiella, Huperzia, Selaginella*
clubmoss, bog *Lycopodiella serpentina*
clubmoss, bushy *Lycopodium deuterodensum*
clubmoss, coral *Lycopodiella cernua*
clubmoss, long *Huperzia varia*
clubmoss, nodding *Lycopodiella cernua*

clubmoss, rainbow *Selaginella uncinata*
clubmoss, scrambling *Lycopodiella cernua*
clubmoss, slender *Lycopodiella lateralis*
clubmoss, spreading *Selaginella kraussiana*
clubmoss, staghorn *Lycopodiella cernua, Lycopodium clavatum*
clubmoss, tree *Lycopodium deuterodensum*
club-rush *Schoenoplectus lacustris, Bolboschoenus fluviatilis, Isolepis platycarpa*
club-rush, knobby *Isolepis nodosa*
club-rush, nodding *Isolepis cernua*
club-rush, river *Schoenoplectus validus*
clumping mat-rush *Lomandra banksii*
cluster fig, broom *Ficus sur*
cluster fishtail palm *Caryota mitis*
cluster pine *Pinus pinaster*
cluster rose *Rosa pisocarpa*
cluster, star *Pentas lanceolata*
clustered bellflower *Campanula glomerata*
clustered clover *Trifolium glomeratum*
clustered dock *Rumex conglomeratus*
clustered everlasting *Chrysocephalum semipapposum*
clustered love grass *Eragrostis elongata*
clustered redcurrant *Ribes fasciculatum*
clustered rush *Juncus vaginatus*
clustered sunray *Rhodanthe microglossa*
cluster-leaf, silver *Terminalia sericea*
coachwhip, devil's *Stachytarpheta jamaicensis*
coachwood *Ceratopetalum apetalum*
coarse dodder-laurel *Cassytha melantha*

coarse-leafed mallee *Eucalyptus grossa*
coast azalea *Rhododendron atlanticum*
coast banksia *Banksia attenuata,*
  B. integrifolia
coast barb grass *Parapholis incurva*
coast bitterbush *Adriana klotzschii*
coast blown grass *Agrostis billardieri*
coast canthium *Canthium*
  coprosmoides
coast ceanothus *Ceanothus ramulosus*
coast coral tree *Erythrina caffra*
coast cottonwood *Hibiscus tiliaceus*
coast gray box *Eucalyptus moluccana*
coast live oak *Quercus agrifolia*
coast lotus *Lotus formosissimus*
coast morning glory *Ipomoea cairica*
coast myall *Acacia binervia*
coast polypody *Polypodium scouleri*
coast redwood *Sequoia sempervirens*
coast rosemary *Westringia fruticosa*
coast saltbush *Atriplex cinerea*
coast saw-sedge *Gahnia trifida*
coast silktassel *Garrya elliptica*
coast silver oak *Brachylaena discolor*
coast speargrass *Austrostipa stipoides*
coast tea-tree *Leptospermum*
  laevigatum
coast tussock *Poa poiformis*
coast white cedar *Chamaecyparis*
  thyoides
coast whitethorn *Ceanothus incanus*
coastal boobialla *Myoporum*
  boninense subsp. *australe,*
  M. insulare
coastal cholla *Cylindropuntia*
  prolifera
coastal gray box *Eucalyptus bosistoana*
coastal jackbean *Canavalia rosea*
coastal jugflower *Adenanthos*
  cuneatus
coastal wattle *Acacia longifolia* subsp.
  sophorae
coastal wattle, western *Acacia cyclops*

coastal woollybush *Adenanthos*
  sericeus
coat flower *Petrorhagia saxifraga*
coat, Jacob's *Acalypha amentacea*
  subsp. *wilkesiana*
coat, Joseph's *Amaranthus tricolor*
cobbler's pegs *Bidens pilosa*
cobnut *Corylus avellana*
cobra lily *Arisaema speciosum,*
  Darlingtonia californica
cobweb aloe *Haworthia arachnoidea*
cobweb houseleek *Sempervivum*
  arachnoideum
coca *Erythroxylum coca*
cocaine *Erythroxylum coca*
cochin turmeric *Curcuma aromatica*
cochineal cactus *Opuntia*
  cochenillifera
cockatoo grass *Alloteropsis semialata*
cockies' tongues *Templetonia retusa*
cocklebur *Agrimonia*
cockroach orchid *Restrepia*
cockscomb *Celosia argentea* Cristata
  Group
cocksfoot *Dactylis glomerata*
cockspur coral tree *Erythrina*
  crista-galli
cockspur flower *Plectranthus*
  parviflorus
cockspur, Maltese *Centaurea*
  melitensis
cockspur thorn *Crataegus crus-galli,*
  Maclura cochinchinensis
cockspur thorn, broad-leafed
  Crataegus prunifolia
cocktail kiwi fruit *Actinidia arguta*
cocky apple *Planchonia careya*
cocky's bootlace *Lomandra effusa*
cocoa *Theobroma cacao*
cocoa, Brazilian *Paullinia cupana*
cocona *Solanum sessiliflorum*
coconut, Buddha's *Pterygota alata*
coconut, double *Lodoicea maldivica*

coconut palm *Cocos nucifera*
coco-plum *Chrysobalanus icaco*
cocos palm *Syagrus romanzoffiana*
cocoyam *Colocasia esculenta*
cocus wood *Brya ebenus*
coffee *Coffea, C. arabica*
coffee, Arabian *Coffea arabica*
coffee bush *Breynia oblongifolia*
coffee, Congo *Coffea canephora*
coffee, Liberian *Coffea liberica*
coffee, robusta *Coffea canephora*
coffee, Sierra Leone *Coffea stenophylla*
coffee tree, Kentucky *Gymnocladus dioica*
coffee, wild *Psychotria capensis*
coffeeberry *Rhamnus californica*
coffin cypress *Cupressus funebris*
coffin juniper *Juniperus recurva*
cogon *Imperata cylindrica*
cogon grass *Imperata cylindrica*
cohosh, red *Actaea rubra*
cohune palm *Attalea cohune*
coigue *Nothofagus dombeyi*
coigue de Magellanes *Nothofagus betuloides*
coil-pod wattle *Acacia pravifolia*
cola, abata *Cola acuminata*
cola nut *Cola nitida*
colane *Owenia acidula*
Colchic ivy *Hedera colchica*
cole, red *Armoracia rusticana*
Colenso's Spaniard *Aciphylla colensoi*
coleus *Solenostemon scutellarioides*
colewort *Crambe cordifolia*
coliseum ivy *Cymbalaria muralis*
collard *Brassica oleracea* Acephala Group
colocynth *Citrullus colocynthis*
colonnaire, pin *Araucaria columnaris*
coloradillo *Hamelia erecta, H. patens*
Colorado blue spruce *Picea pungens*
Colorado spruce *Picea pungens*

Colorado white fir *Abies concolor*
coltsfoot *Tussilago farfara*
coltsfoot, sweet *Petasites*
Columbia lily *Lilium columbianum*
Columbia tiger lily *Lilium columbianum*
Columbian hawthorn *Crataegus columbiana*
columbine *Aquilegia*
columbine, alpine *Aquilegia alpina*
columbine, American wild *Aquilegia canadensis*
columbine, black *Aquilegia atrata*
columbine, blue *Aquilegia caerulea*
columbine, Canada *Aquilegia canadensis*
columbine, feathered *Thalictrum aquilegiifolium*
columbine, golden *Aquilegia chrysantha*
columbine, Rocky Mountain *Aquilegia caerulea*
columbine, western *Aquilegia formosa*
comb fern *Schizaea*
comb fern, branched *Schizaea dichotoma*
comb fern, forked *Schizaea bifida*
comb fern, rock *Schizaea rupestris*
comb grevillea *Grevillea huegelii*
comet orchid *Angraecum*
comfrey *Symphytum, S. officinale*
comfrey, common *Symphytum officinale*
comfrey, English *Symphytum officinale*
comfrey, prickly *Symphytum asperum*
comfrey, Russian *Symphytum × uplandicum*
commiphora, forest *Commiphora woodii*
common alder *Alnus glutinosa*
common bamboo *Bambusa vulgaris*

common bittercress *Cardamine hirsuta*
common bog-rush *Schoenus apogon*
common briar *Rosa canina*
common brookweed *Samolus valerandi*
common broom *Cytisus scoparius*
common buckthorn *Rhamnus cathartica*
common buttercup *Ranunculus ficaria*
common centaury *Centaurium erythraea*
common comfrey *Symphytum officinale*
common corkwood *Commiphora glandulosa*
common corn salad *Valerianella locusta*
common crabapple *Malus sylvestris*
common dogbane *Apocynum androsaemifolium*
common dogwood *Cornus sanguinea*
common elder *Sambucus nigra*
common emu bush *Eremophila glabra*
common evening primrose *Oenothera biennis*
common everlasting *Xerochrysum bracteatum*
common fiddleneck *Amsinckia intermedia*
common filmy fern *Hymenophyllum cupressiforme*
common foxglove *Digitalis purpurea*
common fringe-lily *Thysanotus tuberosus*
common gardenia *Gardenia augusta*
common geissois *Geissois pruinosa*
common ginger *Zingiber officinale*
common globe flower *Trollius europaeus*
common gorse *Ulex europaeus*
common grape vine *Vitis vinifera*

common ground fern *Calochlaena dubia*
common guarri *Euclea undulata*
common hyacinth *Hyacinthus orientalis*
common ivy *Hedera helix*
common jasmine *Jasminum officinale, J. o.* 'Grandiflorum'
common jujube *Ziziphus jujuba*
common juniper *Juniperus communis*
common laburnum *Laburnum anagyroides*
common large monkey flower *Mimulus guttatus*
common lettuce *Lactuca sativa*
common lilac *Syringa vulgaris*
common lime *Tilia* × *europaea*
common linden *Tilia* × *europaea*
common maidenhair *Adiantum capillus-veneris*
common maidenhair fern *Adiantum aethiopicum*
common mallow *Malva sylvestris*
common marigold *Calendula officinalis*
common marjoram *Origanum vulgare*
common matrimony vine *Lycium barbarum*
common milkvine *Marsdenia rostrata*
common mock orange *Philadelphus coronarius*
common moonseed *Menispermum canadense*
common morning glory *Ipomoea purpurea*
common myrtle *Myrtus communis*
common nardoo *Marsilea drummondii*
common net bush *Calothamnus quadrifidus*
common nettle *Urtica dioica*
common ninebark *Physocarpus opulifolius*

common oak *Quercus robur*
common oak fern *Gymnocarpium dryopteris*
common olive *Olea europaea*
common osier *Salix viminalis*
common pear *Pyrus communis*
common pearl bush *Exochorda racemosa*
common pepper *Piper nigrum*
common peppercress *Lepidium africanum*
common pest pear *Opuntia stricta*
common phyllota *Phyllota phylicoides*
common pink *Dianthus plumarius*
common poison bush *Acokanthera oppositifolia*
common polypody *Polypodium vulgare*
common pomegranate *Punica granatum*
common primrose willow *Ludwigia peruviana*
common privet *Ligustrum vulgare*
common pulai *Alstonia angustiloba*
common purslane *Portulaca oleracea*
common reed *Phragmites australis*
common resin tree *Ozoroa paniculosa*
common rock rose *Helianthemum nummularium*
common rose mallow *Hibiscus moscheutos*
common rue *Ruta graveolens*
common ruellia *Ruellia brittoniana*
common rush *Juncus effusus*
common saffron *Cassine papillosa*
common sage *Salvia officinalis*
common sallow *Salix cinerea*
common screwpine *Pandanus utilis*
common shield fern *Dryopteris cristata*
common sida *Sida rhombifolia*
common silkpod *Parsonsia straminea*

common skullcap *Scutellaria galericulata*
common snowball *Viburnum opulus* 'Sterile'
common snowberry *Symphoricarpos albus*
common snowdrop *Galanthus nivalis*
common Solomon's seal *Polygonatum* × *hybridum*
common sow-thistle *Sonchus oleraceus*
common speedwell *Veronica officinalis*
common spleenwort *Asplenium trichomanes*
common spotted orchid *Dactylorhiza fuchsii*
common spruce *Picea abies*
common starwort *Callitriche stagnalis*
common stinkweed *Opercularia aspera*
common storksbill *Erodium cicutarium*
common strangler fig *Ficus thonningii*
common sun rose *Helianthemum nummularium*
common sunflower *Helianthus annuus*
common sunray *Triptilodiscus pygmaeus*
common tassel fern *Huperzia phlegmaria*
common thorn apple *Datura stramonium*
common thyme *Thymus vulgaris*
common tree daisy *Olearia arborescens*
common verbena *Verbena officinalis*
common vervain *Verbena officinalis*
common vetch *Vicia sativa*
common walnut *Juglans regia*
common watercress *Rorippa nasturtium-aquaticum*
common white jasmine *Jasminum officinale*

common wild fig *Ficus thonningii*
common witch hazel *Hamamelis virginiana*
common woadwaxen *Genista tinctoria*
common woollybush *Adenanthos cygnorum*
common wormwood *Artemisia absinthium*
common yew *Taxus baccata*
compass cactus *Ferocactus cylindraceus*
compass plant *Lactuca serriola, Silphium laciniatum*
Compton coral pea *Hardenbergia comptoniana*
comun, Navajita *Bouteloua gracilis*
condurango *Marsdenia condurango*
cone peppers, red *Capsicum annuum* Fasciculatum Group
conebush, karoo *Leucadendron nobile*
coneflower *Echinacea, Ratibida, Rudbeckia, R. laciniata, R. nitida*
coneflower, cut-leaf *Rudbeckia laciniata*
coneflower, gray head *Ratibida pinnata*
coneflower, hedgehog *Echinacea purpurea*
coneflower, long-head *Ratibida columnifera*
coneflower, orange *Rudbeckia fulgida*
coneflower, pale *Echinacea pallida*
coneflower, pale purple *Echinacea pallida*
coneflower, prairie *Ratibida columnifera, R. pinnata*
coneflower, purple *Echinacea purpurea*
coneflower, rose *Isopogon formosus*
coneflower, western *Rudbeckia occidentalis*
coneflower, yellow *Ratibida pinnata*

coneseeds, heath-leafed *Conospermum ericifolium*
coneseeds, long-leaf *Conospermum longifolium*
conesticks *Petrophile pulchella*
conesticks, hoary *Petrophile canescens*
conesticks, stalked *Petrophile pedunculata*
Confederate jasmine *Trachelospermum jasminoides*
Confederate rose *Hibiscus mutabilis*
Confederate vine *Antigonon leptopus*
Confederate violet *Viola sororia* 'Priceana'
confetti bush *Coleonema pulchellum*
confetti bush, white *Coleonema album*
Congo coffee *Coffea canephora*
Congo pea *Cajanus cajan*
conostylis, prickly *Conostylis aculeata*
Constantinople, red peony of *Paeonia peregrina*
contorted willow *Salix babylonica* 'Tortuosa'
convolvulus, blue *Convolvulus sabatius*
convolvulus, broom *Convolvulus scoparius*
convolvulus, shrub *Convolvulus floridus*
cooba *Acacia salicina*
cooba, river *Acacia stenophylla*
coobah *Acacia salicina*
Coochin Hills oak *Grevillea whiteana*
coogera *Arytera divaricata*
coogera, twin-leafed *Arytera distylis*
Cooktown ironwood *Erythrophleum chlorostachys*
Cooktown orchid *Dendrobium bigibbum*
Cooktown paperbark *Melaleuca saligna*
coolabah *Eucalyptus coolabah, E. microtheca*

coolabah apple *Angophora melanoxylon*

coolamon *Syzygium moorei*

Coolatai grass *Hyparrhenia hirta*

coolibah *Eucalyptus coolabah, E. microtheca*

coolibah apple *Angophora melanoxylon*

coolibah grass *Panicum queenslandicum*

coolibah, gum-barked *Eucalyptus intertexta*

Coonavittra wattle *Acacia jennerae*

coondoo, blunt-leafed *Pouteria myrsinoides*

coontie *Zamia integrifolia*

Cooper clover *Trigonella suavissima*

Cootamundra wattle *Acacia baileyana*

copaiba *Copaifera lansdorfii*

copall *Pistacia mexicana*

copey *Clusia major*

copihue *Lapageria rosea*

copper beard-orchid *Calochilus campestris*

copper beech *Fagus sylvatica* 'Purpurea'

copperburr, gray *Sclerolaena diacantha*

copperburr, limestone *Sclerolaena obliquicuspis*

copperburr, long-spined *Sclerolaena longicuspis*

copperburr, mallee *Sclerolaena parviflora*

copperburr, salt *Sclerolaena ventricosa*

copperburr, short-winged *Sclerolaena brachyptera*

copperburr, star *Sclerolaena stelligera*

copperburr, tall *Sclerolaena convexula*

copperburr, tangled *Sclerolaena divaricata*

copperburr, three-spined *Sclerolaena tricuspis*

copperburr, twin-horned *Dissocarpus biflorus*

copperburr, woolly *Sclerolaena lanicuspis*

copperburr, woolly-fruit *Maireana sclerolaenoides*

copperleaf *Acalypha amentacea* subsp. *wilkesiana, Alternanthera*

copper-wire daisy, showy *Podolepis jaceoides*

coppery mesembryanthemum *Malephora crocea*

coprosma, sand *Coprosma acerosa*

coquito palm *Jubaea chilensis*

coracan *Eleusine coracana*

coral aloe *Aloe striata*

coral ardisia *Ardisia crenata*

coral bean *Erythrina herbacea*

coral bean, eastern *Erythrina herbacea*

coral bean, Indian *Erythrina variegata*

coral bells *Heuchera*

coral clubmoss *Lycopodiella cernua*

coral fern *Lycopodiella cernua*

coral fern, pouched *Gleichenia dicarpa*

coral fern, rock *Gleichenia rupestris*

coral fern, scrambling *Gleichenia microphylla*

coral gem *Lotus berthelotii*

coral gum *Eucalyptus torquata*

coral heath *Epacris microphylla*

coral hibiscus *Hibiscus schizopetalus*

coral lily *Lilium pumilum*

coral pea *Abrus precatorius, Kennedia*

coral pea, black *Kennedia nigricans*

coral pea, Compton *Hardenbergia comptoniana*

coral pea, dusky *Kennedia rubicunda*

coral pea, scarlet *Kennedia prostrata*

coral penstemon *Penstemon barbatus*

coral plant *Berberidopsis corallina, Jatropha multifida, Russelia equisetiformis* coral tree *Erythrina, E. corallodendron, E. lysistemon, E. × sykesii, E. variegata*

coral tree, bat's wing *Erythrina vespertilio*

coral tree, Brazilian *Erythrina speciosa*

coral tree, coast *Erythrina caffra*

coral tree, cockspur *Erythrina crista-galli*

coral tree, hybrid *Erythrina × bidwillii*

coral tree, Natal *Erythrina humeana*

coral tree, purple *Erythrina fusca*

coral tree, Senegal *Erythrina senegalensis*

coral tree, South African *Erythrina caffra*

coral tree, Transvaal *Erythrina lysistemon*

coral tree, variegated *Erythrina variegata* 'Parcellii'

coral vine *Antigonon leptopus, Kennedia coccinea*

coralberry *Ardisia crenata, Ilex verticillata, Rivina humilis, Symphoricarpos, S. orbiculatus*

coralberry, chenault *Symphoricarpos × chenaultii*

coralberry, Doorenbos *Symphoricarpos × doorenbosii*

coralberry, Indian currant *Symphoricarpos orbiculatus*

coralberry, white *Ardisia crenata* 'Alba'

corallita *Antigonon leptopus*

coralwood *Adenanthera pavonina*

corango-aco *Pfaffia paniculata*

Corbasson's kauri *Agathis corbassonii*

cord grass *Spartina*

cord grass, freshwater *Spartina pectinata*

cordia *Cordia dichotoma*

cordia, little leaf *Cordia parvifolia*

cord-rush, mountain *Baloskion australe*

cord-rush, pale *Baloskion pallens*

cord-rush, tassel *Baloskion tetraphyllum*

corduroy *Cryptocarya corrugata*

corduroy tamarind *Arytera lautereriana*

coriander *Coriandrum sativum*

coriander, Roman *Nigella sativa*

coriander, Vietnamese *Persicaria odorata*

cork elm *Ulmus thomasii*

cork oak *Quercus suber*

cork tree *Hakea suberea*

cork tree, Amur *Phellodendron amurense*

cork tree, Japanese *Phellodendron japonicum*

cork tree, western *Hakea lorea*

corkbark, gnarled *Hakea fraseri*

corkbark honey-myrtle *Melaleuca suberosa*

corkbark, straggly *Hakea eyreana*

corkbark tree *Hakea ivoryi*

corkbush *Euonymus alatus*

corkscrew flower *Strophanthus speciosus, Vigna caracalla*

corkscrew grass *Austrostipa setacea*

corkscrew hazel *Corylus avellana* 'Contorta'

corkscrew plant *Genlisea*

corkwood *Duboisia myoporoides, Hakea ivoryi, Leitneria floridana, Myoporum acuminatum*

corkwood, common *Commiphora glandulosa*

corkwood, Florida *Leitneria floridana*

corkwood, hard *Endiandra sieberi*

corkwood, long-leaf *Hakea suberea*

corkwood oak *Hakea fraseri*

corkwood, oak-leafed *Commiphora wildii*

corkwood, pink-flowered *Melicope elleryana*
corkwood wattle *Acacia bidwillii*
corky passionflower *Passiflora suberosa*
corky prickle-vine *Caesalpinia subtropica*
corky thorn *Acacia davyi*
corn *Zea mays*
corn, Indian *Zea mays*
corn lily *Ixia*
corn marigold *Chrysanthemum segetum*
corn mignonette *Reseda phyteuma*
corn millet, broom *Panicum miliaceum*
corn mint *Mentha arvensis*
corn poppy *Papaver rhoeas*
corn salad *Valerianella locusta*
corn salad, common *Valerianella locusta*
corn spurrey *Spergula arvensis*
corn, sweet *Zea mays*
corn, turkey *Dicentra eximia*
corn-cockle *Agrostemma githago*
cornel, dwarf *Cornus canadensis*
Cornelian cherry *Cornus mas*
corners, four *Grewia occidentalis*
cornflag, African *Chasmanthe floribunda*
cornflower *Centaurea cyanus*
cornflower, globe *Centaurea macrocephala*
cornflower, perennial *Centaurea montana*
cornflower, Persian *Centaurea dealbata*
Cornish heath *Erica vagans*
cornus, Bentham's *Cornus capitata*
coroba *Schinus lentiscifolius*
corojo *Gastrococos crispa*
Corozo palm *Attalea butyracea, Elaeis oleifera*
correa, chef's-cap *Correa baeuerlenii*

correa, mountain *Correa lawrenciana*
correa, tree *Correa lawrenciana*
correa, white *Correa alba*
correosa *Rhus microphylla*
Corrigin grevillea *Grevillea scapigera*
corrugated sida *Sida corrugata*
Corsican heath *Erica terminalis*
Corsican hellebore *Helleborus argutifolius*
Corsican mint *Mentha requienii*
Corsican pine *Pinus nigra* var. *maritima*
cosmea *Cosmos bipinnatus*
cosmetic bark *Murraya paniculata*
cosmos *Cosmos bipinnatus*
cosmos, black *Cosmos atrosanguineus*
cosmos, chocolate *Cosmos atrosanguineus*
cosmos, yellow *Cosmos sulphureus*
costmary *Tanacetum balsamita*
costus, fiery *Costus igneus*
cotoneaster, bearberry *Cotoneaster dammeri*
cotoneaster, cranberry *Cotoneaster apiculatus*
cotoneaster, creeping *Cotoneaster adpressus*
cotoneaster, European *Cotoneaster integerrimus*
cotoneaster, hedge *Cotoneaster lucidus*
cotoneaster, Himalayan tree *Cotoneaster frigidus*
cotoneaster, rock *Cotoneaster horizontalis*
cotoneaster, rockspray *Cotoneaster horizontalis*
cotoneaster, spreading *Cotoneaster divaricatus*
cotton *Gossypium*
cotton, Australian wild *Gossypium australe*
cotton ball cactus *Espostoa lanata*

cotton bush *Ptilotus obovatus*
cotton bush, balloon *Gomphocarpus fruticosus, G. physocarpus*
cotton bush, black *Maireana decalvans*
cotton bush, eastern *Maireana brevifolia, M. microphylla*
cotton bush, white *Pimelea nivea*
cotton daisy *Celmisia spectabilis*
cotton, devil's *Abroma augusta*
cotton fireweed *Senecio quadridentatus*
cotton grass *Eriophorum, E. vaginatum*
cotton grass, tussock *Eriophorum vaginatum*
cotton gum *Nyssa aquatica*
cotton palm *Washingtonia filifera, W. robusta*
cotton palm, American *Washingtonia filifera*
cotton panic grass *Digitaria brownii*
cotton plant *Celmisia spectabilis*
cotton rose *Hibiscus mutabilis*
cotton, Sea Island *Gossypium barbadense*
cotton thistle *Onopordum acanthium, O. nervosum*
cotton, tree *Gossypium arboreum*
cotton tree, silk *Bombax ceiba*
cottonheads, gray *Conostylis candicans*
cottonleaf physic *Jatropha gossypifolia*
cottonleaf physic nut *Jatropha gossypiifolia*
cottonsedge *Eriophorum vaginatum*
cotton-seed tree *Baccharis halimifolia*
cottonwood *Populus deltoides*
cottonwood, American *Populus deltoides*
cottonwood, black *Populus heterophylla, P. trichocarpa*
cottonwood, coast *Hibiscus tiliaceus*
cottonwood, eastern *Populus deltoides*
cottonwood, Fremont *Populus fremontii*
cottonwood, golden *Cassinia fulvida*
cottonwood, lance-leaf *Populus × acuminata*
cottonwood, narrow-leaf *Populus angustifolia*
cottonwood, northern *Populus deltoides* subsp. *monilifera*
cottonwood, plains *Populus sargentii*
cottonwood, southern *Populus deltoides* subsp. *deltoides*
cottonwood tree *Hibiscus tiliaceus*
cottonwood, western *Populus fremontii*
cotula *Cotula australis*
couch grass *Cynodon dactylon, Elytrigia repens*
couch, Mullumbimby *Cyperus brevifolius*
couch, onion *Arrhenatherum elatius*
couch, prickly *Zoysia macrantha*
couch, rat's-tail *Sporobolus mitchellii*
couch, saltwater *Paspalum vaginatum*
couch, sand *Sporobolus virginicus*
couch, water *Paspalum distichum*
cough-bush *Cassinia laevis*
Coulter pine *Pinus coulteri*
courgette *Cucurbita, C. pepo*
Coventry bells *Campanula trachelium*
coville *Larrea tridentata*
cow okra *Parmentiera aculeata*
cow orchid *Cryptostylis subulata*
cow parsley *Anthriscus sylvestris*
cowberry *Vaccinium vitis-idaea*
cow-itch *Campsis radicans*
cowl, friar's *Arisarum vulgare*
cowpea *Vigna unguiculata*
cow's foot *Piper aduncum*
cow's horn euphorbia *Euphorbia grandicornis*

cowslip *Mertensia virginica, Primula veris*

cowslip, American *Dodecatheon, D. meadia*

cowslip, blue *Pulmonaria angustifolia*

cowslip, Cape *Lachenalia*

cowslip orchid *Diuris lanceolata*

cow's-tail pine *Cephalotaxus harringtonia* 'Fastigiata'

Cox's juniper *Juniperus recurva* 'Coxii'

coyau, palme *Coccothrinax argentea*

coyote brush *Baccharis pilularis*

coyote willow *Salix exigua*

crab, American sweet *Malus coronaria*

crab, bechtel *Malus ioensis* 'Plena'

crab cactus *Schlumbergera truncata*

crab, Chinese *Malus spectabilis*

crab claw plant *Vriesea carinata*

crab grass *Digitaria, Eleusine, Panicum*

crab, Hupeh *Malus hupehensis*

crab, Iowa *Malus ioensis*

crab, Japanese *Malus floribunda*

crab, Oregon *Malus fusca*

crab, prairie *Malus ioensis*

crab, weeping *Malus* (hybrid crabapple) 'Echtermeyer'

crab, wild *Malus sylvestris*

crabapple *Malus pumila, M.* × *purpurea, M. sylvestris, Schizomeria ovata*

crabapple, American *Malus coronaria*

crabapple, American sweet *Malus coronaria*

crabapple, Arnold *Malus* × *arnoldiana*

crabapple, Balkan *Malus florentina*

crabapple, Chinese flowering *Malus spectabilis*

crabapple, common *Malus sylvestris*

crabapple, Hupeh *Malus hupehensis*

crabapple, Iowa *Malus ioensis*

crabapple, Italian *Malus florentina*

crabapple, Japanese flowering *Malus floribunda*

crabapple, Oregon *Malus fusca*

crabapple, pear-leafed *Malus prunifolia*

crabapple, prairie *Malus ioensis*

crabapple, purple-flowered *Malus pumila* 'Niedzwetzkyana'

crabapple, redbud *Malus* × *zumi*

crabapple, Sargent's *Malus sargentii*

crabapple, Siberian *Malus baccata*

crabapple, tea *Malus hupehensis*

crabapple, Tibetan *Malus transitoria*

crabapple, wild *Malus sylvestris*

crab's eyes *Abrus precatorius*

crack willow *Salix fragilis*

cradle lily *Tradescantia spathacea*

craibia, small *Craibia zimmermannii*

crake berry *Empetrum nigrum*

cranberry *Vaccinium macrocarpon*

cranberry, American *Vaccinium macrocarpon*

cranberry, American highbush *Viburnum trilobum*

cranberry bush *Viburnum trilobum*

cranberry bush, American *Viburnum trilobum*

cranberry, Chilean *Ugni molinae*

cranberry cotoneaster *Cotoneaster apiculatus*

cranberry, European *Viburnum opulus*

cranberry, European highbush *Viburnum opulus*

cranberry heath *Astroloma humifusum*

cranberry, highbush *Viburnum trilobum*

cranberry, native *Lissanthe sapida*

cranberry, small *Oxycoccus macrocarpus*

cranberry, wild *Vaccinium oxycoccos*

cranesbill *Geranium*

cranesbill, Armenian *Geranium psilostemon*

cranesbill, bloody *Geranium sanguineum*

cranesbill, dove's-foot *Geranium molle*

cranesbill, meadow *Geranium pratense*

crape fern *Leptopteris fraseri*

crape gardenia *Tabernaemontana divaricata*

crape jasmine *Tabernaemontana divaricata, T. d.* 'Flore Pleno'

crape myrtle *Lagerstroemia fauriei* × *indica, L. indica*

crape myrtle, queen *Lagerstroemia speciosa*

crater onion *Allium cratericola*

Craven gray box *Eucalyptus largeana*

cream silky oak *Athertonia diversifolia*

creambush *Holodiscus discolor, H. dumosus*

creamcups *Platystemon*

creek plum *Prunus rivularis*

creek sandpaper fig *Ficus coronata*

creek wattle *Acacia rivalis*

creeper, bluebell *Sollya heterophylla*

creeper, bower *Pandorea jasminoides*

creeper, canary *Tropaeolum peregrinum*

creeper, cardinal *Ipomoea horsfalliae*

creeper, Carmel *Ceanothus griseus* var. *horizontalis*

creeper, cat's claw *Macfadyena unguis-cati*

creeper, caustic *Chamaesyce drummondii*

creeper, Chinese Virginia *Parthenocissus henryana*

creeper, emerald *Strongylodon macrobotrys*

creeper, flame *Combretum microphyllum, Tropaeolum speciosum*

creeper, Japanese *Parthenocissus tricuspidata*

creeper, love *Comesperma volubile*

creeper, malu *Bauhinia vahlii*

creeper, Mexican *Antigonon leptopus*

creeper, pink foam *Congea tomentosa*

creeper, Point Reyes *Ceanothus gloriosus*

creeper, Port St John *Podranea ricasoliana*

creeper, Rangoon *Quisqualis indica*

creeper, Rodondo *Drosanthemum candens*

creeper, silver vein *Parthenocissus henryana*

creeper, trumpet *Campsis*

creeper, Virginia *Parthenocissus quinquefolia*

creeper, wait-a-while *Smilax australis*

creeping avens *Geum reptans*

creeping banksia *Banksia repens*

creeping bent *Agrostis stolonifera*

creeping blueberry *Vaccinium crassifolium*

creeping boobialla *Eremophila debilis, Myoporum parvifolium*

creeping brookweed *Samolus repens*

creeping buttercup *Ranunculus repens*

creeping Charlie *Pilea nummulariifolia, Plectranthus australis*

creeping cotoneaster *Cotoneaster adpressus*

creeping cudweed *Gnaphalium gymnocephalum*

creeping devil *Stenocereus eruca*

creeping dogwood *Cornus canadensis*

creeping fern *Pyrrosia rupestris*

creeping fig *Ficus pumila*

creeping fog *Holcus mollis*

creeping forget-me-not *Omphalodes verna*

creeping geebung *Persoonia chamaepitys*

creeping Jacob's ladder *Polemonium reptans*

creeping Jenny *Lysimachia nummularia*

creeping juniper *Juniperus horizontalis, J. procumbens*

creeping knotweed *Persicaria prostrata*

creeping lasiandra *Heterocentron elegans*

creeping lily *Gloriosa superba*

creeping mahonia *Mahonia repens*

creeping millotia *Millotia greevesii*

creeping monkey flower *Mimulus repens*

creeping myoporum *Myoporum parvifolium*

creeping myrtle *Vinca minor*

creeping oxalis *Oxalis corniculata*

creeping parakeelya *Calandrinia ptychosperma*

creeping pine *Microcachrys tetragona*

creeping raspwort *Gonocarpus micranthus*

creeping sage *Salvia sonomensis*

creeping St John's wort *Hypericum calycinum*

creeping saltbush *Atriplex semibaccata*

creeping saxifrage *Saxifraga stolonifera*

creeping shield fern *Lastreopsis microsora*

creeping soft grass *Holcus mollis*

creeping speedwell *Veronica persica, V. plebeia, V. repens*

creeping spurge *Euphorbia myrsinites*

creeping thyme *Thymus praecox, T. serpyllum*

creeping velvet grass *Holcus mollis*

creeping vervain *Verbena canadensis*

creeping willow *Salix repens*

creeping willow, Arctic *Salix reptans*

creeping zinnia *Sanvitalia procumbens*

creosote bush *Larrea, L. tridentata*

creosote bush scrub *Prosopis pubescens*

crepe fern *see* crape fern

crepe gardenia *see* crape gardenia

crepe jasmine *see* crape jasmine

crepe myrtle *see* crape myrtle

cress, bitter *Cardamine*

cress, garden *Lepidium sativum*

cress, hairy-pod *Harmsiodoxa blennodioides*

cress, meadow *Cardamine, C. pratensis*

cress, rock *Arabis*

cress, scented *Harmsiodoxa puberula*

cress, short *Harmsiodoxa brevipes*

cress, stone *Aethionema*

cress, upland *Barbarea vulgaris*

crested crumbweed *Chenopodium cristatum*

crested dog's-tail *Cynosurus cristatus*

crested iris *Iris cristata*

crested speargrass *Austrostipa blackii*

crested wattle *Paraserianthes lophantha*

crested wood fern *Dryopteris cristata*

Cretan brake *Pteris cretica*

Cretan date palm *Phoenix theophrasti*

Cretan dittany *Origanum dictamnus*

Cretan mallow *Lavatera cretica*

Cretan maple *Acer sempervirens*

Cretan weed *Hedypnois rhagadioloides* subsp. *cretica*

Cretan zelkova *Zelkova abelicea*

Crete, dittany of *Origanum dictamnus*

cricket ball hakea *Hakea platysperma*

Crimean snowdrop *Galanthus plicatus*
crimson bramble *Rubus arcticus*
crimson foxtail *Ptilotus atriplicifolius*
crimson glory vine *Vitis coignetiae*
crimson sage *Salvia spathacea*
crimson turkey bush *Eremophila latrobei*
crimson yarrow *Achillea millefolium* 'Cerise Queen'
crinkle bush *Lomatia silaifolia*
crinkled hair grass *Deschampsia flexuosa*
crinum, southern swamp *Crinum americanum*
crocus, autumn *Colchicum, C. autumnale, Sternbergia*
crocus, blue *Tecophilaea*
crocus, Chilean *Tecophilaea, T. cyanocrocus*
crocus, Dutch *Crocus vernus*
crocus, saffron *Crocus sativus*
Crofton weed *Ageratina adenophora*
crookneck gourd *Lagenaria siceraria*
crookneck squash *Cucurbita moschata*
crookstem bamboo *Phyllostachys aureosulcata*
cropleaf ceanothus *Ceanothus dentatus*
cross, Jerusalem *Lychnis chalcedonica*
cross, Maltese *Lychnis chalcedonica*
cross-leafed heath *Erica tetralix*
cross-vine *Bignonia capreolata*
crosswort *Phuopsis stylosa*
croton *Codiaeum variegatum*
croton, oil *Croton tiglium*
crow garlic *Allium vineale*
crowberry, black *Empetrum nigrum*
crowberry, Plymouth *Corema conradii*
crowberry, Portuguese *Corema album*
crowberry, South American *Empetrum rubrum*

crowded-leaf wattle *Acacia conferta*
crowfoot *Anemonella thalictroides, Erodium cicutarium*
crowfoot, blue *Erodium crinitum*
crowfoot, native *Erodium crinitum, E. cygnorum*
crowfoot violet *Viola pedata*
crown daisy *Xanthophthalmum coronarium*
crown fern *Blechnum discolor*
crown, flat *Albizia adianthifolia*
crown imperial *Fritillaria imperialis*
crown, king's *Calotropis procera, Dicliptera suberecta*
crown of thorns *Euphorbia milii, Ziziphus spina-christi*
crown of thorns, giant *Euphorbia × lomii*
crown, silver *Cotyledon undulata*
crown vetch *Coronilla varia*
crow's apple *Owenia venosa*
crow's ash *Flindersia australis*
crow's ash, bastard *Pentaceras australe*
crowsfoot *Erodium*
crowsfoot elm *Argyrodendron trifoliolatum*
crowsfoot grass *Eleusine indica*
crowsfoot, water *Ranunculus aquatilis*
crucifix orchid *Epidendrum ibaguense, E.* Obrienianum (grex)
cruel plant *Araujia sericifera*
crumbweed, black *Chenopodium melanocarpum*
crumbweed, crested *Chenopodium cristatum*
crumbweed, green *Chenopodium carinatum, Dysphania rhadinostachya*
crumbweed, small *Chenopodium pumilio*
cryptocarya, three-veined *Cryptocarya triplinervis*
crystal tea *Ledum palustre*

Cuba pink trumpet *Tabebuia pallida*
Cuban bast *Hibiscus elatus*
Cuban lily *Scilla peruviana*
Cuban petticoat palm *Copernicia macroglossa*
Cuban royal palm *Roystonea regia*
cubeb *Piper cubeba*
cuckoo bread *Oxalis acetosella*
cuckoo flower *Cardamine, C. pratensis*
cuckoo pint *Arum maculatum*
cucumber *Cucumis sativus*
cucumber, burr *Cucumis anguria*
cucumber, Jerusalem *Cucumis anguria*
cucumber orchid *Dendrobium cucumerinum*
cucumber, prickly *Cucumis myriocarpus*
cucumber, serpent *Trichosanthes cucumerina*
cucumber, slender *Zehneria cunninghamii*
cucumber, squirting *Ecballium elaterium*
cucumber tree *Magnolia acuminata*
cucumber tree, yellow *Magnolia cordata*
cudgerie *Flindersia schottiana*
cudweed *Artemisia ludoviciana, Gnaphalium coarctatum*
cudweed, creeping *Gnaphalium gymnocephalum*
cudweed, flannel *Actinobole uliginosum*
cudweed, hooked *Stuartina hamata*
cudweed, Jersey *Pseudognaphalium luteoalbum*
cudweed, shining *Gnaphalium nitidulum*
cudweed, silver *Gnaphalium argentifolium*
cudweed, spoon *Stuartina muelleri*

cudweed, star *Gnaphalium involucratum*
culen *Psoralea glandulosa*
Culver's root *Veronicastrum virginicum*
Cumberland azalea *Rhododendron cumberlandense*
Cumberland false rosemary *Conradina verticillata*
cumbungi, broad-leaf *Typha orientalis*
cumbungi, narrow-leaf *Typha domingensis*
cumin *Cuminum cyminum*
cumin, black *Nigella sativa*
cumquat *Citrus japonica*
cumquat, native *Citrus glauca*
cunjevoi *Alocasia brisbanensis*
cunjevoi lily *Alocasia brisbanensis*
cup and saucer *Campanula medium*
cup and saucer plant *Holmskioldia sanguinea*
cup and saucer vine *Cobaea scandens*
cup, claret *Echinocereus triglochidiatus*
cup fern *Dennstaedtia*
cup, golden *Hunnemannia fumariifolia*
cup gum *Eucalyptus cosmophylla*
cup, king *Caltha palustris*
cup of gold *Solandra maxima*
cup plant *Silphium perfoliatum*
cup rosinweed *Silphium perfoliatum*
cupflower *Nierembergia*
cupflower, dwarf *Gnephosis tenuissima*
cupflower, hairy *Angianthus tomentosus*
cupflower, spreading *Angianthus brachypappus*
cupidone, blue *Catananche caerulea*
Cupid's dart *Catananche caerulea*
cups, monkey *Nepenthes*
cups, painted *Castilleja*

cups, wine *Babiana rubrocyanea,*
  Callirhoe involucrata
cupscale grass, Indian *Sacciolepis*
  indica
cupuaçu *Theobroma bicolor*
curare *Strychnos toxifera*
curl tree, ivory *Buckinghamia*
  celsissima
curled dock *Rumex crispus*
curlew berry *Empetrum nigrum*
curls, blue *Trichostema lanatum*
curls, woolly blue *Trichostema*
  lanatum
curly chaff-rush *Lepidobolus*
  drapetocoleus
curly mallee *Eucalyptus gillii*
curly palm *Howea belmoreana*
curly parsley *Petroselinum crispum*
curly pondweed *Potamogeton crispus*
curly ryegrass *Parapholis incurva*
curly windmill grass *Enteropogon*
  acicularis
curly-bark wattle *Acacia curranii*
curly-leafed rock rose *Cistus crispus*
curly-wig *Caustis flexuosa*
curracabah *Acacia concurrens,*
  A. leiocalyx
currajong, Tasmanian *Asterotrichion*
  discolor
currant *Ribes*
currant, alpine *Ribes alpinum*
currant, buffalo *Ribes odoratum*
currant bush *Carissa lanceolata,*
  Apophyllum anomalum
currant bush, prickly *Coprosma*
  quadrifida
currant, chaparral *Ribes malvaceum*
currant, clove *Ribes odoratum*
currant coralberry, Indian
  Symphoricarpos orbiculatus
currant, flowering *Ribes sanguineum*
currant, fuchsia-flowered *Ribes*
  speciosum

currant, garden *Ribes* × *koehneanum*
currant, golden *Ribes aureum,*
  R. odoratum
currant, golden flowering *Ribes*
  aureum
currant, golden buffalo *Ribes*
  odoratum
currant, Indian *Symphoricarpos*
  orbiculatus
currant, mountain *Ribes alpinum*
currant, native *Canthium latifolium,*
  Leptomeria acida
currant, Nordic *Ribes rubrum*
currant, squaw *Ribes cereum*
currant, white-flowered *Ribes*
  indecorum
currant, wild *Rhus pyroides*
currant, winter *Ribes sanguineum*
currawang *Acacia doratoxylon*
curry bush *Hypericum revolutum*
curry leaf *Murraya koenigii*
curry plant *Helichrysum italicum*
curry tree *Murraya koenigii*
curse, Paterson's *Echium*
  plantagineum
cursed cholla *Grusonia emoryi*
curuba *Passiflora mollissima*
curved rice flower *Pimelea curviflora*
cush-cush *Dioscorea trifida*
cushion bush *Leucophyta brownii*
cushion caraway *Oreomyrrhis*
  pulvinifica
cushion daisy, white *Celmisia*
  sessiliflora
cushion knawel *Scleranthus*
  minusculus
cushion pink *Silene acaulis*
cushion plant *Raoulia australis,*
  R. hookeri, R. parkii
cushion plant, hard *Colobanthus*
  pulvinatus
cushion spurge *Euphorbia polychroma*
cushions, grass *Isoetopsis graminifolia*

custard apple *Annona* Atemoya
Group, *A. cherimola, A. squamosa*

custard lily *Hemerocallis lilio-asphodelus*

cutch, black *Acacia catechu*

cut-leaf beech *Fagus sylvatica*
'Rohanii'

cut-leaf birch *Betula pendula*
'Dalecarlica'

cut-leaf burr-daisy *Calotis anthemoides*

cut-leaf coneflower *Rudbeckia laciniata*

cut-leaf daisy *Brachyscome multifida*

cut-leaf germander *Teucrium botrys*

cut-leaf guinea-flower *Hibbertia cuneiformis*

cut-leaf medic *Medicago laciniata*

cut-leaf pear *Pyrus regelii*

cut-leaf peppercress *Lepidium bonariense*

cut-leaf self-heal *Prunella laciniata*

cut-leafed lilac *Syringa laciniata*

cut-leafed mint bush *Prostanthera incisa*

cut-leafed plantain *Plantago coronopus*

cut-leafed stephanandra *Stephanandra incisa*

cut-leafed toothwort *Cardamine laciniata*

cycad, Eastern Cape blue *Encephalartos horridus*

cycad, fern *Bowenia spectabilis, Stangeria eriopus*

cycad, Japanese sago *Cycas revoluta*

cycad, Natal *Encephalartos natalensis*

cycad, prickly *Encephalartos altensteinii*

cycad, sago *Cycas circinalis*

cycad, Thousand Hills *Encephalartos natalensis*

cycad, woolly *Encephalartos friderici-guilielmi*

cyclamen *Cyclamen, C. persicum*

cyclamen cherry *Prunus cyclamina*

cyclamen-leafed violet *Viola koreana*

cylinder snake plant *Sansevieria cylindrica*

cymbidium, native *Cymbidium suave*

cypress *Cupressus*

cypress, Arizona *Cupressus arizonica*

cypress, bald *Taxodium distichum*

cypress, Bhutan *Cupressus cashmeriana, C. torulosa*

cypress, boulevard *Chamaecyparis pisifera* 'Boulevard'

cypress, Brunning's golden
Monterey *Cupressus macrocarpa*
'Brunneana'

cypress, Chinese mourning *Cupressus funebris*

cypress, Chinese swamp
Glyptostrobus pensilis

cypress, Chinese weeping *Cupressus funebris*

cypress, coffin *Cupressus funebris*

cypress, golden Lawson
Chamaecyparis lawsoniana
'Stewartii'

cypress, Gowen *Cupressus goveniana*

cypress, Guadalupe *Cupressus guadalupensis*

cypress, Himalayan *Cupressus torulosa*

cypress, hinoki *Chamaecyparis obtusa*

cypress, Kashmir *Cupressus cashmeriana*

cypress, Lawson *Chamaecyparis lawsoniana*

cypress, Leyland × *Cuprocyparis leylandii*

cypress, Mediterranean *Cupressus sempervirens*

cypress, Mexican *Cupressus lusitanica*

cypress, Modoc *Cupressus bakeri*
cypress, Monterey *Cupressus macrocarpa*
cypress, Montezuma *Taxodium mucronatum*
cypress, moss *Crassula muscosa*
cypress, mountain *Widdringtonia nodiflora*
cypress, Nootka *Chamaecyparis nootkatensis*
cypress, pond *Taxodium ascendens*
cypress, Russian *Microbiota decussata*
cypress, San Pedro Mártir *Cupressus montana*
cypress, Santa Cruz *Cupressus abramsiana*
cypress, Sargent *Cupressus sargentii*
cypress, sawara *Chamaecyparis pisifera*
cypress, Siberian carpet *Microbiota decussata*
cypress, smooth Arizona *Cupressus glabra*
cypress spurge *Euphorbia cyparissias*
cypress, standing *Ipomopsis rubra*
cypress, summer *Bassia scoparia*
cypress, swamp *Taxodium distichum*
cypress, Taiwan *Chamaecyparis formosensis*
cypress, Tecate *Cupressus guadalupensis* var. *forbesii*
cypress, Tsangpo *Cupressus gigantea*
cypress, watch-chain *Crassula muscosa*

cypress, white *Chamaecyparis thyoides*
cypress, Yunnan *Cupressus duclouxiana*
cypress-pine *Callitris*
cypress-pine, Australian *Callitris*
cypress-pine, Bailey's *Callitris baileyi*
cypress-pine, black *Callitris endlicheri*
cypress-pine, mallee *Callitris verrucosa*
cypress-pine, mountain *Callitris monticola*
cypress-pine, Mueller's *Callitris muelleri*
cypress-pine, Murray *Callitris gracilis* subsp. *murrayensis*
cypress-pine, northern *Callitris intratropica*
cypress-pine, Port Jackson *Callitris rhomboidea*
cypress-pine, sand *Callitris columellaris*
cypress-pine, stringybark *Callitris macleayana*
cypress-pine, Tasmanian *Callitris oblonga*
cypress-pine, white *Callitris glaucophylla*
Cyprus cedar *Cedrus brevifolia*
Cyprus, golden oak of *Quercus alnifolia*
Cyprus thyme *Thymus integer*
Cyprus turpentine *Pistacia terebinthus*

D

dacryberry, New Zealand *Dacrycarpus dacrydioides*

daffodil *Narcissus*

daffodil, autumn *Sternbergia*

daffodil garlic *Allium neapolitanum*

daffodil, hoop-petticoat *Narcissus bulbocodium*

daffodil, wild *Narcissus pseudonarcissus*

dagga, wild *Leonotis leonurus*

dagger cholla *Grusonia clavata*

dagger fern *Polystichum acrostichoides*

dagger hakea *Hakea teretifolia*

dagger plant *Yucca aloifolia*

dagger, shin *Agave lechuguilla, A. schottii*

dagger wattle *Acacia siculiformis*

dagger-leafed wattle *Acacia rhigiophylla*

Dahlberg daisy *Thymophylla tenuiloba*

dahlia *Dahlia*

dahlia, tree *Dahlia imperialis*

dahoon holly *Ilex cassine*

dahoon, myrtle *Ilex myrtifolia*

Dahurian buckthorn *Rhamnus dahurica*

Dahurian larch *Larix gmelinii*

daimyo oak *Quercus dentata*

dainty wedge pea *Gompholobium glabratum*

daisy *Bellis perennis*

daisy, African *Arctotis, A. stoechadifolia, Dimorphotheca, Osteospermum*

daisy, Aspen *Erigeron speciosus macranthus*

daisy, Barberton *Gerbera jamesonii*

daisy, bellis *Bellis perennis*

daisy, blackfoot *Melampodium leucanthum*

daisy, blue *Felicia amelloides*

daisy, blue burr *Calotis cuneifolia*

daisy, blue-eyed Africa *Arctotis venusta*

daisy, burr *Calotis*

daisy bush *Olearia albida*

daisy bush, blue-and-white *Osteospermum ecklonis*

daisy bush, blush *Olearia myrsinoides*

daisy bush, downy *Olearia tomentosa*

daisy bush, dusty *Olearia phlogopappa*

daisy bush, golden *Euryops pectinatus*

daisy bush, silky *Olearia erubescens*

daisy bush, snow *Olearia stellulata*

daisy, butter *Melampodium paludosum*

daisy, Cape *Arctotis fastuosa*

daisy, cotton *Celmisia spectabilis*

daisy, crown *Xanthophthalmum coronarium*

daisy, cut-leaf *Brachyscome multifida*

daisy, Dahlberg *Thymophylla tenuiloba*

daisy, dune *Tanacetum camphoratum*

daisy, Easter *Townsendia hookeri*

daisy, grassland *Brachyscome angustifolia*

daisy, Hawkesbury River *Brachyscome multifida*

daisy, large white *Brachyscome campylocarpa*

daisy, lawn *Bellis perennis*

daisy, leafy *Brachyscome rigidula*

daisy, Livingstone *Dorotheanthus, D. bellidiformis*

daisy, marguerite *Argyranthemum frutescens*

daisy, Marlborough rock *Olearia insignis*

daisy, mat *Raoulia*

daisy, Mexican *Erigeron karvinskianus*
daisy, Michaelmas *Aster novi-belgii*
daisy, Miyabe *Chrysanthemum weyrichii*
daisy, Moroccan *Rhodanthemum hosmariense*
daisy, Mossgiel *Brachyscome papillosa*
daisy, mountain *Celmisia*
daisy, oxeye *Leucanthemum vulgare, Telekia speciosa*
daisy, painted *Ismelia carinata*
daisy, paper *Baileya multiradiata*
daisy, Paris *Euryops chrysanthemoides*
daisy, Pilliga *Brachyscome formosa*
daisy, Santa Barbara *Erigeron karvinskianus*
daisy, seaside *Erigeron glaucus, E. karvinskianus*
daisy, Shasta *Leucanthemum × superbum*
daisy, snow *Celmisia*
daisy, star *Lindheimera texana*
daisy, stiff *Brachyscome angustifolia*
daisy, Swan River *Brachyscome iberidifolia*
daisy, Tahoka *Machaeranthera tanacetifolia*
daisy, Transvaal *Gerbera*
daisy, turf mat *Raoulia subsericea*
daisy, wandering *Erigeron peregrinus*
dakua *Agathis macrophylla*
dalea, black *Dalea frutescens*
Dalmatian bellflower *Campanula portenschlagiana*
Dalmatian iris *Iris pallida*
Dalmatian laburnum *Petteria ramentacea*
Dalmatian pyrethrum *Tanacetum cinerariifolium*
damask violet *Hesperis matronalis*
dames violet *Hesperis matronalis*
Damocles, tree of *Oroxylum*

dancing lady orchid *Oncidium, O. varicosum*
dandelion *Taraxacum, T. officinale*
dandelion, Cape *Arctotheca calendula*
Dane's elder *Sambucus ebulus*
danewort *Sambucus ebulus*
dangleberry *Gaylussacia frondosa*
daphne, Australian *Philotheca myoporoides, Pittosporum undulatum*
daphne, Burkwood *Daphne × burkwoodii*
daphne, February *Daphne mezereum*
daphne, garland *Daphne cneorum*
daphne heath *Brachyloma daphnoides*
daphne, lilac *Daphne genkwa*
daphne, native *Philotheca myoporoides*
daphne, New Zealand *Pimelea prostrata*
daphne, rock *Daphne cneorum*
daphne, rose *Daphne cneorum*
daphne, winter *Daphne odora*
dappled willow *Salix integra*
d'arco, pau *Tabebuia impetiginosa*
dark dryandra *Dryandra squarrosa*
dark wiregrass *Aristida calycina*
dark-eye sunflower *Helianthus atrorubens*
dark-leafed willow *Salix nigricans*
Darley Dale heath *Erica × darleyensis*
Darling lily *Crinum flaccidum*
Darling pea *Swainsona purpurea*
Darling pratia *Pratia darlingensis*
darnel *Lolium temulentum*
dart, Cupid's *Catananche caerulea*
Darwin barberry *Berberis darwinii*
Darwin stringybark *Eucalyptus tetrodonta*
Darwin woollybutt *Eucalyptus miniata*
darwinia, lemon-scented *Darwinia citriodora*

dasheen *Colocasia esculenta*
date, African wild *Phoenix reclinata*
date, Chinese *Ziziphus jujuba*
date, dwarf *Phoenix loureiroi*
date, edible *Phoenix dactylifera*
date, Formosan *Phoenix hanceana*
date, Indian wild *Phoenix sylvestris*
date palm *Phoenix dactylifera*
date palm, Canary Island *Phoenix canariensis*
date palm, cliff *Phoenix rupicola*
date palm, Cretan *Phoenix theophrasti*
date palm, dwarf *Phoenix roebelenii*
date palm, Senegal *Phoenix reclinata*
date palm, silver *Phoenix sylvestris*
date plum *Diospyros lotus*
date, Trebizand *Elaeagnus angustifolia*
David's peach *Prunus davidiana*
David's pine *Pinus armandii*
Davidson plum *Davidsonia pruriens*
Davis milkweed *Asclepias speciosa*
dawn, poppy of the *Eomecon chionantha*
dawn redwood *Metasequoia glyptostroboides*
Dawson River fan palm *Livistona nitida*
day flower *Commelina*
day jessamine *Cestrum diurnum*
daylily *Hemerocallis*
de Beuzeville's snow gum *Eucalyptus debeuzevillei*
De Kaap, pride of *Bauhinia galpinii*
dead finish *Acacia tetragonophylla*
dead nettle *Lamium*
deadly nightshade *Atropa belladonna*
Deane's gum *Eucalyptus deanei*
Deane's wattle *Acacia deanei*
death camas *Zigadenus*
Deccan hemp *Hibiscus cannabinus*
deciduous azalea *Rhododendron molle*
deciduous fig *Ficus superba, F. s.* var. *henneana*

deciduous holly *Ilex decidua*
deep yellowwood *Rhodosphaera rhodanthema*
deer brush *Ceanothus integerrimus*
deer fern *Blechnum spicant*
deer oak *Quercus sadleriana*
deerberry *Vaccinium caesium, V. stamineum*
deerhorn cedar *Thujopsis dolabrata*
dekriet *Thamnochortus insignis*
Delavay's fir *Abies delavayi*
delicate hair grass *Aira elegantissima*
delta maidenhair fern *Adiantum raddianum*
dense mat-plant *Herniaria hirsuta*
dense midge orchid *Genoplesium nudiscapum*
dense stonecrop *Crassula colorata*
deodar *Cedrus deodara*
deodar cedar *Cedrus deodara*
Derwent speedwell *Derwentia derwentiana*
desert almond *Prunus fasciculata*
desert apoon *Dasylirion wheeleri*
desert apricot *Prunus fremontii*
desert ash *Fraxinus angustifolia* subsp. *syriaca, F. velutina*
desert baileya *Baileya multiradiata*
desert bean *Phaseolus acutifolius*
desert bluebell *Phacelia campanularia*
desert broom *Baccharis* 'Centennial'
desert broombush *Templetonia egena*
desert candle *Eremurus*
desert Chinese lantern *Abutilon leucopetalum, A. otocarpum*
desert fig *Ficus brachypoda, F. palmeri*
desert fringe-myrtle *Calytrix longiflora*
desert glasswort *Pachycornia triandra*
desert goosefoot *Chenopodium desertorum*
desert grevillea *Grevillea eriostachya*

desert hakea *Hakea mitchellii,
H. muelleriana*
desert heath-myrtle *Baeckea crassifolia*
desert honeysuckle *Anisacanthus
thurberi*
desert ironwood *Olneya tesota*
desert jasmine *Jasminum lineare*
desert kurrajong *Brachychiton
gregorii*
desert lime *Citrus glauca*
desert mahonia *Mahonia fremontii*
desert mallow *Sphaeralcea ambigua*
desert marigold *Baileya multiradiata*
desert olive *Forestiera pubescens*
desert paintbrush *Castilleja
angustifolia*
desert pea, Sturt's *Swainsona formosa*
desert rice flower *Pimelea simplex*
desert rose *Adenium obesum,
Gossypium sturtianum, Rosa stellata*
desert rose, Sturt's *Gossypium
sturtianum*
desert ruellia *Ruellia peninsularis*
desert sage *Salvia dorrii*
desert sage, mountain *Salvia
pachyphylla*
desert saw-sedge *Gahnia lanigera*
desert sneezeweed *Centipeda
thespidioides*
desert spider flower *Grevillea
pterosperma*
desert spoon *Dasylirion wheeleri*
desert sumac *Rhus microphylla*
desert wattle *Acacia victoriae*
desert willow *Chilopsis linearis*
Desmond mallee *Eucalyptus
desmondensis*
dessert kiwi fruit *Actinidia arguta*
deutzia, fuzzy *Deutzia scabra*
deutzia, slender *Deutzia gracilis*
devil cholla *Grusonia emoryi*
devil, creeping *Stenocereus eruca*
devil lily *Lilium lancifolium*

devil, mountain *Lambertia formosa*
devil tree *Alstonia scholaris*
devilpepper, four-leaf *Rauvolfia
tetraphylla*
devil's apple *Podophyllum peltatum*
devil's apples *Mandragora officinarum*
devil's backbone *Pedilanthus
tithymaloides*
devil's bit scabious *Succisa pratensis*
devil's claw *Harpagophytum
procumbens, Ibicella*
devil's club *Oplopanax horridus*
devil's coachwhip *Stachytarpheta
jamaicensis*
devil's cotton *Abroma augusta*
devil's fig *Solanum hispidum*
devil's ivy *Epipremnum pinnatum*
'Aureum'
devil's needles *Solanum stelligerum*
devil's root *Lophophora williamsii*
devil's rope pear *Cylindropuntia
imbricata*
devil's tongue *Amorphophallus konjac,
A. rivieri, Sansevieria zeylanica*
devil's twine *Cassytha pubescens*
devil's walking-stick *Aralia spinosa*
devilwood *Osmanthus americanus*
dew drop, golden *Duranta erecta*
dew plant, purple *Ruschia caroli*
dew thread *Drosera filiformis*
dewberry *Rubus caesius*
dewberry, American *Rubus canadensis*
dewy pine *Drosophyllum lusitanicum*
dhak *Butea monosperma*
dhal *Cajanus cajan*
diamond maidenhair *Adiantum
trapeziforme*
diamond milfoil *Myriophyllum
aquaticum*
diamond-leaf laurel *Auranticarpa
rhombifolia*
dianthus *Dianthus*
didiscus *Trachymene coerulea*

diehard stringybark *Eucalyptus cameronii*
digger pine *Pinus sabiniana*
digger's speedwell *Derwentia perfoliata*
dill *Anethum graveolens*
dillenia, Indian *Dillenia indica*
dillon bush *Nitraria billardierei*
dinner plate fig *Ficus dammaropsis*
Diogenes' lantern *Calochortus amabilis*
diosma, pink *Coleonema pulchellum*
dipelta, rosy *Dipelta floribunda*
dipladenia, white *Mandevilla boliviensis*
dirty Dora *Cyperus difformis*
dirty gum *Eucalyptus chloroclada*
dish fern *Pteris*
dissected Japanese maple *Acer palmatum* Dissectum Group
dita bark *Alstonia scholaris*
ditch millet *Paspalum orbiculare*
dittany *Cunila origanoides, Dictamnus albus*
dittany of Crete *Origanum dictamnus*
divi-divi *Caesalpinia coriaria*
dobo lily *Cyrtanthus brachyscyphus*
dock *Rumex*
dock, gray *Balsamorhiza sagittata*
dock, prairie *Silphium terebinthinaceum*
dock, red-veined *Rumex sanguineus*
dock, sour *Rumex acetosa*
dock, tanner's *Rumex hymenosepalus*
dockmackie *Viburnum acerifolium*
dodder *Cuscuta*
dodder-laurel *Cassytha*
dog fennel *Anthemis*
dog rose *Bauera rubioides, Rosa canina*
dog violet *Viola riviniana*
dog violet, heath *Viola canina*

dog violet, western *Viola adunca*
dogbane *Apocynum*
dogbane, blue *Amsonia tabernaemontana*
dogbane, common *Apocynum androsaemifolium*
dogbane, spreading *Apocynum androsaemifolium*
dogleg ash *Fraxinus greggii*
dogtooth pea *Lathyrus sativus*
dogtooth violet *Erythronium, Erythronium dens-canis*
dogtooth violet, white *Erythronium albidum*
dogwood *Cornus*
dogwood, American *Cornus sericea*
dogwood, Australian *Jacksonia scoparia*
dogwood, bloodwing *Cornus sanguinea*
dogwood, Canadian *Cornus nuttallii*
dogwood, Chinese *Cornus kousa*
dogwood, common *Cornus sanguinea*
dogwood, creeping *Cornus canadensis*
dogwood, dwarf red-tipped *Cornus pumila*
dogwood, European *Cornus sanguinea*
dogwood, flowering *Cornus florida*
dogwood, giant *Cornus controversa*
dogwood, gray *Cornus racemosa*
dogwood, Himalayan *Cornus capitata*
dogwood, Japanese flowering *Cornus kousa*
dogwood, kousa *Cornus kousa*
dogwood, mountain *Cornus nuttallii*
dogwood, pagoda *Cornus alternifolia*
dogwood, panicled *Cornus racemosa*
dogwood, red osier *Cornus stolonifera*
dogwood, red-barked *Cornus alba*
dogwood, round-leafed *Cornus rugosa*

dogwood, silky *Cornus amomum, C. obliqua*
dogwood, South African *Rhamnus prinoides*
dogwood, tabletop *Cornus controversa*
dogwood, tartarian *Cornus alba*
dogwood, white *Ozothamnus diosmifolius*
dolichos pea *Dipogon lignosus*
dollar bush *Zygophyllum stapfii*
dollar plant *Crassula ovata*
dollar, silver *Lunaria annua*
doll's eyes *Actaea alba*
dolly bush *Cassinia aculeata*
domatia tree *Endiandra discolor*
dombeya, forest *Dombeya tiliacea*
dombeya, pink *Dombeya burgessiae*
donkey orchid *Diuris longifolia, D. maculata*
donkey tail *Euphorbia myrsinites*
donkey's tail *Sedum morganianum*
Doorenbos coralberry *Symphoricarpos × doorenbosii*
doronoki *Populus maximowiczii*
Dorothy's wattle *Acacia dorothea*
Dorrigo waratah *Alloxylon pinnatum*
Dorrigo white gum *Eucalyptus dorrigoensis*
Dorset heath *Erica ciliaris*
dotted hawthorn *Crataegus punctata*
doubah *Marsdenia australis*
double Arabian jasmine *Jasminum sambac* 'Grand Duke of Tuscany'
double coconut *Lodoicea maldivica*
double crape fern *Leptopteris superba*
double Japanese wisteria *Wisteria floribunda* 'Violaceo-plena'
double pink flowering plum *Prunus × blireana*
double red poinsettia *Euphorbia pulcherrima* 'Henrietta Ecke'

double Reeves' spiraea *Spiraea cantoniensis* 'Flore Pleno'
double sneezewort *Achillea ptarmica* 'The Pearl'
double soapwort *Saponaria officinalis* 'Roseo-plena'
double tiger lily *Lilium lancifolium* 'Flore Pleno'
double white Banks' rose *Rosa banksiae* 'Alboplena'
doublefile viburnum *Viburnum plicatum*
double-flowered gorse *Ulex europaeus* 'Plenus'
doublegee *Emex australis*
doughwood *Acronychia octandra*
doughwood, pink-flowered *Melicope elleryana*
Douglas fir *Pseudotsuga, P. menziesii*
Douglas fir, Chinese *Pseudotsuga sinensis*
Douglas fir, large-cone *Pseudotsuga macrocarpa*
Douglas fir, Taiwan *Pseudotsuga wilsoniana*
Douglas fir, Yunnan *Pseudotsuga forrestii*
Douglas's triteleia *Triteleia grandiflora*
doum palm *Hyphaene dichotoma, H. thebaica*
doum palm, East African *Hyphaene coriacea*
doum palm, Egyptian *Hyphaene thebaica*
dove orchid *Dendrobium crumenatum*
dove plum *Coccoloba laurifolia*
dove tree *Davidia involucrata*
dove's-foot cranesbill *Geranium molle*
Dowerin rose *Eucalyptus pyriformis*
downs nutgrass *Cyperus bifax*

downy birch *Betula pubescens*
downy cherry *Prunus tomentosa*
downy daisy bush *Olearia tomentosa*
downy Darling pea *Swainsona swainsonioides*
downy hawthorn *Crataegus mollis*
downy manzanita *Arctostaphylos tomentosa*
downy oak *Quercus pubescens*
downy rose *Rosa tomentosa*
downy serviceberry *Amelanchier arborea*
downy skullcap *Scutellaria incana*
downy thorn apple *Datura inoxia*
downy wattle *Acacia pubescens*
downy zieria *Zieria cytisoides*
dracaena, blue *Cordyline indivisa*
dracaena fig *Ficus pseudopalma*
dracaena, gold-dust *Dracaena surculosa*
dracaena, spotted *Dracaena surculosa*
Dracula orchid *Dracula*
dragon arum *Dracunculus vulgaris*
dragon bones *Euphorbia lactea*
dragon fruit *Hylocereus undatus*
dragon, green *Arisaema dracontium*
dragon head, false *Physostegia*
dragon heath *Dracophyllum secundum*
dragon sagewort *Artemisia dracunculus*
dragon spruce *Picea asperata*
dragon tree *Dracaena draco*
dragonroot *Arisaema dracontium*
dragon's mouth *Dracunculus muscivorus*
dragon's-blood tree *Dracaena draco*
dragon's-eye pine *Pinus densiflora* 'Oculus-draconis'
drain flat-sedge *Cyperus eragrostis*
Drakensberg agapanthus *Agapanthus inapertus*

drooping agapanthus *Agapanthus inapertus*
drooping juniper *Juniperus recurva*
drooping mistletoe *Amyema miquelii, A. pendulum*
drooping prickly pear *Opuntia monacantha*
drooping sedge *Carex longebrachiata*
drooping she-oak *Allocasuarina verticillata*
drooping wattle *Acacia difformis*
dropseed *Sporobolus*
dropseed, prairie *Sporobolus heterolepsis*
dropwort *Filipendula, F. vulgaris*
dropwort, water *Oenanthe javanica*
Drummond's wattle *Acacia drummondii*
drumstick primula *Primula denticulata*
drumsticks *Isopogon anemonifolius, I. dawsonii, Pycnosorus globosus*
drumsticks, narrow-leaf *Isopogon anethifolius*
Dryander's grevillea *Grevillea dryanderi*
dryandra, many-headed *Dryandra polycephala*
dryandra, oak-leaf *Dryandra quercifolia*
dryandra, sea urchin *Dryandra praemorsa*
dryandra, shaggy *Dryandra speciosa*
dryandra, showy *Dryandra formosa*
duboisia *Duboisia myoporoides*
duchess protea *Protea eximia*
duck plant *Sutherlandia frutescens*
duckweed *Lemna disperma, Spirodela oligorrhiza, S. pusilla*
duke cherry *Prunus × gondouinii*
Duke of Argyll's tea-tree *Lycium barbarum*
dumb cane *Dieffenbachia*

dumb cane, spotted *Dieffenbachia seguine*
dumpling cactus *Lophophora williamsii*
dumplings *Billardiera scandens*
dune bean *Vigna marina*
dune daisy *Tanacetum camphoratum*
dune fan-flower *Scaevola calendulacea*
dune flax-lily *Dianella congesta*
dune grass, European *Leymus arenarius*
dune knobwood *Zanthoxylum delagoense*
dune manzanita *Arctostaphylos pumila*
dune myrtle *Eugenia capensis*
dune poison bush *Acokanthera oblongifolia*
dune soapberry *Deinbollia oblongifolia*
dune thistle *Actites megalocarpa*
Dunkeld larch *Larix × marschlinsii*
durand oak *Quercus durandii*
Durango pine *Pinus durangensis*
Durban grass *Dactyloctenium australe*
durian *Durio zibethinus*
durmast oak *Quercus dalechampii, Q. petraea*
durobby *Syzygium moorei*
durum wheat *Triticum turgidum* Durum Group
dusky coral pea *Kennedia rubicunda*
duster, fairy *Calliandra eriophylla*
dusty daisy bush *Olearia phlogopappa*
dusty miller *Artemisia stelleriana, Centaurea cineraria, Lychnis coronaria, Senecio cineraria, S. vira-vira*
Dutch case-knife bean *Phaseolus coccineus*
Dutch crocus *Crocus vernus*

Dutch elm *Ulmus × hollandica*
Dutch rush *Equisetum hyemale*
Dutchman's breeches *Dicentra cucullaria*
Dutchman's pipe *Aristolochia*
dwarf Alberta white spruce *Picea glauca* var. *albertiana* 'Conica'
dwarf aluminum plant *Pilea cadierei* 'Minima'
dwarf American cherry *Prunus pumila*
dwarf apple *Angophora hispida*
dwarf balsam fir *Abies balsamea*
dwarf bearded iris *Iris pumila*
dwarf bilberry *Vaccinium caespitosum*
dwarf birch *Betula nana*
dwarf birch, American *Betula pumila*
dwarf blue trumpet *Brunoniella pumilio*
dwarf burning bush *Euonymus nanus*
dwarf buttercup *Ranunculus millanii*
dwarf cherry *Exocarpos strictus*
dwarf Chilean beech *Nothofagus pumilio*
dwarf Chinese mountain ash *Sorbus reducta*
dwarf chinquapin oak *Quercus prinoides*
dwarf cornel *Cornus canadensis*
dwarf cup-flower *Gnephosis tenuissima*
dwarf date *Phoenix loureiroi*
dwarf date palm *Phoenix roebelenii*
dwarf elder *Sambucus ebulus*
dwarf erythrina *Erythrina humeana*
dwarf euonymus *Euonymus nanus*
dwarf fan palm *Livistona muelleri*
dwarf fern-leafed bamboo *Pleioblastus pygmaeus*
dwarf flowering almond *Prunus triloba*
dwarf flowering cherry *Prunus glandulosa*

dwarf fothergilla *Fothergilla gardenii*
dwarf gasteria *Gasteria bicolor*
dwarf genista *Genista lydia*
dwarf gorse *Ulex gallii, U. minor*
dwarf jasmine *Jasminum parkeri*
dwarf jo-jo *Soliva anthemifolia*
dwarf Korean lilac *Syringa meyeri*
dwarf kowhai *Sophora prostrata*
dwarf kurrajong *Brachychiton bidwillii*
dwarf lantern-flower *Abutilon fraseri*
dwarf lemon *Citrus × limon* 'Meyer'
dwarf marigold *Schkuhria pinnata*
dwarf meadow grass *Poa annua*
dwarf mondo grass *Ophiopogon japonicus* 'Nanus'
dwarf mountain pine *Pinus mugo*
dwarf nealie *Acacia wilhelmiana*
dwarf palmetto *Sabal minor*
dwarf panic *Panicum pygmaeum*
dwarf papyrus *Cyperus prolifer*
dwarf phyllota *Phyllota humifusa*
dwarf pine *Microstrobos niphophilus*
dwarf pink hibiscus *Hibiscus pedunculatus*
dwarf pomegranate *Punica granatum* 'Nana'
dwarf red-tipped dogwood *Cornus pumila*
dwarf Russian almond *Prunus tenella*
dwarf sacred bamboo *Nandina domestica* 'Nana'
dwarf she-oak *Allocasuarina nana*
dwarf Siberian pine *Pinus pumila*

dwarf silver-leaf sage *Salvia daghestanica*
dwarf skullcap *Scutellaria humilis*
dwarf snapdragon *Chaenorhinum*
dwarf sour bush *Choretrum pauciflorum*
dwarf Spanish heath *Erica umbellata*
dwarf sumac *Rhus copallina*
dwarf sundrops *Calylophus serrulatus*
dwarf sunray *Hyalosperma demissum*
dwarf Thai chilli *Capsicum annuum* 'Thai Hot Small'
dwarf tree fern *Blechnum gibbum*
dwarf Turk's cap cactus *Melocactus matanzanus*
dwarf twinleaf *Zygophyllum ovatum*
dwarf umbrella tree *Schefflera arboricola*
dwarf wake robin *Trillium pusillum*
dwarf wallflower *Erysimum linariifolium*
dwarf water gum *Tristania neriifolia*
dwarf wedge pea *Gompholobium minus*
dwarf whitebeam *Sorbus chamaemespilus*
dwarf white-striped bamboo *Pleioblastus variegatus*
Dwyer's red gum *Eucalyptus dwyeri*
dye, Indian *Hydrastis canadensis*
dyer's bugloss *Alkanna tinctoria*
dyer's chamomile *Anthemis tinctoria*
dyer's greenweed *Genista tinctoria*
dyer's woad *Isatis tinctoria*

E

eaglewood *Aquilaria malaccensis*
ear, bear's *Cymbonotus lawsonianus,*
Primula auricula
eardrops, ladies' *Fuchsia magellanica*
eared cassia *Senna petersiana*
ear-leafed magnolia *Magnolia fraseri*
ear-leafed umbrella tree *Magnolia*
fraseri
early Dutch honeysuckle *Lonicera*
periclymenum 'Belgica'
early flowering lilac *Syringa* ×
hyacinthiflora
early forsythia *Forsythia ovata*
early marsh orchid *Dactylorhiza*
incarnata
early meadow-rue *Thalictrum*
dioicum
early Nancy *Wurmbaea dioica*
early spring grass *Eriochloa*
pseudoacrotricha
early tamarisk *Tamarix parviflora*
ear-pod wattle *Acacia auriculiformis*
ears, antelope *Platycerium*
ears, cat's *Antennaria, Hypochaeris*
radicata
ears, elephant *Alocasia, Caladium,*
Colocasia, Xanthosoma
ears, lambs' *Stachys byzantina*
ears, sheep's *Helichrysum*
appendiculatum
earth-star, green *Cryptanthus acaulis*
earth-star, rainbow *Cryptanthus*
bromelioides
East African doum palm *Hyphaene*
coriacea
East African juniper *Juniperus*
procera
East Himalayan spruce *Picea*
spinulosa

East Indian holly fern *Arachniodes*
simplicior
Easter cactus *Hatiora gaertneri,*
H. rosea
Easter daisy *Townsendia hookeri*
Easter herald trumpet *Beaumontia*
grandiflora
Easter Island sophora *Sophora*
toromiro
Easter ledges *Persicaria bistorta*
Easter lily *Lilium longiflorum*
Easter lily cactus *Echinopsis*
Easter lily vine *Beaumontia*
grandiflora
eastern arborvitae *Thuja occidentalis*
eastern bitterbush *Adriana glabrata*
eastern bladdernut *Staphylea trifolia*
eastern bog laurel *Kalmia polifolia*
Eastern Cape blue cycad
Encephalartos horridus
eastern coral bean *Erythrina*
herbacea
eastern cottonbush *Maireana*
brevifolia, M. microphylla
eastern cottonwood *Populus deltoides*
eastern flame pea *Chorizema*
parviflorum
eastern flat-top saltbush *Atriplex*
lindleyi
eastern hemlock *Tsuga canadensis*
eastern holly fern *Polystichum*
braunii
eastern hop hornbeam *Ostrya*
virginiana
eastern larch *Larix laricina*
eastern leatherwood *Eucryphia moorei*
eastern maidenhair *Adiantum*
pedatum
eastern pasque flower *Pulsatilla patens*
eastern red cedar *Juniperus virginiana*
eastern redbud *Cercis canadensis*
eastern shooting star *Dodecatheon*
meadia

eastern wahoo *Euonymus atropurpureus*
eastern white pine *Pinus strobus*
eating apple *Malus pumula*
Eaton's firecracker *Penstemon eatonii*
eau-de-cologne mint *Mentha × piperita* var. *citrata*
ebony *Diospyros*
ebony, Ceylon *Diospyros ebenum*
ebony, Jamaica *Brya ebenus*
ebony, Macassar *Diospyros celebica*
ebony, Mexican *Pithecellobium mexicanum*
ebony, myrtle *Diospyros pentamera*
ebony, native *Bauhinia hookeri*
ebony, Queensland *Bauhinia carronii*
ebony, Texas *Pithecellobium flexicaule*
ebony, West Indies *Brya ebenus*
echeveria, blue *Echeveria secunda*
echinacea *Echinacea purpurea*
edelweiss *Leontopodium alpinum*
edelweiss, New Zealand *Leucogenes*
edelweiss, North Island *Leucogenes leontopodium*
edging lobelia *Lobelia erinus*
edible bamboo *Phyllostachys edulis*
edible date *Phoenix dactylifera*
edible fig *Ficus carica*
eelweed *Vallisneria americana*
eggfruit *Pouteria campechiana*
eggplant *Solanum melongena*
eggs, scrambled *Goodenia pinnatifida*
eggs-and-bacon *Dillwynia*
eggs-and-bacon pea *Dillwynia*
eggs-and-bacon pea, prickly *Dillwynia juniperina*
eglantine *Rosa rubiginosa*
Egyptian bean *Lablab purpureus*
Egyptian doum palm *Hyphaene thebaica*
Egyptian pea *Cicer arietinum*
Egyptian reed *Cyperus papyrus*
Egyptian rose *Scabiosa atropurpurea*

Egyptian sycamore *Ficus sycomorus*
Egyptian waterlily *Nymphaea lotus*
elder *Sambucus, S. nigra*
elder, American *Sambucus canadensis*
elder, American red *Sambucus pubens*
elder, black *Sambucus nigra*
elder, blueberry *Sambucus caerulea*
elder, box *Acer negundo*
elder, Dane's *Sambucus ebulus*
elder, dwarf *Sambucus ebulus*
elder, European *Sambucus nigra*
elder, European red *Sambucus racemosa*
elder, forest wild *Nuxia floribunda*
elder, golden *Sambucus canadensis* 'Aurea', *Sambucus nigra* 'Aurea'
elder, ground *Aegopodium podagraria*
elder, poison *Toxicodendron vernix*
elder, red-berried *Sambucus racemosa*
elder, scarlet *Sambucus pubens*
elder, stinking *Sambucus pubens*
elder, sweet *Sambucus canadensis*
elder, wild *Nuxia congesta*
elder, yellow *Tecoma stans*
elderberry *Sambucus, S. nigra*
elderberry, American *Sambucus canadensis*
elderberry panax *Polyscias sambucifolia*
elderberry, red *Sambucus racemosa*
eleagnus, autumn *Eleagnus umbellata*
elecampane *Inula helenium*
elegant bamboo *Phyllostachys vivax*
elemi tree, Queensland *Canarium muelleri*
elephant apple *Dillenia indica*
elephant bush *Portulacaria afra*
elephant climber *Argyreia nervosa*
elephant ear philodendron *Philodendron domesticum*
elephant ear wattle *Acacia dunnii*
elephant ears *Alocasia, Caladium, Colocasia, Xanthosoma*

elephant hedge *Schotia latifolia*
elephant hedge bean tree *Schotia latifolia*
elephant tree *Bursera microphylla*
elephant tree, Baja *Pachycormus discolor*
elephant's food *Portulacaria afra*
elephant's foot *Dioscorea elephantipes*
elephant's foot yam *Amorphophallus paeoniifolius, Dioscorea elephantipes*
eleven o'clock *Portulaca grandiflora*
Elim heath *Erica regia*
elk clover *Aralia californica*
elkhorn fern *Platycerium*
elkhorn fern, silver *Platycerium veitchii*
elm *Ulmus*
elm, American *Ulmus americana*
elm, cedar *Ulmus crassifolia*
elm, cherry-bark *Ulmus villosa*
elm, Chinese *Ulmus parvifolia, U. pumila*
elm, cork *Ulmus thomasii*
elm, crowsfoot *Argyrodendron trifoliolatum*
elm, Dutch *Ulmus* × *hollandica*
elm, English *Ulmus procera*
elm, field *Ulmus carpinifolia*
elm, golden *Ulmus glabra* 'Lutescens'
elm, Huntingdon *Ulmus* × *hollandica* 'Vegeta'
elm, Jersey *Ulmus* 'Sarniensis'
elm, red *Ulmus rubra*
elm, rock *Ulmus thomasii*
elm, Russian *Ulmus laevis*
elm, Scotch *Ulmus glabra*
elm, September *Ulmus serotina*
elm, Siberian *Ulmus pumila*
elm, silver *Ulmus carpinifolia* 'Variegata'
elm, slippery *Ulmus rubra*
elm, smooth-leafed *Ulmus minor*
elm, water *Planera aquatica*
elm, weeping *Ulmus glabra* 'Camperdownii'
elm, Wheatley *Ulmus* 'Sarniensis'
elm, white *Ulmus americana*
elm, winged *Ulmus alata*
elm, wych *Ulmus glabra*
Elvins flowering plum *Prunus cerasifera* 'Elvins'
emblic *Phyllanthus emblica*
emerald creeper *Strongylodon macrobotrys*
emerald duke philodendron *Philodendron domesticum*
emerald fern *Asparagus densiflorus*
emex, spiny *Emex australis*
emilia *Emilia sonchifolia*
emmer wheat *Triticum turgidum* Dicoccom Group
emory oak *Quercus emoryi*
empress tree *Paulownia tomentosa*
emu berry *Eremophila duttonii, Podocarpus drouynianus*
emu bush *Eremophila*
emu bush, common *Eremophila glabra*
emu bush, spotted *Eremophila maculata*
enamel flower *Adenandra uniflora*
endive *Cichorium endivia, C. intybus*
Engelmann aster *Aster engelmannii*
Engelmann pine *Pinus engelmannii*
Engelmann spruce *Picea engelmannii*
English bluebell *Hyacinthoides non-scripta*
English box *Buxus sempervirens*
English comfrey *Symphytum officinale*
English daisy *Bellis perennis*
English elm *Ulmus procera*
English hawthorn *Crataegus laevigata*
English holly *Ilex aquifolium*
English ivy *Hedera helix*

English lavender *Lavandula angustifolia*
English marigold *Calendula officinalis*
English oak *Quercus robur*
English primrose *Primula vulgaris*
English ryegrass *Lolium perenne*
English snowdrop *Galanthus nivalis*
English tamarisk *Tamarix anglica*
English walnut *Juglans regia*
English yew *Taxus baccata*
enkeldoring *Acacia robusta*
enkianthus, red-vein *Enkianthus campanulatus*
ensete *Ensete ventricosum*
epaulette tree *Pterostyrax hispida*
ephedra, green *Ephedra viridis*
ephedra, Torrey *Ephedra torreyana*
erect guinea-flower *Hibbertia riparia*
erect hedgehog grass *Echinopogon intermedius*
erect mallee bluebush *Maireana pentatropis*
erect marsh-flower *Villarsia exaltata*
erect sword fern *Nephrolepis cordifolia*
Erman's birch *Betula ermanii*
erythrina, dwarf *Erythrina humeana*
escabon *Chamaecytisus prolifer*
escallonia, white *Escallonia bifida*
escarole *Cichorium endivia*
Eskimo potatoes *Fritillaria camschatcensis*
espino *Acacia cavenia*
Ethiopian banana *Ensete ventricosum*
Etruscan honeysuckle *Lonicera etrusca*
Ettrema mallee *Eucalyptus sturgissiana*
eucryphia, hardy *Eucryphia glutinosa*
eulalia *Miscanthus sinensis*
eumong *Acacia stenophylla*
euodia, Korean *Tetradium daniellii*
euonymus, dwarf *Euonymus nanus*

euonymus, European *Euonymus europaeus*
euonymus, evergreen *Euonymus japonicus*
euonymus, wintercreeper *Euonymus fortunei*
euonymus, Yeddo *Euonymus hamiltonianus*
euphorbia, Arabian *Euphorbia ammak*
euphorbia, big-horn *Euphorbia grandicornis*
euphorbia, big-toothed *Euphorbia grandidens*
euphorbia, cow's horn *Euphorbia grandicornis*
euphorbia, hedge *Euphorbia neriifolia*
euphorbia, lebombo *Euphorbia confinalis*
euphorbia, lowveld *Euphorbia evansii*
euphorbia, pincushion *Euphorbia pulvinata*
euphorbia, river *Euphorbia triangularis*
euphorbia, tree *Euphorbia ingens*
eurabbie *Eucalyptus bicostata*
eurabbie, bastard *Eucalyptus pseudoglobulus*
eurah *Eremophila bignoniiflora*
Eurasian smokebush *Cotinus coggygria*
Eureka lemon *Citrus × limon* 'Eureka'
European ash *Fraxinus excelsior*
European aspen *Populus tremula*
European basswood *Tilia × europaea*
European beech *Fagus sylvatica*
European bird cherry *Prunus padus*
European bladdernut *Staphylea pinnata*
European box *Buxus sempervirens*
European chain fern *Woodwardia radicans*

European cotoneaster *Cotoneaster integerrimus*
European cranberry *Viburnum opulus*
European dogwood *Cornus sanguinea*
European dune grass *Leymus arenarius*
European elder *Sambucus nigra*
European euonymus *Euonymus europaeus*
European firethorn *Pyracantha coccinea*
European golden ball *Forsythia europaea*
European hazelnut *Corylus avellana*
European highbush cranberry *Viburnum opulus*
European hop *Humulus lupulus*
European hornbeam *Carpinus betulus*
European horse chestnut *Aesculus hippocastanum*
European joint-pine *Ephedra distachya*
European larch *Larix decidua*
European mountain ash *Sorbus aucuparia*
European nettle tree *Celtis australis*
European plum *Prunus × domestica*
European privet *Ligustrum vulgare*
European raspberry *Rubus idaeus*
European red elder *Sambucus racemosa*
European shrubby horsetail *Ephedra distachya*
European silver birch *Betula pendula*
European silver fir *Abies alba*
European snowball *Viburnum opulus* 'Sterile'
European spindle tree *Euonymus europaeus*
European vervain *Verbena officinalis*
European white birch *Betula pendula*
European white lily *Nymphaea alba*

European white lime *Tilia tomentosa*
euryops, Clanwilliam *Euryops speciosissimus*
euryops, gray *Euryops pectinatus*
euryops, gray-haired *Euryops pectinatus*
euryops, honey *Euryops virgineus*
Evans' begonia *Begonia grandis*
evening primrose *Oenothera*
evening primrose, beach *Oenothera drummondii*
evening primrose, common *Oenothera biennis*
evening primrose, fragrant *Oenothera caespitosa*
evening primrose, hairy *Oenothera mollissima*
evening primrose, large-flowered *Oenothera glazioviana*
evening primrose, long-flowered *Oenothera affinis*
evening primrose, pink *Oenothera rosea, O. speciosa, O. s.* 'Rosea'
evening primrose, sweet-scented *Oenothera stricta*
evening primrose, white *Oenothera caespitosa, O. speciosa*
Everglades palm *Acoelorrhaphe wrightii*
evergreen alder *Alnus acuminata*
evergreen ash *Fraxinus uhdei*
evergreen azalea, tall *Rhododendron × mucronatum*
evergreen, Belgian *Dracaena sanderiana*
evergreen chloris *Eustachys distichophylla*
evergreen euonymus *Euonymus japonicus*
evergreen huckleberry *Vaccinium ovatum*
evergreen kangaroo paw *Anigozanthos flavidus*

evergreen kittentail *Synthyris platycarpa*

evergreen maidenhair *Adiantum venustum*

evergreen miscanthus *Miscanthus transmorrisonensis*

evergreen oak, Himalayan *Quercus leucotrichophora*

evergreen oak, Japanese *Quercus acuta, Q. glauca, Q. laevigata*

evergreen pear *Pyrus kawakamii*

evergreen rose *Rosa sempervirens*

evergreen sumac *Rhus virens*

evergreen tree viburnum *Viburnum odoratissimum*

evergreen violet *Viola sempervirens*

everlasting *Antennaria, Helichrysum, Rhodanthe, Syncarpha, Xeranthemum, Xerochrysum*

everlasting, alpine *Xerochrysum subundulatum*

everlasting, button *Helichrysum scorpioides*

everlasting, Cape *Phaenocoma prolifera, Syncarpha vestita*

everlasting, clustered *Chrysocephalum semipapposum*

everlasting, common *Xerochrysum bracteatum*

everlasting, fringed *Chrysocephalum baxteri*

everlasting, golden *Xerochrysum bracteatum × subundulatum*

everlasting, gray *Ozothamnus obcordatus*

everlasting, hill *Chrysocephalum semicalvum*

everlasting pale *Helichrysum rutidolepis*

everlasting pea *Lathyrus grandiflorus, L. latifolius*

everlasting, pearly *Anaphalis, A. margaritacea*

everlasting, satin *Helichrysum leucopsideum*

everlasting, silver *Helichrysum argyrophyllum*

everlasting, snowball *Helichrysum chionosphaerum*

everlasting, sticky *Xerochrysum viscosum*

everlasting sunflower *Heliopsis helianthoides*

everlasting, Swan River *Rhodanthe manglesii*

everlasting, tree *Ozothamnus ferrugineus*

everlasting, white *Chrysocephalum baxteri*

everlasting, winged *Ammobium alatum*

eye root *Hydrastis canadensis*

eye, bird's *Apodytes dimidiata, Gilia tricolor, Veronica chamaedrys*

eye, clear *Salvia sclarea*

eye, pheasant's *Adonis aestivalis, A. amurensis, A. annua, Gilia tricolor*

eyebright *Euphrasia*

eyelash begonia *Begonia bowerae*

eyelash-leafed sage *Salvia blepharophylla*

eyes, angel's *Veronica chamaedrys*

eyes, bright *Euryops pectinatus*

eyes, crab's *Abrus precatorius*

eyes, doll's *Actaea alba*

eyes, green *Berlandiera*

ezo-yama-hagi *Lespedeza bicolor*

F

fairies' thimbles *Campanula cochlearifolia*
fairy aprons *Utricularia dichotoma*
fairy bells *Disporum, Melasphaerula*
fairy bells, Japanese *Disporum sessile*
fairy bells, yellow *Disporum uniflorum*
fairy duster *Calliandra eriophylla*
fairy fan-flower *Scaevola aemula*
fairy foxglove *Erinus alpinus*
fairy grass *Agrostis avenacea, Sporobolus caroli*
fairy lantern *Calochortus*
fairy lantern, rose *Calochortus amoenus*
fairy lantern, white *Calochortus albus*
fairy moss *Azolla*
fairy orchid *Sarcochilus*
fairy spectacles *Menkea australis*
fairy spuds *Claytonia virginica*
fairy wands *Dierama pulcherrimum*
falcate yellowwood *Podocarpus henkelii*
fall poison *Eupatorium rugosum*
falling stars *Campanula isophylla, Crocosmia*
false acacia *Robinia pseudoacacia*
false aralia *Schefflera elegantissima*
false arborvitae *Thujopsis dolabrata*
false bird of paradise *Heliconia*
false bishop's weed *Ammi majus*
false bodhi tree *Ficus rumphii*
false buckthorn *Bumelia lanuginosa*
false chamomile *Boltonia*
false chamomile, sweet *Matricaria recutita*
false daisy *Eclipta prostrata*
false dandelion *Hypochaeris radicata*
false dragon head *Physostegia*

false golden aster, hairy *Heterotheca villosa*
false hair grass *Pentaschistis airoides*
false heather *Cuphea hyssopifolia, Hudsonia ericoides*
false hellebore *Veratrum*
false hellebore, black *Veratrum nigrum*
false hellebore, white *Veratrum album*
false indigo *Amorpha fruticosa, Baptisia*
false indigo, blue *Baptisia australis*
false indigo, prairie *Baptisia lactea*
false indigo, white *Baptisia lactea*
false Jerusalem cherry *Solanum capsicastrum*
false kava *Piper aduncum*
false lily-of-the-valley *Maianthemum bifolium*
false lupin *Thermopsis, T. rhombifolia*
false mallow *Sidalcea, Sphaeralcea*
false mallow, red *Sphaeralcea coccinea*
false matico *Piper aduncum*
false mock orange *Fendlera rupicola*
false monstera *Epipremnum pinnatum*
false oat *Arrhenatherum elatius*
false olive *Cassine orientalis*
false red yucca *Hesperaloe parviflora*
false rhubarb *Thalictrum flavum*
false rosemary, Cumberland *Conradina verticillata*
false rue anemone *Isopyrum*
false saffron *Carthamus tinctorius*
false sandalwood *Eremophila mitchellii, Myoporum platycarpum*
false sarsaparilla *Hardenbergia violacea*
false sea onion *Ornithogalum longibracteatum*
false Solomon's seal *Maianthemum racemosum, Smilacina, S. racemosa*
false spikenard *Smilacina racemosa*

false spiraea *Astilbe, Sorbaria sorbifolia*
false spirea, tree *Sorbaria kirilowii*
false spirea, Ural *Sorbaria kirilowii*
false sumac *Brucea javanica*
false sunflower *Heliopsis, H. helianthoides*
false thorn, paperbark *Albizia tanganyicensis*
false-flag, blue *Neomarica caerulea*
false-flag, North's *Neomarica northiana*
fan aloe *Aloe plicatilis*
fan fern *Schizaea dichotoma*
fan fern, shiny *Sticherus flabellatus*
fan grevillea *Grevillea ramosissima*
fan maidenhair fern *Adiantum tenerum*
fan, ox-killer *Boophone disticha*
fan palm *Livistona, Trachycarpus*
fan palm, Australian *Livistona australis*
fan palm, Blackdown *Livistona fulva*
fan palm, Cape York *Livistona muelleri*
fan palm, Chinese *Livistona chinensis, Trachycarpus fortunei*
fan palm, Dawson River *Livistona nitida*
fan palm, dwarf *Livistona muelleri*
fan palm, Fiji *Pritchardia pacifica*
fan palm, Himalayan *Trachycarpus martianus*
fan palm, Jamaican *Thrinax parviflora*
fan palm, mangrove *Licuala spinosa*
fan palm, Mediterranean *Chamaerops humilis*
fan palm, ribbon *Livistona decipiens*
fan palm, Victoria River *Livistona victoriae*
fan palm, wedge-leaflet *Licuala ramsayi*

fan, veld *Boophone disticha*
fan wattle *Acacia amblygona*
fan-flower *Scaevola*
fan-flower, climbing *Scaevola enantophylla*
fan-flower, dune *Scaevola calendulacea*
fan-flower, fairy *Scaevola aemula*
fan-flower, pale *Scaevola albida*
fan-flower, purple *Scaevola ramosissima*
fan-flower, spiny *Scaevola spinescens*
fan-leafed cabbage palm *Corypha utan*
farewell to spring *Clarkia*
farmer's friend *Bidens pilosa*
farnetto *Quercus frainetto*
fat hen *Atriplex hortensis, Chenopodium album*
fat, macaw *Elaeis guineensis*
Father David's maple *Acer davidii*
fatsia *Fatsia japonica*
fawn lily *Erythronium californicum*
feather flower *Verticordia monadelpha*
feather flower, Morrison *Verticordia nitens*
feather geranium *Chenopodium botrys*
feather grass *Phragmites australis, Stipa*
feather grass, giant *Stipa gigantea*
feather, painted *Vriesea carinata*
feather, parrot *Myriophyllum aquaticum*
feather, prince's *Amaranthus cruentus, A. hybridus* var. *erythrostachyus, Persicaria orientalis*
feather reed grass *Calamagrostis foliosa, C. × acutiflora*
feather speargrass *Austrostipa elegantissima*
feathered columbine *Thalictrum aquilegiifolium*

feather-flower, claw *Verticordia grandiflora*

feathers, Prince of Wales' *Leptopteris superba*

feathertop *Pennisetum villosum*

feathertop Rhodes grass *Chloris virgata*

featherwood *Polyosma cunninghamii*

feathery cassia *Senna artemisioides*

February daphne *Daphne mezereum*

feijoa *Acca sellowiana*

feldmark veronica *Chionohebe densifolia*

felicia, lilac *Felicia fruticosa*

felt fern *Pyrrosia*

felt fern, horseshoe *Pyrrosia confluens*

felt fern, rock *Pyrrosia rupestris*

felt plant *Kalanchoe beharensis*

felt-bush, gray *Hannafordia bissillii*

felted buttercup *Ranunculus muelleri*

female peony *Paeonia officinalis*

fendlerbush, little *Fendlerella utahensis*

Fendler's lip fern *Cheilanthes fendleri*

fennel *Foeniculum vulgare*

fennel, bronze *Foeniculum vulgare* 'Purpurascens'

fennel, dog *Anthemis*

fennel, Florence *Foeniculum vulgare* var. *azoricum*

fennel flower *Nigella*

fennel, wild *Nigella*

fenugreek *Trigonella foenum-graecum*

fenugreek, native *Trigonella suavissima*

fern, adder's *Polypodium vulgare*

fern, American maidenhair *Adiantum pedatum*

fern, American rock *Polypodium virginianum*

fern, Anderson's sword *Polystichum andersoni*

fern, angle-vein *Polypodium triseriale*

fern, asparagus *Asparagus densiflorus, A. setaceus*

fern, Australian shield *Polystichum australiense*

fern, autumn *Dryopteris erythrosora*

fern, bat *Histiopteris incisa*

fern, bat's wing *Histiopteris incisa*

fern, bead *Onoclea sensibilis*

fern, bear's foot *Humata tyermannii*

fern, bear's paw *Aglaomorpha meyeniana*

fern, berry bladder *Cystopteris bulbifera*

fern, bird's nest *Asplenium australasicum, A. nidus*

fern, black-stem water *Blechnum nudum*

fern, blanket *Pleurosorus rutifolius*

fern, blue *Phlebodium aureum* 'Mandaianum'

fern, Boston *Nephrolepis exaltata*

fern, brake *Pteris cretica*

fern, Braun's sword *Polystichum braunii*

fern, bristly cloak *Cheilanthes distans*

fern, brittle maidenhair *Adiantum tenerum*

fern, broad buckler *Dryopteris dilatata*

fern, buckler *Dryopteris*

fern, button *Pellaea rotundifolia*

fern, Byfield *Bowenia serrulata*

fern, California gold *Pityrogramma triangularis*

fern, California rock *Polypodium californicum*

fern, California shield *Polystichum californicum*

fern, Cape *Cyathea capensis*

fern, caterpillar *Goniophlebium subauriculatum, Polypodium formosanum*

fern, chain *Woodwardia*
fern, Christmas *Polystichum acrostichoides*
fern, climbing *Lygodium*
fern, climbing bird's nest *Microsorum punctatum*
fern, climbing swamp *Stenochlaena palustris*
fern, cloak *Cheilanthes*
fern, comb *Schizaea*
fern, common filmy *Hymenophyllum cupressiforme*
fern, common ground *Calochlaena dubia*
fern, common oak *Gymnocarpium dryopteris*
fern, common shield *Dryopteris cristata*
fern, common tassel *Huperzia phlegmaria*
fern, coral *Lycopodiella cernua*
fern, crape *Leptopteris fraseri*
fern, creeping *Pyrrosia rupestris*
fern, crested wood *Dryopteris cristata*
fern, crown *Blechnum discolor*
fern, cup *Dennstaedtia*
fern cycad *Bowenia spectabilis, Stangeria eriopus*
fern, dagger *Polystichum acrostichoides*
fern, deer *Blechnum spicant*
fern, delta maidenhair *Adiantum raddianum*
fern, dish *Pteris*
fern, double crape *Leptopteris superba*
fern, dwarf tree *Blechnum gibbum*
fern, eastern holly *Polystichum braunii*
fern, elkhorn *Platycerium, P. bifurcatum*
fern, emerald *Asparagus densiflorus*
fern, erect sword *Nephrolepis cordifolia*
fern, fan *Schizaea dichotoma*

fern, fan maidenhair *Adiantum tenerum*
fern, felt *Pyrrosia*
fern, Fendler's lip *Cheilanthes fendleri*
fern, fishbone *Nephrolepis cordifolia, N. exaltata*
fern, five-fingered maidenhair *Adiantum pedatum*
fern, flowering *Osmunda regalis*
fern, fragrant *Microsorum scandens*
fern, giant *Angiopteris evecta*
fern, giant chain *Woodwardia fimbriata*
fern, giant hare's foot *Davallia solida*
fern, giant holly *Polystichum munitum*
fern, glade *Diplazium pycnocarpon*
fern, gold and silver *Pityrogramma*
fern, golden male *Dryopteris affinis*
fern, goldenback *Pityrogramma triangularis*
fern, gristle *Blechnum cartilagineum*
fern, hacksaw *Doodia*
fern, hard *Blechnum spicant*
fern, hard shield *Polystichum aculeatum*
fern, hard water *Blechnum wattsii*
fern, hare's foot *Davallia, D. solida* var. *pyxidata, Phlebodium aureum*
fern, hart's tongue *Asplenium scolopendrium*
fern, Hawaiian man *Cibotium chamissoi*
fern, hay-scented *Dennstaedtia punctilobula*
fern, heart *Hemionitis arifolia*
fern, hen and chicken *Asplenium bulbiferum*
fern, holly *Cyrtomium falcatum, Polystichum*
fern, horseshoe *Marattia salicina*
fern, interrupted *Osmunda claytoniana*

fern, iron *Rumohra adiantiformis*

fern, Japanese felt *Pyrrosia lingua*

fern, Japanese wood *Dryopteris sieboldii*

fern, kangaroo *Microsorum pustulatum*

fern, king *Angiopteris evecta, Marattia salicina, Todea barbara*

fern, Korean rock *Polystichum tsussimense*

fern, ladder *Blechnum spicant, Nephrolepis cordifolia*

fern, lady *Athyrium filix-femina*

fern, Lawson's cliff *Woodsia × gracilis*

fern, leather *Rumohra adiantiformis*

fern, leather wood *Dryopteris marginalis*

fern, leatherleaf *Rumohra adiantiformis*

fern, licorice *Polypodium glycyrrhiza*

fern lily, plumosa *Asparagus setaceus*

fern, lip *Cheilanthes*

fern, locust *Osmunda regalis*

fern, macho *Nephrolepis falcata*

fern, maidenhair *Adiantum, A. aethiopicum, A. raddianum*

fern, male *Dryopteris filix-mas*

fern, mangrove *Acrostichum speciosum*

fern, marginal wood *Dryopteris marginalis*

fern, marsh *Thelypteris palustris*

fern, Meyer asparagus *Asparagus densiflorus* 'Meyeri'

fern, mosquito *Azolla*

fern, mule's *Asplenium sagittatum*

fern, mule's foot *Angiopteris evecta*

fern, narrow buckler *Dryopteris carthusiana*

fern, narrow swamp *Dryopteris cristata*

fern, necklace *Asplenium flabellifolium*

fern, netted chain *Woodwardia areolata*

fern, New Zealand water *Blechnum discolor*

fern, oak *Gymnocarpium dryopteris*

fern, ostrich *Matteuccia struthiopteris*

fern palm, Mexican *Dioon edule*

fern, parasol *Gleichenia microphylla*

fern, parsley *Cryptogramma crispa*

fern, Peruvian maidenhair *Adiantum peruvianum*

fern, piggyback *Hemionitis arifolia*

fern pine, African *Afrocarpus gracilior*

fern, potato *Marattia salicina*

fern, prickly shield *Polystichum aculeatum, P. vestitum*

fern, rabbit's-foot *Davallia solida* var. *fejeensis, Phlebodium aureum*

fern, rainbow *Calochlaena dubia*

fern, rasp *Doodia aspera*

fern, resurrection *Polypodium scouleri, Selaginella lepidophylla*

fern, ribbon *Pteris cretica*

fern, robber *Pyrrosia confluens*

fern, rock *Cheilanthes sieberi, C. tenuifolia*

fern, rosy maidenhair *Adiantum hispidulum*

fern, rough maidenhair *Adiantum hispidulum*

fern, roundleaf *Pellaea rotundifolia*

fern, royal *Osmunda regalis*

fern, rush *Schizaea*

fern, scrambling coral *Gleichenia microphylla*

fern, screw *Lindsaea linearis*

fern, sensitive *Onoclea sensibilis*

fern, shaggy shield *Dryopteris cycadina*

fern, shield *Dryopteris, Polystichum*

fern, shuttlecock *Matteuccia struthiopteris*

fern, sickle *Pellaea falcata*

fern, silver *Pityrogramma calomelanos*
fern, silver dollar maidenhair
    Adiantum peruvianum
fern, silver elkhorn *Platycerium
    veitchii*
fern, small rasp *Doodia caudata*
fern, small sickle *Pellaea nana*
fern, snake *Lygodium microphyllum*
fern, soft shield *Polystichum
    setiferum*
fern, soft water *Blechnum minus*
fern, spider *Pteris multifida*
fern, staghorn *Platycerium,
    P. superbum*
fern, strap *Blechnum patersonii*
fern, sweet *Comptonia peregrina*
fern, sword *Nephrolepis, Polystichum*
fern, table *Pteris*
fern, tassel *Huperzia, Polystichum
    polyblepharon*
fern, tongue *Pyrrosia lingua*
fern, tree *Cibotium, Cyathea,
    Dicksonia*
fern tree *Jacaranda mimosifolia*
fern, turnip *Angiopteris evecta*
fern, umbrella *Dipteris conjugata,
    Sticherus flabellatus*
fern, variegated shield *Arachniodes
    simplicior*
fern, Venus maidenhair *Adiantum
    capillus-veneris*
fern, wall *Polypodium vulgare*
fern, Wallich's wood *Dryopteris
    wallichiana*
fern, water *Azolla, Blechnum
    ambiguum, B. camfieldii,
    Histiopteris incisa*
fern, weeping sword *Nephrolepis
    falcata*
fern, western sword *Polystichum
    munitum*
fern, wood *Dryopteris*
fernbush *Chamaebatiaria millefolium*

fern-leaf aralia *Polyscias filicifolia*
fern-leaf bamboo *Bambusa multiplex
    *'Fernleaf'
fern-leaf grevillea *Grevillea
    aspleniifolia, G. caleyii,
    G. pteridifolia*
fern-leaf hopbush *Dodonaea
    boroniifolia*
fern-leaf wattle *Acacia filicifolia*
fern-leafed bamboo, dwarf
    Pleioblastus pygmaeus
ferny azolla *Azolla pinnata*
ferny buttercup *Ranunculus pumilio*
ferny panax *Polyscias sambucifolia*
ferny-leafed bosistoa *Bosistoa
    pentacocca*
fescue *Festuca*
fescue, Atlas *Festuca mairei*
fescue, blue *Festuca glauca*
fescue, California *Festuca californica*
fescue, fine-leafed sheep's *Festuca
    filiformis*
fescue, gray *Festuca glauca*
fescue, hair *Festuca filiformis*
fescue, hard *Festuca longifolia*
fescue, large blue *Festuca amethystina*
fescue, meadow *Festuca pratensis*
fescue, rats-tail *Vulpia muralis,
    V. myuros*
fescue, red *Festuca rubra*
fescue, sheep's *Festuca ovina*
fescue, squirrel-tail *Vulpia bromoides*
fescue, tall *Festuca arundinacea*
fescue, tufted *Festuca amethystina*
fescue, Wallis *Festuca valesiaca*
fescue, western *Festuca pratensis*
festoon moss *Papillaria*
fetter bush *Leucothoe racemosa,
    Lyonia lucida, Pieris floribunda*
fetticus *Valerianella locusta*
fever berry, lavender *Croton
    gratissimus*
fever bush *Garrya fremontii*

fever tree *Acacia xanthophloea,
Pinckneya pubens*
feverfew *Tanacetum parthenium*
few-flowered leek *Allium paradoxum*
fiber palm, spiny *Trithrinax
acanthocoma*
fickle ladybell *Adenophora stricta*
fiddle-leaf fig *Ficus lyrata*
fiddleneck *Phacelia tanacetifolia*
fiddleneck, common *Amsinckia
intermedia*
fiddlewood *Citharexylum spinosum*
fiddlewood, Florida *Citharexylum
fruticosum*
field chickweed *Cerastium arvense*
field elm *Ulmus carpinifolia*
field horsetail *Equisetum arvense*
field madder *Sherardia arvensis*
field maple *Acer campestre*
field marigold *Calendula arvensis*
field mushroom *Agaricus campestris*
field pea *Pisum sativum*
field poppy *Papaver rhoeas*
field scabious *Knautia arvensis*
fiery costus *Costus igneus*
fig *Ficus, F. carica*
fig, Baja *Ficus palmeri*
fig, banana *Ficus pleurocarpa*
fig, banjo *Ficus lyrata*
fig, banyan *Ficus benghalensis,
F. microcarpa*
fig, Barbados *Opuntia ficus-indica*
fig, Bellinger River *Ficus watkinsiana*
fig, Benjamin *Ficus benjamina*
fig, broom cluster *Ficus sur*
fig, bush *Ficus sur*
fig, Cape *Ficus sur*
fig, Cape strangler *Ficus sur*
fig, clown *Ficus aspera* 'Parcellii'
fig, common strangler *Ficus
thonningii*
fig, common wild *Ficus thonningii*
fig, creek sandpaper *Ficus coronata*

fig, creeping *Ficus pumila*
fig, deciduous *Ficus superba, F. s.* var.
henneana
fig, desert *Ficus palmeri,
F. brachypoda*
fig, devil's *Solanum hispidum*
fig, dinner plate *Ficus dammaropsis*
fig, dracaena *Ficus pseudopalma*
fig, edible *Ficus carica*
fig, fiddle-leaf *Ficus lyrata*
fig, Florida strangler *Ficus aurea*
fig, golden *Ficus aurea*
fig, gray *Ficus virens*
fig, Hottentot *Carpobrotus edulis*
fig, Indian *Opuntia ficus-indica*
fig, Indian laurel *Ficus microcarpa*
fig, large-leafed rock *Ficus
abutilifolia*
fig, mistletoe *Ficus deltoidea*
fig, Moreton Bay *Ficus macrophylla*
fig, mosaic *Ficus aspera* 'Parcellii'
fig, mountain *Ficus glumosa*
fig, mulberry *Ficus sycomorus*
fig, Natal *Ficus natalensis*
fig, palm-like *Ficus pseudopalma*
fig pear, Indian *Opuntia ficus-indica*
fig, Philippine *Ficus pseudopalma*
fig, Port Jackson *Ficus rubiginosa*
fig, rock *Ficus brachypoda*
fig, Roxburgh *Ficus auriculata*
fig, rusty *Ficus destruens,
F. rubiginosa*
fig, sacred *Ficus religiosa*
fig, sandpaper *Ficus coronata,
F. fraseri, F. opposita*
fig, sea *Ficus superba*
fig, spotted *Ficus virens*
fig, strangler *Ficus virens*
fig, sycamore *Ficus sycomorus*
fig, triangle *Ficus deltoidea*
fig, Vogel's *Ficus lutea*
fig, Watkins' *Ficus watkinsiana*
fig, weeping *Ficus benjamina*

fig, Zulu *Ficus lutea*
fig-leafed gourd *Cucurbita ficifolia*
figwort *Scrophularia*
figwort, Cape *Phygelius capensis*
figwort, water *Scrophularia auriculata*
Fiji fan palm *Pritchardia pacifica*
Fijian fire plant *Acalypha amentacea* subsp. *wilkesiana*
filbert *Corylus, Corylus avellana, C. maxima*
filbert, American *Corylus americana*
filbert, beaked *Corylus cornuta*
filbert, purple *Corylus maxima* 'Purpurea'
filimoto *Flacourtia rukam*
filmy fern, common *Hymenophyllum cupressiforme*
filmy maidenhair *Adiantum diaphanum*
fine sida *Sida filiformis*
fine-leaf sunray *Hyalosperma praecox*
fine-leaf tussock grass *Poa sieberiana* var. *hirtella*
fine-leafed nassella *Nassella tenuissima*
fine-leafed sheep's fescue *Festuca filiformis*
fine-leafed tuckeroo *Lepiderema pulchella*
finetooth holly *Ilex serrata*
finger cherry *Rhodomyrtus macrocarpa*
finger, five *Pseudopanax arboreus*
finger grass *Dactyloctenium radulans*
finger grass, small-flower *Digitaria parviflora*
finger, lady's *Abelmoschus esculentus*
finger lime *Citrus australasica*
finger millet *Eleusine coracana*
finger panic *Digitaria coenicola*
finger tree *Euphorbia tirucalli*
finger-flower *Cheiranthera cyanea*
fingernail, painted *Neoregelia spectabilis*

fingers, pink *Caladenia carnea, C. catenata*
finish, dead *Acacia tetragonophylla*
fir *Abies*
fir, Algerian *Abies numidica*
fir, alpine *Abies lasiocarpa*
fir, balsam *Abies balsamea*
fir, beautiful *Abies amabilis*
fir, blue *Abies concolor*
fir, bristlecone *Abies bracteata*
fir, California red *Abies magnifica*
fir, Caucasian *Abies nordmanniana*
fir, China *Cunninghamia lanceolata*
fir, Chinese Douglas *Pseudotsuga sinensis*
fir, Colorado white *Abies concolor*
fir, Douglas *Pseudotsuga, P. menziesii*
fir, dwarf balsam *Abies balsamea*
fir, European silver *Abies alba*
fir, Forrest's *Abies forrestii*
fir, giant *Abies grandis*
fir, Greek *Abies cephalonica*
fir, Himalayan *Abies spectabilis*
fir, Japanese *Abies firma*
fir, joint *Ephedra*
fir, Korean *Abies koreana*
fir, large-cone Douglas *Pseudotsuga macrocarpa*
fir, Manchurian *Abies holophylla*
fir, Mexican *Abies religiosa*
fir, min *Abies recurvata*
fir, Nikko *Abies homolepis*
fir, noble *Abies procera*
fir, Pacific *Abies amabilis*
fir, Rocky Mountain *Abies lasiocarpa*
fir, Santa Lucia *Abies bracteata*
fir, Shensi *Abies chensiensis*
fir, Sicilian *Abies nebrodensis*
fir, silver *Abies concolor*
fir, Spanish *Abies pinsapo*
fir, subalpine *Abies lasiocarpa*
fir, Taiwan *Abies kawakamii*

fir, Taiwan Douglas *Pseudotsuga wilsoniana*
fir, West Himalayan *Abies pindrow*
fir, white *Abies concolor*
fir, Yunnan Douglas *Pseudotsuga forrestii*
fire barrel cactus *Ferocactus gracilis*
fire lily *Clivia miniata, Cyrtanthus*
fire lily, greentip *Clivia nobilis*
fire orchid *Renanthera*
fire plant, Fijian *Acalypha amentacea* subsp. *wilkesiana*
fire plant, Mexican *Euphorbia cyathophora*
fire, prairie *Castilleja*
fire vine *Lotus maculatus*
fireball *Bassia scoparia, Boophone disticha*
fireball lily *Scadoxus multiflorus*
firebush *Bassia scoparia, Hamelia erecta, H. patens*
firebush, Chilean *Embothrium coccineum*
firecracker, Eaton's *Penstemon eatonii*
firecracker, floral *Dichelostemma ida-maia*
firecracker flower *Crossandra infundibuliformis*
firecracker, Mexican *Echeveria setosa*
firecracker plant *Cuphea ignea*
firecracker vine *Manettia luteorubra*
fire-on-the-mountain *Euphorbia cyathophora*
firespike *Odontonema callistachyum*
firethorn *Pyracantha, Rhus pyroides*
firethorn, Chinese *Pyracantha atalantioides*
firethorn, European *Pyracantha coccinea*
firethorn, Himalayan *Pyracantha crenulata*
firethorn, narrow-leafed *Pyracantha angustifolia*

firethorn, orange *Pyracantha angustifolia*
firethorn, Rogers' *Pyracantha rogersiana*
firethorn, scarlet *Pyracantha coccinea*
firethorn, Taiwan *Pyracantha koidzumii*
firethorn, Yunnan *Pyracantha crenatoserrata*
fireweed *Bassia scoparia, Epilobium angustifolium, Senecio madagascariensis*
fireweed, Brazilian *Erechtites valerianifolia*
fireweed, cotton *Senecio quadridentatus*
fireweed groundsel *Senecio linearifolius*
fireweed, hill *Senecio hispidulus*
fireweed, purple *Arrhenechtites mixta*
fireweed, rough *Senecio hispidulus*
firewheel *Gaillardia*
firewheel pincushion *Leucospermum tottum*
firewheel tree *Stenocarpus sinuatus*
firewheel tree, Queensland *Stenocarpus sinuatus*
firewood banksia *Banksia menziesii*
fishbone fern *Nephrolepis cordifolia, N. exaltata*
fishbone water fern *Blechnum nudum*
fishing rod, angel's *Dierama*
fish-killer tree *Barringtonia asiatica*
fishpoison tree, Florida *Piscidia piscipula*
fishpole bamboo *Phyllostachys aurea*
fishtail lawyer cane *Calamus caryotoides*
fishtail palm *Caryota*
fishtail palm, Chinese *Caryota ochlandra*
fishtail palm, cluster *Caryota mitis*
fishtail palm, giant *Caryota no*

fishtail palm, Indian *Caryota obtusa*
fishtail palm, Queensland *Caryota rumphiana* var. *albertii*
fishweed *Einadia trigonos*
fissure-weed *Maireana*
fissure-weed, slender *Maireana pentagona*
fissure-weed, wingless *Maireana enchylaenoides*
five corner fruit *Averrhoa carambola*
five finger *Pseudopanax arboreus*
five spot *Nemophila maculata*
fivecorners *Styphelia laeta*
fivecorners, pink *Styphelia triflora, S. tubiflora*
five-fingered jack *Adiantum hispidulum*
five-fingered maidenhair fern *Adiantum pedatum*
five-leaf azalea *Rhododendron quinquefolium*
five-leafed bosistoa *Bosistoa floydii*
five-minute grass *Tripogon loliiformis*
flaccid grass *Pennisetum flaccidum*
flag, African corn *Chasmanthe floribundum*
flag, alligator *Thalia*
flag, butterfly *Diplarrhena*
flag, morning *Orthrosanthus*
flag, myrtle *Acorus calamus*
flag orchid *Masdevallia*
flag, powdery alligator *Thalia dealbata*
flag, Spanish *Ipomoea lobata*
flag, spiral *Costus*
flag, sweet *Acorus calamus*
flag, yellow *Iris pseudoacorus*
flagroot *Acorus calamus*
flamboyant tree *Delonix regia*
flamboyante *Delonix regia*
flame azalea *Rhododendron calendulaceum, R. flammeum*
flame bush, Natal *Alberta magna*

flame creeper *Combretum microphyllum, Tropaeolum speciosum*
flame flower *Tropaeolum speciosum*
flame grevillea *Grevillea dimorpha*
flame, jungle *Ixora*
flame kurrajong *Brachychiton acerifolius*
flame lily *Gloriosa superba*
flame nasturtium *Tropaeolum speciosum*
flame of the forest *Butea monosperma, Delonix regia*
flame of the woods *Ixora coccinea*
flame pea, eastern *Chorizema parviflorum*
flame pea, heart-leafed *Chorizema cordatum*
flame pea, holly *Chorizema ilicifolium*
flame tree, Argentine *Tabebuia impetiginosa*
flame tree, Australian *Brachychiton acerifolius*
flame tree, Chinese *Koelreuteria bipinnata*
flame tree, Illawarra *Brachychiton acerifolius*
flame tree, yellow *Peltophorum pterocarpum*
flame vine *Pyrostegia venusta*
flame vine, Brazilian *Pyrostegia venusta*
flame vine, Mexican *Pseudogynoxys chenopodioides*
flame violet *Episcia cupreata*
flame willow *Salix* 'Flame'
flamegold tree *Koelreuteria elegans*
flaming beauty *Carphalea kirondron*
flaming Katie *Kalanchoe blossfeldiana*
flaming sword *Vriesea splendens*
flamingo flower *Anthurium andraeanum*
Flanders poppy *Papaver rhoeas*

flannel bush *Fremontodendron,*
F. californicum
flannel bush, Mexican
Fremontodendron mexicanum
flannel bush, Pine Hill
Fremontodendron decumbens
flannel bush, southern
Fremontodendron mexicanum
flannel cudweed *Actinobole*
uliginosum
flannel flower *Actinotus, A. helianthi,*
Phylica plumosa
flannel flower, lesser *Actinotus minor*
flat crown *Albizia adianthifolia*
flat pea, angled *Platylobium*
obtusangulum
flat pea, handsome *Platylobium*
formosum
flat spurge *Chamaesyce drummondii*
flat-awned speargrass *Austrostipa*
platychaeta
flat-leaf pine *Pinus krempfii*
flat-leafed parsley *Petroselinum*
crispum var. *neapolitaum*
flat-sedge *Cyperus*
flat-sedge, drain *Cyperus eragrostis*
flat-sedge, flecked *Cyperus gunnii*
flat-sedge, leafy *Cyperus lucidus*
flat-sedge, tall *Cyperus exaltatus*
flat-spine prickly ash *Zanthoxylum*
simulans
flat-stemmed wattle *Acacia*
complanata
flat-top saltbush, eastern *Atriplex*
lindleyi
flatweed *Hypochaeris radicata*
flatwoods plum *Prunus umbellata*
flax *Linum*
flax bush, yellow *Reinwardtia*
indica
flax, flowering *Linum grandiflorum*
flax, French *Linum trigynum*
flax lily *Phormium*

flax, mountain *Phormium cookianum*
flax, native *Linum marginale*
flax, New Zealand *Phormium,*
P. tenax
flax, New Zealand mountain
Phormium cookianum
flax, perennial *Linum perenne*
flax, perennial blue *Linum perenne*
flax, settlers' *Gymnostachys anceps*
flax wattle *Acacia linifolia*
flax, wild *Linum marginale*
flaxleaf fleabane *Conyza bonariensis*
flax-leafed alyssum *Alyssum linifolium*
flax-leafed paperbark *Melaleuca*
linariifolia
flax-lily *Dianella*
flax-lily, big blue *Dianella prunina*
flax-lily, blue *Dianella caerulea,*
D. revoluta, D. tasmanica
flax-lily, dune *Dianella congesta*
flax-lily, inland *Dianella porracea*
flax-lily, mountain *Dianella*
tasmanica
flax-lily, smooth *Dianella longifolia*
flax-lily, spreading *Dianella revoluta*
flax-lily, Tasmanian *Dianella*
tasmanica
flea, Bogan *Calotis hispidula*
fleabane *Conyza, Erigeron*
fleabane, Canadian *Conyza*
canadensis
fleabane, flaxleaf *Conyza bonariensis*
fleabane, small *Conyza parva*
fleabane, tall *Conyza albida*
fleabane, wandering *Erigeron*
peregrinus
fleawort *Plantago psyllium*
flecked flat-sedge *Cyperus gunnii*
fleece, mountain *Persicaria*
amplexicaulis
fleece vine *Fallopia*
fleshy groundsel *Senecio gregorii*
fleshy hawthorn *Crataegus succulenta*

fleshy mistletoe *Amyema miraculosum*

fleur-de-paradis *Delonix regia*

Flinders Range bottlebrush *Callistemon teretifolius*

Flinders Range wattle *Acacia iteaphylla*

Flinders wattle *Acacia notabilis*

flintwood *Scolopia braunii*

floating bladderwort *Utricularia inflata*

floating heart, yellow *Nymphoides peltata*

floating liverwort *Ricciocarpos natans*

floating pondweed *Potamogeton tricarinatus*

flooded gum *Eucalyptus grandis*

flor del volcan *Solanum wendlandii*

floral firecracker *Dichelostemma ida-maia*

Flora's paintbrush *Emilia sonchifolia*

Florence fennel *Foeniculum vulgare* var. *azoricum*

Florida anise tree *Illicium floridanum*

Florida arrowroot *Zamia integrifolia*

Florida azalea *Rhododendron austrinum*

Florida cherry *Eugenia uniflora*

Florida cherry palm *Pseudophoenix sargentii*

Florida corkwood *Leitneria floridana*

Florida fiddlewood *Citharexylum fruticosum*

Florida fishpoison tree *Piscidia piscipula*

Florida orange *Citrus* × *aurantium* Tangor Group

Florida pinxter azalea *Rhododendron canescens*

Florida poison tree *Metopium toxiferum*

Florida royal palm *Roystonea elata*

Florida silver palm *Coccothrinax argentata*

Florida strangler fig *Ficus aurea*

Florida swamp lily *Crinum americanum*

Florida thatch palm *Thrinax radiata*

Florida torreya *Torreya taxifolia*

Florida yew *Taxus floridana*

florist's anemone *Anemone coronaria*

florist's chrysanthemum *Chrysanthemum* × *grandiflorum*

florist's cineraria *Pericallis* × *hybrida*

florist's gloxinia *Sinningia speciosa*

florist's hydrangea *Hydrangea macrophylla*

florist's smilax *Asparagus asparagoides*

florist's willow *Salix caprea*

floss flower *Ageratum houstonianum*

floss-silk tree *Ceiba insignis, C. speciosa*

floss-silk tree, pink *Ceiba speciosa*

flower, bag *Clerodendrum thomsoniae*

flower, balloon *Platycodon grandiflorus*

flower, blanket *Gaillardia, G. pulchella*

flower, butterfly *Bauhinia monandra, Schizanthus, S.* × *wisetonensis*

flower, calico *Aristolochia grandiflora, A. littoralis*

flower, cardinal *Ipomoea* × *multifida, Lobelia cardinalis, Sinningia cardinalis*

flower, carrion *Orbea variegata, Stapelia, S. gigantea*

flower, chaff *Achyranthes, A. aspera*

flower, Chilean glory *Eccremocarpus scaber*

flower, claw *Calothamnus*

flower, cockspur *Plectranthus parviflorus*

flower, feather *Verticordia monadelpha*

flower, fennel *Nigella*

flower, flannel *Actinotus, A. helianthi, Phylica plumosa*
flower, floss *Ageratum houstonianum*
flower, garland *Adenophora, Daphne cneorum, Hedychium coronarium*
flower, gland *Adenanthos terminalis*
flower, globe *Gomphrena globosa, Trollius*
flower, greenbird *Crotalaria cunninghamii*
flower, guinea-hen *Fritillaria meleagris*
flower, harlequin *Sparaxis*
flower, helmet *Aconitum napellus, Scutellaria, Sinningia cardinalis*
flower, monkey *Mimulus, M. moschatus*
flower, narrow-leaf wax *Philotheca linearis*
flower, pagoda *Clerodendrum paniculatum*
flower, paper *Bougainvillea glabra*
flower, pinxter *Rhododendron periclymenoides*
flower, rice *Ozothamnus diosmifolius, Pimelea*
flower, spade *Hybanthus enneaspermus*
flower, spider *Cleome, Gasslferiana, Grevillea*
flower, trinity *Tradescantia virginiana*
flower, velvet *Amaranthus caudatus, Salpiglossis sinuata, Sparaxis tricolor*
flower, wax *Eriostemon, Hoya, Jamesia americana, Philotheca*
flower, wishbone *Torenia fournieri*
flower, woolly rice *Pimelea octophylla*
flower, yellow trumpet *Tecoma stans*
flowering almond *Prunus × amygdalo-persica*
flowering almond, dwarf *Prunus triloba*
flowering apricot, Japanese *Prunus mume* 'Geisha'

flowering ash *Fraxinus ornus*
flowering banana *Musa ornata*
flowering cherry, dwarf *Prunus glandulosa*
flowering cherry, Japanese *Prunus* Sato-zakura Group
flowering crabapple, Chinese *Malus spectabilis*
flowering currant *Ribes sanguineum*
flowering currant, golden *Ribes aureum*
flowering dogwood *Cornus florida*
flowering dogwood, Chinese *Cornus kousa* var. *chinensis*
flowering dogwood, Japanese *Cornus kousa*
flowering fern *Osmunda regalis*
flowering flax *Linum grandiflorum*
flowering lignum *Eremophila polyclada*
flowering onion *Allium neapolitanum*
flowering peach *Prunus persica*
flowering pepper *Peperomia fraseri*
flowering plum *Prunus cerasifera*
flowering plum, double pink *Prunus × blireana*
flowering plum, Elvins *Prunus cerasifera* 'Elvins'
flowering quince *Chaenomeles, C. speciosa*
flowering quince, Chinese *Chaenomeles speciosa*
flowering quince, white *Chaenomeles speciosa* 'Nivalis'
flowering raspberry *Rubus odoratus*
flowering rush *Butomus, B. umbellatus*
flowering spurge *Euphorbia corollata*
flowering tobacco *Nicotiana alata, N. sylvestris*
flower-of-an-hour *Hibiscus trionum*
flowers, hearts and *Aptenia cordifolia*
fluke bog-rush *Schoenus apogon*

fluted-horn mallee *Eucalyptus stowardii*
fly agaric *Amanita muscaria*
fly honeysuckle *Lonicera xylosteum*
fly poison *Amianthium muscitoxicum*
flycatcher *Sarracenia alata*
flying duck orchid *Caleana major*
flytrap, Venus *Dionaea muscipula*
foambark tree *Jagera pseudorhus*
foamflower *Tiarella cordifolia*
fodder burnet *Sanguisorba minor*
fog, creeping *Holcus mollis*
fog, Yorkshire *Holcus lanatus*
Fontainebleau service tree *Sorbus latifolia*
fonteinbos *Psoralea aphylla*
fonteinriet *Elegia capensis*
food, elephant's *Portulacaria afra*
fool's huckleberry *Menziesia ferruginea*
foot, bear's *Alchemilla, Helleborus foetidus*
foot, cow's *Piper aduncum*
foot, elephant's *Dioscorea elephantipes*
foothill lupine *Lupinus succulentus*
foothill penstemon *Penstemon heterophyllus*
footstool palm *Livistona rotundifolia*
forage peanut *Arachis pintoi*
forest bluegrass *Poa chaixii*
forest bride's bush *Pavetta lanceolata*
forest cabbage tree *Cussonia sphaerocephala, Schefflera umbellifera*
forest commiphora *Commiphora woodii*
forest dombeya *Dombeya tiliacea*
forest, flame of the *Butea monosperma, Delonix regia*
forest germander *Teucrium corymbosum*
forest grass tree *Xanthorrhoea arborea*
forest groundsel *Senecio velleioides*

forest hedgehog grass *Echinopogon ovatus*
forest hound's tongue *Austrocynoglossum latifolium*
forest indigo *Indigofera natalensis*
forest lily *Veltheimia bracteata*
forest lobelia *Lobelia trigonocaulis*
forest maidenhair *Adiantum sylvaticum*
forest maple *Cryptocarya rigida*
forest mint *Mentha laxiflora*
forest nightshade *Solanum prinophyllum*
forest oak *Allocasuarina torulosa*
forest olive *Olea woodiana*
forest pennywort *Hydrocotyle geraniifolia*
forest red gum *Eucalyptus tereticornis*
forest she-oak *Allocasuarina torulosa*
forest starwort *Stellaria flaccida*
forest wild elder *Nuxia floribunda*
forget-me-not *Cynoglossum, Myosotis*
forget-me-not, alpine *Eritrichium, Myosotis alpestris*
forget-me-not, bedding *Myosotis sylvatica*
forget-me-not, Chatham Island *Myosotidium hortensia*
forget-me-not, Chinese *Cynoglossum amabile*
forget-me-not, creeping *Omphalodes verna*
forget-me-not, garden *Cynoglossum amabile*
forget-me-not, wood *Myosotis sylvatica*
forget-me-not, yellow *Amsinckia intermedia*
forked comb fern *Schizaea bifida*
forked sundew *Drosera binata*
forked tree *Pandanus forsteri*
fork-fern, skeleton *Psilotum nudum*

Formosa maiden grass *Miscanthus transmorrisonensis*
Formosa toad lily *Tricyrtis formosana*
Formosan date *Phoenix hanceana*
Formosan gum *Liquidambar formosana*
Forrest's fir *Abies forrestii*
forsythia *Forsythia*
forsythia, border *Forsythia × intermedia*
forsythia, early *Forsythia ovata*
forsythia, green stem *Forsythia viridissima*
forsythia, Korean *Forsythia ovata*
forsythia, weeping *Forsythia suspensa*
forsythia, white *Abeliophyllum distichum*
Fort Bragg manzanita *Arctostaphylos nummularia*
Fortune's plum-yew *Cephalotaxus fortunei*
fothergilla, Alabama *Fothergilla major*
fothergilla, dwarf *Fothergilla gardenii*
fothergilla, large *Fothergilla major*
fountain bamboo *Fargesia nitida*
fountain buddleja *Buddleja alternifolia*
fountain grass *Pennisetum alopecuroides, P. setaceum*
fountain grass, African *Pennisetum setaceum*
fountain grass, oriental *Pennisetum orientale*
fountain palm *Livistona chinensis*
fountain rush *Elegia capensis*
four corners *Grewia occidentalis*
four o'clock flower *Mirabilis jalapa*
four seasons rose *Rosa* 'Quatre Saisons'
four-angled bean *Psophocarpus tetragonobolus*

four-leaf allseed *Polycarpon tetraphyllum*
four-leaf devilpepper *Rauvolfia tetraphylla*
four-leafed maidenhair *Adiantum tetraphyllum*
four-wing saltbush *Atriplex canescens*
four-winged mallee *Eucalyptus tetraptera*
fox banksia *Banksia sphaerocarpa*
fox grape *Vitis labrusca, V. rotundifolia*
foxglove *Digitalis, D. purpurea*
foxglove beardtongue *Penstemon digitalis*
foxglove, Chinese *Rehmannia, R. elata*
foxglove, chocolate *Digitalis parviflora*
foxglove, common *Digitalis purpurea*
foxglove, fairy *Erinus alpinus*
foxglove, Grecian *Digitalis lanata*
foxglove, large yellow *Digitalis grandiflora*
foxglove, Mexican *Tetranema roseum*
foxglove, Portuguese *Digitalis purpurea* subsp. *heywoodii*
foxglove, rusty *Digitalis ferruginea*
foxglove, straw *Digitalis lutea*
foxglove, strawberry *Digitalis × mertonensis*
foxglove, willow-leafed *Digitalis obscura*
foxtail barley *Hordeum jubatum*
foxtail brome *Bromus rubens*
foxtail cactus *Escobaria vivipara*
foxtail, crimson *Ptilotus atriplicifolius*
foxtail grass *Alopecurus*
foxtail grass, swamp *Pennisetum alopecuroides*
foxtail lily *Eremurus*
foxtail, marsh *Alopecurus geniculatus*
foxtail, meadow *Alopecurus pratensis*

foxtail millet *Setaria italica*
foxtail palm *Wodyetia bifurcata*
foxtail, paper *Ptilotus gaudichaudii*
foxtail pine *Pinus balfouriana*
foxtail, regal *Ptilotus nobilis*
foxtail shrub *Asparagus densiflorus*
foxtail speargrass *Austrostipa densiflora*
foxtail, water *Alopecurus geniculatus*
foxtail, white *Ptilotus obovatus*
fragrant evening primrose *Oenothera caespitosa*
fragrant fern *Microsorum scandens*
fragrant olive *Osmanthus fragrans*
fragrant pitcher sage *Lepechinia fragrans*
fragrant rondeletia *Rondeletia odorata*
fragrant snowball viburnum *Viburnum* × *carlcephalum*
fragrant snowbell *Styrax obassia*
fragrant sumac *Rhus aromatica*
fragrant waterlily *Nymphaea odorata*
fragrant winter-hazel *Corylopsis glabrescens*
fragrant woodsia *Woodsia ilvensis*
frail birthwort *Aristolochia debilis*
framboise *Rubus idaeus*
France, oeillet de *Dianthus gallicus*
frangipani *Plumeria*
frangipani, Australian *Hymenosporum flavum*
frangipani, Australian native *Hymenosporum flavum*
frangipani, white *Plumeria obtusa*
Franklin tree *Franklinia alatamaha*
franklinia *Franklinia alatamaha*
Fraser photinia *Photinia* × *fraseri*
Fraser's magnolia *Magnolia fraseri*
freesia *Freesia*
freesia, scarlet *Freesia laxa*
freesia, white *Freesia alba*
Fremont cottonwood *Populus fremontii*

Fremont silktassel *Garrya fremontii*
fremontia *Fremontodendron californicum*
fremontia, Mexican *Fremontodendron mexicanum*
French bean *Phaseolus vulgaris*
French catchfly *Silene gallica*
French flax *Linum trigynum*
French heather *Erica* × *hiemalis*
French hybrid lilac *Syringa vulgaris*
French lavender *Lavandula stoechas*
French marigold *Tagetes patula*
French marjoram *Origanum onites*
French meadow-rue *Thalictrum aquilegiifolium*
French physic nut *Jatropha curcas*
French pussy willow *Salix caprea*
French rose *Rosa gallica*
French rye *Arrhenatherum elatius*
French shallot *Allium ascalonicum*
French sorrel *Rumex scutatus*
French spinach *Atriplex hortensis*
French tamarisk *Tamarix gallica*
French tarragon *Artemisia dracunculus* var. *sativa*
French tree *Tamarix gallica*
French willow *Epilobium angustifolium*
freshwater cord grass *Spartina pectinata*
freshwater mangrove *Barringtonia acutangula*
friar's cap *Aconitum napellus*
friar's cowl *Arisarum vulgare*
friend, farmer's *Bidens pilosa*
friendship plant *Billbergia nutans, Pilea involucrata*
friendship tree *Crassula ovata*
frijolito *Sophora secundiflora*
fringe bells *Shortia soldanelloides*
fringe flower *Loropetalum chinense*
fringe flower, pink *Loropetalum chinense* 'Burgundy'

fringe tree *Chionanthus*
fringe tree, American *Chionanthus virginicus*
fringe tree, Chinese *Chionanthus retusus*
fringecups *Tellima grandiflora*
fringed daisy *Brachyscome ciliaris*
fringed everlasting *Chrysocephalum baxteri*
fringed galax *Shortia soldanelloides*
fringed gentian *Gentianopsis*
fringed gentian, greater *Gentianopsis crinita*
fringed heath-myrtle *Micromyrtus ciliata*
fringed helmet-orchid, small *Corybas pruinosus*
fringed hibiscus *Hibiscus schizopetalus*
fringed Indian pink *Silene laciniata*
fringed violet *Thysanotus*
fringed wattle *Acacia fimbriata*
fringe-lily *Thysanotus*
fringe-lily, common *Thysanotus tuberosus*
fringe-lily, mallee *Thysanotus baueri*
fringe-lily, rush *Thysanotus juncifolius*
fringe-lily, twining *Thysanotus patersonii*
fringe-myrtle *Calytrix, C. tetragona*
fringe-myrtle, desert *Calytrix longiflora*
fringe-myrtle, golden *Calytrix aurea*
fringe-myrtle, Grampians *Calytrix alpestris*
fringe-myrtle, pink *Calytrix longiflora*
fritillary *Fritillaria*
fritillary, black *Fritillaria biflora*
fritillary, snake's head *Fritillaria meleagris*
frog bonnets *Sarracenia oreophila*
frogfruit *Phyla*

frogmouth *Philydrum lanuginosum*
frost grape *Vitis riparia, V. vulpina*
frosted hawthorn *Crataegus pruinosa*
frosty wattle *Acacia pruinosa*
fruit, chain *Alyxia ruscifolia*
fruit, champagne *Carica pentagona*
fruit, dragon *Hylocereus undatus*
fruit, five corner *Averrhoa carambola*
fruit, lotus *Ziziphus lotus*
fruit, nipple *Solanum mammosum*
fruit, pearl *Margyricarpus pinnatus*
fruit, pickle *Averrhoa bilimbi*
fruit salad plant *Monstera deliciosa*
fruit, star *Averrhoa carambola*
fruits of youth *Paullinia cupana*
fruit-scented sage *Salvia dorisiana*
frying pans *Eschscholzia lobbii*
fuchsia, Australian *Correa*
fuchsia begonia *Begonia fuchsioides*
fuchsia bush *Eremophila glabra*
fuchsia bush, harlequin *Eremophila duttonii*
fuchsia bush, prickly *Graptophyllum ilicifolium*
fuchsia bush, scarlet *Graptophyllum excelsum*
fuchsia, California *Zauschneria californica*
fuchsia, Cape *Phygelius capensis*
fuchsia grevillea *Grevillea bipinnatifida*
fuchsia gum *Eucalyptus forrestiana*
fuchsia heath *Epacris longiflora*
fuchsia, honeysuckle *Fuchsia triphylla*
fuchsia, native *Correa reflexa*
fuchsia, New Zealand tree *Fuchsia excorticata*
fuchsia, small-leafed *Fuchsia microphylla*
fuchsia, trailing *Fuchsia procumbens*

fuchsia, tree *Fuchsia arborescens,*
Halleria lucida, Schotia
brachypetala
fuchsia, water *Impatiens*
fuchsia-bush, green *Eremophila*
serrulata
fuchsia-flowered currant *Ribes*
speciosum
Fuji cherry *Prunus incisa*
full-moon maple *Acer japonicum*
fumewort *Corydalis solida*
fumitory *Fumaria*
fumitory, Bastard's *Fumaria bastardii*
fumitory, climbing *Fumaria*
capreolata
fumitory, wall *Fumaria muralis*

fungus, bracket *Ganoderma lucidum,*
Poria cocos
fungus, caterpillar *Cordyceps sinensis*
fungus, polypore *Boletellus ananas*
fungus, rainbow *Trametes versicolor*
fungus, starfish *Aseroe rubra*
furrowed wake robin *Trillium*
sulcatum
furze *Ulex europaeus*
furze hakea *Hakea ulicina*
furze, needle *Genista anglica*
fuzzweed *Vittadinia*
fuzzweed, rough *Vittadinia*
pterochaeta
fuzzy box *Eucalyptus conica*
fuzzy deutzia *Deutzia scabra*

G

galangal *Alpinia galanga*
galangal, greater *Alpinia galanga*
galangal, lesser *Alpinia calcarata*
galax, fringed *Shortia soldanelloides*
gale, sweet *Myrica gale*
galenia *Galenia pubescens*
galingale *Cyperus longus*
gall, Chinese *Rhus chinensis*
gall weed *Zygophyllum apiculatum*
gallant soldiers *Galinsoga parviflora*
gallberry *Ilex glabra*
galvanised burr *Sclerolaena birchii*
gambel oak *Quercus gambelii*
gamboge *Garcinia xanthochymus*
ganagra *Rumex hymenosepalus*
gap mouth *Mimulus guttatus*
gaping mint bush *Prostanthera
ringens*
Garambulla cactus *Myrtillocactus
geometrizans*
garambuyo *Pachycereus schottii*
garbanzo bean *Cicer arietinum*
garden abutilon *Abutilon × hybridum*
garden balsam *Impatiens balsamina*
garden burnet *Sanguisorba minor*
garden candytuft *Iberis umbellata*
garden canna *Canna × generalis*
garden cress *Lepidium sativum*
garden currant *Ribes × koehneanum*
garden forget-me-not *Cynoglossum
amabile*
garden heliotrope *Valeriana officinalis*
garden huckleberry *Solanum
melanocerasum*
garden hydrangea *Hydrangea
macrophylla*
garden mint *Mentha spicata*
garden monkshood *Aconitum
napellus*

garden myrrh *Myrrhis odorata*
garden pea *Pisum sativum*
garden pear *Pyrus communis*
garden pink *Dianthus*
garden portulaca *Portulaca
grandiflora*
garden pyrethrum *Tanacetum
coccineum*
garden ranunculus *Ranunculus
asiaticus*
garden sage *Salvia officinalis*
garden sorrel *Rumex acetosa,
R. scutatus*
garden strawberry *Fragaria ×
ananassa*
garden thyme *Thymus vulgaris*
gardener's garters *Phalaris
arundinacea* 'Picta'
gardenia *Gardenia augusta*
gardenia, bell *Rothmannia globosa*
gardenia, common *Gardenia augusta*
gardenia, crape *Tabernaemontana
divaricata*
gardenia, Natal *Gardenia cornuta*
gardenia, starry *Gardenia thunbergia*
gardenia, tree *Rothmannia globosa*
gardenia, wild *Rothmannia capensis*
gargaloo *Parsonsia eucalyptophylla*
garland chrysanthemum
Xanthophthalmum coronarium
garland daphne *Daphne cneorum*
garland flower *Adenophora, Daphne
cneorum, Hedychium coronarium*
garland lily *Calostemma, Hedychium*
garland lily, pink *Calostemma
purpureum*
garland lily, yellow *Calostemma
luteum*
garlic *Allium, A. sativum*
garlic chives *Allium tuberosum*
garlic, crow *Allium vineale*
garlic, daffodil *Allium neapolitanum*
garlic, German *Allium senescens*

garlic, giant *Allium scorodoprasum*
garlic, golden *Allium moly*
garlic, great-headed *Allium ampeloprasum*
garlic, keeled *Allium carinatum*
garlic, Levant *Allium ampeloprasum*
garlic, Naples *Allium neapolitanum*
garlic, rosy *Allium roseum*
garlic, society *Tulbaghia*
garlic, Spanish *Allium scorodoprasum*
garlic, sweet *Tulbaghia fragrans, T. simmleri*
garlic, three-cornered *Allium triquetrum*
garlic, wild *Allium cratericola, Tulbaghia, T. violacea*
garrocha *Tecoma garrocha*
garters, gardener's *Phalaris arundinacea* 'Picta'
gas plant *Dictamnus albus*
gasteria, dwarf *Gasteria bicolor*
gasteria, rice *Gasteria carinata*
gayfeather *Liatris, L. spicata*
gean *Prunus avium*
gebang palm *Corypha utan*
geebung *Persoonia*
geebung, broad-leafed *Persoonia levis*
geebung, creeping *Persoonia chamaepitys*
geebung, laurel *Persoonia laurina*
geebung, myrtle *Persoonia myrtilloides*
geebung, narrow-leaf *Persoonia linearis*
geebung, pine-leaf *Persoonia pinifolia*
geebung, tropical *Persoonia falcata*
geiger tree *Cordia sebestena*
geissois, common *Geissois pruinosa*
gem, coral *Lotus berthelotii*
genista *Genista lydia, G. pilosa*
genista, dwarf *Genista lydia*
gentian *Gentiana, Gentianella, Gentianopsis*

gentian, fringed *Gentianopsis*
gentian, greater fringed *Gentianopsis crinita*
gentian, prairie *Eustoma*
gentian sage *Salvia patens*
gentian, spotted *Gentiana punctata*
gentian, willow *Gentiana asclepiadea*
George lily *Cyrtanthus elatus*
Georgia bark *Pinckneya pubens*
Georgia bush honeysuckle *Diervilla rivularis*
Georgia choke cherry *Prunus cuthbertii*
Georgia hackberry *Celtis tenuifolia*
Georgia oak *Quercus georgiana*
Geraldton wax *Chamelaucium uncinatum*
geranium, almond *Pelargonium quercifolium*
geranium, apple *Pelargonium odoratissimum*
geranium aralia *Polyscias guilfoylei*
geranium, bedding *Pelargonium* Zonal Hybrids
geranium, beefsteak *Begonia* Rex-cultorum Group
geranium, birch-leaf *Pelargonium betulinum*
geranium, cactus *Pelargonium echinatum*
geranium, climbing *Pelargonium peltatum*
geranium, feather *Chenopodium botrys*
geranium, ivy *Pelargonium peltatum*
geranium, ivy-leafed *Pelargonium peltatum*
geranium, lemon-scented *Pelargonium crispum*
geranium, lime-scented *Pelargonium* 'Nervosum'
geranium, Martha Washington *Pelargonium* Regal Hybrid

geranium, native *Geranium homeanum, G. potentilloides, G. solanderi*

geranium, oak-leaf *Pelargonium quercifolium*

geranium, regal *Pelargonium* Regal Hybrids

geranium, rock *Heuchera americana*

geranium, rose *Pelargonium capitatum, P. graveolens*

geranium, rose-scented *Pelargonium graveolens*

geranium, samphire-leafed *Pelargonium crithmifolium*

geranium, southernwood *Pelargonium abrotanifolium*

geranium, sweetheart *Pelargonium echinatum*

geranium, wild *Pelargonium australe*

geranium, zonal *Pelargonium* Zonal Hybrids

gerard, herb *Aegopodium podagraria*

gerbera *Gerbera jamesonii*

German catchfly *Lychnis viscaria*

German chamomile *Matricaria recutita*

German garlic *Allium senescens*

German iris *Iris* × *germanica*

German onion *Ornithogalum longibracteatum*

German primrose *Primula obconica*

German rampion *Oenothera biennis*

German violet *Exacum affine*

germander *Teucrium*

germander, American *Teucrium canadense*

germander, bush *Teucrium fruticans*

germander, cut-leaf *Teucrium botrys*

germander, forest *Teucrium corymbosum*

germander, golden *Teucrium polium*

germander, gray *Teucrium racemosum*

germander sage *Salvia chamaedryoides*

germander, shrubby *Teucrium fruticans*

germander speedwell *Veronica chamaedrys*

germander spiraea *Spiraea chamaedryfolia*

germander, wall *Teucrium chamaedrys*

germander, water *Teucrium scordium*

germander, wood *Teucrium scorodonia*

gewone wildevy *Ficus thonningii*

Geyer's onion *Allium geyeri*

gharab *Populus euphratica*

gherkin *Cucumis sativus*

gherkin, West Indian *Cucumis anguria*

ghost gum *Corymbia papuana*

ghost gum, Central Australian *Corymbia aparrerinja*

ghost gum, rough-leafed *Corymbia aspera*

ghost plant *Graptopetalum paraguayense*

ghost tree *Davidia involucrata*

ghost weed *Euphorbia marginata*

giant allium *Allium giganteum*

giant arborvitae *Thuja plicata*

giant bamboo *Bambusa balcooa*

giant bellflower *Campanula latifolia, C. l.* var. *macrantha*

giant bird of paradise *Strelitzia nicolai*

giant blue waterlily *Nymphaea gigantea*

giant burrawang *Macrozamia moorei*

giant chain fern *Woodwardia fimbriata*

giant chincherinchee *Ornithogalum saundersiae*

giant crown of thorns *Euphorbia* × *lomii*

giant dogwood *Cornus controversa*
giant feather grass *Stipa gigantea*
giant fern *Angiopteris evecta*
giant fir *Abies grandis*
giant fishtail palm *Caryota no*
giant garlic *Allium scorodoprasum*
giant granadilla *Passiflora quadrangularis*
giant groundsel, Mexican *Senecio petasitis*
giant hare's foot fern *Davallia solida*
giant holly fern *Polystichum munitum*
giant honeysuckle *Lonicera hildebrandiana*
giant horsetail *Equisetum giganteum, E. telmateia*
giant hummingbird mint *Agastache barberi*
giant hyssop *Agastache, A. barberi*
giant hyssop, Mexican *Agastache mexicana*
giant hyssop, threadleaf *Agastache rupestris*
giant hyssop, wrinkled *Agastache rugosa*
giant ironwood *Choricarpia subargentea*
giant kalanchoe *Kalanchoe beharensis*
giant leather fern *Acrostichum danaeifolium*
giant lily *Cardiocrinum, Doryanthes excelsa*
giant lily, Himalayan *Cardiocrinum giganteum*
giant lobelia *Lobelia telekii*
giant maidenhair *Adiantum formosum, A. trapeziforme*
giant maidenhair fern *Adiantum formosum*
giant mallee *Eucalyptus socialis*
giant mallow *Hibiscus*
giant mountain fishtail palm *Caryota aequatorialis, C. maxima*

giant mustard *Rapistrum rugosum*
giant Parramatta grass *Sporobolus indicus* var. *major*
giant pepper vine *Piper novae-hollandiae*
giant pigweed *Trianthema portulacastrum*
giant potato creeper *Solanum wendlandii*
giant protea *Protea cynaroides*
giant raisin *Grewia hexamita*
giant reed *Arundo donax*
giant reed, variegated *Arundo donax* 'Versicolor'
giant rhubarb *Gunnera manicata*
giant St John's wort *Hypericum ascyron*
giant salvia *Brillantaisia lamium*
giant scabious *Cephalaria gigantea*
giant sedge *Cyperus exaltatus*
giant sensitive plant *Mimosa pigra*
giant sequoia *Sequoiadendron giganteum*
giant snowdrop *Galanthus elwesii*
giant spider flower *Cleome hassleriana*
giant stapelia *Stapelia gigantea*
giant stinging tree *Dendrocnide excelsa*
giant sunflower *Helianthus giganteus*
giant taro *Alocasia macrorrhizos*
giant thevetia *Thevetia thevetioides*
giant timber bamboo *Phyllostachys bambusoides*
giant umbrella fern *Dipteris conjugata*
giant velvet rose *Aeonium canariense*
giant water gum *Syzygium francisii*
giant water vine *Cissus hypoglauca*
giant waterlily *Victoria*
giant wild rye *Elymus condensatus*
giant yucca *Yucca elephantipes*

giboshi, hyuga *Hosta kikutii*
giboshi, kanzashi *Hosta nakaiana*
giboshi, kirin *Hosta minor*
giboshi, koba *Hosta sieboldii*
giboshi, kuro *Hosta nigrescens*
giboshi, kuronami *Hosta fluctuans*
giboshi, mizu *Hosta longissima*
giboshi, murasaki *Hosta ventricosa*
giboshi, oba *Hosta montana*
giboshi, otafuku *Hosta decorata*
giboshi, otome *Hosta venusta*
giboshi, sazanami *Hosta crispula*
giboshi, suji *Hosta undulata*
giboshi, tokudama *Hosta tokudama*
giboshi, urajiro *Hosta hypoleuca*
Gibraltar candytuft *Iberis
   gibraltarica*
Gibraltar Range waratah *Telopea
   aspera*
gidgee *Acacia cambagei*
gidyea *Acacia cambagei*
gigante, cardón *Pachycereus pringlei*
gigantic lily *Doryanthes palmeri*
Gilead, balm of *Cedronella
   canariensis, Commiphora
   gileadensis, Populus × jackii
   'Gileadensis'*
Giles' net bush *Calothamnus gilesii*
gilgai grass *Panicum subxerophilum*
gillyflower *Matthiola*
gimlet *Eucalyptus salubris*
gimlet, silvertop *Eucalyptus campaspe*
gingelly *Sesamum orientale*
ginger *Zingiber, Z. officinale*
ginger, beehive *Zingiber spectabile*
ginger, blue *Dichorisandra thyrsiflora*
ginger, Brazilian *Dichorisandra
   thyrsiflora*
ginger, canton *Zingiber officinale*
ginger, common *Zingiber officinale*
ginger, Indian *Alpinia calcarata*
ginger, kahili *Hedychium
   gardnerianum*

ginger lily *Alpinia, Hedychium,
   H. coronarium, H. gardnerianum*
ginger lily, scarlet *Hedychium
   coccineum*
ginger, pine-cone *Zingiber zerumbet*
ginger, red *Alpinia purpurata*
ginger, shampoo *Zingiber zerumbet*
ginger, shell *Alpinia zerumbet*
ginger, Siamese *Alpinia galanga*
ginger, snap *Alpinia calcarata*
ginger, spiral *Costus*
ginger, stem *Zingiber officinale*
ginger, torch *Etlingera elatior*
ginger, white *Hedychium coronarium*
ginger, wild *Asarum*
ginger, yellow *Hedychium
   gardnerianum*
gingerbread palm *Hyphaene thebaica*
gingham golf ball *Euphorbia obesa*
ginkgo *Ginkgo biloba*
ginseng *Panax, P. ginseng*
ginseng, American *Panax
   quinquefolius*
ginseng, Asian *Panax ginseng*
ginseng, qi *Panax pseudoginseng*
ginseng, Siberian *Eleutherococcus
   senticosus*
Gippsland waratah *Telopea oreades*
gipsywort *Lycopus europaeus*
Gittins's wattle *Acacia gittinsii*
gladdon *Iris foetidissima*
glade fern *Diplazium pycnocarpon*
glade onion *Allium stellatum*
gladiolus, water *Butomus*
gladiolus, wild *Gladiolus undulatus*
gladwyn *Iris foetidissima*
gladwyn, stinking *Iris foetidissima*
gland flower *Adenanthos terminalis*
glasswort *Salicornia europaea,
   Sarcocornia quinqueflora*
glasswort, desert *Pachycornia triandra*
glassy hyacinth *Triteleia lilacina*
glassy onion *Allium hyalinum*

globe amaranth *Gomphrena globosa*
globe, artichoke *Cynara scolymus*
globe artichoke *Cynara scolymus*
globe cornflower *Centaurea macrocephala*
globe flower *Gomphrena globosa, Trollius europaeus*
globe lily, white *Calochortus albus*
globe mallow *Sphaeralcea, S. coccinea*
globe thistle *Echinops, E. ritro, E. sphaerocephalus*
globe tulip, golden *Calochortus amabilis*
globe-flowered magnolia *Magnolia globosa*
globe-pea, leafless *Sphaerolobium minus, S. vimineum*
gloriosa daisy *Rudbeckia hirta*
glory bean, Java *Clerodendrum speciosissimum*
glory bower *Clerodendrum, C. philippinum*
glory bush *Tibouchina, T. granulosa, T. lepidota, T. urvilleana*
glory bush, large-flowered *Tibouchina macrantha*
glory flower *Clerodendrum bungei*
glory flower, Chilean *Eccremocarpus scaber*
glory lily *Gloriosa superba*
glory, morning *Ipomoea*
glory of the snow *Chionodoxa, C. forbesii, C. luciliae*
glory of the sun *Leucocoryne ixioides, L. odorata*
glory pea *Swainsona formosa*
glory pea, golden *Gompholobium latifolium*
glory plant, purple *Sutera grandiflora*
glory vine, crimson *Vitis coignetiae*
glossy abelia *Abelia × grandiflora*
glossy hawthorn *Crataegus nitida*
glossy laurel *Cryptocarya laevigata*

glossy magnolia *Magnolia nitida*
glossy nightshade *Solanum americanum*
glossy privet *Ligustrum lucidum*
glossyleaf manzanita *Arctostaphylos nummularia*
gloxinia *Sinningia speciosa*
gloxinia, florist's *Sinningia speciosa*
glycine, silky *Glycine canescens*
glycine, twining *Glycine clandestina*
glycine, variable *Glycine tabacina*
gnaingar *Eucalyptus phoenicea*
gnarled corkbark *Hakea fraseri*
gnat orchid *Acianthus fornicatus, Cyrtostylis reniformis*
Goa, cedar of *Cupressus lusitanica*
goat horn cactus *Astrophytum capricorne*
goat nut *Simmondsia chinensis*
goat orchid *Diuris venosa*
goat pepper *Capsicum frutescens*
goat weed, horny *Epimedium sagittatum*
goat willow *Salix caprea*
goathead burr *Sclerolaena bicornis*
goat's beard *Aruncus dioicus, Tragopogon*
goat's rue *Galega officinalis*
goatsfoot morning glory *Ipomoea pes-caprae*
goddess bamboo, Chinese *Bambusa multiplex* var. *riviereorum*
godetia *Clarkia, C. amoena*
gold and silver fern *Pityrogramma*
gold, basket of *Aurinia saxatilis*
gold birch *Betula ermanii*
gold, cup of *Solandra maxima*
gold dust *Aurinia saxatilis*
gold fern, California *Pityrogramma triangularis*
gold medallion flower *Melampodium paludosum*
gold net iris *Iris chrysographes*

gold nuggets *Calochortus luteus*
gold pattern iris *Iris chrysographes*
gold shower *Galphimia glauca*
gold, tree of *Tabebuia argentea*
gold-dust dracaena *Dracaena surculosa*
gold-dust plant *Aucuba japonica* 'Variegata', *Dracaena surculosa*
gold-dust wattle *Acacia acinacea*
golden abelia *Abelia* × *grandiflora* 'Frances Mason'
golden allamanda *Allamanda cathartica, A. hendersonii*
golden angel's trumpet *Brugmansia aurea*
golden arborvitae *Thuja occidentalis* 'Lutea'
golden Arizona cypress *Cupressus glabra* 'Limelight'
golden ash *Fraxinus excelsior* 'Aurea'
golden aster *Heterotheca villosa*
golden aster, hairy *Heterotheca villosa*
golden Atlantic cedar *Cedrus atlantica* 'Aurea'
golden Atlas cedar *Cedrus atlantica* 'Aurea'
golden ball *Leucaena retusa*
golden ball cactus *Echinocactus grusonii, Parodia leninghausii*
golden ball, European *Forsythia europaea*
golden bamboo *Phyllostachys aurea*
golden banner *Thermopsis rhombifolia*
golden barrel cactus *Echinocactus grusonii*
golden bead tree *Duranta erecta*
golden bells *Forsythia* × *intermedia, F. suspensa, F. viridissima*
golden berry *Physalis peruviana*
golden brodiaea *Triteleia ixioides*
golden buffalo currant *Ribes odoratum*

golden buttons *Tanacetum vulgare*
golden California privet *Ligustrum ovalifolium* 'Aureum'
golden calla *Zantedeschia elliottiana*
golden camellia *Camellia nitidissima*
golden candles *Pachystachys lutea*
golden cane palm *Dypsis lutescens*
golden cereus *Bergerocactus emoryi*
golden chain tree *Laburnum anagyroides, L.* × *watereri*
golden chestnut *Chrysolepis chrysophylla*
golden club *Orontium aquaticum*
golden columbine *Aquilegia chrysantha*
golden cottonwood *Cassinia fulvida*
golden crown grass *Paspalum dilatatum*
golden cup *Hunnemannia fumariifolia*
golden currant *Ribes aureum, R. odoratum*
golden daisy bush *Euryops pectinatus*
golden deodar *Cedrus deodara* 'Aurea'
golden dew drop *Duranta erecta*
golden diosma *Coleonema pulchellum* 'Sunset Gold'
golden doubletails *Diuris aurea*
golden elder *Sambucus canadensis* 'Aurea', *Sambucus nigra* 'Aurea'
golden elm *Ulmus glabra* 'Lutescens'
golden everlasting *Xerochrysum bracteatum, X. subundulatum*
golden eye grass *Sisyrinchium californicum*
golden fig *Ficus aurea*
golden flowering currant *Ribes aureum*
golden fringe-myrtle *Calytrix aurea*
golden garlic *Allium moly*
golden germander *Teucrium polium*

golden globe tulip *Calochortus amabilis*

golden glory pea *Gompholobium latifolium*

golden gram *Vigna radiata*

golden grass, Bowles' *Milium effusum* 'Aureum'

golden grevillea *Grevillea chrysophaea*

golden guinea-flower *Hibbertia*

golden heather *Hudsonia ericoides*

golden hinoki cypress *Chamaecyparis obtusa* 'Crippsii'

golden honey locust *Gleditsia triacanthos* 'Sunburst'

golden larch *Pseudolarix amabilis*

golden Lawson cypress *Chamaecyparis lawsoniana* 'Stewartii'

golden lily of the valley *Sandersonia aurantiaca*

golden lobelia *Monopsis lutea*

golden maidenhair *Polypodium vulgare*

golden male fern *Dryopteris affinis*

golden mistletoe *Notothixos subaureus*

golden Monterey cypress *Cupressus macrocarpa* 'Aurea'

golden Monterey cypress, Brunning's *Cupressus macrocarpa* 'Brunneana'

golden moths *Diuris lanceolata*

golden myrtle, Queensland *Thaleropia queenslandica*

golden oak of Cyprus *Quercus alnifolia*

golden oats *Stipa gigantea*

golden oregano *Origanum vulgare* 'Aureum'

golden parrot tree *Grevillea pteridifolia*

golden pearlwort *Sagina subulata* 'Aurea'

golden pencil pine, Swane's *Cupressus sempervirens* 'Swane's Golden'

golden pennants *Glischrocaryon behrii*

golden polypody *Phlebodium aureum*

golden powderpuff *Parodia chrysacanthion*

golden rain tree *Cassia fistula, Koelreuteria paniculata*

golden root *Rhodiola rosea*

golden sage *Salvia aurea*

golden scabweed *Raoulia australis*

golden shallot *Allium ascalonicum*

golden shower *Pyrostegia venusta*

golden shower tree *Cassia fistula*

golden Spaniard *Aciphylla aurea*

golden spider lily *Lycoris aurea*

golden spined cereus *Bergerocactus emoryi*

golden spire azara *Azara integrifolia*

golden star *Chrysogonum virginianum, Hypoxis hygrometrica*

golden sunray *Hyalosperma glutinosum*

golden tauhinu *Cassinia fulvida*

golden tip *Goodia lotifolia*

golden top *Lamarckia aurea*

golden torch cereus *Echinopsis spachiana*

golden totara *Podocarpus totara* 'Aurea'

golden tree *Grevillea pteridifolia*

golden trumpet *Allamanda cathartica*

golden trumpet tree *Tabebuia chrysotricha*

golden vine *Stigmaphyllon ciliatum*

golden wattle *Acacia pycnantha*

golden wattle, Australian *Acacia pycnantha*

golden wattle, Sydney *Acacia longifolia*

golden wattle, western *Acacia decora*

golden wattle, Western Australian *Acacia saligna*

golden weather-glass *Hypoxis hygrometrica*

golden weeping Monterey cypress *Cupressus macrocarpa* 'Aurea Saligna'

golden weeping willow *Salix × sepulcralis* 'Chrysocoma'

golden wreath wattle *Acacia saligna*

golden yarrow *Eriophyllum lanatum*

golden yew *Taxus baccata* 'Aurea'

goldenback fern *Pityrogramma triangularis*

goldenbush *Chrysothamnus graveolens, C. viscidiflorus*

goldenfleece *Ericameria aborescens*

golden-rayed lily *Lilium auratum*

goldenrod *Solidago, S. canadensis*

goldenrod, California *Solidago californica*

goldenrod, rough-stemmed *Solidago rugosa*

goldenrod, southern California *Solidago confinis*

goldenrod, zigzag *Solidago flexicaulis*

goldenseal *Hydrastis canadensis*

golden-tip clover tree *Goodia lotifolia*

golden-top grass *Lamarckia aurea*

golden-top wattle *Acacia tindaleae*

goldenweed *Haplopappus*

goldenweed, Chilean *Haplopappus foliosus*

goldfields *Lasthenia glabrata*

goldfields bottlebrush *Melaleuca coccinea*

goldfields grevillea *Grevillea dryophylla*

goldfish plant *Columnea gloriosa*

goldfussia *Strobilanthes anisophyllus*

Goldilocks' buttercup *Ranunculus auricomus*

gold-leafed lemon thyme *Thymus × citriodorus* 'Aureus'

gold-tip yew *Taxus baccata* 'Fastigiata Aureomarginata'

gold-tipped bottlebrush *Callistemon polandii*

gold-tooth aloe *Aloe mitriformis*

gold-twig willow *Salix alba* 'Aurea'

golf ball, gingham *Euphorbia obesa*

gomphrena *Gomphrena globosa*

gomphrena weed *Gomphrena celosioides, G. flaccida*

gomuti palm *Arenga pinnata*

goober *Arachis hypogaea*

good King Henry *Chenopodium bonus-henricus*

goodenia, ivy *Goodenia hederacea*

goodenia, mallee *Goodenia willisiana*

goodenia, serrated *Goodenia cycloptera*

goodenia, silky *Goodenia fascicularis*

goose grass *Bromus hordeaceus, Eleusine tristachya, Galium aparine*

goose plum *Prunus americana*

gooseberry *Ribes uva-crispa*

gooseberry, Barbados *Pereskia aculeata*

gooseberry, Cape *Physalis peruviana*

gooseberry, Ceylon *Dovyalis hebecarpa*

gooseberry, Chinese *Actinidia chinensis, A. deliciosa*

gooseberry mallee *Eucalyptus calycogona*

gooseberry, mountain *Ribes oxyacanthoides*

gooseberry, northern *Ribes oxyacanthoides*

gooseberry, Otaheite *Phyllanthus acidus*

gooseberry, Siberian *Actinidia arguta*

gooseberry, star *Phyllanthus acidus*

gooseberry, white-stemmed *Ribes inerme*

gooseberry, wild *Solanum ellipticum*

goosefoot *Acer pensylvanicum*

goosefoot, desert *Chenopodium desertorum*

goosefoot, keeled *Chenopodium carinatum*

goosefoot, mallee *Chenopodium desertorum*

goosefoot, nettle-leaf *Chenopodium murale*

goosefoot, nitre *Chenopodium nitrariaceum*

goosefoot, purple *Scleroblitum atriplicinum*

gooseneck loosestrife *Lysimachia clethroides*

Gordon's Bay pincushion *Leucospermum bolusii*

gorse *Ulex europaeus*

gorse bitter pea *Daviesia ulicifolia*

gorse, double-flowered *Ulex europaeus* 'Plenus'

gorse, dwarf *Ulex gallii, U. minor*

gorse, Spanish *Genista hispanica*

Gosford wattle *Acacia prominens*

gotu-kola *Centella asiatica*

gourd *Cucurbita, C. maxima, C. pepo, Lagenaria siceraria*

gourd, bitter *Momordica charantia*

gourd, bottle *Lagenaria siceraria*

gourd, club *Trichosanthes cucumerina*

gourd, crookneck *Lagenaria siceraria*

gourd, fig-leafed *Cucurbita ficifolia*

gourd, Malabar *Cucurbita ficifolia*

gourd, snake *Trichosanthes cucumerina*

gourd, trumpet *Lagenaria siceraria*

gourd, wax *Benincasa hispida*

gourd, white-flowered *Lagenaria siceraria*

gout plant *Jatropha podagrica*

goutweed *Aegopodium podagraria*

gouty vine *Cyphostemma bainesii*

governor's plum *Flacourtia indica, F. rukam*

Gowen cypress *Cupressus goveniana*

grace, herb of *Ruta graveolens*

graceful honey-myrtle *Melaleuca radula*

grain sorghum *Sorghum bicolor* subsp. *bicolor*

grains of paradise *Aframomum melegueta*

gram, black *Vigna mungo*

gram, golden *Vigna radiata*

gram, green *Vigna radiata*

gram, red *Cajanus cajan*

grama *Stenotaphrum secundatum*

grama, blue *Bouteloua gracilis*

grama grass *Bouteloua*

Grampians bauera *Bauera sessiliflora*

Grampians fringe-myrtle *Calytrix alpestris*

Grampians grevillea *Grevillea alpina, G. confertifolia*

Grampians thryptomene *Thryptomene calycina*

granadilla *Passiflora edulis, P. quadrangularis*

granadilla, giant *Passiflora quadrangularis*

granadilla, purple *Passiflora edulis*

granadilla, red *Passiflora coccinea*

granadilla, yellow *Passiflora laurifolia*

grand Somali hemp *Sansevieria grandis*

grand trillium *Trillium grandiflorum*

granite banksia *Banksia verticillata*

granite bluebell *Wahlenbergia graniticola*

granite buttercup *Ranunculus graniticola*

granite wattle *Acacia granitica*

granny's bonnet *Aquilegia, A. vulgaris, Angelonia angustifolia*

granny's cap *Angelonia angustifolia, A. salicariifolia*

Grant's milkbush *Synadenium grantii*

grape *Vitis*
grape, Amur *Vitis amurensis*
grape, bush *Vitis rupestris*
grape, California holly *Mahonia pinnata*
grape, California wild *Vitis californica*
grape, canyon *Vitis arizonica*
grape, Cape *Rhoicissus capensis*
grape, chicken *Vitis vulpina*
grape, fox *Vitis labrusca, V. rotundifolia*
grape, frost *Vitis riparia, V. vulpina*
grape grevillea *Grevillea bipinnatifida*
grape hyacinth *Muscari, M. armeniacum*
grape, Isabella *Vitis labruscana* 'Isabella'
grape ivy *Cissus*
grape ivy, miniature *Cissus striata*
grape, Macquarie *Muehlenbeckia gunnii*
grape, muscadine *Vitis rotundifolia*
grape, native *Cissus hypoglauca*
grape, Oregon *Mahonia aquifolium*
grape, ornamental *Vitis vinifera × rupestris* 'Ganzin Glory'
grape, painted *Cissus discolor*
grape, possum *Cissus trifoliata*
grape, riverbank *Vitis riparia*
grape, sand *Vitis rupestris*
grape, sea *Coccoloba uvifera*
grape, slender *Cayratia clematidea*
grape, tree *Cyphostemma juttae*
grape, veld *Cissus quadrangularis*
grape vine *Vitis vinifera*
grape, wine *Vitis vinifera*
grapefruit *Citrus × paradisi*
grapeleaf anemone *Anemone tomentosa*
grapeleaf begonia *Begonia dregei*
grape-scented sage *Salvia melissodora*

grass, African fountain *Pennisetum setaceum*
grass, African love *Eragrostis curvula*
grass, annual meadow *Poa annua*
grass, autumn moor *Sesleria autumnalis*
grass, Bahama *Cynodon dactylon*
grass, bahia *Paspalum notatum*
grass, bamboo *Eragrostis australasica, Stipa ramosissima*
grass, bandicoot *Monachather paradoxa*
grass, barbed-wire *Cymbopogon refractus*
grass, barley *Hordeum leporinum*
grass, barnyard *Echinochloa crus-galli*
grass, basket *Lomandra longifolia, Oplismenus*
grass, bear *Xerophyllum tenax*
grass, bearskin *Festuca eskia*
grass, bent *Agrostis*
grass, Bermuda *Cynodon dactylon*
grass, birdwood *Cenchrus setiger*
grass, black mondo *Ophiopogon planiscapus* 'Nigrescens'
grass, blady *Imperata cylindrica*
grass, blown *Agrostis aemula, A. avenacea*
grass, blue moor *Sesleria caerulea*
grass, blue mountain *Sesleria caerulea*
grass, blue oat *Helictotrichon sempervirens*
grass, blue-eyed *Sisyrinchium angustifolium, S. graminoides, S. idahoense*
grass, bottlebrush *Hystrix patula*
grass, Bowles' golden *Milium effusum* 'Aureum'
grass, broad-leafed meadow *Poa chaixii*
grass, brome *Bromus*
grass, buffalo *Buchloe, B. dactyloides, Stenotaphrum secundatum*

grass, buffel *Cenchrus ciliaris*
grass, bugle *Sarracenia oreophila*
grass, bulbous oat *Arrhenatherum elatius* var. *bulbosum*
grass, button *Dactyloctenium radulans, Gymnoschoenus sphaerocephalus*
grass, California blue-eyed *Sisyrinchium idahoense*
grass, Canary *Phalaris, P. canariensis*
grass, cane *Eragrostis australasica*
grass, carpet *Axonopus compressus*
grass, cloud *Agrostis nebulosa*
grass, coast barb *Parapholis incurva*
grass, cockatoo *Alloteropsis semialata*
grass, cogon *Imperata cylindrica*
grass, common hair *Deschampsia flexuosa*
grass, Coolatai *Hyparrhenia hirta*
grass, coolibah *Panicum queenslandicum*
grass, cord *Spartina*
grass, corkscrew *Austrostipa setacea*
grass, cotton *Eriophorum*
grass, cotton panic *Digitaria brownii*
grass, couch *Cynodon dactylon, Elytrigia repens*
grass, crab *Digitaria, Eleusine, Panicum*
grass, creeping bent *Agrostis stolonifera*
grass, creeping soft *Holcus mollis*
grass, crinkled hair *Deschampsia flexuosa*
grass, crowsfoot *Eleusine indica*
grass, curly windmill *Enteropogon acicularis*
grass cushions *Isoetopsis graminifolia*
grass, Durban *Dactyloctenium australe*
grass, dwarf meadow *Poa annua*
grass, dwarf mondo *Ophiopogon japonicus* 'Nanus'

grass, European dune *Leymus arenarius*
grass, fairy *Agrostis avenacea, Sporobolus caroli*
grass, false hair *Pentaschistis auroides*
grass, feather *Phragmites australis, Stipa*
grass, feather reed *Calamagrostis foliosa, C. × acutiflora*
grass, feathertop Rhodes *Chloris virgata*
grass, finger *Dactyloctenium radulans*
grass, five-minute *Tripogon loliiformis*
grass, flaccid *Pennisetum flaccidum*
grass, forest hedgehog *Echinopogon ovatus*
grass, Formosa maiden *Miscanthus transmorrisonensis*
grass, fountain *Pennisetum alopecuroides, P. setaceum*
grass, foxtail *Alopecurus*
grass, freshwater cord *Spartina pectinata*
grass, giant feather *Stipa gigantea*
grass, gilgai *Panicum subxerophilum*
grass, golden crown *Paspalum dilatatum*
grass, golden eye *Sisyrinchium californicum*
grass, golden-top *Lamarckia aurea*
grass, goose *Bromus hordeaceus, Eleusine tristachya, Galium aparine*
grass, grama *Bouteloua*
grass, graybeard *Amphipogon strictus*
grass, great quaking *Briza maxima*
grass, Guildford *Romulea rosea* var. *australis*
grass, Guinea *Panicum maximum*
grass, hair *Aira, Deschampsia, Eleocharis acicularis*
grass, hakone *Hakonechloa macra*
grass, hare's-tail *Lagurus ovatus*

grass, herds' *Phleum pratense*
grass, holy *Hierochloe odorata*
grass, hoop Mitchell *Astrebla elymoides*
grass, Indian *Sorghastrum nutans*
grass, Japanese forest *Hakonechloa macra*
grass, Japanese silver *Miscanthus sinensis*
grass, Johnson *Sorghum halepense*
grass, June *Poa pratensis*
grass, kangaroo *Themeda australis*
grass, kikuyu *Pennisetum clandestinum, P. flaccidum*
grass, knottybutt *Paspalidium constrictum*
grass, Korean velvet *Zoysia tenuifolia*
grass, kunai *Imperata cylindrica*
grass, large blue hair *Koeleria glauca*
grass, leafy reed *Calamagrostis foliosa*
grass, lemon *Cymbopogon citratus*
grass lily *Caesia parviflora*
grass lily, blue *Caesia parviflora* var. *vittata*
grass lily, pale *Caesia parviflora*
grass, liverseed *Urochloa panicoides*
grass, long graybeard *Amphipogon caricinus*
grass, love *Eragrostis*
grass, lyme *Leymus arenarius*
grass, Magennis Bermuda *Cynodon* × *magennisii*
grass, manna *Glyceria*
grass, marram *Ammophila arenaria*
grass, marsh *Spartina, S. pectinata*
grass, mascarene *Zoysia tenuifolia*
grass, mat *Hemarthria uncinata*
grass, meadow *Glyceria, Poa pratensis*
grass, Mitchell *Astrebla*
grass, molasses *Melinis minutiflora*
grass, mondo *Ophiopogon japonicus*

grass, moor *Molinia, M. caerulea, Sesleria*
grass, mosquito *Bouteloua gracilis*
grass, Mossman River *Cenchrus echinatus*
grass, mulga *Thyridolepis mitchelliana*
grass, mulka *Eragrostis dielsii*
grass, New Zealand wind *Stipa arundinacea*
grass, oat *Arrhenatherum elatius, Helictotrichon*
grass, onion *Romulea rosea* var. *australis*
grass orchid *Grastidium*
grass, oriental fountain *Pennisetum orientale*
grass, palm *Setaria palmifolia*
grass pampas *Cortaderia jubata, C. selloana*
grass, panic *Panicum*
grass, paradoxa *Phalaris paradoxa*
grass, Parramatta *Sporobolus indicus* var. *capensis*
grass, pepper *Panicum laevinode*
grass, plains *Austrostipa aristiglumis, A. bigeniculata*
grass, plume *Dichelachne crinita, Saccharum ravennae*
grass, plumed tussock *Chionochloa conspicua*
grass, porcupine *Triodia mitchellii, T. scariosa*
grass, poverty *Hudsonia tomentosa*
grass, prairie *Bromus catharticus*
grass, quaking *Briza, B. maxima, B. media*
grass, rabbit-foot *Polypogon monspeliensis*
grass, ravenna *Saccharum ravennae*
grass, red *Bothriochloa macra*
grass, red tussock *Chionochloa rubra*
grass, redhead *Potamogeton perfoliatus*

grass, redleg *Bothriochloa decipiens*
grass, reed *Calamagrostis, Phalaris arundinacea*
grass, reed Canary *Phalaris arundinacea*
grass, reed meadow *Glyceria maxima*
grass, reed sweet *Glyceria maxima*
grass, Rhodes *Chloris gayana*
grass, ribbon *Phalaris arundinacea*
grass, roughtail *Rostraria pumila*
grass, rye *Lolium*
grass, St Augustine *Stenotaphrum secundatum*
grass salt *Spartina pectinata*
grass, satintop *Bothriochloa erianthoides*
grass, scented-top *Capillipedium spicigerum*
grass, scurvy *Oxalis enneaphylla*
grass, sea barley *Hordeum marinum*
grass, sea lyme *Leymus arenarius*
grass, serpent *Persicaria vivipara*
grass, shivery *Briza minor*
grass, sideoats *Bouteloua curtipendula*
grass, silver banner *Miscanthus sacchariflorus*
grass, silvery hair *Aira caryophyllea, A. cupaniana*
grass, small Japanese silver *Miscanthus oligostachyus*
grass, snow *Chionochloa, Poa sieberiana*
grass, spangle *Chasmanthium latifolium*
grass, star *Hypoxis*
grass, summer *Digitaria ciliaris, D. sanguinalis*
grass, swamp foxtail *Pennisetum alopecuroides*
grass, sweet *Glyceria*
grass, switch *Panicum virgatum*
grass, Timothy *Phleum pratense*

grass, toetoe *Cortaderia richardii*
grass, tor *Brachypodium pinnatum*
grass, torpedo *Panicum repens*
grass tree *Kingia australis, Xanthorrhoea*
grass tree, forest *Xanthorrhoea arborea*
grass tree, Mexican *Dasylirion quadrangulatum, D. longissimum*
grass tree, narrow-leafed *Xanthorrhoea glauca*
grass tree, northern *Xanthorrhoea johnsonii*
grass tree, Queensland *Xanthorrhoea johnsonii*
grass tree, southern *Xanthorrhoea australis*
grass tree, square-leaf *Xanthorrhoea quadrangulata*
grass tree, swamp *Xanthorrhoea fulva*
grass tree, Western Australian *Xanthorrhoea preissii*
grass, trembling *Briza media*
grass, tuber oat *Arrhenatherum elatius* var. *bulbosum*
grass, tufted hair *Deschampsia cespitosa*
grass, tussock *Deschampsia cespitosa, Poa labillardierei*
grass, umbrella *Digitaria divaricatissima, D. hystrichoides*
grass, vasey *Paspalum urvillei*
grass, wallaby *Austrodanthonia, Notodanthonia*
grass, wanderrie *Eriachne*
grass, Warrego *Paspalidium jubiflorum*
grass, wavy hair *Deschampsia flexuosa*
grass, weeping *Microlaena stipoides*
grass, weeping love *Eragrostis curvula*
grass, wheat *Elymus*
grass, whisky *Andropogon virginicus*
grass, white star *Hypoxis capensis*
grass, whitlow *Draba*

grass, windmill *Chloris truncata*
grass, winter *Poa annua*
grass, wood *Sorghastrum nutans*
grass, woollybutt *Eragrostis eriopoda*
grass, yadbila *Panicum queenslandicum*
grass, yellow-eyed *Sisyrinchium palmifolium*
grass, zoysia *Zoysia*
grass-flag, branching *Libertia paniculata*
grassland daisy *Brachyscome angustifolia*
grass-leaf hakea *Hakea francisiana, H. multilineata*
grass-leaf sunray *Leucochrysum graminifolium*
grass-leaf trigger plant *Stylidium graminifolium*
grassnut *Triteleia laxa*
grassy bells *Edraianthus*
grassy rush *Butomus umbellatus*
gray alder *Alnus incana*
gray barleria *Barleria albostellata*
gray birch *Betula populifolia*
gray bluebush *Maireana radiata*
gray box, coastal *Eucalyptus bosistoana*
gray box, Craven *Eucalyptus largeana*
gray box, narrow-leafed *Eucalyptus pilligaensis*
gray box, western *Eucalyptus microcarpa*
gray bush-pea *Pultenaea cunninghamii*
gray copperburr *Sclerolaena diacantha*
gray cottonheads *Conostylis candicans*
gray dock *Balsamorhiza sagittata*
gray dogwood *Cornus racemosa*
gray euryops *Euryops pectinatus*
gray everlasting *Ozothamnus obcordatus*

gray felt-bush *Hannafordia bissillii*
gray fescue *Festuca glauca*
gray fig *Ficus virens*
gray germander *Teucrium racemosum*
gray gum *Eucalyptus biturbinata, E. punctata*
gray gum, large-fruited *Eucalyptus canaliculata*
gray gum, mountain *Eucalyptus cypellocarpa*
gray gum, small-fruited *Eucalyptus propinqua*
gray hakea *Hakea cinerea*
gray head coneflower *Ratibida pinnata*
gray honey-myrtle *Melaleuca incana*
gray ironbark *Eucalyptus paniculata, E. siderophloia*
gray ironbark, Queensland *Eucalyptus drepanophylla*
gray mallee *Eucalyptus morrisii*
gray mangrove *Avicennia marina, A. m.* var. *australasica*
gray mistletoe *Amyema quandang*
gray mulga *Acacia brachybotrya*
gray myrtle *Backhousia myrtifolia*
gray oak *Quercus grisea*
gray pine *Pinus sabiniana*
gray poplar *Populus* × *canescens*
gray possumwood *Quintinia verdonii*
gray raspwort *Haloragis glauca*
gray rattle pod *Crotalaria dissitiflora*
gray rush, California *Juncus patens*
gray sage *Salvia leucophylla*
gray saltbush *Atriplex cinerea*
gray samphire *Halosarcia pergranulata*
gray spider flower *Grevillea buxifolia*
gray willow *Salix cinerea*
gray wrinklewort *Rutidosis helichrysoides*
graybeard grass *Amphipogon strictus*

gray-bud snakebark maple *Acer rufinerve*

gray-haired euryops *Euryops pectinatus*

gray-leaf cherry *Prunus canescens*

grease nut *Hernandia bivalvis*

greasewood *Adenostoma fasciculatum, Sarcobatus vermiculatus*

Great Basin blue sage *Salvia dorrii*

Great Basin bristlecone pine *Pinus longaeva*

great bellflower *Campanula latifolia*

great burdock *Arctium lappa*

great burnet *Sanguisorba canadensis, S. officinalis*

great horsetail *Equisetum telmateia*

great laurel magnolia *Magnolia grandiflora*

great laurel rhododendron *Rhododendron maximum*

great merrybells *Uvularia grandiflora*

great millet *Sorghum bicolor*

great mullein *Verbascum thapsus*

great pignut *Bunium bulbocastanum*

great purple monkey flower *Mimulus lewisii*

great quaking grass *Briza maxima*

great St John's wort *Hypericum ascyron*

great willow herb *Epilobium angustifolium*

greater beggar's ticks *Bidens subalternans*

greater burnet saxifrage *Pimpinella major*

greater celandine *Chelidonium majus*

greater fringed gentian *Gentianopsis crinita*

greater galangal *Alpinia galanga*

greater masterwort *Astrantia major*

greater periwinkle *Vinca major*

greater spearwort *Ranunculus lingua*

greater stitchwort *Stellaria holostea*

greater yam *Dioscorea alata*

great-headed garlic *Allium ampeloprasum*

great-spurred violet *Viola selkirkii*

Grecian foxglove *Digitalis lanata*

Grecian strawberry tree *Arbutus andrachne*

Greece, anemone of *Anemone pavonina*

Greek clover *Trigonella foenum-graecum*

Greek fir *Abies cephalonica*

Greek hay *Trigonella foenum-graecum*

Greek juniper *Juniperus excelsa*

Greek maple *Acer heldreichii*

Greek sage *Salvia fruticosa*

Greek valerian *Polemonium caeruleum, P. reptans*

green alder *Alnus viridis*

green amaranth *Amaranthus viridis*

green and gold *Chrysogonum virginianum*

green arrow arum *Peltandra virginica*

green ash *Fraxinus pennsylvanica*

green bark ceanothus *Ceanothus spinosus*

green bean *Phaseolus vulgaris*

green bolly gum *Neolitsea australiensis*

green bottlebrush *Callistemon flavovirens, C. viridiflorus*

green button protea *Protea scolymocephala*

green cascarilla *Croton verreauxii*

green cestrum *Cestrum parqui*

green, cliff *Paxistima canbyi*

green cliff brake *Pellaea viridis*

green crumbweed *Chenopodium carinatum, Dysphania rhadinostachya*

green dragon *Arisaema dracontium*

green earth-star *Cryptanthus acaulis*

green ephedra *Ephedra viridis*

green eyes *Berlandiera*

green fuchsia bush *Eremophila serrulata*
green gram *Vigna radiata*
green grevillea *Grevillea jephcottii*
green hawthorn *Crataegus viridis*
green hellebore *Helleborus viridis*
green ixia *Ixia viridiflora*
green joint-fir *Ephedra viridis*
green kangaroo apple *Solanum vescum*
green kangaroo paw *Anigozanthos viridis*
green lavender *Lavandula viridis*
green mallee *Eucalyptus viridis*
green Mexican rose *Echeveria × gilva*
green osier *Cornus alternifolia*
green pigeon grass *Setaria viridis*
green pitcher plant *Sarracenia oreophila*
green protea *Protea scolymocephala*
green santolina *Santolina rosmarinifolia*
green sapote *Pouteria viridis*
green satinheart *Geijera salicifolia*
green stem forsythia *Forsythia viridissima*
green summer grass *Urochloa subquadripara*
green tamarind *Elattostachys nervosa*
green tea-tree *Leptospermum coriaceum*
green wattle *Acacia deanei, A. irrorata*
green wattle, Sydney *Acacia parramattensis*
green waxberry *Gaultheria appressa*
green-berry nightshade *Solanum opacum*
greenbird flower *Crotalaria cunninghamii*
greenbush *Callistachys lanceolata*
green-flowered mint bush *Prostanthera leichhardtii*

greenhood, baby *Pterostylis parviflora*
greenhood, blunt *Pterostylis obtusa, P. curta*
greenhood, king *Pterostylis baptistii*
greenhood, midget *Pterostylis mutica*
greenhood, nodding *Pterostylis nutans*
greenhood orchid *Pterostylis*
greenhood, sharp *Pterostylis acuminata*
greenhood, superb *Pterostylis grandiflora*
greenhood, tiny *Pterostylis parviflora*
greenleaf Japanese maple *Acer palmatum*
greenleaf manzanita *Arctostaphylos patula*
greens, mustard *Brassica juncea*
greens, warrigal *Tetragonia tetragonioides*
greentip fire lily *Clivia nobilis*
greenweed, dyer's *Genista tinctoria*
grefsheim spiraea *Spiraea × cinerea*
grevillea, alpine *Grevillea australis*
grevillea, Banks' *Grevillea banksii*
grevillea, Bauer's *Grevillea baueri*
grevillea, Burra Range *Grevillea decora*
grevillea, Caley's *Grevillea caleyi*
grevillea, caramel *Grevillea polybotrya*
grevillea, Carrington Falls *Grevillea rivularis*
grevillea, catkin *Grevillea synapheae*
grevillea, comb *Grevillea huegelii*
grevillea, Corrigin *Grevillea scapigera*
grevillea, desert *Grevillea eriostachya*
grevillea, Dryander's *Grevillea dryanderi*
grevillea, fan *Grevillea ramosissima*
grevillea, fern-leaf *Grevillea aspleniifolia, G. caleyi, G. pteridifolia*
grevillea, flame *Grevillea dimorpha*
grevillea, fuchsia *Grevillea bipinnatifida*

grevillea, golden *Grevillea chrysophaea*
grevillea, goldfields *Grevillea dryophylla*
grevillea, Grampians *Grevillea alpina, G. confertifolia*
grevillea, grape *Grevillea bipinnatifida*
grevillea, green *Grevillea jephcottii*
grevillea, gully *Grevillea barklyana*
grevillea, Helms' *Grevillea helmsiae*
grevillea, holly *Grevillea aquifolium, G. ilicifolia*
grevillea, Johnson's *Grevillea johnsonii*
grevillea, juniper-leaf *Grevillea juniperina*
grevillea, laurel-leaf *Grevillea laurifolia*
grevillea, lavender *Grevillea lavandulacea*
grevillea, linear-leaf *Grevillea linearifolia*
grevillea, long-style *Grevillea longistyla*
grevillea, mountain *Grevillea alpina*
grevillea, Mullet Creek *Grevillea shiressii*
grevillea, oak-leaf *Grevillea quercifolia*
grevillea, olive *Grevillea dimorpha, G. olivacea*
grevillea, Omeo *Grevillea willisii*
grevillea, oval-leaf *Grevillea miqueliana*
grevillea, Pine Mountain *Grevillea jephcottii*
grevillea, rattle pod *Grevillea stenobotrya*
grevillea, red *Grevillea heliosperma*
grevillea, rock *Grevillea heliosperma, G. willisii*
grevillea, rosemary *Grevillea rosmarinifolia*
grevillea, royal *Grevillea victoriae*

grevillea, short-styled *Grevillea brachystylis*
grevillea, silky *Grevillea sericea*
grevillea, silvery-leafed *Grevillea argyrophylla*
grevillea, smooth *Grevillea manglesii*
grevillea, southern *Grevillea australis*
grevillea, spider-net *Grevillea thelemanniana*
grevillea, star-leaf *Grevillea asteriscosa*
grevillea, strawberry *Grevillea confertifolia*
grevillea, Wee Jasper *Grevillea iaspicula*
grevillea, white *Grevillea parallela*
grevillea, white plume *Grevillea leucopteris*
grevillea, Wickham's *Grevillea wickhamii*
grevillea, Wilson's *Grevillea wilsonii*
grevillea, woolly *Grevillea lanigera*
grevillea, yellow flame *Grevillea eriostachya*
grey *see* gray
grindelia, Pacific *Grindelia stricta*
gristle fern *Blechnum cartilagineum*
gromwell, red-rooted *Lithospermum erythrorhizon*
gromwell, scrambling *Lithodora diffusa*
ground ash *Aegopodium podagraria*
ground cherry *Physalis, Prunus fruticosa*
ground cherry, Mexican *Physalis ixocarpa*
ground cherry, purple *Physalis philadelphica*
ground elder *Aegopodium podagraria*
ground fern *Calochlaena dubia*
ground fern, harsh *Hypolepis muelleri*
ground fern, lacy *Dennstaedtia davallioides*
ground ivy *Glechoma hederacea*
ground oak *Teucrium chamaedrys*

ground orchid, Chinese *Bletilla striata*
ground pine *Lycopodium clavatum*
ground raspberry *Hydrastis canadensis*
ground rose *Protea pudens*
groundheads *Chthonocephalus pseudevax*
groundnut *Arachis hypogaea*
groundsel *Senecio vulgaris*
groundsel, bigleaf *Telanthophora grandifolia*
groundsel bush *Baccharis halimifolia*
groundsel, fireweed *Senecio linearifolius*
groundsel, fleshy *Senecio gregorii*
groundsel, forest *Senecio velleioides*
groundsel, slender *Senecio glossanthus*
groundsel tree *Baccharis halimifolia*
groundsel, variable *Senecio lautus*
grub fern, white *Goniophlebium subauriculatum*
gruie *Owenia acidula*
grumichama *Eugenia brasiliensis*
Guadalupe cypress *Cupressus guadalupensis*
Guadalupe palm *Brahea edulis*
guado *Isatis tinctoria*
guajillo *Acacia berlandieri*
guajilote *Parmentiera aculeata*
guanabana *Annona muricata*
guano *Coccothrinax argentea, C. spissa*
guaramaco *Brownea coccinea*
guarana *Paullinia cupana*
guarana bread *Paullinia cupana*
guard, cardinal's *Pachystachys coccinea*
guaromo *Cecropia peltata*
guarri *Euclea undulata*
guarri, blue *Euclea crispa*
guarri, large-leafed *Euclea natalensis, E. undulata*
guarri, magic *Euclea divinorum*
guarri, Natal *Euclea natalensis*

Guatemala rhubarb *Jatropha podagrica*
guava *Psidium guajava*
guava, cherry *Psidium cattleianum*
guava, Chilean *Ugni molinae*
guava, native *Rhodomyrtus psidioides*
guava, pineapple *Acca sellowiana*
guava, strawberry *Psidium cattleianum*
guayiga *Zamia pumila*
guelder rose *Viburnum opulus*
guembe *Monstera deliciosa*
Guernsey lily *Nerine sarniensis*
Guildford grass *Romulea rosea* var. *australis*
guinea grass *Panicum maximum*
guinea-flower *Hibbertia*
guinea-flower, cutleaf *Hibbertia cuneiformis*
guinea-flower, erect *Hibbertia riparia*
guinea-flower, golden *Hibbertia*
guinea-flower, prickly *Hibbertia acicularis*
guinea-flower, rough *Hibbertia aspera*
guinea-flower, silky *Hibbertia sericea*
guinea-flower, toothed *Hibbertia dentata*
guinea-flower, trailing *Hibbertia empetrifolia*
guinea-flower, twiggy *Hibbertia virgata*
guinea-flower, twining *Hibbertia scandens*
guinea-hen flower *Fritillaria meleagris*
guioa *Guioa semiglauca*
guisaro *Psidium guineense*
guitar plant *Lomatia tinctoria*
gully grevillea *Grevillea barklyana*
gully gum *Eucalyptus smithii*
gum, alpine cider *Eucalyptus gunnii*
gum, American sweet *Liquidambar styraciflua*
gum, apple *Angophora, Corymbia clavigera*

gum arabic tree *Acacia nilotica,*
  A. seyal
gum arabic tree, Senegal *Acacia*
  senegal
gum arabic tree, Sudan *Acacia senegal*
gum, Baeuerlen's *Eucalyptus*
  baeuerlenii
gum, big badja *Eucalyptus badjensis*
gum, black *Eucalyptus aggregata,*
  Nyssa sylvatica
gum, Blakely's red *Eucalyptus blakelyi*
gum, blue *Eucalyptus globulus*
gum, Bogong *Eucalyptus chapmaniana*
gum, bolly *Litsea reticulata*
gum, brittle *Eucalyptus mannifera,*
  E. praecox
gum, broad-leafed scribbly
  Eucalyptus haemastoma
gum, Brooker's *Eucalyptus brookeriana*
gum bumelia *Bumelia lanuginosa*
gum, Burdett's *Eucalyptus*
  burdettiana
gum, Buxton *Eucalyptus crenulata*
gum, cabbage *Eucalyptus amplifolia*
gum, candlebark *Eucalyptus rubida*
gum, Cape York red *Eucalyptus*
  brassiana
gum, Central Australian ghost
  Corymbia aparrerinja
gum, Chinese sweet *Liquidambar*
  acalycina, L. formosana
gum, cider *Eucalyptus gunnii*
gum cistus *Cistus ladanifer*
gum, coral *Eucalyptus torquata*
gum, cotton *Nyssa aquatica*
gum, cup *Eucalyptus cosmophylla*
gum, de Beuzeville's snow *Eucalyptus*
  debeuzevillei
gum, Deane's *Eucalyptus deanei*
gum, dirty *Eucalyptus chloroclada*
gum, Dorrigo white *Eucalyptus*
  dorrigoensis
gum, dwarf water *Tristania neriifolia*

gum, Dwyer's red *Eucalyptus dwyeri*
gum, flooded *Eucalyptus grandis*
gum, forest red *Eucalyptus tereticornis*
gum, Formosan *Liquidambar*
  formosana
gum, fuchsia *Eucalyptus forrestiana*
gum, ghost *Corymbia papuana*
gum, giant water *Syzygium francisii*
gum, gray *Eucalyptus biturbinata,*
  E. punctata
gum, gully *Eucalyptus smithii*
gum, Hillgrove *Eucalyptus*
  michaeliana
gum, inland scribbly *Eucalyptus rossii*
gum, Kybean *Eucalyptus parvula*
gum, lemon-flowered *Eucalyptus*
  woodwardii
gum, lemon-scented *Corymbia*
  citriodora
gum, Maiden's *Eucalyptus maidenii*
gum, manna *Eucalyptus mannifera,*
  E. viminalis
gum, Mindanao *Eucalyptus deglupta*
gum, mountain *Eucalyptus*
  dalrympleana
gum, mountain gray *Eucalyptus*
  cypellocarpa
gum, Nepean River *Eucalyptus*
  benthamii
gum, northern water *Tristaniopsis*
  exiliflora
gum, Omeo *Eucalyptus neglecta*
gum, orange *Eucalyptus bancroftii*
gum, oriental sweet *Liquidambar*
  orientalis
gum plant *Grindelia, G. camporum*
gum plant, juniper *Tetraclinis*
  articulata
gum, poplar *Eucalyptus alba*
gum, Queensland blue *Eucalyptus*
  tereticornis
gum, red-cap *Eucalyptus erythrocorys*
gum, red-flowering *Corymbia ficifolia*

gum, ribbon *Eucalyptus viminalis*
gum, river red *Eucalyptus camaldulensis*
gum, rough-leafed ghost *Corymbia aspera*
gum, round-leaf blue *Eucalyptus deanei*
gum, round-leafed *Eucalyptus deanei*
gum, rusty *Angophora costata*
gum, salmon *Eucalyptus salmonophloia*
gum, scarlet *Eucalyptus phoenicea*
gum, scarlet pear *Eucalyptus stoatei*
gum, scribbly *Eucalyptus haemastoma*
gum, shining *Eucalyptus nitens*
gum, silver *Eucalyptus cordata*
gum, silver dollar *Eucalyptus polyanthemos*
gum, slaty *Eucalyptus dawsonii*
gum, small-fruited gray *Eucalyptus propinqua*
gum, small-leafed *Eucalyptus parvifolia*
gum, snappy *Eucalyptus racemosa, E. leucophloia*
gum, snow *Eucalyptus niphophila, E. pauciflora*
gum, sour *Nyssa sylvatica*
gum, South Australian blue *Eucalyptus leucoxylon*
gum, spinning *Eucalyptus perriniana*
gum, spotted *Corymbia maculata*
gum, Steedman's *Eucalyptus steedmanii*
gum, Strickland's *Eucalyptus stricklandii*
gum, sugar *Eucalyptus cladocalyx*
gum, swamp *Eucalyptus ovata*
gum, sweet *Liquidambar, L. styraciflua*
gum, Sydney blue *Eucalyptus saligna*
gum, Sydney red *Angophora costata*

gum, Tasmanian blue *Eucalyptus globulus*
gum, Tasmanian snow *Eucalyptus coccifera*
gum, Tingiringi *Eucalyptus glaucescens*
gum, tupelo *Nyssa aquatica*
gum, urn *Eucalyptus urnigera*
gum, varnished *Eucalyptus vernicosa*
gum vine *Aphanopetalum resinosum*
gum, Wallangarra white *Eucalyptus scoparia*
gum, water *Tristaniopsis laurina*
gum, weeping *Eucalyptus sepulcralis*
gum, white *Eucalyptus alba, E. dalrympleana*
gum, Woila *Eucalyptus olsenii*
gum, Wolgan snow *Eucalyptus gregsoniana*
gum, yellow *Eucalyptus cypellocarpa, E. leucoxylon*
gum-barked coolibah *Eucalyptus intertexta*
gumbo *Abelmoschus esculentus*
gumbo-limbo *Bursera simaruba*
gumdigger's soap *Pomaderris kumeraho*
gumweed *Grindelia squarrosa*
gundabluey *Acacia victoriae*
gungurru *Eucalyptus caesia*
Gunn's alpine buttercup *Ranunculus gunnianus*
Gunn's beech *Nothofagus gunnii*
gunyang *Solanum vescum*
gutta percha tree *Eucommia ulmoides*
Guyana arrowroot *Dioscorea alata*
Gymea lily *Doryanthes excelsa*
Gympie *Dendrocnide moroides*
Gympie messmate *Eucalyptus cloeziana*
gynostemma *Gynostemma pentaphyllum*
gypsy weed *Veronica officinalis*

H

hacksaw fern *Doodia*
hack, hard *Spiraea tomentosa*
hackberry, American *Celtis occidentalis*
hackberry, Chinese *Celtis sinensis*
hackberry, Georgia *Celtis tenuifolia*
hackberry, net-leaf *Celtis reticulata*
hackberry, sugar *Celtis laevigata*
hair, angel's *Artemisia schmidtiana*
hair fescue *Festuca filiformis*
hair grass *Aira, Deschampsia,
Eleocharis acicularis*
hair grass, crinkled *Deschampsia
flexuosa*
hair grass, delicate *Aira elegantissima*
hair grass, false *Pentaschistis airoides*
hair grass, silvery *Aira caryophyllea,
A. cupaniana*
hair grass, tufted *Deschampsia
cespitosa*
hair, Venus' *Adiantum capillus-veneris*
hairpin banksia *Banksia spinulosa*
hairy alpenrose *Rhododendron
hirsutum*
hairy arum *Dracunculus muscivorus*
hairy bergenia *Bergenia ciliata*
hairy bird's eye *Alectryon tomentosus*
hairy bird's foot trefoil *Lotus
suaveolens*
hairy bog-rush *Schoenus villosus*
hairy boronia *Boronia pilosa*
hairy brassica *Hirschfeldia incana*
hairy buttercup *Ranunculus plebeius*
hairy clerodendrum *Clerodendrum
tomentosum*
hairy correa *Correa aemula*
hairy cup flower *Angianthus
tomentosus*
hairy daisy, small *Brachyscome
leptocarpa*

hairy evening primrose *Oenothera
mollissima*
hairy false golden aster *Heterotheca
villosa*
hairy golden aster *Heterotheca villosa*
hairy hopbush *Dodonaea boroniifolia*
hairy hound's tooth *Cynoglossum
nervosum*
hairy jugflower *Adenanthos barbigerus*
hairy manzanita *Arctostaphylos
columbiana*
hairy panic *Panicum effusum*
hairy paulownia *Paulownia tomentosa*
hairy rock rose *Cistus creticus*
hairy rosewood *Dysoxylum rufum*
hairy spinifex *Spinifex hirsutus*
hairy starfish flower *Stapelia hirsuta*
hairy toad lily *Tricyrtis hirta*
hairy vetch *Vicia hirsuta*
hairy wattle *Acacia lanigera*
hairy wattle, white *Acacia
centrinervia*
hairy-leafed doughwood *Melicope
micrococca*
hairy-pod cress *Harmsiodoxa
blennodioides*
hakea, ashy *Hakea cinerea*
hakea, broad-leafed *Hakea dactyloides*
hakea, cricket ball *Hakea platysperma*
hakea, dagger *Hakea teretifolia*
hakea, desert *Hakea mitchellii,
H. muelleriana*
hakea, furze *Hakea ulicina*
hakea, grass-leaf *Hakea francisiana,
H. multilineata*
hakea, gray *Hakea cinerea*
hakea, harsh *Hakea prostrata*
hakea, holly-leafed *Hakea varia*
hakea, hood-leafed *Hakea cucullata*
hakea, Ivory's *Hakea ivoryi*
hakea, Macrae's *Hakea macraeana*
hakea, myrtle *Hakea myrtoides*
hakea, pincushion *Hakea laurina*

hakea, pink spike *Hakea coriacea*
hakea, royal *Hakea victoria*
hakea, silky *Hakea sericea*
hakea, small-fruited *Hakea microcarpa*
hakea, striped *Hakea tephrosperma*
hakea, sweet-scented *Hakea drupacea*
hakea, thick-leafed *Hakea crassifolia*
hakea, tree *Hakea eriantha*
hakea, willow *Hakea salicifolia*
hakea, yellow *Hakea arborescens, H. nodosa*
hakone grass *Hakonechloa macra*
hala screwpine *Pandanus odoratissimus*
halberd willow *Salix hastata*
halgania, rough *Halgania cyanea*
halgania, smooth *Halgania andromedifolia, H. lavandulacea*
Hall's honeysuckle *Lonicera japonica* 'Halliana'
Hall's totara *Podocarpus hallii*
Hamburg parsley *Petroselinum crispum* var. *tuberosum*
Hamilton's wattle *Acacia hamiltoniana*
hand tree, Mexican *Chiranthodendron pentadactylon*
handkerchief plant *Mussaenda frondosa*
handkerchief tree *Davidia involucrata*
handsome flat pea *Platylobium formosum*
hanging heliconia *Heliconia collinsiana*
happy plant *Dracaena fragrans*
hapu *Cibotium glaucum*
hara-giri *Kalopanax septemlobus*
hard beech *Nothofagus truncata*
hard beech, New Zealand *Nothofagus truncata*
hard corkwood *Endiandra sieberi*

hard cushion plant *Colobanthus pulvinatus*
hard fern *Blechnum spicant*
hard fescue *Festuca longifolia*
hard hack *Spiraea tomentosa*
hard ironbark *Eucalyptus dura*
hard maple *Acer saccharum*
hard pear *Olinia ventosa*
hard pear, mountain *Olinia emarginata*
hard pear, Transvaal *Olinia emarginata*
hard quandong *Elaeocarpus obovatus*
hard shield fern *Polystichum aculeatum*
hard tack *Cercocarpus montanus*
hard tree fern *Dicksonia squarrosa*
hard water fern *Blechnum wattsii*
hard-headed daisy *Brachycome lineariloba*
hard-leaf, box *Phylica buxifolia*
hard-leafed monkey plum *Diospyros scabrida*
hardy begonia *Begonia grandis*
hardy eucryphia *Eucryphia glutinosa*
hardy kiwi fruit *Actinidia arguta*
harebell *Campanula rotundifolia*
harebell, African *Dierama*
hare's ear *Bupleurum rotundifolium*
hare's ear, shrubby *Bupleurum fructicosum*
hare's foot clover *Trifolium arvense*
hare's foot, Polynesian *Davallia solida*
hare's foot fern *Davallia, D. solida* var. *pyxidata, Phlebodium aureum*
hare's foot fern, giant *Davallia solida*
hare's foot fern, silver *Humata tyermannii*
hare's tail *Eriophorum vaginatum*
hare's-tail grass *Lagurus ovatus*
haricot *Phaseolus vulgaris*
harkness bottlebrush *Callistemon viminalis* 'Harkness'

harlequin flower *Sparaxis*
harlequin fuchsia bush *Eremophila duttonii*
harlequin mistletoe *Lysiana exocarpi*
harrisia cactus *Harrisia martinii*
harrow wattle *Acacia acanthoclada*
Harry Lauder's walking-stick *Corylus avellana* 'Contorta'
harsh ground fern *Hypolepis muelleri*
harsh hakea *Hakea prostrata*
hart's tongue fern *Asplenium scolopendrium*
harvest brodiaea *Brodiaea coronaria*
hastate orache *Atriplex prostrata*
hat, bishop's *Epimedium*
hat, cardinal's *Malvaviscus penduliflorus*
hat palm, Puerto Rico *Sabal causiarum*
hat plant, Chinese *Holmskioldia sanguinea*
hatchet cactus *Pelecyphora aselliformis*
hatpins *Xyris complanata*
hat-rack cactus *Euphorbia lactea*
hau, large-leafed *Hibiscus macrophyllus*
haumakaroa *Pseudopanax simplex*
hautbois strawberry *Fragaria moschata*
Havana cigar *Calathea lutea*
Haviland's wattle *Acacia havilandiorum*
haw, black *Bumelia lanuginosa, Viburnum prunifolium*
haw, summer *Crataegus flava*
Hawaiian elf schefflera *Schefflera arboricola*
Hawaiian hibiscus *Hibiscus rosa-sinensis*
Hawaiian man fern *Cibotium chamissoi*
Hawaiian red hibiscus *Hibiscus kokio*
Hawaiian tree fern *Cibotium glaucum*

Hawaiian white hibiscus *Hibiscus arnottianus*
hawkbit, lesser *Leontodon taraxacoides*
Hawkesbury River daisy *Brachyscome multifida*
hawksbeard, smooth *Crepis capillaris*
hawksbeard, stinking *Crepis foetida*
hawkweed *Crepis incana*
haworthia, zebra *Haworthia fasciata*
hawthorn *Crataegus, C. monogyna*
hawthorn, Arnold *Crataegus arnoldiana*
hawthorn, black *Crataegus douglasii*
hawthorn, cerro *Crataegus rivularis*
hawthorn, Chinese *Crataegus pinnatifida, Photinia serratifolia*
hawthorn, Columbian *Crataegus columbiana*
hawthorn, dotted *Crataegus punctata*
hawthorn, downy *Crataegus mollis*
hawthorn, English *Crataegus laevigata*
hawthorn, fleshy *Crataegus succulenta*
hawthorn, frosted *Crataegus pruinosa*
hawthorn, glossy *Crataegus nitida*
hawthorn, green *Crataegus viridis*
hawthorn, hybrid Indian *Rhaphiolepis* × *delacourii*
hawthorn, Indian *Rhaphiolepis indica*
hawthorn, Kansas *Crataegus coccinioides*
hawthorn, Lavalle *Crataegus* × *lavallei*
hawthorn, Mexican *Crataegus pubescens*
hawthorn, midland *Crataegus laevigata*
hawthorn, parsley-leafed *Crataegus apiifolia*
hawthorn, scarlet *Crataegus laevigata* 'Paul's Scarlet'
hawthorn, thicket *Crataegus intricata*

hawthorn, Washington *Crataegus phaenopyrum*
hawthorn, water *Aponogeton distachyos*
hay, Greek *Trigonella foenum-graecum*
hay-scented fern *Dennstaedtia punctilobula*
hay-scented orchid *Dendrochilum glumaceum*
hazel *Corylus avellana*
hazel alder *Alnus serrulata*
hazel, Chilean *Gevuina avellana*
hazel, Chinese *Corylus chinensis*
hazel, corkscrew *Corylus avellana* 'Contorta'
hazel pomaderris *Pomaderris aspera*
hazel, Turkish *Corylus colurna*
hazel, witch *Hamamellis*
hazelnut, American *Corylus americana*
hazelnut, European *Corylus avellana*
hazelnut, purple-leaf *Corylus maxima*
head, Hottentot's *Stangeria eriopus*
headache tree *Umbellularia californica*
headache vine *Clematis glycinoides*
heal all *Prunella vulgaris*
heart fern *Hemionitis arifolia*
heart, saffron *Halfordia kendack*
heart seed *Cardiospermum*
heartleaf *Bergenia ciliata*
heartleaf ice plant *Aptenia cordifolia*
heartleaf manzanita *Arctostaphylos andersonii*
heartleaf philodendron *Philodendron hederaceum*
heartleaf saxifrage *Bergenia cordifolia*
heart-leafed beard-heath *Leucopogon amplexicaulis*
heart-leafed flame pea *Chorizema cordatum*

heart-leafed pennywort *Centella asiatica, C. cordifolia*
heart-leafed stringybark *Eucalyptus camfieldii*
hearts and flowers *Aptenia cordifolia*
hearts, bleeding *Dicentra spectabilis*
heartsease *Viola, V. tricolor*
heath *Epacris, Erica*
heath, alpine *Erica carnea*
heath aster *Aster ericoides*
heath, Azores *Daboecia azorica*
heath banksia *Banksia ericifolia*
heath, besom *Erica scoparia*
heath, blood-red *Erica cruenta*
heath, blunt-leaf *Epacris obtusifolia*
heath bog-rush *Schoenus ericetorum*
heath, bridal *Erica bauera*
heath, candle *Richea continentis*
heath, Chinese lantern *Erica blenna*
heath, coral *Epacris microphylla*
heath, Cornish *Erica vagans*
heath, Corsican *Erica terminalis*
heath, cranberry *Astroloma humifusum*
heath, cross-leafed *Erica tetralix*
heath, daphne *Brachyloma daphnoides*
heath, Darley Dale *Erica × darleyensis*
heath dog violet *Viola canina*
heath, Dorset *Erica ciliaris*
heath, dragon *Dracophyllum secundum*
heath, Elim *Erica regia*
heath, fuchsia *Epacris longiflora*
heath, kapokkie *Erica peziza*
heath, Kimberley *Calytrix exstipulata*
heath, mealie *Erica patersonia*
heath milkwort *Comesperma ericinum*
heath, mountain *Leucopogon suaveolens*
heath, Mueller's *Epacris muelleri*
heath, peach *Lissanthe strigosa*
heath, pine *Astroloma pinifolium*

heath, pink *Epacris impressa*
heath, pink swamp *Sprengelia incarnata*
heath, Portugal *Erica lusitanica*
heath, Prince of Wales' *Erica perspicua*
heath red *Erica rubens*
heath, St Dabeoc's *Daboecia cantabrica*
heath, sea *Frankenia*
heath, snow *Erica carnea*
heath, southern *Erica australis*
heath, Spanish *Erica australis, E. lusitanica*
heath, Spanish dwarf *Erica umbellata*
heath speedwell *Veronica officinalis*
heath, swamp *Epacris paludosa*
heath, tree *Erica arborea, Richea pandanifolia, Trochocarpa laurina*
heath, urn *Melichrus urceolatus*
heath violet *Viola canina*
heath, wandering *Erica vagans*
heath, water *Erica curviflora*
heath, winter *Erica carnea*
heather *Calluna vulgaris*
heather, beach *Hudsonia tomentosa*
heather, bell *Erica cinerea*
heather, false *Cuphea hyssopifolia, Hudsonia ericoides*
heather, French *Erica × hiemalis*
heather, golden *Hudsonia ericoides*
heather, Irish *Erica erigena*
heather, Mexican *Cuphea hyssopifolia*
heather, mock *Ericameria ericoides*
heather, purple *Phyllodoce breweri*
heath-leafed banksia *Banksia ericifolia*
heath-leafed coneseeds *Conospermum ericifolium*
heath-myrtle, desert *Baeckea crassifolia*
heath-myrtle, fringed *Micromyrtus ciliata*
heath-myrtle, short-leafed *Baeckea brevifolia*
heath-myrtle, twiggy *Babingtonia pluriflora*
heaven, tree of *Ailanthus altissima*
heavenly bamboo *Nandina domestica*
hebe, blue gem *Hebe × franciscana* 'Blue Gem'
hebe, showy *Hebe speciosa*
hebe, whipcord *Hebe cupressoides*
hedge bamboo *Bambusa multiplex*
hedge bean tree, elephant *Schotia latifolia*
hedge cotoneaster *Cotoneaster lucidus*
hedge, elephant *Schotia latifolia*
hedge euphorbia *Euphorbia neriifolia*
hedge maple *Acer campestre*
hedge mustard *Sisymbrium officinale*
hedge mustard, Indian *Sisymbrium orientale*
hedge nettle *Stachys*
hedge nettle, scarlet *Stachys coccinea*
hedge, rubber *Euphorbia tirucalli*
hedge thorn *Carissa bispinosa*
hedge woundwort *Stachys sylvatica*
hedgehog broom *Erinacea anthyllis*
hedgehog cactus *Echinocereus*
hedgehog cactus, strawberry *Echinocereus engelmannii*
hedgehog coneflower *Echinacea purpurea*
hedgehog grass, erect *Echinopogon intermedius*
hedgehog grass, forest *Echinopogon ovatus*
hedgehog grass, tufted *Echinopogon caespitosus*
hedgehog holly *Ilex aquifolium* 'Ferox'
hedge-thorn *Carissa bispinosa*
hediondo *Bosea yervamora*

he-huckleberry *Lyonia ligustrina*
Heldreich's maple *Acer heldreichii*
heliconia, beefsteak *Heliconia mariae*
heliconia, hanging *Heliconia collinsiana*
heliotrope *Heliotropium, H. arborescens*
hellebore, black *Veratrum nigrum*
hellebore, Corsican *Helleborus argutifolius*
hellebore, false *Veratrum*
hellebore, green *Helleborus viridis*
hellebore, stinking *Helleborus foetidus*
helmet flower *Aconitum napellus, Scutellaria, Sinningia cardinalis*
helmet orchid *Corybas*
helmet orchid, small fringed *Corybas pruinosus*
helmet orchid, spurred *Corybas aconitiflorus*
helmet, policeman's *Impatiens glandulifera*
Helms' grevillea *Grevillea helmsiae*
hembra, yarey *Copernicia baileyana*
hemlock *Conium maculatum*
hemlock, Canadian *Tsuga canadensis*
hemlock, Carolina *Tsuga caroliniana*
hemlock, Chinese *Tsuga chinensis*
hemlock, eastern *Tsuga canadensis*
hemlock, mountain *Tsuga mertensiana*
hemlock, North Japanese *Tsuga diversifolia*
hemlock, southern Japanese *Tsuga sieboldii*
hemlock spruce *Tsuga*
hemlock, western *Tsuga heterophylla*
hemp *Cannabis sativa*
hemp, African *Sparmannia africana*
hemp agrimony *Agrimonia eupatoria*
hemp, bowstring *Sansevieria, S. hyacinthoides*

hemp, Ceylon bowstring *Sansevieria zeylanica*
hemp, Deccan *Hibiscus cannabinus*
hemp, Indian *Cannabis sativa*
hemp, Indian bowstring *Sansevieria roxburghiana*
hemp, New Zealand *Phormium tenax*
hemp, pygmy bowstring *Sansevieria intermedia*
hemp willow *Salix viminalis*
hempweed, climbing *Mikania scandens*
hen and chicken fern *Asplenium bulbiferum*
hen and chickens *Chlorophytum comosum, Sempervivum, S. tectorum*
henbane *Hyoscyamus niger*
henbane, black *Hyoscyamus niger*
henna *Lawsonia inermis*
heptacodium, Chinese *Heptacodium miconioides*
herald's trumpet *Beaumontia grandiflora*
herb bennet *Geum urbanum*
herb gerard *Aegopodium podagraria*
herb, great willow *Epilobium angustifolium*
herb of grace *Ruta graveolens*
herb Paris *Paris quadrifolia*
herb Robert *Geranium robertianum*
herb, rosebay willow *Epilobium angustifolium*
herb, willow *Epilobium*
Herbert River cherry *Antidesma dallachyana*
Hercules club *Aralia spinosa*
herds' grass *Phleum pratense*
heronsbill *Erodium, E. cicutarium*
hesper palm *Brahea, B. armata*
hesper palm, Brandegee *Brahea brandegeei*
Hexham scent *Melilotus indica*
hiba *Thujopsis dolabrata*

hiba cedar *Thujopsis dolabrata*
hibiscus, beach *Hibiscus tiliaceus*
hibiscus, blue *Alyogyne huegelii,*
Hibiscus syriacus
hibiscus, Chinese *Hibiscus*
rosa-sinensis
hibiscus, coral *Hibiscus schizopetalus*
hibiscus, dwarf pink *Hibiscus*
pedunculatus
hibiscus, fringed *Hibiscus*
schizopetalus
hibiscus, Hawaiian *Hibiscus*
rosa-sinensis
hibiscus, Hawaiian white *Hibiscus*
arnottianus
hibiscus, hill *Hibiscus sturtii*
hibiscus, Japanese *Hibiscus*
schizopetalus
hibiscus, mangrove *Hibiscus tiliaceus*
hibiscus, native *Hibiscus diversifolius*
hibiscus, Norfolk Island *Lagunaria*
patersonia
hibiscus, Phillip Island *Hibiscus*
insularis
hibiscus, red-centered *Alyogyne*
hakeifolia
hibiscus, scarlet *Hibiscus coccineus*
hibiscus, sleeping *Malvaviscus*
penduliflorus
hibiscus, swamp *Hibiscus coccineus,*
H. diversifolius
hibiscus, Syrian *Hibiscus syriacus*
hibiscus, tree *Hibiscus tiliaceus*
hibiscus, variegated *Hibiscus*
rosa-sinensis 'Cooperi'
hiccup nut *Combretum bracteosum*
hickory *Carya*
hickory, big shellbark *Carya laciniosa*
hickory, bigbud *Carya tomentosa*
hickory, bitternut *Carya cordiformis*
hickory, black *Carya texana*
hickory, broad-leafed *Acacia*
falciformis

hickory, Chinese *Carya cathayensis*
hickory, hognut broom *Carya glabra*
hickory, little shellbark *Carya ovata*
hickory, mockernut *Carya tomentosa*
hickory, mountain *Acacia penninervis*
hickory, New England *Acacia*
nova-anglica
hickory, nutmeg *Carya*
myristiciformis
hickory, pale *Carya pallida*
hickory, pignut *Carya glabra*
hickory, red *Carya ovalis*
hickory, sand *Carya pallida*
hickory, scrub *Carya floridana*
hickory, shagbark *Carya ovata*
hickory, swamp *Carya cordiformis*
hickory, two-veined *Acacia*
binervata
hickory, water *Carya aquatica*
hickory wattle *Acacia implexa*
hickory wattle, mountain *Acacia*
obliquinervia
hickory, white hart *Carya tomentosa*
hierbamora *Bosea yervamora*
high mallow *Malva sylvestris*
highbush cranberry *Viburnum*
trilobum
highbush cranberry, European
Viburnum opulus
Highclere holly *Ilex × altaclerensis*
highland basswood *Tilia truncata*
highveld cabbage tree *Cussonia*
paniculata
hill banksia *Banksia spinulosa* var.
collina
hill daisy *Brachyscome aculeata*
hill everlasting *Chrysocephalum*
semicalvum
hill fireweed *Senecio hispidulus*
hill hibiscus *Hibiscus sturtii*
hill raspwort *Gonocarpus elatus*
hill wallaby grass *Austrodanthonia*
eriantha

Hillgrove gum *Eucalyptus michaeliana*
hillock bush *Melaleuca hypericifolia*
Hill's weeping fig *Ficus microcarpa* var. *hillii*
hillside burrgrass *Cenchrus caliculatus*
Himalayan balsam *Impatiens glandulifera*
Himalayan birch *Betula utilis*
Himalayan bird cherry *Prunus cornuta*
Himalayan black juniper *Juniperus indica*
Himalayan box *Buxus wallichiana*
Himalayan catmint *Nepeta clarkei*
Himalayan cherry *Prunus rufa*
Himalayan cinquefoil *Potentilla atrosanguinea*
Himalayan cypress *Cupressus torulosa*
Himalayan dogwood *Cornus capitata*
Himalayan evergreen oak *Quercus leucotrichophora*
Himalayan fan palm *Trachycarpus martianus*
Himalayan fir *Abies spectabilis*
Himalayan firethorn *Pyracantha crenulata*
Himalayan giant lily *Cardiocrinum giganteum*
Himalayan holly *Ilex dipyrena*
Himalayan honeysuckle *Leycesteria formosa*
Himalayan hornbeam *Carpinus viminea*
Himalayan ivy *Hedera nepalensis*
Himalayan juniper *Juniperus recurva*
Himalayan longleaf pine *Pinus roxburghii*
Himalayan maidenhair *Adiantum venustum*
Himalayan manna ash *Fraxinus floribunda*
Himalayan May apple *Podophyllum hexandrum*

Himalayan pear *Pyrus pashia*
Himalayan pine *Pinus wallichiana*
Himalayan poplar *Populus ciliata*
Himalayan privet *Ligustrum confusum*
Himalayan rhubarb *Rheum australe*
Himalayan strawberry tree *Cornus capitata*
Himalayan tree cotoneaster *Cotoneaster frigidus*
Himalayan whitebeam *Sorbus vestita*
Himalayan yew *Taxus wallichiana*
hinau *Elaeocarpus dentatus*
Hinds' black walnut *Juglans hindsii*
hinojo *Bupleurum salicifolium*
hinoki cypress *Chamaecyparis obtusa*
hinoki cypress, golden *Chamaecyparis obtusa* 'Crippsii'
hippo, wild *Euphorbia corollata*
Hispaniolan palmetto *Sabal domingensis*
Hispaniolan silver thatch *Coccothrinax argentea*
Hispaniolan wine palm *Pseudophoenix vinifera*
hoary basil *Ocimum canum*
hoary cherry *Prunus canescens*
hoary conesticks *Petrophile canescens*
hoary manzanita *Arctostaphylos canescens*
hoary rush *Juncus radula*
hoary sunray *Leucochrysum albicans, L. molle*
hoary vervain *Verbena stricta*
hoary willow *Salix elaeagnos*
hoary-leafed ceanothus *Ceanothus crassifolius*
hobble bush *Viburnum lantanoides*
hog apple *Podophyllum peltatum*
hog millet *Panicum miliaceum*
hog plum *Prunus americana*
hognut broom hickory *Carya glabra*

hog's bean *Hyoscyamus niger*
hogweed, tree *Polygonum patulum*
hoho *Pseudopanax chathamicus*
Holford pine *Pinus × holfordiana*
hollowleaf annual lupine *Lupinus succulentus*
holly *Ilex, I. aquifolium*
holly, African *Solanum giganteum*
holly, American *Ilex opaca*
holly, Barbados *Malpighia coccigera*
holly, blue *Ilex × meserveae*
holly, box-leafed *Ilex crenata*
holly, California *Heteromeles arbutifolia*
holly, Canary Island *Ilex perado*
holly, Cape *Ilex mitis*
holly, Chinese *Ilex cornuta*
holly, Dahoon *Ilex cassine*
holly, deciduous *Ilex decidua*
holly, English *Ilex aquifolium*
holly fern *Cyrtomium falcatum, Polystichum*
holly fern, Alaskan *Polystichum × setigerum, P. andersoni*
holly fern, Anderson's *Polystichum andersoni*
holly fern, East Indian *Arachniodes simplicior*
holly fern, eastern *Polystichum braunii*
holly fern, giant *Polystichum munitum*
holly fern, Tsu-shima *Polystichum tsussimense*
holly, finetooth *Ilex serrata*
holly flame pea *Chorizema ilicifolium*
holly grape, California *Mahonia pinnata*
holly grape, Oregon *Mahonia aquifolium*
holly grevillea *Grevillea aquifolium, G. ilicifolia*

holly, hedgehog *Ilex aquifolium* 'Ferox'
holly, Highclere *Ilex × altaclerensis*
holly, Himalayan *Ilex dipyrena*
holly, horned *Ilex cornuta*
holly, hybrid blue *Ilex × meserveae*
holly, Japanese *Ilex crenata*
holly, Madeira *Ilex perado*
holly, Meserve *Ilex × meserveae*
holly, Michigan *Ilex verticillata*
holly, miniature *Malpighia coccigera*
holly, mountain *Ilex montana, Olearia ilicifolia*
holly, myrtle *Ilex myrtifolia*
holly, Nepal *Ilex integra*
holly oak *Quercus ilex*
holly, Okinawa *Ilex dimorphophylla*
holly osmanthus *Osmanthus heterophyllus*
holly, Perny's *Ilex pernyi*
holly, sea *Eryngium maritimum*
holly, Singapore *Malpighia coccigera*
holly, summer *Arctostaphylos diversifolia*
holly, topal *Ilex × attenuata*
holly, variegated *Ilex aquifolium* 'Argenteomarginata'
holly, West Indian *Leea coccinea*
holly wood *Auranticarpa rhombifolia, Heteromeles arbutifolia*
hollyhock *Alcea, A. rosea*
hollyhock, Antwerp *Alcea ficifolia*
hollyhock, Australian *Lavatera plebeia*
hollyhock begonia *Begonia gracilis*
holly-leaf banksia *Banksia ilicifolia*
holly-leaf ceanothus *Ceanothus purpureus*
holly-leaf sweetspire *Itea ilicifolia*
holly-leafed cherry *Prunus ilicifolia*
holly-leafed fuchsia bush *Graptophyllum ilicifolium*
holly-leafed hakea *Hakea varia*

holly-leafed lomatia *Lomatia ilicifolia*
holly-leafed mirbelia *Mirbelia dilatata*
Hollywood juniper *Juniperus squamata*
holm oak *Quercus ilex*
holy basil *Ocimum tenuiflorum*
holy grass *Hierochloe odorata*
holywood lignum-vitae *Guaiacum sanctum*
Honduran sarsaparilla *Smilax officinalis*
Honduras mahogany *Swietenia macrophylla*
honesty *Lunaria annua*
honewort *Cryptotaenia canadensis*
honey euryops *Euryops virgineus*
honey locust *Gleditsia triacanthos*
honey locust, golden *Gleditsia triacanthos* 'Sunburst'
honey locust, thornless *Gleditsia triacanthos* f. *inermis*
honey mesquite *Prosopis glandulosa*
honey protea *Protea repens*
honey reed *Lomandra longifolia*
honey sage *Salvia mellifera*
honey spurge *Euphorbia mellifera*
honeybell bush *Freylinia lanceolata*
honeybells *Hermannia, H. incana*
honeybush *Hakea lissocarpha*
honeydew melon *Cucumis melo* Inodorus Group
honeyflower *Lambertia formosa, L. multiflora, Lonicera, Melianthus major*
honey-myrtle *Melaleuca*
honey-myrtle, ball *Melaleuca nodosa*
honey-myrtle, bracelet *Melaleuca armillaris*
honey-myrtle, broom *Melaleuca uncinata*
honey-myrtle, chenille *Melaleuca huegelii*

honey-myrtle, cork bark *Melaleuca suberosa*
honey-myrtle, graceful *Melaleuca radula*
honey-myrtle, gray *Melaleuca incana*
honey-myrtle, Rottnest *Melaleuca lanceolata*
honey-myrtle, rough *Melaleuca scabra*
honey-myrtle, scarlet *Melaleuca fulgens*
honey-myrtle, showy *Melaleuca nesophila*
honey-myrtle, slender *Melaleuca gibbosa*
honey-myrtle, Steedman's *Melaleuca fulgens* subsp. *steedmanii*
honey-myrtle, thyme *Melaleuca thymifolia*
honeysuckle *Lonicera*
honeysuckle, box *Lonicera nitida*
honeysuckle, box-leafed *Lonicera nitida*
honeysuckle, bush *Diervilla lonicera, D. rivularis, D. sessilifolia*
honeysuckle, Cape *Tecoma capensis*
honeysuckle, chuparosa *Justicia californica*
honeysuckle, desert *Anisacanthus thurberi*
honeysuckle, Etruscan *Lonicera etrusca*
honeysuckle, fly *Lonicera xylosteum*
honeysuckle fuchsia *Fuchsia triphylla*
honeysuckle, Georgia bush *Diervilla rivularis*
honeysuckle, giant *Lonicera hildebrandiana*
honeysuckle, Hall's *Lonicera japonica* 'Halliana'
honeysuckle, Himalayan *Leycesteria formosa*

honeysuckle, hybrid *Lonicera* ×
americana
honeysuckle, Italian *Lonicera*
caprifolium
honeysuckle, Japanese *Lonicera*
japonica
honeysuckle Mexican *Justicia*
spicigera
honeysuckle, Minorca *Lonicera*
implexa
honeysuckle, New Zealand *Knightia*
excelsa
honeysuckle, Pyrenees *Lonicera*
pyrenaica
honeysuckle, redgold *Lonicera* ×
tellmanniana
honeysuckle, scarlet trumpet
Lonicera × *brownii*
honeysuckle, silver *Grevillea striata*
honeysuckle, southern bush *Diervilla*
sessilifolia
honeysuckle spider flower *Grevillea*
juncifolia
honeysuckle, swamp *Rhododendron*
viscosum
honeysuckle, Tatarian *Lonicera*
tatarica
honeysuckle, Tellmann *Lonicera* ×
tellmanniana
honeysuckle tree, lesser *Turraea*
obtusifolia
honeysuckle tree, small *Turraea*
obtusifolia
honeysuckle, trumpet *Lonicera*
sempervirens
honeysuckle, wild *Turraea floribunda*
honeysuckle, winter *Lonicera*
fragrantissima
honeywort *Cerinthe, C. major*
Hong Kong camellia *Camellia*
hongkongensis
Hong Kong orchid tree *Bauhinia* ×
blakeana

Honolulu rose *Clerodendrum chinense*
hooded pitcher plant *Sarracenia*
minor
hood-leafed hakea *Hakea cucullata*
hook sedge *Uncinia*
hooked cudweed *Stuartina hamata*
hooked needlewood *Hakea*
tephrosperma
hooked-spur violet *Viola adunca*
Hooker's maple *Acer sikkimense*
Hooker's onion *Allium acuminatum*
hook-thorn, common *Acacia caffra*
hoop Mitchell grass *Astrebla*
elymoides
hoop pine *Araucaria cunninghamii*
hoop-petticoat daffodil *Narcissus*
bulbocodium
hop bitter pea *Daviesia latifolia*
hop clover *Trifolium campestre*
hop, common *Humulus lupulus*
hop, European *Humulus lupulus*
hop marjoram *Origanum dictamnus*
hop tree, common *Ptelea trifoliata*
hop tree, western *Ptelea angustifolia*
hop wattle *Acacia stricta*
hopbush *Dodonaea triquetra,*
D. viscosa
hopbush, brilliant *Dodonaea*
microzyga
hopbush, Camfield's *Dodonaea*
camfieldii
hopbush, fern-leaf *Dodonaea*
boroniifolia
hopbush, hairy *Dodonaea boroniifolia*
hopbush, lobed-leaf *Dodonaea*
lobulata
hopbush, narrow-leaf *Dodonaea*
viscosa subsp. *angustissima*
hopbush, pinnate *Dodonaea pinnata*
hopbush, purple *Dodonaea viscosa*
'Purpurea'
hopbush, stalked *Dodonaea*
peduncularis

hop-hornbeam *Ostrya, O. carpinifolia*
hop-hornbeam, American *Ostrya virginiana*
hop-hornbeam, eastern *Ostrya virginiana*
hop-hornbeam, Japanese *Ostrya japonica*
hop-hornbeam, western *Ostrya knowltonii*
hops *Humulus lupulus*
hops, native *Dodonaea triquetra*
horehound *Marrubium vulgare*
horehound, black *Ballota nigra*
horehound, common *Marrubium vulgare*
horehound, white *Marrubium vulgare*
horizontal juniper *Juniperus horizontalis*
hornbeam *Carpinus*
hornbeam, American *Carpinus caroliniana*
hornbeam, common *Carpinus betulus*
hornbeam, European *Carpinus betulus*
hornbeam, Himalayan *Carpinus viminea*
hornbeam, Japanese *Carpinus japonica*
hornbeam, Korean *Carpinus eximia*
hornbeam maple *Acer carpinifolium*
hornbeam, oriental *Carpinus orientalis*
hornbeam, Turkish *Carpinus orientalis*
horned holly *Ilex cornuta*
horned maple *Acer diabolicum*
horned orchid *Orthoceras strictum*
horned poppy *Glaucium*
horned poppy, yellow *Glaucium flavum*
horned rampion *Phyteuma*
horned thorn *Acacia grandicornuta*
horned tulip *Tulipa acuminata*

horned violet *Viola cornuta*
horns, soft *Malacocera tricornis*
horny goat weed *Epimedium sagittatum*
horoeka *Pseudopanax crassifolius*
horopito *Pseudowintera axillaris, P. colorata*
horrid Spaniard *Aciphylla horrida*
horror, midnight *Oroxylum*
horse bean *Vicia faba*
horse chestnut *Aesculus, A. hippocastanum*
horse chestnut, Chinese *Aesculus chinensis*
horse chestnut, common *Aesculus hippocastanum*
horse chestnut, European *Aesculus hippocastanum*
horse chestnut, Indian *Aesculus indica*
horse chestnut, Japanese *Aesculus turbinata*
horse chestnut, red *Aesculus × carnea*
horse mulga *Acacia ramulosa*
horse parsley *Smyrnium olusatrum*
horsemint *Mentha longifolia, Monarda*
horsemint, sweet *Cunila origanoides*
horseradish *Armoracia rusticana*
horseradish tree *Moringa oleifera*
horseshoe felt fern *Pyrrosia confluens*
horseshoe fern *Marattia salicina*
horsetail *Equisetum*
horsetail, common *Equisetum arvense*
horsetail, European shrubby *Ephedra distachya*
horsetail, field *Equisetum arvense*
horsetail, giant *Equisetum giganteum, E. telmateia*
horsetail, great *Equisetum telmateia*
horsetail, marsh *Equisetum palustre*
horsetail, rough *Equisetum hyemale*
horsetail rush *Equisetum hyemale*
horsetail, shady *Equisetum pratense*

horsetail, water *Equisetum fluviatile*
horsetail, wood *Equisetum sylvaticum*
hortensia *Hydrangea macrophylla*
  Hortensia Group
hortulan plum *Prunus hortulana*
hosta, miniature *Hosta* 'Saishu Jima'
hot water plant *Achimenes*
hotbark, Lord Howe *Zygogynum*
  howeanum
Hottentot bean *Schotia brachypetala*
Hottentot fig *Carpobrotus edulis*
Hottentot's head *Stangeria eriopus*
Hottentot's lilac *Ehretia rigida*
houhere *Hoheria populnea*
hound's tongue *Cynoglossum*
hound's tongue, forest
  Austrocynoglossum latifolium
hound's tongue, native *Cynoglossum*
  australe, C. suaveolens
hound's tooth, hairy *Cynoglossum*
  nervosum
houpara *Pseudopanax lessonii*
house lime *Sparmannia*
house, meeting *Aquilegia canadensis*
houseleek *Sempervivum montanum,*
  S. tectorum
houseleek, cobweb *Sempervivum*
  arachnoideum
houses, Chinese *Collinsia bicolor*
hovea, lance-leaf *Hovea lanceolata*
hovea, long-leaf *Hovea longifolia*
hovea, mountain *Hovea montana*
hovea, narrow-leaf *Hovea linearis*
hovea, velvet *Hovea pannosa*
Howell's triteleia *Triteleia grandiflora*
Howitt's wattle *Acacia howittii*
huckleberry *Vaccinium angustifolium*
huckleberry, black *Gaylussacia*
  baccata, Vaccinium atrococcum
huckleberry, box *Gaylussacia*
  brachycera
huckleberry, evergreen *Vaccinium*
  ovatum

huckleberry, fool's *Menziesia*
  ferruginea
huckleberry, garden *Solanum*
  melanocerasum
huckleberry, red *Vaccinium*
  parvifolium
huckleberry, squaw *Vaccinium*
  caesium
Hudson Bay rose *Rosa blanda*
huigen *Schinus polygamus*
humea *Calomeria amaranthoides*
hummingbird bush *Hamelia erecta,*
  H. patens, Justicia candicans
hummingbird plant *Agastache cana,*
  Dicliptera suberecta
hummingbird sage *Salvia spathacea*
hunangamoho *Chionochloa conspicua*
Hungarian clover *Trifolium*
  pannonicum
Hungarian lilac *Syringa josikaea*
Hungarian oak *Quercus frainetto*
Huntingdon elm *Ulmus* × *hollandica*
  'Vegeta'
huntsman's cap *Sarracenia purpurea*
huo xiang *Agastache rugosa*
Huon pine *Lagarostrobos franklinii*
Hupeh crab *Malus hupehensis*
Hupeh crabapple *Malus hupehensis*
hurricane lily *Lycoris aurea*
hurricane palm *Dictyosperma album*
huru *Hura crepitans*
husk tomato *Physalis*
hutan, salac *Salacca affinis*
hyacinth *Hyacinthus, H. orientalis*
hyacinth bean *Lablab purpureus*
hyacinth, bog *Monochoria cyanea*
hyacinth, Cape *Galtonia candicans*
hyacinth, common *Hyacinthus*
  orientalis
hyacinth, glassy *Triteleia lilacina*
hyacinth, grape *Muscari,*
  M. armeniacum
hyacinth, Kenya *Sansevieria parva*

hyacinth lilac *Syringa* × *hyacinthiflora*
hyacinth of Peru *Scilla peruviana*
hyacinth orchid *Bletilla striata,*
Dipodium punctatum
hyacinth scilla *Scilla hyacinthoides*
hyacinth, summer *Galtonia candicans*
hyacinth, water *Eichhornia crassipes*
hyacinth, wild *Hyacinthoides non-*
scripta, Lachenalia contaminata
hybrid astilbe *Astilbe* × *arendsii*
hybrid blue holly *Ilex* × *meserveae*
hybrid catmint *Nepeta* × *faassenii*
hybrid coral tree *Erythrina* × *bidwillii*
hybrid dombeya *Dombeya* × *cayeuxii*
hybrid honeysuckle *Lonicera* ×
americana
hybrid Indian hawthorn *Rhaphiolepis*
× *delacourii*
hybrid kurrajong *Brachychiton* ×
roseus
hybrid larch *Larix* × *marschlinsii*
hybrid lavender *Lavandula* × *allardii*
hybrid lilac, Skinner *Syringa* ×
hyacinthiflora
hybrid poplar *Populus* × *canadensis*
hybrid purple barberry *Berberis* ×
ottawensis 'Superba'
hybrid rock rose *Cistus* × *purpureus*
hybrid strawberry tree *Arbutus* ×
andrachnoides
hybrid trumpet tree *Tecoma* × *smithii*
hybrid witch hazel *Hamamelis* ×
intermedia
hybrid yew *Taxus* × *media*
hydrangea *Hydrangea macrophylla*
hydrangea, bigleaf *Hydrangea*
macrophylla

hydrangea, climbing *Hydrangea*
petiolaris
hydrangea, florist's *Hydrangea*
macrophylla
hydrangea, garden *Hydrangea*
macrophylla
hydrangea, lacecap *Hydrangea*
macrophylla Lacecap Group
hydrangea, mophead *Hydrangea*
macrophylla Hortensia Group
hydrangea, oak-leafed *Hydrangea*
quercifolia
hydrangea, panicle *Hydrangea*
paniculata
hydrangea, peegee *Hydrangea*
paniculata 'Grandiflora'
hydrangea, smooth *Hydrangea*
arborescens
hydrangea vine, Japanese
Schizophragma hydrangeoides
hyssop *Hyssopsus officinalis*
hyssop, anise *Agastache foeniculum*
hyssop giant *Agastache, A. barberi*
hyssop loosestrife *Lythrum*
hyssopifolia
hyssop, Mexican *Agastache mexicana*
hyssop, Mexican giant *Agastache*
mexicana
hyssop, sunset *Agastache rupestris*
hyssop, threadleaf giant *Agastache*
rupestris
hyssop, water *Bacopa caroliniana*
hyssop, wild *Pycnanthemum*
virginianum
hyssop, wrinkled giant *Agastache*
rugosa
hyuga giboshi *Hosta kikutii*

I

icaco *Chrysobalanus icaco*
ice plant *Lampranthus, Malephora, Mesembryanthemum, Ruschia, Sedum spectabile*
ice plant, bicolored *Drosanthemum bicolor*
ice plant, heartleaf *Aptenia cordifolia*
ice plant, purple *Lampranthus productus*
ice plant, trailing *Lampranthus filicaulis*
ice-cream bean *Inga edulis*
Iceland moss *Cetraria islandica*
Iceland poppy *Papaver nudicaule*
ichant papeda *Citrus ichangensis*
idolatrica palm *Elaeis guineensis* f. *idolatrica*
ifafa lily *Cyrtanthus mackenii*
igname *Dioscorea esculenta*
Ilam azalea *Rhododendron* Ilam Hybrids
ilama *Annona diversifolia*
Illawarra flame tree *Brachychiton acerifolius*
Illawarra lily *Doryanthes excelsa*
illyarrie *Eucalyptus erythrocorys*
Illyrian thistle *Onopordum illyricum*
immortelle *Xeranthemum annuum*
immortelle, orange *Waitzia acuminata*
impala lily *Adenium obesum*
impatiens, New Guinea *Impatiens hawkeri*
imperial, crown *Fritillaria imperialis*
Inca wheat *Chenopodium quinoa*
Incas, lily of the *Alstroemeria*
Incas, sacred flower of the *Cantua buxifolia*

Incas, sacred lily of the *Hymenocallis, H. narcissiflora*
incense bush *Calomeria amaranthoides*
incense cedar *Anthocarapa nitidula, Calocedrus decurrens*
incense cedar, Chilean *Austrocedrus chilensis*
incense plant *Calomeria amaranthoides*
incense rose *Rosa primula*
incense tree *Bursera simaruba*
inch plant *Callisia elegans*
inch plant, striped *Callisia elegans* 'Variegata'
incienso *Encelia farinosa*
India, pride of *Lagerstroemia speciosa*
India rubber vine *Strophanthus gratus*
Indian abutilon *Abutilon indicum*
Indian almond *Sterculia foetida, Terminalia catappa*
Indian apple *Datura inoxia, Podophyllum peltatum*
Indian arrowwood *Philadelphus lewisii*
Indian azalea *Rhododendron indicum, R. simsii*
Indian banyan *Ficus benghalensis*
Indian basil *Ocimum gratissimum*
Indian bead tree *Elaeocarpus sphaericus*
Indian bean *Lablab purpureus*
Indian bean tree *Catalpa bignonioides*
Indian beech *Pongamia pinnata*
Indian blanket *Gaillardia pulchella*
Indian bowstring hemp *Sansevieria roxburghiana*
Indian breadroot *Psoralea esculenta*
Indian chocolate *Geum rivale*
Indian coral bean *Erythrina variegata*
Indian corn *Zea mays*
Indian cupscale grass *Sacciolepis indica*

Indian currant *Symphoricarpos orbiculatus*
Indian currant coralberry *Symphoricarpos orbiculatus*
Indian dill *Anethum graveolens* subsp. *sowa*
Indian dillenia *Dillenia indica*
Indian dye *Hydrastis canadensis*
Indian fig *Opuntia ficus-indica*
Indian fig pear *Opuntia ficus-indica*
Indian fishtail palm *Caryota obtusa*
Indian ginger *Alpinia calcarata*
Indian grass *Sorghastrum nutans*
Indian hawthorn *Rhaphiolepis indica*
Indian hawthorn, hybrid *Rhaphiolepis × delacourii*
Indian hedge mustard *Sisymbrium orientale*
Indian hemp *Cannabis sativa*
Indian horse chestnut *Aesculus indica*
Indian laburnum *Cassia fistula*
Indian laurel *Ficus microcarpa*
Indian laurel fig *Ficus microcarpa*
Indian long pepper *Piper longum*
Indian madder *Rubia cordifolia*
Indian mulberry *Morinda citrifolia*
Indian mustard *Brassica juncea*
Indian oak *Barringtonia acutangula*
Indian paintbrush *Castilleja, C. coccinea*
Indian pea *Lathyrus sativus*
Indian physic *Gillenia trifoliata*
Indian plum *Flacourtia rukam*
Indian prune *Flacourtia rukam*
Indian rhododendron *Melastoma malabathricum*
Indian sandalwood *Santalum album*
Indian senna *Cassia fistula*
Indian shot *Canna, C. indica*
Indian snakeroot *Rauvolfia serpentina*
Indian strawberry *Duchesnea indica*
Indian tobacco *Eriogonum*

Indian turnip *Arisaema triphyllum*
Indian umbrella tree *Schefflera pueckleri*
Indian weed *Sigesbeckia orientalis*
Indian weed, pale *Sigesbeckia australiensis*
Indian wild date *Phoenix sylvestris*
Indian willow *Polyalthia longifolia*
Indian wood apple *Limonia acidissima*
India-rubber tree *Ficus elastica*
indigo, Atlantic wild *Baptisia lactea*
indigo, Australian *Indigofera australis*
indigo, bastard *Amorpha fruticosa*
indigo bush *Dalea*
indigo, false *Amorpha fruticosa, Baptisia*
indigo, forest *Indigofera natalensis*
indigo, tree *Indigofera cylindrica*
indigo, wild *Baptisia*
injerto *Pouteria viridis*
injerto, zapote *Pouteria viridis*
inkberry *Cestrum diurnum, Ilex glabra*
inkweed *Phytolacca octandra*
inland ceanothus *Ceanothus ovatus*
inland flax-lily *Dianella porracea*
inland pigface *Carpobrotus modestus*
inland red box *Eucalyptus intertexta*
inland scribbly gum *Eucalyptus rossii*
innocence *Collinsia bicolor*
insect flower *Tanacetum cinerariifolium*
interior live oak *Quercus wislizeni*
interrupted fern *Osmunda claytoniana*
invisible plant *Podolepis capillaris*
Ione manzanita *Arctostaphylos myrtifolia*
Iowa crab *Malus ioensis*
Iowa crabapple *Malus ioensis*
ipe roxo *Tabebuia heptaphylla, T. impetiginosa*
ipecac *Cephaelis ipecacuanha*

ipecac, wild *Euphorbia corollata*
ipecacuanha, bastard *Asclepias curassavica*
ipomoea, yellow *Ochna natalitia*
Iranian tulip *Tulipa montana*
Ireland, bells of *Moluccella laevis*
iris, African *Dietes*
iris, Algerian *Iris unguicularis*
iris, Australian *Patersonia*
iris, bearded *Iris × germanica*
iris, butterfly *Dietes bicolor, D. grandiflora, D. iridioides*
iris, crested *Iris cristata*
iris, Dalmatian *Iris pallida*
iris, Dutch *Iris* Dutch Hybrids
iris, dwarf bearded *Iris pumila*
iris, German *Iris × germanica*
iris, gold net *Iris chrysographes*
iris, gold pattern *Iris chrysographes*
iris, Japanese water *Iris ensata, I. laevigata*
iris, morning *Orthrosanthus*
iris, mourning *Iris susiana*
iris, New Zealand *Libertia grandiflora, L. ixioides*
iris, peacock *Moraea aristata, M. villosa, Tigridia pavonia*
iris, rabbit-ear *Iris laevigata*
iris, roof *Iris tectorum*
iris, snake's head *Hermodactylus tuberosus*
iris, Trojan *Iris trojana*
iris, walking *Neomarica northiana*
iris, widow *Hermodactylus tuberosus*
iris, wild *Dietes grandiflora*
iris, winter *Iris unguicularis*
iris, woodland *Iris ensata*
Irish heather *Erica erigena*
Irish ivy *Hedera hibernica*
Irish juniper *Juniperus communis* 'Hibernica'
Irish lace *Tagetes filifolia*
Irish strawberry tree *Arbutus unedo*

Irish yew *Taxus baccata* 'Fastigiata'
Irishman, wild *Discaria toumatou*
Iron Cross begonia *Begonia masoniana*
iron fern *Rumohra adiantiformis*
iron tree *Parrotia persica*
ironbark, Beyer's *Eucalyptus beyeriana*
ironbark, blue-leafed *Eucalyptus nubila*
ironbark, broad-leafed red *Eucalyptus fibrosa*
ironbark, Caley's *Eucalyptus caleyi*
ironbark, gray *Eucalyptus paniculata, E. siderophloia*
ironbark, hard *Eucalyptus dura*
ironbark, narrow-leafed *Eucalyptus crebra*
ironbark, Queensland gray *Eucalyptus drepanophylla*
ironbark red *Eucalyptus sideroxylon*
ironbark, silver-leafed *Eucalyptus melanophloia, E. shirleyi*
ironbox, black *Eucalyptus raveretiana*
irongrass *Lomandra effusa, L. patens*
ironplant *Haplopappus*
ironwood *Acacia estrophiolata, A. excelsa, Backhousia myrtifolia, Carpinus caroliniana, Mesua ferrea, Ostrya virginiana*
ironwood, black *Olea capensis*
ironwood, Brazilian *Caesalpinia ferrea*
ironwood, Catalina *Lyonothamnus floribundus*
ironwood, Cooktown *Erythrophleum chlorostachys*
ironwood, desert *Olneya tesota*
ironwood, giant *Choricarpia subargentea*
ironwood, Persian *Parrotia persica*
ironwood, South African *Millettia grandis*
ironwood, white *Vepris lanceolata*
Isabella grape *Vitis labruscana* 'Isabella'

island manzanita *Arctostaphylos insularis*
island oak *Quercus tomentella*
island snapdragon *Galvezia speciosa*
islay *Prunus ilicifolia*
isotome, showy *Isotoma axillaris*
isotome, swamp *Isotoma fluviatilis*
isu tree *Distylium racemosum*
itala palm *Hyphaene coriacea*
Italian alder *Alnus cordata*
Italian bellflower *Campanula isophylla*
Italian buckthorn *Rhamnus alaternus*
Italian crabapple *Malus florentina*
Italian honeysuckle *Lonicera caprifolium*
Italian jasmine *Jasminum humile*
Italian lavender *Lavandula stoechas*
Italian maple *Acer opalus*
Italian millet *Setaria italica*
Italian parsley *Petroselinum crispum* var. *neapolitaum*
Italian ryegrass *Lolium multiflorum*
Italian yellow jasmine *Jasminum humile*
ivory curl tree *Buckinghamia celsissima*
ivory palm, vegetable *Phytelephas*
Ivory's hakea *Hakea ivoryi*
ivy *Hedera, H. helix*
ivy, Algerian *Hedera canariensis*
ivy, Atlantic *Hedera hibernica*
ivy, Boston *Parthenocissus tricuspidata*
ivy, bullock's heart *Hedera colchica*
ivy, Canary Island *Hedera canariensis*
ivy, Cape *Delairea odorata, Senecio macroglossus*
ivy, Colchic *Hedera colchica*
ivy, coliseum *Cymbalaria muralis*

ivy, common *Hedera helix*
ivy, devil's *Epipremnum pinnatum* 'Aureum'
ivy, English *Hedera helix*
ivy geranium *Pelargonium peltatum*
ivy goodenia *Goodenia hederacea*
ivy, grape *Cissus*
ivy, ground *Glechoma hederacea*
ivy, Himalayan *Hedera nepalensis*
ivy, Irish *Hedera hibernica*
ivy, Japanese *Parthenocissus tricuspidata*
ivy, Kenilworth *Cymbalaria muralis*
ivy, marine *Cissus trifoliata*
ivy, Mexican *Cobaea scandens*
ivy, miniature grape *Cissus striata*
ivy, Natal *Senecio macroglossus*
ivy, Nepal *Hedera nepalensis*
ivy, North African *Hedera canariensis*
ivy palm, Australian *Schefflera actinophylla*
ivy, Persian *Hedera colchica*
ivy red *Hemigraphis alternata*
ivy, Swedish *Plectranthus australis, P. verticillatus*
ivy, switch *Leucothoe fontanesiana*
ivy tree *Schefflera heptaphylla*
ivy, variegated *Hedera canariensis* 'Variegata'
ivy-leaf pepper *Peperomia griseoargentea*
ivy-leafed geranium *Pelargonium peltatum*
ivy-leafed toadflax *Cymbalaria muralis*
ivy-leafed violet *Viola hederacea*
ixia *Ixia*
ixia, green *Ixia viridiflora*
izote *Yucca filifera*

J

jaboncillo *Clethra mexicana*
jaborandi *Pilocarpus microphyllus*
jaboticaba *Myrciaria cauliflora*
jacaranda *Jacaranda mimosifolia*
jack, brown *Cryptocarya microneura*
jack, five-fingered *Adiantum hispidulum*
jack, long *Flindersia xanthoxyla*
jack pine *Pinus banksiana*
jack wattle, jumping *Acacia enterocarpa*
jackal's food *Euphorbia mauritanica*
jackbean *Canavalia ensiformis*
jackbean, coastal *Canavalia rosea*
jacket, leather *Barklya syringifolia, Geissois benthamii*
jacket plum *Pappea capensis*
jackfruit *Artocarpus heterophyllus*
Jack-in-the-pulpit *Arisaema triphyllum, Arum maculatum*
jackwood *Cryptocarya glaucescens*
Jacobean lily *Sprekelia formosissima*
jacobinia, scarlet *Libonia floribunda*
Jacob's coat *Acalypha amentacea* subsp. *wilkesiana*
Jacob's ladder *Polemonium, P. caeruleum*
Jacob's ladder, creeping *Polemonium reptans*
Jacob's ladder, northern *Polemonium boreale*
Jacob's rod *Asphodeline lutea*
jade, Chinese *Portulacaria afra*
jade orchid *Magnolia denudata*
jade plant *Crassula arborescens, C. ovata, Portulacaria afra*
jade plant, Chinese *Portulacaria afra*
jade plant, silver *Crassula arborescens*
jade tree *Crassula ovata*

jade tree, variegated *Crassula ovata* 'Sunset'
jade vine *Strongylodon macrobotrys*
jakfruit *Artocarpus heterophyllus*
jalap *Anredera cordifolia, Ipomoea purga*
jalapeno chilli *Capsicum annuum* 'Jalapeno'
Jamaica caper tree *Capparis cynophallophora*
Jamaica dogwood *Piscidia piscipula*
Jamaica ebony *Brya ebenus*
Jamaica pepper *Pimenta dioica*
Jamaica royal palm *Roystonea altissima*
Jamaica silver palm *Coccothrinax argentata*
Jamaica sorrel *Hibiscus sabdariffa*
Jamaican fan palm *Thrinax parviflora*
Jamaican king *Coccoloba uvifera*
Jamaican oak *Catalpa longissima*
Jamaican thatch palm *Thrinax parviflora*
jamberry *Physalis ixocarpa, P. philadelphica*
jambhiri orange *Citrus × jambhiri*
jambolan *Syzygium cumini*
jambosa *Syzygium samarangense*
jambu *Syzygium, S. cumini*
Jamestown weed *Datura stramonium*
jammy-mouth *Ruttya fruticosa*
Jane, salvation *Echium plantagineum*
Japan wood oil tree *Aleurites cordata*
Japanese alder *Alnus firma, A. japonica*
Japanese allspice *Chimonanthus praecox*
Japanese alpine cherry *Prunus nipponica*
Japanese anemone *Anemone hupehensis* var. *japonica, A. × hybrida*
Japanese angelica tree *Aralia elata*

Japanese anise *Illicium anisatum*
Japanese apricot *Prunus mume*
Japanese aralia *Fatsia japonica*
Japanese arborvitae *Thuja standishii*
Japanese arrowroot *Pueraria lobata*
Japanese aspen *Populus sieboldii*
Japanese aucuba *Aucuba japonica*
Japanese barberry *Berberis thunbergii*
Japanese beauty berry *Callicarpa japonica*
Japanese beauty bush *Callicarpa japonica*
Japanese beech *Fagus crenata*
Japanese big-leafed magnolia *Magnolia hypoleuca*
Japanese bird cherry *Prunus grayana*
Japanese bitter orange *Poncirus trifoliata*
Japanese black pine *Pinus thunbergii*
Japanese bladdernut *Staphylea bumalda*
Japanese blue beech *Fagus japonica*
Japanese box *Buxus microphylla,
B. m.* var. *japonica*
Japanese bunching onion *Allium fistulosum*
Japanese cedar *Cryptomeria japonica*
Japanese cherry birch *Betula grossa*
Japanese cherry tree *Prunus pseudocerasus*
Japanese chestnut *Castanea crenata*
Japanese chestnut oak *Quercus acutissima*
Japanese chilli *Capsicum frutescens* 'Yatsufusa'
Japanese clethra *Clethra barbinervis*
Japanese climbing fern *Lygodium japonicum*
Japanese cork-tree *Phellodendron japonicum*
Japanese cornelian cherry *Cornus officinalis*
Japanese crab *Malus floribunda*

Japanese creeper *Parthenocissus tricuspidata*
Japanese date plum *Diospyros kaki*
Japanese dead nettle *Meehania*
Japanese dodder *Cuscuta japonica*
Japanese evergreen azalea *Rhododendron indicum*
Japanese fairy bells *Disporum sessile*
Japanese felt fern *Pyrrosia lingua*
Japanese fir *Abies firma*
Japanese flowering apricot *Prunus mume* 'Geisha'
Japanese flowering cherry *Prunus* Sato-zakura Group, *P. serrulata*
Japanese flowering crabapple *Malus floribunda*
Japanese flowering dogwood *Cornus kousa*
Japanese flowering quince *Chaenomeles japonica*
Japanese forest grass *Hakonechloa macra*
Japanese garden juniper *Juniperus procumbens*
Japanese hemlock, southern *Tsuga sieboldii*
Japanese hibiscus *Hibiscus schizopetalus*
Japanese holly *Ilex crenata*
Japanese honeysuckle *Lonicera japonica*
Japanese hop-hornbeam *Ostrya japonica*
Japanese hornbeam *Carpinus japonica*
Japanese horse chestnut *Aesculus turbinata*
Japanese hydrangea vine *Schizophragma hydrangeoides*
Japanese ivy *Parthenocissus tricuspidata*
Japanese juniper *Juniperus procumbens*

Japanese knotweed *Fallopia japonica*

Japanese lacquer tree *Toxicodendron vernicifluum*

Japanese lantern *Hibiscus schizopetalus*

Japanese larch *Larix kaempferi*

Japanese laurel *Aucuba japonica*

Japanese leek *Allium fistulosum*

Japanese lime *Tilia japonica*

Japanese linden *Tilia japonica*

Japanese locust *Gleditsia japonica*

Japanese maple *Acer palmatum*

Japanese maple, dissected *Acer palmatum* Dissectum Group

Japanese maple, greenleaf *Acer palmatum*

Japanese maple, purple-leafed *Acer palmatum* 'Atropurpureum'

Japanese maple, red-stemmed *Acer palmatum* 'Senkaki'

Japanese millet *Echinochloa esculenta*

Japanese mint *Mentha arvensis* var. *piperascens*

Japanese nutmeg yew *Torreya nucifera*

Japanese oak *Quercus acutissima, Q. mongolica* var. *grosseserrata*

Japanese pachysandra *Pachysandra terminalis*

Japanese pagoda tree *Sophora japonica*

Japanese painted fern *Athyrium niponicum, A. n.* 'Pictum'

Japanese parsley *Cryptotaenia canadensis* subsp. *japonica*

Japanese pepper *Zanthoxylum piperitum*

Japanese photinia *Photinia glabra*

Japanese pieris *Pieris japonica*

Japanese pittosporum *Pittosporum tobira*

Japanese plum *Prunus salicina*

Japanese plum-yew *Cephalotaxus harringtonia, C. h.* var. *drupacea*

Japanese poplar *Populus maximowiczii*

Japanese primula *Primula japonica*

Japanese privet *Ligustrum japonicum*

Japanese raisin tree *Hovenia dulcis*

Japanese red pine *Pinus densiflora*

Japanese rose *Rosa multiflora, R. rugosa*

Japanese rowan *Sorbus commixta*

Japanese sago cycad *Cycas revoluta*

Japanese shore juniper *Juniperus conferta*

Japanese silver grass *Miscanthus sinensis*

Japanese snowball *Viburnum plicatum* 'Sterile'

Japanese snowdrop tree *Styrax japonicus*

Japanese spikenard *Aralia cordata*

Japanese spiraea *Spiraea japonica*

Japanese spurge *Pachysandra terminalis*

Japanese star jasmine *Trachelospermum asiaticum*

Japanese star-anise *Illicium anisatum*

Japanese stewartia *Stewartia pseudocamellia*

Japanese stone pine *Pinus pumila*

Japanese thistle *Cirsium japonicum*

Japanese timber bamboo *Phyllostachys bambusoides*

Japanese tree lilac *Syringa reticulata*

Japanese umbrella pine *Sciadopitys verticillata*

Japanese varnish tree *Firmiana simplex*

Japanese walnut *Juglans ailanthifolia*

Japanese water iris *Iris ensata, I. laevigata*

Japanese white birch *Betula platyphylla* var. *japonica*

Japanese white pine *Pinus parviflora*
Japanese willow *Salix integra*
Japanese wingnut *Pterocarya rhoifolia*
Japanese winterberry *Ilex serrata*
Japanese wisteria *Wisteria floribunda*
Japanese wisteria, double *Wisteria floribunda* 'Violaceo-plena'
Japanese witch hazel *Hamamelis japonica*
Japanese wood fern *Dryopteris sieboldii*
Japanese yellowwood *Cladrastis platycarpa*
Japanese yew *Taxus cuspidata*
Japanese zelkova *Zelkova serrata*
japonica *Chaenomeles, C. speciosa*
jarrah *Eucalyptus marginata*
jasmine *Jasminum*
jasmine, angel wing *Jasminum nitidum*
jasmine, Arabian *Jasminum sambac*
jasmine, Azores *Jasminum azoricum*
jasmine, Brazilian *Mandevilla sanderi*
jasmine, Canary Island *Jasminum odoratissimum*
jasmine, Cape *Gardenia augusta, Rothmannia globosa*
jasmine, Carolina *Gelsemium sempervirens*
jasmine, Chilean *Mandevilla laxa*
jasmine, Chinese *Jasminum polyanthum*
jasmine, Chinese star *Trachelospermum jasminoides*
jasmine, common *Jasminum officinale, J. o.* 'Grandiflorum'
jasmine, common white *Jasminum officinale*
jasmine, Confederate *Trachelospermum asminoides*
jasmine, crape *Tabernaemontana divaricata, T. d.* 'Flore Pleno'

jasmine, desert *Jasminum lineare*
jasmine, double Arabian *Jasminum sambac* 'Grand Duke of Tuscany'
jasmine, dwarf *Jasminum parkeri*
jasmine, Italian *Jasminum humile*
jasmine, Italian yellow *Jasminum humile*
jasmine, native *Jasminum volubile*
jasmine orange *Murraya paniculata*
jasmine, poet's *Jasminum officinale*
jasmine, primrose *Jasminum mesnyi*
jasmine, rock *Androsace*
jasmine, Spanish *Clerodendrum chinense*
jasmine, spicy *Jasminum suavissimum*
jasmine, star *Trachelospermum, T. jasminoides*
jasmine, sweet *Jasminum suavissimum*
jasmine tobacco *Nicotiana alata*
jasmine, true *Jasminum officinale*
jasmine, wild *Schrebera alata*
jasmine, winter *Jasminum nudiflorum*
jasmine, yellow *Jasminum mesnyi*
jata de guanboca *Copernicia macroglossa*
jatropha, spicy *Jatropha integerrima*
jaundice root *Hydrastis canadensis*
Java apple *Syzygium samarangense*
Java cedar *Bischofia javanica*
Java glory bean *Clerodendrum speciosissimum*
Java olive *Sterculia foetida*
Java plum *Syzygium cumini*
Java willow *Ficus virens*
jaws, tiger *Faucaria tigrina*
Jeffrey pine *Pinus jeffreyi*
jelly palm *Butia capitata*
jelutong *Dyera costulata*
Jenny, creeping *Lysimachia nummularia*
Jericho wiregrass *Aristida jerichoensis*
jerry-jerry *Ammannia multiflora*

Jersey cudweed *Pseudognaphalium luteoalbum*
Jersey elm *Ulmus* 'Sarniensis'
Jersey lily *Amaryllis*
Jerusalem artichoke *Helianthus tuberosus*
Jerusalem cherry *Solanum pseudocapsicum*
Jerusalem cherry, false *Solanum capsicastrum*
Jerusalem cross *Lychnis chalcedonica*
Jerusalem cucumber *Cucumis anguria*
Jerusalem oak *Chenopodium botrys*
Jerusalem sage *Phlomis fruticosa, Pulmonaria officinalis, P. saccharata*
Jerusalem thorn *Parkinsonia aculeata*
jessamine, Carolina *Gelsemium sempervirens*
jessamine, day *Cestrum diurnum*
jessamine, night-scented *Cestrum nocturnum*
jessamine, orange *Murraya paniculata*
jessamine, yellow *Gelsemium sempervirens*
Jessie, black *Pithecellobium unguis-cati*
Jesuits' nut *Trapa natans*
Jew, wandering *Tradescantia albiflora, T. fluminensis*
jewel daisy *Ursinia anthemoides*
jewel orchid *Ludisia*
jewel weed *Impatiens capensis*
jeweled aloe *Aloe distans*
jewels of Opar *Talinum paniculatum*
jewels, tower of *Echium wildprettii*
Jew's apple *Solanum melongena*
jicama *Pachyrhizus erosus, P. tuberosus*
Jillaga ash *Eucalyptus stenostoma*
Jim sage *Salvia clevelandii*
Jimson's weed *Datura stramonium*
Job's tears *Coix lacryma-jobi*
jockey's cap *Tigridia pavonia*

Joe Pye weed *Eupatorium purpureum*
joey palm *Johannesteijsmannia altifrons*
Johnny jump-up *Viola tricolor*
Johnson grass *Sorghum halepense*
Johnson's grevillea *Grevillea johnsonii*
jointed charlock *Raphanus raphanistrum*
jointed rush *Juncus articulatus*
jointed twig-rush *Baumea articulata*
joint-fir *Ephedra*
joint-fir, green *Ephedra viridis*
joint-pine *Ephedra*
joint-pine, European *Ephedra distachya*
jointwood *Piper aduncum*
jo-jo *Soliva sessilis, S. stolonifera*
jo-jo, dwarf *Soliva anthemifolia*
jojoba *Simmondsia chinensis*
joker's hat chilli *Capsicum baccatum* 'Bi-Bell'
jonquil *Narcissus jonquilla*
Josephine's lily *Brunsvigia josephinae*
Joseph's coat *Amaranthus tricolor*
Joshua tree *Yucca brevifolia*
joy, simpler's *Verbena hastata*
joyweed *Alternanthera, A. denticulata*
Juçara palm *Euterpe edulis*
Judas tree *Cercis siliquastrum*
judd viburnum *Viburnum* × *juddii*
jugflower, coastal *Adenanthos cuneatus*
jugflower, hairy *Adenanthos barbiger*
jugflower, Scott River *Adenanthos detmoldii*
jugflower, yellow *Adenanthos detmoldii*
jujube, Chinese *Ziziphus jujuba*
jujube, common *Ziziphus jujuba*
jumping cholla *Cylindropuntia bigelovii, C. prolifera*
jumping jack wattle *Acacia enterocarpa*
jump-up, Johnny *Viola tricolor*

June grass *Poa pratensis*
juneberry *Amelanchier alnifolia,
A. canadensis*
juneberry, running *Amelanchier
stolonifera*
junegrass *Koeleria*
jungle bells *Fieldia australis*
jungle brake *Pteris umbrosa*
jungle flame *Ixora*
jungle vine *Cissus hypoglauca*
juniper, African *Juniperus procera*
juniper, alligator *Juniperus deppeana,
J. deppeana* var. *pachyphlaea*
juniper, Bonin Island *Juniperus
procumbens*
juniper, California *Juniperus
californica*
juniper, Canary Island *Juniperus
cedrus*
juniper, chequerboard *Juniperus
deppeana*
juniper, cherrystone *Juniperus
monosperma*
juniper, Chinese *Juniperus chinensis*
juniper, coffin *Juniperus recurva*
juniper, common *Juniperus communis*
juniper, Cox's *Juniperus recurva* var.
coxii
juniper, creeping *Juniperus
horizontalis, J. procumbens*
juniper, drooping *Juniperus recurva*
juniper, East African *Juniperus
procera*
juniper, Greek *Juniperus excelsa*
juniper gum plant *Tetraclinis
articulata*
juniper, Himalayan *Juniperus recurva*
juniper, Himalayan black *Juniperus
indica*

juniper, Hollywood *Juniperus
squamata*
juniper, horizontal *Juniperus
horizontalis*
juniper, Irish *Juniperus communis*
'Hibernica'
juniper, Japanese *Juniperus
procumbens*
juniper, Japanese garden *Juniperus
procumbens*
juniper, Mexican *Juniperus flaccida*
juniper, Meyer *Juniperus squamata*
'Meyeri'
juniper, needle *Juniperus rigida*
juniper, one-seed *Juniperus
monosperma*
juniper, pinchot *Juniperus pinchotii*
juniper, prickly *Juniperus oxycedrus*
juniper, redberry *Juniperus
monosperma*
juniper, Rocky Mountain *Juniperus
scopulorum*
juniper, Ryukyu *Juniperus taxifolia*
juniper, savin *Juniperus sabina*
juniper, shore *Juniperus conferta*
juniper, singleseed *Juniperus
squamata*
juniper, Spanish *Juniperus thurifera*
juniper, Syrian *Juniperus drupacea*
juniper, Taiwan *Juniperus formosana*
juniper, Utah *Juniperus osteosperma*
juniper, western *Juniperus occidentalis*
juniper-leaf grevillea *Grevillea
juniperina*
Jupiter's beard *Anthyllis barba-jovis,
Centranthus ruber*
Jupiter's distaff *Salvia glutinosa*
jusquaime *Hyoscyamus niger*
justicia, red *Justicia candicans*

K

ka, kyein *Calamus viminalis*
kabong *Arenga pinnata*
Kaempfer azalea *Rhododendron kaempferi*
kaffir lily *Clivia miniata, Schizostylis, S. coccinea*
kaffir lily, greentip *Clivia nobilis*
kaffir lime *Citrus hystrix*
kaffir plum *Harpephyllum caffrum*
kaffirboom *Erythrina caffra*
kaffirboom, dwarf *Erythrina humeana*
kaffirboom, Transvaal *Gardenia volkensii*
kahikatea *Dacrycarpus dacrydioides*
kahili ginger *Hedychium gardnerianum*
kai kai *Ipomoea batatas*
kai tsoi *Brassica juncea*
kaitha *Limonia acidissima*
kaka beak *Clianthus puniceus*
kaki *Diospyros kaki*
Kalahari Christmas tree *Dichrostachys cinerea*
kalanchoe, giant *Kalanchoe beharensis*
kale *Brassica oleracea* Acephala Group
kale, ornamental *Brassica oleracea* Acephala Group
kale, sea *Crambe maritima*
kale, Siberian *Brassica napus* Pabularia Group
kalgan boronia *Boronia heterophylla*
kamahi *Weinmannia racemosa*
kamala, red *Mallotus philippensis*
kamarere *Eucalyptus deglupta*
Kamchatka stonecrop *Sedum kamtschaticum*
kan-chiku *Chimonobambusa marmorea*

kangaroo apple *Solanum aviculare*
kangaroo apple, green *Solanum vescum*
kangaroo apple, large *Solanum laciniatum*
kangaroo apple, mountain *Solanum linearifolium*
kangaroo fern *Microsorum pustulatum*
kangaroo grass *Themeda australis*
kangaroo paw *Anigozanthos*
kangaroo paw, black *Macropidia fulginosa*
kangaroo paw, evergreen *Anigozanthos flavidus*
kangaroo paw, green *Anigozanthos viridis*
kangaroo paw, Mangles' *Anigozanthos manglesii*
kangaroo paw, red *Anigozanthos rufus*
kangaroo paw, red and green *Anigozanthos manglesii*
kangaroo paw, tall *Anigozanthos flavidus*
kangaroo paw, yellow *Anigozanthos flavidus*
kangaroo thorn *Acacia paradoxa*
kangaroo vine *Cissus antarctica*
kangkong *Ipomoea aquatica*
Kansas hawthorn *Crataegus coccinioides*
kanska *Abutilon indicum*
kanuka *Kunzea ericoides*
kanuka box *Tristaniopsis laurina*
kanzashi giboshi *Hosta nakaiana*
kapok bush *Cochlospermum fraseri, Eriocephalus*
kapok bush, western *Cochlospermum fraseri*
kapok, native *Cochlospermum gillivraei*
kapok tree *Ceiba pentandra, Cochlospermum gillivraei*

kapok, yellow *Cochlospermum fraseri*
kapokkie heath *Erica peziza*
kapuka *Griselinia littoralis*
karaka *Corynocarpus laevigatus*
karamu *Coprosma lucida, C. robusta*
karee *Rhus lancea*
karee, mountain *Rhus leptodictya*
karee, white *Rhus viminalis*
karkalla *Carpobrotus rossii*
karo *Pittosporum crassifolium*
karoo conebush *Leucadendron nobile*
karoo rose *Lapidaria margaretae*
karri *Eucalyptus diversicolor*
karroo thorn *Acacia karroo*
Karwinski's sage *Salvia karwinskii*
kashgaer tree *Tamarix hispida*
Kashmir cypress *Cupressus cashmeriana*
kassod tree *Senna siamea*
Katie *Pseudophoenix vinifera*
Katie, flaming *Kalanchoe blossfeldiana*
katsura tree *Cercidiphyllum japonicum*
katsura tree, Chinese *Cercidiphyllum japonicum* var. *sinense*
kauri *Agathis, A. australis*
kauri, Corbasson's *Agathis corbassonii*
kauri, Mont Panie *Agathis montana*
kauri, New Guinea *Agathis robusta* subsp. *nesophila*
kauri, New Zealand *Agathis australis*
kauri, Pacific Islands *Agathis macrophylla*
kauri, Queensland *Agathis robusta*
kauri, scrub *Agathis ovata*
kauri, Vanikoro *Agathis macrophylla*
kauri, western New Guinea *Agathis labillardierei*
kava *Piper methysticum*
kava, false *Piper aduncum*
kava-kava *Piper methysticum*
kawaka *Libocedrus plumosa*

kawakawa *Macropiper excelsum*
kawmaka *Bactris major*
kaya nut *Torreya nucifera*
keck *Anthriscus sylvestris*
keeled garlic *Allium carinatum*
keeled goosefoot *Chenopodium carinatum*
kei apple *Dovyalis caffra*
kelp *Ecklonia, Laminaria, Macrocystis*
kembang *Clerodendrum buchananii*
kenaf *Hibiscus cannabinus*
Kenai birch *Betula kenaica*
Kenilworth ivy *Cymbalaria muralis*
kentan *Lilium lancifolium*
kentia palm *Howea forsteriana*
kentia palm, Belmore *Howea belmoreana*
Kentucky bluegrass *Poa pratensis*
Kentucky coffee tree *Gymnocladus dioica*
Kentucky wisteria *Wisteria macrostachya*
Kenya hyacinth *Sansevieria parva*
ke-oroshima-chiku *Pleioblastus pygmaeus*
Kermadec pohutukawa *Metrosideros kermadecensis*
kermes oak *Quercus coccifera*
kerosene bush *Ozothamnus hookeri, O. ledifolius, Richea scoparia*
kerrawang *Rulingia dasyphylla*
ketmia, bladder *Hibiscus trionum*
khat *Catha edulis*
kiaat *Pterocarpus angolensis*
kidney bean *Phaseolus vulgaris*
kidney begonia *Begonia* × *erythrophylla*
kidney vetch *Anthyllis vulneraria*
kidney-weed *Dichondra micrantha, D. repens*
kikuyu grass *Pennisetum clandestinum, P. flaccidum*

Kilimanjaro, snows of *Euphorbia leucocephala*
Kimberley heath *Calytrix exstipulata*
king begonia *Begonia rex*
King Billy pine *Athrotaxis selaginoides*
king cup *Caltha palustris*
king fern *Angiopteris evecta, Marattia salicina, Todea barbara*
king greenhood *Pterostylis baptistii*
king, Jamaican *Coccoloba uvifera*
king mandarin *Citrus* × *aurantium* Tangor Group
king orchid *Dendrobium speciosum*
king protea *Protea cynaroides*
King William pine *Athrotaxis selaginoides*
king's crown *Calotropis procera, Dicliptera suberecta*
king's mantle *Thunbergia erecta*
king's spear *Asphodeline lutea*
kinnikinick *Arctostaphylos uva-ursi*
kirin giboshi *Hosta minor*
kiss-me-over-the-garden-gate *Persicaria orientalis*
kite tree *Nuxia floribunda*
kittatinny blackberry *Rubus bellobatus*
kittentail *Synthyris*
kittentail, evergreen *Synthyris platycarpa*
kiwi fruit *Actinidia deliciosa*
kiwi fruit, cocktail *Actinidia arguta*
kiwi fruit, dessert *Actinidia arguta*
kiwi fruit, hardy *Actinidia arguta*
kleinbergaalwyn *Aloe melanacantha*
klinki pine *Araucaria hunsteinii*
klipnoors *Euphorbia obesa*
knapweed *Centaurea*
knawel, cushion *Scleranthus minusculus*
knawel, prickly *Scleranthus pungens*

knawel, twin-flowered *Scleranthus biflorus*
kneed Darling pea *Swainsona oroboides*
knife-leaf wattle *Acacia cultriformis*
knight's star lily *Hippeastrum*
knight's star lily, long-styled *Hippeastrum stylosum*
knitbone *Symphytum*
knob sedge *Carex inversa*
knob thorn *Acacia nigrescens*
knobby club-rush *Isolepis nodosa*
knobcone pine *Pinus attenuata*
knobwood *Zanthoxylum davyi*
knobwood, dune *Zanthoxylum delagoense*
knobwood, kundanyoka *Zanthoxylum chalybeum*
knobwood, large-leafed *Zanthoxylum gilletii*
knobwood, rusty *Zanthoxylum trijugum*
knobwood, sand *Zanthoxylum leprieurii*
knobwood, small *Zanthoxylum capense*
knotted clover *Trifolium striatum*
knotted marjoram *Origanum majorana*
knottybutt grass *Paspalidium constrictum*
knotweed *Fallopia, Persicaria, Polygonum*
knotweed, bristly *Persicaria strigosa*
knotweed, creeping *Persicaria prostrata*
knotweed, Japanese *Fallopia japonica*
knotweed, lesser *Persicaria campanulata*
knotweed, pale *Persicaria lapathifolia*
knotweed, slender *Persicaria decipiens*
knotweed, small *Polygonum plebeium*
koa *Acacia koa*

koba giboshi *Hosta sieboldii*
kobus magnolia *Magnolia kobus*
kochia *Bassia scoparia*
koda *Ehretia acuminata*
kodo wood *Ehretia acuminata*
kohlrabi *Brassica oleracea* Gongylodes
  Group
kohuhu *Pittosporum tenuifolium*
kokio *Kokia drynarioides*
koko tree *Maytenus undulata*
kokuwa *Actinidia arguta*
kooboo berry *Cassine sphaerophylla*
kooboo berry, Transvaal *Cassine
  burkeana*
Korean arborvitae *Thuja koraiensis*
Korean azalea *Rhododendron yedoense*
Korean barberry *Berberis koreana*
Korean box *Buxus microphylla*
Korean boxwood *Buxus microphylla*
  var. *koreana*
Korean devil's club *Oplopanax elatus*
Korean euodia *Tetradium daniellii*
Korean fir *Abies koreana*
Korean forsythia *Forsythia ovata*
Korean hornbeam *Carpinus eximia*
Korean lilac, dwarf *Syringa meyeri*
Korean linden *Tilia insularis*
Korean mint *Agastache rugosa*
Korean mountain ash *Sorbus alnifolia*
Korean mulberry *Morus australis*
Korean pearl bush *Exochorda
  serratifolia*
Korean pine *Pinus koraiensis*
Korean raspberry *Rubus crataegifolius*
Korean rhododendron *Rhododendron
  mucronulatum*
Korean rock fern *Polystichum
  tsussimense*
Korean spice viburnum *Viburnum
  carlesii*
Korean spiraea *Spiraea fritschiana,
  S. trichocarpa*
Korean velvet grass *Zoysia tenuifolia*

korokio *Corokia buddlejoides*
koromiko *Hebe salicifolia, H. stricta*
koromiko, mountain *Hebe subalpina*
koru *Pratia physaloides*
Kosciuszko rose *Pimelea ligustrina*
  subsp. *ciliata*
kosi palm *Raphia australis*
koso *Hagenia abyssinica*
Koster blue spruce *Picea pungens*
  'Koster'
kotamba *Terminalia catappa*
kotukutuku *Fuchsia excorticata*
kou *Cordia subcordata*
kousa dogwood *Cornus kousa*
kowhai *Sophora microphylla,
  S. tetraptera*
kowhai, dwarf *Sophora prostrata*
kowhai, yellow *Sophora tetraptera*
kraalaalwyn *Aloe claviflora*
krans aalwyn *Aloe mitriformis*
krantz aloe *Aloe arborescens*
kris plant *Alocasia sanderiana*
kudzu *Pueraria lobata*
kudzu vine *Pueraria lobata*
kulcha *Corymbia terminalis*
kuma zasa *Sasa veitchii*
kumara *Ipomoea batatas*
kumarahou *Pomaderris kumeraho*
kumquat *Citrus japonica*
kunai grass *Imperata cylindrica*
kundanyoka knobwood *Zanthoxylum
  chalybeum*
kunibush *Rhus undulata*
kunkerberry *Carissa lanceolata,
  C. ovata*
kunzea, pink *Kunzea capitata*
kunzea, scarlet *Kunzea baxteri*
kunzea, violet *Kunzea parvifolia*
kunzea, yellow *Kunzea muelleri*
kurakkan *Eleusine coracana*
kuro giboshi *Hosta nigrescens*
kuronami giboshi *Hosta fluctuans*
kurrajong *Brachychiton populneus*

kurrajong, brown *Commersonia bartramia*

kurrajong, brush *Commersonia fraseri*

kurrajong, desert *Brachychiton gregorii*

kurrajong, dwarf *Brachychiton bidwillii*

kurrajong, flame *Brachychiton acerifolius*

kurrajong, hybrid *Brachychiton × roseus*

kurrajong, lacebark *Brachychiton discolor*

kurrajong, red-fruited *Sterculia quadrifida*

kurrajong, scrub *Hibiscus heterophyllus*

kurrat *Allium ampeloprasum*

kurume azalea *Rhododendron × obtusum*

kusamaki *Podocarpus macrophyllus*

kuskoraalboom *Erythrina caffra*

Kybean gum *Eucalyptus parvula*

Kybean mallee *Eucalyptus kybeanensis*

Kybean wattle *Acacia kybeanensis*

kyein ka *Calamus viminalis*

Kyushu azalea *Rhododendron kiusianum*

Kyushu linden *Tilia kiusiana*

L

la Purisima *Arctostaphylos purissima*
labdanum *Cistus ladanifer*
lablab bean *Lablab purpureus*
Labrador tea *Ledum groenlandicum*
Labrador violet *Viola labradorica*
laburnum *Laburnum × watereri*
laburnum, Cape *Crotalaria capensis*
laburnum, common *Laburnum anagyroides*
laburnum, Dalmatian *Petteria ramentacea*
laburnum, Indian *Cassia fistula*
laburnum, Natal *Calpurnia aurea*
laburnum, Scotch *Laburnum alpinum*
laburnum, Voss *Laburnum × watereri* 'Vossii'
lace aloe *Aloe aristata*
lace cactus *Mammillaria elongata*
lace flower, blue *Trachymene coerulea*
lace flower, pink *Archidendron grandiflorum*
lace flower, veiny *Archidendron muellerianum*
lace flower, white *Archidendron hendersonii*
lace, Irish *Tagetes filifolia*
lace, St Catherine's *Eriogonum giganteum*
lace shrub *Stephanandra incisa*
lace vine, silver *Fallopia aubertii*
lacebark *Hoheria*
lacebark kurrajong *Brachychiton discolor*
lacebark, New Zealand *Hoheria lyallii, H. populnea*
lacebark pine *Pinus bungeana*
lacecap hydrangea *Hydrangea macrophylla* Lacecap Group
lacecap hydrangea, variegated *Hydrangea macrophylla* 'Maculata'
lace-flower vine *Episcia dianthiflora*
lacquer tree, Chinese *Toxicodendron vernicifluum*
lacquer tree, Japanese *Toxicodendron vernicifluum*
lacy ground fern *Dennstaedtia davallioides*
lacy ragweed *Ambrosia tenuifolia*
lacy wedge-fern *Lindsaea microphylla*
ladanum *Cistus ladanifer*
ladder fern *Blechnum spicant, Nephrolepis cordifolia*
ladder, Jacob's *Polemonium, P. caeruleum*
ladies' eardrops *Fuchsia magellanica*
ladies, naked *Amaryllis belladonna, Colchicum*
ladies' purses *Calceolaria* Herbeohybrida Group
ladies' smock *Cardamine, C. pratensis*
ladies' tobacco *Antennaria*
lad's love *Artemisia abrotanum*
Lady Banks' rose *Rosa banksiae*
lady fern *Athyrium filix-femina*
lady finger cactus *Echinocereus pentalophus*
lady of the night *Brunfelsia americana, Cestrum nocturnum*
lady of the night orchid *Brassavola*
lady, painted *Gladiolus carneus*
lady palm *Rhapis excelsa*
lady palm, miniature *Rhapis subtilis*
lady palm, slender *Rhapis humilis*
lady tulip *Tulipa clusiana*
ladybell, fickle *Adenophora stricta*
ladybells *Adenophora*
ladybells, lilyleaf *Adenophora liliifolia*
lady's bedstraw *Galium verum*
lady's finger *Abelmoschus esculentus*
lady's leek *Allium cernuum*
lady's mantle *Alchemilla*

lady's mantle, alpine *Alchemilla alpina*
lady's slipper orchid *Cypripedium, Paphiopedilum*
lady's slipper, sand *Calceolaria uniflora*
lalang *Imperata cylindrica*
Lamarck serviceberry *Amelanchier lamarckii*
lamb's ears *Stachys byzantina*
lamb's lettuce *Valerianella locusta*
lamb's tail *Anredera cordifolia*
lamb's tails *Ptilotus semilanatus*
lamb's tongue *Scleroblitum atriplicinum*
Lamington's silky oak *Helicia lamingtoniana*
lampwick plant *Phlomis lychnitis*
lance-leaf beard-heath *Leucopogon lanceolatus*
lance-leaf cottonwood *Populus × acuminata*
lance-leaf hovea *Hovea lanceolata*
lance-leaf sundew *Drosera adelae*
lance-leaf waxberry *Myrica serrata*
lancewood *Acacia doratoxylon, Pseudopanax crassifolius*
lancewood, toothed *Pseudopanax ferox*
langkap *Arenga obtusifolia*
lantana *Lantana camara*
lantana, trailing *Lantana montevidensis*
lantern, Chinese *Abutilon, A. × hybridum, A. megapotamicum, A. pictum, Nymania capensis, Physalis alkekengi*
lantern, Diogenes' *Calochortus amabilis*
lantern heath, Chinese *Erica blenna*
lantern, Japanese *Hibiscus schizopetalus*
lantern lily, Chinese *Sandersonia aurantiaca*
lantern tree, Chile *Crinodendron hookerianum*

lantern-flower, dwarf *Abutilon fraseri*
lanterns, fairy *Calochortus*
larch *Larix*
larch, American *Larix laricina*
larch, Chinese *Larix potannii*
larch, Dahurian *Larix gmelinii*
larch, Dunkeld *Larix × marschlinsii*
larch, eastern *Larix laricina*
larch, European *Larix decidua*
larch, golden *Pseudolarix amabilis*
larch, hybrid *Larix × marschlinsii*
larch, Japanese *Larix kaempferi*
larch, Prince Rupprecht *Larix principis-rupprechtii*
larch, Siberian *Larix sibirica*
larch, Sikkim *Larix griffithiana*
larch, subalpine *Larix lyallii*
larch, tamarack *Larix laricina*
larch, western *Larix occidentalis*
large applemint *Mentha alopecuroides*
large beardtongue *Penstemon grandiflorus*
large blue fescue *Festuca amethystina*
large blue hair grass *Koeleria glauca*
large fothergilla *Fothergilla major*
large kangaroo apple *Solanum laciniatum*
large merrybells *Uvularia grandiflora*
large mudwort *Limosella curdieana*
large plantain *Plantago major*
large poroporo *Solanum laciniatum*
large prickle-vine *Caesalpinia scortechinii*
large self-heal *Prunella grandiflora*
large sour-plum *Ximenia caffra*
large thyme *Thymus pulegioides*
large tick-trefoil *Desmodium brachypodum*
large tongue-orchid *Cryptostylis subulata*
large white daisy *Brachyscome campylocarpa*
large white petunia *Petunia axillaris*

large yellow foxglove *Digitalis grandiflora*

large-cone Douglas fir *Pseudotsuga macrocarpa*

large-flowered bellwort *Uvularia grandiflora*

large-flowered bundy *Eucalyptus nortonii*

large-flowered calamint *Calamintha grandiflora*

large-flowered chickweed *Cerastium arvense*

large-flowered evening primrose *Oenothera glazioviana*

large-flowered glory bush *Tibouchina macrantha*

large-flowered ochna *Ochna atropurpurea, O. mossambicensis*

large-flowered plectranthus *Plectranthus ambiguus*

large-flowered wood-sorrel *Oxalis purpurea*

large-flowered yellow oleander *Thevetia thevetioides*

large-fruited blackbutt *Eucalyptus pyrocarpa*

large-fruited bushwillow *Combretum zeyheri*

large-fruited gray gum *Eucalyptus canaliculata*

large-fruited orange mangrove *Bruguiera gymnorhiza*

large-fruited red mahogany *Eucalyptus scias*

large-fruited tea-tree *Leptospermum macrocarpum*

large-fruited whitebeam *Sorbus megalocarpa*

large-fruited yellowjacket *Corymbia watsoniana*

large-leafed banksia *Banksia robur*

large-leafed bush-pea *Pultenaea daphnoides*

large-leafed canthium *Canthium lamprophyllum*

large-leafed guarri *Euclea natalensis, E. undulata*

large-leafed hau *Hibiscus macrophyllus*

large-leafed knobwood *Zanthoxylum gilletii*

large-leafed maidenhair *Adiantum macrophyllum*

large-leafed rock fig *Ficus abutilifolia*

large-leafed spotted gum *Corymbia henryi*

large-veined sun orchid *Thelymitra venosa*

larkspur *Consolida, C. ajacis, C. orientalis*

lasiandra *Tibouchina*

lasiandra, creeping *Heterocentron elegans*

lasiandra, trailing *Heterocentron elegans*

latan palm, blue *Latania loddigesii*

latan palm, red *Latania lontaroides*

latanier balai *Coccothrinax barbadensis*

late black wattle *Acacia mearnsii*

late tamarisk *Tamarix ramosissima*

laurel *Laurus, L. nobilis*

laurel, Alexandrian *Calophyllum inophyllum, Danäe racemosa*

laurel, alpine *Kalmia microphylla*

laurel, Arizona mountain *Sophora arizonica*

laurel, Australian *Auranticarpa rhombifolia*

laurel, bay *Laurus nobilis*

laurel, bog *Kalmia polifolia*

laurel, California *Umbellularia californica*

laurel, camphor *Cinnamomum camphora*

laurel, canary *Laurus azorica*

laurel, Chinese *Antidesma bunius*
laurel, diamond-leaf *Auranticarpa rhombifolia*
laurel, eastern bog *Kalmia polifolia*
laurel fig, Indian *Ficus microcarpa*
laurel geebung *Persoonia laurina*
laurel, glossy *Cryptocarya laevigata*
laurel, Indian *Ficus microcarpa*
laurel, Japanese *Aucuba japonica*
laurel, Macleay *Anopterus macleayanus*
laurel magnolia, great *Magnolia grandiflora*
laurel, mountain *Kalmia latifolia*
laurel oak *Quercus laurifolia*
laurel poplar *Populus laurifolia*
laurel, Portugal *Prunus lusitanica*
laurel rhododendron, great *Rhododendron maximum*
laurel, sheep *Kalmia angustifolia*
laurel, Sierra *Leucothoe davisiae*
laurel, small-leafed *Cryptocarya williwilliana*
laurel, spurge *Daphne laureola*
laurel, swamp *Kalmia polifolia, Magnolia virginiana*
laurel, Tasmanian *Anopterus glandulosus*
laurel, Texas mountain *Sophora secundiflora*
laurel, true *Laurus nobilis*
laurel willow *Salix pentandra*
laurel-cherry *Prunus laurocerasus*
laurel-cherry, Carolina *Prunus caroliniana*
laurel-cherry, West Indian *Prunus myrtifolia*
laurel-leaf grevillea *Grevillea laurifolia*
laurel-leafed rock rose *Cistus laurifolius*
laurustinus *Viburnum tinus*
Lavalle hawthorn *Crataegus × lavallei*
lavatera, tree *Lavatera olbia*

lavender *Lavandula, L. angustifolia*
lavender, Canary Island *Lavandula canariensis, L. pinnata*
lavender, English *Lavandula angustifolia*
lavender fever berry *Croton gratissimus*
lavender, French *Lavandula stoechas*
lavender, green *Lavandula viridis*
lavender grevillea *Grevillea lavandulacea*
lavender, hybrid *Lavandula × allardii*
lavender, Italian *Lavandula stoechas*
lavender pebbles *Graptopetalum amethystinum*
lavender, sea *Limonium*
lavender, Spanish *Lavandula stoechas*
lavender, spike *Lavandula latifolia*
lavender, toothed *Lavandula dentata*
lavender tree *Heteropyxis natalensis*
lavender, woolly *Lavandula lanata*
lavender-cotton *Santolina chamaecyparissus*
lawn chamomile *Chamaemelum nobile* 'Treneague'
lawn daisy *Bellis perennis*
Lawson cypress *Chamaecyparis lawsoniana*
Lawson cypress, golden *Chamaecyparis lawsoniana* 'Stewartii'
Lawson's cliff fern *Woodsia × gracilis*
lawyer, bush *Calamus muelleri*
lawyer cane *Calamus*
lawyer cane, fishtail *Calamus caryotoides*
lawyer cane, southern *Calamus muelleri*
lawyer palm *Calamus muelleri*
lawyer vine *Smilax australis*
lead tree *Leucaena leucocephala*
lead tree, little-leaf *Leucaena retusa*
leadplant *Amorpha canescens*

leadwort *Plumbago*
leadwort, Cape *Plumbago auriculata*
leadwort, scarlet *Plumbago indica*
leaf, blanket *Blandfordia arborescens*
leaf celery *Apium graveolens* var.
   secalinum
leaf, platter *Coccoloba uvifera*
leaf, rusty *Menziesia ferruginea*
leafless ballart *Exocarpos aphyllus*
leafless bird of paradise *Strelitzia
   juncea*
leafless globe-pea *Sphaerolobium
   minus, S. vimineum*
leafless sourbush *Omphacomeria
   acerba*
leafy bossiaea *Bossiaea foliosa*
leafy cactus *Pereskia bahiensis*
leafy daisy *Brachyscome rigidula*
leafy flat-sedge *Cyperus lucidus*
leafy lichen *Lobaria*
leafy nineawn *Enneapogon polyphyllus*
leafy panic *Urochloa foliosa*
leafy purple-flag *Patersonia glabrata*
leafy reed grass *Calamagrostis foliosa*
leafy twig-rush *Cladium procerum*
leather fern *Rumohra adiantiformis*
leather fern, giant *Acrostichum
   danaeifolium*
leather jacket *Barklya syringifolia,
   Geissois benthamii*
leather vine *Clematis*
leather wood fern *Dryopteris
   marginalis*
leatherleaf *Chamaedaphne calyculata*
leatherleaf fern *Rumohra
   adiantiformis*
leatherleaf mahonia *Mahonia bealei*
leatherwood *Cyrilla racemiflora,
   Dirca, D. palustris*
leatherwood, American *Cyrilla*
leatherwood, eastern *Eucryphia moorei*
leatherwood, mountain *Eucryphia
   milliganii*

leatherwood, Tasmanian *Eucryphia
   lucida*
leatherwood, western *Dirca
   occidentalis*
leathery polypody *Polypodium
   scouleri*
Lebanon, cedar of *Cedrus libani*
Lebanon oak *Quercus libani*
lebombo euphorbia *Euphorbia
   confinalis*
ledges, Easter *Persicaria bistorta*
ledum boronia *Boronia ledifolia*
ledum, marsh *Ledum palustre*
leech lime *Citrus hystrix*
leek *Allium ampeloprasum* Porrum
   Group
leek, few-flowered *Allium paradoxum*
leek, Japanese *Allium fistulosum*
leek, lady's *Allium cernuum*
leek lily *Bulbine semibarbata*
leek, native *Bulbine bulbosa*
leek orchid *Prasophyllum*
leek orchid, tall *Prasophyllum elatum*
leek orchid, yellow *Prasophyllum
   flavum*
leek, round-headed *Allium
   sphaerocephalon*
leek, sand *Allium scorodoprasum*
leek, wild *Allium ampeloprasum*
lehua, ohi'a *Metrosideros polymorpha*
Leichhardt bean *Cassia brewsteri*
Leichhardt tree *Nauclea orientalis*
lelo palm *Pritchardia hillebrandii*
lemoendoring *Cassinopsis ilicifolia*
lemon *Citrus* × *limon*
lemon balm *Melissa officinalis*
lemon bergamot *Monarda citriodora*
lemon bottlebrush *Callistemon
   pallidus*
lemon, bush *Citrus jambhiri*
lemon, dwarf *Citrus* × *limon* 'Meyer'
lemon, Eureka *Citrus* × *limon*
   'Eureka'

lemon grass *Cymbopogon citratus*
lemon lily *Hemerocallis dumortieri*
lemon, Lisbon *Citrus* × *limon* 'Lisbon'
lemon, Meyer *Citrus* × *meyeri* 'Meyer'
lemon mint *Mentha* × *piperita* var. *citrata*
lemon pistol bush *Duvernoia aconitiflora*
lemon, rough *Citrus jambhiri*
lemon starbush *Asterolasia asteriscophora*
lemon sumach *Rhus aromatica*
lemon, sweet *Citrus limetta*
lemon thyme *Thymus* × *citriodorus*
lemon thyme, gold-leafed *Thymus* × *citriodorus* 'Aureus'
lemon thyme, variegated *Thymus* × *citriodorus* 'Silver Queen'
lemon vine *Pereskia aculeata*
lemon, wild *Canthium latifolium, C. oleifolium*
lemonade sumac *Rhus integrifolia*
lemonball *Leucaena retusa*
lemon-flowered gum *Eucalyptus woodwardii*
lemon-scented darwinia *Darwinia citriodora*
lemon-scented geranium *Pelargonium crispum*
lemon-scented gum *Corymbia citriodora*
lemon-scented myrtle *Backhousia citriodora*
lemon-scented tea-tree *Leptospermum petersonii*
lemon-scented thyme *Thymus* × *citriodorus*
lemon-scented verbena *Aloysia citriodora, A. triphylla*
lemonwood *Pittosporum eugenioides*
lenga *Nothofagus pumilio*
Lent lily *Narcissus pseudonarcissus*

Lenten rose *Helleborus, H. orientalis*
lentil *Lens culinaris*
lentisco *Pistacia lentiscus, P. texana, Rhus virens*
leopard ash *Flindersia collina*
leopard lily *Belamcanda chinensis*
leopard orchid *Diuris maculata*
leopard plant *Farfugium japonicum* 'Aureo-maculatum'
leopard tree *Caesalpinia ferrea*
leopard tree, broad-leafed *Flindersia collina*
leopard's bane *Doronicum, D. orientale*
leopardwood *Flindersia maculosa*
leper lily *Fritillaria meleagris*
leschenaultia, blue *Leschenaultia biloba*
leschenaultia, red *Lechenaultia formosa*
leschenaultia, wreath *Leschenaultia macrantha*
lespedeza, perennial *Lespedeza juncea*
Lesser Antilles silver thatch *Coccothrinax barbadensis*
lesser bottlebrush *Callistemon phoeniceus*
lesser calamint *Calamintha nepeta*
lesser Canary grass *Phalaris minor*
lesser celandine *Ranunculus ficaria*
lesser chickweed *Stellaria pallida*
lesser flannel flower *Actinotus minor*
lesser galangal *Alpinia calcarata*
lesser hawkbit *Leontodon taraxacoides*
lesser honeysuckle tree *Turraea obtusifolia*
lesser joyweed *Alternanthera denticulata*
lesser knotweed *Persicaria campanulata*
lesser periwinkle *Vinca minor*
lesser spearwort *Ranunculus flammula*

lesser swinecress *Coronopus didymus*
lesser tree mallow *Lavatera cretica*
lesser yam *Dioscorea esculenta*
lettuce *Lactuca*
lettuce, chalk *Dudleya pulverulenta*
lettuce, common *Lactuca sativa*
lettuce, lamb's *Valerianella locusta*
lettuce, miner's *Montia perfoliata*
lettuce, oakleaf *Lactuca sativa*
 'Oakleaf'
lettuce, prickly *Lactuca serriola*
lettuce, sea *Scaevola taccada*
lettuce, water *Pistia stratiotes*
lettuce, willow-leafed *Lactuca saligna*
Levant garlic *Allium ampeloprasum*
Lewis mock orange *Philadelphus
 lewisii*
Lewis syringa *Philadelphus lewisii*
Leyland cypress × *Cuprocyparis
 leylandii*
Liberian coffee *Coffea liberica*
libertia, showy *Libertia formosa*
lichen, leafy *Lobaria*
licorice *Glycyrrhiza glabra*
licorice, Chinese *Glycyrrhiza uralensis*
licorice fern *Polypodium glycyrrhiza*
licorice mint *Agastache rupestris*
licorice, native *Glycyrrhiza
 acanthocarpa*
licorice plant *Helichrysum petiolare*
lifebuoy plant *Huernia zebrina*
lightwood *Acacia implexa*
lignum *Muehlenbeckia florulenta*
lignum, climbing *Muehlenbeckia
 adpressa*
lignum, flowering *Eremophila
 polyclada*
lignum-vitae *Guaiacum officinale*
lignum-vitae, holywood *Guaiacum
 sanctum*
ligularia, Shavalski's *Ligularia
 przewalskii*
Lijiang spruce *Picea likiangensis*

lilac *Syringa, S. vulgaris*
lilac, Afghan *Syringa protolaciniata*
lilac, American hybrid *Syringa ×
 hyacinthiflora*
lilac, Australian *Hardenbergia
 comptoniana*
lilac bottlebrush *Callistemon
 'Lilacinus'*
lilac, broadleaf *Syringa oblata*
lilac, California *Ceanothus,
 C. thyrsiflorus*
lilac, Cape *Virgilia oroboides*
lilac, Catalina mountain *Ceanothus
 arboreus*
lilac, Chinese *Syringa × chinensis*
lilac, Chinese tree *Syringa pekinensis*
lilac, common *Syringa vulgaris*
lilac, cut-leafed *Syringa laciniata*
lilac daphne *Daphne genkwa*
lilac, dwarf Korean *Syringa meyeri*
lilac, early flowering *Syringa ×
 hyacinthiflora*
lilac felicia *Felicia fruticosa*
lilac, French hybrid *Syringa vulgaris*
lilac, Hottentot's *Ehretia rigida*
lilac, Hungarian *Syringa josikaea*
lilac, hyacinth *Syringa ×
 hyacinthiflora*
lilac, Japanese tree *Syringa reticulata*
lilac lily *Schelhammera undulata*
lilac, Meyer *Syringa meyeri*
lilac, New Zealand *Heliohebe hulkeana*
lilac, nodding *Syringa × prestoniae*
lilac, Peking *Syringa pekinensis*
lilac, Persian *Melia azedarach,
 Syringa × persica*
lilac, Preston *Syringa × prestoniae*
lilac sage *Salvia verticillata*
lilac, St Vincent *Solanum
 seaforthianum*
liilac, Skinner hybrid *Syringa ×
 hyacinthiflora*
lilac, summer *Buddleja colvilei*

lilac, wild *Ceanothus sanguineus*
lilac, Yunnan *Syringa yunnanensis*
lilian, blonde *Erythronium albidum*
lilies, straw *Uvularia sessilifolia*
lillypilly *Acmena smithii*
lillypilly, blue *Syzygium oleosum*
lillypilly, broad-leafed *Acmena hemilampra*
lillypilly, powderpuff *Syzygium wilsonii*
lillypilly, red *Syzygium hodgkinsoniae*
lillypilly, small-leafed *Syzygium luehmannii*
lillypilly, weeping *Waterhousea floribunda*
lily *Lilium*
lily, Abyssinian sword *Gladiolus callianthus*
lily, African *Agapanthus, A. africanus*
lily, African corn *Ixia*
lily, Amazon *Eucharis*
lily, American Turk's cap *Lilium superbum*
lily, arum *Zantedeschia, Z. aethiopica*
lily, Asiatic poison *Crinum asiaticum*
lily, atamasco *Zephyranthes atamasco*
lily, August *Hosta plantaginea*
lily, Aztec *Sprekelia formosissima*
lily, bamboo *Lilium japonicum*
lily, Barbados *Hippeastrum puniceum*
lily, beach *Crinum pedunculatum*
lily, belladona *Amaryllis belladonna*
lily, Bermuda *Lilium longiflorum*
lily, blackberry *Belamcanda chinensis*
lily, blood *Haemanthus coccineus, Scadoxus, S. multiflorus*
lily, blue grass *Caesia parviflora* var. *vittata*
lily, blueberry *Dianella caerulea*
lily, boat *Tradescantia spathacea*
lily, bog *Monochoria cyanea*
lily, broad-leaf palm *Cordyline petiolaris*

lily, bugle *Watsonia*
lily, bulbine *Bulbine bulbosa*
lily, butterfly *Hedychium coronarium*
lily cactus, Easter *Echinopsis*
lily, calla *Zantedeschia, Z. aethiopica*
lily, canna *Canna*
lily, chequered *Fritillaria meleagris*
lily, Chinese lantern *Sandersonia aurantiaca*
lily, climbing *Gloriosa superba*
lily, club-fruit *Corynotheca lateriflora, C. licrota*
lily, cobra *Arisaema speciosum, Darlingtonia californica*
lily, Columbia *Lilium columbianum*
lily, Columbia tiger *Lilium columbianum*
lily, coral *Lilium pumilum*
lily, corn *Ixia*
lily, cradle *Tradescantia spathacea*
lily, creeping *Gloriosa superba*
lily, Cuban *Scilla peruviana*
lily, cunjevoi *Alocasia brisbanensis*
lily, custard *Hemerocallis lilio-asphodelus*
lily, darling *Crinum flaccidum*
lily, devil *Lilium lancifolium*
lily, dobo *Cyrtanthus brachyscyphus*
lily, double tiger *Lilium lancifolium* 'Flore Pleno'
lily, Easter *Lilium longiflorum*
lily, European white *Nymphaea alba*
lily, fawn *Erythronium californicum*
lily, fire *Clivia miniata, Cyrtanthus*
lily, fireball *Scadoxus multiflorus*
lily, flame *Gloriosa superba*
lily, flax *Phormium*
lily, Florida swamp *Crinum americanum*
lily, forest *Veltheimia bracteata*
lily, formosa toad *Tricyrtis formosana*
lily, foxtail *Eremurus*
lily, garland *Calostemma, Hedychium*

lily, George *Cyrtanthus elatus*
lily, giant *Cardiocrinum, Doryanthes excelsa*
lily, gigantic *Doryanthes palmeri*
lily, ginger *Alpinia, Hedychium, H. coronarium, H. gardnerianum*
lily, glory *Gloriosa superba*
lily, golden spider *Lycoris aurea*
lily, golden-rayed *Lilium auratum*
lily, grass *Caesia parviflora*
lily, greentip fire *Clivia nobilis*
lily, Guernsey *Nerine sarniensis*
lily, Gymea *Doryanthes excelsa*
lily, hairy toad *Tricyrtis hirta*
lily, Himalayan giant *Cardiocrinum giganteum*
lily, hurricane *Lycoris aurea*
lily, ifafa *Cyrtanthus mackenii*
lily, Illawarra *Doryanthes excelsa*
lily, impala *Adenium obesum*
lily, Jacobean *Sprekelia formosissima*
lily, Jersey *Amaryllis belladonna*
lily, Josephine's *Brunsvigia josephinae*
lily, kaffir *Clivia miniata, Schizostylis coccinea*
lily, knight's star *Hippeastrum*
lily, leek *Bulbine semibarbata*
lily, lemon *Hemerocallis dumortieri*
lily, Lent *Narcissus pseudonarcissus*
lily, leopard *Belamcanda chinensis*
lily, leper *Fritillaria meleagris*
lily, lilac *Schelhammera undulata*
lily, madonna *Lilium candidum*
lily, magic *Lycoris squamigera*
lily, March *Amaryllis belladonna*
lily, May *Maianthemum bifolium*
lily, Mexican *Hippeastrum reginae*
lily, Mount Cook *Ranunculus lyallii*
lily, November *Lilium longiflorum*
lily of the Incas *Alstroemeria*
lily of the Nile *Agapanthus, A. praecox*
lily of the palace *Hippeastrum aulicum*

lily of the valley *Convallaria majalis*
lily of the valley, false *Maianthemum bifolium*
lily of the valley, golden *Sandersonia aurantiaca*
lily of the valley, pampas *Salpichroa origanifolia*
lily of the valley, star-flowered *Smilacina stellata*
lily, Oregon *Lilium columbianum*
lily, palm *Cordyline petiolaris, C. rubra, Molineria capitulata, Yucca gloriosa*
lily, paradise *Paradisea liliastrum*
lily, peace *Spathiphyllum*
lily, Peruvian *Alstroemeria*
lily, pineapple *Eucomis*
lily, pink porcelain *Alpinia zerumbet*
lily, plantain *Hosta, H. plantaginea*
lily, plumosa fern *Asparagus setaceus*
lily, pond *Nymphaea odorata*
lily, Poor Knights *Xeronema callistemon*
lily, queen *Phaedranassa*
lily, red ginger *Hedychium coccineum*
lily, regal *Lilium regale*
lily, resurrection *Lycoris squamigera*
lily, rock *Arthropodium cirratum, Dendrobium speciosum*
lily, St Bernard's *Anthericum liliago*
lily, St Bruno's *Paradisea liliastrum*
lily, St James' *Sprekelia formosissima*
lily, St Joseph's *Hippeastrum vittatum*
lily, sand *Corynotheca lateriflora*
lily, Scarborough *Cyrtanthus elatus*
lily, scarlet ginger *Hedychium coccineum*
lily, scrambling *Geitonoplesium cymosum*
lily, Siberian *Ixiolirion tataricum*
lily, Siskiyou *Fritillaria glauca*
lily, slender palm *Cordyline stricta*
lily, snake's head *Fritillaria meleagris*

lily, spear *Doryanthes palmeri*
lily, spider *Hymenocallis, Lycoris, Nerine, Tradescantia*
lily, spoon *Alocasia brisbanensis*
lily, star *Zigadenus fremontii*
lily, stink *Typhonium brownii*
lily, swamp *Ottelia ovalifolia*
lily, sword *Gladiolus*
lily, tartar *Ixiolirion tataricum*
lily, tiger *Lilium lancifolium*
lily, toad *Tricyrtis, T. hirta*
lily, torch *Kniphofia, Veltheimia bracteata*
lily, triplet *Triteleia laxa*
lily, trout *Erythronium*
lily tree *Magnolia denudata*
lily, trumpet *Lilium longiflorum*
lily, Turk's-cap *Lilium martagon*
lily, vanilla *Arthropodium milleflorum, Sowerbaea juncea*
lily vine, Easter *Beaumontia grandiflora*
lily, voodoo *Sauromatum venosum*
lily, white *Lilium candidum*
lily, white pineapple *Eucomis autumnalis*
lily, wood *Trillium*
lily-flowered magnolia *Magnolia liliiflora*
lilyleaf ladybells *Adenophora liliifolia*
lily-of-the-valley bush *Pieris japonica*
lily-of-the-valley tree *Clethra arborea*
lily-turf *Liriope, Ophiopogon*
lima bean *Phaseolus lunatus*
limber pine *Pinus flexilis*
lime *Citrus × aurantiifolia*
lime, Australian finger *Citrus australasica*
lime berry *Triphasia trifolia*
lime, broad-leafed *Tilia platyphyllos*
lime, caffre *Citrus hystrix*
lime, common *Tilia × europaea*
lime, desert *Citrus glauca*

lime, European white *Tilia tomentosa*
lime, finger *Citrus australasica*
lime, house *Sparmannia*
lime, Japanese *Tilia japonica*
lime, kaffir *Citrus hystrix*
lime, leech *Citrus hystrix*
lime, mock *Aglaia odorata*
lime, Mongolian *Tilia mongolica*
lime, myrtle *Triphasia trifolia*
lime, Oliver's *Tilia oliveri*
lime, pendent silver *Tilia* 'Petiolaris'
lime, Rangpur *Citrus × limonia*
lime, Siberian *Tilia sibirica*
lime, silver *Tilia tomentosa*
lime, small-leafed *Tilia cordata*
lime, sweet *Citrus limetta*
lime, Tahitian *Citrus × latifolia*
lime tree, bird *Pisonia umbellifera*
lime, weeping silver *Tilia* 'Petiolaris'
limebush *Citrus glauca*
lime-leafed maple *Acer distylum*
lime-scented geranium *Pelargonium* 'Nervosum'
limestone bugle *Ajuga pyramidalis*
limestone copperburr *Sclerolaena obliquicuspis*
limestone spleenwort *Asplenium trichomanes*
linaria *Linaria maroccana*
Lincoln weed *Diplotaxis tenuifolia*
linden *Tilia, T. × europaea, T. platyphyllos*
linden, African *Sparmannia africana*
linden, American *Tilia americana*
linden, Amur *Tilia amurensis*
linden, bigleaf *Tilia platyphyllos*
linden, broad-leafed *Tilia platyphyllos*
linden, Caucasian *Tilia caucasica*
linden, common *Tilia × europaea*
linden, Japanese *Tilia japonica*
linden, Korean *Tilia insularis*
linden, Kyushu *Tilia kiusiana*
linden, Mongolian *Tilia mongolica*

linden, silver *Tilia tomentosa*
linden, small-leafed *Tilia cordata*
linden viburnum *Viburnum dilatatum*
linear-leaf grevillea *Grevillea linearifolia*
ling *Calluna vulgaris*
ling nut *Trapa bicornis*
lion's beard *Geum triflorum*
lion's foot *Alchemilla*
lion's tail *Leonotis leonurus*
lip fern *Cheilanthes*
lippia *Phyla nodiflora*
lipstick palm *Cyrtostachys renda*
lipstick plant *Aeschynanthus radicans, Bixa orellana*
liquidambar *Liquidambar styraciflua*
liquidambar, Chinese *Liquidambar formosana*
liquidambar, Turkish *Liquidambar orientalis*
liquorice *see* licorice
Lisbon lemon *Citrus* × *limon* 'Lisbon'
lisianthus *Eustoma grandiflorum*
little fendlerbush *Fendlerella utahensis*
little gem sarchochilus *Sarcochilus hillii*
little leaf cordia *Cordia parvifolia*
little merrybells *Uvularia sessilifolia*
little mountain palm *Lepidorrhachis mooreana*
little owl *Huernia zebrina*
little pickles *Othonna capensis*
little shellbark hickory *Carya ovata*
Little Sur manzanita *Arctostaphylos edmundsii*
little sword-sedge *Lepidosperma lineare*
little-leaf lead tree *Leucaena retusa*
little-leaf linden *Tilia cordata*
little-leaf pussytoes *Antennaria microphylla*

little-leafed sage *Salvia microphylla*
live oak *Quercus virginiana*
live oak, California *Quercus agrifolia*
live oak, canyon *Quercus chrysolepis*
live oak, coast *Quercus agrifolia*
live oak, interior *Quercus wislizeni*
live oak, shrub *Quercus turbinella*
live plant *Bryophyllum pinnatum*
live-forever *Sedum telephium*
liverseed grass *Urochloa panicoides*
liverwort, floating *Ricciocarpos natans*
living stones *Lithops*
Livingstone daisy *Dorotheanthus bellidiformis*
lizard's tail *Crassula muscosa, Saururus cernuus*
lobed wallaby grass *Austrodanthonia auriculata*
lobed-leaf hopbush *Dodonaea lobulata*
lobed-seeded daisy *Brachyscome heterodonta*
lobelia, angled *Lobelia alata*
lobelia, bedding *Lobelia erinus*
lobelia, big blue *Lobelia siphilitica*
lobelia, Chinese *Lobelia chinensis*
lobelia, edging *Lobelia erinus*
lobelia, forest *Lobelia trigonocaulis*
lobelia, giant *Lobelia telekii*
lobelia, golden *Monopsis lutea*
lobelia, milky *Pratia concolor*
lobelia, scarlet *Lobelia splendens*
lobelia, tall *Lobelia gibbosa*
lobelia, torch *Lobelia laxiflora*
lobelia, trailing *Lobelia gracilis*
loblolly bay *Gordonia lasianthus*
loblolly pine *Pinus taeda*
lobster claw *Heliconia*
lobster pot *Sarracenia psittacina*
lobster's claw *Clianthus puniceus*
locust, black *Robinia pseudoacacia*
locust, bristly *Robinia fertilis*
locust, Caspian *Gleditsia caspica*

locust, Chinese *Gleditsia sinensis*
locust, clammy *Robinia viscosa*
locust fern *Osmunda regalis*
locust, honey *Gleditsia triacanthos*
locust, Japanese *Gleditsia japonica*
locust, water *Gleditsia aquatica*
lodgepole pine *Pinus contorta,*
P. c. var. *latifolia*
Loebner magnolia *Magnolia* ×
loebneri
loganberry *Rubus loganobaccus*
logania, narrow-leaf *Logania albiflora*
logania, tiny *Logania pusilla*
lohan pine *Podocarpus macrophyllus*
lolly bush *Clerodendrum floribundum*
lomatia, river *Lomatia myricoides*
lomatium, Bradshaw's *Lomatium*
bradshawii
Lombardy poplar *Populus nigra*
'Italica'
Lompoc manzanita *Arctostaphylos*
purissima
London plane *Platanus* × *hispanica*
London pride *Saxifraga* × *urbium*
London rocket *Sisymbrium irio*
long clubmoss *Huperzia varia*
long graybeard grass *Amphipogon*
caricinus
long jack *Flindersia xanthoxyla*
long pepper, Indian *Piper longum*
longan *Dimocarpus longan*
long-flowered beard-heath
Leucopogon juniperinus
long-flowered evening primrose
Oenothera affinis
long-fruited bloodwood *Corymbia*
dolichocarpa
long-haired plume grass *Dichelachne*
crinita
long-head coneflower *Ratibida*
columnifera
long-leaf coneseeds *Conospermum*
longifolium

long-leaf corkwood *Hakea suberea*
long-leaf hovea *Hovea longifolia*
long-leaf mahonia *Mahonia nervosa*
long-leaf pine *Pinus palustris*
long-leaf pine, Himalayan *Pinus*
roxburghii
long-leaf star-hair *Astrotricha*
longifolia
long-leaf wallaby grass
Notodanthonia longifolia
long-leaf wax flower *Philotheca*
myoporoides
long-spined copperburr *Sclerolaena*
longicuspis
long-style grevillea *Grevillea longistyla*
long-styled knight's star lily
Hippeastrum stylosum
lontar palm *Borassus flabellifer,*
B. sundaicus
loofah *Luffa cylindrica*
looking-glass plant *Coprosma repens*
loose silky bent *Apera spica-venti*
loose-flower bush-pea *Pultenaea*
laxiflora
loosestrife *Lysimachia, Lythrum*
loosestrife, gooseneck *Lysimachia*
clethroides
loosestrife, hyssop *Lythrum hyssopifolia*
loosestrife, purple *Lythrum salicaria,*
L. virgatum
loosestrife, small *Lythrum hyssopifolia*
loosestrife, striped *Lythrum salicaria*
loquat *Eriobotrya japonica*
Lord Howe blue plum *Chionanthus*
quadristamineus
Lord Howe hotbark *Zygogynum*
howeanum
Lord Howe mountain rose
Metrosideros nervulosa
Lord Howe pittosporum *Pittosporum*
erioloma
Lord Howe tea-tree *Leptospermum*
polygalifolium subsp. *howense*

Lord Howe wedding lily *Dietes robinsoniana*
lords and ladies *Arum maculatum*
lotus *Nymphaea lotus*
lotus, American *Nelumbo lutea*
lotus, bicolored *Lotus formosissimus*
lotus, coast *Lotus formosissimus*
lotus fruit *Ziziphus lotus*
lotus, red-flowering *Lotus cruentus*
lotus, sacred *Nelumbo nucifera*
lotus, scarlet *Lotus berthelotii*
loulou *Pritchardia hillebrandii*
lovage *Levisticum officinale*
lovage, black *Smyrnium olusatrum*
lovage, Sichuan *Ligusticum wallichii*
love apple *Lycopersicon esculentum, Mandragora officinarum*
love, chain of *Antigonon leptopus*
love creeper *Comesperma volubile*
love grass *Eragrostis*
love grass, African *Eragrostis curvula*
love grass, Brown's *Eragrostis brownii*
love grass, clustered *Eragrostis elongata*
love grass, mallee *Eragrostis dielsii*
love grass, Mexican *Eragrostis mexicana*
love grass, paddock *Eragrostis leptostachya*
love grass, purple *Eragrostis lacunaria*
love grass, weeping *Eragrostis curvula*
love parsley *Levisticum officinale*
love-in-a-mist *Nigella damascena, Passiflora foetida*
love-in-a-puff *Cardiospermum grandiflorum*
love-in-idleness *Viola tricolor*
love-lies-bleeding *Amaranthus caudatus*
lovely penstemon *Penstemon venustus*
love's chain *Antigonon leptopus*
low poppy mallow *Callirhoe involucrata*

lowbush blueberry *Vaccinium angustifolium*
lowveld cabbage tree *Cussonia spicata*
lowveld chestnut *Sterculia murex*
lowveld euphorbia *Euphorbia evansii*
lucerne *Medicago sativa*
lucerne, Paddy's *Sida rhombifolia*
lucerne, tree *Chamaecytisus palmensis*
lucky bean tree *Erythrina lysistemon*
lucky nut *Thevetia peruviana*
Lucuba palm *Dypsis lucubensis*
ludo wild oats *Avena ludoviciana*
lulo *Solanum quitoense*
Lumholtz pine *Pinus lumholtzii*
lung ngaan *Dimocarpus longan*
lungwort *Pulmonaria*
lungwort, blue *Pulmonaria angustifolia*
lupin *Lupinus*
lupin, Carolina *Thermopsis villosa*
lupin, false *Thermopsis, T. rhombifolia*
lupin, tree *Lupinus arboreus*
lupine *Lupinus*
lupine, arroyo *Lupinus succentulus*
lupine, blue *Lupinus perennis*
lupine, blue-pod *Lupinus polyphyllus*
lupine, foothill *Lupinus succulentus*
lupine, hollowleaf annual *Lupinus succulentus*
lupine, silver *Lupinus albifrons*
lupine, silver bush *Lupinus albifrons*
lupine, sundial *Lupinus perennis*
lupine, wild *Lupinus perennis*
lupine, yellow bush *Lupinus arboreus*
lupins, Russell *Lupinus* Russell Hybrids
Lusitanian oak *Quercus faginea*
lychee *Litchi chinensis*
lyme grass *Leymus arenarius*
lyme grass, sea *Leymus arenarius*
lyonia, rusty *Lyonia ferruginea*
lyre-leaf green eyes *Berlandiera lyrata*

M

ma tai *Eleocharis dulcis*
maackia, Amur *Maackia amurensis*
Mabel's wattle *Acacia mabellae*
mabie *Colubrina arborescens*
mabola *Diospyros blancoi*
macadamia nut *Macadamia
    tetraphylla*
macadamia nut, smooth-shelled
    Macadamia integrifolia
macap, rotan *Daemonorops longipes*
Macarthur palm *Ptychosperma
    macarthurii*
Macartney rose *Rosa bracteata*
Macassar ebony *Diospyros celebica*
macaw fat *Elaeis guineensis*
macaw flower *Heliconia bihai*
macaw palm *Acrocomia aculeata,
    A. totai, A. vinifera, Aiphanes erosa*
mace *Myristica fragrans*
mace sedge *Carex grayi*
mace, sweet *Tagetes lucida*
Macedonian oak *Quercus trojana*
Macedonian pine *Pinus peuce*
macho fern *Nephrolepis falcata*
Mackay cedar *Paraserianthes toona*
McKie's stringybark *Eucalyptus
    mckieana*
Macleay laurel *Anopterus macleayanus*
McMinn's manzanita *Arctostaphylos
    viridissima*
Macquarie grape *Muehlenbeckia
    gunnii*
Macquarie Island cabbage *Stilbocarpa
    polaris*
Macquarie vine *Muehlenbeckia
    gunnii*
Macrae's hakea *Hakea macraeana*
Madagascar doum palm *Hyphaene
    schatan*

Madagascar ordeal tree *Cerbera
    venenifera*
Madagascar pepper *Piper nigrum*
Madagascar periwinkle *Catharanthus
    roseus*
Madagascar plum *Flacourtia indica*
Madagascar ragwort *Senecio
    madagascariensis*
Madagascar rubber vine *Cryptostegia
    madagascariensis*
Madagascar spur flower *Plectranthus
    madagascariensis*
madake bamboo *Phyllostachys
    bambusoides*
madder *Rubia tinctorum*
madder, field *Sherardia arvensis*
madder, Indian *Rubia cordifolia*
madder, stinking *Putoria calabrica*
mad-dog skullcap *Scutellaria
    lateriflora*
Madeira broom *Genista tenera*
Madeira holly *Ilex perado*
Madeira, pride of *Echium candicans*
Madeira vine *Anredera cordifolia*
Madeira wax-myrtle *Myrica faya*
Madeira whortleberry *Vaccinium
    padifolium*
Madeiran orchid *Dactylorhiza
    foliosa*
maden *Weinmannia trichosperma*
madonna lily *Lilium candidum*
madre *Gliricidia sepium*
madre de cacao *Gliricidia sepium*
madreselva *Arctostaphylos pungens*
Madrid brome *Bromus madritensis*
madrone *Arbutus menziesii,
    A. xalapensis*
madrone, Pacific *Arbutus menziesii*
madwort *Alyssum*
Magellan wheatgrass *Elymus
    magellanicus*
Magellanes, coigue de *Nothofagus
    betuloides*

Magennis Bermuda grass *Cynodon ×
magennisii*

magenta brush cherry *Syzygium
paniculatum*

magenta cherry *Syzygium
paniculatum*

magenta storksbill *Pelargonium
rodneyanum*

magic flower *Cantua buxifolia*

magic guarri *Euclea divinorum*

magic lily *Lycoris squamigera*

magnificent mint-bush *Prostanthera
magnifica*

magnolia, anise *Magnolia salicifolia*

magnolia, Ashe *Magnolia ashei*

magnolia, bigleaf *Magnolia
macrophylla*

magnolia, bull bay *Magnolia
grandiflora*

magnolia, Campbell's *Magnolia
campbellii*

magnolia, ear-leafed *Magnolia fraseri*

magnolia, Fraser's *Magnolia fraseri*

magnolia, globe-flowered *Magnolia
globosa*

magnolia, glossy *Magnolia nitida*

magnolia, great laurel *Magnolia
grandiflora*

magnolia, Japanese big-leafed
Magnolia hypoleuca

magnolia, kobus *Magnolia kobus*

magnolia, lily-flowered *Magnolia
liliiflora*

magnolia, Loebner *Magnolia ×
loebneri*

magnolia, medicinal *Magnolia
officinalis*

magnolia, oyama *Magnolia sieboldii*

magnolia, port-wine *Michelia figo*

magnolia, pyramid *Magnolia
pyramidata*

magnolia, saucer *Magnolia ×
soulangeana*

magnolia, Siebold's *Magnolia
sieboldii*

magnolia, southern *Magnolia
grandiflora*

magnolia, Sprenger's *Magnolia
sprengeri*

magnolia, star *Magnolia stellata*

magnolia, tulip *Magnolia ×
soulangeana*

magnolia, umbrella *Magnolia
tripetala*

magnolia, Veitch's *Magnolia ×
veitchii*

magnolia, whitebark *Magnolia
hypoleuca*

magnolia, willow-leafed *Magnolia
salicifolia*

magnolia, Wilson's *Magnolia wilsonii*

magnolia, yulan *Magnolia denudata*

maguey de pulque *Agave salmiana*

Mahala mats *Ceanothus prostratus*

mahaleb cherry *Prunus mahaleb*

maharajah palm *Cyrtostachys renda*

mahoe *Hibiscus elatus, H. tiliaceus,
Melicytus ramiflorus*

mahoe wao *Melicytus lanceolatus*

mahogany *Swietenia*

mahogany, broad-leafed white
Eucalyptus umbra

mahogany, brush *Geissois benthamii*

mahogany, Honduras *Swietenia
macrophylla*

mahogany, mountain *Cercocarpus
montanus, Eucalyptus notabilis*

mahogany, Natal *Trichilia emetica*

mahogany, red *Eucalyptus resinifera*

mahogany, swamp *Eucalyptus robusta*

mahogany, thick-leafed *Eucalyptus
carnea*

mahogany, Tom Russell's *Lysicarpus
angustifolius*

mahogany, West Indian *Swietenia
mahogani*

mahogany, white *Eucalyptus acmenoides*
mahon stock *Malcolmia maritima*
mahonia, creeping *Mahonia repens*
mahonia, desert *Mahonia fremontii*
mahonia, leatherleaf *Mahonia bealei*
mahonia, longleaf *Mahonia nervosa*
mahuang *Ephedra sinica*
maiden grass, Formosa *Miscanthus transmorrisonensis*
maiden pink *Dianthus deltoides*
maidenbush *Andrachne phyllanthoides*
maidenhair, American *Adiantum pedatum*
maidenhair, Australian *Adiantum formosum*
maidenhair, black stem *Adiantum formosum*
maidenhair, brittle *Adiantum concinnum*
maidenhair, California *Adiantum jordanii*
maidenhair, Chilean *Adiantum excisum*
maidenhair, climbing *Lygodium microphyllum*
maidenhair, common *Adiantum capillus-veneris*
maidenhair, diamond *Adiantum trapeziforme*
maidenhair, eastern *Adiantum pedatum*
maidenhair, evergreen *Adiantum venustum*
maidenhair fern *Adiantum, A. aethiopicum, A. raddianum*
maidenhair fern, American *Adiantum pedatum*
maidenhair fern, brittle *Adiantum tenerum*
maidenhair fern, common *Adiantum aethiopicum*

maidenhair fern, delta *Adiantum raddianum*
maidenhair fern, fan *Adiantum tenerum*
maidenhair fern, five-fingered *Adiantum pedatum*
maidenhair fern, giant *Adiantum formosum*
maidenhair fern, Peruvian *Adiantum peruvianum*
maidenhair fern, rosy *Adiantum hispidulum*
maidenhair fern, rough *Adiantum hispidulum*
maidenhair fern, silver dollar *Adiantum peruvianum*
maidenhair, filmy *Adiantum diaphanum*
maidenhair, forest *Adiantum sylvaticum*
maidenhair, four-leafed *Adiantum tetraphyllum*
maidenhair, giant *Adiantum formosum, A. trapeziforme*
maidenhair, golden *Polypodium vulgare*
maidenhair, Himalayan *Adiantum venustum*
maidenhair, large-leafed *Adiantum macrophyllum*
maidenhair, plumed *Adiantum formosum*
maidenhair, southern *Adiantum capillus-veneris*
maidenhair spleenwort *Asplenium trichomanes*
maidenhair tree *Ginkgo biloba*
maidenhair, true *Adiantum capillus-veneris*
maidenhair, Venus *Adiantum capillus-veneris*
maidenhair vine *Muehlenbeckia complexa*

maiden's blush *Sloanea australis*
Maiden's gum *Eucalyptus maidenii*
Maiden's wattle *Acacia maidenii*
mairehau *Phebalium nudum*
maiten *Maytenus boaria*
maize *Zea mays*
Majorcan peony *Paeonia cambessedesii*
makaka *Plagianthus divaricatus*
makomako *Aristotelia serrata*
Malabar gourd *Cucurbita ficifolia*
Malabar nut *Justicia adhatoda*
Malabar spinach *Basella rubra*
Malay apple *Syzygium malaccense*
Malay tea *Psoralea corylifolia*
Malcolm stock *Malcolmia maritima*
male berry *Lyonia ligustrina*
male fern *Dryopteris filix-mas*
male peony *Paeonia mascula*
mallee ash, cliff *Eucalyptus cunninghamii*
mallee ash, whipstick *Eucalyptus multicaulis*
mallee, Barren Mountain *Eucalyptus approximans*
mallee, bell-fruited *Eucalyptus preissiana*
mallee bitterbush *Adriana hookeri*
mallee, blue *Eucalyptus gamophylla, E. polybractea*
mallee, Blue Mountains *Eucalyptus stricta*
mallee bluebush, erect *Maireana pentatropis*
mallee, blue-leafed *Eucalyptus gamophylla*
mallee, bookleaf *Eucalyptus kruseana*
mallee box *Eucalyptus porosa*
mallee, bull *Eucalyptus behriana*
mallee, coarse-leafed *Eucalyptus grossa*
mallee copperburr *Sclerolaena parviflora*

mallee, curly *Eucalyptus gillii*
mallee cypress-pine *Callitris verrucosa*
mallee, Desmond *Eucalyptus desmondensis*
mallee, Ettrema *Eucalyptus sturgissiana*
mallee, fluted-horn *Eucalyptus stowardii*
mallee fringe-lily *Thysanotus baueri*
mallee, giant *Eucalyptus socialis*
mallee goodenia *Goodenia willisiana*
mallee, gooseberry *Eucalyptus calycogona*
mallee goosefoot *Chenopodium desertorum*
mallee, gray *Eucalyptus morrisii*
mallee, green *Eucalyptus viridis*
mallee, Kybean *Eucalyptus kybeanensis*
mallee love grass *Eragrostis dielsii*
mallee, many-flowered *Eucalyptus cooperiana*
mallee, Mount Le Grand *Eucalyptus aquilina*
mallee, narrow-leafed *Eucalyptus angustissima*
mallee, pear-fruited *Eucalyptus pyriformis*
mallee pine *Callitris tuberculata*
mallee, Plunkett *Eucalyptus curtisii*
mallee, pointed *Eucalyptus socialis*
mallee, Pokolbin *Eucalyptus pumila*
mallee, Port Jackson *Eucalyptus obstans*
mallee, red *Eucalyptus oleosa, E. socialis*
mallee red gum *Eucalyptus nandewarica*
mallee, redbud *Eucalyptus oleosa, E. pachyphylla*
mallee, red-flowered *Eucalyptus erythronema*

mallee, ridge-fruited *Eucalyptus costata*
mallee, rose *Eucalyptus rhodantha*
mallee, round-leafed *Eucalyptus orbifolia*
mallee, sandplain *Eucalyptus ebbanoensis*
mallee, silver *Eucalyptus crucis*
mallee, Suggan Buggan *Eucalyptus saxatilis*
mallee tea-tree *Leptospermum coriaceum*
mallee, twin-leafed *Eucalyptus gamophylla*
mallee wattle *Acacia montana*
mallee, white *Eucalyptus dumosa*
mallet, swamp *Eucalyptus spathulata*
malletwood, white *Rhodamnia whiteana*
mallow *Lavatera, Malva*
mallow, annual *Lavatera trimestris*
mallow, common *Malva sylvestris*
mallow, Cretan *Lavatera cretica*
mallow, desert *Sphaeralcea ambigua*
mallow, false *Sidalcea, Sphaeralcea*
mallow, giant *Hibiscus*
mallow, globe *Sphaeralcea, S. coccinea*
mallow, high *Malva sylvestris*
mallow, musk *Malva moschata*
mallow, poppy *Callirhoe*
mallow, prairie *Sphaeralcea coccinea*
mallow, red-flower *Modiola caroliniana*
mallow, regal *Lavatera trimestris*
mallow, rose *Hibiscus moscheutos, Lavatera trimestris*
mallow, royal *Lavatera trimestris*
mallow, sea *Lavatera maritima*
mallow, small-flower *Malva parviflora*
mallow, tree *Lavatera, L. arborea*
mallow, wax *Malvaviscus arboreus*
mallow, white *Althaea officinalis*
Maltese cockspur *Centaurea melitensis*

Maltese cross *Lychnis chalcedonica*
Maltese cross rose *Rosa sericea*
malu creeper *Bauhinia vahlii*
Malva rose *Lavatera assurgentiflora*
mamey sapote *Pouteria sapota*
manac *Euterpe oleracea*
manaco *Euterpe*
manchineel *Hippomane mancinella*
Manchu cherry *Prunus tomentosa*
Manchurian alder *Alnus hirsuta*
Manchurian apricot *Prunus mandshurica*
Manchurian ash *Fraxinus mandshurica*
Manchurian bean *Glycine max*
Manchurian birch *Betula mandschurica*
Manchurian cherry *Prunus maackii*
Manchurian fir *Abies holophylla*
Manchurian maple *Acer mandshuricum*
Manchurian walnut *Juglans mandshurica*
Manchurian white birch *Betula platyphylla* var. *platyphylla*
mandarin *Citrus reticulata*
mandarin, king *Citrus × aurantium* Tangor Group
mandrake *Mandragora officinarum*
mandrake, American *Podophyllum peltatum*
mangle bobo *Bontia daphnoides*
Mangles' kangaroo paw *Anigozanthos manglesii*
mango *Mangifera indica*
mango bark *Canarium australasicum*
mangosteen *Garcinia mangostana*
mangosteen, African *Garcinia livingstonei*
mangosteen, yellow *Garcinia xanthochymus*
mangrove *Avicennia, Rhizophora, R. mangle*

mangrove acanthus *Acanthus ilicifolius*
mangrove, American *Rhizophora mangle*
mangrove, black *Bruguiera gymnorhiza*
mangrove, button *Conocarpus erecta*
mangrove fan palm *Licuala spinosa*
mangrove fern *Acrostichum speciosum*
mangrove, freshwater *Barringtonia acutangula*
mangrove, gray *Avicennia marina, A. m. var. australasica*
mangrove hibiscus *Hibiscus tiliaceus*
mangrove, milky *Excoecaria agallocha*
mangrove, red *Rhizophora mangle*
mangrove, river *Aegiceras corniculatum*
mangrove, spider *Rhizophora stylosa*
mangrove, white *Avicennia alba*
mangrove, yellow *Ceriops australis*
Manila palm *Veitchia merrillii*
manioc *Manihot esculenta*
Manitoba maple *Acer negundo*
manna ash *Fraxinus ornus*
manna grass *Glyceria*
manna gum *Eucalyptus mannifera, E. viminalis*
manna plant *Tamarix gallica*
manna wattle *Acacia microcarpa*
mansa, yerba *Anemopsis californica*
mantle, alpine lady's *Alchemilla alpina*
mantle, king's *Thunbergia erecta*
mantle, lady's *Alchemilla*
mantle, woolly *Eriochlamys behrii*
manuka *Leptospermum scoparium*
many-flowered mallee *Eucalyptus cooperiana*
many-flowered mat-rush *Lomandra multiflora*
many-headed dryandra *Dryandra polycephala*

manzanilla *Arctostaphylos pungens*
manzanita *Arctostaphylos manzanita*
manzanita, Baker's *Arctostaphylos bakeri*
manzanita bigberry *Arctostaphylos glauca*
manzanita, downy *Arctostaphylos tomentosa*
manzanita, dune *Arctostaphylos pumila*
manzanita, Fort Bragg *Arctostaphylos nummularia*
manzanita, greenleaf *Arctostaphylos patula*
manzanita, hairy *Arctostaphylos columbiana*
manzanita, heartleaf *Arctostaphylos andersonii*
manzanita, hoary *Arctostaphylos canescens*
manzanita, Ione *Arctostaphylos myrtifolia*
manzanita, island *Arctostaphylos insularis*
manzanita, Little Sur *Arctostaphylos edmundsii*
manzanita, Lompoc *Arctostaphylos purissima*
manzanita, McMinn's *Arctostaphylos viridissima*
manzanita, Monterey *Arctostaphylos hookeri*
manzanita, Pajaro *Arctostaphylos pajaroensis*
manzanita, pointed-leaf *Arctostaphylos pungens*
manzanita, sandmat *Arctostaphylos pumila*
manzanita, Santa Catalina *Arctostaphylos catalinae*
manzanita, Santa Margarita *Arctostaphylos pilosula*

manzanita, Santa Rosa *Arctostaphylos confertiflora*

manzanita, serpentine *Arctostaphylos obispoensis*

manzanita, shaggy-bark *Arctostaphylos tomentosa*

manzanita, Wells' *Arctostaphylos wellsii*

manzanita, woolly *Arctostaphylos tomentosa*

mao, chiang *Schefflera heptaphylla*

mao zhu *Phyllostachys edulis*

maple *Acer, A. saccharum*

maple, Amur *Acer tataricum*

maple, bigtooth *Acer grandidentatum*

maple, box-elder *Acer negundo*

maple, Canadian *Acer rubrum*

maple, Cappadocian *Acer cappadocicum*

maple, chalk *Acer saccharum* subsp. *leucoderme*

maple, Chinese paperbark *Acer griseum*

maple, Cretan *Acer sempervirens*

maple, dissected Japanese *Acer palmatum* Dissectum Group

maple, Father David's *Acer davidii*

maple, field *Acer campestre*

maple, forest *Cryptocarya rigida*

maple, full-moon *Acer japonicum*

maple, gray-bud snakebark *Acer rufinerve*

maple, Greek *Acer heldreichii*

maple, greenleaf Japanese *Acer palmatum*

maple, hard *Acer saccharum*

maple, hedge *Acer campestre*

maple, Heldreich's *Acer heldreichii*

maple, Hooker's *Acer sikkimense*

maple, hornbeam *Acer carpinifolium*

maple, horned *Acer diabolicum*

maple, Italian *Acer opalus*

maple, Japanese *Acer palmatum*

maple, lime-leafed *Acer distylum*

maple, Manchurian *Acer mandshuricum*

maple, Manitoba *Acer negundo*

maple, Montpelier *Acer monspessulanum*

maple, mountain *Acer spicatum*

maple, Nikko *Acer maximowiczianum, A. nikoense*

maple, Norway *Acer platanoides*

maple, Oregon *Acer macrophyllum*

maple, paperbark *Acer griseum*

maple, Père David's *Acer davidii*

maple, Queensland *Flindersia brayleyana*

maple, red *Acer rubrum*

maple, red snakebark *Acer capillipes*

maple, red-vein *Acer rufinerve*

maple, river *Acer saccharinum*

maple, rock *Acer glabrum, A. saccharum*

maple, Rocky Mountain *Acer glabrum*

maple, scarlet *Acer rubrum*

maple, Shantung *Acer truncatum*

maple, silver *Acer saccharinum*

maple, soft *Acer saccharinum*

maple, striped *Acer pensylvanicum*

maple, sugar *Acer saccharum*

maple, swamp *Acer rubrum*

maple, sycamore *Acer pseudoplatanus*

maple, Tatarian *Acer tataricum*

maple, three-flower *Acer triflorum*

maple, trident *Acer buergerianum*

maple, velvet *Acer velutinum*

maple, vine *Acer circinnatum*

maple, vine-leaf *Acer cissifolium*

maple, white *Acer saccharinum*

maple-leafed bayur *Pterospermum acerifolium*

maple-leafed begonia *Begonia dregei*

maracaibo lignum-vitae *Bulnesia arborea*

marara, rose-leaf *Caldcluvia paniculosa*
marara, southern *Vesselowskya rubifolia*
marble sheath bamboo *Chimonobambusa marmorea*
marble tree, blue *Elaeocarpus grandis*
March lily *Amaryllis belladonna*
mareer *Cordia subcordata*
marer *Cordia subcordata*
marginal wood fern *Dryopteris marginalis*
Marguerite *Argyranthemum frutescens*
Marguerite, blue *Felicia amelloides*
Marguerite daisy *Argyranthemum frutescens*
Marguerite, winter *Coreopsis maritima*
Marguerite, yellow *Argyranthemum maderense*
marigold *Calendula, Tagetes*
marigold, burr *Bidens*
marigold, Cape *Dimorphotheca pluvialis*
marigold, common *Calendula officinalis*
marigold, corn *Xanthophthalmum segetum*
marigold, desert *Baileya multiradiata*
marigold, dwarf *Schkuhria pinnata*
marigold, English *Calendula officinalis*
marigold, field *Calendula arvensis*
marigold, French *Tagetes patula*
marigold, marsh *Caltha palustris*
marigold, pot *Calendula officinalis*
marigold, Scotch *Calendula officinalis*
marigold, signet *Tagetes tenuifolia*
marigold, striped *Tagetes tenuifolia*
marigold, sweet-scented *Tagetes lucida*
marigold, wild *Baileya multiradiata*
marijuana *Cannabis sativa*

marine ivy *Cissus trifoliata*
marine vine *Cissus trifoliata*
Mariposa, proud *Calochortus superbus*
Mariposa tulip *Calochortus*
Mariposa tulip, yellow *Calochortus luteus*
maritime ceanothus *Ceanothus maritimus*
maritime pine *Pinus pinaster*
marjoram *Origanum majorana*
marjoram, common *Origanum vulgare*
marjoram, French *Origanum onites*
marjoram, hop *Origanum dictamnus*
marjoram, knotted *Origanum majorana*
marjoram, pot *Origanum onites*
marjoram, sweet *Origanum majorana*
marjoram, wild *Origanum vulgare*
marking nut *Semecarpus anacardium*
marlberry *Ardisia escallonioides*
Marlborough rock daisy *Olearia insignis*
marmalade bush *Streptosolen jamesonii*
marmalade plum *Pouteria sapota*
marn *Ulmus villosa*
maroela *Sclerocarya birrea*
maron, ti palmis *Pseudophoenix lediniana*
Maroola plum *Sclerocarya birrea*
maroon tree peony *Paeonia delavayi*
maroon-stemmed banana *Musa banksii*
marram grass *Ammophila arenaria*
marri *Corymbia calophylla*
marron, palme *Pseudophoenix lediniana*
marrow *Cucurbita, C. pepo*
marrow, vegetable *Cucurbita pepo*
marsh Afrikaner *Gladiolus tristis*
marsh Afrikaner, summer *Gladiolus tristis* var. *aestivalis*

marsh andromeda *Andromeda polifolia*
marsh blue violet *Viola cucullata*
marsh fern *Thelypteris palustris*
marsh foxtail *Alopecurus geniculatus*
marsh grass *Spartina, S. pectinata*
marsh horsetail *Equisetum palustre*
marsh ledum *Ledum palustre*
marsh mallow *Althaea officinalis*
marsh marigold *Caltha palustris*
marsh orchid *Dactylorhiza*
marsh orchid, broad-leafed *Dactylorhiza majalis*
marsh orchid, early *Dactylorhiza incarnata*
marsh orchid, robust *Dactylorhiza elata*
marsh pitcher *Heliamphora*
marsh reed *Phleum*
marsh samphire *Salicornia europaea*
marsh trefoil *Menyanthes trifoliata*
marsh watercress *Rorippa palustris*
marsh-cress, perennial *Rorippa laciniata*
marsh-flower, erect *Villarsia exaltata*
marshwort, wavy *Nymphoides crenata*
martagon *Lilium martagon*
Martha Washington geranium *Pelargonium* Regal Hybrid
maruba *Hosta plantaginea*
marula *Sclerocarya birrea*
marvel of Peru *Mirabilis jalapa*
Mary, blue-eyed *Collinsia parviflora, Omphalodes verna*
Mary, tears of *Fritillaria imperialis*
mascarene grass *Zoysia tenuifolia*
mask flower *Alonsoa, A. warscewiczii*
masterwort *Astrantia*
masterwort, greater *Astrantia major*
mastic, Atlas *Pistacia atlantica*
mastic tree *Pistacia lentiscus*
masusa *Renealmia alpinia*
mat daisy *Raoulia*

mat grass *Hemarthria uncinata*
mat saltbush *Atriplex prostrata*
mat, Siskiyou *Ceanothus pumilus*
mata *Histiopteris incisa*
mata ajam *Clerodendrum buchananii, C. speciosissimum*
matai *Prumnopitys taxifolia*
matchstick plant *Aechmea gamosepala*
maté *Ilex paraguariensis*
matgrass *Hemarthria uncinata, Phyla nodiflora*
matico, false *Piper aduncum*
Matilija poppy *Romneya coulteri*
mat-plant, dense *Herniaria hirsuta*
matrimony vine *Lycium*
matrimony vine, common *Lycium barbarum*
mat-rush *Lomandra*
mat-rush, clumping *Lomandra banksii*
mat-rush, many-flowered *Lomandra multiflora*
mat-rush, needle *Lomandra cylindrica*
mat-rush, pale *Lomandra glauca*
mat-rush, small-flowered *Lomandra micrantha*
mat-rush, spiny-headed *Lomandra longifolia*
mat-rush, tufted *Lomandra brevis*
mat-rush, wattle *Lomandra filiformis*
mat-rush, woolly-head *Lomandra leucocephala*
mats, Mahala *Ceanothus prostratus*
matted brooklime *Gratiola nana*
matted bush-pea *Pultenaea pedunculata*
matted pratia *Pratia pedunculata*
matted St John's wort *Hypericum japonicum*
mattipaul *Ailanthus triphysa*
mattress vine *Muehlenbeckia complexa*
mau *Hibiscus tiliaceus*
maul oak *Quercus chrysolepis*

Maule, roble del *Nothofagus glauca*
Mauritius papeda *Citrus hystrix*
Mauritius raspberry *Rubus rosifolius*
mauve candytuft *Harmsiodoxa puberula*
may *Crataegus laevigata, C. monogyna*
May apple *Passiflora incarnata, Podophyllum, P. peltatum*
May apple, Himalayan *Podophyllum hexandrum*
May lily *Maianthemum bifolium*
May pops *Passiflora incarnata*
May rose *Rosa cinnamomea*
Maya palm *Gaussia maya*
maybush *Spiraea cantoniensis*
Mayday tree *Prunus padus*
mayflower *Epigaea repens*
mayfly orchid *Acianthus caudatus*
Mayne's pest *Verbena tenuisecta*
mayten *Maytenus boaria*
mayweed *Anthemis cotula*
mayweed, scented *Matricaria recutita*
mayweed, scentless *Tripleurospermum inodorum*
mazus, swamp *Mazus pumilio*
mazzard *Prunus avium*
meadow buttercup *Ranunculus acris*
meadow chickweed *Cerastium arvense*
meadow clary *Salvia pratensis*
meadow cranesbill *Geranium pratense*
meadow cress *Cardamine, C. pratensis*
meadow fescue *Festuca pratensis*
meadow foxtail *Alopecurus pratensis*
meadow grass *Glyceria, Poa pratensis*
meadow grass, annual *Poa annua*
meadow grass, broad-leafed *Poa chaixii*
meadow grass, dwarf *Poa annua*
meadow grass, reed *Glyceria maxima*
meadow phlox *Phlox maculata*

meadow rice-grass *Microlaena stipoides*
meadow rose *Rosa blanda*
meadow saffron *Colchicum*
meadow sage *Salvia pratensis*
meadow-rue *Thalictrum*
meadow-rue, early *Thalictrum dioicum*
meadow-rue, French *Thalictrum aquilegiifolium*
meadow-rue, yellow *Thalictrum flavum*
meadows, queen of the *Filipendula ulmaria*
meadowsweet *Filipendula, F. ulmaria, Spiraea alba, S. latifolia*
mealie *Zea mays*
mealie heath *Erica patersonia*
mealy sage *Salvia farinacea*
mealy saltbush *Atriplex pseudocampanulata*
mealy stringybark *Eucalyptus cephalocarpa*
mealy-cup sage *Salvia farinacea*
medallion flower, gold *Melampodium paludosum*
medic *Medicago*
medic, barrel *Medicago truncatula*
medic, black *Medicago lupulina*
medic, burr *Medicago polymorpha*
medic, cut-leaf *Medicago laciniata*
medic, purple *Medicago sativa*
medicinal magnolia *Magnolia officinalis*
medicine bush *Pogonolobus reticulatus*
Mediterranean barley *Hordeum hystrix*
Mediterranean catchfly *Silene nocturna*
Mediterranean cypress *Cupressus sempervirens*
Mediterranean fan palm *Chamaerops humilis*

Mediterranean turnip *Brassica
tournefortii*
medlar *Mespilus germanica*
medlar, Bronvaux + *Crataegomespilus
dardarii*
medlar, mountain *Tapiphyllum
parvifolium*
medlar, wild *Vangueria infausta*
Medusa's head *Euphorbia caput-
medusae*
meeting houses *Aquilegia canadensis*
mei *Prunus mume*
melegueta pepper *Aframomum
melegueta*
melic *Melica*
melic, Siberian *Melica altissima*
melilot, sweet *Melilotus indica*
melon *Cucumis melo*
melon, bitter *Citrullus lanatus*
melon cactus *Melocactus*
melon, camel *Citrullus lanatus*
melon, Chinese preserving *Benincasa
hispida*
melon, honeydew *Cucumis melo*
Inodorus Group
melon, netted *Cucumis melo*
Reticulatus Group
melon pear *Solanum muricatum*
melon shrub *Solanum muricatum*
melon, wild *Citrullus lanatus*
memorial rose *Rosa wichurana*
menziesia, Allegheny *Menziesia pilosa*
meranti *Shorea*
Mercury Bay weed *Dichondra repens*
mermaid, snowy *Libertia formosa*
merrin *Typhonium brownii*
merrit *Eucalyptus flocktoniae*
merrybells *Uvularia*
merrybells, big *Uvularia grandiflora*
merrybells, great *Uvularia grandiflora*
merrybells, large *Uvularia grandiflora*
merrybells, little *Uvularia sessilifolia*
merrybells, wood *Uvularia perfoliata*

meryta, broad-leafed *Meryta latifolia*
mesa oak *Quercus engelmannii*
mescal *Agave neomexicana*
mescal bean *Sophora secundiflora*
mescal button *Lophophora williamsii*
mesembryanthemum, coppery
Malephora crocea
Meserve holly *Ilex* × *meserveae*
Mesopotamian poplar *Populus
euphratica*
mespilus, snowy *Amelanchier ovalis*
mesquite *Prosopis juliflora*
mesquite, Argentine *Prosopis alba*
mesquite, honey *Prosopis glandulosa*
mesquite, mock *Calliandra eriophylla*
mesquite, screwbean *Prosopis
pubescens*
mesquite, velvet *Prosopis velutina*
messmate *Eucalyptus exserta,
E. obliqua*
messmate, Gympie *Eucalyptus
cloeziana*
metake *Pseudosasa japonica*
metal leaf *Hemigraphis alternata*
Mexican alder *Alnus acuminata,
A. jorullensis*
Mexican ash *Fraxinus greggii*
Mexican aster *Cosmos bipinnatus*
Mexican bald cypress *Taxodium
mucronatum*
Mexican bamboo *Fallopia japonica*
Mexican bird cherry *Prunus
salicifolia*
Mexican blood flower *Distictis
buccinatoria*
Mexican blood trumpet *Distictis
buccinatoria*
Mexican breadfruit *Monstera deliciosa*
Mexican bush sage *Salvia leucantha*
Mexican campion *Silene laciniata*
Mexican creeper *Antigonon leptopus*
Mexican cypress *Cupressus lusitanica*
Mexican daisy *Erigeron karvinskianus*

Mexican ebony *Pithecellobium mexicanum*

Mexican fence post cactus *Pachycereus marginatus*

Mexican fern palm *Dioon edule*

Mexican fir *Abies religiosa*

Mexican fire plant *Euphorbia cyathophora*

Mexican firecracker *Echeveria setosa*

Mexican flame vine *Pseudogynoxys chenopodioides*

Mexican flannel bush *Fremontodendron mexicanum*

Mexican foxglove *Tetranema roseum*

Mexican fremontia *Fremontodendron mexicanum*

Mexican giant groundsel *Senecio petasitis*

Mexican giant hyssop *Agastache mexicana*

Mexican grass tree *Dasylirion quadrangulatum, D. longissimum*

Mexican ground cherry *Physalis ixocarpa*

Mexican hand tree *Chiranthodendron pentadactylon*

Mexican hat *Ratibida columnifera*

Mexican hat plant *Kalanchoe daigremontiana*

Mexican hawthorn *Crataegus pubescens*

Mexican heather *Cuphea hyssopifolia*

Mexican honeysuckle *Justicia spicigera*

Mexican hyssop *Agastache mexicana*

Mexican ivy *Cobaea scandens*

Mexican juniper *Juniperus flaccida*

Mexican lily *Hippeastrum reginae*

Mexican love grass *Eragrostis mexicana*

Mexican mint *Tagetes lucida*

Mexican mock orange *Philadelphus mexicanus*

Mexican nut pine *Pinus cembroides*

Mexican orange *Choisya ternata*

Mexican orange blossom *Choisya ternata*

Mexican oregano *Lippia graveolens*

Mexican palmetto *Sabal mexicana*

Mexican pine *Pinus patula*

Mexican pine, rough-barked *Pinus montezumae*

Mexican pine, smooth-barked *Pinus pseudostrobus*

Mexican plane *Platanus mexicana*

Mexican plum *Prunus mexicana*

Mexican poppy *Argemone mexicana*

Mexican potato *Pachyrhizus erosus*

Mexican rose, green *Echeveria × gilva*

Mexican rose, white *Echeveria elegans*

Mexican sage *Salvia mexicana*

Mexican shrub lobelia *Lobelia laxiflora*

Mexican snowball *Echeveria elegans*

Mexican sunflower *Tithonia*

Mexican swamp cypress *Taxodium mucronatum*

Mexican tea *Chenopodium ambrosioides, Ephedra*

Mexican tree celandine *Bocconia frutescens*

Mexican tree daisy *Montanoa bipinnatifida*

Mexican tree fern *Cibotium schiedei*

Mexican tree groundsel *Telanthophora grandifolia*

Mexican tulip poppy *Hunnemannia fumariifolia*

Mexican turnip *Pachyrhizus erosus*

Mexican violet *Tetranema roseum*

Mexican washingtonia palm *Washingtonia robusta*

Mexican white pine *Pinus ayacahuite*

Mexican zinnia *Zinnia haageana*

Mexico, old man of *Cephalocereus senilis, Pilosocereus leucocephalus*

Meyer asparagus fern *Asparagus densiflorus* 'Meyeri'
Meyer juniper *Juniperus squamata* 'Meyeri'
Meyer lemon *C.* × *meyeri* 'Meyer'
Meyer lilac *Syringa meyeri*
Meyer spruce *Picea meyeri*
mezereon *Daphne mezereum*
Michaelmas daisy *Aster novi-belgii*
Michigan holly *Ilex verticillata*
Michoacan pine *Pinus devoniana*
Mickey Mouse plant *Ochna serrulata*
midge orchid, dense *Genoplesium nudiscapum*
midgenberry *Austromyrtus dulcis*
midgenberry, narrow-leafed *Austromyrtus tenuifolia*
midget greenhood *Pterostylis mutica*
midland hawthorn *Crataegus laevigata*
midnight horror *Oroxylum*
midsummer aster *Erigeron speciosus*
mignonette *Reseda, R. odorata*
mignonette, corn *Reseda phyteuma*
mignonette tree *Lawsonia inermis*
mignonette, white *Reseda alba*
mignonette, wild *Reseda lutea*
mignonette, yellow *Reseda lutea*
migum *Eucalyptus leucophloia*
mikoikoi *Libertia grandiflora, L. ixioides*
mile-a-minute plant *Fallopia aubertii*
mile-a-minute vine *Fallopia baldschuanica*
milfoil *Achillea, A. millefolium, Myriophyllum*
milfoil, diamond *Myriophyllum aquaticum*
milfoil, water *Myriophyllum*
miljee *Acacia oswaldii*
milk barrel *Euphorbia cereiformis*
milk thistle *Silybum marianum, Sonchus oleraceus*

milk thistle, Our Lady's *Silybum marianum*
milk thistle, rough *Sonchus asper*
milk tree, African *Euphorbia trigona*
milk tree, Brazilian *Mimusops elengi*
milkbush *Euphorbia tirucalli, Sarcostemma australe*
milkbush, African *Synadenium grantii*
milkbush, Grant's *Synadenium grantii*
milkbush, yellow *Euphorbia mauritanica*
milkmaids *Burchardia umbellata*
milkvetch *Astragalus membranaceus*
milkvine, common *Marsdenia rostrata*
milkvine, scented *Marsdenia suaveolens*
milkweed *Asclepias, Gomphocarpus*
milkweed, Davis *Asclepias speciosa*
milkweed, pine-leaf *Asclepias linaria*
milkweed, pine-needle *Asclepias linaria*
milkweed, scarlet *Asclepias curassavica*
milkweed, showy *Asclepias speciosa*
milkweed, threadleaf *Asclepias linaria*
milkwood, red *Mimusops obovata*
milkwood, Transvaal red *Mimusops zeyheri*
milkwood, white *Sideroxylon inerme*
milkwort, broom *Comesperma sphaerocarpum*
milkwort, heath *Comesperma ericinum*
milkwort, myrtle-leaf *Comesperma retusum*
milkwort, Siberian *Polygala tenuifolia*
milkwort, twining *Comesperma volubile*
milky bellflower *Campanula lactiflora*
milky lobelia *Pratia concolor*
milky mangrove *Excoecaria agallocha*

miller, dusty *Artemisia stelleriana,
Centaurea cineraria, Lychnis
coronaria, Senecio cineraria,
S. vira-vira*
millet *Echinochloa, Panicum
miliaceum, Setaria, Sorghum*
millet, broom *Sorghum vulgare*
Technicum Group
millet, broom-corn *Panicum
miliaceum*
millet, ditch *Paspalum orbiculare*
millet, finger *Eleusine coracana*
millet, foxtail *Setaria italica*
millet, great *Sorghum bicolor*
millet, hog *Panicum miliaceum*
millet, Italian *Setaria italica*
millet, Japanese *Echinochloa esculenta*
millet, Siberian *Echinochloa
frumentacea*
millet, swamp *Isachne globosa*
millet, wood *Milium effusum*
millotia, broad-leaf *Millotia
myosotidifolia*
millotia, creeping *Millotia greevesii*
Millstream palm *Livistona alfredii*
mimosa *Acacia dealbata*
mimosa bush *Acacia farnesiana*
mimosa, catclaw *Mimosa pigra*
min fir *Abies recurvata*
Mindanao gum *Eucalyptus deglupta*
mind-your-own-business *Soleirolia
soleirolii*
miner's lettuce *Montia*
Ming aralia *Polyscias fruticosa*
mingimingi *Leucopogon fasciculatus*
mini protea *Protea scolymocephala*
miniature agapanthus *Agapanthus
praecox* 'Baby Blue'
miniature Chilean lily *Rhodophiala
bifida*
miniature grape ivy *Cissus striata*
miniature holly *Malpighia coccigera*
miniature hosta *Hosta* 'Saishu Jima'

miniature lady palm *Rhapis subtilis*
miniature thyme *Thymus* 'Minimus'
miniature tree fern *Blechnum
gibbum*
miniature umbrella tree *Schefflera
arboricola*
mink, pink *Protea neriifolia*
minnie bush *Menziesia pilosa*
minnie daisy *Minuria leptophylla*
Minorca honeysuckle *Lonicera
implexa*
mint, American mountain
Pycnanthemum
mint, apple *Mentha suaveolens*
mint, Bowles' *Mentha × villosa*
mint bush *Prostanthera*
mint bush, alpine *Prostanthera
cuneata*
mint bush, blotchy *Prostanthera
walteri*
mint bush, blue *Prostanthera caerulea*
mint bush, cut-leafed *Prostanthera
incisa*
mint bush, gaping *Prostanthera
ringens*
mint bush, green-flowered
Prostanthera leichhardtii
mint bush, magnificent *Prostanthera
magnifica*
mint bush, purple *Prostanthera
ovalifolia*
mint bush, red *Prostanthera calycina*
mint bush, rough *Prostanthera
denticulata*
mint bush, round-leafed *Prostanthera
rotundifolia*
mint bush, scarlet *Prostanthera
aspalathoides*
mint bush, snowy *Prostanthera nivea*
mint bush, Somersby *Prostanthera
junonis*
mint bush, splendid *Prostanthera
magnifica*

mint bush, streaked *Prostanthera striatiflora*

mint bush, thyme-leafed *Prostanthera serpyllifolia*

mint, corn *Mentha arvensis*

mint, Corsican *Mentha requienii*

mint, eau-de-cologne *Mentha* × *piperita* var. *citrata*

mint, forest *Mentha laxiflora*

mint, garden *Mentha spicata*

mint, giant hummingbird *Agastache barberi*

mint, Japanese *Mentha arvensis* var. *piperascens*

mint, Korean *Agastache rugosa*

mint, lemon *Mentha* × *piperita* var. *citrata*

mint, licorice *Agastache rupestris*

mint, Mexican *Tagetes lucida*

mint, mountain *Pycnanthemum muticum, P. virginianum*

mint, orange hummingbird *Agastache aurantiaca*

mint, pennyroyal *Mentha pulegium*

mint, river *Mentha australis*

mint, slender *Mentha diemenica*

mint, Vietnamese *Persicaria odorata*

mint, water *Mentha aquatica*

mint, whorled *Mentha* × *verticillata*

mint, winter *Mentha* × *villosa*

mint, woolly *Mentha suaveolens*

mintleaf *Plectranthus madagascariensis*

miracle berry *Synsepalum dulcificum*

miraguama *Coccothrinax miraguama*

miraguama, rose-fruited *Coccothrinax miraguama* subsp. *roseocarpa*

Mirbeck's oak *Quercus canariensis*

mirbelia, holly-leafed *Mirbelia dilatata*

miro *Prumnopitys ferruginea*

mirror bush *Coprosma repens*

miscanthus, evergreen *Miscanthus transmorrisonensis*

misery, southern mountain *Chamaebatia australis*

mishmii bitter *Coptis chinensis*

Miss Willmott's ghost *Eryngium giganteum*

Miss Willmott's rose *Rosa willmottiae*

mission bells *Fritillaria biflora*

Missouri primrose *Oenothera macrocarpa*

mistflower *Ageratina riparia, Conoclinium*

mistletoe *Viscum album*

mistletoe, Australian *Amyena*

mistletoe, box *Amyema miquelii*

mistletoe, broad-leafed *Dendrophthoe vitellina*

mistletoe, cactus *Korthalsella disticha*

mistletoe, drooping *Amyema miquelii, A. pendulum*

mistletoe fig *Ficus deltoidea*

mistletoe, fleshy *Amyema miraculosum*

mistletoe, golden *Notothixos subaureus*

mistletoe, gray *Amyema quandang*

mistletoe, harlequin *Lysiana exocarpi*

mistletoe, mulga *Lysiana murrayi*

mistletoe, northern *Lysiana subfalcata*

mistletoe, pale-leaf *Amyema maidenii*

mistletoe, paperbark *Amyema gaudichaudii*

mistletoe, round-leaf *Amyema miraculosum*

mistletoe, she-oak *Amyema cambagei*

Mitchell grass *Astrebla*

Mitchell grass, hoop *Astrebla elymoides*

Mitchell's wattle *Acacia mitchellii*

miter, bishop's *Astrophytum myriostigma, Epimedium*

miter weed *Mitrasacme polymorpha*

miterwort *Mitella*
mitsuba *Cryptotaenia canadensis*
 subsp. *japonica*
miyabe daisy *Chrysanthemum*
 weyrichii
miyagino-hagi *Lespedeza thunbergii*
miyama cherry *Prunus maximowiczii*
mizu giboshi *Hosta longissima*
Mlanje cedar *Widdringtonia nodiflora*
mock heather *Ericameria ericoides*
mock lime *Aglaia odorata*
mock mesquite *Calliandra eriophylla*
mock olive *Notelaea*
mock olive, veined *Notelaea venosa*
mock orange *Philadelphus*
mock orange, common *Philadelphus*
 coronarius
mock orange, false *Fendlera rupicola*
mock orange, Lewis *Philadelphus*
 lewisii
mock orange, Mexican *Philadelphus*
 mexicanus
mock orange, sweet *Philadelphus*
 coronarius
mock privet *Phillyrea latifolia*
mock strawberry *Duchesnea indica*
mockernut hickory *Carya tomentosa*
Modoc cypress *Cupressus bakeri*
mogil-mogil *Canthium latifolium*
Mohave yucca *Yucca schidigera*
mohintli *Justicia spicigera*
molasses grass *Melinis minutiflora*
mold, slime *Fuligo septica*
molle *Schinus latifolius,*
 S. lentiscifolius
Molly the witch *Paeonia*
 mlokosewitschii
Molucca bramble *Rubus moluccana*
monarch birch *Betula*
 maximovicziana
monarch of the veldt *Arctotis fastuosa*
monarch-of-the-east *Sauromatum*
 venosum

mondo grass *Ophiopogon japonicus*
mondo grass, black *Ophiopogon*
 planiscapus 'Nigrescens'
mondo grass, dwarf *Ophiopogon*
 japonicus 'Nanus'
money plant *Lunaria annua*
money tree *Crassula ovata*
moneywort *Lunaria annua,*
 Lysimachia nummularia
Monga waratah *Telopea mongaensis*
Mongolian lime *Tilia mongolica*
Mongolian linden *Tilia mongolica*
Mongolian oak *Quercus mongolica*
Mongolian pear *Pyrus ussuriensis*
monkey cups *Nepenthes*
monkey flower *Mimulus,*
 M. moschatus
monkey flower, Allegheny *Mimulus*
 ringens
monkey flower, bush *Mimulus*
 aurantiacus
monkey flower, common large
 Mimulus guttatus
monkey flower, creeping *Mimulus*
 repens
monkey flower, great purple
 Mimulus lewisii
monkey flower, salmon bush
 Mimulus longiflorus
monkey flower, scarlet *Mimulus*
 cardinalis
monkey flower, small *Mimulus*
 prostratus
monkey flower, yellow *Mimulus luteus*
monkey musk *Mimulus luteus*
monkey pistol *Hura crepitans*
monkey plant *Ruellia makoyana*
monkey plum, hard-leafed *Diospyros*
 scabrida
monkey pod *Albizia saman, Senna*
 petersiana
monkey pod tree *Samanea saman*
monkey pot tree *Lecythis ollaria*

monkey puzzle *Araucaria araucana*
monkey puzzle pine *Araucaria araucana*
monkey rope *Parsonsia straminea*
monkey thorn *Acacia galpinii*
monkey thorn, black *Acacia burkei*
monkey vine *Parsonsia eucalyptophylla*
monkey's brush *Combretum aubletii*
monkey's rice pot *Nepenthes albomarginata*
monk's rhubarb *Rumex alpinus*
monkshood *Aconitum, A. napellus*
monkshood, garden *Aconitum napellus*
monoao *Halocarpus kirkii*
monox *Empetrum nigrum*
monstera, false *Epipremnum pinnatum*
Mont Panie kauri *Agathis montana*
montbretia *Crocosmia, C. × crocosmiiflora*
Monterey ceanothus *Ceanothus rigidus*
Monterey cenizo *Leucophyllum langmaniae*
Monterey cypress *Cupressus macrocarpa*
Monterey cypress, Brunning's golden *Cupressus macrocarpa* 'Brunneana'
Monterey cypress, golden *Cupressus macrocarpa* 'Aurea'
Monterey cypress, golden weeping *Cupressus macrocarpa* 'Aurea Saligna'
Monterey manzanita *Arctostaphylos hookeri*
Monterey pine *Pinus radiata*
Montezuma cypress *Taxodium mucronatum*
Montezuma pine *Pinus montezumae*
Montpelier broom *Genista monspessulana*
Montpelier maple *Acer monspessulanum*

Montpelier rock rose *Cistus monspeliensis*
moon cactus *Harrisia* 'Jusbertii', *H. martinii, Selenicereus*
moon trefoil *Medicago arborea*
moon violet *Viola dissecta*
moonah *Melaleuca lanceolata, M. preissiana*
Moonbi apple box *Eucalyptus malacoxylon*
moonflower *Ipomoea alba*
moonseed *Menispermum*
moonseed, common *Menispermum canadense*
moor grass *Molinia, M. caerulea, Sesleria*
moor grass, autumn *Sesleria autumnalis*
moor grass, blue *Sesleria caerulea*
moor grass, purple *Molinia caerulea*
moorei palm *Lepidorrhachis mooreana*
moort, round-leafed *Eucalyptus platypus*
moosewood *Acer pensylvanicum*
mophead hydrangea *Hydrangea macrophylla* Hortensia Group
mop-headed acacia *Robinia pseudoacacia* 'Umbraculifera'
mops, pixie *Petrophile linearis*
morass royal palm *Roystonea princeps*
morel *Morchella elata*
Moreton Bay ash *Corymbia tessellaris*
Moreton Bay chestnut *Castanospermum, C. australe*
Moreton Bay fig *Ficus macrophylla*
moringo *Moringa oleifera*
Mormon tea *Ephedra viridis*
morning flag *Orthrosanthus*
morning glory *Ipomoea*
morning glory, beach *Ipomoea pes-caprae*

morning glory, blue *Ipomoea indica*
morning glory, coast *Ipomoea cairica*
morning glory, common *Ipomoea purpurea*
morning glory, goatsfoot *Ipomoea pes-caprae*
morning glory plant, purple *Sutera grandiflora*
morning glory, shrub *Ipomoea carnea* subsp. *fistulosa*
morning glory, tree *Ipomoea arborescens*
morning glory, yellow *Ipomoea ochracea*
morning iris *Orthrosanthus*
morning star sedge *Carex grayi*
Moroccan daisy *Rhodanthemum hosmariense*
Moroccan toadflax *Linaria maroccana*
Moroccan wallflower *Erysimum mutabile*
morrel *Eucalyptus socialis*
Morrison feather flower *Verticordia nitens*
mosaic fig *Ficus aspera* 'Parcellii'
mosaic plant *Fittonia albivenis*
moschosma *Tetradenia riparia*
Moses, prickly *Acacia brownii, A. ulicifolia, A. verticillata*
Moses-in-his-cradle *Tradescantia spathacea*
moso *Phyllostachys edulis*
mosquito bills *Dodecatheon hendersonii*
mosquito fern *Azolla*
mosquito flower *Lopezia coronata*
mosquito grass *Bouteloua gracilis*
mosquito plant *Agastache cana*
moss, Allegheny *Robinia kelseyi*
moss, ball *Tillandsia recurvata*
moss campion *Silene acaulis*
moss cypress *Crassula muscosa*

moss, fairy *Azolla*
moss, festoon *Papillaria*
moss, Iceland *Cetraria islandica*
moss, peacock *Selaginella uncinata*
moss phlox *Phlox subulata*
moss rose *Portulaca grandiflora*
moss, Spanish *Tillandsia usneoides*
moss, sphagnum *Sphagnum cristatum*
moss verbena *Verbena tenuisecta*
Mossgiel daisy *Brachyscome papillosa*
Mossman River grass *Cenchrus echinatus*
mossycup oak *Quercus macrocarpa*
moth catcher *Araujia sericifera*
moth mullein *Verbascum blattaria*
moth mullein, nettle-leaf *Verbascum chaixii*
moth orchid *Phalaenopsis*
moth vine *Araujia sericifera*
mother shield fern *Polystichum proliferum*
mother spleenwort *Asplenium bulbiferum*
mother-in-law's chair *Echinocactus grusonii*
mother-in-law's tongue *Dieffenbachia, Sansevieria, S. trifasciata*
mother-of-millions *Bryophyllum daigremontianum, B. delagoense*
mother-of-pearl plant *Graptopetalum paraguayense*
mother-of-thousands *Saxifraga stolonifera, Tolmiea menziesii*
mother-of-thyme *Thymus serpyllum*
mother-of-thyme, woolly *Thymus pseudolanuginosus*
motherumbah *Acacia cheelii*
motherwort *Leonurus cardiaca*
moths, golden *Diuris lanceolata*
mottlecah *Eucalyptus macrocarpa*
mottled spurge *Euphorbia lactea*

mound of pebbles *Aloinopsis schooneesii*

moundlily yucca *Yucca gloriosa*

Mount Buffalo sally *Eucalyptus mitchelliana*

Mount Cook buttercup *Ranunculus lyallii*

Mount Cook lily *Ranunculus lyallii*

Mount Etna broom *Genista aetnensis*

Mount Le Grand mallee *Eucalyptus aquilina*

Mount Lewis palm *Archontophoenix purpurea*

mountain aciphyll *Aciphylla simplicifolia*

mountain alder *Alnus tenuifolia*

mountain arnica *Arnica latifolia*

mountain ash *Eucalyptus regnans, Sorbus, S. aucuparia*

mountain ash, American *Sorbus americana*

mountain ash, dwarf Chinese *Sorbus reducta*

mountain ash, European *Sorbus aucuparia*

mountain ash, Korean *Sorbus alnifolia*

mountain ash, oak-leafed *Sorbus × thuringiaca*

mountain ash, showy *Sorbus decora*

mountain ash, Swedish *Sorbus intermedia*

mountain avens *Dryas octopetala*

mountain baeckea *Baeckea utilis*

mountain banksia *Banksia canei*

mountain beard-heath *Leucopogon suaveolens*

mountain beech *Nothofagus solanderi*

mountain beech, New Zealand *Nothofagus cliffortioides*

mountain berry, pink *Leucopogon parviflorus*

mountain blue gum *Eucalyptus deanei*

mountain bluet *Centaurea montana*

mountain bottlebrush *Callistemon pityoides*

mountain cabbage tree *Cordyline indivisa*

mountain cedar *Widdringtonia nodiflora*

mountain celery *Aciphylla glacialis*

mountain cherry, Syrian *Prunus prostrata*

mountain cord-rush *Baloskion australe*

mountain correa *Correa lawrenciana*

mountain currant *Ribes alpinum*

mountain cypress *Widdringtonia nodiflora*

mountain cypress pine *Callitris monticola*

mountain daisy *Celmisia*

mountain desert sage *Salvia pachyphylla*

mountain devil *Lambertia formosa*

mountain dogwood *Cornus nuttallii*

mountain ebony *Bauhinia hookeri*

mountain fig *Ficus glumosa*

mountain fishtail palm, giant *Caryota aequatorialis, C. maxima*

mountain flax *Phormium cookianum*

mountain flax, New Zealand *Phormium cookianum*

mountain flax-lily *Dianella tasmanica*

mountain fleece *Persicaria amplexicaulis*

mountain gooseberry *Ribes oxyacanthoides*

mountain gray gum *Eucalyptus cypellocarpa*

mountain grevillea *Grevillea alpina*

mountain gum *Eucalyptus dalrympleana*

mountain gum, small-fruited
Eucalyptus oresbia
mountain hard pear *Olinia*
emarginata
mountain heath *Leucopogon suaveolens*
mountain heather, pink *Phyllodoce*
empetriformis
mountain hemlock *Tsuga mertensiana*
mountain hickory *Acacia penninervis*
mountain hickory wattle *Acacia*
obliquinervia
mountain holly *Ilex montana,*
Olearia ilicifolia
mountain hovea *Hovea montana*
mountain kangaroo apple *Solanum*
linearifolium
mountain karee *Rhus leptodictya*
mountain koromiko *Hebe subalpina*
mountain laurel *Kalmia latifolia*
mountain laurel, Arizona *Sophora*
arizonica
mountain laurel, Texas *Sophora*
secundiflora
mountain leatherwood *Eucryphia*
milliganii
mountain mahogany *Cercocarpus*
montanus, Eucalyptus notabilis
mountain maple *Acer spicatum*
mountain medlar *Tapiphyllum*
parvifolium
mountain mint *Pycnanthemum*
muticum, P. virginianum
mountain needlewood *Hakea*
lissosperma
mountain neinei *Dracophyllum*
traversii
mountain ninebark *Physocarpus*
monogynus
mountain oak *Brachylaena*
rotundata
mountain palm, little *Lepidorrhachis*
mooreana
mountain papaya *Carica × heilbornii*

mountain pawpaw *Carica pubescens*
mountain pepper *Tasmannia*
lanceolata
mountain phlox *Phlox subulata*
mountain pine *Pinus mugo*
mountain pine, dwarf *Pinus mugo*
mountain pine, Swiss *Pinus mugo*
mountain pink *Rhododendron*
prinophyllum
mountain plum pine *Podocarpus*
lawrencei
mountain pride *Penstemon*
newberryi
mountain ribbonwood *Hoheria*
glabrata, H. lyallii
mountain rose *Protea nana*
mountain rose, Lord Howe
Metrosideros nervulosa
mountain rosebay *Rhododendron*
catawbiense
mountain sage *Salvia regla, Teucrium*
scorodonia
mountain saxifrage, purple *Saxifraga*
oppositifolia
mountain silkpod *Parsonsia brownii*
mountain silver oak *Brachylaena*
rotundata
mountain silverbell *Halesia monticola*
mountain, snow on the *Euphorbia*
marginata
mountain snowdrop tree *Halesia*
monticola
mountain spinach *Atriplex hortensis*
mountain spiraea *Spiraea densiflora*
mountain spray *Holodiscus dumosus*
mountain stewartia *Stewartia ovata*
mountain sumach *Rhus copallina*
mountain sundew *Drosera montana*
mountain swamp gum *Eucalyptus*
camphora
mountain sweet *Ceanothus*
americanus
mountain tea *Gaultheria procumbens*

mountain thistle *Acanthus montanus*
mountain toatoa *Phyllocladus alpinus*
mountain tulip *Tulipa montana*
mountain water gum *Tristaniopsis collina*
mountain wild rye *Elymus canadensis*
mountain wineberry *Aristotelia australasica*
mountain winterberry *Ilex montana*
mountain woodruff *Asperula gunnii*
mountain yapunyah *Eucalyptus thozetiana*
mountain yucca *Yucca schottii*
mountain-lover *Paxistima canbyi*
mournful widow *Scabiosa atropurpurea*
mourning iris *Iris susiana*
mouse plant *Arisarum proboscideum glomeratum*
mouse-ear, alpine *Cerastium alpinum*
mouse-ear chickweed *Cerastium fontanum, C. glomeratum*
mousetail *Myosurus minimus*
mousou chiku *Phyllostachys edulis*
moustache, cat's *Orthosiphon aristatus*
moutan *Paeonia suffruticosa*
mouth, dragon's *Dracunculus muscivorus*
mouth, gap *Mimulus guttatus*
mu, po *Fokienia hodginsii*
mu, zhi *Anemarrhena asphodeloides*
Mudgee wattle *Acacia spectabilis*
mudgrass, slender *Pseudoraphis paradoxa*
mudgrass, spiny *Pseudoraphis spinescens*
mudmat, small *Glossostigma diandrum, G. elatinoides*
mudwort, large *Limosella curdieana*
Mueller's cypress-pine *Callitris muelleri*

Mueller's daisy-bush *Olearia muelleri*
Mueller's heath *Epacris muelleri*
Mueller's silky oak *Austromuellera trinervia*
Mueller's wattle *Acacia muelleriana*
mugga *Eucalyptus sideroxylon*
mugga, South Coast *Eucalyptus tricarpa*
Mugo pine *Pinus mugo*
mugwort *Artemisia verlotiorum, A. vulgaris*
mugwort, western *Artemisia ludoviciana*
mugwort, white *Artemisia lactiflora*
muicle *Anisacanthus thurberi*
muira-puama *Liriosma ovata*
mulberry *Morus, M. nigra*
mulberry, black *Morus nigra*
mulberry fig *Ficus sycomorus*
mulberry, Indian *Morinda citrifolia*
mulberry, Korean *Morus australis*
mulberry, native *Hedycarya angustifolia, Pipturus argenteus*
mulberry, paper *Broussonetia papyrifera*
mulberry, red *Morus rubra*
mulberry, Texan *Morus microphylla*
mulberry, white *Morus alba*
mule, white *Lophophora williamsii*
mule's fern *Asplenium sagittatum*
mule's foot fern *Angiopteris evecta*
mulga *Acacia aneura*
mulga, bastard *Acacia stowardii*
mulga grass *Thyridolepis mitchelliana*
mulga, gray *Acacia brachybotrya*
mulga, horse *Acacia ramulosa*
mulga mistletoe *Lysiana murrayi*
mulga, umbrella *Acacia brachystachya*
mulka grass *Eragrostis dielsii*
mulla mulla *Ptilotus*
mulla mulla, pink *Ptilotus exaltatus, P. manglesii*
mulla mulla, tall *Ptilotus exaltatus*

mullein *Verbascum*
mullein, great *Verbascum thapsus*
mullein, moth *Verbascum blattaria*
mullein, nettle-leafed moth *Verbascum chaixii*
mullein nightshade *Solanum erianthum*
mullein, purple *Verbascum phoeniceum*
mullein, twiggy *Verbascum virgatum*
mullein, woolly *Verbascum thapsus*
Mullet Creek grevillea *Grevillea shiressii*
Mullumbimby couch *Cyperus brevifolius*
mundi, rosa *Rosa gallica* 'Versicolor'
mung bean *Vigna radiata*
muntries *Kunzea pomifera*
Munz's sage *Salvia munzii*
mu-oil tree *Aleurites montana*
Mupin willow *Salix moupinensis*
murasaki giboshi *Hosta ventricosa*
Murray cypress-pine *Callitris gracilis* subsp. *murrayensis*
murrnong *Microseris lanceolata*
murrogun *Cryptocarya microneura*
muscadine *Vitis rotundifolia*
muscadine grape *Vitis rotundifolia*
musclewood *Carpinus caroliniana*
musengera *Afrocarpus gracilior*
mushroom, field *Agaricus campestris*
musk *Mimulus*
musk mallow *Malva moschata*
musk mallow, pink *Malva moschata* 'Rosea'
musk mallow, white *Malva moschata* 'Alba'
musk, monkey *Mimulus luteus*
musk rose *Rosa moschata*
musk storksbill *Erodium moschatum*
musk sunray *Rhodanthe moschata*
musk tree *Olearia argophylla*
musk willow *Salix aegyptiaca*

muskmallow *Abelmoschus moschatus*
muskmelon *Cucumis melo*
muskwood *Alangium villosum*
musky caladenia *Caladenia gracilis*
mustard, black *Brassica nigra*
mustard, brown *Brassica juncea*
mustard, Chinese *Brassica juncea*
mustard, giant *Rapistrum rugosum*
mustard greens *Brassica juncea*
mustard, hedge *Sisymbrium officinale*
mustard, Indian *Brassica juncea*
mustard, smooth *Sisymbrium erysimoides*
mustard tree *Nicotiana glauca*
mustard, white *Sinapis alba*
muttonwood *Rapanea variabilis*
muttonwood, brush *Rapanea howittiana*
myall, coast *Acacia binervia*
myall, weeping *Acacia pendula*
myall, western *Acacia papyrocarpa*
myoporum, creeping *Myoporum parvifolium*
myrobalan *Phyllanthus emblica, Prunus cerasifera, Terminalia chebula*
myrrh *Commiphora myrrha*
myrrh, garden *Myrrhis odorata*
myrtle *Myrtus communis*
myrtle, apple *Angophora*
myrtle beech *Nothofagus cunninghamii*
myrtle, bog *Myrica gale*
myrtle, brown *Choricarpia leptopetala*
myrtle, California wax *Myrica californica*
myrtle, Cape *Myrsine africana*
myrtle, common *Myrtus communis*
myrtle, crape *Lagerstroemia fauriei* × *indica, L. indica*
myrtle, creeping *Vinca minor*
myrtle, crepe *see* myrtle, crape
myrtle dahoon *Ilex myrtifolia*
myrtle, dune *Eugenia capensis*
myrtle ebony *Diospyros pentamera*

myrtle flag *Acorus calamus*
myrtle geebung *Persoonia myrtilloides*
myrtle, gray *Backhousia myrtifolia*
myrtle hakea *Hakea myrtoides*
myrtle holly *Ilex myrtifolia*
myrtle, lemon-scented *Backhousia citriodora*
myrtle lime *Triphasia trifolia*
myrtle, northern fringe *Calytrix exstipulata*
myrtle oak *Quercus myrtifolia*
myrtle, peach *Uromyrtus australis*
myrtle, prickly *Rhaphithamnus spinosus*
myrtle, Queensland golden *Thaleropia queenslandica*
myrtle, rose *Archirhodomyrtus beckleri, Rhodomyrtus tomentosa*

myrtle, sand *Leiophyllum buxifolium*
myrtle, silky *Decaspermum humile*
myrtle, snow *Calytrix alpestris*
myrtle spurge *Euphorbia lathyris*
myrtle, Swan River *Hypocalymma robustum*
myrtle, true *Myrtus communis*
myrtle, velvet *Lenwebbia prominens*
myrtle wattle *Acacia myrtifolia*
myrtle, wax *Myrica cerifera*
myrtle, white *Hypocalymma angustifolium, Rhodamnia argentea*
myrtle, willow *Agonis flexuosa*
myrtle-leaf milkwort *Comesperma retusum*
myrtle-leaf orange *Citrus aurantium* 'Myrtifolia'
Mysore thorn *Caesalpinia decapetala*

N

naboom *Euphorbia grandidens,*
  E. ingens
nagi *Nageia nagi*
naidi *Euterpe oleracea*
naked ladies *Amaryllis belladonna,*
  Colchicum
nana-berry *Rhus dentata*
Nancy, early *Wurmbaea dioica*
Nancy, sweet *Achillea ageratum*
Nanking cherry *Prunus tomentosa*
nanmu *Persea nanmu*
nannyberry *Viburnum lentago*
Naples garlic *Allium neapolitanum*
Naples plum *Prunus cocomilia*
napunya *Eucalyptus thozetiana*
naranjilla *Solanum quitoense*
narcissus, bunch-flowered *Narcissus*
  tazetta
narcissus, paper white *Narcissus*
  papyraceus
narcissus, pheasant's eye *Narcissus*
  poeticus
narcissus, poet's *Narcissus poeticus*
narcissus, polyanthus *Narcissus*
  tazetta
nardoo *Marsilea*
nardoo, banded *Marsilea mutica*
nardoo, common *Marsilea*
  drummondii
nardoo, narrow-leafed *Marsilea*
  angustifolia
nardoo, striped *Marsilea mutica*
narihira bamboo *Semiarundinaria*
  fastuosa
Narrawa burr *Solanum cinereum*
narrow buckler fern *Dryopteris*
  carthusiana
narrow swamp fern *Dryopteris*
  cristata

narrow thread-petal *Stenopetalum*
  lineare
narrow-leaf bitter pea *Daviesia*
  mimosoides
narrow-leaf bower wattle *Acacia*
  cognata
narrow-leaf cottonwood *Populus*
  angustifolia
narrow-leaf cumbungi *Typha*
  domingensis
narrow-leaf drumsticks *Isopogon*
  anethifolius
narrow-leaf geebung *Persoonia linearis*
narrow-leaf hopbush *Dodonaea*
  viscosa subsp. *angustissima*
narrow-leaf hovea *Hovea linearis*
narrow-leaf logania *Logania albiflora*
narrow-leaf wax flower *Philotheca*
  linearis
narrow-leaf yucca *Yucca angustissima*
narrow-leafed apple *Angophora bakeri*
narrow-leafed ash *Fraxinus*
  angustifolia
narrow-leafed basket grass
  Oplismenus imbecillis
narrow-leafed black peppermint
  Eucalyptus nicholii
narrow-leafed bottlebrush
  Callistemon linearis
narrow-leafed carpet grass *Axonopus*
  affinis
narrow-leafed clover *Trifolium*
  angustifolium
narrow-leafed firethorn *Pyracantha*
  angustifolia
narrow-leafed grass tree *Xanthorrhoea*
  glauca
narrow-leafed gray box *Eucalyptus*
  pilligaensis
narrow-leafed ironbark *Eucalyptus*
  crebra
narrow-leafed mallee *Eucalyptus*
  angustissima

narrow-leafed midgenberry
Austromyrtus tenuifolia
narrow-leafed nardoo *Marsilea
angustifolia*
narrow-leafed peppermint *Eucalyptus
radiata*
narrow-leafed phebalium *Phebalium
stenophyllum*
narrow-leafed red gum *Eucalyptus
seeana*
narrow-leafed red mallee *Eucalyptus
leptophylla*
narrow-leafed reedmace *Typha
angustifolia*
narrow-leafed spleenwort *Diplazium
pycnocarpon*
narrow-leafed stringybark *Eucalyptus
oblonga, E. sparsifolia*
narrow-leafed trigger plant *Stylidium
lineare*
narrow-leafed valerian *Centranthus
angustifolius*
narrow-leafed vetch *Vicia sativa*
subsp. *angustifolia*
narrow-leafed white mahogany
Eucalyptus tenuipes
nassella, fine-leafed *Nassella
tenuissima*
nasturtium *Tropaeolum majus*
nasturtium, flame *Tropaeolum
speciosum*
nasturtium, wreath *Tropaeolum
polyphyllum*
Natal bauhinia *Bauhinia natalensis*
Natal bottlebrush *Greyia sutherlandii*
Natal camwood *Baphia racemosa*
Natal Christmas bell *Sandersonia
aurantiaca*
Natal coral tree *Erythrina humeana*
Natal cycad *Encephalartos natalensis*
Natal fig *Ficus natalensis*
Natal flame bush *Alberta magna*
Natal gardenia *Gardenia cornuta*

Natal grass, red *Melinis repens*
Natal guarri *Euclea natalensis*
Natal ivy *Senecio macroglossus*
Natal laburnum *Calpurnia aurea*
Natal mahogany *Trichilia emetica*
Natal orange *Strychnos spinosa*
Natal plum *Carissa macrocarpa*
Natal red-top *Melinis repens*
Natal shellflower bush *Bowkeria
verticillata*
Natal wedding flower *Dombeya
tiliacea*
Natal wild banana *Strelitzia nicolai*
native annual sorghum *Sorghum
stipoideum*
native banana *Musa banksii*
native bindweed *Convolvulus
erubescens*
native brome *Bromus arenarius*
native broom, Australian *Viminaria
juncea*
native bugle *Ajuga australis*
native caraway *Oreomyrrhis eriopoda*
native cascarilla *Croton verreauxii*
native chamomile *Gnephosis
eriocarpa*
native cherry *Exocarpos cupressiformis*
native cranberry *Lissanthe sapida*
native crowfoot *Erodium crinitum,
E. cygnorum*
native cumquat *Citrus glauca*
native currant *Canthium latifolium,
Leptomeria acida*
native cymbidium *Cymbidium suave*
native daphne *Philotheca myoporoides*
native ebony *Bauhinia hookeri*
native elder *Sambucus australasica,
S. gaudichaudiana*
native fenugreek *Trigonella
suavissima*
native flax *Linum marginale*
native frangipani, Australian
Hymenosporum flavum

native fuchsia, Australian *Correa reflexa*
native geranium *Geranium homeanum, G. potentilloides, G. solanderi*
native grape *Cissus hypoglauca*
native guava *Rhodomyrtus psidioides*
native hibiscus *Hibiscus diversifolius*
native holly *Alchornea ilicifolia, Podolobium ilicifolium*
native hollyhock *Lavatera plebeia*
native hops *Dodonaea triquetra*
native hound's-tongue *Cynoglossum australe, C. suaveolens*
native hydrangea *Abrophyllum ornans*
native indigo *Indigofera australis*
native iris *Patersonia glabrata, P. sericea*
native iris, white *Diplarrena moraea*
native jasmine *Jasminum volubile*
native kapok *Cochlospermum gillivraei*
native leek *Bulbine bulbosa*
native licorice *Glycyrrhiza acanthocarpa*
native lilac *Hardenbergia comptoniana*
native lucerne *Glycyrrhiza acanthocarpa*
native mulberry *Hedycarya angustifolia, Pipturus argenteus*
native orange *Capparis mitchellii*
native parsley *Lomatia silaifolia*
native passionflower *Passiflora aurantia*
native passionfruit *Passiflora herbertiana*
native peach *Trema aspera*
native pear *Marsdenia viridiflora, Planchonia careya*
native pellitory *Parietaria debilis*
native pennyroyal *Mentha satureioides*
native poplar *Codonocarpus cotinifolius, Omalanthus populifolius*

native poppy *Papaver aculeatum*
native quince *Alectryon subcinereus*
native raspberry *Rubus hillii, R. parvifolius, R. rosifolius*
native rose, Australian *Boronia serrulata*
native rosella, Australian *Hibiscus heterophyllus*
native rosemary *Westringia fruticosa*
native sowthistle *Sonchus hydrophilus*
native spinach *Tetragonia tetragonioides*
native stock *Blennodia canescens*
native storksbill *Pelargonium australe*
native tamarind *Diploglottis australis*
native tobacco *Nicotiana occidentalis, N. suaveolens*
native turmeric *Curcuma australasica*
native violet, Australian *Viola hederacea*
native willow *Acacia salicina, A. stenophylla, Callistachys lanceolata*
native wisteria *Millettia megasperma*
native yam *Dioscorea transversa*
Navajita azul *Bouteloua gracilis*
Navajita comun *Bouteloua gracilis*
Navajo yucca *Yucca navajoa*
navel orange *Citrus × aurantium*
Navel Group
navelseed *Omphalodes*
navelwort *Omphalodes, O. cappadocica*
navelwort, Venus' *Omphalodes linifolia*
nealie *Acacia loderi*
nealie, dwarf *Acacia wilhelmiana*
necklace, Arizona *Sophora arizonica*
necklace fern *Asplenium flabellifolium*
necklace poplar, Chinese *Populus lasiocarpa*
necklace spleenwort *Asplenium flabellifolium*

necklace vine *Muehlenbeckia
complexa*
nectarine *Prunus persica* var. *nectarina*
née tree *Quercus rugosa*
needle, Adam's *Yucca*
needle burr *Amaranthus spinosus*
needle furze *Genista anglica*
needle juniper *Juniperus rigida*
needle mat-rush *Lomandra cylindrica*
needle palm *Rhapidophyllum hystrix*
needle, Spanish *Yucca gloriosa*
needle spike rush *Eleocharis acicularis*
needle wattle *Acacia carnei,
A. havilandiorum, A. rigens*
needle-and-thread, Adam's *Yucca
filamentosa*
needlebush *Hakea gibbosa, H.
leucoptera, H. sericea, H. teretifolia*
needlegrass *Stipa*
needlegrass, nodding *Nassella cernua*
needlegrass, snake *Oldenlandia
diffusa*
needle-leafed bottlebrush *Callistemon
teretifolius*
needles, devil's *Solanum stelligerum*
needles, Spanish *Bidens*
needlewood *Hakea leucoptera*
needlewood, hooked *Hakea
tephrosperma*
needlewood, mountain *Hakea
lissosperma*
neem *Azadirachta indica*
neinei, mountain *Dracophyllum
traversii*
nekbudu *Ficus lutea*
nemesia, perennial *Nemesia caerulea*
Nepal alder *Alnus nepalensis*
Nepal holly *Ilex integra*
Nepal ivy *Hedera nepalensis*
Nepean River gum *Eucalyptus
benthamii*
nepenthes, winged *Nepenthes alata*
nerine *Nerine bowdenii*

net bush *Calothamnus*
net bush, common *Calothamnus
quadrifidus*
net bush, Giles' *Calothamnus gilesii*
net-leaf hackberry *Celtis reticulata*
net-leaf oak *Quercus reticulata,
Q. rugosa*
net-leaf willow *Salix reticulata*
netted chain fern *Woodwardia
areolata*
netted melon *Cucumis melo*
Reticulatus Group
netted shaggy pea *Podolobium
scandens*
nettle, big stinging *Urtica dioica*
nettle, common *Urtica dioica*
nettle, dead *Lamium*
nettle, hedge *Stachys*
nettle, Japanese dead *Meehania*
nettle, painted *Solenostemon
scutellarioides*
nettle, scarlet hedge *Stachys coccinea*
nettle, scrub *Urtica incisa*
nettle, small *Urtica urens*
nettle, stinging *Urtica*
nettle tree *Celtis australis*
nettle tree, caucasian *Celtis caucasica*
nettle tree, Chinese *Celtis sinensis*
nettle tree, European *Celtis australis*
nettle-leaf bellflower *Campanula
trachelium*
nettle-leaf goosefoot *Chenopodium
murale*
nettle-leaf moth mullein *Verbascum
chaixii*
never never plant *Ctenanthe
oppenheimiana*
neverfail *Eragrostis setifolia*
New Caledonian pine *Araucaria
columnaris*
New England aster *Aster novae-angliae*
New England blackbutt *Eucalyptus
andrewsii, E. campanulata*

New England hickory *Acacia nova-anglica*

New England peppermint *Eucalyptus nova-anglica*

New England tea-tree *Leptospermum novae-angliae*

New Guinea impatiens *Impatiens hawkeri*

New Guinea kauri *Agathis robusta* subsp. *nesophila*

New Jersey tea *Ceanothus americanus*

New Mexico privet *Forestiera pubescens*

New South Wales Christmas bush *Ceratopetalum gummiferum*

New South Wales sassafras *Doryphora sassafras*

new year flower, Chinese *Enkianthus quinqueflorus*

New York aster *Aster novi-belgii*

New Zealand beech *Nothofagus solanderi*

New Zealand black pine *Prumnopitys taxifolia*

New Zealand burr *Acaena*

New Zealand cabbage tree *Cordyline australis*

New Zealand celery-top pine *Phyllocladus trichomanoides*

New Zealand Christmas tree *Metrosideros excelsa*

New Zealand dacryberry *Dacrycarpus dacrydioides*

New Zealand daphne *Pimelea prostrata*

New Zealand edelweiss *Leucogenes*

New Zealand flax *Phormium, P. tenax*

New Zealand hard beech *Nothofagus truncata*

New Zealand hemp *Phormium tenax*

New Zealand honeysuckle *Knightia excelsa*

New Zealand iris *Libertia grandiflora, L. ixioides*

New Zealand kauri *Agathis australis*

New Zealand lacebark *Hoheria lyallii, H. populnea*

New Zealand lilac *Heliohebe hulkeana*

New Zealand mountain beech *Nothofagus cliffortioides*

New Zealand mountain flax *Phormium cookianum*

New Zealand pink broom *Carmichaelia cormichaeliae*

New Zealand pink tree broom *Carmichaelia glabrescens*

New Zealand red beech *Nothofagus fusca*

New Zealand red pine *Dacrydium cupressinum*

New Zealand rock lily *Arthropodium cirratum*

New Zealand scented broom *Carmichaelia odorata*

New Zealand silver beech *Nothofagus menziesii*

New Zealand silver pine *Manoao colensoi*

New Zealand skullcap *Scutellaria novae-zelandiae*

New Zealand spinach *Tetragonia tetragonioides*

New Zealand tree fuchsia *Fuchsia excorticata*

New Zealand water fern *Blechnum discolor*

New Zealand white pine *Dacrycarpus dacrydioides*

New Zealand wind grass *Stipa arundinacea*

New Zealand yam *Oxalis tuberosa*

ngaan, lung *Dimocarpus longan*

ngaio *Myoporum laetum*

nibung palm *Oncosperma tigillarium*
Nicaraguan cacao-shade *Gliricidia sepium*
nicker nut *Caesalpinia bonduc*
nicodemia *Buddleja madagascariensis*
nicotiana *Nicotiana alata*
night, lady of the *Brunfelsia americana, Cestrum nocturnum*
night, queen of the *Hylocereus undatus, Selenicereus*
night-blooming cactus *Hylocereus undatus*
night-closing flower *Magnolia coco*
night-flowering cactus *Epiphyllum oxypetalum*
night-scented jessamine *Cestrum nocturnum*
night-scented stock *Matthiola longipetala*
nightshade, blackberry *Solanum americanum, S. nigrum*
nightshade, Brazilian *Solanum seaforthianum*
nightshade, Catalina *Solanum wallacei*
nightshade, climbing *Solanum jasminoides*
nightshade, deadly *Atropa belladonna*
nightshade, forest *Solanum prinophyllum*
nightshade, green-berry *Solanum opacum*
nightshade, mullein *Solanum erianthum*
nightshade, Paraguay *Solanum rantonnetii*
nightshade, purple *Solanum xantii*
nightshade, stinking *Hyoscyamus niger*
nightshade, three-flowered *Solanum triflorum*
nightshade, velvet *Solanum ellipticum*
nightshade, violet *Solanum brownii*

nightshade, white-tip *Solanum chenopodioides*
nijanda *Sansevieria zeylanica*
Nikau palm *Rhopalostylis sapida*
Nikko fir *Abies homolepis*
Nikko maple *Acer maximowiczianum*
Nile, lily of the *Agapanthus, A. praecox*
nim *Azadirachta indica*
nineawn, leafy *Enneapogon polyphyllus*
ninebark *Physocarpus, P. opulifolius*
ninebark, common *Physocarpus opulifolius*
ninebark, mountain *Physocarpus monogynus*
nin-sin *Panax ginseng*
nipa palm *Nypa fruticans*
nipah *Nypa fruticans*
nipple fruit *Solanum mammosum*
Nippon spiraea *Spiraea nipponica*
nirre *Nothofagus antarctica*
nirrhe *Eucryphia glutinosa*
nitre bush *Nitraria billardierei*
nitre goosefoot *Chenopodium nitrariaceum*
noble fir *Abies procera*
noche, reina de la *Selenicereus grandiflorus*
nodding banksia *Banksia nutans*
nodding blue-lily *Stypandra glauca*
nodding catchfly *Silene pendula*
nodding chocolate-lily *Dichopogon fimbriatus*
nodding clubmoss *Lycopodiella cernua*
nodding club-rush *Isolepis cernua*
nodding greenhood *Pterostylis nutans*
nodding lilac *Syringa × prestoniae*
nodding needlegrass *Nassella cernua*
nodding onion *Allium cernuum*
nodding pincushion *Leucospermum cordifolium*

nodding thistle *Carduus nutans*
nogal *Juglans major*
nonda plum *Parinari nonda*
Noogoora burr *Xanthium occidentale*
noon flower *Lampranthus glaucus*
noor *Euphorbia coerulescens*
noor, sweet *Euphorbia coerulescens*
Nootka cypress *Chamaecyparis
nootkatensis*
Nordic currant *Ribes rubrum*
Norfolk Island palm *Rhopalostylis
baueri*
Norfolk Island hibiscus *Lagunaria
patersonia*
Norfolk Island pine *Araucaria
heterophylla*
Norfolk Island tree fern *Cyathea
brownii*
North African ivy *Hedera canariensis*
North American tulip tree
Liriodendron tulipifera
North American wild oats
Chasmanthium latifolium
North Island edelweiss *Leucogenes
leontopodium*
North Island rata *Metrosideros robusta*
North Japanese hemlock *Tsuga
diversifolia*
northern barley grass *Hordeum
glaucum*
northern blue violet *Viola
septentrionalis*
northern bottle tree *Brachychiton
australis*
northern catalpa *Catalpa speciosa*
northern cottonwood *Populus
deltoides* subsp. *monilifera*
northern cypress-pine *Callitris
intratropica*
northern fringe myrtle *Calytrix
exstipulata*
northern gooseberry *Ribes
oxyacanthoides*

northern grass-tree *Xanthorrhoea
johnsonii*
northern Jacob's ladder *Polemonium
boreale*
northern mistletoe *Lysiana subfalcata*
northern pepperbush *Tasmannia
purpurascens*
northern pin oak *Quercus ellipsoidalis*
northern pitch pine *Pinus rigida*
northern pitcher plant *Sarracenia
purpurea*
northern prickly ash *Zanthoxylum
americanum*
northern red oak *Quercus rubra*
northern sandalwood *Santalum
lanceolatum*
northern silver wattle *Acacia
leucoclada*
northern snappy gum *Eucalyptus
brevifolia*
northern stinging tree *Dendrocnide
moroides*
northern water gum *Tristaniopsis
exiliflora*
northern wedding bush *Ricinocarpos
bowmannii*
North's false-flag *Neomarica
northiana*
Norway maple *Acer platanoides*
Norway maple, Schwedler's *Acer
platanoides* 'Schwedleri'
Norway spruce *Picea abies*
notched sundew *Drosera schizandra*
November lily *Lilium longiflorum*
nuestro, padre *Myrtillocactus
geometrizans*
Nuevo Leon spruce *Picea
engelmannii* subsp. *mexicana*
nuggets, gold *Calochortus luteus*
num-num *Carissa bispinosa*
num-num, small *Carissa edulis*
nut, ball *Floydia praealta*
nut, Barbados *Jatropha curcas*

nut, bopple *Macadamia tetraphylla*
nut, Brazil *Bertholletia excelsa*
nut, bull *Trapa natans*
nut, Chile *Gevuina avellana*
nut, cola *Cola nitida*
nut, cottonleaf physic *Jatropha gossypiifolia*
nut, French physic *Jatropha curcas*
nut, goat *Simmondsia chinensis*
nut, grease *Hernandia bivalvis*
nut hiccup *Combretum bracteosum*
nut, Jesuits' *Trapa natans*
nut, kaya *Torreya nucifera*
nut, ling *Trapa bicornis*
nut, lucky *Thevetia peruviana*
nut, macadamia *Macadamia tetraphylla*
nut, Malabar *Justicia adhatoda*
nut, marking *Semecarpus anacardium*
nut, nicker *Caesalpinia bonduc*
nut palm *Cycas media*
nut, Para *Bertholletia excelsa*
nut, paradise *Lecythis zabucajo*
nut, physic *Jatropha multifida, Justicia adhatoda*
nut, pili *Canarium ovatum*
nut pine *Pinus edulis*

nut, pistachio *Pistacia vera*
nut, purging *Jatropha curcas*
nut, Queensland *Macadamia tetraphylla*
nut, red bopple *Hicksbeachia pinnatifolia*
nut, sapucaia *Lecythis zabucajo*
nut sedge *Cyperus esculentus*
nut, smooth-shelled macadamia *Macadamia integrifolia*
nut, union *Bouchardatia neurococca*
nutgall *Rhus chinensis*
nutgrass *Cyperus rotundus*
nutgrass, downs *Cyperus bifax*
nut-heads, sprawling *Epaltes australis*
nutmeg *Myristica fragrans*
nutmeg bush *Tetradenia riparia*
nutmeg, California *Torreya californica*
nutmeg flower *Nigella sativa*
nutmeg hickory *Carya myristiciformis*
nutmeg yew, California *Torreya californica*
nutmeg yew, Yunnan *Torreya yunnanense*
nutwood *Terminalia arostrata*

O

oak *Quercus*
oak, Algerian *Quercus canariensis*
oak, American turkey *Quercus laevis*
oak, American white *Quercus alba*
oak, Arkansas *Quercus arkansana*
oak, Armenian *Quercus pontica*
oak, Atherton *Athertonia diversifolia*
oak, bamboo-leafed *Quercus bambusifolia*
oak, Bartram's *Quercus × heterophylla*
oak, basket *Quercus prinus*
oak, bear *Quercus ilicifolia*
oak, black *Quercus velutina*
oak, blackjack *Quercus marilandica*
oak, blue *Quercus douglasii*
oak, bluejack *Quercus incana*
oak, bootlace *Hakea lorea*
oak, bottom *Quercus × runcinata*
oak, Brazilian *Posqueria latifolia*
oak, bull *Allocasuarina luehmannii*
oak, burr *Quercus macrocarpa*
oak, Bush's *Quercus × bushii*
oak, California live *Quercus agrifolia*
oak, California poison *Toxicodendron diversilobum*
oak, California scrub *Quercus dumosa*
oak, California white *Quercus lobata*
oak, Cambridge *Quercus warburgii*
oak, Canary *Quercus canariensis*
oak, canyon live *Quercus chrysolepis*
oak, Caucasian *Quercus macranthera*
oak, Chapman *Quercus chapmanii*
oak, chestnut *Quercus montana*
oak, chestnut-leafed *Quercus castaneifolia*
oak, Chinese cork *Quercus variabilis*
oak, chinquapin *Quercus muehlenbergii*

oak, coast live *Quercus agrifolia*
oak, coast silver *Brachylaena discolor*
oak, common *Quercus robur*
oak, Coochin Hills *Grevillea whiteana*
oak, cork *Quercus suber*
oak, corkwood *Hakea fraseri*
oak, cream silky *Athertonia diversifolia*
oak, Daimyo *Quercus dentata*
oak, deer *Quercus sadleriana*
oak, downy *Quercus pubescens*
oak, durand *Quercus durandii*
oak, durmast *Quercus dalechampii, Q. petraea*
oak, dwarf chinquapin *Quercus prinoides*
oak, emory *Quercus emoryi*
oak, English *Quercus robur*
oak fern *Gymnocarpium dryopteris*
oak fern, common *Gymnocarpium dryopteris*
oak, forest *Allocasuarina torulosa*
oak, gambel *Quercus gambelii*
oak, Georgia *Quercus georgiana*
oak, gray *Quercus grisea*
oak, ground *Teucrium chamaedrys*
oak, holly *Quercus ilex*
oak, holm *Quercus ilex*
oak, Hungarian *Quercus frainetto*
oak, Indian *Barringtonia acutangula*
oak, interior live *Quercus wislizeni*
oak, island *Quercus tomentella*
oak, Jamaican *Catalpa longissima*
oak, Japanese *Quercus acutissima, Q. mongolica* var. *grosseserrata*
oak, Japanese chestnut *Quercus acutissima*
oak, Jerusalem *Chenopodium botrys*
oak, kermes *Quercus coccifera*
oak, laurel *Quercus laurifolia*
oak, Lebanon *Quercus libani*
oak, live *Quercus virginiana*

oak, Lusitanian *Quercus faginea*
oak, Macedonian *Quercus trojana*
oak, maul *Quercus chrysolepis*
oak, mesa *Quercus engelmannii*
oak, Mirbeck's *Quercus canariensis*
oak, Mongolian *Quercus mongolica*
oak, mossycup *Quercus macrocarpa*
oak, mountain *Brachylaena rotundata*
oak, mountain silver *Brachylaena rotundata*
oak, myrtle *Quercus myrtifolia*
oak, net-leaf *Quercus reticulata, Q. rugosa*
oak, northern pin *Quercus ellipsoidalis*
oak, northern red *Quercus rubra*
oak, Oregon *Quercus garryana*
oak, Oregon white *Quercus garryana*
oak, overcup *Quercus lyrata*
oak, Palestine *Quercus coccifera* subsp. *calliprinos*
oak, pedunculate *Quercus robur*
oak, Persian *Quercus macranthera*
oak, pin *Quercus palustris*
oak, Pontine *Quercus pontica*
oak, Portuguese *Quercus faginea, Q. lusitanica*
oak, post *Quercus stellata*
oak, Pyrenean *Quercus pyrenaica*
oak, red *Quercus rubra*
oak, river *Casuarina cunninghamiana*
oak, rock *Quercus montana*
oak, Rocky Mountain white *Quercus gambelii*
oak, scarlet *Quercus coccinea*
oak, sessile *Quercus petraea*
oak, shingle *Quercus imbricaria*
oak, shumard *Quercus shumardii*
oak, silky *Grevillea robusta*
oak, silver *Grevillea parallela*
oak, silver-leaf *Quercus hypoleucoides*
oak, Sind *Quercus coccifera* subsp. *calliprinos*

oak, southern red *Quercus falcata*
oak, Spanish *Quercus falcata, Q. texana, Q. × hispanica*
oak, stave *Quercus alba*
oak, stone *Quercus alba*
oak, Stone Mountain *Quercus georgiana*
oak, swamp *Casuarina glauca, Quercus palustris*
oak, swamp chestnut *Quercus michauxii, Q. prinus*
oak, swamp white *Quercus bicolor*
oak, tanbark *Lithocarpus densiflorus*
oak, tanner's *Quercus alba*
oak, thick-leaf *Quercus crassifolia*
oak, Turkey *Quercus cerris*
oak, valley *Quercus lobata*
oak, vallonea *Quercus ithaburensis*
oak walnut *Cryptocarya corrugata*
oak, water *Quercus nigra*
oak, wavy-leaf *Quercus undulata*
oak, western poison *Toxicodendron diversilobum*
oak, white *Athertonia diversifolia, Lagunaria patersonia, Quercus alba*
oak, willow-leafed *Quercus phellos*
oak, yellow *Quercus muehlenbergii*
oak, yellow bark *Quercus velutina*
oak, yellow chestnut *Quercus muehlenbergii*
Oakland star tulip *Calochortus umbellatus*
oak-leaf dryandra *Dryandra quercifolia*
oak-leaf geranium *Pelargonium quercifolium*
oak-leaf grevillea *Grevillea quercifolia*
oak-leaf lettuce *Lactuca sativa* 'Oakleaf'
oak-leafed corkwood *Commiphora wildii*
oak-leafed hydrangea *Hydrangea quercifolia*

oak-leafed mountain ash *Sorbus* ×
thuringiaca
oat, bearded *Avena barbata*
oat, false *Arrhenatherum elatius*
oat grass *Arrhenatherum elatius,
Helictotrichon*
oat grass, blue *Helictotrichon
sempervirens*
oat grass, bulbous *Arrhenatherum
elatius* var. *bulbosum*
oat grass, tuber *Arrhenatherum
elatius* var. *bulbosum*
oat spear grass *Anisopogon avenaceus*
oats *Avena sativa*
oats, golden *Stipa gigantea*
oats, North American wild
Chasmanthium latifolium
oats, sea *Chasmanthium latifolium*
oats, wild *Avena fatua, Uvularia
sessilifolia*
Oaxaca palmetto *Sabal mexicana*
oba giboshi *Hosta montana*
obeche *Triplochiton scleroxylon*
obedience plant *Maranta arundinacea,
Physostegia virginiana*
oca *Oxalis tuberosa*
ocean spray *Holodiscus discolor*
ochna, large-flowered *Ochna
atropurpurea, O. mossambicensis*
o'clock, eleven *Portulaca grandiflora*
o'clock, four *Mirabilis jalapa*
Oconee bells *Shortia galacifolia*
Ocote pine *Pinus oocarpa*
ocotillo *Fouquieria diguetii,
F. splendens*
ocotillo, tall *Fouquieria diguetii*
octopus agave *Agave vilmoriniana*
octopus tree *Schefflera actinophylla*
oeillet de France *Dianthus gallicus*
ogeechee tupelo *Nyssa ogeche*
ohi'a lehua *Metrosideros polymorpha*
Ohio buckeye *Aesculus glabra,
A. ohioensis*

oil bush *Geijera linearifolia*
oil camellia *Camellia oleifera*
oil croton *Croton tiglium*
oil palm *Elaeis, E. guineensis*
oil palm, African *Elaeis guineensis*
oil palm, American *Elaeis oleifera*
oil tea *Camellia oleifera*
oil-nut tree *Calophyllum inophyllum*
oil-seed rape *Brassica napus* subsp.
oleifera
Okinawa holly *Ilex dimorphophylla*
Okinawa pine *Pinus luchuensis*
Oklahoma plum *Prunus gracilis*
okra *Abelmoschus esculentus*
okra, cow *Parmentiera aculeata*
olax *Olax stricta*
old lady cactus *Mammillaria
hahniana*
old man *Artemisia abrotanum,
A. absinthium*
old man banksia *Banksia serrata*
old man cactus *Cephalocereus senilis,
Pilosocereus leucocephalus*
old man of Mexico *Cephalocereus
senilis, Pilosocereus leucocephalus*
old man of the Andes *Espostoa
lanata, Oreocereus celsianus*
old man palm *Coccothrinax crinita*
old man saltbush *Atriplex
nummularia*
old man's beard *Clematis, Tillandsia
usneoides*
old man's whiskers *Caustis flexuosa,
Geum triflorum*
old warrior *Artemisia pontica*
old woman *Artemisia stelleriana*
old woman cactus *Mammillaria
hahniana*
old-fashioned weigela *Weigela
florida*
Oldham bamboo *Bambusa oldhamii*
oldwood *Leucosidea sericea*
oleander *Nerium oleander*

oleander, climbing *Strophanthus gratus*
oleander, large-flowered yellow *Thevetia thevetioides*
oleander spurge *Euphorbia neriifolia*
oleander wattle *Acacia neriifolia*
oleander, yellow *Thevetia peruviana*
oleander-leafed protea *Protea neriifolia*
oleaster *Elaeagnus angustifolia*
olive *Olea, O. europaea*
olive, Australian *Olea paniculata*
olive, autumn *Elaeagnus umbellata*
olive, bastard *Buddleja saligna*
olive, common *Olea europaea*
olive, desert *Forestiera pubescens*
olive, false *Cassine orientalis*
olive, forest *Olea woodiana*
olive, fragrant *Osmanthus fragrans*
olive grevillea *Grevillea dimorpha, G. olivacea*
olive, Java *Sterculia foetida*
olive, mock *Notelaea*
olive plum, red *Cassine australis*
olive, Russian *Elaeagnus angustifolia*
olive, small-fruited *Olea europaea* subsp. *africana*
olive, spurge *Cneorum tricoccon*
olive, sweet *Osmanthus fragrans*
olive, Texas *Cordia boissieri*
oliveberry, black *Elaeocarpus holopetalus*
Oliver's lime *Tilia oliveri*
Oliver's sassafras *Cinnamomum oliveri*
olivewood bark, Bermuda *Cassine laneana*
olor, roble de *Catalpa punctata*
ombu *Phytolacca dioica*
Omeo grevillea *Grevillea willisii*
Omeo gum *Eucalyptus neglecta*
one-flowered clover *Trifolium uniflorum*

one-seed juniper *Juniperus monosperma*
one-sided bottlebrush *Calothamnus quadrifidus*
one-spiked paspalum *Paspalum ciliatifolium*
onion *Allium, A. cepa*
onion, bog *Owenia cepiodora*
onion, bunching *Allium cepa* Aggregatum Group
onion, cascade *Allium cratericola*
onion couch *Arrhenatherum elatius*
onion, crater *Allium cratericola*
onion, flowering *Allium neapolitanum*
onion, German *Ornithogalum longibracteatum*
onion, Geyer's *Allium geyeri*
onion, glade *Allium stellatum*
onion, glassy *Allium hyalinum*
onion grass *Romulea rosea* var. *australis*
onion, Hooker's *Allium acuminatum*
onion, Japanese bunching *Allium fistulosum*
onion, nodding *Allium cernuum*
onion orchid *Dendrobium canaliculatum, Microtis unifolia*
onion orchid, slender *Microtis parviflora*
onion, pink wild *Allium acuminatum*
onion, prairie *Allium stellatum*
onion, purple *Allium cepa* 'Purple Sensation'
onion, sea *Ornithogalum longibracteatum*
onion, shallot *Allium cepa*
onion, Siskiyou *Allium siskiyouense*
onion, small yellow *Allium flavum*
onion, spring *Allium cepa*
onion, tapertip *Allium acuminatum*
onion, tree *Allium cepa* Proliferum Group

onion, volcanic *Allium cratericola*
onion weed *Asphodelus fistulosus,*
Nothoscordum gracile
onion, Welsh *Allium fistulosum*
onion, wild *Allium cernuum*
Opar, jewels of *Talinum*
paniculatum
opium poppy *Papaver somniferum*
opium poppy, wild *Papaver*
somniferum subsp. *setigerum*
orach *Atriplex hortensis*
orache *Atriplex hortensis*
orache, hastate *Atriplex prostrata*
orache, prostrate *Atriplex australasica*
orache, spear-leafed *Atriplex*
prostrata
orange ball tree *Buddleja globosa*
orange, bergamot *Citrus × bergamia*
orange, bitter *Citrus × aurantium,*
Poncirus trifoliata
orange, blood *Citrus × aurantium*
'Blood'
orange blossom, Mexican *Choisya*
ternata
orange blossom orchid *Sarcochilus*
falcatus
orange browallia *Streptosolen*
jamesonii
orange, calamondin *Citrus ×*
microcarpa
orange cestrum *Cestrum aurantiacum*
orange clock vine *Thunbergia*
gregorii
orange coneflower *Rudbeckia fulgida*
orange darling pea *Swainsona*
stipularis
orange firethorn *Pyracantha*
angustifolia
orange, Florida *Citrus × aurantium*
Tangor Group
orange gum *Eucalyptus bancroftii*
orange hook sedge *Uncinia*
egmontiana

orange hummingbird mint *Agastache*
aurantiaca
orange immortelle *Waitzia*
acuminata
orange, jambhiri *Citrus × jambhiri*
orange, Japanese bitter *Poncirus*
trifoliata
orange, jasmine *Murraya paniculata*
orange jessamine *Murraya paniculata*
orange mangrove, large-fruited
Bruguiera gymnorhiza
orange, Mexican *Choisya ternata*
orange, mock *Philadelphus*
orange, myrtle-leaf *Citrus ×*
aurantium 'Myrtifolia'
orange, Natal *Strychnos spinosa*
orange, native *Capparis mitchellii*
orange, navel *Citrus × aurantium*
Navel Group
orange, Osage *Maclura pomifera*
orange, Panama *Citrus × microcarpa*
orange peel clematis *Clematis*
tibetana subsp. *vernayi*
orange, Seville *Citrus × aurantium*
orange stars *Hibbertia stellaris*
orange sunray *Hyalosperma semisterile*
orange, sweet *Citrus sinensis*
orange thorn *Cassinopsis ilicifolia,*
Pittosporum pauciflorum
orange, trifoliate *Poncirus trifoliata*
orange trumpet creeper *Pyrostegia*
venusta
orange, Valencia *Citrus × aurantium*
'Valencia'
orange vygie *Lampranthus aureus*
orange wattle *Acacia saligna*
orange, wild *Capparis canescens,*
C. mitchellii, Prunus caroliniana
orange wisteria shrub *Sesbania*
punicea
orangeglow vine *Pseudogynoxys*
chenopodioides
orangeroot *Hydrastis canadensis*

orchard apple *Malus pumila*
orchid, angel *Coelogyne cristata*
orchid, antelope *Dendrobium antennatum*
orchid, bamboo *Arundina, Thunia alba*
orchid, beech *Dendrobium falcorostrum*
orchid, bird *Chiloglottis*
orchid, bird's mouth *Orthoceras strictum*
orchid, blue *Vanda* Rothschildiana (grex)
orchid, bottlebrush *Dendrobium smillieae*
orchid, bridal veil *Dockrillia teretifolia*
orchid, broad leafed marsh *Dactylorhiza majalis*
orchid bush, South African *Bauhinia galpinii*
orchid, butterfly *Psychopsis papilio*
orchid, button *Dischidia nummularia*
orchid cactus, red *Disocactus ackermannii*
orchid, candle *Arpophyllum*
orchid, chain *Dendrochilum*
orchid, cherry *Mediocalcar*
orchid, Chinese ground *Bletilla striata*
orchid, Christmas *Calanthe triplicata*
orchid, climbing *Erythrorchis cassythoides*
orchid, cockroach *Restrepia*
orchid, comet *Angraecum*
orchid, common spotted *Dactylorhiza fuchsii*
orchid, Cooktown *Dendrobium bigibbum*
orchid, cow *Cryptostylis subulata*
orchid, cowslip *Diuris lanceolata*
orchid, crucifix *Epidendrum ibaguense, E.* Obrienianum (grex)

orchid, cucumber *Dendrobium cucumerinum*
orchid, dancing lady *Oncidium, O. varicosum*
orchid, dense midge *Genoplesium nudiscapum*
orchid, donkey *Diuris longifolia, D. maculata*
orchid, dove *Dendrobium crumenatum*
orchid, Dracula *Dracula*
orchid, early marsh *Dactylorhiza incarnata*
orchid, fairy *Sarcochilus*
orchid, fire *Renanthera*
orchid, flag *Masdevallia*
orchid, flying duck *Caleana major*
orchid, gnat *Acianthus fornicatus, Cyrtostylis reniformis*
orchid, goat *Diuris venosa*
orchid, grass *Grastidium*
orchid, greenhood *Pterostylis*
orchid, hay-scented *Dendrochilum glumaceum*
orchid, helmet *Corybas*
orchid, horned *Orthoceras strictum*
orchid, hyacinth *Bletilla striata, Dipodium punctatum*
orchid, jade *Magnolia denudata*
orchid, jewel *Ludisia*
orchid, king *Dendrobium speciosum*
orchid, lady of the night *Brassavola*
orchid, lady's slipper *Cypripedium, Paphiopedilum*
orchid, leek *Prasophyllum*
orchid, leopard *Diuris maculata*
orchid, Madeiran *Dactylorhiza foliosa*
orchid, marsh *Dactylorhiza*
orchid, mayfly *Acianthus caudatus*
orchid, moth *Phalaenopsis*
orchid, onion *Dendrobium canaliculatum, Microtis unifolia*

orchid, orange blossom *Sarcochilus falcatus*
orchid, pansy *Miltoniopsis*
orchid, peacock *Gladiolus callianthus*
orchid, pencil *Dockrillia teretifolia*
orchid, pigeon *Dendrobium crumenatum*
orchid, poor man's *Schizanthus × wisetonensis*
orchid, raspy root *Rhinerrhiza divitiflora*
orchid, rat's-tail *Dockrillia teretifolia*
orchid, robust marsh *Dactylorhiza elata*
orchid, rock *Dendrobium speciosum*
orchid, scented leek *Prasophyllum odoratum*
orchid, shower *Congea tomentosa*
orchid, slipper *Cypripedium, Paphiopedilum*
orchid, small fringed helmet *Corybas pruinosus*
orchid, snake *Diuris lanceolata*
orchid, South American slipper *Phragmipedium*
orchid, spider *Brassia, Caladenia*
orchid, spurred helmet *Corybas aconitiflorus*
orchid, sun *Thelymitra, T. ixioides*
orchid, swamp *Phaius, P. tankervilliae*
orchid, thumbnail *Dockrillia linguiformis*
orchid, tiger *Diuris sulphurea*
orchid, tongue *Dockrillia linguiformis*
orchid tree *Bauhinia variegata*
orchid tree, Hong Kong *Bauhinia × blakeana*
orchid tree, white *Bauhinia variegata* 'Candida'
orchid, tulip *Anguloa*
orchid, underground *Rhizanthella*
orchid, upside-down *Stanhopea*
orchid, vanilla *Vanilla planifolia*

orchid, wallflower *Diuris longifolia*
orchid, wax-lip *Glossodia major*
ordeal tree, Madagascar *Cerbera venenifera*
ordeal tree, Swazi *Erythrophleum lasianthum*
oregano *Origanum vulgare*
oregano, golden *Origanum vulgare* 'Aureum'
oregano, Mexican *Lippia graveolens*
oregano, pizza *Origanum heracleoticum*
Oregon alder *Alnus rubra*
Oregon ash *Fraxinus latifolia*
Oregon bitter cherry *Prunus emarginata*
Oregon boxwood *Paxistima myrtifolia*
Oregon cedar *Chamaecyparis lawsoniana*
Oregon crab *Malus fusca*
Oregon crabapple *Malus fusca*
Oregon grape *Mahonia aquifolium*
Oregon holly grape *Mahonia aquifolium*
Oregon lily *Lilium columbianum*
Oregon maple *Acer macrophyllum*
Oregon oak *Quercus garryana*
Oregon plum *Oemleria cerasiformis, Prunus subcordata*
Oregon sunshine *Eriophyllum lanatum*
Oregon tea *Ceanothus sanguineus*
Oregon white oak *Quercus garryana*
organ pipe cactus *Stenocereus thurberi*
oriental alder *Alnus orientalis*
oriental beech *Fagus orientalis*
oriental bittersweet *Celastrus orbiculatus*
oriental bush cherry *Prunus japonica*
oriental cashew nut *Semecarpus anacardium*

oriental cherry *Prunus serrulata*
oriental fountain grass *Pennisetum orientale*
oriental hornbeam *Carpinus orientalis*
oriental persicary *Persicaria orientalis*
oriental photinia *Photinia villosa*
oriental plane *Platanus orientalis*
oriental poppy *Papaver orientale*
oriental sweet gum *Liquidambar orientalis*
oriental thorn *Crataegus laciniata*
ornamental chillies *Capsicum annuum* Conoides Group
ornamental grape *Vitis vinifera* × *rupestris* 'Ganzin Glory'
ornamental kale *Brassica oleracea* Acephala Group
ornamental raspberry *Rubus odoratus*
orpine *Sedum telephium*
orris *Iris* × *germanica* var. *florentina*
Osage orange *Maclura pomifera*
osha *Ligusticum porteri*
Oshima cherry *Prunus speciosa*
osier *Salix*
osier, common *Salix viminalis*
osier dogwood, red *Cornus stolonifera*
osier, green *Cornus alternifolia*
osier, purple *Salix purpurea*
osmanthus, holly *Osmanthus heterophyllus*
osmanthus, sweet *Osmanthus fragrans*
oso berry *Oemleria cerasiformis*
ostrich fern *Matteuccia struthiopteris*
oswego tea *Monarda didyma*
otafuku giboshi *Hosta decorata*
Otaheite gooseberry *Phyllanthus acidus*
Otaheite potato *Dioscorea bulbifera*

Otaheite yam *Dioscorea bulbifera*
otome giboshi *Hosta venusta*
oudehout *Leucosidea sericea*
ouhout *Leucosidea sericea*
Our Lady's milk thistle *Silybum marianum*
Our Lord's candle *Yucca whipplei*
Outeniqua yellowwood *Afrocarpus falcatus*
oval-leaf buchu *Agathosma ovata*
oval-leaf grevillea *Grevillea miqueliana*
oval-leafed privet *Ligustrum ovalifolium*
ovens wattle *Acacia pravissima*
overcup oak *Quercus lyrata*
owl-eyes *Huernia zebrina*
oxalis, barber's pole *Oxalis versicolor*
oxalis, candy-cane *Oxalis versicolor*
oxalis, creeping *Oxalis corniculata*
oxalis, pink *Oxalis debilis* var. *corymbosa*
oxalis, shamrock *Oxalis articulata*
oxeye *Heliopsis*
oxeye daisy *Leucanthemum vulgare, Telekia speciosa*
oxeye, smooth *Heliopsis helianthoides*
oxhorn bucida *Bucida buceras*
ox-killer fan *Boophone disticha*
oxlip *Primula elatior*
oyama magnolia *Magnolia sieboldii*
Oyster Bay pine *Callitris rhomboidea*
oyster plant *Mertensia simplicissima, Tragopogon porrifolius*
oyster, vegetable *Tragopogon porrifolius*
Ozark chinkapin *Castanea ozarkensis*
Ozark sundrops *Oenothera macrocarpa*
Ozark witch hazel *Hamamelis vernalis*

P

pacaya palm *Chamaedorea tepejilote*
pachistima *Paxistima canbyi*
pachysandra, Allegheny *Pachysandra procumbens*
pachysandra, Japanese *Pachysandra terminalis*
Pacific azolla *Azolla filiculoides* var. *rubra*
Pacific fir *Abies amabilis*
Pacific gold and silver chrysanthemum *Ajania pacifica*
Pacific grindelia *Grindelia stricta*
Pacific Islands kauri *Agathis macrophylla*
Pacific madrone *Arbutus menziesii*
Pacific plum *Prunus subcordata*
Pacific serviceberry *Amelanchier alnifolia* var. *semiintegrifolia*
Pacific white fir *Abies concolor* var. *lowiana*
Pacific yew *Taxus brevifolia*
paddock love grass *Eragrostis leptostachya*
paddymelon, prickly *Cucumis myriocarpus*
Paddy's lucerne *Sida rhombifolia*
Paddys River box *Eucalyptus macarthurii*
padouk *Pterocarpus soyauxii*
padre nuestro *Myrtillocactus geometrizans*
pagoda dogwood *Cornus alternifolia*
pagoda flower *Clerodendrum paniculatum*
pagoda tree *Plumeria obtusa, Sophora japonica*
pagoda tree, Japanese *Sophora japonica*
pahautea *Libocedrus bidwillii*

pai tong *Dendrocalamus asper*
paintbrush, desert *Castilleja angustifolia*
paintbrush, Flora's *Emilia sonchifolia*
paintbrush, Indian *Castilleja, C. coccinea*
paintbrush, scarlet *Castilleja coccinea, Crassula falcata*
painted brake *Pteris tricolor*
painted cups *Castilleja*
painted daisy *Ismelia carinata*
painted drop-tongue *Aglaonema crispum*
painted feather *Vriesea carinata*
painted fern, Japanese *Athyrium niponicum, A. n.* 'Pictum'
painted fingernail *Neoregelia spectabilis*
painted grape *Cissus discolor*
painted lady *Gladiolus carneus*
painted leaf *Caladium bicolor, Euphorbia cyathophora*
painted nettle *Solenostemon scutellarioides*
painted pitcher plant *Nepenthes burbidgeae*
painted sage *Salvia viridis*
painted spurge *Euphorbia cyathophora*
painted sundew *Drosera zonaria*
painted tongue *Salpiglossis sinuata*
painted-leaf begonia *Begonia rex*
Pajaro manzanita *Arctostaphylos pajaroensis*
pak choi *Brassica rapa* Chinensis Group
pal *Pseudophoenix lediniana*
palace, lily of the *Hippeastrum aulicum*
palasa *Butea monosperma*
pale appleberry *Billardiera versicolor*
pale beauty-heads *Calocephalus sonderi*

pale bloodwood *Corymbia terminalis*
pale coneflower *Echinacea pallida*
pale cord-rush *Baloskion pallens*
pale everlasting *Helichrysum rutidolepis*
pale fan-flower *Scaevola albida*
pale grass lily *Caesia parviflora*
pale hickory *Carya pallida*
pale Indian weed *Sigesbeckia australiensis*
pale knotweed *Persicaria lapathifolia*
pale mat-rush *Lomandra glauca*
pale pigeon grass *Setaria pumila*
pale pink boronia *Boronia floribunda*
pale pitcher plant *Sarracenia alata*
pale purple coneflower *Echinacea pallida*
pale spike-rush *Eleocharis pallens*
pale sundew *Drosera peltata*
pale turpentine bush *Beyeria leschenaultii*
pale wedge pea *Gompholobium huegelii*
pale wolfberry *Lycium pallidum*
pale-fruited ballart *Exocarpos strictus*
pale-leaf mistletoe *Amyema maidenii*
pale-pink boronia *Boronia floribunda*
palestine oak *Quercus coccifera* subsp. *calliprinos*
palm, African oil *Elaeis guineensis*
palm, Alexandra *Archontophoenix alexandrae*
palm, American cotton *Washingtonia filifera*
palm, American oil *Elaeis oleifera*
palm, Assai *Euterpe oleracea*
palm, Atherton *Laccospadix australasicus*
palm, Australian fan *Livistonia australis*
palm, Australian ivy *Schefflera actinophylla*

palm, bamboo *Chamaedorea costaricana*
palm, Bangalow *Archontophoenix cunninghamiana*
palm, Barbassu *Attalea cohune*
palm, barbel *Acanthophoenix crinita, A. rubra*
palm, Belmore *Howea belmoreana*
palm, betel *Areca catechu*
palm, big mountain *Hedyscepe canterburyana*
palm, Blackdown fan *Livistona fulva*
palm, blue hesper *Brahea armata*
palm, blue latan *Latania loddigesii*
palm, bottle *Hyophorbe lagenicaulis*
palm, Brandegee hesper *Brahea brandegeei*
palm, Brazilian sand *Allagoptera arenaria*
palm, brittle thatch *Thrinax morrisii*
palm, buccaneer *Pseudophoenix sargentii, P. vinifera*
palm, buri *Corypha utan, Polyandrococos caudescens*
palm, butia *Butia, B. capitata*
palm, butterfly *Dypsis lutescens*
palm, cabbage *Livistona australis, Sabal palmetto*
palm, cabbage tree *Livistona australis*
palm, Canary Island date *Phoenix canariensis*
palm, candy *Syagrus comosa*
palm, Cape York fan *Livistona muelleri*
palm, caranda *Copernicia alba*
palm, carandai *Trithrinax brasiliensis*
palm, caranday *Copernicia alba*
palm, cardboard *Zamia furfuracea*
palm, Caribbean royal *Roystonea oleracea*
palm, Carpentaria *Carpentaria acuminata*

palm, cascade *Chamaedorea atrovirens*
palm, cherry *Pseudophoenix*
palm, Chilean wine *Jubaea chilensis*
palm, Chinese fan *Livistona chinensis, Trachycarpus fortunei*
palm, Chinese fishtail *Caryota ochlandra*
palm, Chinese windmill *Trachycarpus fortunei*
palm, Christmas *Veitchia merrillii*
palm, chusan *Trachycarpus fortunei*
palm, cliff date *Phoenix rupicola*
palm, cluster fishtail *Caryota mitis*
palm, coconut *Cocos nucifera*
palm, cocos *Syagrus romanzoffiana*
palm, cohune *Attalea cohune*
palm, coquito *Jubaea chilensis*
palm, Corozo *Attalea butyracea, Elaeis oleifera*
palm, cotton *Washingtonia filifera, W. robusta*
palm, Cretan date *Phoenix theophrasti*
palm, Cuban petticoat *Copernicia macroglossa*
palm, Cuban royal *Roystonea regia*
palm, curly *Howea belmoreana*
palm, date *Phoenix dactylifera*
palm, Dawson River fan *Livistona nitida*
palm, doum *Hyphaene dichotoma, H. thebaica*
palm, dwarf date *Phoenix roebelenii*
palm, dwarf fan *Livistona muelleri*
palm, East African doum *Hyphaene coriacea*
palm, Egyptian doum *Hyphaene thebaica*
palm, Everglades *Acoelorrhaphe wrightii*
palm, fan *Livistona, Trachycarpus*
palm, Fiji fan *Pritchardia pacifica*

palm, fishtail *Caryota*
palm, Florida cherry *Pseudophoenix sargentii*
palm, Florida royal *Roystonea elata*
palm, Florida silver *Coccothrinax argentata*
palm, Florida thatch *Thrinax radiata*
palm, footstool *Livistona rotundifolia*
palm, fountain *Livistona chinensis*
palm, foxtail *Wodyetia bifurcata*
palm, gebang *Corypha utan*
palm, giant fishtail *Caryota no*
palm, gingerbread *Hyphaene thebaica*
palm, golden cane *Dypsis lutescens*
palm, gomuti *Arenga pinnata*
palm grass *Setaria palmifolia*
palm, Guadalupe *Brahea edulis*
palm, hesper *Brahea, B. armata*
palm, Himalayan fan *Trachycarpus martianus*
palm, hurricane *Dictyosperma album*
palm, idolatrica *Elaeis guineensis f. idolatrica*
palm, Indian fishtail *Caryota obtusa*
palm, itala *Hyphaene coriacea*
palm, Jamaica royal *roystonea altissima*
palm, Jamaica silver *Coccothrinax argentata*
palm, Jamaican fan *Thrinax parviflora*
palm, Jamaican thatch *Thrinax parviflora*
palm, jelly *Butia capitata*
palm, joey *Johannesteijsmannia altifrons*
palm, Juçara *Euterpe edulis*
palm, kentia *Howea forsteriana*
palm, kosi *Raphia australis*
palm, lady *Rhapis excelsa*
palm, lawyer *Calamus muelleri*

palm, lelo *Pritchardia hillebrandii*
palm lily *Cordyline petiolaris,*
    Cordyline rubra, Molineria
    capitulata, Yucca gloriosa
palm lily, broad-leaf *Cordyline*
    petiolaris
palm lily, slender *Cordyline stricta*
palm, lipstick *Cyrtostachys renda*
palm, little mountain *Lepidorrhachis*
    mooreana
palm, lontar *Borassus flabellifer,*
    B. sundaicus
palm, Lucuba *Dypsis lucubensis*
palm, Macarthur *Ptychosperma*
    macarthurii
palm, macaw *Acrocomia aculeata,*
    A. totai, A. vinifera
palm, maharajah *Cyrtostachys renda*
palm, mangrove fan *Licuala spinosa*
palm, Manila *Veitchia merrillii*
palm, Maya *Gaussia maya*
palm, Mediterranean fan *Chamaerops*
    humilis
palm, Mexican fern *Dioon edule*
palm, Mexican washingtonia
    Washingtonia robusta
palm, Millstream *Livistona alfredii*
palm, moorei *Lepidorrhachis*
    mooreana
palm, Mount Lewis *Archontophoenix*
    purpurea
palm, needle *Rhapidophyllum*
    hystrix
palm, nibung *Oncosperma tigillarium*
palm, nikau *Rhopalostylis sapida*
palm, nipa *Nypa fruticans*
palm, Norfolk Island *Rhopalostylis*
    baueri
palm, nut *Cycas media*
palm, oil *Elaeis, E. guineensis*
palm, old man *Coccothrinax crinita*
palm, pacaya *Chamaedorea tepejilote*
palm, Palmyra *Borassus flabellifer*

palm, paradise *Howea forsteriana*
palm, parlor *Chamaedorea elegans*
palm, paurotis *Acoelorrhaphe wrightii*
palm, peaberry *Thrinax morrisii*
palm, peach *Bactris gasipaes*
palm, petticoat *Washingtonia filifera*
palm, piccabeen *Archontophoenix*
    cunninghamiana
palm, Pondoland *Jubaeopsis caffra*
palm, ponytail *Beaucarnea recurvata*
palm, prickly *Bactris major*
palm, princess *Dictyosperma album*
palm, Puerto Rico hat *Sabal*
    causiarum
palm, Puerto Rico royal *Roystonea*
    borinquena
palm, queen *Syagrus romanzoffiana*
palm, raphia *Raphia vinifera*
palm, red latan *Latania lontaroides*
palm, red-leafed *Livistona mariae*
palm, redneck *Dypsis leptocheilos*
palm, rhapis *Rhapis excelsa*
palm, ribbon fan *Livistona decipiens*
palm, rock *Brahea dulcis*
palm, royal *Roystonea*
palm, ruffle *Aiphanes caryotifolia*
palm, sago *Cycas circinalis,*
    Metroxylon sagu
palm, San José hesper *Brahea*
    brandegeei
palm, sand *Livistona humilis*
palm, Sargent's *Pseudophoenix*
    sargentii
palm, seaforthia *Ptychosperma elegans*
palm, sealing-wax *Cyrtostachys renda*
palm sedge *Carex muskingumensis*
palm, Senegal date *Phoenix reclinata*
palm, sentry *Howea belmoreana*
palm, silver *Coccothrinax,*
    C. argentata
palm, silver date *Phoenix sylvestris*
palm, silver joey *Johannesteijsmannia*
    magnifica

palm, silver saw *Acoelorrhaphe wrightii*
palm, slender lady *Rhapis humilis*
palm, snake *Amorphophallus konjac*
palm, solitaire *Ptychosperma elegans*
palm, spindle *Hyophorbe verschaffeltii*
palm, spiny fiber *Trithrinax acanthocoma*
palm, sugar *Arenga pinnata*
palm, talipot *Corypha umbraculifera*
palm, taraw *Livistona saribus*
palm, teddy bear *Dypsis leptocheilos*
palm, thatch *Coccothrinax, C. crinita, Thrinax*
palm, thread *Washingtonia robusta*
palm, three-cornered *Dypsis decaryi*
palm, toddy *Caryota urens*
palm, travelers' *Ravenala madagascariensis*
palm, triangle *Dypsis decaryi*
palm, umbrella *Hedyscepe canterburyana*
palm, vegetable ivory *Phytelephas*
palm, Victoria River fan *Livistona victoriae*
palm, walking-stick *Linospadix monostachya*
palm, wanga *Pigafetta filaris*
palm, Washingtonia *Washingtonia filifera*
palm, wax *Copernicia*
palm, wedge-leaflet fan *Licuala ramsayi*
palm, windmill *Trachycarpus fortunei*
palm, window *Reinhardtia gracilis*
palm, wine *Pseudophoenix vinifera*
palm, yatay *Butia yatay*
palm, yellow latan *Latania verschaffeltii*
palm, zamia *Cycas media, Macrozamia moorei, M. riedlei*
palm, zombi *Zombia antillarum*
palma amarga *Sabal mauritiiformis*

palma pita *Yucca treculeana*
palme coyau *Coccothrinax argentea*
palme marron *Pseudophoenix lediniana*
palmella *Yucca elata*
palmetto *Sabal, S. palmetto*
palmetto, Bermuda *Sabal bermudana*
palmetto, dwarf *Sabal minor*
palmetto, Hispaniolan *Sabal domingensis*
palmetto, Mexican *Sabal mexicana*
palmetto, Oaxaca *Sabal mexicana*
palmetto, Rio Grande *Sabal mexicana*
palmetto, saw *Serenoa repens*
palmetto, scrub *Sabal etonia, S. minor*
palmetto, Sonoran *Sabal uresana*
palmito *Euterpe edulis*
palmito do campo *Syagrus flexuosa*
palm-like fig *Ficus pseudopalma*
Palmyra palm *Borassus flabellifer*
palo brea *Parkinsonia praecox*
palo Colorado *Luma apiculata*
palo verde *Parkinsonia aculeata, P. florida*
Pamirian winterfat *Krascheninnikovia ceratoides*
pampas grass *Cortaderia jubata, C. selloana*
pampas lily of the valley *Salpichroa origanifolia*
pan *Piper betle*
Panama hat plant *Carludovica palmata*
Panama orange *Citrus × microcarpa*
Panama rubber tree *Castilla elastica*
Panama tree *Sterculia apetala*
panamica *Pilea involucrata*
panax, climbing *Cephalaralia cephalobotrys*
panax, elderberry *Polyscias sambucifolia*

panax, ferny *Polyscias sambucifolia*
panda plant *Kalanchoe tomentosa*
pandang *Pandanus odoratissimus*
pandani *Richea pandanifolia*
paniala *Flacourtia jangomas*
panic, blackseed *Panicum bisulcatum*
panic, bordered *Entolasia marginata*
panic, dwarf *Panicum pygmaeum*
panic, finger *Digitaria coenicola*
panic, hairy *Panicum effusum*
panic grass *Panicum*
panic grass, cotton *Digitaria brownii*
panic, leafy *Urochloa foliosa*
panic, rigid *Homopholis proluta*
panic, slender *Paspalidium gracile*
panic, sweet *Panicum gilvum*
panic, two-color *Panicum simile*
panic, white water *Panicum obseptum*
panic, wiry *Entolasia stricta*
panicle hydrangea *Hydrangea paniculata*
panicled dogwood *Cornus racemosa*
pansy *Viola × wittrockiana*
pansy, bedding *Viola cornuta*
pansy orchid *Miltoniopsis*
pansy, tricolor *Viola tricolor*
pansy violet *Viola pedata*
papauma *Griselinia littoralis*
papaya *Carica papaya*
papaya de monte *Carica parviflora*
papaya, mountain *Carica × heilbornii*
papayuelo *Carica goudetiana*
papeda, ichant *Citrus ichangensis*
papeda, Mauritius *Citrus hystrix*
paper birch *Betula papyrifera*
paper birch, Alaskan *Betula kenaica*
paper bush *Edgeworthia chrysantha*
paper daisy *Baileya multiradiata, Rhodanthe floribunda*
paper flower *Bougainvillea glabra*
paper foxtail *Ptilotus gaudichaudii*

paper mulberry *Broussonetia papyrifera*
paper tree, bronze *Commiphora harveyi*
paper white narcissus *Narcissus papyraceus*
paperbark *Melaleuca nervosa, M. quinquenervia*
paperbark albizia *Albizia tanganyicensis*
paperbark, broad-leafed *Melaleuca quinquenervia, M. viridiflora*
paperbark, Cooktown *Melaleuca saligna*
paperbark false thorn *Albizia tanganyicensis*
paperbark, flax-leafed *Melaleuca linariifolia*
paperbark maple *Acer griseum*
paperbark maple, Chinese *Acer griseum*
paperbark mistletoe *Amyema gaudichaudii*
paperbark, prickly *Melaleuca styphelioides*
paperbark, river *Melaleuca trichostachya*
paperbark, saltwater *Melaleuca cuticularis*
paperbark, scented *Melaleuca squarrosa*
paperbark, swamp *Melaleuca ericifolia, M. rhaphiophylla*
paperbark tea-tree *Leptospermum trinervium*
paperbark thorn *Acacia sieberiana*
paperbark, weeping *Melaleuca leucadendra*
paper-spined cactus *Tephrocactus articulatus*
paper-spined cholla *Tephrocactus articulatus*
paprika *Capsicum annuum* Longum Group

papyrus *Cyperus papyrus*
papyrus, dwarf *Cyperus prolifer*
para *Marattia salicina*
Para nut *Bertholletia excelsa*
Para rubber tree *Hevea brasiliensis*
parachute plant *Ceropegia sandersonii*
paradise flower *Solanum wendlandii*
paradise, grains of *Aframomum melegueta*
paradise lily *Paradisea liliastrum*
paradise nut *Lecythis zabucajo*
paradise palm *Howea forsteriana*
paradise tree *Simarouba glauca*
paradoxa grass *Phalaris paradoxa*
Paraguay burr *Acanthospermum australe*
Paraguay nightshade *Solanum rantonnetii*
parakeelya *Calandrinia polyandra*
parakeelya, broad-leaf *Calandrinia balonensis*
parakeelya, creeping *Calandrinia ptychosperma*
parakeelya, small-leaf *Calandrinia calyptrata*
parakeelya, twining *Calandrinia volubilis*
parakeet flower *Heliconia psittacorum*
Parana pine *Araucaria angustifolia*
parapara *Pisonia brunoniana*
parasol fern *Gleichenia microphylla*
parasol tree *Firmiana simplex*
parasol tree, Chinese *Firmiana simplex*
pareira *Chondodendron tomentosum*
parilla, yellow *Menispermum canadense*
Paris daisy *Euryops chrysanthemoides*
Paris, herb *Paris quadrifolia*
parlor palm *Chamaedorea elegans*
Parramatta grass *Sporobolus indicus* var. *capensis*

Parramatta grass, giant *Sporobolus indicus* var. *major*
Parramatta red gum *Eucalyptus parramattensis*
parrot alstroemeria *Alstroemeria pulchella*
parrot bush *Dryandra sessilis*
parrot feather *Myriophyllum aquaticum*
parrot flower *Heliconia psittacorum*
parrot pea *Crotalaria cunninghamii, Dillwynia retorta*
parrot pea, showy *Dillwynia sericea*
parrot pitcher plant *Sarracenia purpurea, S. p.* × *psittacina*
parrot tree, golden *Grevillea pteridifolia*
parrotia, Persian *Parrotia persica*
parrot's beak *Lotus berthelotii*
parrot's bill *Clianthus puniceus*
Parry's beargrass *Nolina parryi*
Parry's buckeye *Aesculus parryi*
Parry's pinyon *Pinus quadrifolia*
Parry's townsendia *Townsendia parryi*
parsley *Petroselinum, P. crispum*
parsley, Chinese *Coriandrum sativum*
parsley, cow *Anthriscus sylvestris*
parsley, curly *Petroselinum crispum*
parsley fern *Cryptogramma crispa*
parsley, flat-leafed *Petroselinum crispum* var. *neapolitaum*
parsley, Hamburg *Petroselinum crispum* var. *tuberosum*
parsley, horse *Smyrnium olusatrum*
parsley, Italian *Petroselinum crispum* var. *neapolitaum*
parsley, Japanese *Cryptotaenia canadensis* subsp. *japonica*
parsley, love *Levisticum officinale*
parsley, native *Lomatia silaifolia*
parsley, rock *Petroselinum*
parsley tree *Heteromorpha trifoliolata*

parsley, turnip-rooted *Petroselinum crispum* var. *tuberosum*

parsley, wild *Hydrocotyle trachycarpa*

parsley-leafed hawthorn *Crataegus apiifolia*

parsley-leafed thorn *Crataegus apiifolia, C. marshallii*

parsley-piert *Aphanes arvensis*

parsnip *Pastinaca sativa*

parsnip, purple *Trachymene cyanopetala*

parsnip tree *Heteromorpha trifoliolata*

parsnip, white *Trachymene ochracea*

parsnip, wild *Trachymene ochracea*

parson's bands *Eriochilus cucullatus*

partridge berry *Mitchella repens*

partridge breast aloe *Aloe variegata*

pascuita *Euphorbia leucocephala*

paspalum *Paspalum dilatatum*

paspalum, one-spiked *Paspalum ciliatifolium*

pasque flower *Pulsatilla*

pasque flower, alpine *Pulsatilla alpina*

pasque flower, eastern *Pulsatilla patens*

passionflower *Passiflora, P. incarnata*

passionflower, banana *Passiflora mollissima*

passionflower, blue *Passiflora caerulea*

passionflower, blue crown *Passiflora caerulea*

passionflower, corky *Passiflora suberosa*

passionflower, native *Passiflora aurantia*

passionflower, red *Passiflora cinnabarina, P. coccinea, P. manicata, P. racemosa*

passionflower, scarlet *Passiflora coccinea*

passionflower, wild *Passiflora incarnata*

passionfruit *Passiflora, P. edulis*

passionfruit, banana *Passiflora mollissima*

passionfruit, native *Passiflora herbertiana*

passionfruit, white *Passiflora subpeltata*

patashte *Theobroma bicolor*

pataxte *Theobroma bicolor*

patchouli *Pogostemon cablin, P. heyneanus*

pate *Schefflera digitata*

paternoster beans *Abrus precatorius*

Paterson's curse *Echium plantagineum*

patrinia, scabious *Patrinia scabiosifolia*

pau d'arco *Tabebuia avellanedae, T. impetiginosa*

pau rosa *Aniba rosaeodora*

paulownia, hairy *Paulownia tomentosa*

paulownia, Sichuan *Paulownia fargesii*

paulownia, Taiwan *Paulownia kawakamii*

paulownia, white-flowered *Paulownia fortunei*

paurotis palm *Acoelorrhaphe wrightii*

pavatta *Justicia adhatoda*

pavi *Phaseolus acutifolius*

paw, bear's *Cotyledon tomentosa*

paw, cat's *Anigozanthos humilis, Ptilotus spathulatus*

paw, kangaroo *Anigozanthos*

pawpaw *Asimina triloba, Carica papaya*

pawpaw, mountain *Carica pubescens*

pe tsaie *Brassica rapa* Pekinensis Group

pea *Pisum sativum*

pea, angled flat *Platylobium obtusangulum*

pea, Ashburton *Swainsona macullochiana*
pea, balloon *Sutherlandia, S. frutescens*
pea, blue *Clitoria ternatea, Psoralea pinnata*
pea, bluebush *Crotalaria eremaea*
pea, butterfly *Clitoria ternatea*
pea, cactus *Bossiaea walkeri*
pea, Cape bladder *Sutherlandia frutescens*
pea, catjang *Cajanus cajan*
pea, centipede *Bossiaea scolopendria*
pea, Congo *Cajanus cajan*
pea, coral *Abrus precatorius, Kennedia*
pea, dainty wedge *Gompholobium glabratum*
pea, Darling *Swainsona purpurea*
pea, dogtooth *Lathyrus sativus*
pea, dolichos *Dipogon lignosus*
pea, downy Darling *Swainsona swainsonioides*
pea, dusky coral *Kennedia rubicunda*
pea, eggs-and-bacon *Dillwynia*
pea, Egyptian *Cicer arietinum*
pea, everlasting *Lathyrus grandiflorus, L. latifolius*
pea, field *Pisum sativum*
pea, garden *Pisum sativum*
pea, glory *Swainsona formosa*
pea, golden glory *Gompholobium latifolium*
pea, gorse bitter *Daviesia ulicifolia*
pea, handsome flat *Platylobium formosum*
pea, heart-leafed flame *Chorizema cordatum*
pea, holly flame *Chorizema ilicifolium*
pea, hop bitter *Daviesia latifolia*
pea, Indian *Lathyrus sativus*
pea, narrow-leaf bitter *Daviesia mimosoides*
pea, parrot *Crotalaria cunninghamii, Dillwynia retorta*
pea, perennial *Lathyrus latifolius*
pea, pigeon *Cajanus cajan*
pea, poison *Gastrolobium*
pea, shamrock *Parochetus communis*
pea shrub *Caragana*
pea shrub, Russian *Caragana frutex*
pea shrub, Siberian *Caragana arborescens*
pea, Sturt *Swainsona formosa*
pea, sugar *Pisum sativum*
pea, Swan River *Brachysema celsianum*
pea tree *Caragana*
pea tree, Siberian *Caragana arborescens*
pea, two-flowered *Lathyrus grandiflorus*
pea, violet *Baphia racemosa*
pea, wedge *Gompholobium grandiflorum*
pea, wild *Lathyrus*
pea, yellow *Senna clavigera*
peaberry palm *Thrinax morrisii*
pea-bush, matted *Pultenaea pedunculata*
pea-bush, Swan River *Brachysema lanceolatum*
peace lily *Spathiphyllum*
peach *Prunus persica*
peach, David's *Prunus davidiana*
peach, flowering *Prunus persica* (double cultivars)
peach heath *Lissanthe strigosa*
peach, native *Trema aspera*
peach myrtle *Uromyrtus australis*
peach palm *Bactris gasipaes*
peach, poison *Trema aspera*
peach protea *Protea grandiceps*
peach sage *Salvia dorisiana*
peach-flowered tea-tree *Leptospermum squarrosum*

peach-leaf poison bush *Trema aspera*
peach-leafed bellflower *Campanula persicifolia*
peach-leafed willow *Salix amygdaloides*
peachwood *Caesalpinia echinata*
peacock flower *Caesalpinia pulcherrima*
peacock iris *Moraea aristata, M. villosa, Tigridia pavonia*
peacock moss *Selaginella uncinata*
peacock orchid *Gladiolus callianthus*
peacock plant *Calathea makoyana*
peanut *Arachis hypogaea*
peanut cactus *Echinopsis chamaecereus*
peanut, forage *Arachis pintoi*
peanut, pinto *Arachis pintoi*
peanut tree *Sterculia quadrifida*
pear *Pyrus*
pear, alligator *Persea americana*
pear, almond-leafed *Pyrus amygdaliformis*
pear, balsam *Momordica charantia*
pear, birch-leaf *Pyrus betulifolia*
pear, Bradford *Pyrus calleryana* 'Bradford'
pear, Callery *Pyrus calleryana*
pear, China *Pyrus pyrifolia, P. p.* var. *culta*
pear, common *Pyrus communis*
pear, common pest *Opuntia stricta*
pear, cut-leaf *Pyrus regelii*
pear, devil's rope *Cylindropuntia imbricata*
pear, evergreen *Pyrus kawakamii*
pear, garden *Pyrus communis*
pear gum, scarlet *Eucalyptus stoatei*
pear, hard *Olinia ventosa*
pear, Himalayan *Pyrus pashia*
pear, melon *Solanum muricatum*
pear, Mongolian *Pyrus ussuriensis*

pear, native *Marsdenia viridiflora, Planchonia careya*
pear, pink wild *Dombeya burgessiae*
pear, prickly *Opuntia stricta, O. tomentosa*
pear, red *Scolopia mundii*
pear, sand *Pyrus pyrifolia*
pear, silver *Pyrus salicifolia*
pear, silver-leafed *Pyrus salicifolia*
pear, snow *Pyrus nivalis*
pear, South African white *Apodytes dimidiata*
pear, South African wild *Dombeya rotundifolia*
pear, spiny pest *Opuntia dillenii*
pear thorn *Crataegus calpodendron*
pear, Transvaal hard *Olinia emarginata*
pear, Ussurian *Pyrus ussuriensis*
pear, wild *Dombeya rotundifolia, Pyrus pyraster*
pear, willow-leafed *Pyrus salicifolia*
pear, woody *Xylomelum pyriforme*
pear-fruit, woolly *Mischocarpus lachnocarpus*
pear-fruit, yellow *Mischocarpus pyriformis*
pear-fruited mallee *Eucalyptus pyriformis*
pearl bluebush *Maireana sedifolia*
pearl bush *Exochorda, E. racemosa*
pearl bush, common *Exochorda racemosa*
pearl bush, Korean *Exochorda serratifolia*
pearl fruit *Margyricarpus pinnatus*
pearl vine *Sarcopetalum harveyanum*
pear-leafed crabapple *Malus prunifolia*
pearlwort *Sagina, S. subulata*
pearlwort, golden *Sagina subulata* 'Aurea'

pearlwort, procumbent *Sagina procumbens*

pearly everlasting *Anaphalis, A. margaritacea*

pearwood, brown *Amorphospermum antilogum*

peawood *Craibia zimmermannii*

pebbles, lavender *Graptopetalum amethystinum*

pecan *Carya illinoinensis*

pecan, scrub *Carya floridana*

pedunculate oak *Quercus robur*

peebeen *Syncarpia hillii*

peegee hydrangea *Hydrangea paniculata* 'Grandiflora'

peeling plane *Ochna pulchra*

peepul tree *Ficus religiosa*

pegs, cobbler's *Bidens pilosa*

pegunny *Bauhinia hookeri*

pejibaye *Bactris gasipaes*

Peking cabbage *Brassica rapa* Pekinensis Group

Peking lilac *Syringa pekinensis*

Peking willow *Salix babylonica*

pelargonium, birch leaf *Pelargonium betulinum*

pelargonium, regal *Pelargonium* Regal Hybrid

pelican flower *Aristolochia grandiflora*

pelican's beak *Lotus berthelotii*

pellitory *Parietaria*

pellitory, native *Parietaria debilis*

pellitory, spreading *Parietaria judaica*

pellitory, wall *Parietaria judaica*

pencil bush *Euphorbia tirucalli*

pencil cedar *Juniperus virginiana, Polyscias murrayi*

pencil orchid *Dockrillia teretifolia*

pencil pine *Cupressus sempervirens* 'Stricta'

pencil pine, Tasmanian *Athrotaxis cupressoides*

pencil tree *Euphorbia tirucalli*

pencil willow *Salix humboldtiana*

penda, black *Xanthostemon chrysanthus*

pendent silver lime *Tilia* 'Petiolaris'

pennants, golden *Glischrocaryon behrii*

pennisetum, Chinese *Pennisetum alopecuroides*

pennyroyal *Mentha pulegium*

pennyroyal mint *Mentha pulegium*

pennyroyal, native *Mentha satureioides*

pennywort *Hydrocotyle*

pennywort, beach *Hydrocotyle bonariensis*

pennywort, forest *Hydrocotyle geraniifolia*

pennywort, heart-leafed *Centella asiatica, C. cordifolia*

pennywort, stinking *Hydrocotyle laxiflora*

penstemon, blue bedder *Penstemon heterophyllus*

penstemon, climbing *Keckiella ternata*

penstemon, coral *Penstemon barbatus*

penstemon, foothill *Penstemon heterophyllus*

penstemon, lovely *Penstemon venustus*

penstemon, scented *Penstemon palmeri*

penstemon, shrubby *Penstemon fruticosus*

penstemon, small-flowered *Penstemon procerus*

pentas *Pentas lanceolata*

peony *Paeonia*

peony, Caucasian *Paeonia mlokosewitschii*

peony, Chinese *Paeonia lactiflora*

peony, female *Paeonia officinalis*

peony, Majorcan *Paeonia cambessedesii*

peony, male *Paeonia mascula*

peony, Rock's *Paeonia rockii*

peony rose *Paeonia* (herbaceous) double cultivars

peony, tree *Paeonia lutea, P. suffruticosa*

pepa *Calamus viminalis*

peperomia, watermelon *Peperomia argyreia*

pepino *Solanum muricatum*

pepper *Capsicum*

pepper, banana *Capsicum annuum* Longum Group

pepper, bell *Capsicum annuum*

pepper, betle *Piper betle*

pepper, black or white *Piper nigrum*

pepper bush, sweet *Clethra alnifolia*

pepper, cayenne *Capsicum annuum* Longum Group

pepper, cherry *Capsicum annuum* Cerasiforme Group

pepper, chilli *Capsicum annuum*

pepper, common *Piper nigrum*

pepper, flowering *Peperomia fraseri*

pepper, goat *Capsicum frutescens*

pepper grass *Panicum laevinode*

pepper, ivy-leaf *Peperomia griseoargentea*

pepper, Jamaican *Pimenta dioica*

pepper, Japanese *Zanthoxylum piperitum*

pepper, Madagascar *Piper nigrum*

pepper, melegueta *Aframomum melegueta*

pepper, mountain *Tasmannia lanceolata*

pepper plant *Piper nigrum*

pepper, platinum *Peperomia griseoargentea*

pepper root *Cardamine laciniata*

pepper, silver-leaf *Peperomia griseoargentea*

pepper, spiked *Piper aduncum*

pepper, spur *Capsicum frutescens*

pepper, sweet *Capsicum annuum* Grossum Group

pepper, Tabasco *Capsicum frutescens*

pepper tree *Macropiper excelsum, Pseudowintera colorata, Schinus molle*

pepper tree, alpine *Pseudowintera colorata*

pepper tree, Brazilian *Schinus terebinthifolia*

pepper vine, giant *Piper novae-hollandiae*

pepper, wall *Sedum acre*

pepper, water *Persicaria hydropiper*

pepper, watermelon *Peperomia argyreia*

pepperberry tree *Cryptocarya obovata*

pepperbush, alpine *Tasmannia xerophila*

pepperbush, brush *Tasmannia insipida*

pepperbush, northern *Tasmannia purpurascens*

peppercorn *Schinus molle*

peppercress *Lepidium*

peppercress, common *Lepidium africanum*

peppercress, cut-leaf *Lepidium bonariense*

peppercress, veined *Lepidium phlebopetalum*

peppercress, warty *Lepidium papillosum*

peppercress, winged *Lepidium monoplocoides*

pepper-face *Peperomia obtusifolia*

peppermint *Mentha* × *piperita*

peppermint box *Eucalyptus odorata*

peppermint, broad-leafed *Eucalyptus dives*

peppermint, narrow-leafed *Eucalyptus radiata*

peppermint, narrow-leafed black *Eucalyptus nicholii*

peppermint, New England *Eucalyptus nova-anglica*

peppermint, river *Eucalyptus elata*

peppermint, Smithton *Eucalyptus nitida*

peppermint, swamp *Eucalyptus rodwayi*

peppermint, Sydney *Eucalyptus piperita*

peppermint tree *Agonis flexuosa*

peppers *Capsicum annuum*

pepperwort *Marsilea*

Père David's maple *Acer davidii*

peregrina *Jatropha integerrima*

perennial aster *Aster novi-belgii*

perennial aster, white *Aster ericoides*

perennial beardgrass *Polypogon littoralis*

perennial blue flax *Linum perenne*

perennial candytuft *Iberis sempervirens*

perennial cornflower *Centaurea montana*

perennial flax *Linum perenne*

perennial lespedeza *Lespedeza juncea*

perennial marsh-cress *Rorippa laciniata*

perennial nemesia *Nemesia caerulea*

perennial pea *Lathyrus latifolius*

perennial petunia *Calibrachoa*

perennial phlox *Phlox paniculata*

perennial ragweed *Ambrosia psilostachya*

perennial ryegrass *Lolium perenne*

perennial sea lavender *Limonium sinuatum*

perennial veld grass *Ehrharta calycina*

perennial wallflower *Erysimum mutabile*

perfoliate bellwort *Uvularia perfoliata*

perfoliate pondweed *Potamogeton perfoliatus*

perican *Tagetes lucida*

perilla *Perilla frutescens*

periwinkle *Catharanthus, Vinca*

periwinkle, greater *Vinca major*

periwinkle, lesser *Vinca minor*

periwinkle, Madagascar *Catharanthus roseus*

periwinkle, pink *Catharanthus roseus*

periwinkle, rose *Catharanthus roseus*

periwinkle, rosy *Catharanthus roseus*

periwinkle, variegated *Vinca major* 'Variegata'

Pernambuco wood *Caesalpinia echinata*

Perny's holly *Ilex pernyi*

perpetual-flowering carnation *Dianthus* × *allwoodii*

Persia, star of *Allium cristophii*

Persian buttercup *Ranunculus asiaticus*

Persian cornflower *Centaurea dealbata*

Persian ironwood *Parrotia persica*

Persian ivy *Hedera colchica*

Persian lilac *Melia azederach, Syringa* × *persica*

Persian oak *Quercus macranthera*

Persian parrotia *Parrotia persica*

Persian silk tree *Albizia julibrissin*

Persian violet *Cyclamen, Exacum affine*

Persian walnut *Juglans regia*

Persian witch hazel *Parrotia persica*

persicary, oriental *Persicaria orientalis*

persimmon *Diospyros, D. kaki, D. virginiana*

persimmon, American *Diospyros virginiana*
persimmon, black *Diospyros digyna*
persimmon, Texas *Diospyros texana*
Peru, apple of *Nicandra physalodes*
Peru, hyacinth of *Scilla peruviana*
Peru, marvel of *Mirabilis jalapa*
Peruvian balsam *Myroxylon balsamum* var. *pereirae*
Peruvian lily *Alstroemeria*
Peruvian maidenhair fern *Adiantum peruvianum*
Peruvian primrose willow *Ludwigia peruviana*
Peruvian squill *Scilla peruviana*
pest, Mayne's *Verbena tenuisecta*
pest pear, common *Opuntia stricta*
pest pear, spiny *Opuntia dillenii*
petai *Parkia speciosa*
petals, rusty *Lasiopetalum ferrugineum*
petrea, blue *Petrea arborea*
petrea, tree *Petrea arborea*
petticoat palm *Washingtonia filifera*
petticoat palm, Cuban *Copernicia macroglossa*
petty spurge *Euphorbia peplus*
petty whin *Genista anglica*
petunia *Petunia* × *hybrida*
petunia, large white *Petunia axillaris*
petunia, perennial *Calibrachoa*
peyote *Lophophora, L. williamsii*
peyote verde *Echinocereus knippelianus*
pfaffia *Pfaffia paniculata*
phacelia, tansy *Phacelia tanacetifolia*
phalaris *Phalaris aquatica*
phanera *Bauhinia corymbosa*
phasey bean *Macroptilium lathyroides*
pheasant's eye *Adonis aestivalis, A. amurensis, A. annua, Gilia tricolor*

pheasant's eye narcissus *Narcissus poeticus*
phebalium, club-leafed *Phebalium obcordatum*
phebalium, narrow-leafed *Phebalium stenophyllum*
phebalium, pink *Phebalium nottii*
phebalium, scaly *Phebalium squamulosum*
phebalium, wallum *Phebalium woombye*
Philippine fig *Ficus pseudopalma*
Philippine violet *Barleria cristata*
Philippine wax flower *Etlingera elatior*
Phillip Island hibiscus *Hibiscus insularis*
phillyrea, Cape *Cassine capensis*
philodendron, blushing *Philodendron erubescens*
philodendron, elephant's ear *Philodendron domesticum*
philodendron, emerald duke *Philodendron domesticum*
philodendron, heartleaf *Philodendron hederaceum*
philodendron, red-leaf *Philodendron erubescens*
philodendron, tree *Philodendron bipinnatifidum*
phlox *Phlox drummondii*
phlox, annual *Phlox drummondii*
phlox, blue *Phlox divaricata*
phlox, border *Phlox paniculata*
phlox, meadow *Phlox maculata*
phlox, moss *Phlox subulata*
phlox mountain *Phlox subulata*
phlox, perennial *Phlox paniculata*
phlox, prairie *Phlox pilosa*
phlox, prickly *Leptodactylon californicum*
phlox, sand *Phlox bifida*
phlox, Santa Fe *Phlox nana*

phlox, summer *Phlox paniculata*
phlox, thick-leaf *Phlox carolina*
phlox, trailing *Phlox nivalis*
phlox, woodland *Phlox adsurgens*
phoenix tree *Firmiana simplex*
photinia, Fraser *Photinia × fraseri*
photinia, Japanese *Photinia glabra*
photinia, oriental *Photinia villosa*
phyllota, common *Phyllota phylicoides*
phyllota, dwarf *Phyllota humifusa*
physic, cottonleaf *Jatropha gossypifolia*
physic, Indian *Gillenia trifoliata*
physic nut *Jatropha multifida, Justicia adhatoda*
physic nut, cottonleaf *Jatropha gossypiifolia*
physic nut, French *Jatropha curcas*
Piccabeen palm *Archontophoenix cunninghamiana*
pichi *Fabiana imbricata*
pickaback plant *Tolmiea menziesii*
pickerel rush *Pontederia cordata*
pickerel weed *Pontederia, P. cordata*
pickle fruit *Averrhoa bilimbi*
pie, cherry *Heliotropium arborescens*
pie plant, red-veined *Rheum australe*
Piedmont azalea *Rhododendron canescens*
pieris, Japanese *Pieris japonica*
pigeon berry *Duranta erecta*
pigeon grass *Setaria*
pigeon grass, green *Setaria viridis*
pigeon grass, pale *Setaria pumila*
pigeon grass, slender *Setaria gracilis*
Pigeon House ash *Eucalyptus triflora*
pigeon orchid *Dendrobium crumenatum*
pigeon pea *Cajanus cajan*
pigeon seagrape *Coccoloba laurifolia*
pigeonwings, Asian *Clitoria ternatea*
pigface *Carpobrotus*

pigface, annual *Portulaca grandiflora*
pigface, inland *Carpobrotus modestus*
pigface, round-leafed *Disphyma crassifolium*
pigface, small-flowered *Carpobrotus modestus*
pigface, Western Australian *Carpobrotus virescens*
piggyback fern *Hemionitis arifolia*
piggyback plant *Tolmiea menziesii*
pignut, great *Bunium bulbocastanum*
pignut hickory *Carya glabra*
pignut, sweet *Carya ovalis*
pigroot, blue *Sisyrinchium iridifolium*
pigsqueak *Bergenia, B. cordifolia*
pigweed *Portulaca oleracea*
pigweed, black *Trianthema portulacastrum*
pigweed, giant *Trianthema portulacastrum*
pilewort *Ranunculus ficaria*
pili nut *Canarium ovatum*
pill flower *Ozothamnus diosmifolius*
Pilliga daisy *Brachyscome formosa*
pillo-pillo *Ovidia pillopillo*
pillwort *Pilularia globulifera*
pillwort, Australian *Pilularia novae-hollandiae*
pimelea, poison *Pimelea decora*
pimento *Pimenta dioica*
pimpernel *Anagallis, A. arvensis*
pimpernel, blue *Anagallis arvensis, A. monellii*
pimpernel, bog *Anagallis tenella*
pimpernel, scarlet *Anagallis arvensis*
pimpernel, water *Samolus valerandi*
pin cherry *Prunus pensylvanica*
pin colonnaire *Araucaria columnaris*
pin oak *Quercus palustris*
pin oak, northern *Quercus ellipsoidalis*
pin sida *Sida fibulifera*

pinbush wattle *Acacia burkittii*
pinchot juniper *Juniperus pinchotii*
pinckneya *Pinckneya pubens*
pincushion *Leucospermum, Scabiosa atropurpurea*
pincushion, blue *Brunonia australis*
pincushion, Bolus *Leucospermum bolusii*
pincushion cactus *Mammillaria*
pincushion, Cape *Scabiosa africana*
pincushion, Catherine's *Leucospermum catherinae*
pincushion euphorbia *Euphorbia pulvinata*
pincushion, firewheel *Leucospermum tottum*
pincushion flower *Astrantia*
pincushion, Gordon's Bay *Leucospermum bolusii*
pincushion hakea *Hakea laurina*
pincushion, nodding *Leucospermum cordifolium*
pincushion, showy *Escobaria vivipara*
pincushion, skyrocket *Leucospermum reflexum*
pincushion tree *Hakea laurina*
pine *Pinus*
pine, African fern *Afrocarpus gracilior*
pine, Aleppo *Pinus halapensis*
pine, alpine celery *Phyllocladus alpinus*
pine, ancient *Pinus longaeva*
pine, Apache *Pinus engelmannii*
pine, Armand *Pinus armandii*
pine, arolla *Pinus cembra*
pine, Australian *Casuarina, C. equisetifolia*
pine, Austrian *Pinus nigra*
pine, Austrian black *Pinus nigra*
pine, beach *Pinus contorta*
pine, Bhutan *Pinus wallichiana*
pine, big-cone *Pinus coulteri*
pine, bishop *Pinus muricata*

pine, black *Pinus nigra, Prumnopitys ladei*
pine, blue *Pinus wallichiana*
pine, bog *Halocarpus bidwillii*
pine, Bosnian *Pinus heldreichii, P. h.* var. *leucodermis*
pine, Bribie Island *Callitris columellaris*
pine, bristlecone *Pinus aristata*
pine, brown *Podocarpus elatus*
pine, bunya *Araucaria bidwillii*
pine, bunya bunya *Araucaria bidwillii*
pine, Canary Island *Pinus canariensis*
pine, Caribbean *Pinus caribaea*
pine, celery *Phyllocladus, P. trichomanoides*
pine, celery-top *Phyllocladus aspleniifolius*
pine, Cheshunt *Diselma archeri*
pine, chiapas white *Pinus chiapensis*
pine, chilgoza *Pinus gerardiana*
pine, Chinese red *Pinus massoniana, P. tabuliformis*
pine, Chinese white *Pinus armandii*
pine, chir *Pinus roxburghii*
pine, cluster *Pinus pinaster*
pine, Corsican *Pinus nigra* var. *maritima*
pine, Coulter *Pinus coulteri*
pine, cow's-tail *Cephalotaxus harringtonia* 'Fastigiata'
pine, creeping *Microcachrys, M. tetragona*
pine, David's *Pinus armandii*
pine, dewy *Drosophyllum lusitonicum*
pine, digger *Pinus sabiniana*
pine, dragon's-eye *Pinus densiflora* 'Oculus-draconis'
pine, Durango *Pinus durangensis*
pine, dwarf *Microstrobos niphophilus*
pine, dwarf mountain *Pinus mugo*
pine, dwarf Siberian *Pinus pumila*

pine, eastern white *Pinus strobus*
pine, Engelmann *Pinus engelmannii*
pine, European joint *Ephedra distachya*
pine, flat-leaf *Pinus krempfii*
pine, foxtail *Pinus balfouriana*
pine, gray *Pinus sabiniana*
pine, Great Basin bristlecone *Pinus longaeva*
pine, ground *Lycopodium clavatum*
pine heath *Astroloma pinifolium*
Pine Hill flannel bush *Fremontodendron decumbens*
pine, Himalayan *Pinus wallichiana*
pine, Himalayan long-leaf *Pinus roxburghii*
pine, Holford *Pinus × holfordiana*
pine, hoop *Araucaria cunninghamii*
pine, Huon *Lagarostrobos franklinii*
pine, jack *Pinus banksiana*
pine, Japanese black pine *Pinus thunbergii*
pine, Japanese red *Pinus densiflora*
pine, Japanese stone *Pinus pumila*
pine, Japanese umbrella *Sciadopitys verticillata*
pine, Japanese white *Pinus parviflora*
pine, Jeffrey *Pinus jeffreyi*
pine, King Billy *Athrotaxis selaginoides*
pine, King William *Athrotaxis selaginoides*
pine, klinki *Araucaria hunsteinii*
pine, knobcone *Pinus attenuata*
pine, Korean *Pinus koraiensis*
pine, lacebark *Pinus bungeana*
pine, limber *Pinus flexilis*
pine, loblolly *Pinus taeda*
pine, lodgepole *Pinus contorta, P. c.* var. *latifolia*
pine, lohan *Podocarpus macrophyllus*
pine, longleaf *Pinus palustris*
pine, Lumholtz *Pinus lumholtzii*

pine, Macedonian *Pinus peuce*
pine, mallee *Callitris tuberculata*
pine, maritime *Pinus pinaster*
pine, Mexican *Pinus patula*
pine, Mexican nut *Pinus cembroides*
pine, Mexican white *Pinus ayacahuite*
pine, Michoacan *Pinus devoniana*
pine, monkey puzzle *Araucaria araucana*
pine, Monterey *Pinus radiata*
pine, Montezuma *Pinus montezumae*
pine, mountain *Pinus mugo*
Pine Mountain grevillea *Grevillea jephcottii*
pine, mountain plum *Podocarpus lawrencei*
pine, Mugo *Pinus mugo*
pine, New Caledonian *Araucaria columnaris*
pine, New Zealand black *Prumnopitys taxifolia*
pine, New Zealand celery-top *Phyllocladus trichomanoides*
pine, New Zealand red *Dacrydium cupressinum*
pine, New Zealand silver *Manoao colensoi*
pine, New Zealand white *Dacrycarpus dacrydioides*
pine, Norfolk Island *Araucaria heterophylla*
pine, northern pitch *Pinus rigida*
pine, nut *Pinus edulis*
pine, Ocote *Pinus oocarpa*
pine, Okinawa *Pinus luchuensis*
pine, Oyster Bay *Callitris rhomboidea*
pine, Parana *Araucaria angustifolia*
pine, pencil *Cupressus sempervirens* 'Stricta'
pine, pitch *Pinus palustris*
pine, plum *Podocarpus elatus*
pine, pond *Pinus serotina*

pine, ponderosa *Pinus ponderosa*
pine, pygmy *Lepidothamnus laxifolius*
pine, radiata *Pinus radiata*
pine, red *Pinus resinosa*
pine, remarkable *Pinus radiata*
pine, Rocky Mountain bristlecone
 Pinus aristata
pine, Roman *Pinus pinea*
pine, Rottnest Island *Callitris preissii*
pine, rough-barked Mexican *Pinus
 montezumae*
pine, running *Lycopodium clavatum*
pine, sand *Pinus clausa*
pine, Scotch *Pinus sylvestris*
pine, Scots *Pinus sylvestris*
pine, scrub *Pinus virginiana*
pine, shore *Pinus contorta*
pine, shortleaf *Pinus echinata*
pine, shortstraw *Pinus echinata*
pine, silver *Manoao colensoi*
pine, slash *Pinus elliottii*
pine, smooth-barked Mexican *Pinus
 pseudostrobus*
pine, smooth-leaf *Pinus leiophylla*
pine, Soledad *Pinus torreyana*
pine, South Esk *Callitris oblonga*
pine, spreading-leafed *Pinus patula*
pine, spruce *Pinus glabra*
pine, stone *Pinus pinea*
pine, sugar *Pinus lambertiana*
pine sugar bush *Protea aristata*
pine, Sumatran *Pinus merkusii*
pine, Swiss mountain *Pinus mugo*
pine, Swiss stone *Pinus cembra*
pine, Table Mountain *Pinus pungens*
pine, Tasmanian pencil *Athrotaxis
 cupressoides*
pine, tenasserim *Pinus merkusii*
 subsp. *latteri*
pine, thin-leaf *Pinus maximinoi*
pine, Torrey *Pinus torreyana*
pine, Turkish *Pinus brutia*
pine, twisted-leaf *Pinus teocote*

pine, umbrella *Pinus pinea,
 Sciadopitys verticillata*
pine, Virginia *Pinus virginiana*
pine, weeping *Pinus patula*
pine, western white *Pinus monticola*
pine, western yellow *Pinus ponderosa*
pine, white *Pinus strobus*
pine, whitebark *Pinus albicaulis*
pine, Wollemi *Wollemia nobilis*
pine, yellow *Halocarpus biformis*
pine, yellow silver *Lepidothamnus
 intermedius*
pine, Yunnan *Pinus yunnanensis*
pineapple *Ananas, A. comosus*
pineapple guava *Acca sellowiana*
pineapple lily *Eucomis*
pineapple lily, white *Eucomis
 autumnalis*
pineapple, red *Ananas bracteatus*
pineapple sage *Salvia elegans*
pineapple, variegated *Ananas
 bracteatus* 'Tricolor', *A. comosus*
 'Variegatus'
pineapple, wild *Ananas bracteatus*
pine-cone cactus *Pelecyphora
 strobiliformis*
pine-cone ginger *Zingiber zerumbet*
pine-leaf geebung *Persoonia pinifolia*
pine-leaf milkweed *Asclepias linaria*
pine-leafed bottlebrush *Callistemon
 pinifolius*
pine-mat *Ceanothus diversifolius*
pine-needle milkweed *Asclepias
 linaria*
pine-needle she-oak *Allocasuarina
 pinaster*
pings *Pinguicula*
pinguin *Bromelia pinguin*
pink *Dianthus*
pink agapanthus *Tulbaghia simmleri*
pink allamanda *Allamanda blanchetii*
pink anemone clematis *Clematis
 montana* 'Rubens'

pink arum *Zantedeschia rehmannii*
pink bells *Tetratheca ciliata,*
T. ericifolia
pink bignonia *Clytostoma*
callistegioides
pink bindweed *Convolvulus erubescens*
pink bloodwood *Corymbia*
intermedia
pink breath of heaven *Coleonema*
pulchellum
pink broom *Notospartium*
carmichaeliae
pink broom, New Zealand
Carmichaelia carmichaeliae
pink, Carthusian *Dianthus*
carthusianorum
pink cassia *Cassia javanica*
pink cedar *Acrocarpus fraxinifolius*
pink, cheddar *Dianthus*
gratianopolitanus
pink, common *Dianthus plumarius*
pink, cushion *Silene acaulis*
pink diosma *Coleonema pulchellum*
pink dombeya *Dombeya burgessiae*
pink evening primrose *Oenothera*
rosea, O. speciosa, O. s. 'Rosea'
pink fingers *Caladenia carnea,*
C. catenata
pink fivecorners *Styphelia triflora,*
S. tubiflora
pink floss-silk tree *Ceiba speciosa*
pink foam creeper *Congea tomentosa*
pink fringe flower *Loropetalum*
chinense 'Burgundy'
pink, fringed Indian *Silene laciniata*
pink fringe-myrtle *Calytrix*
longiflora
pink, garden *Dianthus*
pink garland lily *Calostemma*
purpureum
pink heath *Epacris impressa*
pink hibiscus, dwarf *Hibiscus*
pedunculatus

pink kunzea *Kunzea capitata*
pink lace flower *Archidendron*
grandiflorum
pink, maiden *Dianthus deltoides*
pink mink *Protea neriifolia*
pink, mountain *Rhododendron*
prinophyllum
pink mountain berry *Leucopogon*
parviflorus
pink mountain heather *Phyllodoce*
empetriformis
pink mulla mulla *Ptilotus exaltatus,*
P. manglesii
pink musk mallow *Malva moschata*
'Rosea'
pink oxalis *Oxalis debilis* var.
corymbosa
pink periwinkle *Catharanthus roseus*
pink phebalium *Phebalium nottii*
pink pokers *Grevillea petrophiloides*
pink porcelain lily *Alpinia zerumbet*
pink poui *Tabebuia rosea*
pink, proliferous *Petrorhagia*
nanteuilii, P. velutina
pink pussytoes *Antennaria*
microphylla
pink rock orchid *Dendrobium*
kingianum
pink, saxifrage *Petrorhagia saxifraga*
pink, sea *Armeria*
pink shower *Cassia grandis,*
C. javanica
pink silk tree *Albizia julibrissin*
'Rosea'
pink siris *Albizia julibrissin*
pink snakeweed *Stachytarpheta*
mutabilis
pink spider flower *Grevillea sericea*
pink spike hakea *Hakea coriacea*
pink sundew *Drosera capillaris*
pink, swamp *Helonias bullata*
pink swamp heath *Sprengelia*
incarnata

pink tips *Callistemon salignus*
pink tree broom, New Zealand *Carmichaelia glabrescens*
pink trumpet tree *Tabebuia heterophylla*
pink trumpet vine *Podranea ricasoliana*
pink tulip tree *Magnolia campbellii*
pink velvet bush *Lasiopetalum behrii*
pink vygie *Lampranthus blandus*
pink wax flower *Eriostemon australasius*
pink wild onion *Allium acuminatum*
pink wild pear *Dombeya burgessiae*
pink-and-white powderpuff *Calliandra surinamensis*
pink-flowered corkwood *Melicope elleryana*
pink-flowered doughwood *Melicope elleryana*
pinkheart *Medicosma cunninghamii*
pinkpussy willow *Salix caprea*
pink-shell azalea *Rhododendron vaseyi*
pinkwood *Eucryphia lucida, E. moorei*
pinnate boronia *Boronia pinnata*
pinnate hopbush *Dodonaea pinnata*
pinnate wedge pea *Gompholobium pinnatum*
pinot *Euterpe oleracea*
pint, cuckoo *Arum maculatum*
pinto peanut *Arachis pintoi*
pinuela *Bromelia pinguin*
pinwheel *Aeonium haworthii*
pinwheel flower *Tabernaemontana divaricata*
pinxter azalea *Rhododendron periclymenoides*
pinxter flower *Rhododendron periclymenoides*
pinxterbloom azalea *Rhododendron periclymenoides*

pinyon *Pinus cembroides, P. edulis*
pinyon, Parry's *Pinus quadrifolia*
pinyon, Rocky Mountain *Pinus edulis*
pinyon, single-leaf *Pinus monophylla*
pinyon, weeping *Pinus pinceana*
pipe, Dutchman's *Aristolochia*
pipestem clematis *Clematis lasiantha*
pipsissewa *Chimaphila, C. umbellata*
pirri-pirri *Acaena novae-zelandiae*
pistachio *Pistacia vera*
pistachio, American *Pistacia texana*
pistachio, Chinese *Pistacia chinensis*
pistachio nut *Pistacia vera*
pistol bush *Duvernoia adhatodoides*
pistol bush, lemon *Duvernoia aconitiflora*
pistol, monkey *Hura crepitans*
pita, palma *Yucca treculeana*
pitanga *Eugenia pitanga, E. uniflora*
pitch pine *Pinus palustris*
pitch pine, northern *Pinus rigida*
pitcher, marsh *Heliamphora*
pitcher plant *Nepenthes, Sarracenia*
pitcher plant, Albany *Cephalotus follicularis*
pitcher plant, American *Sarracenia*
pitcher plant, California *Darlingtonia californica*
pitcher plant, green *Sarracenia oreophila*
pitcher plant, hooded *Sarracenia minor*
pitcher plant, northern *Sarracenia purpurea*
pitcher plant, painted *Nepenthes burbidgeae*
pitcher plant, pale *Sarracenia alata*
pitcher plant, parrot *Sarracenia purpurea, S. p. × psittacina*
pitcher plant, Western Australian *Cephalotus follicularis*

pitcher plants, tropical *Nepenthes*
pitcher sage *Salvia spathacea*
pitcher, sun *Heliamphora*
pitcher, trumpet *Sarracenia*
pitcheri *Duboisia hopwoodii*
pitchforks *Bidens*
pithy sword-sedge *Lepidosperma longitudinale*
pitted bluegrass *Bothriochloa decipiens*
pittosporum, Cape *Pittosporum viridiflorum*
pittosporum, Japanese *Pittosporum tobira*
pittosporum, Lord Howe *Pittosporum erioloma*
pittosporum, sweet *Pittosporum undulatum*
pittosporum, thorny *Pittosporum oreillyanum*
pittosporum, weeping *Pittosporum phylliraeoides*
pittosporum, yellow *Pittosporum revolutum*
pituri *Duboisia hopwoodii*
pixie mops *Petrophile linearis*
pizza oregano *Origanum heracleoticum*
plains acacia *Acacia berlandieri*
plains cottonwood *Populus sargentii*
plains grass *Austrostipa aristiglumis, A. bigeniculata*
plains plover-daisy *Ixiolaena brevicompta*
plains prickly pear *Opuntia polyacantha*
plains soapweed *Yucca glauca*
plains spurge *Euphorbia planiticola*
plains yellow primrose *Calylophus serrulatus*
plane, American *Platanus occidentalis*
plane, Arizona *Platanus wrightii*
plane, California *Platanus racemosa*

plane, London *Platanus hispanica*
plane, Mexican *Platanus mexicana*
plane, oriental *Platanus orientalis*
plane, peeling *Ochna pulchra*
plane tree *Platanus*
planer tree *Planera aquatica*
plant, beef *Iresine herbstii*
plant, bootlace *Pimelea axiflora*
plant, cigarette *Cuphea ignea*
plant, cotton *Celmisia spectabilis*
plant, cruel *Araujia sericifera*
plant, curry *Helichrysum italicum*
plant, fruit salad *Monstera deliciosa*
plant, gum *Grindelia*
plant, ice *Lampranthus, Mesembryanthemum, Ruschia, Sedum spectabile*
plant, kris *Alocasia sanderiana*
plant, mile-a-minute *Fallopia aubertii*
plant, Panama hat *Carludovica palmata*
plant, pitcher *Nepenthes* hybrid, *Nepenthes mirabilis, Sarracenia*
plant, seersucker *Geogenanthus undatus*
plant, sensitive *Mimosa pudica, Neptunia dimorphantha*
plant, spider *Chlorophytum comosum*
plant, Swiss cheese *Monstera deliciosa*
plant, velvet *Gynura aurantiaca*
plant, wax *Eriostemon australasius, Hoya carnosa, Philotheca*
plant, Western Australian pitcher *Cephalotus, Follicularis*
plant, window *Fenestraria aurantiaca, F. rhopalophylla*
plantain *Musa* × *paradisiaca, Plantago, P. lanceolata*
plantain, buck's-horn *Plantago coronopus*

plantain, cut-leafed *Plantago coronopus*
plantain, large *Plantago major*
plantain lily *Hosta, H. plantaginea*
plantain lily, blue *Hosta ventricosa*
plantain, rat's-tail *Plantago major*
plantain, robin's *Erigeron pulchellus*
plantain, variable *Plantago varia*
plantain, water *Alisma plantago-aquatica*
plantain, wild *Heliconia, Heliconia bihai, H. caribaea*
platinum pepper *Peperomia griseoargentea*
platter leaf *Coccoloba uvifera*
plectranthus, large-flowered *Plectranthus ambiguus*
pleurisy root *Asclepias tuberosa*
ploughbreaker *Erythrina zeyheri*
ploughshare wattle *Acacia cultriformis, A. gunnii*
plover-daisy, plains *Ixiolaena brevicompta*
plover-daisy, stalked *Ixiolaena leptolepis*
plum *Prunus domestica*
plum, Allegheny *Prunus alleghaniensis*
plum, American *Prunus americana*
plum, American red *Prunus americana*
plum, Assyrian *Cordia myxa*
plum, batoko *Flacourtia indica*
plum, beach *Prunus maritima*
plum, big-tree *Prunus mexicana*
plum, black *Diospyros australis*
plum, black cherry *Prunus cerasifera* 'Nigra'
plum, Blireana *Prunus × blireana*
plum boxwood *Amorphospermum whitei*
plum, Burdekin *Pleiogynium timorense*

plum, Canadian *Prunus nigra*
plum, cherry *Prunus cerasifera*
plum, chickasaw *Prunus angustifolia*
plum, creek *Prunus rivularis*
plum, date *Diospyros lotus*
plum, Davidson *Davidsonia pruriens*
plum, double pink flowering *Prunus × blireana*
plum, dove *Coccoloba laurifolia*
plum, European *Prunus × domestica*
plum, flatwoods *Prunus umbellata*
plum, flowering *Prunus cerasifera*
plum, goose *Prunus americana*
plum, governor's *Flacourtia indica, F. rukam*
plum, hard-leafed monkey *Diospyros scabrida*
plum, hog *Prunus americana*
plum, hortulan *Prunus hortulana*
plum, Indian *Flacourtia rukam*
plum, jacket *Pappea capensis*
plum, Japanese *Prunus salicina*
plum, Japanese date *Diospyros kaki*
plum, Java *Syzygium cumini*
plum, Madagascar *Flacourtia indica*
plum, marmalade *Pouteria sapota*
plum, Maroola *Sclerocarya birrea*
plum, Mexican *Prunus mexicana*
plum, Naples *Prunus cocomilia*
plum, Natal *Carissa macrocarpa*
plum, nonda *Parinari nonda*
plum, Oklahoma *Prunus gracilis*
plum, Oregon *Oemleria cerasiformis, Prunus subcordata*
plum, Pacific *Prunus subcordata*
plum pine *Podocarpus elatus*
plum pine, mountain *Podocarpus lawrencei*
plum, purple-leafed *Prunus cerasifera* 'Nigra'
plum, red olive *Cassine australis*
plum, red-leaf *Prunus × cistena*

plum, rusty *Amorphospermum whitei*

plum, sand *Prunus maritima*

plum, small date *Diospyros lotus*

plum, South African wild *Harpephyllum caffrum*

plum, tulip *Pleiogynium timorense*

plum, wild *Podocarpus drouynianus, Pouteria australis, Prunus americana*

plum, wild goose *Prunus munsoniana*

plumbago *Plumbago auriculata*

plumbago, blue *Plumbago auriculata*

plumbago, Chinese *Ceratostigma willmottianum*

plumbago, white *Plumbago auriculata* 'Alba'

plume, Apache *Fallugia paradoxa*

plume, Brazilian *Justicia carnea*

plume grass *Dichelachne crinita, Saccharum ravennae*

plume grass, long-haired *Dichelachne crinita*

plume grass, short-haired *Dichelachne micrantha*

plume grass, sparse *Dichelachne rara*

plume poppy *Macleaya, M. cordata*

plume, scarlet *Euphorbia fulgens*

plume, Solomon's *Smilacina*

plume, southern *Elliottia racemosa*

plumed maidenhair *Adiantum formosum*

plumed tussock grass *Chionochloa conspicua*

plum-fruited yew *Prumnopitys andina*

plum-leaf azalea *Rhododendron pruniflorum*

plumosa fern lily *Asparagus setaceus*

plumwood, yellow *Pouteria myrsinoides*

plum-yew *Cephalotaxus*

plum-yew, Chinese *Cephalotaxus sinensis*

plum-yew, Fortune's *Cephalotaxus fortunei*

plum-yew, Japanese *Cephalotaxus harringtonia, C. h.* var. *drupacea*

Plunkett mallee *Eucalyptus curtisii*

plush plant *Echeveria pulvinata*

Plymouth crowberry *Corema conradii*

po mu *Fokienia hodginsii*

poa, scaly *Poa fax*

poached egg daisy *Myriocephalus stuartii*

pocketbook plant *Calceolaria* Herbeohybrida Group

pod, monkey *Albizia saman, Senna petersiana*

pod, rusty *Hovea longifolia*

pod, sjambok *Cassia abbreviata*

podocarp, blackleaf *Podocarpus neriifolius*

podocarp, cloud *Podocarpus nubigenus*

podocarp, Tasmanian *Podocarpus lawrencei*

podocarp, willow *Podocarpus salignus*

poet's jasmine *Jasminum officinale*

poet's narcissus *Narcissus poeticus*

pohutukawa *Metrosideros excelsus*

pohutukawa, Kermadec *Metrosideros kermadecensis*

poinciana *Delonix regia*

poinciana, royal *Delonix regia*

poinciana, thorny *Caesalpinia decapetala*

poinsettia *Euphorbia pulcherrima*

poinsettia, double red *Euphorbia pulcherrima* 'Henrietta Ecke'

Point Reyes creeper *Ceanothus gloriosus*

pointed mallee *Eucalyptus socialis*

pointed-leaf manzanita *Arctostaphylos pungens*

poison bulb *Crinum asiaticum*

poison bulb, bushman's *Boophone disticha*
poison bush, common *Acokanthera oppositifolia*
poison bush, dune *Acokanthera oblongifolia*
poison bush, peach-leaf *Trema aspera*
poison bush, round-leafed *Acokanthera schimperi*
poison, bushman's *Acokanthera oppositifolia*
poison buttercup *Ranunculus sceleratus*
poison elder *Toxicodendron vernix*
poison, fall *Eupatorium rugosum*
poison, fly *Amianthium muscitoxicum*
poison lily, Asiatic *Crinum asiaticum*
poison oak, California *Toxicodendron diversilobum*
poison oak, western *Toxicodendron diversilobum*
poison pea *Gastrolobium*
poison peach *Trema aspera*
poison pimelea *Pimelea decora*
poison pratia *Pratia concolor*
poison primrose *Primula obconica, P. sinensis*
poison rice flower *Pimelea pauciflora*
poison, rock *Gastrolobium callistachys*
poison sumac *Rhus vernix, Toxicodendron succedaneum, T. vernix*
poison tree, brush *Excoecaria dallachyana*
poison tree, Florida *Metopium toxiferum*
pokaka *Elaeocarpus hookerianus*
poke *Phytolacca americana*
pokeberry *Phytolacca americana*
poker, red-hot *Kniphofia*
poker tree, red-hot *Erythrina abyssinica*
poker, winter *Kniphofia ensifolia*
pokers, pink *Grevillea petrophiloides*

pokers, red *Hakea bucculenta*
pokeweed *Phytolacca americana*
Pokolbin mallee *Eucalyptus pumila*
polecat bush *Rhus aromatica*
polecat tree *Illicium floridanum*
polemonium, Arctic *Polemonium boreale*
polemonium, showy *Polemonium pulcherrimum*
polemonium, skunk *Polemonium viscosum*
polemonium, sticky *Polemonium viscosum*
policeman's helmet *Impatiens glandulifera*
polished willow *Salix laevigata*
polka-dot plant *Hypoestes phyllostachya*
pollia *Pollia crispata*
polyanthus *Primula × pruhonicensis* hybrids
polyanthus narcissus *Narcissus tazetta*
polyanthus primula *Primula × pruhonicensis*
polymeria *Polymeria calycina*
Polynesian arrowroot *Tacca leontopetaloides*
Polynesian hare's foot *Davallia solida*
polypody *Polypodium*
polypody, California *Polypodium californicum*
polypody, coast *Polypodium scouleri*
polypody, common *Polypodium vulgare*
polypody, golden *Phlebodium aureum*
polypody, leathery *Polypodium scouleri*
polypody, southern *Polypodium cambricum*
polypody, Welsh *Polypodium cambricum*
polypore fungus *Boletellus ananas*
pomaderris, hazel *Pomaderris aspera*

pomaderris, velvet *Pomaderris velutina*
pomaderris, woolly *Pomaderris lanigera*
pomax *Pomax umbellata*
pomegranate *Punica granatum*
pomegranate, common *Punica granatum*
pomegranate, dwarf *Punica granatum* 'Nana'
pomegranate, South African *Burchellia bubalina*
pomelo *Citrus maxima*
pomme blanche *Psoralea esculenta*
pomme de prairie *Psoralea esculenta*
pommelo *Citrus maxima*
pomodoro *Lycopersicon esculentum*
pompon tree *Dais cotinifolia*
pond apple *Annona glabra*
pond cypress *Taxodium ascendens*
pond lily *Nymphaea odorata*
pond pine *Pinus serotina*
ponderosa pine *Pinus ponderosa*
Pondo waterwood *Syzygium pondoense*
Pondoland palm *Jubaeopsis caffra*
pondweed *Potamogeton*
pondweed, blunt *Potamogeton ochreatus*
pondweed, Canadian *Elodea canadensis*
pondweed, Cape *Aponogeton distachyos*
pondweed, clasped *Potamogeton perfoliatus*
pondweed, clasping leaf *Potamogeton perfoliatus*
pondweed, curly *Potamogeton crispus*
pondweed, floating *Potamogeton tricarinatus*
pondweed, perfoliate *Potamogeton perfoliatus*
pondweed, sago *Potamogeton pectinatus*

ponga *Cyathea dealbata*
pongam *Pongamia pinnata*
pongamia *Pongamia pinnata*
Pontic azalea *Rhododendron luteum*
Pontic rhododendron *Rhododendron ponticum*
Pontine oak *Quercus pontica*
ponytail palm *Beaucarnea recurvata*
Poor Knights lily *Xeronema callistemon*
poor man's orchid *Schizanthus ×wisetonensis*
poor man's umbrella *Gunnera insignis*
pop saltbush *Atriplex holocarpa, A. spongiosa*
popinac, white *Leucaena leucocephala*
poplar *Populus*
poplar, American black *Populus deltoides*
poplar, balsam *Populus balsamifera*
poplar, Berlin *Populus × berolinensis*
poplar, black *Populus nigra*
poplar, bolleana *Populus alba* 'Pyramidalis'
poplar box *Eucalyptus populnea*
poplar, Canadian *Populus × canadensis*
poplar, Carolina *Populus × canadensis*
poplar, Chinese necklace *Populus lasiocarpa*
poplar, gray *Populus × canescens*
poplar gum *Eucalyptus alba*
poplar, Himalayan *Populus ciliata*
poplar, hybrid *Populus × canadensis*
poplar, Japanese *Populus maximowiczii*
poplar, laurel *Populus laurifolia*
poplar, Lombardy *Populus nigra* 'Italica'
poplar, Mesopotamian *Populus euphratica*
poplar, native *Codonocarpus cotinifolius, Omalanthus populifolius*

poplar, silver *Populus alba*
poplar, swamp *Populus heterophylla*
poplar, Theves *Populus nigra*
'Afghanica'
poplar, tower *Populus × canescens*
poplar, white *Populus alba*
poplar, Yunnan *Populus yunnanensis*
poppy *Papaver*
poppy, alpine *Papaver alpinum*
poppy, Arctic *Papaver nudicaule*
poppy, blue *Meconopsis*
betonicifolia
poppy, California *Eschscholzia,*
E. californica, Platystemon
poppy, celandine *Stylophorum*
diphyllum
poppy, Chinese celandine
Stylophorum lasiocarpum
poppy, corn *Papaver rhoeas*
poppy, field *Papaver rhoeas*
poppy, Flanders *Papaver rhoeas*
poppy, horned *Glaucium*
poppy, Iceland *Papaver nudicaule*
poppy mallow *Callirhoe*
poppy mallow, low *Callirhoe*
involucrata
poppy mallow, prairie *Callirhoe*
involucrata
poppy mallow, purple *Callirhoe*
involucrata
poppy, Matilija *Romneya coulteri*
poppy, Mexican *Argemone*
mexicana
poppy, Mexican tulip *Hunnemannia*
fumariifolia
poppy, native *Papaver aculeatum*
poppy of the dawn *Eomecon*
chionantha
poppy, opium *Papaver somniferum*
poppy, oriental *Papaver orientale*
poppy, plume *Macleaya, M. cordata*
poppy, prickly *Argemone, Papaver*
argemone

poppy, rough *Papaver × hybridum*
poppy, satin *Meconopsis napaulensis*
poppy, sea *Glaucium*
poppy, Shirley *Papaver rhoeas*
cultivar
poppy, snow *Eomecon chionantha*
poppy, tree *Dendromecon rigida*
poppy, tufted California *Eschscholzia*
caespitosa
poppy, Welsh *Meconopsis cambrica*
poppy, western *Papaver californicum*
poppy, wild *Papaver × hybridum*
poppy, wind *Anemone coronaria,*
Stylomecon heterophyllus
poppy, wood *Stylophorum diphyllum*
poppy, yellow horned *Glaucium*
flavum
pops, May *Passiflora incarnata*
poranthera, small *Poranthera*
microphylla
porcelain lily, pink *Alpinia zerumbet*
porcupine grass *Triodia mitchellii,*
T. scariosa
poroporo *Solanum aviculare*
poroporo, large *Solanum laciniatum*
Port Jackson *Callitris rhomboidea*
Port Jackson cypress-pine *Callitris*
rhomboidea
Port Jackson fig *Ficus rubiginosa*
Port Jackson mallee *Eucalyptus*
obstans
Port Jackson willow *Acacia saligna*
Port Orford cedar *Chamaecyparis*
lawsoniana
Port St John creeper *Podranea*
ricasoliana
portia tree *Thespesia populnea*
Portugal heath *Erica lusitanica*
Portugal laurel *Prunus lusitanica*
Portuguese broom *Chamaecytisus*
albus, Cytisus multiflorus
Portuguese crowberry *Corema*
album

Portuguese foxglove *Digitalis purpurea* subsp. *heywoodii*
Portuguese heath *Erica lusitanica*
Portuguese oak *Quercus faginea, Q. lusitanica*
Portuguese sundew *Drosophyllum lusitanicum*
portulaca *Portulaca grandiflora*
portulaca, garden *Portulaca grandiflora*
port-wine magnolia *Michelia figo*
possum banksia *Banksia baueri*
possum grape *Cissus trifoliata*
possum-haw *Ilex decidua, Viburnum acerifolium*
possum-haw viburnum *Viburnum nudum*
possumwood *Quintinia sieberi*
possumwood, gray *Quintinia verdonii*
post oak *Quercus stellata*
postman, running *Kennedia prostrata*
posy, rosy *Rhodohypoxis baurii*
pot marigold *Calendula officinalis*
pot marjoram *Origanum onites*
potato *Solanum tuberosum*
potato, air *Dioscorea bulbifera*
potato bush, blue *Solanum rantonnetii*
potato bush, spiny *Solanum ferocissimum*
potato bush, velvet *Solanum ellipticum*
potato, Chinese *Dioscorea batatas*
potato creeper, giant *Solanum wendlandii*
potato fern *Marattia salicina*
potato, Mexican *Pachyrhizus erosus*
potato, Otaheite *Dioscorea bulbifera*
potato, sweet *Ipomoea batatas*
potato, Telingo *Amorphophallus paeoniifolius*
potato tree *Solanum erianthum*

potato tree, Brazilian *Solanum wrightii*
potato vine *Solanum jasminoides, S. wendlandii*
potato vine, Chilean *Solanum crispum*
potato weed *Heliotropium europaeum*
potato yam *Dioscorea esculenta*
potatoes, Eskimo *Fritillaria camschatcensis*
potentilla *Potentilla*
potentilla, scarlet *Potentilla atrosanguinea*
pouched coral fern *Gleichenia dicarpa*
poui, pink *Tabebuia rosea*
poverty grass *Hudsonia tomentosa*
poverty wattle *Acacia dawsonii*
poverty-bush, streaked *Sclerolaena tricuspis*
poverty-bush, tangled *Sclerolaena intricata*
powderpuff cactus *Mammillaria bocasana*
powderpuff lillypilly *Syzygium wilsonii*
powderpuff, golden *Parodia chrysacanthion*
powderpuff, pink-and-white *Calliandra surinamensis*
powderpuff tree *Barringtonia racemosa, Calliandra haematocephala*
powderpuff, white *Calliandra portoricensis*
powdery alligator flag *Thalia dealbata*
powdery strap airplant *Catopsis berteroniana*
powton *Paulownia fortunei*
prairie aster *Machaeranthera tanacetifolia*
prairie chickweed *Cerastium arvense*
prairie clover, purple *Dalea purpurea*
prairie coneflower *Ratibida columnifera, R. pinnata*

prairie crab *Malus ioensis*
prairie crabapple *Malus ioensis*
prairie dock *Silphium terebinthinaceum*
prairie dropseed *Sporobolus heterolepsis*
prairie false indigo *Baptisia lactea*
prairie fire *Castilleja*
prairie gentian *Eustoma*
prairie grass *Bromus catharticus*
prairie mallow *Sphaeralcea coccinea*
prairie onion *Allium stellatum*
prairie phlox *Phlox pilosa*
prairie, pomme de *Psoralea esculenta*
prairie poppy mallow *Callirhoe involucrata*
prairie, queen of the *Filipendula rubra*
prairie rose *Rosa arkansana, R. setigera*
prairie smoke *Geum triflorum*
prairie zinnia *Zinnia grandiflora*
pratia, Darling *Pratia darlingensis*
pratia, matted *Pratia pedunculata*
pratia, poison *Pratia concolor*
prayer plant *Maranta leuconeura*
prayer plant, red-veined *Maranta leuconeura* 'Erythroneura'
precatory bean *Abrus precatorius*
preserving melon, Chinese *Benincasa hispida*
Preston lilac *Syringa* × *prestoniae*
pretty face *Triteleia ixioides*
pretty sundew *Drosera pulchella*
pricklefoot *Eryngium vesiculosum*
prickle-vine, corky *Caesalpinia subtropica*
prickle-vine, large *Caesalpinia scortechinii*
prickly alyxia *Alyxia ruscifolia*
prickly ash *Zanthoxylum americanum, Z. simulans*

prickly ash, northern *Zanthoxylum americanum*
prickly bottlebrush *Callistemon brachyandrus*
prickly broom-heath *Monotoca scoparia*
prickly cardinal *Erythrina zeyheri*
prickly comfrey *Symphytum asperum*
prickly conostylis *Conostylis aculeata*
prickly couch *Zoysia macrantha*
prickly cucumber *Cucumis myriocarpus*
prickly currant bush *Coprosma quadrifida*
prickly cycad *Encephalartos altensteinii*
prickly eggs-and-bacon pea *Dillwynia juniperina*
prickly fuchsia bush *Graptophyllum ilicifolium*
prickly guinea-flower *Hibbertia acicularis*
prickly juniper *Juniperus oxycedrus*
prickly knawel *Scleranthus pungens*
prickly lettuce *Lactuca serriola*
prickly Moses *Acacia brownii, A. ulicifolia, A. verticillata*
prickly Moses, western *Acacia pulchella*
prickly myrtle *Rhaphithamnus spinosus*
prickly paddymelon *Cucumis myriocarpus*
prickly palm *Bactris major*
prickly paperbark *Melaleuca styphelioides*
prickly pear *Opuntia stricta, O. tomentosa*
prickly pear, black-spine *Opuntia macrocentra*
prickly pear, brittle *Opuntia fragilis*
prickly pear cactus *Opuntia humifusa*

prickly pear, chenille *Opuntia aciculata*

prickly pear, drooping *Opuntia monacantha*

prickly pear, Indian fig *Opuntia ficus-indica*

prickly pear, plains *Opuntia polyacantha*

prickly pear, purple-fruited *Opuntia phaeacantha*

prickly pear, starvation *Opuntia polyacantha*

prickly pear, velvet *Opuntia tomentosa*

prickly pear, white-spined *Opuntia leucotricha*

prickly phlox *Leptodactylon californicum*

prickly poppy *Argemone, Papaver argemone*

prickly rasp fern *Doodia aspera*

prickly saltwort *Salsola kali*

prickly shaggy pea *Podolobium ilicifolium*

prickly shield fern *Polystichum aculeatum, P. vestitum*

prickly sow-thistle *Sonchus asper*

prickly spider flower *Grevillea juniperina*

prickly starwort *Stellaria pungens*

prickly supplejack *Ripogonum discolor*

prickly tea-tree *Leptospermum juniperinum*

prickly thrift *Acantholimon*

prickly tree fern *Cyathea leichhardtiana*

prickly waterlily *Euryale ferox*

prickly wattle *Acacia ulicifolia, A. victoriae*

prickly wax flower *Philotheca pungens*

prickly woodruff *Asperula scoparia*

pricklybark *Eucalyptus todtiana*

pride, Barbados *Caesalpinia pulcherrima*

pride, Christmas *Ruellia macrantha*

pride, London *Saxifraga × urbium*

pride, mountain *Penstemon newberryi*

pride of Bolivia *Tipuana tipu*

pride of Burma *Amherstia nobilis*

pride of California *Lathyrus splendens*

pride of China *Koelreuteria bipinnata*

pride of De Kaap *Bauhinia galpinii*

pride of India *Lagerstroemia speciosa*

pride of Madeira *Echium candicans*

primrose *Primula, P. vulgaris*

primrose, Abyssinian *Primula verticillata*

primrose, Balkan *Ramonda myconi*

primrose, bird's eye *Primula farinosa*

primrose, Cape *Streptocarpus*

primrose, English *Primula vulgaris*

primrose, evening *Oenothera*

primrose, German *Primula obconica*

primrose jasmine *Jasminum mesnyi*

primrose, Missouri *Oenothera macrocarpa*

primrose, plains yellow *Calylophus serrulatus*

primrose, poison *Primula obconica, P. sinensis*

primrose, Scottish *Primula scotica*

primrose, water *Ludwigia peploides*

primrose, willow *Ludwigia octovalvis*

primrose willow, common *Ludwigia peruviana*

primula, drumstick *Primula denticulata*

primula, Japanese *Primula japonica*

primula, polyanthus *Primula × pruhonicensis*

Prince Albert's yew *Saxegothaea conspicua*

Prince of Wales' feathers *Leptopteris superba*
Prince of Wales' heath *Erica perspicua*
prince protea *Protea compacta*
Prince Rupprecht larch *Larix principis-rupprechtii*
prince's feather *Amaranthus cruentus, A. hybridus* var. *erythrostachyus, Persicaria orientalis*
prince's pine *Chimaphila*
princess flower *Tibouchina urvilleana*
princess gum, silver *Eucalyptus caesia* subsp. *magna*
princess palm *Dictyosperma album*
princess palm, small *Dictyosperma album* var. *conjugatum*
princess protea *Protea grandiceps*
princess tree *Paulownia tomentosa*
princess vine *Cissus sicyoides*
pring betung *Dendrocalamus asper*
prinsepia, cherry *Prinsepia sinensis*
prism cactus *Leuchtenbergia principis*
privet *Ligustrum*
privet, Amur *Ligustrum amurense*
privet, broad-leafed *Ligustrum lucidum*
privet, California *Ligustrum ovalifolium*
privet, Chinese *Ligustrum sinense*
privet, common *Ligustrum vulgare*
privet, European *Ligustrum vulgare*
privet, glossy *Ligustrum lucidum*
privet, Himalayan *Ligustrum confusum*
privet, Japanese *Ligustrum japonicum*
privet, mock *Phillyrea latifolia*
privet, New Mexico *Forestiera pubescens*
privet, oval-leafed *Ligustrum ovalifolium*
privet, small-leafed *Ligustrum sinense*
privet, swamp *Forestiera acuminata*

privet, Transvaal *Galpinia transvaalica*
privet, variegated *Ligustrum lucidum* 'Tricolor'
privet, waxleaf *Ligustrum lucidum*
privet-leafed stringybark *Eucalyptus ligustrina*
procumbent pearlwort *Sagina procumbens*
proliferous pink *Petrorhagia nanteuilii, P. velutina*
propeller bush *Dodonaea heteromorpha*
propeller plant *Crassula falcata*
propeller tree *Gyrocarpus americanus*
prostrate blue devil *Eryngium vesiculosum*
prostrate broom *Cytisus decumbens*
prostrate orache *Atriplex australasica*
prostrate rosemary *Rosmarinus officinalis* 'Prostratus'
prostrate snowberry *Gaultheria macrostigma*
protea, bearded *Protea magnifica*
protea, black *Protea lepidocarpodendron*
protea, Bot River *Protea compacta*
protea, Christmas *Protea aristata*
protea, duchess *Protea eximia*
protea, giant *Protea cynaroides*
protea, green *Protea scolymocephala*
protea, green button *Protea scolymocephala*
protea, honey *Protea repens*
protea, king *Protea cynaroides*
protea, mini *Protea scolymocephala*
protea, oleander-leafed *Protea neriifolia*
protea, peach *Protea grandiceps*
protea, prince *Protea compacta*
protea, princess *Protea grandiceps*
protea, queen *Protea magnifica*
protea, ray-flowered *Protea eximia*

protea, river *Protea compacta*
protea, Sir Lowry's Pass *Protea longifolia*
proud Mariposa *Calochortus superbus*
prune, Indian *Flacourtia rukam*
puccoon, red *Sanguinaria canadensis*
puccoon, yellow *Hydrastis canadensis*
pudding-pipe tree *Cassia fistula*
Puerto Rico hat palm *Sabal causiarum*
Puerto Rico royal palm *Roystonea borinquena*
puff, silver *Chaptalia nutans*
puka *Griselinia lucida, Meryta sinclairii*
pukanui *Meryta sinclairii*
pukatea *Laurelia novae-zelandiae*
pulai, common *Alstonia angustiloba*
pulasan *Nephelium mutabile, N. ramboutan-ake*
pummelo *Citrus maxima*
pumpkin *Cucurbita, C. maxima, C. moschata*
pumpkin ash *Fraxinus tomentosa*
pumpkin, butternut *Cucurbita moschata* 'Butternut'
pumpkin, Canada *Cucurbita moschata*
pumpkin tree *Negria rhabdothamnoides*
pumpkin, winter *Cucurbita maxima*
puniu *Polystichum vestitum*
punty bush *Senna artemisioides*
purau *Hibiscus tiliaceus*
purging nut *Jatropha curcas*
puriri *Vitex lucens*
Purisima, la *Arctostaphylos purissima*
purple allamanda *Allamanda blanchetii*
purple amaranth *Amaranthus cruentus*
purple anise *Illicium floridanum*

purple apple-berry *Billardiera longiflora*
purple aster *Aster tataricus*
purple avens *Geum triflorum*
purple barberry *Berberis thunbergii* 'Atropurpurea'
purple barberry, hybrid *Berberis × ottawensis* 'Superba'
purple beauty berry *Callicarpa dichotoma*
purple beauty bush *Callicarpa dichotoma*
purple beech *Fagus sylvatica* 'Purpurea'
purple beech, Rivers' *Fagus sylvatica* 'Riversii'
purple beech, weeping *Fagus sylvatica* 'Purpurea Pendula'
purple bell vine *Rhodochiton atrosanguineus*
purple bougainvillea *Bougainvillea glabra*
purple broom, Cape *Polygala virgata*
purple burr-daisy *Calotis cuneifolia*
purple castor oil plant *Ricinus communis* 'Cambodgensis'
purple cestrum *Cestrum × cultum*
purple cherry *Syzygium crebrinerve*
purple coneflower *Echinacea purpurea*
purple coral tree *Erythrina fusca*
purple dampiera *Dampiera purpurea*
purple dew plant *Ruschia caroli*
purple donkey orchid *Diuris punctata*
purple fan-flower *Scaevola ramosissima*
purple filbert *Corylus maxima* 'Purpurea'
purple fireweed *Arrhenechtites mixta*
purple glory plant *Sutera grandiflora*

purple goosefoot *Scleroblitum atriplicinum*
purple granadilla *Passiflora edulis*
purple ground cherry *Physalis philadelphica*
purple heather *Phyllodoce breweri*
purple hopbush *Dodonaea viscosa* 'Purpurea'
purple ice plant *Lampranthus productus*
purple loosestrife *Lythrum salicaria, L. virgatum*
purple love grass *Eragrostis lacunaria*
purple medic *Medicago sativa*
purple mint bush *Prostanthera ovalifolia*
purple moor grass *Molinia caerulea*
purple morning glory plant *Sutera grandiflora*
purple mountain saxifrage *Saxifraga oppositifolia*
purple mullein *Verbascum phoeniceum*
purple nightshade *Solanum xantii*
purple onion *Allium cepa* 'Purple Sensation'
purple osier *Salix purpurea*
purple owl clover *Castilleja exserta*
purple parsnip *Trachymene cyanopetala*
purple poppy mallow *Callirhoe involucrata*
purple prairie clover *Dalea purpurea*
purple rangiora *Brachyglottis repanda* 'Purpurea'
purple robe *Solanum xantii*
purple rock brake *Pellaea atropurpurea*
purple sage *Salvia dorrii, S. leucophylla*
purple spider plant *Tradescantia pallida* 'Purpurea'
purple spurge *Euphorbia dulcis*

purple stonecrop *Crassula peduncularis*
purple tails *Ptilotus semilanatus*
purple taro *Colocasia esculenta* 'Fontanesiana'
purple toadflax *Linaria purpurea*
purple top *Verbena bonariensis*
purple velvet plant *Gynura aurantiaca*
purple verbena *Verbena rigida*
purple violet *Viola adunca*
purple viper's bugloss *Echium plantagineum*
purple wiregrass *Aristida ramosa*
purple wreath *Petrea volubilis*
purple-coned spruce *Picea purpurea*
purple-flag *Patersonia*
purple-flag, leafy *Patersonia glabrata*
purple-flag, short *Patersonia fragilis*
purple-flag, silky *Patersonia sericea*
purple-flowered crabapple *Malus pumila* 'Niedzwetzkyana'
purple-flowering raspberry *Rubus odoratus*
purple-fruited prickly pear *Opuntia phaeacantha*
purple-leaf hazelnut *Corylus maxima*
purple-leafed Japanese maple *Acer palmatum* 'Atropurpureum'
purple-leafed plum *Prunus cerasifera* 'Nigra'
purple-leafed sand cherry *Prunus × cistena*
purple-leafed smoke tree *Cotinus coggygria* 'Purpureus'
purple-star, climbing *Rhyncharrhena linearis*
purple-top *Salvia viridis*
purple-top verbena *Verbena bonariensis*
purple-vein rocket *Eruca sativa*
purplish beard-orchid *Calochilus robertsonii*

purse, shepherd's *Capsella bursa-pastoris*
purses, ladies' *Calceolaria* Herbeohybrida Group
purslane *Claytonia, Portulaca, P. oleracea*
purslane, common *Portulaca oleracea*
purslane, sea *Atriplex hortensis*
purslane, small *Calandrinia eremaea*
purslane, tree *Atriplex halimus*
purslane, white *Neopaxia australasica*
purslane, winter *Montia perfoliata*
pussley *Portulaca oleracea*
pussy willow *Salix caprea, S. cinerea*
pussy willow, American *Salix discolor*
pussy willow, French *Salix caprea*
pussy willow, rosegold *Salix gracilistyla*
pussy-ears *Cyanotis somaliensis*
pussy-tails *Ptilotus exaltatus, P. spathulatus*
pussy-tails, tall *Ptilotus exaltatus*
pussy-toes *Antennaria*
pussy-toes, littleleaf *Antennaria microphylla*

pussy-toes, pink *Antennaria microphylla*
putaputaweta *Carpodetus serratus*
puzzle bush *Ehretia rigida*
pygmy bamboo *Pleioblastus pygmaeus*
pygmy bowstring hemp *Sansevieria intermedia*
pygmy pine *Lepidothamnus laxifolius*
pygmy sundew *Drosera pygmaea*
pygmy sunray *Rhodanthe pygmaea*
pygmy waterlily *Nymphaea tetragona*
pyramid bugle *Ajuga pyramidalis*
pyramid magnolia *Magnolia pyramidata*
Pyrenean oak *Quercus pyrenaica*
Pyrenean squill *Scilla liliohyacinthus*
Pyrenean violet *Viola pyrenaica*
Pyrenees honeysuckle *Lonicera pyrenaica*
Pyrenees saxifrage *Saxifraga longifolia*
pyrethrum *Tanacetum cinerariifolium, T. coccineum, T. parthenicum*
pyrethrum, Dalmatian *Tanacetum cinerariifolium*
pyrethrum, garden *Tanacetum coccineum*

Q/R

qat *Catha edulis*
qi ginseng *Panax pseudoginseng*
quail bush *Atriplex lentiformis*
quaking aspen *Populus tremula,
P. tremuloides*
quaking grass *Briza, B. maxima,
B. media*
quaking grass, great *Briza maxima*
Qualup bells *Pimelea physodes*
quamash *Camassia*
quandong *Santalum acuminatum*
quandong, bitter *Santalum
murrayanum*
quandong, blue *Elaeocarpus grandis*
quandong, hard *Elaeocarpus obovatus*
quandong, silver *Elaeocarpus kirtonii*
quandong, sweet *Santalum
acuminatum*
quandong, white *Elaeocarpus kirtonii*
quarter vine *Bignonia capreolata*
quassia wood *Picrasma excelsa*
quebracho *Aspidosperma quebracho-
colorado*
queen anthurium *Anthurium
warocqueanum*
queen crape myrtle *Lagerstroemia
speciosa*
queen lily *Phaedranassa*
queen of the meadows *Filipendula
ulmaria*
queen of the night *Hylocereus
undatus, Selenicereus*
queen of the night, Arizona
Peniocereus greggii
queen of the prairie *Filipendula
rubra*
queen palm *Syagrus romanzoffiana*
queen protea *Protea magnifica*
queen, snow *Synthyris reniformis*

queen's delight *Stillingia sylvatica*
queen's tears *Billbergia nutans*
queen's wreath *Petrea volubilis*
Queensland arrowroot *Canna indica*
Queensland bamboo *Bambusa
moreheadiana*
Queensland black bean
Castanospermum australe
Queensland black bean tree
Castanospermum australe
Queensland black palm *Normanbya
normanbyi*
Queensland black wattle *Acacia
leiocalyx*
Queensland blue couch *Digitaria
didactyla*
Queensland blue gum *Eucalyptus
tereticornis*
Queensland bottle tree *Brachychiton
rupestris*
Queensland brittlewood *Claoxylon
tenerifolium*
Queensland candlenut tree *Aleurites
rockinghamensis*
Queensland ebony *Bauhinia carronii*
Queensland elemi tree *Canarium
muelleri*
Queensland firewheel tree
Stenocarpus sinuatus
Queensland fishtail palm *Caryota
rumphiana* var. *albertii*
Queensland golden myrtle
Thaleropia queenslandica
Queensland grass tree *Xanthorrhoea
johnsonii*
Queensland gray ironbark *Eucalyptus
drepanophylla*
Queensland kauri *Agathis robusta*
Queensland maple *Flindersia
brayleyana*
Queensland nut *Macadamia
tetraphylla*
Queensland red beech *Dillenia alata*

Queensland umbrella tree *Schefflera
actinophylla*
Queensland wattle *Acacia
podalyriifolia*
Queensland white gum *Eucalyptus
argophloia*
quena *Solanum esuriale*
quéñoa *Polylepis tomentella*
quick-set thorn *Crataegus laevigata*
quickthorn *Crataegus monogyna*
quince *Cydonia oblonga*
quince, Chinese *Pseudocydonia
sinensis*
quince, Chinese flowering
Chaenomeles speciosa
quince, flowering *Chaenomeles,
C. speciosa*
quince, Japanese flowering
Chaenomeles japonica
quince, native *Alectryon subcinereus*
quinine *Cinchona officinalis*
quinine bush *Garrya fremontii,
Petalostigma pubescens*
quinine tree *Alstonia constricta,
Rauvolfia caffra*
quinoa *Chenopodium quinoa*
rabbit tails *Ptilotus seminudus*
rabbit tracks *Maranta leuconeura*
rabbitbrush *Chrysothamnus,
C. graveolens, C. viscidiflorus*
rabbitbrush *Chrysothamnus*
rabbitbrush, sticky-leafed
Chrysothamnus viscidiflorus
rabbit-ear iris *Iris laevigata*
rabbiteye blueberry *Vaccinium ashei*
rabbit-foot grass *Polypogon
monspeliensis*
rabbit's-foot fern *Davallia solida* var.
fejeensis, Phlebodium aureum
radiata pine *Pinus radiata*
radiator plant *Peperomia*
radicchio *Cichorium intybus*
'Red Treviso'

radish *Raphanus sativus*
radish, wild *Raphanus raphanistrum*
radium plant *Euphorbia peplus*
ragged daisy-bush *Olearia nernstii*
ragged robin *Lychnis flos-cuculi*
ragi *Eleusine coracana*
ragweed, lacy *Ambrosia tenuifolia*
ragweed, perennial *Ambrosia
psilostachya*
ragwort, Madagascar *Senecio
madagascariensis*
ragwort, sea *Senecio cineraria*
railway fence bauhinia *Bauhinia
pauletia*
rain tree *Albizia saman, Brunfelsia
undulata*
rain tree, golden *Cassia fistula,
Koelreuteria paniculata*
rainbow clubmoss *Selaginella
uncinata*
rainbow earth-star *Cryptanthus
bromelioides*
rainbow fern *Calochlaena dubia*
rainbow fungus *Trametes versicolor*
rainbow shower *Cassia javanica,
C. × nealiae*
raisin, giant *Grewia hexamita*
raisin tree, Japanese *Hovenia dulcis*
raisin, wild *Viburnum cassinoides,
V. lentago*
tamanas rose *Rosa rugosa*
ramarama *Lophomyrtus bullata*
rambling dock *Rumex sagittatus*
rambutan *Nephelium lappaceum*
rambutan, smooth *Alectryon
subcinereus*
rambutan, woolly *Alectryon
tomentosus*
ramontchi *Flacourtia indica*
rampion *Campanula rapunculus*
rampion, German *Oenothera biennis*
rampion, horned *Phyteuma*
rampion, spiked *Phyteuma spicatum*

ramsons *Allium ursinum*
rangiora *Brachyglottis repanda*
rangiora, purple *Brachyglottis repanda* 'Purpurea'
Rangoon creeper *Quisqualis indica*
Rangpur lime *Citrus × limonia*
ranunculus, garden *Ranunculus asiaticus*
rape *Brassica napus* subsp. *oleifera*
rape, bird *Brassica rapa*
rape, oil-seed *Brassica napus* subsp. *oleifera*
raphia palm *Raphia vinifera*
raphia palm, South African *Raphia australis*
raphia, southern *Raphia australis*
rapier-sedge *Lepidosperma flexuosum*
rapier-sedge, stiff *Lepidosperma neesii*
rapier-sedge, thread *Lepidosperma filiforme*
rapier-sedge, twisted *Lepidosperma tortuosum*
rasp fern *Doodia aspera*
rasp fern, prickly *Doodia aspera*
rasp fern, small *Doodia caudata*
raspberry *Rubus idaeus*
raspberry, black *Rubus occidentalis*
raspberry, European *Rubus idaeus*
raspberry, flowering *Rubus odoratus*
raspberry, ground *Hydrastis canadensis*
raspberry, Korean *Rubus crataegifolius*
raspberry, Mauritius *Rubus rosifolius*
raspberry, native *Rubus hillii, R. parvifolius, R. rosifolius*
raspberry, ornamental *Rubus odoratus*
raspberry, purple-flowering *Rubus odoratus*
raspberry, red *Rubus idaeus*
raspberry, Rocky Mountain *Rubus deliciosus*

raspberry, wild *Rubus idaeus*
raspwort *Gonocarpus, Haloragis*
raspwort, creeping *Gonocarpus micranthus*
raspwort, gray *Haloragis glauca*
raspwort, hill *Gonocarpus elatus*
raspwort, rough *Haloragis aspera*
raspwort, toothed *Haloragis odontocarpa*
raspy root orchid *Rhinerrhiza divitiflora*
rata *Metrosideros robusta*
rata, North Island *Metrosideros robusta*
rata, southern *Metrosideros umbellata*
rat's-tail cactus *Aporocactus flagelliformis*
rat's-tail couch *Sporobolus mitchellii*
rats-tail fescue *Vulpia muralis, V. myuros*
rat's-tail grass, slender *Sporobolus creber, S. elongatus*
rat's-tail orchid *Dockrillia teretifolia*
rat's-tail plantain *Plantago major*
rattan *Calamus*
rattan, bitter *Calamus viminalis*
rattan cane *Calamus rotang*
rattlebox *Crotalaria*
rattle pod *Crotalaria mitchellii*
rattle pod, gray *Crotalaria dissitiflora*
rattle pod grevillea *Grevillea stenobotrya*
rattle pod, yellow *Crotalaria mitchellii*
rattle, snap and *Eucalyptus gracilis*
rattlesnake master *Eryngium yuccifolium*
rattlesnake plant *Calathea lancifolia*
rattlesnake tail *Crassula barklyi*
rattleweed *Crotalaria retusa*
raukumara *Brachyglottis perdicioides*
rauli *Nothofagus procera*
rautini *Brachyglottis huntii*

ravenna grass *Saccharum ravennae*
ray-flowered protea *Protea eximia*
razor sedge *Lepidosperma limicola*
red alder *Alnus rubra*
red alga *Chondrus, Gelidium*
red amaranth *Amaranthus cruentus*
red and green kangaroo paw *Anigozanthos manglesii*
red angel's trumpet *Brugmansia sanguinea*
red apple *Acmena ingens*
red ash *Alphitonia excelsa, Fraxinus pennsylvanica*
red banana *Musa acuminata* 'Red'
red baneberry *Actaea rubra*
Red Bay persea *Persea borbonia*
red bead tree *Adenanthera pavonina*
red bean *Dysoxylum mollissimum, Geissois benthamiana*
red beard-orchid *Calochilus paludosus*
red beech *Dillenia alata, Nothofagus fusca*
red beech, New Zealand *Nothofagus fusca*
red beech, Queensland *Dillenia alata*
red birch, American *Betula fontinalis*
red birch, Chinese *Betula albosinensis*
red bloodwood *Corymbia gummifera*
red bopple nut *Hicksbeachia pinnatifolia*
red boronia *Boronia heterophylla*
red bouvardia *Bouvardia ternifolia*
red box *Eucalyptus polyanthemos*
red box, inland *Eucalyptus intertexta*
red brome *Bromus rubens*
red buckeye *Aesculus pavia*
red campion *Lychnis coronaria, Silene dioica*
red carabeen *Geissois benthamiana*
red cardinal flower *Lobelia fulgens*
red carpet *Crassula radicans*
red carrabeen *Geissois benthamii*

red cat-tails *Acalypha reptans*
red caustic weed *Chamaesyce prostrata*
red cedar *Juniperus virginiana, Thuja plicata*
red cedar, Australian *Toona ciliata*
red cedar, eastern *Juniperus virginiana*
red cedar, western *Thuja plicata*
red cestrum *Cestrum* 'Newellii'
red cherry *Prunus pensylvanica*
red chokeberry *Aronia arbutifolia*
red cinquefoil *Potentilla atrosanguinea*
red cloak, Brazilian *Megaskepasma erythrochlamys*
red clover *Trifolium pratense*
red cohosh *Actaea rubra*
red cole *Armoracia rusticana*
red cone peppers *Capsicum annuum* Fasciculatum Group
red elder, American *Sambucus pubens*
red elder, European *Sambucus racemosa*
red elderberry *Sambucus racemosa*
red elm *Ulmus rubra*
red false mallow *Sphaeralcea coccinea*
red fescue *Festuca rubra*
red fir, California *Abies magnifica*
red ginger *Alpinia purpurata*
red ginger lily *Hedychium coccineum*
red gram *Cajanus cajan*
red granadilla *Passiflora coccinea*
red grass *Bothriochloa macra*
red grevillea *Grevillea heliosperma*
red gum, Blakely's *Eucalyptus blakelyi*
red gum, Cape York *Eucalyptus brassiana*
red gum, Dwyer's *Eucalyptus dwyeri*
red gum, forest *Eucalyptus tereticornis*
red gum, mallee *Eucalyptus nandewarica*
red gum, narrow-leafed *Eucalyptus seeana*

red gum, Parramatta *Eucalyptus parramattensis*

red gum, river *Eucalyptus camaldulensis*

red gum, slaty *Eucalyptus glaucina*

red gum, Sydney *Angophora costata*

red gum, tumbledown *Eucalyptus dealbata*

red gum, Williamtown *Eucalyptus parramattensis* subsp. *decadens*

red heath *Erica rubens*

red heath, blood *Erica cruenta*

red hibiscus, Hawaiian *Hibiscus kokio*

red hickory *Carya ovalis*

red hook sedge *Uncinia rubra*

red horse chestnut *Aesculus* × *carnea*

red huckleberry *Vaccinium parvifolium*

red ironbark *Eucalyptus sideroxylon*

red ironbark, broad-leafed *Eucalyptus fibrosa*

red ivy *Hemigraphis alternata*

red justicia *Justicia candicans*

red kamala *Mallotus philippensis*

red kangaroo paw *Anigozanthos rufus*

red latan *Latania lontaroides*

red latan palm *Latania lontaroides*

red leschenaultia *Lechenaultia formosa*

red lillypilly *Syzygium hodgkinsoniae*

red mahogany *Eucalyptus resinifera*

red mahogany, large-fruited *Eucalyptus scias*

red mallee *Eucalyptus oleosa, E. socialis*

red mallee, narrow-leafed *Eucalyptus leptophylla*

red mangrove *Rhizophora mangle*

red maple *Acer rubrum*

red milkwood *Mimusops obovata*

red milkwood, Transvaal *Mimusops zeyheri*

red mint bush *Prostanthera calycina*

red mulberry *Morus rubra*

red Natal grass *Melinis repens*

red oak *Quercus rubra*

red oak, northern *Quercus rubra*

red oak, southern *Quercus falcata*

red oak, swamp *Quercus falcata*

red olive plum *Cassine australis*

red orchid cactus *Disocactus ackermannii*

red osier dogwood *Cornus stolonifera*

red passionflower *Passiflora cinnabarina, P. coccinea, P. manicata, P. racemosa*

red pear *Scolopia mundii*

red peony of Constantinople *Paeonia peregrina*

red pine *Pinus resinosa*

red pine, Chinese *Pinus massoniana, P. tabuliformis*

red pine, Japanese *Pinus densiflora*

red pine, New Zealand *Dacrydium cupressinum*

red pineapple *Ananas bracteatus*

red poinsettia, double *Euphorbia pulcherrima* 'Henrietta Ecke'

red pokers *Hakea bucculenta*

red puccoon *Sanguinaria canadensis*

red raspberry *Rubus idaeus*

red rocket *Leucospermum reflexum*

red rose *Rosa gallica*

red rusty-petals *Lasiopetalum rufum*

red sandalwood *Pterocarpus santalinus*

red silky oak *Carnarvonia araliifolia, Grevillea banksii, Stenocarpus salignus*

red snakebark maple *Acer capillipes*

red sorrel *Hibiscus sabdariffa*

red spider flower *Grevillea speciosa*

red spider lily *Lycoris radiata*

red star *Rhodohypoxis baurii*

red stinkwood *Prunus africana*

red stopper *Eugenia confusa*
red stringybark *Eucalyptus macrorhyncha*
red stringybark, Rylstone *Eucalyptus cannonii*
red sugarbush *Protea grandiceps*
red swamp banksia *Banksia occidentalis*
red tassel flower *Calliandra tweedii*
red thorn *Acacia gerrardii*
red tingle *Eucalyptus jacksonii*
red trillium, southern *Trillium sulcatum*
red tussock grass *Chionochloa rubra*
red twig *Leucothoe recurva*
red valerian *Centranthus ruber*
red verbena, trailing *Verbena peruviana*
red vygie *Lampranthus coccineus*
red water milfoil *Myriophyllum verrucosum*
red wedge pea *Gompholobium uncinatum*
red whortleberry *Vaccinium parvifolium*
red willow *Salix laevigata*
red wood sorrel *Oxalis oregana*
red yucca, false *Hesperaloe parviflora*
red-anther wallaby grass *Joycea pallida*
red-barked dogwood *Cornus alba*
red-berried elder *Sambucus racemosa*
redberry *Rhamnus crocea*
redberry juniper *Juniperus monosperma*
redbud *Cercis canadensis*
redbud, California *Cercis occidentalis*
redbud, Chinese *Cercis chinensis*
redbud crabapple *Malus* × *zumi*
redbud, eastern *Cercis canadensis*
redbud, mallee *Eucalyptus oleosa, E. pachyphylla*

redbud, Texas *Cercis canadensis* var. *texensis, C. reniformis*
redbud, western *Cercis occidentalis*
red-cap gum *Eucalyptus erythrocorys*
red-centered hibiscus *Alyogyne hakeifolia*
redcoat *Utricularia menziesii*
redcurrant *Rhus chirindensis, Ribes rubrum, R. sativum, R. silvestre*
redcurrant, clustered *Ribes fasciculatum*
red-eyed baboon flower *Babiana rubrocyanea*
red-flower mallow *Modiola caroliniana*
red-flowered mallee *Eucalyptus erythronema*
red-flowering gum *Corymbia ficifolia*
red-flowering lotus *Lotus cruentus*
red-fruit saw-sedge *Gahnia sieberiana*
red-fruited kurrajong *Sterculia quadrifida*
redgold honeysuckle *Lonicera* × *tellmanniana*
redhead grass *Potamogeton perfoliatus*
red-heat *Ceanothus spinosus*
red-hot cat-tail *Acalypha hispida*
red-hot poker *Kniphofia*
red-hot poker tree *Erythrina abyssinica*
red-ink sundew *Drosera erythrorhiza*
red-leaf philodendron *Philodendron erubescens*
red-leaf plum *Prunus* × *cistena*
redleaf rose *Rosa glauca*
red-leafed palm *Livistona mariae*
red-leafed rock fig *Ficus ingens*
red-leafed wattle, small *Acacia nana*
redleg grass *Bothriochloa decipiens*
redneck palm *Dypsis leptocheilos*
redoul *Coriaria myrtifolia*
redroot *Ceanothus ovatus*

red-rooted gromwell *Lithospermum erythrorhizon*

redshanks *Adenostoma sparsifolium*

red-stemmed Japanese maple *Acer palmatum* 'Senkaki'

red-stemmed wattle *Acacia rubida*

red-tipped dogwood, dwarf *Cornus pumila*

redtop bent *Agrostis gigantea*

red-top, Natal *Melinis repens*

red-vein enkianthus *Enkianthus campanulatus*

red-vein maple *Acer rufinerve*

red-veined dock *Rumex sanguineus*

red-veined pie plant *Rheum australe*

red-veined prayer plant *Maranta leuconeura* 'Erythroneura'

redwood *Sequoia sempervirens*

redwood, California *Sequoia sempervirens*

redwood, coast *Sequoia sempervirens*

redwood, dawn *Metasequoia glyptostroboides*

redwood, Sierra *Sequoiadendron giganteum*

redwood violet *Viola sempervirens*

reed *Phragmites australis*

reed bent grass *Deyeuxia quadriseta*

reed Canary grass *Phalaris arundinacea*

reed, cane *Arundinaria gigantea*

reed, common *Phragmites australis*

reed, Egyptian *Cyperus papyrus*

reed, giant *Arundo donax*

reed grass *Calamagrostis, Phalaris arundinacea*

reed grass, feather *Calamagrostis foliosa, C.* × *acutiflora*

reed grass, leafy *Calamagrostis foliosa*

reed, honey *Lomandra longifolia*

reed, marsh *Phleum*

reed meadow grass *Glyceria maxima*

reed sweet grass *Glyceria maxima*

reed, thatching *Thamnochortus insignis*

reedmace *Typha*

reedmace, narrow-leafed *Typha angustifolia*

Reeves' spiraea *Spiraea cantoniensis*

Reeves' spiraea, double *Spiraea cantoniensis* 'Flore Pleno'

regal foxtail *Ptilotus nobilis*

regal geranium *Pelargonium* Regal Hybrids

regal lily *Lilium regale*

regal mallow *Lavatera trimestris*

regal pelargonium *Pelargonium* Regal Hybrids

reina de la noche *Selenicereus grandiflorus*

remarkable pine *Pinus radiata*

rengarenga *Arthropodium cirratum*

reseda, sweet *Reseda odorata*

resin birch *Betula glandulosa*

resin tree, common *Ozoroa paniculosa*

rest-harrow, shrubby *Ononis fruticosa*

resurrection fern *Polypodium scouleri, Selaginella lepidophylla*

resurrection lily *Lycoris squamigera*

resurrection plant *Bryophyllum pinnatum*

retam *Retama raetam*

retinospora *Chamaecyparis pisifera* 'Squarrosa'

rewarewa *Knightia excelsa*

rex begonias *Begonia* Rex-cultorum Hybrids

rhapis palm *Rhapis excelsa*

rhatany *Krameria triandra*

rhella *Ammi visnaga*

rheumatism root *Jeffersonia diphylla*

rhinograss *Sansevieria desertii*

rhodanthe *Rhodanthe manglesii*

Rhodes grass *Chloris gayana*

Rhodes grass, feathertop *Chloris virgata*
rhododendron *Rhododendron*
rhododendron, Australian *Rhododendron lochiae*
rhododendron, Catawba *Rhododendron catawbiense*
rhododendron, great laurel *Rhododendron maximum*
rhododendron, Indian *Melastoma malabathricum*
rhododendron, Korean *Rhododendron mucronulatum*
rhododendron, Pontic *Rhododendron ponticum*
rhododendron, rosebay *Rhododendron maximum*
rhododendron, Turkish *Rhododendron smirnowii*
rhodoleia *Rhodoleia championii*
rhodora *Rhododendron canadense*
rhubarb *Rheum, R. × hybridum*
rhubarb, Chilean *Gunnera chilensis*
rhubarb, false *Thalictrum flavum*
rhubarb, giant *Gunnera manicata*
rhubarb, Guatemala *Jatropha podagrica*
rhubarb, Himalayan *Rheum australe*
rhubarb, monk's *Rumex alpinus*
rhubarb, Turkey *Rheum palmatum*
rhubarb, wild *Rumex hymenosepalus*
rhus tree *Toxicodendron succedaneum*
rhus, willow *Rhus lancea*
ribbed spike-rush *Eleocharis plana*
ribbon bush *Homalocladium platycladium, Hypoestes aristata*
ribbon fan palm *Livistona decipiens*
ribbon fern *Pteris cretica*
ribbon grass *Phalaris arundinacea*
ribbon gum *Eucalyptus viminalis*
ribbon plant *Dracaena sanderiana*
ribbons, water *Triglochin procerum*

ribbonweed *Vallisneria*
ribbonwood *Adenostoma sparsifolium, Euroschinus falcata, Hoheria, Plagianthus*
ribbonwood, mountain *Hoheria glabrata, H. lyallii*
ribbonwood, shore *Plagianthus divaricatus*
riberry *Syzygium luehmannii*
ribwort *Plantago lanceolata*
rice *Oryza sativa*
rice flower *Ozothamnus diosmifolius, Pimelea linifolia*
rice flower, alpine *Pimelea alpina*
rice flower, curved *Pimelea curviflora*
rice flower, desert *Pimelea simplex*
rice flower, poison *Pimelea pauciflora*
rice flower, rosy *Pimelea ferruginea*
rice flower, shrubby *Pimelea microcephala*
rice flower, slender *Pimelea linifolia*
rice flower, spiked *Pimelea trichostachya*
rice flower, tall *Pimelea ligustrina*
rice flower, tough *Pimelea axiflora*
rice flower, woolly *Pimelea octophylla*
rice gasteria *Gasteria carinata*
rice, wild *Zizania aquatica*
ricegrain flower *Aglaia odorata*
rice-grass, meadow *Microlaena stipoides*
rice-grass, wiry *Tetrarrhena juncea*
rice-paper plant *Tetrapanax papyrifer*
Rice's wattle *Acacia riceana*
ridge sida *Sida cunninghamii*
ridge-fruited mallee *Eucalyptus costata*
rigid panic *Homopholis proluta*
rimu *Dacrydium cupressinum*
ring bellflower *Symphyandra*
ringed wallaby grass *Austrodanthonia caespitosa*
ringwood *Anetholea anisata*

ringworm cassia *Senna alata*
Rio Bravo sage *Leucophyllum langmaniae*
Rio Grande palmetto *Sabal mexicana*
ripgut brome *Bromus diandrus*
river birch *Betula nigra*
river bluebell *Wahlenbergia fluminalis*
river bottlebrush *Callistemon sieberi*
river bushwillow *Combretum erythrophyllum*
river buttercup *Ranunculus inundatus*
river club-rush *Schoenoplectus validus*
river cooba *Acacia stenophylla*
river euphorbia *Euphorbia triangularis*
river lomatia *Lomatia myricoides*
river mangrove *Aegiceras corniculatum*
river maple *Acer saccharinum*
river mint *Mentha australis*
river oak *Casuarina cunninghamiana*
river paperbark *Melaleuca trichostachya*
river peppermint *Eucalyptus elata*
river protea *Protea compacta*
river red gum *Eucalyptus camaldulensis*
river rose *Bauera rubioides*
river she-oak *Casuarina cunninghamiana*
river tea-tree *Melaleuca bracteata*
riverbank grape *Vitis riparia*
Rivers' purple beech *Fagus sylvatica* 'Riversii'
Roanoke bells *Mertensia virginica*
roast beef plant *Iris foetidissima*
robber fern *Pyrrosia confluens*
robe, purple *Solanum xantii*
Robert, herb *Geranium robertianum*
robillo *Catalpa punctata*
robin, dwarf wake *Trillium pusillum*
robin, ragged *Lychnis flos-cuculi*

robin redbreast bush *Melaleuca lateritia*
robin, wake *Trillium, T. ovatum*
robin, yellow wake *Trillium luteum*
robin's plantain *Erigeron pulchellus*
roble *Nothofagus obliqua*
roble beech *Nothofagus obliqua*
roble de Chile *Eucryphia cordifolia*
roble de olor *Catalpa punctata*
roble del Maule *Nothofagus glauca*
robust marsh orchid *Dactylorhiza elata*
robusta coffee *Coffea canephora*
rock araucaria *Araucaria scopulorum*
rock bells *Aquilegia canadensis*
rock, birch, Russian *Betula ermanii*
rock boronia *Boronia bipinnata*
rock bulbine lily *Bulbine glauca*
rock comb fern *Schizaea rupestris*
rock coral fern *Gleichenia rupestris*
rock cotoneaster *Cotoneaster horizontalis*
rock cress *Arabis*
rock daisy, Marlborough *Olearia insignis*
rock daphne *Daphne cneorum*
rock elm *Ulmus thomasii*
rock felt fern *Pyrrosia rupestris*
rock fern *Cheilanthes sieberi, C. tenuifolia*
rock fern, American *Polypodium virginianum*
rock fern, California *Polypodium californicum*
rock fern, Korean *Polystichum tsussimense*
rock fern, tropical *Paraceterach muelleri*
rock fig *Ficus brachypoda*
rock fig, Baja *Ficus palmeri*
rock fig, large-leafed *Ficus abutilifolia*
rock fig, red-leafed *Ficus ingens*

rock geranium *Heuchera americana*
rock grevillea *Grevillea heliosperma,*
  G. willisii
rock jasmine *Androsace*
rock lily *Arthropodium cirratum,*
  Dendrobium speciosum
rock lily, New Zealand *Arthropodium*
  cirratum
rock maple *Acer glabrum,*
  A. saccharum
rock oak *Quercus montana*
rock orchid *Dendrobium speciosum*
rock orchid, pink *Dendrobium*
  kingianum
rock palm *Brahea dulcis*
rock poison *Gastrolobium callistachys*
rock rose *Cistus, Helianthemum*
rock rose, common *Helianthemum*
  nummularium
rock rose, curly-leafed *Cistus crispus*
rock rose, hairy *Cistus creticus*
rock rose, laurel-leafed *Cistus*
  laurifolius
rock rose, Montpelier *Cistus*
  monspeliensis
rock rose, sage-leafed *Cistus*
  salviifolius
rock samphire *Crithmum*
  maritimum
rock selinen *Petroselinum*
rock sida *Sida petrophila*
rock soapwort *Saponaria ocymoides*
rock speedwell *Veronica fruticans*
rock spiraea *Holodiscus dumosus,*
  Petrophytum
rock tassel fern *Huperzia squarrosa*
rock thryptomene *Thryptomene*
  saxicola
rock violet *Boea hygroscopica*
rockberry *Empetrum eamesii*
rocket *Eruca vesicaria*
rocket, bastard *Reseda odorata*
rocket, London *Sisymbrium irio*

rocket, purple-vein *Eruca sativa*
rocket, red *Leucospermum reflexum*
rocket, sand *Diplotaxis tenuifolia*
rocket, sea *Cakile maritima*
rocket, sweet *Hesperis matronalis*
rocket, wall *Diplotaxis muralis*
rocket, white *Diplotaxis erucoides*
rocket, yellow *Leucospermum*
  reflexum
rock-lily *Dendrobium speciosum*
rockmelon *Cucumis melo*
  Cantalupenis Group
rock-rose, hybrid *Cistus × purpureus*
Rock's peony *Paeonia rockii*
rockspray cotoneaster *Cotoneaster*
  horizontalis
Rocky Mountain bristlecone pine
  Pinus aristata
Rocky Mountain cherry *Prunus*
  besseyi
Rocky Mountain columbine
  Aquilegia caerulea
Rocky Mountain fir *Abies lasiocarpa*
Rocky Mountain juniper *Juniperus*
  scopulorum
Rocky Mountain maple *Acer*
  glabrum
Rocky Mountain pinyon *Pinus edulis*
Rocky Mountain raspberry *Rubus*
  deliciosus
Rocky Mountain white oak *Quercus*
  gambelii
rocoto *Capsicum pubescens*
rocoto chilli *Capsicum pubescens*
rod, Aaron's *Verbascum thapsus*
rod, blue *Morgania floribunda*
rod, Jacob's *Asphodeline lutea*
rod, white *Viburnum cassinoides*
Rodondo creeper *Drosanthemum*
  candens
Roger, stinking *Tagetes minuta*
Rogers' firethorn *Pyracantha*
  rogersiana

rohutu *Lophomyrtus obcordata,*
Neomyrtus pedunculata
roly-poly *Salsola kali*
rolypoly, black *Sclerolaena muricata*
var. *semiglabra*
Roman candle *Yucca gloriosa*
Roman chamomile *Chamaemelum*
nobile
Roman coriander *Nigella sativa*
Roman pine *Pinus pinea*
Roman wormwood *Artemisia*
pontica
Romanesco broccoli *Brassica oleracea*
'Romanesco'
rondeletia, fragrant *Rondeletia*
odorata
roof iris *Iris tectorum*
rooibosch *Aspalathus linearis*
rooikrans *Acacia cyclops*
rooistompie *Mimetes cucullatus*
rooster flower *Aristolochia labiata*
root, alum *Heuchera*
root, balsam *Balsamorhiza*
sagittata
root, bitter *Lewisia rediviva*
root, Bowman's *Gillenia trifoliata,*
Veronicastrum virginicum
root, Culver's *Veronicastrum*
virginicum
root, devil's *Lophophora williamsii*
root, eye *Hydrastis canadensis*
root, golden *Rhodiola rosea*
root, jaundice *Hydrastis canadensis*
root, pepper *Cardamine laciniata*
root, pleurisy *Asclepias tuberosa*
root, senga *Polygala senega*
root, snake *Liatris*
rope, monkey *Parsonsia straminea*
rope pear, devil's *Cylindropuntia*
imbricata
ropebark *Dirca palustris*
rope-rush, tassel *Hypolaena fastigiata*
roquette *Eruca vesicaria*

rosa mundi *Rosa gallica* 'Versicolor'
rosa, pau *Aniba rosaeodora*
rosary vine *Ceropegia linearis* subsp.
woodii
rose *Rosa*
rose acacia *Robinia hispida*
rose, Afghan yellow *Rosa primula*
rose, alpine *Rhododendron*
ferrugineum
rose, apple *Rosa pomifera*
rose apple *Syzygium jambos,*
S. moorei
rose apple, water *Syzygium aqueum*
rose, Australian native *Boronia*
serrulata
rose, Austrian yellow *Rosa foetida*
rose, baby *Rosa* (Dwarf China)
'Cécile Brunner'
rose, banksia *Rosa banksiae*
rose, beach *Rosa rugosa*
rose, blackberry *Rosa rubus*
rose, briar *Rosa rubiginosa*
rose, broad-spined *Rosa sericea* var.
pteracantha
rose, buffalo *Callirhoe involucrata*
rose, burnet *Rosa spinosissima*
rose, burr *Rosa roxburghii*
rose campion *Lychnis coronaria*
rose, Cape stock *Sparmannia*
africana
rose, Cherokee *Rosa laevigata*
rose, chestnut *Rosa roxburghii*
rose, China *Hibiscus rosa-sinensis,*
Rosa chinensis
rose, Christmas *Helleborus niger*
rose, cinnamon *Rosa cinnamomea*
rose, cliff *Cowania mexicana,*
C. plicata
rose, cluster *Rosa pisocarpa*
rose, common rock *Helianthemum*
nummularium
rose, common sun *Helianthemum*
nummularium

rose coneflower *Isopogon formosus*
rose, Confederate *Hibiscus mutabilis*
rose, cotton *Hibiscus mutabilis*
rose daphne *Daphne cneorum*
rose, desert *Adenium obesum,
Gossypium sturtianum, Rosa stellata*
rose, dog *Bauera rubioides, Rosa
canina*
rose, double white Banks' *Rosa
banksiae* 'Alboplena'
rose, Dowerin *Eucalyptus pyriformis*
rose, downy *Rosa tomentosa*
rose, Egyptian *Scabiosa atropurpurea*
rose, evergreen *Rosa sempervirens*
rose fairy lantern *Calochortus
amoenus*
rose, four seasons *Rosa* 'Quatre
Saisons'
rose, French *Rosa gallica*
rose geranium *Pelargonium
capitatum, P. graveolens*
rose, giant velvet *Aeonium canariense*
rose, green Mexican *Echeveria
× gilva*
rose, ground *Protea pudens*
rose, guelder *Viburnum opulus*
rose, Honolulu *Clerodendrum
chinense*
rose, Hudson Bay *Rosa blanda*
rose, incense *Rosa primula*
rose, Japanese *Rosa multiflora,
R. rugosa*
rose, karoo *Lapidaria margaretae*
rose, Kosciuszko *Pimelea ligustrina*
subsp. *ciliata*
rose, Lady Banks' *Rosa banksiae*
rose, Lenten *Helleborus, H. orientalis*
rose, Macartney *Rosa bracteata*
rose mallee *Eucalyptus rhodantha*
rose mallow *Hibiscus moscheutos,
Lavatera trimestris*
rose mallow, common *Hibiscus
moscheutos*

rose mallow, scarlet *Hibiscus
coccineus*
rose mallow, swamp *Hibiscus
moscheutos*
rose, Maltese cross *Rosa sericea*
rose, Malva *Lavatera assurgentiflora*
rose, May *Rosa cinnamomea*
rose, meadow *Rosa blanda*
rose, memorial *Rosa wichurana*
rose, Miss Willmott's *Rosa
willmottiae*
rose, Montpelier rock *Cistus
monspeliensis*
rose, moss *Portulaca grandiflora*
rose, mountain *Protea nana*
rose, musk *Rosa moschata*
rose myrtle *Archirhodomyrtus
beckleri, Rhodomyrtus tomentosa*
rose, native *Boronia serrulata*
rose of China *Hibiscus rosa-sinensis*
rose of Sharon *Hibiscus syriacus,
Hypericum calycinum*
rose of Venezuela *Brownea ariza*
rose, peony *Paeonia* (herbaceous)
double cultivars
rose periwinkle *Catharanthus roseus*
rose, prairie *Rosa arkansana,
R. setigera*
rose, Ramana's *Rosa rugosa*
rose, red *Rosa gallica*
rose, redleaf *Rosa glauca*
rose, river *Bauera rubioides*
rose, rock *Cistus, Helianthemum*
rose sage *Salvia pachyphylla*
rose shower *Cassia roxburghii*
rose, smooth *Rosa blanda*
rose, sulfur *Rosa hemisphaerica*
rose, sun *Helianthemum*
rose, swamp *Rosa palustris*
rose tamarind *Arytera divaricata*
rose, threepenny-bit *Rosa elegantula*
'Persetosa'
rose tree of China *Prunus triloba*

rose, velvet *Aeonium canariense*
rose vervain *Verbena canadensis*
rose, Virginia *Rosa virginiana*
rose walnut *Endiandra discolor*
rose, western wild *Rosa woodsii*
rose, winter *Helleborus*
rose, wood *Rosa gymnocarpa*
roseau, black *Bactris major*
rosebay, mountain *Rhododendron catawbiense*
rosebay rhododendron *Rhododendron maximum*
rosebay willow herb *Epilobium angustifolium*
rose-fruited miraguama *Coccothrinax miraguama* subsp. *roseocarpa*
rosegold pussy willow *Salix gracilistyla*
rose-leaf bramble *Rubus rosifolius*
rose-leaf marara *Caldcluvia paniculosa*
roseleaf sage *Salvia involucrata*
rosella *Hibiscus sabdariffa*
rosella, Australian *Hibiscus heterophyllus*
roselle *Hibiscus sabdariffa*
roselle sorrell *Hibiscus sabdariffa*
rose-mallow *Hibiscus lasiocarpus*
rosemary *Rosmarinus officinalis*
rosemary, Australian *Westringia fruticosa*
rosemary, bog *Andromeda, A. glaucophylla, A. polifolia*
rosemary, coast *Westringia fruticosa*
rosemary grevillea *Grevillea rosmarinifolia*
rosemary, native *Westringia fruticosa*
rosemary, prostrate *Rosmarinus officinalis* 'Prostratus'
rosemary, slender western *Westringia eremicola*
rosemary, Tennessee *Conradina verticillata*

rosemary, wild *Eriocephalus africanus, Ledum palustre*
rosemary willow *Salix elaeagnos*
rose-root *Rhodiola rosea*
rose-scented geranium *Pelargonium graveolens*
roseshell azalea *Rhododendron prinophyllum*
rose-walnut, rusty *Endiandra hayesii*
rosewood *Dysoxylum fraserianum*
rosewood, Brazilian *Dalbergia nigra*
rosewood, Burmese *Pterocarpus indicus*
rosewood, hairy *Dysoxylum rufum*
rosewood, scentless *Synoum glandulosum*
rosewood, western *Alectryon oleifolius*
rosin weed *Grindelia*
rosinweed, cup *Silphium perfoliatum*
rosy baeckea *Baeckea ramosissima, Euryomyrtus ramosissima*
rosy dipelta *Dipelta floribunda*
rosy dock *Rumex vesicarius*
rosy garlic *Allium roseum*
rosy maidenhair fern *Adiantum hispidulum*
rosy periwinkle *Catharanthus roseus*
rosy posy *Rhodohypoxis baurii*
rosy rice flower *Pimelea ferruginea*
rotan macap *Daemonorops longipes*
rotang *Calamus*
Rottnest honey-myrtle *Melaleuca lanceolata*
Rottnest Island pine *Callitris preissii*
rough blazing star *Liatris aspera*
rough burr-daisy *Calotis scabiosifolia*
rough bush-pea *Pultenaea scabra*
rough daisy bush *Olearia asterotricha*
rough dog's-tail *Cynosurus echinatus*
rough fireweed *Senecio hispidulus*
rough fuzzweed *Vittadinia pterochaeta*
rough guinea-flower *Hibbertia aspera*

rough halgania *Halgania cyanea*
rough honey-myrtle *Melaleuca scabra*
rough horsetail *Equisetum hyemale*
rough lemon *Citrus jambhiri*
rough maidenhair fern *Adiantum hispidulum*
rough milk thistle *Sonchus asper*
rough mint bush *Prostanthera denticulata*
rough poppy *Papaver × hybridum*
rough raspwort *Haloragis aspera*
rough speargrass *Austrostipa scabra*
rough tree fern *Cyathea australis*
rough verbena *Verbena hispida*
rough wattle *Acacia aspera*
rough wheatgrass *Elymus scaber*
rough-barked apple *Angophora floribunda*
rough-barked Mexican pine *Pinus montezumae*
rough-leafed ghost gum *Corymbia aspera*
rough-leafed saw-sedge *Gahnia aspera*
rough-leafed wax-flower *Philotheca hispidula*
rough-stemmed goldenrod *Solidago rugosa*
roughtail grass *Rostraria pumila*
round-headed leek *Allium sphaerocephalon*
round-leaf blue gum *Eucalyptus deanei*
round-leaf buchu *Agathosma betulina*
roundleaf buffalo berry *Shepherdia rotundifolia*
roundleaf fern *Pellaea rotundifolia*
round-leaf mistletoe *Amyema miraculosum*
round-leaf vine *Legnephora moorei*
round-leaf wattle *Acacia uncinata*
round-leafed dogwood *Cornus rugosa*

round-leafed gum *Eucalyptus deanei*
round-leafed mallee *Eucalyptus orbifolia*
round-leafed mint bush *Prostanthera rotundifolia*
round-leafed moort *Eucalyptus platypus*
round-leafed pigface *Disphyma crassifolium*
round-leafed poison bush *Acokanthera schimperi*
round-leafed sundew *Drosera rotundifolia*
round-leafed teak *Pterocarpus rotundifolius*
round-leafed tea-tree *Leptospermum rotundifolium*
rowan *Sorbus aucuparia*
rowan, Japanese *Sorbus commixta*
rowan, Sargent's *Sorbus sargentiana*
Roxburgh fig *Ficus auriculata*
roxo, ipe *Tabebuia heptaphylla, T. impetiginosa*
royal azalea *Rhododendron schlippenbachii*
royal fern *Osmunda regalis*
royal grevillea *Grevillea victoriae*
royal hakea *Hakea victoria*
royal mallow *Lavatera trimestris*
royal palm *Roystonea*
royal palm, Caribbean *Roystonea oleracea*
royal palm, Cuban *Roystonea regia*
royal palm, Florida *Roystonea elata*
royal palm, Jamaica *Roystonea altissima*
royal palm, morass *Roystonea princeps*
royal palm, Puerto Rico *Roystonea borinquena*
royal palmetto *Thrinax parviflora*
royal poinciana *Delonix regia*
royal velvet plant *Gynura aurantiaca*
royal waterlily *Victoria amazonica*

rubber hedge *Euphorbia tirucalli*

rubber plant, American *Peperomia obtusifolia*

rubber plant, baby *Peperomia obtusifolia*

rubber tree *Calotropis procera, Ficus elastica, Howea brassiliensis*

rubber tree, India *Ficus elastica*

rubber tree, Panama *Castilla elastica*

rubber tree, Para *Hevea brasiliensis*

rubber tree, variegated *Ficus elastica* 'Doescheri'

rubber vine *Cryptostegia grandiflora*

rubber vine, India *Strophanthus gratus*

rubber vine, Madagascar *Cryptostegia madagascariensis*

ruby saltbush *Enchylaena tomentosa*

Rudder's box *Eucalyptus rudderi*

rue *Ruta graveolens*

rue anenome *Anemonella thalictroides*

rue anemone, false *Isopyrum*

rue, common *Ruta graveolens*

rue, early meadow *Thalictrum dioicum*

rue, French meadow *Thalictrum aquilegiifolium*

rue, goat's *Galega officinalis*

ruellia, common *Ruellia brittoniana*

ruellia, desert *Ruellia peninsularis*

ruffle palm *Aiphanes caryotifolia*

ruffles, silver *Cotyledon undulata*

ruil *Nothofagus alessandrii*

rukam *Flacourtia jangomas, F. rukam*

Rule araucaria *Araucaria rulei*

rum cherry *Prunus serotina*

runner bean, scarlet *Phaseolus coccineus*

running juneberry *Amelanchier stolonifera*

running pine *Lycopodium clavatum*

running pop *Passiflora foetida*

running postman *Kennedia prostrata*

running serviceberry *Amelanchier stolonifera*

rush *Juncus*

rush, African thatching *Elegia*

rush, bog *Schoenus pauciflorus*

rush, branching *Juncus prismatocarpus*

rush, broad *Juncus planifolius*

rush, bulbous *Juncus bulbosus*

rush, California gray *Juncus patens*

rush, clustered *Juncus vaginatus*

rush, common *Juncus effusus*

rush, Dutch *Equisetum hyemale*

rush fern *Schizaea*

rush, flowering *Butomus umbellatus*

rush, fountain *Elegia capensis*

rush fringe-lily *Thysanotus juncifolius*

rush, grassy *Butomus*

rush, hoary *Juncus radula*

rush, horsetail *Equisetum hyemale*

rush, jointed *Juncus articulatus*

rush, mat *Lomandra*

rush, May *Lomandra banksii*

rush lily, yellow *Tricoryne elatior*

rush, needle spike *Eleocharis acicularis*

rush, pickerel *Pontederia cordata*

rush, sea *Juncus kraussii*

rush, spike *Eleocharis*

rush, spiny *Juncus acutus*

rush, tassel *Baloskion tetraphyllum*

rush, toad *Juncus bufonius*

rush, tussock *Juncus usitatus*

rushgrass *Sporobolus*

rush-leaf wattle *Acacia juncifolia*

Russell lupins *Lupinus* Russell Hybrids

Russian almond, dwarf *Prunus tenella*

Russian borage *Trachystemon orientalis*

Russian comfrey *Symphytum* ×
  uplandicum
Russian cypress *Microbiota decussata*
Russian elm *Ulmus laevis*
Russian olive *Elaeagnus angustifolia*
Russian pea shrub *Caragana frutex*
Russian rock birch *Betula ermanii*
Russian sage *Perovskia atriplicifolia*
Russian vetch *Vicia villosa*
Russian vine *Fallopia baldschuanica*
rust-hood *Pterostylis rufa*
rusty blackhaw viburnum *Viburnum
  rufidulum*
rusty fig *Ficus destruens, F. rubiginosa*
rusty foxglove *Digitalis ferruginea*
rusty gum *Angophora costata*
rusty knobwood *Zanthoxylum
  trijugum*
rusty leaf *Menziesia ferruginea*
rusty lyonia *Lyonia ferruginea*
rusty petals *Lasiopetalum ferrugineum*
rusty petals, shrubby *Lasiopetalum
  macrophyllum*
rusty plum *Amorphospermum whitei*
rusty pod *Hovea longifolia*
rusty rose-walnut *Endiandra hayesii*
rusty spider-flower *Grevillea
  floribunda*

rusty velvet bush *Lasiopetalum
  ferrugineum*
rusty woodsia *Woodsia ilvensis*
rusty-petals, red *Lasiopetalum rufum*
rutabaga *Brassica napus*
rye *Secale cereale*
rye, Canada wild *Elymus canadensis*
rye, cereal *Secale cereale*
rye, French *Arrhenatherum elatius*
rye, giant wild *Elymus condensatus*
rye grass *Lolium*
rye, mountain wild *Elymus
  canadensis*
rye, western wild *Elymus canadensis*
rye, wild *Elymus*
ryegrass *Lolium*
ryegrass, annual *Lolium multiflorum*
ryegrass, curly *Parapholis incurva*
ryegrass, English *Lolium perenne*
ryegrass, Italian *Lolium multiflorum*
ryegrass, perennial *Lolium perenne*
ryegrass, stiff *Lolium loliaceum*
ryegrass, Wimmera *Lolium rigidum*
Rylstone red stringybark *Eucalyptus
  cannonii*
Ryukyu juniper *Juniperus taxifolia*
Ryukyu viburnum *Viburnum
  suspensum*

S

Sabi star *Adenium obesum*
sabra spike sage *Salvia confertiflora*
sacahuista *Nolina bigelovii,*
   N. microcarpa
sacred bamboo *Nandina domestica*
sacred bamboo, dwarf *Nandina*
   domestica 'Nana'
sacred basil *Ocimum tenuiflorum*
sacred fig *Ficus religiosa*
sacred flower of the Incas *Cantua*
   buxifolia
sacred lily of the Incas *Hymenocallis,*
   H. narcissiflora
sacred lotus *Nelumbo nucifera*
safflower *Carthamus tinctorius*
saffron *Crocus sativus*
saffron, common *Cassine papillosa*
saffron crocus *Crocus sativus*
saffron, false *Carthamus tinctorius*
saffron heart *Halfordia kendack*
saffron, meadow *Colchicum*
saffron spike *Aphelandra squarrosa*
saffron thistle *Carthamus lanatus*
saf-saf *Populus euphratica*
sage *Salvia, S. officinalis*
sage, African blue *Salvia aurita*
sage, Andean *Salvia discolor*
sage, Andean silver *Salvia discolor*
sage, anise-scented *Salvia guaranitica*
sage, annual *Salvia viridis*
sage, Austrian *Salvia austriaca*
sage, autumn *Salvia greggii*
sage, bastard *Eriogonum wrightii*
sage, beach *Salvia aurea*
sage, bee *Salvia apiana*
sage, bicolor *Salvia semiatrata*
sage, black *Salvia mellifera*
sage, blue *Eranthemum pulchellum,*
   Salvia pachyphylla

sage, blue ball *Salvia clevelandii*
sage, bog *Salvia uliginosa*
sage, Buchanan's *Salvia buchananii*
sage, cacalia *Salvia cacaliifolia*
sage, California blue *Salvia*
   clevelandii
sage, California white *Salvia apiana*
sage, Canary Island *Salvia canariensis*
sage, cardinal *Salvia fulgens*
sage, cedar *Salvia roemeriana*
sage, Channel Island *Lepechinia*
   fragrans
sage, chaparral *Salvia leucophylla*
sage, cherry *Salvia microphylla*
sage, Chiapas *Salvia chiapensis*
sage, clary *Salvia sclarea*
sage, Cleveland *Salvia clevelandii*
sage, common *Salvia officinalis*
sage, creeping *Salvia sonomensis*
sage, crimson *Salvia spathacea*
sage, desert *Salvia dorrii*
sage, dwarf silver-leaf *Salvia*
   daghestanica
sage, eyelash-leafed *Salvia*
   blepharophylla
sage, fragrant pitcher *Lepechinia*
   fragrans
sage, fruit-scented *Salvia dorisiana*
sage, garden *Salvia officinalis*
sage, gentian *Salvia patens*
sage, germander *Salvia*
   chamaedryoides
sage, golden *Salvia aurea*
sage, grape-scented *Salvia melissodora*
sage, gray *Salvia leucophylla*
sage, Great Basin blue *Salvia dorrii*
sage, Greek *Salvia fruticosa*
sage, honey *Salvia mellifera*
sage, hummingbird *Salvia spathacea*
sage, Jerusalem *Phlomis fruticosa,*
   Pulmonaria officinalis, P. saccharata
sage, Jim *Salvia clevelandii*
sage, Karwinski's *Salvia karwinskii*

sage, lilac *Salvia verticillata*
sage, little-leafed *Salvia microphylla*
sage, meadow *Salvia pratensis*
sage mealy *Salvia farinacea*
sage, mealy-cup *Salvia farinacea*
sage, Mexican *Salvia mexicana*
sage, Mexican bush *Salvia leucantha*
sage, mountain *Salvia regla, Teucrium scorodonia*
sage, mountain desert *Salvia pachyphylla*
sage, Munz's *Salvia munzii*
sage, painted *Salvia viridis*
sage, peach *Salvia dorisiana*
sage, pineapple *Salvia elegans*
sage, pitcher *Salvia spathacea*
sage, purple *Salvia dorrii, S. leucophylla*
sage, Rio Bravo *Leucophyllum langmaniae*
sage, rose *Salvia pachyphylla*
sage, roseleaf *Salvia involucrata*
sage, Russian *Perovskia atriplicifolia*
sage, sabra spike *Salvia confertiflora*
sage, San Miguel *Salvia munzii*
sage, scarlet *Salvia coccinea, S. splendens*
sage, silver *Salvia argentea*
sage, Sonoma *Salvia sonomensis*
sage, Spanish *Salvia lavandulifolia*
sage, steppe *Salvia nemorosa*
sage, sticky *Salvia glutinosa*
sage, Texas *Salvia coccinea*
sage, triloba *Salvia fruticosa*
sage, tropical *Salvia coccinea*
sage, two-tone *Salvia semiatrata*
sage, variegated *Salvia officinalis* 'Tricolor'
sage, velvet *Salvia leucantha*
sage, Wagner *Salvia wagneriana*
sage weed *Sida corrugata*
sage weeping *Buddleja auriculata*

sage, white *Artemisia ludoviciana*
sage, wild *Salvia verbenaca*
sage willow *Salix candida*
sage, wood *Teucrium canadense, T. scorodonia*
sagebrush, big *Seriphidium tridentatum*
sagebrush, California *Artemisia californica*
sage-leafed rock rose *Cistus salviifolius*
sagewood, South African *Buddleja salviifolia*
sagewort, dragon *Artemisia dracunculus*
sagg *Lomandra longifolia*
sago cycad *Cycas circinalis*
sago palm *Cycas circinalis, Metroxylon sagu*
sago pondweed *Potamogeton pectinatus*
sago-weed *Plantago cunninghamii, P. hispida*
sago-weed, small *Plantago turrifera*
sagrada, cascara *Rhamnus purshiana*
saguaro cactus *Carnegiea gigantea*
saho *Trithrinax brasiliensis*
sailor-boy daisy *Osteospermum ecklonis*
sailor's cap *Dodecatheon hendersonii*
sails, white *Spathiphyllum wallisii*
St Augustine grass *Stenotaphrum secundatum*
St Barnaby's thistle *Centaurea solstitialis*
St Bernard's lily *Anthericum liliago*
St Bruno's lily *Paradisea liliastrum*
St Catherine's lace *Eriogonum giganteum*
St Dabeoc's heath *Daboecia cantabrica*
St James' lily *Sprekelia formosissima*
St John's bread *Ceratonia siliqua*

St John's wort *Hypericum perforatum*

St John's wort, Chinese *Hypericum monogynum*

St John's wort, creeping *Hypericum calycinum*

St John's wort, giant *Hypericum ascyron*

St John's wort, great *Hypericum ascyron*

St John's wort, matted *Hypericum japonicum*

St John's wort, small *Hypericum gramineum*

St John's wort, tree *Hypericum revolutum*

St Joseph's lily *Hippeastrum vittatum*

St Lucie cherry *Prunus mahaleb*

St Martin's flower *Alstroemeria ligtu*

St Patrick's cabbage *Saxifraga spathularis, Sempervivum tectorum*

St Thomas tree *Bauhinia tomentosa*

St Vincent lilac *Solanum seaforthianum*

sakaki *Cleyera japonica*

sal *Shorea robusta*

salac hutan *Salacca affinis*

salad burnet *Sanguisorba minor*

salad, corn *Valerianella locusta*

salal *Gaultheria shallon*

saligot *Trapa natans*

sallow *Salix*

sallow, common *Salix cinerea*

sally, black *Eucalyptus stellulata*

sally, broad-leafed *Eucalyptus aquatica, E. camphora*

sally, Mount Buffalo *Eucalyptus mitchelliana*

sally wattle *Acacia floribunda*

sally, white *Eucalyptus pauciflora*

salmon bush monkey flower *Mimulus longiflorus*

salmon gum *Eucalyptus salmonophloia*

salmonberry *Rubus parviflorus, R. spectabilis*

salsify *Tragopogon porrifolius*

salsify, black *Scorzonera hispanica*

salt cedar *Tamarix chinensis*

salt copperburr *Sclerolaena ventricosa*

salt grass *Spartina pectinata*

salt sandspurry *Spergularia marina*

salt tree *Halimodendron halodendron*

saltbush *Atriplex*

saltbush, berry *Einadia hastata*

saltbush, bitter *Atriplex stipitata*

saltbush, bladder *Atriplex vesicaria*

saltbush, Brewer's *Atriplex lentiformis* subsp. *breweri*

saltbush, climbing *Einadia nutans*

saltbush, coast *Atriplex cinerea*

saltbush, creeping *Atriplex semibaccata*

saltbush, gray *Atriplex cinerea*

saltbush, mat *Atriplex prostrata*

saltbush, mealy *Atriplex pseudocampanulata*

saltbush, old man *Atriplex nummularia*

saltbush, pop *Atriplex holocarpa, A. spongiosa*

saltbush, ruby *Enchylaena tomentosa*

saltbush, spiny *Rhagodia spinescens*

saltbush, spiny-fruit *Atriplex spinibractea*

saltwater couch *Paspalum vaginatum*

saltwater paperbark *Melaleuca cuticularis*

saltwort, prickly *Salsola kali*

salvation Jane *Echium plantagineum*

salvia, beach *Salvia aurea*

salvia, blue *Salvia*

salvia, brown *Salvia aurea*

salvia, giant *Brillantaisia lamium*

salvinia *Salvinia molesta*

salwood, southern *Acacia disparrima*

saman *Albizia saman*
samphire *Salicornia, Sarcocornia*
samphire, gray *Halosarcia pergranulata*
samphire, marsh *Salicornia europaea*
samphire, rock *Crithmum maritimum*
samphire-leafed geranium *Pelargonium crithmifolium*
San Diego ceanothus *Ceanothus cyaneus*
San Diego County viguiera *Viguiera laciniata*
San José hesper palm *Brahea brandegeei*
San Miguel sage *Salvia munzii*
San Pedro Mártir cypress *Cupressus montana*
sand bottlebrush *Beaufortia squarrosa*
sand brome *Bromus arenarius*
sand cherry *Prunus besseyi, P. pumila*
sand cherry, purple-leafed *Prunus × cistena*
sand coprosma *Coprosma acerosa*
sand couch *Sporobolus virginicus*
sand cypress-pine *Callitris columellaris*
sand grape *Vitis rupestris*
sand hickory *Carya pallida*
sand knobwood *Zanthoxylum leprieurii*
sand lady's slipper *Calceolaria uniflora*
sand leek *Allium scorodoprasum*
sand lily *Corynotheca lateriflora*
sand myrtle *Leiophyllum buxifolium*
sand palm *Livistona humilis*
sand palm, Brazilian *Allagoptera arenaria*
sand pear *Pyrus pyrifolia*
sand phlox *Phlox bifida*
sand pine *Pinus clausa*
sand plum *Prunus maritima*
sand rocket *Diplotaxis tenuifolia*

sand sida *Sida ammophila*
sand sunray *Rhodanthe tietkensii*
sand verbena *Abronia, A. maritima, A. umbellata*
sandalwood *Santalum album*
sandalwood, false *Eremophila mitchellii, Myoporum platycarpum*
sandalwood, Indian *Santalum album*
sandalwood, northern *Santalum lanceolatum*
sandalwood, red *Pterocarpus santalinus*
sandalwood, white *Santalum album*
sandbar willow *Salix exigua, S. interior*
sandbox tree *Hura crepitans*
sandfly zieria *Zieria smithii*
sandhill buffel grass *Cenchrus pennisetiformis*
sandhill canegrass *Zygochloa paradoxa*
sandhill spider flower *Grevillea stenobotrya*
sandhill wattle *Acacia acuminata* subsp. *burkittii, A. ligulata*
sandmat manzanita *Arctostaphylos pumila*
sandpaper bush *Ehretia amoena*
sandpaper fig *Ficus coronata, F. fraseri, F. opposita*
sandpaper vine *Petrea volubilis*
sandplain bitter-pea *Daviesia acicularis*
sandplain mallee *Eucalyptus ebbanoensis*
sandplain woody pear *Xylomelum angustifolium*
sandspurry *Spergularia rubra*
sandspurry, salt *Spergularia marina*
sandspurry, small *Spergularia diandra*
sandwort *Arenaria, Minuartia*
sansevieria, blue *Sansevieria ehrenbergii*

sansevieria, star *Sansevieria grandicuspis*

Santa Barbara ceanothus *Ceanothus impressus*

Santa Barbara daisy *Erigeron karvinskianus*

Santa Catalina manzanita *Arctostaphylos catalinae*

Santa Cruz cypress *Cupressus abramsiana*

Santa Cruz Island buckwheat *Eriogonum arborescens*

Santa Fe phlox *Phlox nana*

Santa Lucia fir *Abies bracteata*

Santa Margarita manzanita *Arctostaphylos pilosula*

Santa Rosa manzanita *Arctostaphylos confertiflora*

santa, yerba *Eriodictyon californicum, Eryngium foetidum*

santol *Sandoricum koetjape*

santolina *Santolina chamaecyparissus*

santolina, green *Santolina rosmarinifolia*

sapirangy *Tabernaemontana catharinensis*

sapodilla *Manilkara zapota*

sapote *Pouteria sapota*

sapote, black *Diospyros digyna*

sapote borracho *Pouteria campechiana*

sapote, green *Pouteria viridis*

sapote, mamey *Pouteria sapota*

sapote, white *Casimiroa edulis*

sappanwood *Caesalpinia sappan*

sapphire berry *Symplocos paniculata*

sapree-wood *Widdringtonia cupressoides*

sapucaia nut *Lecythis zabucajo*

sarana, black *Fritillaria camschatcensis*

sarchochilus, little gem *Sarcochilus hillii*

Sargasso weed *Sargassum fusiforme*

Sargent barberry *Berberis sargentiana*

Sargent cherry *Prunus sargentii*

Sargent cypress *Cupressus sargentii*

Sargent spruce *Picea brachytyla*

Sargent viburnum *Viburnum sargentii*

Sargent's crabapple *Malus sargentii*

Sargent's palm *Pseudophoenix sargentii*

Sargent's rowan *Sorbus sargentiana*

saro *Trithrinax brasiliensis*

sarsaparilla *Smilax glabra*

sarsaparilla, Australian *Smilax glyciphylla*

sarsaparilla, false *Hardenbergia violacea*

sarsaparilla, Honduran *Smilax officinalis*

sarsaparilla, sweet *Smilax glyciphylla*

sarsaparilla, wild *Hardenbergia comptoniana*

sarvis tree *Amelanchier laevis*

Saskatoon serviceberry *Amelanchier alnifolia*

sassafras *Doryphora sassafras, Sassafras albidum*

sassafras, black *Atherosperma moschatum*

sassafras, New South Wales *Doryphora sassafras*

sassafras, Oliver's *Cinnamomum oliveri*

sassafras, southern *Atherosperma moschatum*

satin everlasting *Helichrysum leucopsideum*

satin flower *Clarkia amoena*

satin poppy *Meconopsis napaulensis*

satinay *Syncarpia hillii*

satinheart, green *Geijera salicifolia*

satinheart, yellow *Acradenia euodiiformis*

satintop grass *Bothriochloa erianthoides*
satinwood *Nematolepis squamea*
satsuma *Citrus reticulata*
saucer magnolia *Magnolia* × *soulangeana*
saucer plant *Aeonium undulatum*
sausage tree *Kigelia africana*
savin juniper *Juniperus sabina*
savory *Satureja*
savory, summer *Satureja hortensis*
savory, thyme-leafed *Satureja thymbra*
savory, winter *Satureja montana*
saw banksia *Banksia serrata*
saw palm, silver *Acoelorrhaphe wrightii*
saw palmetto *Serenoa repens*
sawara cypress *Chamaecyparis pisifera*
sawgrass *Cladium jamaicense, Nolina bigelovii, N. microcarpa*
saw-sedge *Gahnia*
saw-sedge, black-fruit *Gahnia melanocarpa*
saw-sedge, chaffy *Gahnia filum*
saw-sedge, coast *Gahnia trifida*
saw-sedge, desert *Gahnia lanigera*
saw-sedge, red-fruit *Gahnia sieberiana*
saw-sedge, rough-leafed *Gahnia aspera*
saw-sedge, slender *Gahnia microstachya*
saw-sedge, tall *Gahnia clarkei*
saw-sedge, thatch *Gahnia radula*
saxaul *Haloxylon ammodendron, H. aphyllum, H. persicum*
saxifrage, burnet *Pimpinella saxifraga*
saxifrage, creeping *Saxifraga stolonifera*
saxifrage, heartleaf *Bergenia cordifolia*
saxifrage pink *Petrorhagia saxifraga*

saxifrage, purple mountain *Saxifraga oppositifolia*
saxifrage, Pyrenees *Saxifraga longifolia*
saxifrage, snail *Saxifraga cochlearis*
sazanami giboshi *Hosta crispula*
scabious *Scabiosa, S. atropurpurea*
scabious, devil's bit *Succisa pratensis*
scabious, field *Knautia arvensis*
scabious, giant *Cephalaria gigantea*
scabious, patrinia *Patrinia scabiosifolia*
scabious, shepherd's *Jasione laevis*
scabious, small *Scabiosa columbaria*
scabious, sweet *Scabiosa atropurpurea*
scabweed *Raoulia, R. hookeri*
scabweed, golden *Raoulia australis*
scale-rush *Lepyrodia scariosa*
scale-shedder *Lepidobolus drapetocoleus*
scallion *Allium cepa*
scallops *Hakea cucullata*
scaly bark *Eucalyptus squamosa*
scaly buttons *Leptorhynchos squamatus*
scaly phebalium *Phebalium squamulosum*
scaly poa *Poa fax*
scaly tree fern *Cyathea cooperi*
scaly zamia *Lepidozamia peroffskyana*
scalybark *Cleistocalyx fullageri*
Scarborough lily *Cyrtanthus elatus*
scarlet avens *Geum chiloense*
scarlet banksia *Banksia coccinea*
scarlet bottlebrush *Callistemon citrinus, C. macropunctatus, C. rugulosus*
scarlet bouvardia *Bouvardia glaberrima*
scarlet bugler *Penstemon centranthifolius*
scarlet bush *Hamelia erecta, H. patens*

scarlet coral pea *Kennedia prostrata*
scarlet elder *Sambucus pubens*
scarlet firethorn *Pyracantha coccinea*
scarlet freesia *Freesia laxa*
scarlet fuchsia bush *Graptophyllum excelsum*
scarlet ginger lily *Hedychium coccineum*
scarlet gum *Eucalyptus phoenicea*
scarlet hawthorn *Crataegus laevigata* 'Paul's Scarlet'
scarlet hedge nettle *Stachys coccinea*
scarlet hibiscus *Hibiscus coccineus*
scarlet honey-myrtle *Melaleuca fulgens*
scarlet jacobinia *Libonia floribunda*
scarlet kunzea *Kunzea baxteri*
scarlet leadwort *Plumbago indica*
scarlet lobelia *Lobelia splendens*
scarlet lotus *Lotus berthelotii*
scarlet maple *Acer rubrum*
scarlet milkweed *Asclepias curassavica*
scarlet mint bush *Prostanthera aspalathoides*
scarlet monkey flower *Mimulus cardinalis*
scarlet oak *Quercus coccinea*
scarlet paintbrush *Castilleja coccinea, Crassula falcata*
scarlet passionflower *Passiflora coccinea*
scarlet pear gum *Eucalyptus stoatei*
scarlet pimpernel *Anagallis arvensis*
scarlet plume *Euphorbia fulgens*
scarlet potentilla *Potentilla atrosanguinea*
scarlet rose mallow *Hibiscus coccineus*
scarlet runner bean *Phaseolus coccineus*
scarlet sage *Salvia coccinea, S. splendens*
scarlet silky oak *Alloxylon flammeum*

scarlet skullcap *Scutellaria costaricana*
scarlet sumac *Rhus glabra*
scarlet trumpet honeysuckle *Lonicera* × *brownii*
scarlet wisteria tree *Sesbania grandiflora*
scent, Hexham *Melilotus indica*
scented bells *Rothmannia manganjae*
scented bouvardia *Bouvardia longiflora*
scented broom *Carmichaelia odorata*
scented broom, New Zealand *Carmichaelia odorata*
scented cress *Harmsiodoxa puberula*
scented leek orchid *Prasophyllum odoratum*
scented mayweed *Matricaria recutita*
scented milkvine *Marsdenia suaveolens*
scented paperbark *Melaleuca squarrosa*
scented penstemon *Penstemon palmeri*
scented thorn *Acacia nilotica*
scented-top grass *Capillipedium spicigerum*
scentless mayweed *Tripleurospermum inodorum*
scentless rosewood *Synoum glandulosum*
sceptre banksia *Banksia sceptrum*
schefflera, Hawaiian elf *Schefflera arboricola*
scholar tree *Sophora japonica*
scholar tree, Chinese *Sophora japonica*
Schott's yucca *Yucca schottii*
Schumann's abelia *Abelia schumannii*
Schwedler's Norway maple *Acer platanoides* 'Schwedleri'
scilla, hyacinth *Scilla hyacinthoides*

scollies *Asplenium scolopendrium*
scorpion senna *Hippocrepis emerus*
scorpion weed *Phacelia*
scorzonera *Scorzonera hispanica*
Scotch briar *Rosa spinosissima*
Scotch broom *Cytisus scoparius*
Scotch elm *Ulmus glabra*
Scotch laburnum *Laburnum alpinum*
Scotch marigold *Calendula officinalis*
Scotch pine *Pinus sylvestris*
Scotch thistle *Onopordum acanthium*
Scotia bush *Eremophila scoparia*
Scots pine *Pinus sylvestris*
Scott River jugflower *Adenanthos detmoldii*
Scottish primrose *Primula scotica*
scouring-rush *Equisetum, E. hyemale*
scouring-rush, winter *Equisetum hyemale*
scourweed *Sisyrinchium micranthum*
scrambled eggs *Goodenia pinnatifida*
scrambling cassia *Senna acclinis*
scrambling clubmoss *Lycopodiella cernua*
scrambling coral fern *Gleichenia microphylla*
scrambling gromwell *Lithodora diffusa*
scrambling lily *Geitonoplesium cymosum*
screw fern *Lindsaea linearis*
screwbean *Prosopis pubescens*
screwbean mesquite *Prosopis pubescens*
screwpine *Pandanus*
screwpine, beach *Pandanus tectorius*
screwpine, common *Pandanus utilis*
screwpine, hala *Pandanus odoratissimus*
scribbly gum *Eucalyptus haemastoma*
scribbly gum, broad-leafed *Eucalyptus haemastoma*

scribbly gum, inland *Eucalyptus rossii*
scribbly gum, wallum *Eucalyptus signata*
scrobic *Paspalum scrobiculatum*
scrub arum *Typhonium brownii*
scrub beefwood *Grevillea baileyana, Stenocarpus salignus*
scrub boonaree *Alectryon diversifolius*
scrub bottle tree *Brachychiton discolor*
scrub, creosote bush *Prosopis pubescens*
scrub hickory *Carya floridana*
scrub kauri *Agathis ovata*
scrub kurrajong *Hibiscus heterophyllus*
scrub nettle *Urtica incisa*
scrub oak, California *Quercus dumosa*
scrub oak, seaside *Quercus myrtifolia*
scrub palmetto *Sabal minor, S. etonia*
scrub pecan *Carya floridana*
scrub pine *Pinus virginiana*
scrub she-oak *Allocasuarina distyla*
scrub stringybark *Rhodamnia rubescens*
scrub sumac *Rhus microphylla*
scrubwood *Commidendrum rugosum*
scurf-pea, African *Psoralea pinnata*
scurvy grass *Cochlearia officinalis, Oxalis enneaphylla*
sea barley grass *Hordeum marinum*
sea bindweed *Calystegia soldanella*
sea box *Alyxia buxifolia*
sea buckthorn *Hippophae rhamnoides*
sea buckthorn, Chinese *Hippophae sinensis*
sea campion *Silene uniflora*
sea celery *Apium prostratum*
sea daffodil *Chlidanthus fragrans*
sea fig *Ficus superba*
sea grape *Coccoloba uvifera*

sea heath *Frankenia*
sea holly *Eryngium maritimum*
sea holly, amethyst *Eryngium
    amethystinum*
Sea Island cotton *Gossypium
    barbadense*
sea kale *Crambe maritima*
sea lavender *Limonium*
sea lavender, perennial *Limonium
    sinuatum*
sea lavender, winged *Limonium
    lobatum*
sea lettuce *Scaevola taccada*
sea lyme grass *Leymus arenarius*
sea mallow *Lavatera maritima*
sea oats *Chasmanthium latifolium*
sea onion *Ornithogalum
    longibracteatum*
sea onion, false *Ornithogalum
    longibracteatum*
sea pink *Armeria*
sea poppy *Glaucium*
sea purslane *Atriplex hortensis*
sea ragwort *Senecio cineraria*
sea rocket *Cakile maritima*
sea rush *Juncus kraussii*
sea tassel *Ruppia maritima*
seablite *Suaeda australis*
seaforthia palm *Ptychosperma
    elegans*
seagrape, pigeon *Coccoloba laurifolia*
seal, Solomon's *Polygonatum*
sealing-wax palm *Cyrtostachys renda*
seaside alder *Alnus maritima*
seaside bird's foot *Lotus formosissimus*
seaside brome *Bromus arenarius*
seaside daisy *Erigeron glaucus,
    E. karvinskianus*
seaside scrub oak *Quercus myrtifolia*
sea-urchin cactus *Astrophytum
    asterias, Echinopsis*
sea-urchin dryandra *Dryandra
    praemorsa*

sea-urchin hakea *Hakea laurina*
sedge *Carex, Cladium mariscus*
sedge, blue *Carex riparia*
sedge, bog *Schoenus pauciflorus*
sedge, button *Gymnoschoenus
    sphaerocephalus*
sedge, drooping *Carex longebrachiata*
sedge, giant *Cyperus exaltatus*
sedge, hook *Uncinia*
sedge, knob *Carex inversa*
sedge, mace *Carex grayi*
sedge, morning star *Carex grayi*
sedge, nut *Cyperus esculentus*
sedge, orange hook *Uncinia
    egmontiana*
sedge, palm *Carex muskingumensis*
sedge, razor *Lepidosperma limicola*
sedge, red hook *Uncinia rubra*
sedge, slender *Cyperus gracilis*
sedge, spiny *Cyperus gymnocaulos*
sedge, sticky *Cyperus fulvus*
sedge, strand *Carex pumila*
sedge, tall *Carex appressa*
sedge, tufted *Carex gaudichaudiana*
sedge, umbrella *Cyperus eragrostis*
sedum, silver *Sedum treleasei*
seed, black *Nigella sativa*
seed, heart *Cardiospermum*
seersucker plant *Geogenanthus
    undatus*
sego, swamp *Camassia quamash*
seleb *Sansevieria ehrenbergii*
self-heal *Prunella, P. vulgaris*
self-heal, cut-leaf *Prunella laciniata*
self-heal, large *Prunella grandiflora*
selinen, rock *Petroselinum*
selu *Cordia myxa*
seneca snakeroot *Polygala senega*
Senegal coral tree *Erythrina
    senegalensis*
Senegal date palm *Phoenix reclinata*
Senegal gum arabic tree *Acacia
    senegal*

senga root *Polygala senega*
senita *Pachycereus schottii*
senna *Senna clavigera*
senna, bladder *Colutea arborescens*
senna, Indian *Cassia fistula*
senna, scorpion *Hippocrepis emerus*
senna, smooth *Senna barclayana*
senna, white *Senna glutinosa*
senna, wild *Senna hebecarpa*
sensitive fern *Onoclea sensibilis*
sensitive plant *Mimosa pudica,
Neptunia dimorphantha*
sensitive plant, giant *Mimosa pigra*
sentry palm *Howea belmoreana*
sentul *Sandoricum koetjape*
septee *Cordia caffra*
September bells *Rothmannia globosa*
September elm *Ulmus serotina*
sequoia, giant *Sequoiadendron
giganteum*
Serbian bellflower *Campanula
poscharskyana*
Serbian spruce *Picea omorika*
serpent cucumber *Trichosanthes
cucumerina*
serpent grass *Persicaria vivipara*
serpentine manzanita *Arctostaphylos
obispoensis*
serrated goodenia *Goodenia
cycloptera*
serrated tussock *Nassella trichotoma*
service tree *Sorbus domestica*
service tree, Arran *Sorbus
pseudofennica*
service tree, Fontainebleau *Sorbus
latifolia*
service tree, wild *Sorbus torminalis*
serviceberry *Amelanchier,
A. canadensis, A. × grandiflora*
serviceberry, alderleaf *Amelanchier
alnifolia*
serviceberry, Allegheny *Amelanchier
laevis*

serviceberry, apple *Amelanchier ×
grandiflora*
serviceberry, downy *Amelanchier
arborea*
serviceberry, Lamarck *Amelanchier
lamarckii*
serviceberry, Pacific *Amelanchier
alnifolia* var. *semiintegrifolia*
serviceberry, running *Amelanchier
stolonifera*
serviceberry, Saskatoon *Amelanchier
alnifolia*
serviceberry, shadblow *Amelanchier
canadensis*
serviceberry, Utah *Amelanchier
utahensis*
sesame *Sesamum orientale*
sesame bush, Transvaal
Sesamothamnus lugardii
sesame, wild *Perilla frutescens*
sessile bellwort *Uvularia sessilifolia*
sessile oak *Quercus petraea*
settlers' flax *Gymnostachys anceps*
settlers' twine *Gymnostachys anceps*
seven son flower *Heptacodium
miconioides*
Seville orange *Citrus aurantium*
shadblow serviceberry *Amelanchier
canadensis*
shaddock *Citrus maxima*
shade nettle, small *Australina pusilla*
shady horsetail *Equisetum pratense*
shagbark hickory *Carya ovata*
shaggy dryandra *Dryandra speciosa*
shaggy pea, netted *Podolobium
scandens*
shaggy pea, prickly *Podolobium
ilicifolium*
shaggy shield fern *Dryopteris
cycadina*
shaggy-bark manzanita *Arctostaphylos
tomentosa*
shaking brake *Pteris tremula*

shallon *Gaultheria shallon*
shallot *Allium cepa*
shallot, French *Allium ascalonicum*
shallot, golden *Allium ascalonicum*
shamel ash *Fraxinus uhdei*
shampoo ginger *Zingiber zerumbet*
shamrock oxalis *Oxalis articulata*
shamrock pea *Parochetus communis*
Shantung maple *Acer truncatum*
Sharon, rose of *Hibiscus syriacus,*
Hypericum calycinum
sharp greenhood *Pterostylis*
acuminata
sharp-leafed willow *Salix acutifolia*
Shasta daisy *Leucanthemum* ×
superbum
shatterwood *Backhousia sciadophora*
Shavalski's ligularia *Ligularia*
przewalskii
shaving-brush tree *Pachira aquatica,*
Pseudobombax ellipticum
shawl, Spanish *Heterocentron*
elegans
shawnee wood *Catalpa speciosa*
sheathed cholla *Cylindropuntia*
tunicata
sheep bush *Geijera linearifolia*
sheep laurel *Kalmia angustifolia*
sheep sorrel *Rumex acetosella*
sheep, vegetable *Raoulia*
sheepberry *Viburnum lentago*
sheep's bit *Jasione laevis*
sheep's burnet *Sanguisorba minor*
sheep's burr *Acaena, A. agnipila,*
A. echinata, A. ovina
sheep's ears *Helichrysum*
appendiculatum
sheep's fescue *Festuca ovina*
sheep's fescue, fine-leafed *Festuca*
filiformis
shell flower *Chelone, Pistia*
shell ginger *Alpinia zerumbet*
shell ginger, small *Alpinia mutica*

shellflower *Bowkeria*
shellflower bush, Natal *Bowkeria*
verticillata
shellflower bush, yellow *Bowkeria*
citrina
Shensi fir *Abies chensiensis*
she-oak *Allocasuarina*
she-oak, beach *Casuarina*
equisetifolia
she-oak, black *Allocasuarina littoralis*
she-oak, drooping *Allocasuarina*
verticillata
she-oak, dwarf *Allocasuarina nana*
she-oak, forest *Allocasuarina torulosa*
she-oak, mistletoe *Amyema cambagei*
she-oak, pine-needle *Allocasuarina*
pinaster
she-oak, river *Casuarina*
cunninghamiana
she-oak, scrub *Allocasuarina distyla*
she-oak, swamp *Casuarina glauca*
she-oak, thready-barked
Allocasuarina inophloia
shepherd's purse *Capsella bursa-*
pastoris
shepherd's scabious *Jasione laevis*
shield fern *Dryopteris, Polystichum*
shield fern, Australian *Polystichum*
australiense
shield fern, California *Polystichum*
californicum
shield fern, common *Dryopteris*
cristata
shield fern, creeping *Lastreopsis*
microsora
shield fern, hard *Polystichum*
aculeatum
shield fern, mother *Polystichum*
proliferum
shield fern, prickly *Polystichum*
aculeatum, P. vestitum
shield fern, shaggy *Dryopteris*
cycadina

shield fern, shiny *Lastreopsis
acuminata*
shield fern, soft *Polystichum setiferum*
shield fern, spreading *Sticherus
lobatus*
shield fern, trim *Lastreopsis
decomposita*
shield fern, variegated *Arachniodes
simplicior*
shikakudake *Chimonobambusa
quadrangularis*
shin dagger *Agave lechuguilla,
A. schottii*
shingle oak *Quercus imbricaria*
shingle tree *Acrocarpus fraxinifolius*
shining cudweed *Gnaphalium
nitidulum*
shining gum *Eucalyptus nitens*
shining sumac *Rhus copallina*
shino-chiku *Chimonobambusa
quadrangularis*
shiny cassinia *Cassinia longifolia*
shiny dock *Rumex crystallinus,
R. tenax*
shiny fan fern *Sticherus flabellatus*
shiny shield fern *Lastreopsis
acuminata*
shiny willow *Salix lucida*
Shiress's bottlebrush *Callistemon
shiressii*
Shirley poppy *Papaver rhoeas*
shisham *Dalbergia sissoo*
shiso *Perilla frutescens*
shittimwood *Bumelia lycioides*
shivergrass *Briza*
shivery grass *Briza minor*
shoe black *Hibiscus rosa-sinensis*
shoe button spiraea *Spiraea
prunifolia*
shoo fly *Nicandra physalodes*
shooting star *Dodecatheon, D. meadia*
shooting star, eastern *Dodecatheon
meadia*

shore juniper *Juniperus conferta*
shore juniper, Japanese *Juniperus
conferta*
shore pine *Pinus contorta*
shore ribbonwood *Plagianthus
divaricatus*
shore spleenwort *Asplenium
obtusatum*
short cress *Harmsiodoxa brevipes*
short purple-flag *Patersonia fragilis*
short-haired plume grass *Dichelachne
micrantha*
shortleaf pine *Pinus echinata*
short-leafed heath-myrtle *Baeckea
brevifolia*
short-leafed westringia *Westringia
brevifolia*
shortstraw pine *Pinus echinata*
short-styled grevillea *Grevillea
brachystylis*
short-winged copperburr *Sclerolaena
brachyptera*
shot, Indian *Canna, C. indica*
shower, gold *Galphimia glauca*
shower orchid *Congea tomentosa*
shower, pink *Cassia grandis,
C. javanica*
shower, rose *Cassia roxburghii*
showy banksia *Banksia speciosa*
showy bossiaea *Bossiaea cinerea*
showy copper-wire daisy *Podolepis
jaceoides*
showy daisy-bush *Olearia pimeleoides*
showy dryandra *Dryandra formosa*
showy hebe *Hebe speciosa*
showy honey-myrtle *Melaleuca
nesophila*
showy isotome *Isotoma axillaris*
showy libertia *Libertia formosa*
showy milkweed *Asclepias speciosa*
showy mountain ash *Sorbus decora*
showy parrot pea *Dillwynia sericea*
showy pincushion *Escobaria vivipara*

showy polemonium *Polemonium pulcherrimum*

showy tick-trefoil *Desmodium canadense*

showy trillium *Trillium grandiflorum*

showy violet *Viola betonicifolia*

showy wattle *Acacia decora*

shrimp begonia *Begonia radicans*

shrimp plant *Justicia brandegeeana*

shrub althea *Hibiscus syriacus*

shrub convolvulus *Convolvulus floridus*

shrub, foxtail *Asparagus densiflorus*

shrub germander *Teucrium fruticans*

shrub, lace *Stephanandra incisa*

shrub live oak *Quercus turbinella*

shrub lobelia, Mexican *Lobelia laxiflora*

shrub morning glory *Ipomoea carnea* subsp. *fistulosa*

shrub, silver *Olearia argophylla*

shrub, tassel *Leucopogon verticillatus*

shrub vinca *Kopsia fruticosa*

shrub wormwood *Artemisia arborescens*

shrubby allamanda *Allamanda schottii*

shrubby cinquefoil *Potentilla fruticosa*

shrubby germander *Teucrium fruticans*

shrubby hare's ear *Bupleurum fructicosum*

shrubby horsetail, European *Ephedra distachya*

shrubby penstemon *Penstemon fruticosus*

shrubby rest-harrow *Ononis fruticosa*

shrubby rice flower *Pimelea microcephala*

shrubby rusty petals *Lasiopetalum macrophyllum*

shrubby trumpet flower *Tecoma stans*

shrubby twinleaf *Zygophyllum aurantiacum*

shrubby wild buckwheat *Eriogonum wrightii*

shumard oak *Quercus shumardii*

shuttlecock fern *Matteuccia struthiopteris*

Siamese ginger *Alpinia galanga*

Siberian apricot *Prunus sibirica*

Siberian bluebells *Mertensia sibirica*

Siberian carpet cypress *Microbiota decussata*

Siberian crabapple *Malus baccata*

Siberian elm *Ulmus pumila*

Siberian ginseng *Eleutherococcus senticosus*

Siberian gooseberry *Actinidia arguta*

Siberian kale *Brassica napus* Pabularia Group

Siberian larch *Larix sibirica*

Siberian lily *Ixiolirion tataricum*

Siberian lime *Tilia sibirica*

Siberian melic *Melica altissima*

Siberian milkwort *Polygala tenuifolia*

Siberian millet *Echinochloa frumentacea*

Siberian pea shrub *Caragana arborescens*

Siberian pea tree *Caragana arborescens*

Siberian pine, dwarf *Pinus pumila*

Siberian spruce *Picea obovata*

Siberian squill *Scilla siberica*

Sichuan lovage *Ligusticum wallichii*

Sichuan paulownia *Paulownia fargesii*

Sicilian fir *Abies nebrodensis*

sickle bush *Dichrostachys cinerea*

sickle fern *Pellaea falcata*

sickle fern, small *Pellaea nana*

sickle wattle *Acacia falcata*

sida, common *Sida rhombifolia*

sida, corrugated *Sida corrugata*

sida, fine *Sida filiformis*
sida, pin *Sida fibulifera*
sida, ridge *Sida cunninghamii*
sida, rock *Sida petrophila*
sida, sand *Sida ammophila*
sideoats grass *Bouteloua curtipendula*
sidesaddle plant *Sarracenia purpurea*
Siebold's magnolia *Magnolia sieboldii*
Sierra globe tulip *Calochortus amoenus*
Sierra laurel *Leucothoe davisiae*
Sierra Leone coffee *Coffea stenophylla*
Sierra redwood *Sequoiadendron giganteum*
sifton bush *Cassinia arcuata*
sigaton *Carica stipulata*
signet marigold *Tagetes tenuifolia*
Sikkim larch *Larix griffithiana*
Sikkim spruce *Picea spinulosa*
silk cotton tree *Bombax ceiba*
silk tree *Albizia julibrissin*
silk tree, Persian *Albizia julibrissin*
silk tree, pink *Albizia julibrissin* 'Rosea'
silkpod, common *Parsonsia straminea*
silkpod, mountain *Parsonsia brownii*
silktassel bush *Garrya elliptica*
silktassel, coast *Garrya elliptica*
silktassel, Fremont *Garrya fremontii*
silkweed *Asclepias curassavica*
silky acacia *Acacia rehmanniana*
silky bent *Apera*
silky bent, loose *Apera spica-venti*
silky bluegrass *Dichanthium sericeum*
silky brome *Bromus molliformis*
silky browntop *Eulalia aurea*
silky camellia *Stewartia malacodendron*
silky daisy bush *Olearia erubescens*
silky dogwood *Cornus amomum, C. obliqua*

silky glycine *Glycine canescens*
silky goodenia *Goodenia fascicularis*
silky grevillea *Grevillea sericea*
silky guinea-flower *Hibbertia sericea*
silky hakea *Hakea sericea*
silky leaf woadwaxen *Genista pilosa*
silky myrtle *Decaspermum humile*
silky oak *Grevillea robusta*
silky oak, brown *Darlingia darliniana, Grevillea baileyana*
silky oak, cream *Athertonia diversifolia*
silky oak, Lamington's *Helicia lamingtoniana*
silky oak, Mueller's *Austromuellera trinervia*
silky oak, red *Carnarvonia araliifolia, Grevillea banksii, Stenocarpus salignus*
silky oak, scarlet *Alloxylon flammeum*
silky oak, white *Grevillea hilliana*
silky purple-flag *Patersonia sericea*
silky spinifex *Spinifex sericeus*
silky umbrella grass *Digitaria ammophila*
silky willow *Salix sericea*
silky wisteria *Wisteria brachybotrys*
silky woadwaxen *Genista pilosa*
silky-heads *Cymbopogon obtectus*
silver aspen *Acronychia wilcoxiana*
silver ball cactus *Parodia scopa*
silver banksia *Banksia marginata*
silver banner grass *Miscanthus sacchariflorus*
silver beech, New Zealand *Nothofagus menziesii*
silver beet *Beta vulgaris*
silver birch *Betula pendula*
silver birch, European *Betula pendula*
silver birch, weeping *Betula pendula* 'Dalecarlica'
silver brake *Pteris argyraea*

silver broom *Argyrocytisus battandieri, Retama monosperma*
silver buffalo berry *Shepherdia argentea*
silver bush *Ptilotus obovatus*
silver bush lupine *Lupinus albifrons*
silver cassia *Senna artemisioides, S. phyllodinea*
silver cluster-leaf *Terminalia sericea*
silver crown *Cotyledon undulata*
silver cudweed *Gnaphalium argentifolium*
silver date palm *Phoenix sylvestris*
silver dollar *Lunaria annua*
silver dollar gum *Eucalyptus polyanthemos*
silver dollar maidenhair fern *Adiantum peruvianum*
silver dollar tree *Eucalyptus cinerea, E. polyanthemos*
silver elkhorn fern *Platycerium veitchii*
silver elm *Ulmus carpinifolia* 'Variegata'
silver everlasting *Helichrysum argyrophyllum*
silver fern *Pityrogramma calomelanos*
silver fir *Abies concolor*
silver fir, European *Abies alba*
silver grass, Amur *Miscanthus sacchariflorus*
silver grass, Japanese *Miscanthus sinensis*
silver grass, small Japanese *Miscanthus oligostachyus*
silver gum *Eucalyptus cordata*
silver hare's foot fern *Humata tyermannii*
silver honeysuckle *Grevillea striata*
silver jade plant *Crassula arborescens*
silver joey palm *Johannesteijsmannia magnifica*

silver lace vine *Fallopia*
silver leaf cassia *Senna phyllodinea*
silver lime *Tilia tomentosa*
silver lime, pendent *Tilia* 'Petiolaris'
silver lime, weeping *Tilia* 'Petiolaris'
silver linden *Tilia tomentosa*
silver linden, weeping *Tilia* 'Petiolaris'
silver lupine *Lupinus albifrons*
silver mallee *Eucalyptus crucis*
silver maple *Acer saccharinum*
silver oak *Grevillea parallela*
silver oak, mountain *Brachylaena rotundata*
silver palm *Coccothrinax, C. argentata*
silver palm, Florida *Coccothrinax argentata*
silver palm, Jamaica *Coccothrinax argentata*
silver pear *Pyrus salicifolia*
silver pine *Manoao colensoi*
silver pine, New Zealand *Manoao colensoi*
silver pine, yellow *Lepidothamnus intermedius*
silver poplar *Populus alba*
silver princess gum *Eucalyptus caesia* subsp. *magna*
silver puff *Chaptalia nutans*
silver quandong *Elaeocarpus kirtonii*
silver ruffles *Cotyledon undulata*
silver sage *Salvia argentea*
silver sage, Andean *Salvia discolor*
silver saw palm *Acoelorrhaphe wrightii*
silver sedum *Sedum treleasei*
silver shrub *Olearia argophylla*
silver snow daisy *Celmisia asteliifolia, C. costiniana, C. tomentella*
silver tails *Ptilotus obovatus*
silver tansy *Tanacetum niveum*
silver thatch, Hispaniolan *Coccothrinax argentea*

silver thatch, Lesser Antilles
Coccothrinax barbadensis
silver thatch palm *Coccothrinax
argentata*
silver thatch, swollen *Coccothrinax
spissa*
silver torch cactus *Cleistocactus strausii*
silver tree *Leucadendron argenteum,
Terminalia sericea*
silver tree fern *Cyathea dealbata*
silver trumpet tree *Tabebuia argentea*
silver tussock *Poa cita*
silver vein creeper *Parthenocissus
henryana*
silver vine *Actinidia polygama*
silver wattle *Acacia dealbata,
A. neriifolia, A. retinodes*
silver wattle, northern *Acacia
leucoclada*
silver wattle, western *Acacia
polybotrya*
silver weed *Potentilla anserina*
silver wormwood *Artemisia
ludoviciana*
silverbell *Halesia, H. carolina*
silverbell, Carolina *Halesia carolina*
silverbell, mountain *Halesia
monticola*
silverbell, two-wing *Halesia diptera*
silverberry *Elaeagnus commutata,
E. pungens, Shepherdia argentea*
silverbush *Convolvulus cneorum,
Sophora tomentosa*
silvergrass, Amur *Miscanthus
sacchariflorus*
silver-leaf oak *Quercus hypoleucoides*
silver-leaf pepper *Peperomia
griseoargentea*
silver-leaf sage, dwarf *Salvia
daghestanica*
silver-leafed broom *Genista linifolia*
silver-leafed ironbark *Eucalyptus
melanophloia, E. shirleyi*

silver-leafed pear *Pyrus salicifolia*
silver-rod *Solidago bicolor*
silver-stemmed wattle *Acacia
parvipinnula*
silvertop ash *Eucalyptus sieberi*
silvertop gimlet *Eucalyptus campaspe*
silvertop stringybark *Eucalyptus
laevopinea*
silvery hair grass *Aira caryophyllea,
A. cupaniana*
silvery spleenwort *Diplazium
pycnocarpon*
silvery wormwood *Artemisia filifolia*
silvery-leafed grevillea *Grevillea
argyrophylla*
simpler's joy *Verbena hastata*
Sind oak *Quercus coccifera* subsp.
calliprinos
Singapore holly *Malpighia
coccigera*
single-leaf ash *Fraxinus anomala*
single-leaf pinyon *Pinus monophylla*
singleseed juniper *Juniperus
squamata*
sinicuichi *Heimia myrtifolia*
sinita *Pachycereus schottii*
Sir Lowry's Pass protea *Protea
longifolia*
siris, pink *Albizia julibrissin*
siris, white *Ailanthus triphysa,
Albizia lebbeck*
Siskiyou lily *Fritillaria glauca*
Siskiyou mat *Ceanothus pumilus*
Siskiyou onion *Allium siskiyouense*
sissoo *Dalbergia sissoo*
Sitka alder *Alnus sinuata*
Sitka spruce *Picea sitchensis*
six row barley *Hordeum vulgare*
sjambok pod *Cassia abbreviata*
skeleton fork-fern *Psilotum nudum*
skeleton weed *Chondrilla juncea*
Skinner hybrid lilac *Syringa ×
hyacinthiflora*

skirret *Sium sisarum*
skullcap *Scutellaria*
skullcap, common *Scutellaria galericulata*
skullcap, downy *Scutellaria incana*
skullcap, dwarf *Scutellaria humilis*
skullcap, mad-dog *Scutellaria lateriflora*
skullcap, New Zealand *Scutellaria novae-zelandiae*
skullcap, scarlet *Scutellaria costaricana*
skullcap, Virginian *Scutellaria lateriflora*
skunk bush *Garrya fremontii*
skunk cabbage *Lysichiton*
skunk cabbage, yellow *Lysichiton americanus*
skunk polemonium *Polemonium viscosum*
skunkbush *Garrya fremontii*
skunkbush sumac *Rhus trilobata*
skunkweed *Navarretia squarrosa*
sky pilot *Polemonium, P. viscosum*
sky pilot, western *Polemonium pulcherrimum*
sky vine *Thunbergia grandiflora*
skyflower *Duranta erecta, Thunbergia grandiflora*
skyflower, Brazilian *Duranta stenostachya*
skyrocket pincushion *Leucospermum reflexum*
slash pine *Pinus elliottii*
slaty gum *Eucalyptus dawsonii*
slaty red gum *Eucalyptus glaucina*
sleeping hibiscus *Malvaviscus penduliflorus*
slender bamboo grass *Austrostipa verticillata*
slender banksia *Banksia attenuata*
slender bird's foot trefoil *Lotus angustissimus*

slender bittercress *Cardamine tenuifolia*
slender bitter-pea *Daviesia leptophylla*
slender celery *Ciclospermum leptophyllum*
slender cherry *Exocarpos sparteus*
slender clubmoss *Lycopodiella lateralis*
slender cucumber *Zehneria cunninghamii*
slender daisy bush *Olearia passerinoides*
slender deutzia *Deutzia gracilis*
slender dock *Rumex brownii*
slender fissure-weed *Maireana pentagona*
slender grape *Cayratia clematidea*
slender groundsel *Senecio glossanthus*
slender honey-myrtle *Melaleuca gibbosa*
slender knotweed *Persicaria decipiens*
slender lady palm *Rhapis humilis*
slender mint *Mentha diemenica*
slender mudgrass *Pseudoraphis paradoxa*
slender onion orchid *Microtis parviflora*
slender palm lily *Cordyline stricta*
slender panic *Paspalidium gracile*
slender pigeon grass *Setaria gracilis*
slender rat's-tail grass *Sporobolus creber, S. elongatus*
slender rice flower *Pimelea linifolia*
slender saw-sedge *Gahnia microstachya*
slender sedge *Cyperus gracilis*
slender spike rush *Eleocharis acicularis*
slender stackhousia *Stackhousia viminea*
slender sun orchid *Thelymitra pauciflora*

slender sunray *Rhodanthe stricta*
slender thistle *Carduus pycnocephalus*
slender thistle, winged *Carduus tenuiflorus*
slender tick-trefoil *Desmodium varians*
slender vetch *Vicia tetrasperma*
slender violet bush *Hybanthus monopetalus*
slender wallaby grass *Austrodanthonia penicillata*
slender western rosemary *Westringia eremicola*
slender westringia *Westringia eremicola*
slender wire lily *Laxmannia gracilis*
slender yellow-eye *Xyris gracilis*
slender-leafed stringybark *Eucalyptus tenella*
slime mold *Fuligo septica*
slipper flower *Calceolaria* Herbeohybrida Group
slipper orchid *Cypripedium, Paphiopedilum*
slipper orchid, lady's *Cypripedium, Paphiopedilum*
slipper orchid, South American *Phragmipedium*
slippery elm *Ulmus rubra*
sloe *Prunus spinosa*
small balloon vine *Cardiospermum halicacabum*
small bolwarra *Eupomatia bennettii*
small burrgrass *Tragus australianus*
small bush violet *Barleria repens*
small craibia *Craibia zimmermannii*
small cranberry *Oxycoccus macrocarpus*
small crumbweed *Chenopodium pumilio*
small date plum *Diospyros lotus*
small fleabane *Conyza parva*
small fringed helmet orchid *Corybas pruinosus*
small hairy daisy *Brachyscome leptocarpa*
small honeysuckle tree *Turraea obtusifolia*
small Japanese silver grass *Miscanthus oligostachyus*
small knobwood *Zanthoxylum capense*
small knotweed *Polygonum plebeium*
small loosestrife *Lythrum hyssopifolia*
small monkey flower *Mimulus prostratus*
small mudmat *Glossostigma diandrum, G. elatinoides*
small nettle *Urtica urens*
small num-num *Carissa edulis*
small poranthera *Poranthera microphylla*
small princess palm *Dictyosperma album* var. *conjugatum*
small purslane *Calandrinia eremaea*
small rasp fern *Doodia caudata*
small red-leafed wattle *Acacia nana*
small sago-weed *Plantago turrifera*
small St John's wort *Hypericum gramineum*
small sandspurry *Spergularia diandra*
small scabious *Scabiosa columbaria*
small shade nettle *Australina pusilla*
small shell ginger *Alpinia mutica*
small sickle fern *Pellaea nana*
small supplejack *Ripogonum fawcettianum*
small tongue orchid *Cryptostylis leptochila*
small vanilla lily *Arthropodium minus*
small wax-lip orchid *Glossodia minor*
small white sunray *Rhodanthe corymbiflora*
small woolly burr-medic *Medicago minima*
small yellow onion *Allium flavum*

small-flower finger grass *Digitaria parviflora*
small-flower mallow *Malva parviflora*
small-flowered Australian buttercup *Ranunculus sessiliflorus*
small-flowered beetle grass *Diplachne parviflora*
small-flowered dombeya *Dombeya cymosa*
small-flowered mat-rush *Lomandra micrantha*
small-flowered penstemon *Penstemon procerus*
small-flowered pigface *Carpobrotus modestus*
small-flowered wallaby grass *Austrodanthonia setacea*
small-fruited gray gum *Eucalyptus propinqua*
small-fruited hakea *Hakea microcarpa*
small-fruited mountain gum *Eucalyptus oresbia*
small-fruited olive *Olea europaea* subsp. *africana*
small-fruited twinleaf *Zygophyllum humillimum*
small-leaf parakeelya *Calandrinia calyptrata*
small-leafed apple *Angophora bakeri*
small-leafed basil *Ocimum basilicum* 'Minimum'
small-leafed begonia *Begonia fuchsioides*
small-leafed boronia *Boronia microphylla*
small-leafed clematis *Clematis microphylla*
small-leafed fuchsia *Fuchsia microphylla*
small-leafed gum *Eucalyptus parvifolia*
small-leafed laurel *Cryptocarya williwilliana*

small-leafed lillypilly *Syzygium luehmannii*
small-leafed lime *Tilia cordata*
small-leafed linden *Tilia cordata*
small-leafed native tamarind *Diploglottis campbellii*
small-leafed privet *Ligustrum sinense*
small-leafed tamarind *Diploglottis campbellii*
small-leafed tea-tree *Leptospermum parvifolium*
small-leafed wax flower *Philotheca difformis*
smart weed *Persicaria bistortoides*
smilax, florist's *Asparagus asparagoides*
Smithton peppermint *Eucalyptus nitida*
smock, ladies' *Cardamine, C. pratensis*
smoke, prairie *Geum triflorum*
smoke tree *Cotinus coggygria, C. obovatus*
smoke tree, American *Cotinus obovatus*
smoke tree, purple-leafed *Cotinus coggygria* 'Purpureus'
smokebush *Conospermum stoechadis, C. taxifolium, Cotinus, C. coggygria, Ptilotus obovatus*
smokebush, blue *Conospermum tenuifolium*
smokebush, Canary Island *Bystropogon origanifolius*
smokebush, Eurasian *Cotinus coggygria*
smokebush, spider *Conospermum teretifolium*
smokebush, sprawling *Conospermum tenuifolium*
smooth alder *Alnus serrulata*
smooth Arizona cypress *Cupressus glabra*
smooth brome *Bromus racemosus*

smooth cat's-ears *Hypochaeris glabra*
smooth chain-fruit cholla
Cylindropuntia fulgida
smooth clerodendrum *Clerodendrum floribundum*
smooth daisy *Brachyscome trachycarpa*
smooth darling pea *Swainsona galegifolia*
smooth flax-lily *Dianella longifolia*
smooth grevillea *Grevillea manglesii*
smooth halgania *Halgania andromedifolia, H. lavandulacea*
smooth hawksbeard *Crepis capillaris*
smooth hydrangea *Hydrangea arborescens*
smooth mustard *Sisymbrium erysimoides*
smooth oxeye *Heliopsis helianthoides*
smooth rambutan *Alectryon subcinereus*
smooth rose *Rosa blanda*
smooth senna *Senna barclayana*
smooth sumac *Rhus glabra*
smooth sunray *Rhodanthe laevis*
smooth wallaby bush *Beyeria opaca*
smooth willow-herb *Epilobium billardierianum*
smooth winterberry *Ilex laevigata*
smooth withe-rod *Viburnum nudum*
smooth-barked Mexican pine *Pinus pseudostrobus*
smooth-leaf pine *Pinus leiophylla*
smooth-leafed elm *Ulmus carpinifolia, U. minor*
smooth-shelled macadamia nut *Macadamia integrifolia*
snail bean *Vigna caracalla*
snail flower *Vigna caracalla*
snail saxifrage *Saxifraga cochlearis*
snail vine *Vigna caracalla*
snake arum *Amorphophallus rivieri*
snake fern *Lygodium microphyllum*
snake gourd *Trichosanthes cucumerina*

snake head *Chelone glabra*
snake needlegrass *Oldenlandia diffusa*
snake orchid *Diuris lanceolata*
snake palm *Amorphophallus konjac*
snake plant, cylinder *Sansevieria cylindrica*
snake vine *Hemiandra pungens*
snake wood *Colubrina arborescens*
snakebark maple, gray-bud *Acer rufinerve*
snakeberry *Actaea rubra*
snakebush *Hemiandra pungens*
snakeroot *Liatris*
snakeroot, button *Liatris pycnostachya, L. spicata*
snakeroot, Indian *Rauvolfia serpentina*
snakeroot, seneca *Polygala senega*
snakeroot, Virginia *Aristolochia serpentaria*
snakeroot, white *Eupatorium rugosum*
snake's head fritillary *Fritillaria meleagris*
snake's head iris *Hermodactylus tuberosus*
snake's head lily *Fritillaria meleagris*
snakeweed *Persicaria bistorta*
snakeweed, pink *Stachytarpheta mutabilis*
snakewood tree *Cecropia palmata*
snap and rattle *Eucalyptus gracilis*
snap ginger *Alpinia calcarata*
snapdragon *Antirrhinum, A. majus*
snapdragon, Baja bush *Galvezia juncea*
snapdragon, dwarf *Chaenorhinum*
snapdragon, island *Galvezia speciosa*
snapdragon, spurred *Linaria*
snapdragon, twining *Asarina*
snappy gum *Eucalyptus racemosa, E. leucophloia*

snappy gum, northern *Eucalyptus brevifolia*

sneezeweed *Centipeda, Helenium autumnale*

sneezeweed, bitter *Helenium amarum*

sneezeweed, desert *Centipeda thespidioides*

sneezeweed, spreading *Centipeda minima*

sneezewood *Ptaeroxylon obliquum*

sneezewort *Achillea ptarmica*

sneezewort, double *Achillea ptarmica* 'The Pearl'

snow aciphyll *Aciphylla glacialis*

snow bush *Breynia disticha* 'Roseo-picta', *Leucophyta brownii*

snow buttercup *Ranunculus niphophilus*

snow camellia *Camellia rusticana*

snow daisy *Brachyscome nivalis, Celmisia, C. costiniana*

snow daisy bush *Olearia stellulata*

snow daisy, silver *Celmisia asteliifolia, C. costiniana, C. tomentella*

snow daisy, Tasmanian *Celmisia saxifraga*

snow, glory of the *Chionodoxa, C. forbesii, C. luciliae*

snow grass *Chionochloa, Poa sieberiana*

snow grass, blue *Poa sieberiana* var. *cyanophylla*

snow gum *Eucalyptus niphophila, E. pauciflora*

snow gum, de Beuzeville's *Eucalyptus debeuzevillei*

snow gum, Tasmanian *Eucalyptus coccifera*

snow gum, Wolgan *Eucalyptus gregsoniana*

snow heath *Erica carnea*

snow in summer *Melaleuca linariifolia*

snow myrtle *Calytrix alpestris*

snow on the mountain *Euphorbia marginata*

snow pear *Pyrus nivalis*

snow poppy *Eomecon chionantha*

snow queen *Synthyris reniformis*

snow thoroughwort *Eupatorium rugosum*

Snow White spiraea *Spiraea* 'Snow White'

snowball bush *Viburnum opulus*

snowball bush, Chinese *Viburnum macrocephalum* 'Sterile'

snowball, Chinese *Viburnum macrocephalum* 'Sterile'

snowball, common *Viburnum opulus* 'Sterile'

snowball, European *Viburnum opulus*

snowball everlasting *Helichrysum chionosphaerum*

snowball, Japanese *Viburnum plicatum* 'Sterile'

snowball, Mexican *Echeveria elegans*

snowball Spaniard *Aciphylla congesta*

snowball tree *Viburnum opulus* 'Sterile'

snowball tree, Chinese *Viburnum macrocephalum* 'Sterile'

snowbell, alpine *Soldanella alpina*

snowbell, bigleaf *Styrax grandifolia*

snowbell, big-leafed *Styrax grandifolius*

snowbell, fragrant *Styrax obassia*

snowbell tree *Styrax japonica*

snowberry *Gaultheria, G. hispida, Symphoricarpos, S. albus, S. rivularis*

snowberry, common *Symphoricarpos albus*

snowberry, prostrate *Gaultheria macrostigma*

snowbird *Nolana humifusa*

snowdrop *Galanthus, G. nivalis*

snowdrop anemone *Anemone sylvestris*
snowdrop, common *Galanthus nivalis*
snowdrop, Crimean *Galanthus plicatus*
snowdrop, English *Galanthus nivalis*
snowdrop, giant *Galanthus elwesii*
snowdrop tree *Halesia carolina*
snowdrop tree, Japanese *Styrax japonicus*
snowdrop tree, mountain *Halesia monticola*
snowdrop windflower *Anemone sylvestris*
snowflake *Leucojum, L. aestivum*
snowflake, autumn *Leucojum autumnale*
snowflake, spring *Leucojum vernum*
snowflake, summer *Leucojum aestivale*
snowflake tree *Trevesia palmata* 'Micholitzii'
snow-in-summer *Melaleuca linariifolia*
snows of Kilimanjaro *Euphorbia leucocephala*
snow-wood *Pararchidendron pruinosum*
snow-wreath, Alabama *Neviusia alabamensis*
snowy daisy-bush *Olearia stellulata*
snowy mermaid *Libertia formosa*
snowy mespilus *Amelanchier ovalis*
snowy mint bush *Prostanthera nivea*
snuff box tree *Oncoba spinosa*
snuffweed *Centipeda racemosa*
soap aloe *Aloe maculata*
soap, gumdigger's *Pomaderris kumeraho*
soap tree *Gymnocladus chinensis*
soap weed *Yucca elata*

soapbark tree *Quillaja saponaria*
soapberry *Sapindus saponaria*
soapberry, Chinese *Sapindus mukorossi*
soapberry, dune *Deinbollia oblongifolia*
soapberry tree *Sapindus mukorossi*
soapberry, western *Sapindus drummondii*
soapberry, wing-leaf *Sapindus saponaria*
soap-pod tree, Chinese *Gleditsia sinensis*
soaptree yucca *Yucca elata*
soapweed, plains *Yucca glauca*
soapweed yucca *Yucca glauca*
soapwort *Saponaria, S. officinalis*
soapwort, double *Saponaria officinalis* 'Roseo-plena'
soapwort, rock *Saponaria ocymoides*
society garlic *Tulbaghia*
socketwood *Daphnandra micrantha*
soft boronia *Boronia mollis*
soft bracken *Calochlaena dubia*
soft brome *Bromus hordeaceus, B. molliformis*
soft dogwood *Ozothamnus rufescens*
soft grass, creeping *Holcus mollis*
soft horns *Malacocera tricornis*
soft maple *Acer saccharinum*
soft shield fern *Polystichum setiferum*
soft speargrass *Austrostipa mollis*
soft tree fern *Dicksonia antarctica*
soft twig-rush *Baumea rubiginosa*
soft water fern *Blechnum minus*
soja bean *Glycine max*
soldiers, gallant *Galinsoga parviflora*
Soledad pine *Pinus torreyana*
solitaire palm *Ptychosperma elegans*
Solomon's plume *Smilacina*
Solomon's seal *Polygonatum*
Solomon's seal, angular *Polygonatum odoratum*

Solomon's seal, common
Polygonatum × *hybridum*
Solomon's seal, false *Maianthemum
racemosum, Smilacina, S. racemosa*
Solomon's seal, two-leafed
Maianthemum canadense
Solomon's zigzag *Smilacina racemosa*
Somali hemp, grand *Sansevieria
grandis*
Somersby mint bush *Prostanthera
junonis*
Sonoma sage *Salvia sonomensis*
Sonoran palmetto *Sabal uresana*
sophora, Easter Island *Sophora
toromiro*
sophora, Texas *Sophora affinis*
sorghum *Sorghum, S. bicolor*
sorghum, grain *Sorghum bicolor*
subsp. *bicolor*
sorrel *Rumex, R. acetosella*
sorrel, buckler-leafed *Rumex scutatus*
sorrel, French *Rumex scutatus*
sorrel, garden *Rumex acetosa,
R. scutatus*
sorrel, Jamaica *Hibiscus sabdariffa*
sorrel, red *Hibiscus sabdariffa*
sorrel, sheep *Rumex acetosella*
sorrel tree *Oxydendrum arboreum*
sorrel, wood *Oxalis acetosella*
sorrell, roselle *Hibiscus sabdariffa*
sorrowless tree *Saraca indica*
sotol *Dasylirion texanum,
D. wheeleri*
sour bush, dwarf *Choretrum
pauciflorum*
sour cherry *Prunus cerasus, Syzygium
corynanthum*
sour dock *Rumex acetosa*
sour gum *Nyssa sylvatica*
sour tupelo *Nyssa ogeche*
sourberry *Rhus integrifolia*
sourbush, leafless *Omphacomeria
acerba*

sour-plum, large *Ximenia caffra*
soursob *Oxalis pes-caprae*
soursop *Annona muricata*
sourwood *Oxydendrum arboreum*
South African cabbage tree *Cussonia
spicata*
South African coral tree *Erythrina
caffra*
South African dogwood *Rhamnus
prinoides*
South African ironwood *Millettia
grandis*
South African orchid bush *Bauhinia
galpinii*
South African pomegranate
Burchellia bubalina
South African raphia palm *Raphia
australis*
South African sagewood *Buddleja
salviifolia*
South African white pear *Apodytes
dimidiata*
South African wild almond *Brabejum
stellatifolium*
South African wild peach *Kiggelaria
africana*
South African wild pear *Dombeya
rotundifolia*
South African wild plum
Harpephyllum caffrum
South American basil *Ocimum selloi*
South American bottle tree *Ceiba
insignis*
South American crowberry
Empetrum rubrum
South American slipper orchid
Phragmipedium
South American vervain *Verbena
bonariensis*
South American willow *Salix
humboldtiana*
South Australian blue gum
Eucalyptus leucoxylon

South Coast mugga *Eucalyptus tricarpa*
South Esk pine *Callitris oblonga*
southern arrowwood *Viburnum dentatum*
southern bearclover *Chamaebatia australis*
southern beech *Nothofagus*
southern black haw *Viburnum rufidulum*
southern buckthorn *Bumelia lycioides*
southern bush honeysuckle *Diervilla sessilifolia*
southern California goldenrod *Solidago confinis*
southern catalpa *Catalpa bignonioides*
southern cottonwood *Populus deltoides* subsp. *deltoides*
southern flannel bush *Fremontodendron mexicanum*
southern grass tree *Xanthorrhoea australis*
southern grevillea *Grevillea australis*
southern heath *Erica australis*
southern Japanese hemlock *Tsuga sieboldii*
southern lawyer cane *Calamus muelleri*
southern magnolia *Magnolia grandiflora*
southern maidenhair *Adiantum capillus-veneris*
southern marara *Vesselowskya rubifolia*
southern mountain misery *Chamaebatia australis*
southern plains banksia *Banksia media*
southern plume *Elliottia racemosa*
southern polypody *Polypodium cambricum*
southern raphia *Raphia australis*
southern rata *Metrosideros umbellata*

southern red oak *Quercus falcata*
southern red trillium *Trillium sulcatum*
southern salwood *Acacia disparrima*
southern sassafras *Atherosperma moschatum*
southern swamp crinum *Crinum americanum*
southern white stringybark *Eucalyptus yangoura*
southern witch hazel *Hamamelis macrophylla*
southernwood *Artemisia abrotanum*
southernwood geranium *Pelargonium abrotanifolium*
southwestern beardtongue *Penstemon laevis*
sowbread *Cyclamen*
sow-thistle, common *Sonchus oleraceus*
sow-thistle, native *Sonchus hydrophilus*
sow-thistle, prickly *Sonchus asper*
soya *Glycine max*
soya bean *Glycine max*
soybean *Glycine, G. max*
spade flower *Hybanthus enneaspermus*
spangle grass *Chasmanthium latifolium*
Spaniard *Aciphylla*
Spaniard, Colenso's *Aciphylla colensoi*
Spaniard, golden *Aciphylla aurea*
Spaniard, horrid *Aciphylla horrida*
Spaniard, snowball *Aciphylla congesta*
Spaniard, wild *Aciphylla colensoi*
Spanish bayonet *Yucca aloifolia, Y. baccata, Y. glauca*
Spanish bluebell *Hyacinthoides hispanica*
Spanish broom *Genista hispanica, Spartium junceum*
Spanish broom, white *Cytisus multiflorus*

Spanish cherry *Mimusops elengi*
Spanish chestnut *Castanea sativa*
Spanish dagger *Yucca aloifolia,*
Y. torreyi
Spanish fir *Abies pinsapo*
Spanish fir, blue *Abies pinsapo*
'Glauca'
Spanish flag *Ipomoea lobata*
Spanish garlic *Allium scorodoprasum*
Spanish gorse *Genista hispanica*
Spanish heath *Erica australis,*
E. lusitanica
Spanish jasmine *Clerodendrum*
chinense
Spanish juniper *Juniperus thurifera*
Spanish lavender *Lavandula stoechas*
Spanish moss *Tillandsia usneoides*
Spanish needle *Yucca gloriosa*
Spanish needles *Bidens*
Spanish oak *Quercus falcata,*
Q. texana, Q. × hispanica
Spanish sage *Salvia lavandulifolia*
Spanish shawl *Heterocentron elegans*
Spanish tarragon *Tagetes lucida*
sparkleberry, tree *Vaccinium*
arboreum
sparse plume grass *Dichelachne*
rara
spear, cardinal *Erythrina herbacea*
spear grass, oat *Anisopogon avenaceus*
spear, king's *Asphodeline lutea*
spear lily *Doryanthes palmeri*
spear thistle *Cirsium vulgare*
speargrass *Aciphylla squarrosa,*
Austrostipa, Poa, Stipa
speargrass, bamboo *Austrostipa*
ramosisssima
speargrass, coast *Austrostipa stipoides*
speargrass, crested *Austrostipa blackii*
speargrass, feather *Austrostipa*
elegantissima
speargrass, flat-awned *Austrostipa*
platychaeta

speargrass, foxtail *Austrostipa*
densiflora
speargrass, rough *Austrostipa scabra*
speargrass, soft *Austrostipa mollis*
speargrass, tall *Austrostipa*
bigeniculata, A. pubescens
speargrass, Tucker's *Austrostipa*
tuckeri
spear-leafed orache *Atriplex*
australasica
spearmint *Mentha spicata*
spearwood *Acacia doratoxylon*
spearwood bush *Pandorea pandorana*
spearwort, greater *Ranunculus lingua*
spearwort, lesser *Ranunculus*
flammula
speckled alder *Alnus rugosa*
spectacles, fairy *Menkea australis*
speedwell *Veronica*
speedwell, American alpine *Veronica*
wormskjoldii
speedwell, common *Veronica*
officinalis
speedwell, creeping *Veronica persica,*
V. plebeia, V. repens
speedwell, Derwent *Derwentia*
derwentiana
speedwell, digger's *Derwentia*
perfoliata
speedwell, germander *Veronica*
chamaedrys
speedwell, heath *Veronica officinalis*
speedwell, rock *Veronica fruticans*
speedwell, spiked *Veronica spicata*
speedwell, wall *Veronica arvensis*
speedwell, wandering *Veronica*
peregrina
speedwell, water *Veronica anagallis-*
aquatica
spekboom *Portulacaria afra*
sphagnum moss *Sphagnum*
spice, three-in-one *Solenostemon*
amboinicus

spice viburnum, Korean *Viburnum carlesii*
spicy jasmine *Jasminum suavissimum*
spicy jatropha *Jatropha integerrima*
spider fern *Pteris multifida*
spider flower *Cleome, Gassleriana, Grevillea*
spider flower, desert *Grevillea pterosperma*
spider flower, giant *Cleome hassleriana*
spider flower, gray *Grevillea buxifolia*
spider flower, honeysuckle *Grevillea juncifolia*
spider flower, pink *Grevillea sericea*
spider flower, prickly *Grevillea juniperina*
spider flower, red *Grevillea speciosa*
spider flower, rusty *Grevillea floribunda*
spider flower, sandhill *Grevillea stenobotrya*
spider lily *Hymenocallis, Lycoris, Nerine, Tradescantia*
spider lily, golden *Lycoris aurea*
spider lily, red *Lycoris radiata*
spider mangrove *Rhizophora stylosa*
spider orchid *Brassia, Caladenia*
spider plant *Chlorophytum comosum*
spider plant, purple *Tradescantia pallida* 'Purpurea'
spider smokebush *Conospermum teretifolium*
spider tree *Crateva religiosa*
spider-net grevillea *Grevillea thelemanniana*
spiderwort *Tradescantia*
spiderwort, blue *Commelina cyanea*
spignel *Meum*
spike centaury *Centaurium spicatum*
spike hakea, pink *Hakea coriacea*
spike lavender *Lavandula latifolia*
spike, saffron *Aphelandra squarrosa*

spike wattle *Acacia oxycedrus*
spike winter-hazel *Corylopsis spicata*
spiked pepper *Piper aduncum*
spiked rampion *Phyteuma spicatum*
spiked rice flower *Pimelea trichostachya*
spiked speedwell *Veronica spicata*
spikemoss, trailing *Selaginella kraussiana*
spikenard *Aralia californica, Nardostachys jatamansi*
spikenard, American *Aralia racemosa*
spikenard, false *Smilacina racemosa*
spikenard, Japanese *Aralia cordata*
spike-rush *Eleocharis*
spike-rush, pale *Eleocharis pallens*
spike-rush, ribbed *Eleocharis plana*
spike-rush, slender *Eleocharis acicularis*
spike-rush, tall *Eleocharis sphacelata*
spiky wattle *Acacia maitlandii*
spinach *Spinacia oleracea*
spinach, Ceylon *Basella rubra*
spinach, Chinese *Amaranthus tricolor*
spinach, French *Atriplex hortensis*
spinach, Malabar *Basella rubra*
spinach, mountain *Atriplex hortensis*
spinach, native *Tetragonia tetragonioides*
spinach, New Zealand *Tetragonia tetragonioides*
spinach, water *Ipomoea aquatica*
spindle palm *Hyophorbe verschaffeltii*
spindle tree *Euonymus europaeus*
spindle tree, European *Euonymus europaeus*
spindle tree, winged *Euonymus alatus*
spineless caltrop *Tribulus microccus*
spineless yucca *Yucca elephantipes*
spinifex *Triodia basedowii*
spinifex beach *Spinifex hirsutus*
spinifex, buck *Triodia mitchellii*

spinifex, cane *Zygochloa paradoxa*
spinifex, hairy *Spinifex hirsutus*
spinifex, silky *Spinifex sericeus*
spinning gum *Eucalyptus perriniana*
spiny acanthus *Acanthus spinosus*
spiny amaranth *Amaranthus spinosus*
spiny bossiaea *Bossiaea obcordata*
spiny broom *Calicotome spinosa*
spiny burrgrass *Cenchrus incertus,*
  C. longispinus
spiny emex *Emex australis*
spiny fan-flower *Scaevola spinescens*
spiny fiber palm *Trithrinax*
  acanthocoma
spiny mudgrass *Pseudoraphis*
  spinescens
spiny pest pear *Opuntia dillenii*
spiny potato bush *Solanum*
  ferocissimum
spiny rush *Juncus acutus*
spiny saltbush *Rhagodia spinescens*
spiny sedge *Cyperus gymnocaulos*
spiny star cactus *Escobaria vivipara*
spiny-fruit saltbush *Atriplex*
  spinibractea
spiny-headed mat-rush *Lomandra*
  longifolia
spiraea *Spiraea*
spiraea, birch-leaf *Spiraea betulifolia*
spiraea, blue *Caryopteris incana,*
  C. × clandonensis
spiraea, bridal wreath *Spiraea*
  prunifolia, S. × vanhouttei
spiraea, double Reeves' *Spiraea*
  cantoniensis 'Flore Pleno'
spiraea, false *Astilbe, Sorbaria*
  sorbifolia
spiraea, germander *Spiraea*
  chamaedryfolia
spiraea grefsheim *Spiraea × cinerea*
spiraea, Japanese *Spiraea japonica*
spiraea, Korean *Spiraea fritschiana,*
  S. trichocarpa

spiraea, mountain *Spiraea densiflora*
spiraea, Nippon *Spiraea nipponica*
spiraea, Reeves' *Spiraea cantoniensis*
spiraea, rock *Holodiscus dumosus,*
  Petrophytum
spiraea, shoe button *Spiraea*
  prunifolia
spiraea, Snow White *Spiraea* 'Snow
  White'
spiraea, three-lobed *Spiraea trilobata*
spiraea, Thunberg *Spiraea thunbergii*
spiraea, Ural false *Sorbaria kirilowii*
spiraea, Van Houtte *Spiraea ×*
  vanhouttei
spiraea, western *Spiraea douglasii*
spiral flag *Costus*
spiral ginger *Costus*
spire azalea, golden *Azara integrifolia*
spleenwort *Asplenium*
spleenwort, common *Asplenium*
  trichomanes
spleenwort, limestone *Asplenium*
  trichomanes
spleenwort, maidenhair *Asplenium*
  trichomanes
spleenwort, mother *Asplenium*
  bulbiferum
spleenwort, narrow-leafed *Diplazium*
  pycnocarpon
spleenwort, necklace *Asplenium*
  flabellifolium
spleenwort, shore *Asplenium*
  obtusatum
spleenwort, silvery *Diplazium*
  pycnocarpon
spleenwort, weeping *Asplenium*
  flaccidum
splendid mint bush *Prostanthera*
  magnifica
sponge-fruit *Trachymene ornata*
spoon bush *Cunonia capensis*
spoon cudweed *Stuartina muelleri*
spoon, desert *Dasylirion wheeleri*

spoon lily *Alocasia brisbanensis*
spot, five *Nemophila maculata*
spotted burr medic *Medicago arabica*
spotted dead-nettle *Lamium maculatum*
spotted dracaena *Dracaena surculosa*
spotted dumbcane *Dieffenbachia seguine*
spotted emu bush *Eremophila maculata*
spotted fig *Ficus virens*
spotted gentian *Gentiana punctata*
spotted gum *Corymbia maculata*
spotted gum, large-leafed *Corymbia henryi*
spotted orchid, common *Dactylorhiza fuchsii*
spotted sun orchid *Thelymitra ixioides*
spotted wintergreen *Chimaphila umbellata*
sprawling cactus *Bergerocactus emoryi*
sprawling nut-heads *Epaltes australis*
sprawling smokebush *Conospermum tenuifolium*
sprawling trigger plant *Stylidium productum*
spray, mountain *Holodiscus dumosus*
spray, ocean *Holodiscus discolor*
spreading bush-pea *Pultenaea microphylla*
spreading clubmoss *Selaginella kraussiana*
spreading cotoneaster *Cotoneaster divaricatus*
spreading cupflower *Angianthus brachypappus*
spreading daisy *Brachycome whitei*
spreading dogbane *Apocynum androsaemifolium*
spreading flax-lily *Dianella revoluta*
spreading pellitory *Parietaria judaica*
spreading shield fern *Sticherus lobatus*

spreading sneezeweed *Centipeda minima*
spreading stonecrop *Crassula decumbens*
spreading wattle *Acacia genistifolia*
spreading-leafed pine *Pinus patula*
Sprenger asparagus *Asparagus densiflorus* 'Sprengeri'
Sprenger's magnolia *Magnolia sprengeri*
spring beauty *Claytonia, C. virginica*
spring cherry *Prunus × subhirtella*
spring cinquefoil *Potentilla neumanniana, P. tabernaemontani*
spring, farewell to *Clarkia*
spring grass, early *Eriochloa pseudoacrotricha*
spring onion *Allium cepa*
spring queen *Synthyris reniformis*
spring snowflake *Leucojum vernum*
spring squill *Scilla verna*
spring star flower *Ipheion uniflorum*
spring vetch *Lathyrus vernus*
sprouts, Brussels *Brassica oleracea* Gemmifera Group
spruce *Picea*
spruce, Alaska *Picea sitchensis*
spruce, Alcock's *Picea alcoquiana*
spruce, American black *Picea mariana*
spruce, American red *Picea rubens*
spruce, blue *Picea pungens* 'Glauca'
spruce, Brewer's *Picea breweriana*
spruce, Brewer's weeping *Picea breweriana*
spruce, Caucasian *Picea orientalis*
spruce, Chihuahua *Picea chihuahuana*
spruce, Colorado *Picea pungens*
spruce, Colorado blue *Picea pungens*
spruce, common *Picea abies*
spruce, dragon *Picea asperata*
spruce, dwarf Alberta *Picea glauca*

spruce, dwarf Alberta white *Picea glauca* var. *albertiana* 'Conica'

spruce, East Himalayan *Picea spinulosa*

spruce, Engelmann *Picea engelmannii*

spruce, hemlock *Tsuga*

spruce, Koster blue *Picea pungens* 'Koster'

spruce, Lijiang *Picea likiangensis*

spruce, Meyer *Picea meyeri*

spruce, Norway *Picea abies*

spruce, Nuevo Leon *Picea engelmannii* subsp. *mexicana*

spruce pine *Pinus glabra*

spruce, purple-coned *Picea purpurea*

spruce, Sargent *Picea brachytyla*

spruce, Serbian *Picea omorika*

spruce, Siberian *Picea obovata*

spruce, Sikkim *Picea spinulosa*

spruce, Sitka *Picea sitchensis*

spruce, Taiwan *Picea morrisonicola*

spruce, tiger-tail *Picea torano*

spruce, weeping *Picea breweriana*

spruce, West Himalayan *Picea smithiana*

spruce, white *Picea glauca*

spruce, Wilson's *Picea wilsonii*

spruce, Yezo *Picea jezoensis*

spuds, fairy *Claytonia virginica*

spur flower, blue *Plectranthus ecklonii*

spur flower, Madagascar *Plectranthus madagascariensis*

spur pepper *Capsicum frutescens*

spur velleia *Velleia lyrata, V. paradoxa*

spurge, Allegheny *Pachysandra procumbens*

spurge, blunt *Phyllanthus gasstroemii, P. gunnii*

spurge, bottle-tree *Euphorbia stevenii*

spurge, broom *Amperea xiphoclada*

spurge, caper *Euphorbia lathyris*

spurge, Caucasian *Andrachne colchica*

spurge, cliff *Euphorbia misera*

spurge, creeping *Euphorbia myrsinites*

spurge, cushion *Euphorbia polychroma*

spurge, cypress *Euphorbia cyparissias*

spurge, flat *Chamaesyce drummondii*

spurge, flowering *Euphorbia corollata*

spurge honey *Euphorbia mellifera*

spurge, Japanese *Pachysandra terminalis*

spurge laurel *Daphne laureola*

spurge, mottled *Euphorbia lactea*

spurge, myrtle *Euphorbia lathyris*

spurge olive *Cneorum tricoccon*

spurge, painted *Euphorbia cyathophora*

spurge, petty *Euphorbia peplus*

spurge, plains *Euphorbia planiticola*

spurge, purple *Euphorbia dulcis*

spurge, thyme *Phyllanthus hirtellus*

spurge, tramp's *Euphorbia corollata*

spurge, wood *Euphorbia amygdaloides*

spurred arrowgrass *Triglochin calcitrapum*

spurred helmet orchid *Corybas aconitiflorus*

spurred snapdragon *Linaria*

spurrey, corn *Spergula arvensis*

spurwing wattle *Acacia triptera*

square bamboo *Chimonobambusa quadrangularis*

square cicendia *Cicendia quadrangularis*

square-leaf grass tree *Xanthorrhoea quadrangulata*

squash *Cucurbita maxima, Cucurbita moschata, C. pepo*

squash, autumn *Curcurbita maxima*

squash, crookneck *Cucurbita moschata*

squash, summer *Cucurbita pepo*

squash, winter *Cucurbita maxima*

squaw carpet *Ceanothus prostratus*

squaw currant *Ribes cereum*
squaw huckleberry *Vaccinium
caesium*
squill *Scilla*
squill, African *Ledebouria*
squill, blue *Scilla natalensis,
S. siberica*
squill, Peruvian *Scilla peruviana*
squill, Pyrenean *Scilla liliohyacinthus*
squill, Siberian *Scilla siberica*
squill, spring *Scilla verna*
squill, striped *Puschkinia scilloides*
squill, two-leafed *Scilla bifolia*
squirreltail *Hordeum jubatum*
squirreltail barley *Hordeum jubatum*
squirreltail fescue *Vulpia bromoides*
squirting cucumber *Ecballium
elaterium*
stackhousia, slender *Stackhousia
viminea*
stagger weed *Dicentra eximia, Stachys
arvensis*
staghorn clubmoss *Lycopodiella
cernua, Lycopodium clavatum*
staghorn fern *Platycerium,
P. superbum*
staghorn sumac *Rhus typhina*
stalked brooklime *Gratiola
pedunculata*
stalked conesticks *Petrophile
pedunculata*
stalked hopbush *Dodonaea
peduncularis*
stalked plover-daisy *Ixiolaena
leptolepis*
stamvrug *Bequaertiodendron
magalismontanum*
standing cypress *Ipomopsis rubra*
stapelia, giant *Stapelia gigantea*
star anise *Illicium verum*
star apple *Chrysophyllum cainito*
star, blazing *Liatris, L. aspera,
L. spicata, Tritonia crocata*

star, blue *Amsonia tabernaemontana*
star bush *Asterolasia correifolia*
star cactus, spiny *Escobaria vivipara*
star cluster *Pentas lanceolata*
star copperburr *Sclerolaena stelligera*
star cudweed *Gnaphalium
involucratum*
star daisy *Lindheimera texana*
star, eastern shooting *Dodecatheon
meadia*
star flower, spring *Ipheion uniflorum*
star fruit *Averrhoa carambola*
star, golden *Chrysogonum
virginianum, Hypoxis hygrometrica*
star gooseberry *Phyllanthus acidus*
star grass *Hypoxis*
star grass, white *Hypoxis capensis*
star jasmine *Trachelospermum,
T. jasminoides*
star jasmine, Chinese
Trachelospermum jasminoides
star jasmine, Japanese
Trachelospermum asiaticum
star lily *Zigadenus fremontii*
star lily, knight's *Hippeastrum*
star magnolia *Magnolia stellata*
star of Bethlehem *Campanula
isophylla, Ornithogalum,
O. umbellatum*
star of Persia *Allium cristophii*
star, red *Rhodohypoxis baurii*
star, Sabi *Adenium obesum*
star sansevieria *Sansevieria
grandicuspis*
star, shooting *Dodecatheon,
D. meadia*
star, Texas *Lindheimera texana*
star thistle *Centaurea calcitrapa*
star, yellow *Lindheimera texana*
star zygadene *Zigadenus fremontii*
star-anise, Japanese *Illicium anisatum*
starbush, alpine *Asterolasia
trymalioides*

starbush, lemon *Asterolasia asteriscophora*
starfish flower *Stapelia*
starfish flower, hairy *Stapelia hirsuta*
starfish fungus *Aseroe rubra*
star-flower *Calytrix, Hypoxis, Scabiosa stellata, Smilacina stellata*
star-flowered lily of the valley *Smilacina stellata*
starfruit *Damasonium minus*
star-hair, broad-leaf *Astrotricha latifolia*
star-hair, longleaf *Astrotricha longifolia*
star-hair, woolly *Astrotricha floccosa*
star-leaf grevillea *Grevillea asteriscosa*
starry cerastium *Cerastium arvense*
starry gardenia *Gardenia thunbergia*
stars, falling *Campanula isophylla, Crocosmia*
stars, orange *Hibbertia stellaris*
stars, yellow *Hypoxis villosa*
starvation prickly pear *Opuntia polyacantha*
starwort, bushy *Aster subulatus*
starwort, common *Callitriche stagnalis*
starwort, forest *Stellaria flaccida*
starwort, prickly *Stellaria pungens*
statice *Limonium sinuatum, Psylliostachys*
statice, Cape *Limonium peregrinum*
stave oak *Quercus alba*
Steedman's gum *Eucalyptus steedmanii*
Steedman's honey-myrtle *Melaleuca fulgens* subsp. *steedmanii*
steel acacia *Acacia macracantha*
steel box *Eucalyptus rummeryi*
steelwood *Sarcopteryx stipata*
steeple tree *Markhamia lutea*
steeplebush *Spiraea tomentosa*
stem ginger *Zingiber officinale*

stemless thistle *Onopordum acaulon*
stemona *Stemona tuberosa*
stephanandra, cut-leafed *Stephanandra incisa*
steppe cherry *Prunus fruticosa*
steppe sage *Salvia nemorosa*
stewartia, Chinese *Stewartia sinensis*
stewartia, Japanese *Stewartia pseudocamellia*
stewartia, mountain *Stewartia ovata*
stewartia, tall *Stewartia monadelpha*
stewartia, Virginia *Stewartia malacodendron*
stick tight *Bidens*
sticklewort *Agrimonia*
stickseed, burr *Omphalolappula concava*
sticky boronia *Boronia anemonifolia*
sticky cassinia *Cassinia uncata*
sticky cinquefoil *Potentilla glandulosa*
sticky daisy-bush *Olearia elliptica, O. viscidula*
sticky everlasting *Xerochrysum viscosum*
sticky flower *Orphium frutescens*
sticky polemonium *Polemonium viscosum*
sticky sage *Salvia glutinosa*
sticky sedge *Cyperus fulvus*
sticky sword-sedge *Lepidosperma viscidum*
sticky wallaby bush *Beyeria viscosa*
sticky weed *Parietaria. judaica*
sticky-heads *Podotheca angustifolia*
sticky-leafed rabbitbrush *Chrysothamnus viscidiflorus*
stiff beardtongue *Penstemon strictus*
stiff boronia *Boronia rigens*
stiff bottlebrush *Callistemon rigidus*
stiff daisy *Brachyscome angustifolia*
stiff rapier-sedge *Lepidosperma neesii*
stiff ryegrass *Lolium loliaceum*

stiff western rosemary *Westringia
rigida*
stinging nettle *Urtica*
stinging tree, giant *Dendrocnide
excelsa*
stinging tree, northern *Dendrocnide
moroides*
stink bell *Fritillaria agrestis*
stink lily *Typhonium brownii*
stinkgrass *Eragrostis cilianensis*
stinking bean trefoil *Anagyris foetida*
stinking cedar *Torreya taxifolia*
stinking chamomile *Anthemis cotula*
stinking elder *Sambucus pubens*
stinking gladwyn *Iris foetidissima*
stinking hawksbeard *Crepis foetida*
stinking hellebore *Helleborus foetidus*
stinking madder *Putoria calabrica*
stinking nightshade *Hyoscyamus niger*
stinking pennywort *Hydrocotyle
laxiflora*
stinking Roger *Tagetes minuta*
stinkweed *Opercularia*
stinkweed, common *Opercularia
aspera*
stinkwood *Coprosma putida,
Pararchidendron pruinosum, Zieria
arborescens, Z. smithii*
stinkwood, red *Prunus africana*
stinkwood, white *Celtis africana*
stinkwort *Dittrichia graveolens,
Helleborus foetidus*
stitchwort *Stellaria*
stitchwort, greater *Stellaria holostea*
stock *Matthiola*
stock, Brompton *Matthiola incana*
stock, Cape *Heliophila*
stock, mahon *Malcolmia maritima*
stock, Malcolm *Malcolmia maritima*
stock, native *Blennodia canescens*
stock, night-scented *Matthiola
longipetala*
stock, Virginia *Malcolmia maritima*

stock, wild *Blennodia canescens*
stocks *Matthiola incana*
Stokes' aster *Stokesia laevis*
stompies *Brunia albiflora*
stone cress *Aethionema*
Stone Mountain oak *Quercus
georgiana*
stone oak *Quercus alba*
stone pine *Pinus pinea*
stone pine, Swiss *Pinus cembra*
stonecrop *Sedum, S. acre*
stonecrop, dense *Crassula colorata*
stonecrop, Kamchatka *Sedum
kamtschaticum*
stonecrop, purple *Crassula
peduncularis*
stonecrop, spreading *Crassula
decumbens*
stonecrop, swamp *Crassula helmsii*
stopper *Eugenia*
stopper, red *Eugenia confusa*
storax, bigleaf *Styrax obassia*
storksbill *Erodium, Pelargonium*
storksbill, common *Erodium
cicutarium*
storksbill, magenta *Pelargonium
rodneyanum*
storksbill, musk *Erodium moschatum*
storksbill, native *Pelargonium australe*
stormflower *Zephyranthes candida*
straggly corkbark *Hakea eyreana*
strand sedge *Carex pumila*
strangler fig *Ficus virens*
strangler fig, Cape *Ficus sur*
strangler fig, common *Ficus
thonningii*
strangler fig, Florida *Ficus aurea*
strap airplant, powdery *Catopsis
berteroniana*
strap fern *Blechnum patersonii*
strap water fern *Blechnum patersonii*
strapleaf bloodroot *Haemodorum
planifolium*

straw bell *Uvularia perfoliata*
straw foxglove *Digitalis lutea*
straw lilies *Uvularia sessilifolia*
straw tree fern *Cyathea cooperi*
strawberry *Fragaria, F. × ananassa*
strawberry, alpine *Fragaria vesca*
strawberry, barren *Potentilla sterilis, Waldsteinia fragarioides*
strawberry, beach *Fragaria chiloensis*
strawberry begonia *Saxifraga stolonifera*
strawberry bush *Euonymus americanus*
strawberry cactus *Mammillaria prolifera*
strawberry, Chilean *Fragaria chiloensis*
strawberry foxglove *Digitalis × mertonensis*
strawberry, garden *Fragaria × ananassa*
strawberry grevillea *Grevillea confertifolia*
strawberry guava *Psidium cattleianum*
strawberry, hautbois *Fragaria moschata*
strawberry hedgehog cactus *Echinocereus engelmannii*
strawberry, Indian *Duchesnea, D. indica*
strawberry, mock *Duchesnea indica*
strawberry shrub *Calycanthus floridus*
strawberry tomato *Physalis ixocarpa*
strawberry, tree *Cephalanthus natalensis*
strawberry tree *Arbutus unedo*
strawberry tree, Chinese *Myrica rubra*
strawberry tree, Grecian *Arbutus andrachne*
strawberry tree, Himalayan *Cornus capitata*

strawberry tree, hybrid *Arbutus × andrachnoides*
strawberry tree, Irish *Arbutus unedo*
strawberry, wild *Fragaria vesca*
strawflower *Rhodanthe, Xerochrysum bracteatum*
streaked mint bush *Prostanthera striatiflora*
streaked poverty-bush *Sclerolaena tricuspis*
stream violet *Viola glabella*
Strickland's gum *Eucalyptus stricklandii*
string bean *Phaseolus vulgaris*
string of beads *Senecio rowleyanus*
stringbark, brown *Eucalyptus baxteri, E. capitellata*
stringybark, Bailey's *Eucalyptus baileyana*
stringybark, Blue Mountains *Eucalyptus blaxlandii*
stringybark, blue-leafed *Eucalyptus agglomerata*
stringybark, broad-leafed *Eucalyptus caliginosa*
stringybark cypress-pine *Callitris macleayana*
stringybark, Darwin *Eucalyptus tetrodonta*
stringybark, diehard *Eucalyptus cameronii*
stringybark, heart-leafed *Eucalyptus camfieldii*
stringybark, McKie's *Eucalyptus mckieana*
stringybark, mealy *Eucalyptus cephalocarpa*
stringybark, narrow-leafed *Eucalyptus oblonga, E. sparsifolia*
stringybark, privet-leafed *Eucalyptus ligustrina*
stringybark, red *Eucalyptus macrorhyncha*

stringybark, scrub *Rhodamnia rubescens*

stringybark, silvertop *Eucalyptus laevopinea*

stringybark, slender-leafed *Eucalyptus tenella*

stringybark, thin-leafed *Eucalyptus eugenioides*

stringybark, white *Eucalyptus globoidea*

stringybark, yellow *Eucalyptus muelleriana*

stringybark, Youman's *Eucalyptus youmanii*

striped hakea *Hakea tephrosperma*

striped inch plant *Callisia elegans* 'Variegata'

striped loosestrife *Lythrum salicaria*

striped maple *Acer pensylvanicum*

striped marigold *Tagetes tenuifolia*

striped nardoo *Marsilea mutica*

striped squill *Puschkinia scilloides*

strophanthus *Strophanthus gratus*

strychnine tree *Strychnos arborea*

Sturt pea *Swainsona formosa*

Sturt's desert pea *Swainsona formosa*

Sturt's desert rose *Gossypium sturtianum*

subalpine beard-heath *Leucopogon maccraei*

subalpine fir *Abies lasiocarpa*

subalpine larch *Larix lyallii*

subterranean clover *Trifolium subterraneum*

succory, blue *Catananche caerulea*

suckling clover, yellow *Trifolium dubium*

Sudan gum arabic tree *Acacia senegal*

sugar banana *Musa acuminata* 'Ladyfinger'

sugar bush *Protea repens, Rhus ovata*

sugar cane *Saccharum officinarum*

sugar gum *Eucalyptus cladocalyx*

sugar hackberry *Celtis laevigata*

sugar maple *Acer saccharum*

sugar palm *Arenga pinnata*

sugar pea *Pisum sativum*

sugar pine *Pinus lambertiana*

sugar sumac *Rhus ovata*

sugarberry *Celtis laevigata*

sugarbush *Protea gaguedi, P. repens*

sugarbush, blue *Protea neriifolia*

sugarbush, brown bearded *Protea speciosa*

sugarbush, pine *Protea aristata*

sugarbush, red *Protea grandiceps*

sugarcane *Saccharum officinarum*

sugarwood *Myoporum platycarpum*

Suggan Buggan mallee *Eucalyptus saxatilis*

sugi *Cryptomeria japonica*

suji giboshi *Hosta undulata*

sulfur flower *Eriogonum umbellatum*

sulfur rose *Rosa hemisphaerica*

sulphur cinquefoil *Potentilla recta*

sumac *Rhus*

sumac, African *Rhus lancea*

sumac, desert *Rhus microphylla*

sumac, dwarf *Rhus copallina*

sumac, evergreen *Rhus virens*

sumac, false *Brucea javanica*

sumac, fragrant *Rhus aromatica*

sumac, lemonade *Rhus integrifolia*

sumac, poison *Toxicodendron succedaneum, T. vernix*

sumac, scarlet *Rhus glabra*

sumac, scrub *Rhus microphylla*

sumac, shining *Rhus copallina*

sumac, skunkbush *Rhus trilobata*

sumac, smooth *Rhus glabra*

sumac, staghorn *Rhus typhina*

sumac, sugar *Rhus ovata*

sumac, three-lobe *Rhus trilobata*

sumac, tobacco *Rhus virens*

sumach, lemon *Rhus aromatica*

sumach, mountain *Rhus copallina*
sumach, Venetian *Cotinus coggygria*
Sumatran pine *Pinus merkusii*
summer cypress *Bassia scoparia*
summer grass *Digitaria ciliaris,*
D. sanguinalis
summer grass, green *Urochloa*
subquadripara
summer haw *Crataegus flava*
summer holly *Arctostaphylos*
diversifolia
summer hyacinth *Galtonia candicans*
summer lilac *Buddleja colvilei*
summer marsh Afrikaner *Gladiolus*
tristis var. *aestivalis*
summer phlox *Phlox paniculata*
summer savory *Satureja hortensis*
summer, snow in *Melaleuca*
linariifolia
summer snowflake *Leucojum aestivale*
summer squash *Cucurbita pepo*
summersweet clethra *Clethra*
alnifolia
sun, glory of the *Leucocoryne ixioides,*
L. odorata
sun, glossy *Solanum americanum*
sun orchid *Thelymitra, T. ixioides*
sun orchid, large-veined *Thelymitra*
venosa
sun orchid, slender *Thelymitra*
pauciflora
sun orchid, spotted *Thelymitra*
ixioides
sun pitcher *Heliamphora*
sun plant *Portulaca grandiflora*
sun rose *Helianthemum*
sun rose, common *Helianthemum*
nummularium
sunbonnets *Chaptalia*
sundew *Drosera*
sundew, Cape *Drosera capensis*
sundew, forked *Drosera binata*
sundew, lance-leaf *Drosera adelae*

sundew, mountain *Drosera montana*
sundew, notched *Drosera schizandra*
sundew, painted *Drosera zonaria*
sundew, pale *Drosera peltata*
sundew, pink *Drosera capillaris*
sundew, Portuguese *Drosophyllum*
lusitanicum
sundew, pretty *Drosera pulchella*
sundew, pygmy *Drosera pygmaea*
sundew, red-ink *Drosera erythrorhiza*
sundew, round-leafed *Drosera*
rotundifolia
sundew, threadleaf *Drosera filiformis*
sundew, woolly *Drosera petiolaris*
sundial lupine *Lupinus perennis*
sundrops *Oenothera fruticosa,*
O. perennis
sundrops, bush *Calylophus serrulatus*
sundrops, dwarf *Calylophus serrulatus*
sundrops, Ozark *Oenothera*
macrocarpa
sunflower *Balsamorhiza sagittata,*
Helianthus, H. annuus
sunflower, common *Helianthus*
annuus
sunflower, dark-eye *Helianthus*
atrorubens
sunflower, everlasting *Heliopsis*
helianthoides
sunflower, false *Heliopsis,*
H. helianthoides
sunflower, giant *Helianthus giganteus*
sunflower, Mexican *Tithonia*
sunflower, swamp *Helianthus*
angustifolius
sunflower, telekia *Telekia speciosa*
sunflower, thin-leaf *Helianthus*
decapetalus
sunflower, woolly *Eriophyllum*
lanatum
sunray *Leucochrysum albicans*
sunray, ascending *Rhodanthe*
diffusa

sunray, brilliant *Rhodanthe polygalifolia*
sunray, chamomile *Rhodanthe anthemoides*
sunray, clay *Rhodanthe stuartiana*
sunray, clustered *Rhodanthe microglossa*
sunray, common *Triptilodiscus pygmaeus*
sunray, dwarf *Hyalosperma demissum*
sunray, fine-leaf *Hyalosperma praecox*
sunray, golden *Hyalosperma glutinosum*
sunray, grass-leaf *Leucochrysum graminifolium*
sunray, hoary *Leucochrysum albicans, L. molle*
sunray, musk *Rhodanthe moschata*
sunray, orange *Hyalosperma semisterile*
sunray, pygmy *Rhodanthe pygmaea*
sunray, sand *Rhodanthe tietkensii*
sunray, slender *Rhodanthe stricta*
sunray, smooth *Rhodanthe laevis*
sunray, western *Rhodanthe troedelii*
sunray, white *Rhodanthe floribunda*
sunray, woolly *Rhodanthe uniflora*
sunset hyssop *Agastache rupestris*
sunshine, Oregon *Eriophyllum lanatum*
sunshine wattle *Acacia terminalis*
suntwood *Acacia nilotica*
superb greenhood *Pterostylis grandiflora*
supplejack *Flagellaria indica, Ventilago viminalis*
supplejack, prickly *Ripogonum discolor*
supplejack, small *Ripogonum fawcettianum*
supplejack, white *Ripogonum album*
Surinam cherry *Eugenia uniflora*

Susan, black-eyed *Rudbeckia, Tetratheca, Thunbergia alata*
Susan, brown-eyed *Rudbeckia triloba*
swallow wort *Asclepias curassavica*
swamp ash *Fraxinus caroliniana, F. nigra*
swamp azalea *Rhododendron viscosum*
swamp azalea, white *Rhododendron viscosum*
swamp baeckea *Baeckea linifolia*
swamp banksia *Banksia littoralis, B. robur*
swamp banksia, red *Banksia occidentalis*
swamp bloodwood *Corymbia ptychocarpa*
swamp bluebush *Maireana microcarpa*
swamp boronia *Boronia parviflora*
swamp bottlebrush *Beaufortia sparsa, Callistemon sieberi*
swamp box *Lophostemon suaveolens*
swamp canegrass *Eragrostis australasica*
swamp chestnut oak *Quercus michauxii, Q. prinus*
swamp cypress *Taxodium distichum*
swamp cypress, Chinese *Glyptostrobus pensilis*
swamp cypress, Mexican *Taxodium mucronatum*
swamp fern, climbing *Stenochlaena palustris*
swamp fern, narrow *Dryopteris cristata*
swamp foxtail grass *Pennisetum alopecuroides*
swamp grass tree *Xanthorrhoea fulva*
swamp gum *Eucalyptus ovata*
swamp gum, mountain *Eucalyptus camphora*
swamp heath *Epacris paludosa*

swamp heath, pink *Sprengelia incarnata*

swamp hibiscus *Hibiscus coccineus, H. diversifolius*

swamp hickory *Carya cordiformis*

swamp honeysuckle *Rhododendron viscosum*

swamp isotome *Isotoma fluviatilis*

swamp laurel *Kalmia polifolia, Magnolia virginiana*

swamp lily *Ottelia ovalifolia*

swamp lily, Florida *Crinum americanum*

swamp mahogany *Eucalyptus robusta*

swamp mallet *Eucalyptus spathulata*

swamp maple *Acer rubrum*

swamp mazus *Mazus pumilio*

swamp millet *Isachne globosa*

swamp oak *Casuarina glauca, Quercus palustris*

swamp orchid *Phaius, P. tankervilliae*

swamp orchid, yellow *Phaius barnaysii*

swamp paperbark *Melaleuca ericifolia, M. rhaphiophylla*

swamp peppermint *Eucalyptus rodwayi*

swamp pink *Helonias bullata*

swamp poplar *Populus heterophylla*

swamp privet *Forestiera acuminata*

swamp red oak *Quercus falcata*

swamp rose *Rosa palustris*

swamp rose mallow *Hibiscus moscheutos*

swamp sego *Camassia quamash*

swamp she-oak *Casuarina glauca*

swamp stonecrop *Crassula helmsii*

swamp sunflower *Helianthus angustifolius*

swamp tea-tree *Leptospermum myrtifolium*

swamp turpentine *Lophostemon suaveolens*

swamp violet *Viola caleyana*

swamp wallaby grass *Amphibromus macrorhinus, A. neesii*

swamp water fern *Blechnum indicum*

swamp wattle *Acacia elongata, A. retinodes*

swamp white oak *Quercus bicolor*

swan plant *Gomphocarpus, G. physocarpus*

Swan River daisy *Brachyscome iberidifolia*

Swan River everlasting *Rhodanthe manglesii*

Swan River myrtle *Hypocalymma robustum*

Swan River pea *Brachysema celsianum*

Swan River pea-bush *Brachysema lanceolatum*

Swane's golden pencil pine *Cupressus sempervirens* 'Swane's Golden'

swarthaak *Acacia mellifera*

Swazi ordeal tree *Erythrophleum lasianthum*

swede *Brassica napus*

Swedish aspen *Populus tremula*

Swedish begonia *Plectranthus australis*

Swedish ivy *Plectranthus australis, P. verticillatus*

Swedish mountain ash *Sorbus intermedia*

Swedish turnip *Brassica napus*

Swedish whitebeam *Sorbus intermedia*

sweet alyssum *Lobularia maritima*

sweet azalea *Rhododendron canescens*

sweet bamboo *Dendrocalamus asper*

sweet basil *Ocimum basilicum*

sweet bay *Laurus nobilis, Magnolia virginiana*

sweet bells *Leucothoe racemosa*

sweet Betsy *Trillium cuneatum*

sweet birch *Betula lenta*

sweet box *Sarcococca*

sweet briar *Rosa rubiginosa*
sweet buckeye *Aesculus flava*
sweet calamus *Acorus calamus*
sweet cherry *Prunus avium*
sweet chestnut *Castanea sativa*
sweet cicely *Myrrhis odorata*
sweet coltsfoot *Petasites*
sweet corn *Zea mays*
sweet crab, American *Malus coronaria*
sweet elder *Sambucus canadensis*
sweet false chamomile *Matricaria recutita*
sweet fern *Comptonia peregrina*
sweet flag *Acorus calamus*
sweet gale *Myrica gale*
sweet garlic *Tulbaghia fragrans, T. simmleri*
sweet grass *Glyceria*
sweet grass, reed *Glyceria maxima*
sweet gum *Liquidambar, L. styraciflua*
sweet gum, American *Liquidambar styraciflua*
sweet gum, Chinese *Liquidambar acalycina, L. formosana*
sweet gum, oriental *Liquidambar orientalis*
sweet horsemint *Cunila origanoides*
sweet jasmine *Jasminum suavissimum*
sweet lemon *Citrus limetta*
sweet lime *Citrus limetta*
sweet mace *Tagetes lucida*
sweet marjoram *Origanum majorana*
sweet melilot *Melilotus indica*
sweet mock orange *Philadelphus coronarius*
sweet, mountain *Ceanothus americanus*
sweet Nancy *Achillea ageratum*
sweet noor *Euphorbia coerulescens*
sweet olive *Osmanthus fragrans*
sweet orange *Citrus sinensis*

sweet osmanthus *Osmanthus fragrans*
sweet panic *Panicum gilvum*
sweet pea *Lathyrus, L. odoratus*
sweet pea bush *Podalyria calyptrata*
sweet pepper *Capsicum annuum* Grossum Group
sweet pepper bush *Clethra alnifolia*
sweet pignut *Carya ovalis*
sweet pittosporum *Pittosporum undulatum*
sweet potato *Ipomoea batatas*
sweet potato cactus *Peniocereus greggii*
sweet quandong *Santalum acuminatum*
sweet reseda *Reseda odorata*
sweet rocket *Hesperis matronalis*
sweet sarsaparilla *Smilax glyciphylla*
sweet scabious *Scabiosa atropurpurea*
sweet tea plant *Smilax glyciphylla*
sweet thorn *Acacia karroo*
sweet verbena tree *Backhousia citriodora*
sweet vernal grass *Anthoxanthum odoratum*
sweet viburnum *Viburnum odoratissimum*
sweet violet *Viola odorata*
sweet wattle *Acacia suaveolens*
sweet white violet *Viola blanda*
sweet William *Dianthus barbatus*
sweet William catchfly *Silene armeria*
sweet William, wild *Phlox divaricata, P. maculata*
sweet winter grape *Vitis cinerea*
sweet woodruff *Galium odoratum*
sweetberry, velvet *Bridelia mollis*
sweetheart geranium *Pelargonium echinatum*
sweetheart tree *Euscaphis japonica*
sweetleaf *Symplocos tinctoria*
sweet-scented evening-primrose *Oenothera stricta*

sweet-scented hakea *Hakea drupacea*
sweet-scented marigold *Tagetes lucida*
sweetshoot bamboo *Phyllostachys dulcis*
sweetsop *Annona squamosa*
sweetspire *Itea, I. virginica*
sweetspire, Chinese *Itea chinensis*
sweetspire, holly-leaf *Itea ilicifolia*
sweetwood *Glycyrrhiza glabra*
swinecress, lesser *Coronopus didymus*
Swiss chard *Beta vulgaris*
Swiss cheese plant *Monstera deliciosa*
Swiss mountain pine *Pinus mugo*
Swiss stone pine *Pinus cembra*
Swiss willow *Salix helvetica*
switch grass *Panicum virgatum*
switch ivy *Leucothoe fontanesiana*
swollen silver thatch *Coccothrinax spissa*
sword brake *Pteris ensiformis*
sword fern *Nephrolepis, Polystichum*
sword fern, Anderson's *Polystichum andersoni*
sword fern, Braun's *Polystichum braunii*
sword fern, erect *Nephrolepis cordifolia*
sword fern, weeping *Nephrolepis falcata*
sword fern, western *Polystichum munitum*
sword, flaming *Vriesea splendens*
sword lily *Gladiolus*
sword lily, Abyssinian *Gladiolus callianthus*
sword-sedge *Lepidosperma laterale, L. squamatum*

sword-sedge, little *Lepidosperma lineare*
sword-sedge, pithy *Lepidosperma longitudinale*
sword-sedge, sticky *Lepidosperma viscidum*
sword-sedge, tall *Lepidosperma elatius*
sword-sedge, variable *Lepidosperma laterale*
sycamore *Ficus sycomorus, Platanus occidentalis*
sycamore, California *Platanus racemosa*
sycamore, Egyptian *Ficus sycomorus*
sycamore fig *Ficus sycomorus*
sycamore maple *Acer pseudoplatanus*
sycamore maple, variegated *Acer pseudoplatanus* 'Leopoldii', *A. p.* 'Luteovirens'
sycamore, western *Platanus racemosa*
Sydney blue gum *Eucalyptus saligna*
Sydney boronia *Boronia ledifolia*
Sydney golden wattle *Acacia longifolia*
Sydney green wattle *Acacia parramattensis*
Sydney peppermint *Eucalyptus piperita*
Sydney red gum *Angophora costata*
Syrian alder *Alnus orientalis*
Syrian hibiscus *Hibiscus syriacus*
Syrian juniper *Juniperus drupacea*
Syrian mountain cherry *Prunus prostrata*
syringa *Philadelphus coronarius, P. pubescens*
syringa, Lewis *Philadelphus lewisii*

T

Tabasco pepper *Capsicum frutescens*
table dogwood *Cornus controversa*
table fern *Pteris*
Table Mountain pine *Pinus pungens*
tabletop dogwood *Cornus controversa*
tacamahac *Populus balsamifera*
tagasaste *Chamaecytisus palmensis*
Tahitian lime *Citrus* × *latifolia*
Tahoka daisy *Machaeranthera tanacetifolia*
tai, ma *Eleocharis dulcis*
tail, donkey *Euphorbia myrsinites*
tail, donkey's *Sedum morganianum*
tail, lizard's *Crassula muscosa, Saururus cernuus*
tail-grape *Artabotrys hexapetalus*
tailor's patch *Crassula lactea*
tails, lamb's *Anredera cordifolia, Ptilotus semilanatus*
tails, purple *Ptilotus semilanatus*
tails, rabbit *Ptilotus seminudus*
tails, silver *Ptilotus obovatus*
tailwort *Borago*
Taiwan azalea *Rhododendron oldhamii*
Taiwan cherry *Prunus campanulata*
Taiwan cypress *Chamaecyparis formosensis*
Taiwan Douglas fir *Pseudotsuga wilsoniana*
Taiwan fir *Abies kawakamii*
Taiwan firethorn *Pyracantha koidzumii*
Taiwan juniper *Juniperus formosana*
Taiwan paulownia *Paulownia kawakamii*
Taiwan spruce *Picea morrisonicola*
taiwania *Taiwania cryptomerioides*
talipot palm *Corypha umbraculifera*

tall baeckea *Baeckea virgata*
tall bluebell *Wahlenbergia stricta*
tall boronia *Boronia molloyae*
tall copperburr *Sclerolaena convexula*
tall evergreen azalea *Rhododendron* × *mucronatum*
tall fescue *Festuca arundinacea*
tall flat-sedge *Cyperus exaltatus*
tall fleabane *Conyza albida*
tall kangaroo paw *Anigozanthos flavidus*
tall leek orchid *Prasophyllum elatum*
tall lobelia *Lobelia gibbosa*
tall mulla mulla *Ptilotus exaltatus*
tall ocotillo *Fouquieria diguetii*
tall pussy-tails *Ptilotus exaltatus*
tall rice flower *Pimelea ligustrina*
tall saw-sedge *Gahnia clarkei*
tall sedge *Carex appressa*
tall speargrass *Austrostipa bigeniculata, A. pubescens*
tall spike-rush *Eleocharis sphacelata*
tall stewartia *Stewartia monadelpha*
tall sword-sedge *Lepidosperma elatius*
tall tails *Pennisetum orientale*
tall twig-rush *Cladium procerum*
tall verbena *Verbena bonariensis*
tall windmill grass *Chloris ventricosa*
tall yellow-eye *Xyris operculata*
tallerack *Eucalyptus tetragona*
tallow tree, Chinese *Sapium sebiferum, Triadica sebifera*
tallowwood *Eucalyptus microcorys*
tallowwood, bastard *Eucalyptus planchoniana*
tamalan *Dalbergia oliveri*
tamarack *Larix laricina*
tamarack larch *Larix laricina*
tamarillo *Solanum betaceum*
tamarind *Tamarindus indica*
tamarind, brown *Castanospora alphandii*

tamarind, corduroy *Arytera lautereriana*

tamarind, green *Elattostachys nervosa*

tamarind, native *Diploglottis australis*

tamarind, rose *Arytera divaricata*

tamarind, small-leafed *Diploglottis campbellii*

tamarind, white *Elattostachys xylocarpa*

tamarisk *Tamarix*

tamarisk, Chinese *Tamarix chinensis*

tamarisk, early *Tamarix parviflora*

tamarisk, English *Tamarix anglica*

tamarisk, French *Tamarix gallica*

tamarisk, late *Tamarix ramosissima*

tamarisk salt cedar *Tamarix*

tamarix *Tamarix pentandra, T. ramosissima*

tambookie thorn *Erythrina acanthocarpa*

tampala *Amaranthus tricolor*

tanbark oak *Lithocarpus densiflorus*

tanekaha *Phyllocladus trichomanoides*

tanga-poo *Pyrostegia venusta*

tangelo *Citrus* × *tangelo*

tangerine *Citrus reticulata*

tanghin *Cerbera venenifera*

tangle, turkey *Phyla nodiflora*

tangled burr-daisy *Calotis erinacea*

tangled copperburr *Sclerolaena divaricata*

tangled poverty-bush *Sclerolaena intricata*

tanglefoot *Empodisma minus, Nothofagus gunnii*

tanglefoot beech *Nothofagus gunnii*

tango poi *Pyrostegia venusta*

tangor *Citrus* × *aurantium* Tangor Group

tanguru *Olearia albida*

tanjong tree *Mimusops elengi*

Tanner's dock *Rumex hymenosepalus*

tanner's oak *Quercus alba*

tannia *Xanthosoma sagittifolium*

tansy *Tanacetum vulgare*

tansy phacelia *Phacelia tanacetifolia*

tansy, silver *Tanacetum niveum*

tansyleaf aster *Machaeranthera tanacetifolia*

tansy-leafed thorn *Crataegus tanacetifolia*

tantoon tea-tree *Leptospermum polygalifolium*

tapertip onion *Allium acuminatum*

tapeworm plant *Homalocladium platycladium*

tapioca *Manihot esculenta*

tapioca plant, variegated *Manihot esculenta* 'Variegata'

tar bush *Eremophila glabra*

tar vine *Boerhavia coccinea, B. dominii*

tar weed *Grindelia*

tara vine *Actinidia arguta*

tarajo *Ilex latifolia*

taramea *Aciphylla aurea*

tarata *Pittosporum eugenioides*

taraw palm *Livistona saribus*

taro *Colocasia esculenta*

taro, blue *Xanthosoma violaceum*

taro, purple *Colocasia esculenta* 'Fontanesiana'

tarragon *Artemisia dracunculus*

tarragon, French *Artemisia dracunculus* var. *sativa*

tarragon, Spanish *Tagetes lucida*

tartan flower *Billbergia nutans*

tartan tongue orchid *Cryptostylis erecta*

tartar lily *Ixiolirion tataricum*

tartarian dogwood *Cornus alba*

tartogo *Jatropha podagrica*

Tasmanian beech *Nothofagus cunninghamii*

Tasmanian black peppermint *Eucalyptus amygdalina*

Tasmanian blue gum *Eucalyptus globulus*

Tasmanian bottlebrush *Callistemon viridiflorus*

Tasmanian Christmas bell *Blandfordia punicea*

Tasmanian currajong *Asterotrichion discolor*

Tasmanian cypress-pine *Callitris oblonga*

Tasmanian deciduous beech *Nothofagus gunnii*

Tasmanian flax-lily *Dianella tasmanica*

Tasmanian laurel *Anopterus glandulosus*

Tasmanian leatherwood *Eucryphia lucida*

Tasmanian pencil pine *Athrotaxis cupressoides*

Tasmanian podocarp *Podocarpus lawrencei*

Tasmanian snow daisy *Celmisia saxifraga*

Tasmanian snow gum *Eucalyptus coccifera*

Tasmanian tree fern *Dicksonia antarctica*

Tasmanian waratah *Telopea truncata*

Tasmanian wax flower *Philotheca virgata*

Tasmanian yellow gum *Eucalyptus johnstonii*

tassel berry *Antidesma venosum*

tassel cherry *Prunus litigiosa*

tassel cord-rush *Baloskion tetraphyllum*

tassel fern *Huperzia, Polystichum polyblepharon*

tassel fern, common *Huperzia phlegmaria*

tassel fern, rock *Huperzia squarrosa*

tassel flower *Amaranthus caudatus, Emilia sonchifolia*

tassel flower, blood-red *Calliandra haematocephala*

tassel flower, red *Calliandra tweedii*

tassel flower, white *Calliandra portoricensis*

tassel rope-rush *Hypolaena fastigiata*

tassel rush *Baloskion tetraphyllum*

tassel, sea *Ruppia maritima*

tassel shrub *Leucopogon verticillatus*

Tatarian honeysuckle *Lonicera tatarica*

Tatarian maple *Acer tataricum*

tauhinu, golden *Cassinia fulvida*

taupata *Coprosma repens*

tavoy cardamom *Amomum xanthioides*

tawhero *Weinmannia silvicola*

tea *Camellia sinensis*

tea, Arabian *Catha edulis*

tea, Carolina *Ilex vomitoria*

tea crabapple *Malus hupehensis*

tea, crystal *Ledum palustre*

tea, Labrador *Ledum groenlandicum*

tea, Malay *Psoralea corylifolia*

tea, Mexican *Chenopodium ambrosioides, Ephedra*

tea, Mormon *Ephedra viridis*

tea, mountain *Gaultheria procumbens*

tea, New Jersey *Ceanothus americanus*

tea, oil *Camellia oleifera*

tea, Oregon *Ceanothus sanguineus*

tea, oswego *Monarda didyma*

tea plant, sweet *Smilax glyciphylla*

tea, trappers' *Ledum glandulosum*

teaberry *Gaultheria procumbens*

teak *Tectona grandis*

teak, Australian *Flindersia australis*

teak, Cape *Strychnos decussata*

teak, round-leafed *Pterocarpus rotundifolius*

teak, Transvaal *Pterocarpus angolensis*

tears, angel's *Narcissus triandrus, Soleirolia soleirolii*

tears, baby's *Soleirolia soleirolii*

tears, Christ's *Coix lacryma-jobi*

tears, Job's *Coix lacryma-jobi*

tears of Mary *Fritillaria imperialis*

tears, queen's *Billbergia nutans*

tears, widow's *Commelina*

tea-tree *Leptospermum scoparium, Melaleuca alternifolia*

tea-tree, Australian *Leptospermum laevigatum*

tea-tree, black *Melaleuca bracteata, M. lanceolata*

tea-tree, blood-red *Leptospermum spectabile*

tea-tree, coast *Leptospermum laevigatum*

tea-tree, Duke of Argyll's *Lycium barbarum*

tea-tree, green *Leptospermum coriaceum*

tea-tree, large-fruited *Leptospermum macrocarpum*

tea-tree, lemon-scented *Leptospermum petersonii*

tea-tree, Lord Howe *Leptospermum polygalifolium* subsp. *howense*

tea-tree, mallee *Leptospermum coriaceum*

tea-tree, New England *Leptospermum novae-angliae*

tea-tree, paperbark *Leptospermum trinervium*

tea-tree, peach-flowered *Leptospermum squarrosum*

tea-tree, prickly *Leptospermum juniperinum*

tea-tree, river *Melaleuca bracteata*

tea-tree, round-leafed *Leptospermum rotundifolium*

tea-tree, small-leafed *Leptospermum parvifolium*

tea-tree, swamp *Leptospermum myrtifolium*

tea-tree, tantoon *Leptospermum polygalifolium*

tea-tree, woolly *Leptospermum grandifolium, L. lanigerum*

tea-tree, yellow *Leptospermum polygalifolium*

Tecate cypress *Cupressus guadalupensis* var. *forbesii*

tecoma, Argentine *Tecoma garrocha*

teddy bear banksia *Banksia baueri*

teddy bear cholla *Cylindropuntia bigelovii*

teddy bear palm *Dypsis leptocheilos*

tejocote *Crataegus baroussana*

telegraph weed *Heterotheca grandiflora*

telekia sunflower *Telekia speciosa*

Telingo potato *Amorphophallus paeoniifolius*

Tellmann honeysuckle *Lonicera* × *tellmanniana*

temu *Luma apiculata*

ten commandments *Maranta leuconeura*

tenasserim pine *Pinus merkusii* subsp. *latteri*

tender brake *Pteris tremula*

Tenerife broom *Cytisus supranubius*

Tennessee rosemary *Conradina verticillata*

Tenterfield woollybutt *Eucalyptus banksii*

teparee *Physalis peruviana*

tepary bean *Phaseolus acutifolius* var. *latifolius*

terebinth tree *Pistacia terebinthus*

Texan walnut *Juglans microcarpa*

Texas bean *Phaseolus acutifolius*

Texas bluebell *Eustoma*

Texas bluebonnet *Lupinus texensis*
Texas ebony *Pithecellobium flexicaule*
Texas mountain laurel *Sophora
  secundiflora*
Texas mulberry *Morus microphylla*
Texas olive *Cordia boissieri*
Texas persimmon *Diospyros texana*
Texas redbud *Cercis canadensis* var.
  texensis, C. reniformis
Texas sage *Salvia coccinea*
Texas sophora *Sophora affinis*
Texas star *Lindheimera texana*
Thai basil *Ocimum basilicum*
  'Anise'
Thai chilli, dwarf *Capsicum annuum*
  'Thai Hot Small'
thatch, Bahamian *Coccothrinax
  inaguensis*
thatch palm *Coccothrinax, C. crinita,
  Thrinax*
thatch palm, brittle *Thrinax morrisii*
thatch palm, Florida *Thrinax radiata*
thatch palm, Jamaican *Thrinax
  parviflora*
thatch palm, silver *Coccothrinax
  argentata*
thatch saw-sedge *Gahnia radula*
thatching reed *Thamnochortus
  insignis*
Theves poplar *Populus nigra*
  'Afghanica'
thevetia, giant *Thevetia thevetioides*
thicket hawthorn *Crataegus intricata*
thickhead *Crassocephalum crepidioides*
thick-leaf oak *Quercus crassifolia*
thick-leaf phlox *Phlox carolina*
thick-leafed hakea *Hakea crassifolia*
thick-leafed mahogany *Eucalyptus
  carnea*
thimbleberry *Rubus odoratus,
  R. parviflorus*
thimbles, fairies' *Campanula
  cochlearifolia*

thinleaf alder *Alnus tenuifolia*
thin-leaf pine *Pinus maximinoi*
thin-leaf sunflower *Helianthus
  decapetalus*
thin-leafed bottlebrush *Callistemon
  acuminatus*
thin-leafed stringybark *Eucalyptus
  eugenioides*
thistle, blessed *Silybum marianum*
thistle, cotton *Onopordum
  acanthium, O. nervosum*
thistle, dune *Actites megalocarpa*
thistle, globe *Echinops, E. ritro,
  E. sphaerocephalus*
thistle, Illyrian *Onopordum illyricum*
thistle, Japanese *Cirsium japonicum*
thistle, milk *Silybum marianum,
  Sonchus oleraceus*
thistle, mountain *Acanthus
  montanus*
thistle, nodding *Carduus nutans*
thistle, saffron *Carthamus lanatus*
thistle, St Barnaby's *Centaurea
  solstitialis*
thistle, Scotch *Onopordum
  acanthium*
thistle, slender *Carduus
  pycnocephalus*
thistle, spear *Cirsium vulgare*
thistle, star *Centaurea calcitrapa*
thistle, stemless *Onopordum acaulon*
thistle, variegated *Silybum marianum*
thistle, white *Atriplex lentiformis*
thora *Carpentaria acuminata*
thorn, African box *Lycium
  ferocissimum*
thorn apple, common *Datura
  stramonium*
thorn, black monkey *Acacia burkei*
thorn, blue *Acacia erubescens*
thorn, box *Lycium*
thorn, camel *Acacia erioloba,
  A. giraffae*

thorn, Christ's *Paliurus spina-christi*

thorn, cockspur *Crataegus crus-galli, Maclura cochinchinensis*

thorn, corky *Acacia davyi*

thorn, hedge *Carissa bispinosa*

thorn, horned *Acacia grandicornuta*

thorn, Jerusalem *Parkinsonia aculeata*

thorn, kangaroo *Acacia paradoxa*

thorn, karroo *Acacia karroo*

thorn, knob *Acacia nigrescens*

thorn, monkey *Acacia galpinii*

thorn, Mysore *Caesalpinia decapetala*

thorn, orange *Cassinopsis ilicifolia, Pittosporum pauciflora*

thorn, oriental *Crataegus laciniata*

thorn, paperbark *Acacia sieberiana*

thorn, parsley-leafed *Crataegus apiifolia, C. marshallii*

thorn, pear *Crataegus calpodendron*

thorn, quick-set *Crataegus laevigata*

thorn, red *Acacia gerrardii*

thorn, scented *Acacia nilotica*

thorn, sweet *Acacia karroo*

thorn, tambookie *Erythrina acanthocarpa*

thorn, tansy-leafed *Crataegus tanacetifolia*

thorn, umbrella *Acacia tortilis*

thorn, Washington *Crataegus phaenopyrum*

thorn wattle *Acacia continua*

thorn, white *Acacia polyacantha, Crataegus laevigata*

thorn, yellow-fruited *Crataegus flava*

thornless honey locust *Gleditsia triacanthos* f. *inermis*

thorns, crown of *Euphorbia milii, Ziziphus spina-christi*

thorny pittosporum *Pittosporum oreillyanum*

thorny poinciana *Caesalpinia decapetala*

thorny yellowwood *Zanthoxylum brachyacanthum*

thoroughwort *Conoclinium greggii, Eupatorium fortunei, E. perfoliatum*

thoroughwort, snow *Eupatorium rugosum*

thorowax *Bupleurum rotundifolium*

Thousand Hills cycad *Encephalartos natalensis*

Thozet's box *Eucalyptus thozetiana*

thread, dew *Drosera filiformis*

thread palm *Washingtonia robusta*

thread rapier-sedge *Lepidosperma filiforme*

threadleaf giant hyssop *Agastache rupestris*

threadleaf milkweed *Asclepias linaria*

threadleaf sundew *Drosera filiformis*

thread-petal, narrow *Stenopetalum lineare*

thready-barked she-oak *Allocasuarina inophloia*

three-birds-flying *Linaria triornithophora*

three-cornered garlic *Allium triquetrum*

three-cornered palm *Dypsis decaryi*

three-flower maple *Acer triflorum*

three-flowered nightshade *Solanum triflorum*

three-horned acacia *Acacia senegal*

three-in-one spice *Solenostemon amboinicus*

three-leafed bosistoa *Bosistoa transversa*

three-lobe sumac *Rhus trilobata*

three-lobed spiraea *Spiraea trilobata*

threepenny-bit rose *Rosa elegantula* 'Persetosa'

three-spined copperburr *Sclerolaena tricuspis*

three-veined cryptocarya *Cryptocarya triplinervis*

three-veined wattle *Acacia trinervata*
three-wing bluebush *Maireana triptera*
thrift *Armeria, A. maritima*
thrift, prickly *Acantholimon*
throatwort *Campanula trachelium*
thryptomene, Grampians *Thryptomene calycina*
thryptomene, rock *Thryptomene saxicola*
thumbnail orchid *Dockrillia linguiformis*
Thunberg bush clover *Lespedeza thunbergii*
Thunberg spiraea *Spiraea thunbergii*
thyme *Thymus, T. vulgaris*
thyme, basil *Acinos arvensis*
thyme, camphor *Thymus camphoratus*
thyme, caraway *Thymus herba-barona*
thyme, cat *Teucrium marum*
thyme, common *Thymus vulgaris*
thyme, creeping *Thymus praecox, T. serpyllum*
thyme, Cyprus *Thymus integer*
thyme, garden *Thymus vulgaris*
thyme honey-myrtle *Melaleuca thymifolia*
thyme, large *Thymus pulegioides*
thyme, lemon *Thymus × citriodorus*
thyme, lemon-scented *Thymus × citriodorus*
thyme, miniature *Thymus* 'Minimus'
thyme spurge *Phyllanthus hirtellus*
thyme, wild *Thymus serpyllum*
thyme, woolly *Thymus pseudolanuginosus*
thyme-leaf azalea *Rhododendron serpyllifolium*
thyme-leafed willow *Salix serpyllifolia*

thyme-leafed mint bush *Prostanthera serpyllifolia*
thyme-leafed savory *Satureja thymbra*
ti *Cordyline fruticosa*
ti palmis maron *Pseudophoenix lediniana*
ti parae *Cordyline banksii*
ti plant *Cordyline fruticosa*
tiare *Gardenia taitensis*
Tibetan cherry *Prunus mugus, P. serrula*
Tibetan crabapple *Malus transitoria*
tibouchina, Alstonville *Tibouchina lepidota* 'Alstonville'
tick-bush *Kunzea ambigua*
tickseed *Bidens, Coreopsis*
tick-trefoil *Desmodium rhytidophyllum*
tick-trefoil, large *Desmodium brachypodum*
tick-trefoil, showy *Desmodium canadense*
tick-trefoil, slender *Desmodium varians*
tiger aloe *Aloe variegata*
tiger cacao *Theobroma bicolor*
tiger flower *Tigridia*
tiger jaws *Faucaria tigrina*
tiger lily *Lilium lancifolium*
tiger lily, Columbia *Lilium columbianum*
tiger lily, double *Lilium lancifolium* 'Flore Pleno'
tiger orchid *Diuris sulphurea*
tiger's claw *Erythrina variegata*
tiger-tail spruce *Picea torano*
tigerwood *Loxostylis alata*
tight, stick *Bidens*
tilt-head aloe *Aloe speciosa*
timbe *Acacia angustissima*
timber bamboo, giant *Phyllostachys bambusoides*

Timor black bamboo *Bambusa lako*
Timothy grass *Phleum pratense*
Tinaroo bottlebrush *Callistemon recurvus*
tinder plant *Gomphocarpus physocarpus*
tineo *Weinmannia trichosperma*
Tingiringi gum *Eucalyptus glaucescens*
tingle, red *Eucalyptus jacksonii*
tingletongue *Dinosperma erythrococcum*
tinsel-lily, blue *Calectasia*
tiny bow-flower *Millotia perpusilla*
tiny greenhood *Pterostylis parviflora*
tiny logania *Logania pusilla*
tip, golden *Goodia lotifolia*
tipu tree *Tipuana tipu*
titan arum *Amorphophallus titanum*
titoki *Alectryon excelus*
tjilka-tjilka *Grevillea spinosa*
toa toa *Phyllocladus glaucus*
toad lily *Tricyrtis, T. hirta*
toad lily, Formosa *Tricyrtis formosana*
toad rush *Juncus bufonius*
toad shade *Trillium cuneatum, T. sessile*
toad tree *Tabernaemontana elegans*
toadflax *Linaria, L. vulgaris*
toadflax, annual *Linaria maroccana*
toadflax, ivy-leafed *Cymbalaria muralis*
toadflax, Moroccan *Linaria maroccana*
toadflax, purple *Linaria purpurea*
toadflax, wall *Cymbalaria muralis*
toatoa *Phyllocladus glaucus*
toatoa, mountain *Phyllocladus alpinus*
tobacco *Nicotiana tabacum*
tobacco brush *Ceanothus velutinus*
tobacco, flowering *Nicotiana alata, N. sylvestris*
tobacco, Indian *Eriogonum*

tobacco, jasmine *Nicotiana alata*
tobacco, ladies' *Antennaria*
tobacco, native *Nicotiana occidentalis, N. suaveolens*
tobacco sumac *Rhus virens*
tobacco tree *Solanum erianthum*
tobacco, tree *Nicotiana glauca, Solanum mauritianum*
tobacco, velvet *Nicotiana velutina*
tobacco, wild *Solanum mauritianum*
tobira *Pittosporum tobira*
toddy palm *Caryota urens*
toes, baby *Fenestraria aurantiaca, F. rhopalophylla*
toetoe grass *Cortaderia richardii*
toi *Cordyline indivisa*
toitoi *Cortaderia richardii*
tokudama giboshi *Hosta tokudama*
Tokyo cherry *Prunus × yedoensis*
tollon *Heteromeles arbutifolia*
tolu balsam *Myroxylon balsamum*
Tom Russell's mahogany *Lysicarpus angustifolius*
tomatillo *Lycium pallidum, Physalis ixocarpa, P. philadelphica*
tomato *Lycopersicon esculentum*
tomato, bush *Solanum ellipticum*
tomato, cherry *Lycopersicum esculentum* var. *cerasiforme, L. pimpinellifolium*
tomato husk *Physalis*
tomato, strawberry *Physalis ixocarpa*
tomato, tree *Solanum betaceum*
tongue, adder's *Erythronium americanum*
tongue, blue *Melastoma affine*
tongue, devil's *Amorphophallus konjac, A. rivieri, Sansevieria zeylanica*
tongue fern *Pyrrosia lingua*
tongue, lamb's *Scleroblitum atriplicinum*

tongue, mother-in-law's *Dieffenbachia, Sansevieria, S. trifasciata*
tongue orchid *Dockrillia linguiformis*
tongue orchid, large *Cryptostylis subulata*
tongue orchid, small *Cryptostylis leptochila*
tongue orchid, tartan *Cryptostylis erecta*
tongue, painted *Salpiglossis sinuata*
tonka bean *Dipteryx odorata*
toog *Bischofia javanica*
toon, Chinese *Toona sinensis*
toothache tree *Zanthoxylum americanum*
toothbrush tree *Salvadora persica*
toothbrushes, black *Grevillea hookeriana*
toothed brake *Pteris dentata*
toothed guinea-flower *Hibbertia dentata*
toothed lancewood *Pseudopanax ferox*
toothed lavender *Lavandula dentata*
toothed raspwort *Haloragis odontocarpa*
toothless spoon *Dasylirion longissimum*
toothpick cactus *Stetsonia coryne*
toothpick weed *Ammi visnaga*
toothwort, cut-leafed *Cardamine laciniata*
top, brown *Agrostis capillaris*
top cactus *Strombocactus disciformis*
top, golden *Lamarckia aurea*
top, yellow *Calocephalus platycephalus*
topal holly *Ilex × attenuata*
tor grass *Brachypodium pinnatum*
torch cactus *Cereus hildmannianus* subsp. *uruguayanus*
torch cactus, silver *Cleistocactus strausii*

torch ginger *Etlingera elatior*
torch lily *Kniphofia, Veltheimia bracteata*
torch lobelia *Lobelia laxiflora*
torch plant *Aloe aristata*
torenia *Torenia fournieri*
tornillo *Prosopis pubescens*
toronche *Carica monoica*
torpedo grass *Panicum repens*
Torrey ephedra *Ephedra torreyana*
Torrey pine *Pinus torreyana*
Torrey yucca *Yucca torreyi*
torreya, Florida *Torreya taxifolia*
tortuous beech *Fagus sylvatica* 'Tortuosa'
totara *Podocarpus totara*
totara, alpine *Podocarpus nivalis*
totara, golden *Podocarpus totara* 'Aurea'
totara, Hall's *Podocarpus hallii*
tough rice flower *Pimelea axiflora*
tous-les-mois *Canna edulis*
towai *Weinmannia silvicola*
tower of jewels *Echium wildprettii*
tower poplar *Populus × canescens*
tower tree *Schizolobium parahybum*
townsendia, Parry's *Townsendia parryi*
toyon *Heteromeles arbutifolia*
tragacanth *Astragalus gummifera*
trailing abutilon *Abutilon megapotamicum*
trailing arbutus *Epigaea repens*
trailing bellflower *Cyananthus*
trailing fuchsia *Fuchsia procumbens*
trailing guinea-flower *Hibbertia empetrifolia*
trailing ice plant *Lampranthus filicaulis*
trailing lantana *Lantana montevidensis*
trailing lasiandra *Heterocentron elegans*

trailing lobelia *Lobelia gracilis*
trailing phlox *Phlox nivalis*
trailing red verbena *Verbena peruviana*
trailing spikemoss *Selaginella kraussiana*
trailing velvet plant *Ruellia makoyana*
trailing violet *Viola hederacea*
tramp's spurge *Euphorbia corollata*
Transcaucasian birch *Betula medwedewii*
Transvaal beech *Faurea saligna*
Transvaal bottlebrush *Greyia radlkoferi*
Transvaal candelabra tree *Euphorbia cooperi*
Transvaal coral tree *Erythrina lysistemon*
Transvaal daisy *Gerbera*
Transvaal hard pear *Olinia emarginata*
Transvaal kaffirboom *Erythrina lysistemon*
Transvaal kooboo berry *Cassine burkeana*
Transvaal privet *Galpinia transvaalica*
Transvaal red milkwood *Mimusops zeyheri*
Transvaal sesame bush *Sesamothamnus lugardii*
Transvaal teak *Pterocarpus angolensis*
trappers' tea *Ledum glandulosum*
traveler's joy *Clematis*
traveler's palm *Ravenala madagascariensis*
traveler's tree *Ravenala madagascariensis*
treasure flower *Gazania, G. rigens*
Trebizond date *Elaeagnus angustifolia*
tree, African milk *Euphorbia trigona*
tree, African tulip *Spathodea campanulata*

tree aloe *Aloe bainesii*
tree, alpine pepper *Pseudowintera colorata*
tree, American angelica *Aralia spinosa*
tree, American fringe *Chionanthus virginicus*
tree, American smoke *Cotinus obovatus*
tree, Amur cork *Phellodendron amurense*
tree anemone *Carpenteria californica*
tree, angelica *Aralia elata, Dendropanax arboreus*
tree, anise *Illicium*
tree, aniseed *Anetholea anisata*
tree, apple blossom *Cassia javanica*
tree aralia *Kalopanax septemlobus*
tree, Argentine flame *Tabebuia impetiginosa*
tree, Arran service *Sorbus pseudofennica*
tree, athel *Tamarix aphylla*
tree, Australian flame *Brachychiton acerifolius*
tree, Australian tea *Leptospermum laevigatum*
tree, autograph *Clusia major*
tree, Baja elephant *Pachycormus discolor*
tree, balsam *Clusia alba*
tree, bastard cabbage *Schefflera umbellifera*
tree, bat's wing coral *Erythrina vespertilio*
tree, bay *Laurus nobilis*
tree, bay rum *Pimenta racemosa*
tree, bayur *Pterospermum acerifolium*
tree, bead *Melia azedarach*
tree, bean *Catalpa bignonioides, Schotia latifolia*
tree begonia *Begonia coccinea*

tree, bell bean *Markhamia zanzibarica*

tree, bella sombra *Phytolacca dioica*

tree, bellfruit *Codonocarpus attenuatus*

tree, Benjamin *Ficus benjamina*

tree, ben-oil *Moringa oleifera*

tree, be-still *Thevetia thevetioides*

tree, big *Sequoiadendron giganteum*

tree, birdcatcher *Pisonia brunoniana, P. umbelliffera*

tree, birdlime *Cordia dichotoma, Pisonia grandis, P. umbellifera*

tree, black bean *Castanospermum australe*

tree, bleeding heart *Omalanthus populifolius*

tree, blue haze *Jacaranda mimosifolia*

tree, blue marble *Elaeocarpus grandis*

tree, bo *Ficus religiosa*

tree, boojum *Idria columnaris*

tree, bootlace *Hakea lorea*

tree, bottle *Adansonia gibbosa*

tree, Brazilian pepper *Schinus terebinthifolia*

tree, broad-leaf bottle *Brachychiton australis*

tree, bronze paper *Commiphora harveyi*

tree broom, New Zealand pink *Carmichaelia glabrescens*

tree broom-heath *Monotoca elliptica*

tree, buckwheat *Cliftonia monophylla*

tree, calabash *Crescentia cujete*

tree, camphor *Cinnamomum camphora*

tree, candelabra *Araucaria angustifolia*

tree, candle *Parmentiera cereifera*

tree, candlenut *Aleurites moluccana*

tree, cannonball *Couroupita guianensis*

tree, Caucasian nettle *Celtis caucasica*

tree ceanothus *Ceanothus arboreus*

tree celandine *Bocconia frutescens, Macleaya cordata*

tree celandine, Mexican *Bocconia frutescens*

tree, chaste *Vitex agnus-castus*

tree, cheese *Glochidion ferdinandi*

tree, chequer *Sorbus torminalis*

tree, Chile lantern *Crinodendron hookerianum*

tree, China *Koelreuteria paniculata*

tree, Chinese angelica *Aralia chinensis*

tree, Chinese bottle *Firmiana simplex*

tree, Chinese flame *Koelreuteria bipinnata*

tree, Chinese fringe *Chionanthus retusus*

tree, Chinese katsura *Cercidiphyllum japonicum* var. *sinense*

tree, Chinese lacquer *Toxicodendron vernicifluum*

tree, Chinese nettle *Celtis sinensis*

tree, Chinese scholar *Sophora japonica*

tree, Chinese snowball *Viburnum macrocephalum* 'Sterile'

tree, Chinese strawberry *Myrica rubra*

tree, Chinese tallow *Sapium sebiferum*

tree, Chinese wayfaring *Viburnum veitchii*

tree, chocolate pudding *Diospyros digyna*

tree, clover *Goodia lotifolia*

tree clubmoss *Lycopodium deuterodensum*

tree, coast coral *Erythrina caffra*

tree, cockspur coral *Erythrina crista-galli*

tree, common cabbage *Cussonia spicata*

tree, common coral *Erythrina crista-galli, E. lysistemon*

tree, common hop *Ptelea trifoliata*

tree, common resin *Ozoroa paniculosa*

tree, coral *Erythrina, E. corallodendron, E. × sykesii, E. variegata*

tree, cork *Hakea suberea*

tree, corkbark *Hakea ivoryi*

tree correa *Correa lawrenciana*

tree cotoneaster, Himalayan *Cotoneaster frigidus*

tree cotton *Gossypium arboreum*

tree, cotton-seed *Baccharis halimifolia*

tree, cottonwood *Hibiscus tiliaceus*

tree, cucumber *Magnolia acuminata*

tree, curry *Murraya koenigii*

tree dahlia *Dahlia imperialis*

tree daisy, common *Olearia arborescens*

tree daisy, Mexican *Montanoa bipinnatifida*

tree, devil *Alstonia scholaris*

tree, domatia *Endiandra discolor*

tree, dove *Davidia involucrata*

tree, dragon *Dracaena draco*

tree, dragon's-blood *Dracaena draco*

tree, dwarf umbrella *Schefflera arboricola*

tree, ear-leafed umbrella *Magnolia fraseri*

tree, elephant *Bursera microphylla*

tree, empress *Paulownia tomentosa*

tree, epaulette *Pterostyrax hispida*

tree euphorbia *Euphorbia ingens*

tree, European nettle *Celtis australis*

tree, European spindle *Euonymus europaeus*

tree everlasting *Ozothamnus ferrugineus*

tree, false bodhi *Ficus rumphii*

tree false spiraea *Sorbaria kirilowii*

tree, fern *Jacaranda mimosifolia*

tree fern *Cibotium, Cyathea, Dicksonia*

tree fern, Australian *Cyathea cooperi*

tree fern, black *Cyathea medullaris*

tree fern, Brazilian *Blechnum brasiliense*

tree fern, bristly *Dicksonia youngiae*

tree fern, Cape *Cyathea dregei*

tree fern, dwarf *Blechnum gibbum*

tree fern, hard *Dicksonia squarrosa*

tree fern, Hawaiian *Cibotium glaucum*

tree fern, Mexican *Cibotium schiedei*

tree fern, miniature *Blechnum gibbum*

tree fern, Norfolk Island *Cyathea brownii*

tree fern, prickly *Cyathea leichhardtiana*

tree fern, rough *Cyathea australis*

tree fern, scaly *Cyathea cooperi*

tree fern, silver *Cyathea dealbata, C. medullaris*

tree fern, soft *Dicksonia antarctica*

tree fern, straw *Cyathea cooperi*

tree fern, Tasmanian *Dicksonia antarctica*

tree fern, West Indian *Cyathea arborea*

tree fern, woolly *Cyathea woollsiana*

tree, fever *Acacia xanthophloea, Pinckneya pubens*

tree, finger *Euphorbia tirucalli*

tree, firewheel *Stenocarpus sinuatus*

tree, fish-killer *Barringtonia asiatica*

tree, flamboyant *Delonix regia*
tree, flamegold *Koelreuteria elegans*
tree, Florida anise *Illicium floridanum*
tree, floss-silk *Ceiba insignis, C. speciosa*
tree, foambark *Jagera pseudorhus*
tree, Fontainebleau service *Sorbus latifolia*
tree, forest cabbage *Cussonia sphaerocephala, Schefflera umbellifera*
tree, forest grass *Xanthorrhoea arborea*
tree, forked *Pandanus forsteri*
tree, Franklin *Franklinia alatamaha*
tree, French *Tamarix gallica*
tree, friendship *Crassula ovata*
tree, fringe *Chionanthus*
tree fuchsia *Fuchsia arborescens, Halleria lucida, Schotia brachypetala*
tree fuchsia, New Zealand *Fuchsia excorticata*
tree gardenia *Rothmannia globosa*
tree, geiger *Cordia sebestena*
tree, ghost *Davidia involucrata*
tree, golden *Grevillea pteridifolia*
tree, golden bead *Duranta erecta*
tree, golden chain *Laburnum anagyroides, L. × watereri*
tree, golden parrot *Grevillea pteridifolia*
tree, golden rain *Koelreuteria paniculata*
tree, golden shower *Cassia fistula*
tree, golden trumpet *Tabebuia chrysotricha*
tree grape *Cyphostemma juttae*
tree, grass *Kingia australis, Xanthorrhoea*
tree, Grecian strawberry *Arbutus andrachne*
tree, groundsel *Baccharis halimifolia*

tree groundsel, Mexican *Telanthophora grandifolia*
tree, gum arabic *Acacia nilotica, A. seyal*
tree, gutta percha *Eucommia ulmoides*
tree hakea *Hakea eriantha*
tree, handkerchief *Davidia involucrata*
tree, headache *Umbellularia californica*
tree heath *Erica arborea, Richea pandanifolia, Trochocarpa laurina*
tree hibiscus *Hibiscus tiliaceus*
tree, highveld cabbage *Cussonia paniculata*
tree hogweed *Polygonum patulum*
tree, Hong Kong orchid *Bauhinia × blakeana*
tree, horseradish *Moringa oleifera*
tree, hybrid coral *Erythrina × bidwillii*
tree, hybrid strawberry *Arbutus × andrachnoides*
tree, Illawarra flame *Brachychiton acerifolius*
tree, incense *Bursera simaruba*
tree, Indian bead *Elaeocarpus sphaericus*
tree, Indian bean *Catalpa bignonioides*
tree, Indian umbrella *Schefflera pueckleri*
tree, India-rubber *Ficus elastica*
tree indigo *Indigofera cylindrica*
tree, Irish strawberry *Arbutus unedo*
tree, iron *Parrotia persica*
tree, isu *Distylium racemosum*
tree, ivory curl *Buckinghamia celsissima*
tree, ivy *Schefflera heptaphylla*
tree, jade *Crassula ovata*
tree, Jamaican caper *Capparis cynophallophora*

tree, Japanese angelica *Aralia elata*
tree, Japanese cherry *Prunus pseudocerasus*
tree, Japanese lacquer *Toxicodendron vernicifluum*
tree, Japanese pagoda *Sophora japonica*
tree, Japanese raisin *Hovenia dulcis*
tree, Japanese snowdrop *Styrax japonicus*
tree, Japanese varnish *Firmiana simplex*
tree, Joshua *Yucca brevifolia*
tree, Judas *Cercis siliquastrum*
tree, kapok *Ceiba pentandra, Cochlospermum gillivraei*
tree, kapok yellow *Cochlospermum fraseri*
tree, kashgaer *Tamarix hispida*
tree, kassod *Senna siamea*
tree, katsura *Cercidiphyllum japonicum*
tree, Kentucky coffee *Gymnocladus dioica*
tree, kite *Nuxia floribunda*
tree, koko *Maytenus undulata*
tree lavatera *Lavatera olbia*
tree, lavender *Heteropyxis natalensis*
tree, lead *Leucaena leucocephala, L. retusa*
tree, Leichhardt *Nauclea orientalis*
tree, leopard *Caesalpinia ferrea*
tree, lesser honeysuckle *Turraea obtusifolia*
tree lilac, Chinese *Syringa pekinensis*
tree lilac, Japanese *Syringa reticulata*
tree, lily *Magnolia denudata*
tree, lily-of-the-valley *Clethra arborea*
tree, little-leaf lead *Leucaena retusa*
tree lucerne *Chamaecytisus palmensis*
tree, lucky bean *Erythrina lysistemon*

tree lupin *Lupinus arboreus*
tree, Madagascar ordeal *Cerbera venenifera*
tree, maidenhair *Ginkgo biloba*
tree mallow *Lavatera, L. arborea*
tree mallow, California *Lavatera assurgentiflora*
tree mallow, lesser *Lavatera cretica*
tree, mastic *Pistacia lentiscus*
tree, Mayday *Prunus padus*
tree, Mexican grass *Dasylirion longissimum*
tree, Mexican hand *Chiranthodendron pentadactylon*
tree, mignonette *Lawsonia inermis*
tree, money *Crassula ovata*
tree, monkey pod *Samanea saman*
tree, monkey pot *Lecythis ollaria*
tree morning glory *Ipomoea arborescens*
tree, mountain cabbage *Cordyline indivisa*
tree, mountain snowdrop *Halesia monticola*
tree, mu-oil *Aleurites montana*
tree, musk *Olearia argophylla*
tree, mustard *Nicotiana glauca*
tree, narrow-leafed grass *Xanthorrhoea glauca*
tree, Natal coral *Erythrina humeana*
tree, née *Quercus rugosa*
tree, nettle *Celtis australis*
tree, New Zealand cabbage *Cordyline australis*
tree, New Zealand Christmas *Metrosideros excelsa*
tree, North American tulip *Liriodendron tulipifera*
tree, northern bottle *Brachychiton australis*
tree, octopus *Schefflera actinophylla*
tree of Damocles *Oroxylum*
tree of gold *Tabebuia argentea*

tree of heaven *Ailanthus altissima*
tree, oil-nut *Calophyllum inophyllum*
tree onion *Allium cepa* Proliferum
  Group
tree, orange ball *Buddleja globosa*
tree, orchid *Bauhinia variegata*
tree, pagoda *Plumeria obtusa,*
  Sophora japonica
tree palm, cabbage *Livistona*
  australis
tree, Panama *Sterculia apetala*
tree, Panama rubber *Castilla elastica*
tree, Para rubber *Hevea brasiliensis*
tree, paradise *Simarouba glauca*
tree, parasol *Firmiana simplex*
tree, parsley *Heteromorpha trifoliolata*
tree, parsnip *Heteromorpha*
  trifoliolata
tree, pea *Caragana*
tree, peanut *Sterculia quadrifida*
tree pear, velvet *Opuntia tomentosa*
tree, peepul *Ficus religiosa*
tree, pench *Euphorbia tirucalli*
tree, pencil *Euphorbia tirucalli*
tree peony *Paeonia lutea,*
  P. suffruticosa
tree peony, maroon *Paeonia delavayi*
tree peony, yellow *Paeonia lutea*
tree, pepper *Macropiper excelsum,*
  Pseudowintera colorata, Schinus
  molle
tree, pepperberry *Cryptocarya*
  obovata
tree, peppermint *Agonis flexuosa*
tree, Persian silk *Albizia julibrissin*
tree petrea *Petrea arborea*
tree philodendron *Philodendron*
  bipinnatifidum
tree, phoenix *Firmiana simplex*
tree, pincushion *Hakea laurina*
tree, pink floss-silk *Ceiba speciosa*
tree, pink trumpet *Tabebuia*
  heterophylla

tree, pink tulip *Magnolia campbellii*
tree, plane *Platanus*
tree, planer *Planera aquatica*
tree, polecat *Illicium floridanum*
tree, pompon *Dais cotinifolia*
tree poppy *Dendromecon rigida*
tree poppy, California *Romneya*
  coulteri
tree, portia *Thespesia populnea*
tree, potato *Solanum erianthum*
tree, powderpuff *Barringtonia*
  racemosa, Calliandra haematocephala
tree, princess *Paulownia tomentosa*
tree, propeller *Gyrocarpus americanus*
tree, pudding-pipe *Cassia fistula*
tree, pumpkin *Negria*
  rhabdothamnoides
tree purslane *Atriplex halimus*
tree, Queensland black bean
  Castanospermum australe
tree, Queensland bottle *Brachychiton*
  rupestris
tree, Queensland elemi *Canarium*
  muelleri
tree, quinine *Alstonia constricta,*
  Rauvolfia caffra
tree, rain *Albizia saman, Brunfelsia*
  undulata
tree, red bead *Adenanthera pavonina*
tree, red-hot poker *Erythrina*
  abyssinica
tree, rhus *Toxicodendron succedaneum*
tree, rubber *Calotropis procera, Ficus*
  elastica, Hevea brasiliensis
tree St John's wort *Hypericum*
  revolutum
tree, St Thomas *Bauhinia tomentosa*
tree, salt *Halimodendron halodendron*
tree, sandbox *Hura crepitans*
tree, sarvis *Amelanchier laevis*
tree, sausage *Kigelia africana*
tree, scarlet wisteria *Sesbania*
  grandiflora

tree, scholar *Sophora japonica*
tree, scrub bottle *Brachychiton discolor*
tree, Senegal gum arabic *Acacia senegal*
tree, service *Sorbus domestica*
tree, shaving-brush *Pachira aquatica, Pseudobombax ellipticum*
tree, shingle *Acrocarpus fraxinifolius*
tree, Siberian pea *Caragana arborescens*
tree, silk *Albizia julibrissin*
tree, silver *Leucadendron argenteum, Terminalia sericea*
tree, silver dollar *Eucalyptus cinerea, E. polyanthemos*
tree, silver trumpet *Tabebuia argentea*
tree, small honeysuckle *Turraea obtusifolia*
tree, smoke *Cotinus coggygria, C. obovatus*
tree, snakewood *Cecropia palmata*
tree, snowball *Viburnum opulus* 'Sterile'
tree, snowbell *Styrax japonica*
tree, snowdrop *Halesia carolina*
tree, snowflake *Trevesia palmata* 'Micholitzii'
tree, snuff box *Oncoba spinosa*
tree, soap *Gymnocladus chinensis*
tree, soapbark *Quillaja saponaria*
tree, soapberry *Sapindus mukorossi*
tree, sorrel *Oxydendrum arboreum*
tree, sorrowless *Saraca indica*
tree, South African coral *Erythrina caffra*
tree, South American bottle *Ceiba insignis*
tree, southern grass *Xanthorrhoea australis*
tree sparkleberry *Vaccinium arboreum*
tree, spider *Crateva religiosa*

tree, spindle *Euonymus europaeus*
tree, square-leaf grass *Xanthorrhoea quadrangulata*
tree, steeple *Markhamia lutea*
tree strawberry *Cephalanthus natalensis*
tree, strawberry *Arbutus unedo*
tree, strychnine *Strychnos arborea*
tree, Sudan gum arabic *Acacia senegal*
tree, Swazi ordeal *Erythrophleum lasianthum*
tree, sweet verbena *Backhousia citriodora*
tree, sweetheart *Euscaphis japonica*
tree, tanjong *Mimusops elengi*
tree tobacco *Nicotiana glauca, Solanum mauritianum*
tree, tobacco *Solanum erianthum*
tree tomato *Solanum betaceum*
tree, toothbrush *Salvadora persica*
tree, tower *Echium wildprettii*
tree, traveler's *Ravenala madagascariensis*
tree tutu *Coriaria arborea*
tree, twirly whirly *Gyrocarpus americanus*
tree, umbrella *Polyscias murrayi*
tree, umbrella cheese *Glochidion sumatranum*
tree, vanilla *Azara microphylla*
tree, varnish *Koelreuteria paniculata, Toxicendron vernicifluum*
tree viburnum, evergreen *Viburnum odoratissimum*
tree vine, Venezuela *Cissus rhombifolia*
tree, vinegar *Rhus glabra*
tree, violet *Polygala cowellii*
tree, wahoo *Leucaena retusa*
tree, waratah *Alloxylon flammeum*
tree, wax *Toxicodendron succedaneum*
tree, wayfaring *Viburnum lantana*

tree, Western Australian Christmas *Nuytsia floribunda*
tree, Western Australian grass *Xanthorrhoea preissii*
tree, western cork *Hakea lorea*
tree, western hop *Ptelea angustifolia*
tree, whalebone *Streblus brunonianus*
tree, wheel *Trochodendron aralioides*
tree, whistling *Acacia seyal*
tree, white cloud *Melaleuca decora*
tree, white orchid *Bauhinia variegata* 'Candida'
tree, wild China *Sapindus drummondii*
tree, wild service *Sorbus torminalis*
tree, winged spindle *Euonymus alatus*
tree wisteria *Bolusanthus, B. speciosus*
tree wisteria, African *Bolusanthus*
tree, woman's tongue *Albizia lebbeck*
tree, wonder *Idesia polycarpa*
tree, wood-oil *Aleurites montana*
tree, yellow cucumber *Magnolia cordata*
tree, yellow flame *Peltophorum pterocarpum*
tree, yellow trumpet *Tecoma stans*
tree-in-a-hurry *Virgilia oroboides*
tree-of-heaven *Ailanthus altissima*
trefoil, Australian *Lotus australis*
trefoil, bird's foot *Lotus corniculatus, L. uliginosus*
trefoil, hairy bird's foot *Lotus suaveolens*
trefoil, marsh *Menyanthes trifoliata*
trefoil, moon *Medicago arborea*
trefoil, slender birds' foot *Lotus angustissimus*
trefoil, stinking bean *Anagyris foetida*
trembling aspen *Populus tremuloides*
trembling grass *Briza media*

triangle fig *Ficus deltoidea*
triangle palm *Dypsis decaryi*
tricolor pansy *Viola tricolor*
trident maple *Acer buergerianum*
trifoliate orange *Poncirus trifoliata*
trigger plant *Stylidium, S. graminifolium*
trigger plant, climbing *Stylidium scandens*
trigger plant, grass-leaf *Stylidium graminifolium*
trigger plant, narrow-leafed *Stylidium lineare*
trigger plant, sprawling *Stylidium productum*
trillium, bent *Trillium flexipes*
trillium, grand *Trillium grandiflorum*
trillium, showy *Trillium grandiflorum*
trillium, southern red *Trillium sulcatum*
trillium, western *Trillium ovatum*
trillium, wood *Trillium luteum*
triloba sage *Salvia fruticosa*
trim shield fern *Lastreopsis decomposita*
trinity flower *Tradescantia virginiana*
triplet lily *Triteleia laxa*
triteleia *Ipheion uniflorum*
triteleia, Douglas's *Triteleia grandiflora*
triteleia, Howell's *Triteleia grandiflora*
triticale × *Triticale*
tritonia *Tritonia crocata*
Trojan iris *Iris trojana*
tropical banksia *Banksia dentata*
tropical birch *Betula nigra*
tropical black bamboo *Bambusa lako*
tropical blue bamboo *Chimonobambusa falcata*
tropical geebung *Persoonia falcata*
tropical pitcher plants *Nepenthes*

tropical rock fern *Paraceterach muelleri*
tropical sage *Salvia coccinea*
trout lily *Erythronium*
trout lily, American *Erythronium americanum*
true cedar *Cedrus*
true jasmine *Jasminum officinale*
true laurel *Laurus nobilis*
true maidenhair *Adiantum capillus-veneris*
true myrtle *Myrtus communis*
true valerian *Valeriana officinalis*
trumpet, angel's *Brugmansia aurea, B. × candida, B. suaveolens, Datura inoxia*
trumpet, blue *Brunoniella australis*
trumpet creeper *Campsis*
trumpet creeper, Chinese *Campsis grandiflora*
trumpet creeper, orange *Pyrostegia venusta*
trumpet, Cuba pink *Tabebuia pallida*
trumpet, dwarf blue *Brunoniella pumilio*
trumpet, Easter herald *Beaumontia grandiflora*
trumpet flower *Bignonia capreolata*
trumpet flower, shrubby *Tecoma stans*
trumpet flower, yellow *Tecoma stans*
trumpet, golden *Allamanda cathartica*
trumpet, golden angel's *Brugmansia aurea*
trumpet gourd *Lagenaria siceraria*
trumpet, herald's *Beaumontia grandiflora*
trumpet honeysuckle *Lonicera sempervirens*
trumpet honeysuckle, scarlet *Lonicera × brownii*
trumpet lily *Lilium longiflorum*

trumpet, Mexican blood *Distictis buccinatoria*
trumpet pitcher *Sarracenia*
trumpet, red angel's *Brugmansia sanguinea*
trumpet tree *Cecropia peltata*
trumpet tree, golden *Tabebuia, T. chrysotricha*
trumpet tree, hybrid *Tecoma × smithii*
trumpet tree, pink *Tabebuia heterophylla*
trumpet tree, silver *Tabebuia argentea*
trumpet tree, yellow *Tecoma stans*
trumpet vine *Campsis, C. radicans*
trumpet vine, Argentine *Clytostoma callistegioides*
trumpet vine, blood-red *Distictis buccinatoria*
trumpet vine, blue *Thunbergia grandiflora*
trumpet vine, Chinese *Campsis grandiflora*
trumpet vine, pink *Podranea ricasoliana*
trumpet, violet *Clytostoma callistegioides*
trumpet weed *Eupatorium purpureum*
trumpet, white *Sarracenia leucophylla*
trumpet, yellow *Sarracenia flava*
trumpetilla *Bouvardia glaberrima*
tsaie, pe *Brassica rapa* Pekinensis Group
Tsangpo cypress *Cupressus gigantea*
Tsu-shima holly fern *Polystichum tsussimense*
tuart *Eucalyptus gomphocephala*
tube flower tree *Clerodendrum minahassae*
tuber oat grass *Arrhenatherum elatius* var. *bulbosum*

tuberose *Polianthes tuberosa*
tuckahoe *Peltandra virginica*
tuckeroo *Cupaniopsis anacardioides*
tuckeroo, fine-leafed *Lepiderema pulchella*
Tucker's speargrass *Austrostipa tuckeri*
tufted blue-lily *Thelionema caespitosum*
tufted burr-daisy *Calotis scapigera*
tufted California poppy *Eschscholzia caespitosa*
tufted fescue *Festuca amethystina*
tufted hair grass *Deschampsia cespitosa*
tufted hedgehog grass *Echinopogon caespitosus*
tufted mat-rush *Lomandra brevis*
tufted sedge *Carex gaudichaudiana*
tuftroot *Dieffenbachia*
tukauki *Libertia grandiflora, L. ixioides*
tule *Schoenoplectus lacustris*
tulip *Tulipa*
tulip, candia *Tulipa saxatilis*
tulip, candy-stick *Tulipa clusiana*
tulip, Cape *Homeria*
tulip, golden globe *Calochortus amabilis*
tulip, horned *Tulipa acuminata*
tulip, Iranian *Tulipa montana*
tulip, lady *Tulipa clusiana*
tulip magnolia *Magnolia × soulangeana*
tulip, Mariposa *Calochortus*
tulip, mountain *Tulipa montana*
tulip, Oakland star *Calochortus umbellatus*
tulip orchid *Anguloa*
tulip plum *Pleiogynium timorense*
tulip poppy, Mexican *Hunnemannia fumariifolia*
tulip, Sierra globe *Calochortus amoenus*

tulip tree *Liriodendron tulipifera*
tulip tree, African *Spathodea campanulata*
tulip tree, Chinese *Liriodendron chinense*
tulip tree, North American *Liriodendron tulipifera*
tulip tree, pink *Magnolia campbellii*
tulip, waterlily *Tulipa kaufmanniana*
tulip, yellow Mariposa *Calochortus luteus*
tulipwood *Harpullia pendula*
tulipwood, yellow *Drypetes australasica*
tumble weed *Boophone disticha*
tumbledown red gum *Eucalyptus dealbata*
tuna *Cylindropuntia tunicata*
tuna colorada *Opuntia stenopetala*
tung-oil tree *Aleurites fordii*
tupaculo *Carica cauliflora*
tupelo *Nyssa sylvatica*
tupelo, black *Nyssa sylvatica*
tupelo, Chinese *Nyssa sinensis*
tupelo gum *Nyssa aquatica*
tupelo, ogeechee *Nyssa ogeche*
tupelo, sour *Nyssa ogeche*
tupelo, water *Nyssa aquatica*
turban, Arab's *Crassula hemisphaerica*
turf mat daisy *Raoulia subsericea*
Turkestan burning bush *Euonymus nanus*
turkey bush *Calytrix exstipulata, Eremophila deserti*
turkey bush, crimson *Eremophila latrobei*
turkey corn *Dicentra eximia*
Turkey oak *Quercus cerris*
Turkey rhubarb *Rheum palmatum*
turkey tangle *Phyla nodiflora*
Turkish cedar *Cedrus libani* subsp. *stenocoma*

Turkish hazel *Corylus colurna*
Turkish hornbeam *Carpinus orientalis*
Turkish liquidambar *Liquidambar orientalis*
Turkish pine *Pinus brutia*
Turkish rhododendron *Rhododendron smirnowii*
Turkish willow cherry *Prunus incana*
Turk's cap *Lilium martagon, Malvaviscus arboreus*
Turk's cap cactus, dwarf *Melocactus matanzanus*
Turk's cap lily *Lilium martagon*
Turk's cap lily, American *Lilium superbum*
turmeric *Curcuma longa, Hydrastis canadensis*
turmeric, cochin *Curcuma aromatica*
turmeric, native *Curcuma australasica*
turmeric, wild *Curcuma aromatica*
turnip *Brassica rapa*
turnip fern *Angiopteris evecta*
turnip, Indian *Arisaema triphyllum*
turnip, Mediterranean *Brassica tournefortii*
turnip, Mexican *Pachyrhizus erosus*
turnip, Swedish *Brassica napus*
turnip, twiggy *Brassica fruticulosa*
turnip weed *Rapistrum rugosum*
turnip-rooted parsley *Petroselinum crispum* var. *tuberosum*
turnipwood *Akania bidwillii*
turpentine *Syncarpia glomulifera*
turpentine bush *Eremophila sturtii*
turpentine, brush *Choricarpia leptopetala, Rhodamnia rubescens*
turpentine bush, pale *Beyeria leschenaultii*
turpentine, Cyprus *Pistacia terebinthus*
turpentine, swamp *Lophostemon suaveolens*

turquoise berry *Drymophila cyanocarpa*
turtle's head *Chelone, C. glabra*
tussock bellflower *Campanula carpatica*
tussock, coast *Poa poiformis*
tussock cotton grass *Eriophorum vaginatum*
tussock grass *Deschampsia cespitosa, Poa labillardierei*
tussock grass, blue-leaf *Poa sieberiana* var. *cyanophylla*
tussock grass, fine-leaf *Poa sieberiana* var. *hirtella*
tussock grass, plumed *Chionochloa conspicua*
tussock grass, red *Chionochloa rubra*
tussock rush *Juncus usitatus*
tussock, serrated *Nassella trichotoma*
tussock, silver *Poa cita*
tutahuna *Raoulia eximia*
tutsan *Hypericum androsaemum*
tutu, tree *Coriaria arborea*
twig, red *Leucothoe recurva*
twiggy bush-pea *Pultenaea largiflorens*
twiggy guinea-flower *Hibbertia virgata*
twiggy heath-myrtle *Babingtonia pluriflora*
twiggy mullein *Verbascum virgatum*
twiggy turnip *Brassica fruticulosa*
twig-rush, bare *Baumea juncea*
twig-rush, jointed *Baumea articulata*
twig-rush, leafy *Cladium procerum*
twig-rush, soft *Baumea rubiginosa*
twig-rush, tall *Cladium procerum*
twig-rush, wrinklenut *Baumea teretifolia*
twinberry *Lonicera involucrata*
twine, devil's *Cassytha pubescens*
twine, settlers' *Gymnostachys anceps*
twin-flower *Diascia rigescens*

twin-flowered knawel *Scleranthus biflorus*

twin-heads, yellow *Eclipta platyglossa*

twin-horned copperburr *Dissocarpus biflorus*

twining fringe-lily *Thysanotus patersonii*

twining glycine *Glycine clandestina*

twining guinea-flower *Hibbertia scandens*

twining milkwort *Comesperma volubile*

twining parakeelya *Calandrinia volubilis*

twining snapdragon *Asarina*

twinleaf *Jeffersonia, Zygophyllum*

twinleaf, climbing *Zygophyllum eremaeum*

twinleaf, dwarf *Zygophyllum ovatum*

twinleaf, shrubby *Zygophyllum aurantiacum*

twinleaf, small-fruited *Zygophyllum humillimum*

twinleaf, violet *Zygophyllum iodocarpum*

twin-leafed coogera *Arytera distylis*

twin-leafed mallee *Eucalyptus gamophylla*

twinspur *Diascia*

twirly whirly tree *Gyrocarpus americanus*

twisted rapier-sedge *Lepidosperma tortuosum*

twisted-leaf pine *Pinus teocote*

two-color panic *Panicum simile*

two-flowered pea *Lathyrus grandiflorus*

two-leafed Solomon's seal *Maianthemum canadense*

two-leafed squill *Scilla bifolia*

two-tone sage *Salvia semiatrata*

two-toothed amaranthus *Achyranthes bidentata*

two-veined hickory *Acacia binervata*

two-wing silverbell *Halesia diptera*

U

uabano *Paullinia*
uaranzeiro *Paullinia*
ubutake giboshi *Hosta pulchella*
udo *Aralia cordata*
ulmo *Eucryphia cordifolia*
umbrella arum *Amorphophallus konjac*
umbrella bamboo *Fargesia murielae*
umbrella cheese tree *Glochidion sumatranum*
umbrella fern *Dipteris conjugata, Sticherus flabellatus*
umbrella fern, giant *Dipteris conjugata*
umbrella flower *Ceropegia sandersonii*
umbrella grass *Digitaria divaricatissima, D. hystrichoides*
umbrella grass, silky *Digitaria ammophila*
umbrella magnolia *Magnolia tripetala*
umbrella mulga *Acacia brachystachya*
umbrella palm *Hedyscepe canterburyana*
umbrella pine *Pinus pinea*
umbrella pine, Japanese *Sciadopitys verticillata*
umbrella, poor man's *Gunnera insignis*

umbrella sedge *Cyperus eragrostis*
umbrella thorn *Acacia tortilis*
umbrella tree *Magnolia macrophylla*
umbrella tree, dwarf *Schefflera arboricola*
umbrella tree, ear-leafed *Magnolia fraseri*
umbrella tree, Indian *Schefflera pueckleri*
umbrella tree, miniature *Schefflera arboricola*
umbrella tree, Queensland *Schefflera actinophylla*
underground orchid *Rhizanthella*
union nut *Bouchardatia neurococca*
upas *Antiaris toxicaria*
upland cress *Barbarea vulgaris*
upright bugle *Ajuga genevensis*
upside-down orchid *Stanhopea*
urahagusa *Hakonechloa macra*
urajiro giboshi *Hosta hypoleuca*
Ural false spirea *Sorbaria kirilowii*
urn gum *Eucalyptus urnigera*
urn heath *Melichrus urceolatus*
usambara violet *Saintpaulia ionantha*
Ussurian pear *Pyrus ussuriensis*
Utah ash *Fraxinus anomala*
Utah juniper *Juniperus osteosperma*
Utah serviceberry *Amelanchier utahensis*

V

Valencia orange *Citrus × aurantium*
'Valencia'
valerian *Centranthus, Valeriana,
V. officinalis*
valerian, Greek *Polemonium
caeruleum, P. reptans*
valerian, narrow-leafed *Centranthus
angustifolius*
valerian, red *Centranthus ruber*
valerian, true *Valeriana officinalis*
valley, lily of the *Convallaria majalis*
valley oak *Quercus lobata*
vallonea oak *Quercus ithaburensis*
Van Houtte spiraea *Spiraea ×
vanhouttei*
Vanikoro kauri *Agathis macrophylla*
vanilla *Vanilla planifolia*
vanilla lily *Arthropodium milleflorum,
Sowerbaea juncea*
vanilla lily, small *Arthropodium
minus*
vanilla orchid *Vanilla planifolia*
vanilla tree *Azara microphylla*
variable daisy *Brachyscome ciliaris*
variable darling pea *Swainsona
oroboides*
variable glycine *Glycine tabacina*
variable groundsel *Senecio lautus*
variable plantain *Plantago varia*
variable sword-sedge *Lepidosperma
laterale*
variegated apple mint *Mentha
suaveolens* 'Variegata'
variegated basket grass *Oplismenus
africanus* 'Variegatus'
variegated bougainvillea
Bougainvillea glabra 'Variegata'
variegated box *Buxus sempervirens*
'Argentea', *B. s.* 'Marginata'

variegated box elder *Acer negundo*
'Variegatum'
variegated cassava *Manihot esculenta*
'Variegata'
variegated coral tree *Erythrina
variegata* 'Parcellii'
variegated giant reed *Arundo donax*
'Versicolor'
variegated hibiscus *Hibiscus
rosa-sinensis* 'Cooperi'
variegated holly *Ilex aquifolium*
'Argenteomarginata'
variegated ivy *Hedera canariensis*
'Variegata'
variegated jade tree *Crassula ovata*
'Sunset'
variegated lacecap hydrangea
Hydrangea macrophylla 'Maculata'
variegated lemon thyme *Thymus ×
citriodorus* 'Silver Queen'
variegated periwinkle *Vinca major*
'Variegata'
variegated pineapple *Ananas
bracteatus* 'Tricolor', *A. comosus*
'Variegatus'
variegated privet *Ligustrum lucidum*
'Tricolor'
variegated rubber tree *Ficus elastica*
'Doescheri'
variegated sage *Salvia officinalis*
'Tricolor'
variegated shield fern *Arachniodes
simplicior*
variegated sycamore maple *Acer
pseudoplatanus* 'Leopoldii',
A. p. 'Luteovirens'
variegated tapioca plant *Manihot
esculenta* 'Variegata'
variegated thistle *Silybum marianum*
variegated wintersweet *Acokanthera
oblongifolia* 'Variegata'
varnish tree *Koelreuteria paniculata,
Toxicendron vernicifluum*

varnish tree, Japanese *Firmiana simplex*
varnish wattle *Acacia verniciflua*
varnished gum *Eucalyptus vernicosa*
vasey grass *Paspalum urvillei*
vegetable ivory palm *Phytelephas*
vegetable marrow *Cucurbita pepo*
vegetable oyster *Tragopogon porrifolius*
vegetable sheep *Raoulia*
veined doubletail *Diuris venosa*
veined mock olive *Notelaea venosa*
veined peppercress *Lepidium phlebopetalum*
veined verbena *Verbena rigida*
veiny lace flower *Archidendron muellerianum*
veiny wilkiea *Wilkiea huegeliana*
Veitch's magnolia *Magnolia × veitchii*
veld fan *Boophone disticha*
veld grape *Cissus quadrangularis*
veld grass, perennial *Ehrharta calycina*
velleia, spur *Velleia lyrata, V. paradoxa*
velvet ash *Fraxinus velutina*
velvet banana *Musa velutina*
velvet, black *Colubrina arborescens*
velvet bush, pink *Lasiopetalum behrii*
velvet bush, rusty *Lasiopetalum ferrugineum*
velvet bushwillow *Combretum molle*
velvet flower *Amaranthus caudatus, Salpiglossis sinuata, Sparaxis tricolor*
velvet grass, creeping *Holcus mollis*
velvet grass, Korean *Zoysia tenuifolia*
velvet hovea *Hovea pannosa*
velvet maple *Acer velutinum*
velvet mesquite *Prosopis velutina*
velvet myrtle *Lenwebbia prominens*
velvet nightshade *Solanum ellipticum*

velvet plant *Gynura aurantiaca*
velvet plant, purple *Gynura aurantiaca*
velvet plant, royal *Gynura aurantiaca*
velvet plant, trailing *Ruellia makoyana*
velvet pomaderris *Pomaderris velutina*
velvet potato bush *Solanum ellipticum*
velvet prickly pear *Opuntia tomentosa*
velvet rose *Aeonium canariense*
velvet rose, giant *Aeonium canariense*
velvet sage *Salvia leucantha*
velvet sweetberry *Bridelia mollis*
velvet tobacco *Nicotiana velutina*
velvet tree pear *Opuntia tomentosa*
velvet wallaby grass *Austrodanthonia pilosa*
velvet, white *Tradescantia sillamontana*
velvety buttercup *Ranunculus velutinus*
Venetian sumach *Cotinus coggygria*
Venezuela, rose of *Brownea ariza*
Venezuela tree vine *Cissus rhombifolia*
Venus flytrap *Dionaea muscipula*
Venus maidenhair *Adiantum capillus-veneris*
Venus maidenhair fern *Adiantum capillus-veneris*
Venus' hair *Adiantum capillus-veneris*
Venus' navelwort *Omphalodes linifolia*
verbena *Verbena*
verbena, beach sand *Abronia umbellata*
verbena, common *Verbena officinalis*
verbena, lemon-scented *Aloysia triphylla*
verbena, moss *Verbena tenuisecta*
verbena, purple *Verbena rigida*

verbena, purple-top *Verbena bonariensis*
verbena, rough *Verbena hispida*
verbena, sand *Abronia, A. maritima, A. umbellata*
verbena, tall *Verbena bonariensis*
verbena tree, sweet *Backhousia citriodora*
verbena, veined *Verbena rigida*
verde, peyote *Echinocereus knippelianus*
vernal grass, sweet *Anthoxanthum odoratum*
vernal witch hazel *Hamamelis vernalis*
Veronica *Hebe, Veronica*
veronica, feldmark *Chionohebe densifolia*
vervain *Verbena*
vervain, blue *Verbena hastata*
vervain, common *Verbena officinalis*
vervain, creeping *Verbena canadensis*
vervain, European *Verbena officinalis*
vervain, hoary *Verbena stricta*
vervain, rose *Verbena canadensis*
vervain, South American *Verbena bonariensis*
vetch *Vicia*
vetch, common *Vicia sativa* subsp. *sativa*
vetch, crown *Coronilla varia*
vetch, hairy *Vicia hirsuta*
vetch, kidney *Anthyllis vulneraria*
vetch, narrow-leafed *Vicia sativa* subsp. *angustifolia*
vetch, Russian *Vicia villosa*
vetch, slender *Vicia tetrasperma*
vetch, spring *Lathyrus vernus*
vetchling *Lathyrus*
viburnum, blackhaw *Viburnum prunifolium*
viburnum, Burkwood *Viburnum × burkwoodii*

viburnum, Canary Island *Viburnum rigidum*
viburnum, doublefile *Viburnum plicatum*
viburnum, evergreen tree *Viburnum odoratissimum*
viburnum, fragrant snowball *Viburnum × carlcephalum*
viburnum, judd *Viburnum × juddii*
viburnum, Korean spice *Viburnum carlesii*
viburnum, linden *Viburnum dilatatum*
viburnum, possum-haw *Viburnum nudum*
viburnum, Ryukyu *Viburnum suspensum*
viburnum, Sargent *Viburnum sargentii*
viburnum, sweet *Viburnum odoratissimum*
viburnum, Walters *Viburnum obovatum*
Victoria River fan palm *Livistona victoriae*
Victorian box *Pittosporum undulatum*
Victorian Christmas bush *Prostanthera lasianthos*
Vietnamese coriander *Persicaria odorata*
Vietnamese mint *Persicaria odorata*
viguiera, San Diego County *Viguiera laciniata*
vinca, shrub *Kopsia fruticosa*
vine, Allegheny *Adlumia fungosa*
vine, Amazon *Stigmaphyllon ciliatum*
vine, arrowhead *Syngonium podophyllum*
vine, balloon *Cardiospermum, C. grandiflorum*
vine, bead *Crassula rupestris*
vine, Bengal clock *Thunbergia grandiflora*

vine, bitter *Piptocalyx moorei*
vine, black-eyed Susan *Thunbergia alata*
vine, bleeding heart *Clerodendrum thomsoniae*
vine, blood *Austrosteenisia blackii*
vine, blood-red trumpet *Distictis buccinatoria*
vine, bluebird *Petrea*
vine, bower *Actinidia arguta, Pandorea jasminoides*
vine, Brazilian flame *Pyrostegia venusta*
vine, canary bird *Tropaeolum peregrinum*
vine, caustic *Sarcostemma australe, S. brunonianum*
vine, chain of hearts *Ceropegia linearis* subsp. *woodii*
vine, chalice *Solandra maxima*
vine, Chilean potato *Solanum crispum*
vine, Chinese matrimony *Lycium chinense*
vine, chocolate *Akebia*
vine, cinnamon *Dioscorea batatas*
vine, clock *Thunbergia grandiflora*
vine, Confederate *Antigonon leptopus*
vine, coral *Antigonon leptopus, Kennedia coccinea*
vine, cup and saucer *Cobaea scandens*
vine, Easter lily *Beaumontia grandiflora*
vine, fire *Lotus maculatus*
vine, firecracker *Manettia luteorubra*
vine, flame *Pyrostegia venusta*
vine, fleece *Fallopia*
vine, golden *Stigmaphyllon ciliatum*
vine, gouty *Cyphostemma bainesii*
vine, gum *Aphanopetalum resinosum*
vine, headache *Clematis glycinoides*
vine, India rubber *Strophanthus gratus*

vine, jade *Strongylodon macrobotrys*
vine, jungle *Cissus hypoglauca*
vine, kangaroo *Cissus antarctica*
vine, kudzu *Pueraria lobata*
vine, lace-flower *Episcia dianthiflora*
vine, lawyer *Smilax australis*
vine, leather *Clematis*
vine, lemon *Pereskia aculeata*
vine, Macquarie *Muehlenbeckia gunnii*
vine, Madeira *Anredera cordifolia*
vine, maidenhair *Muehlenbeckia complexa*
vine maple *Acer circinnatum*
vine, marine *Cissus trifoliata*
vine, matrimony *Lycium*
vine, mattress *Muehlenbeckia complexa*
vine, mile-a-minute *Fallopia baldschuanica*
vine, monkey *Parsonsia eucalyptophylla*
vine, moth *Araujia sericifera*
vine, necklace *Muehlenbeckia complexa*
vine, orange clock *Thunbergia gregorii*
vine, orangeglow *Pseudogynoxys chenopodioides*
vine, pearl *Sarcopetalum harveyanum*
vine, potato *Solanum jasminoides, S. wendlandii*
vine, princess *Cissus sicyoides*
vine, quarter *Bignonia capreolata*
vine, rosary *Ceropegia linearis* subsp. *woodii*
vine, round-leaf *Legnephora moorei*
vine, rubber *Cryptostegia grandiflora*
vine, Russian *Fallopia baldschuanica*
vine, sandpaper *Petrea volubilis*
vine, silver *Actinidia polygama*
vine, silver lace *Fallopia aubertii*
vine, sky *Thunbergia grandiflora*

vine, snail *Vigna caracalla*
vine, snake *Hemiandra pungens*
vine, tar *Boerhavia coccinea,*
B. dominii
vine, tara *Actinidia arguta*
vine that ate the south *Pueraria lobata*
vine, trumpet *Campsis, C. radicans*
vine, water *Cissus hypoglauca*
vine, whip *Flagellaria indica*
vine, wire *Muehlenbeckia complexa*
vine, wonga *Pandorea pandorana*
vine, wonga wonga *Pandorea*
pandorana
vine, yellow *Tribulus micrococcus*
vinegar tree *Rhus glabra*
vine-leaf maple *Acer cissifolium*
viola *Viola* Hybrid Cultivars, Viola
Group
viola, bird's foot *Viola pedata*
violet *Viola, V. odorata*
violet, African *Saintpaulia,*
S. ionantha
violet, Australian native *Viola*
hederacea
violet, bird's foot *Viola pedata*
violet, bush *Barleria obtusa,*
Browallia speciosa
violet bush, slender *Hybanthus*
monopetalus
violet, Confederate *Viola sororia*
'Priceana'
violet, crowfoot *Viola pedata*
violet, cyclamen-leafed *Viola koreana*
violet, damask *Hesperis matronalis*
violet, dames *Hesperis matronalis*
violet, dog *Viola riviniana*
violet, dog's tooth *Erythronium,*
E. dens-canis
violet, evergreen *Viola sempervirens*
violet, flame *Episcia cupreata*
violet, fringed *Thysanotus*
violet, German *Exacum affine*
violet, great-spurred *Viola selkirkii*

violet, heath *Viola canina*
violet, heath dog *Viola canina*
violet, hooked-spur *Viola adunca*
violet, horned *Viola cornuta*
violet, ivy-leafed *Viola hederacea*
violet kunzea *Kunzea parvifolia*
violet, Labrador *Viola labradorica*
violet, marsh blue *Viola cucullata*
violet, Mexican *Tetranema roseum*
violet, moon *Viola dissecta*
violet nightshade *Solanum brownii*
violet, Northern blue *Viola*
septentrionalis
violet, pansy *Viola pedata*
violet pea *Baphia racemosa*
violet, Persian *Cyclamen, Exacum*
affine
violet prairie clover *Dalea purpurea*
violet, purple *Viola adunca*
violet, Pyrenean *Viola pyrenaica*
violet, redwood *Viola sempervirens*
violet, rock *Boea hygroscopica*
violet, showy *Viola betonicifolia*
violet, small bush *Barleria repens*
violet, stream *Viola glabella*
violet, swamp *Viola caleyana*
violet, sweet *Viola odorata*
violet, sweet white *Viola blanda*
violet, trailing *Viola hederacea*
violet tree *Polygala cowellii*
violet trumpet *Clytostoma*
callistegioides
violet twinleaf *Zygophyllum*
iodocarpum
violet, usambara *Saintpaulia ionantha*
violet westringia *Westringia glabra*
violet, Willdenow *Viola blanda*
violet willow *Salix daphnoides*
violet, wood *Viola riviniana*
violet, woodland white *Viola blanda*
viper's bugloss *Echium vulgare*
Virginia bluebells *Mertensia*
virginica

Virginia creeper *Parthenocissus,
P. quinquefolia*
Virginia creeper, Chinese
Parthenocissus henryana
Virginia pine *Pinus virginiana*
Virginia rose *Rosa virginiana*
Virginia snakeroot *Aristolochia
serpentaria*
Virginia stewartia *Stewartia
malacodendron*
Virginia stock *Malcolmia maritima*
Virginia willow *Itea virginica*
Virginian bugleweed *Lycopus
virginicus*
Virginian skullcap *Scutellaria
lateriflora*

Virginian stock *Malcolmia
maritima*
virgin's bower *Clematis*
viscaria *Lychnis viscaria, Silene
coeli-rosa*
vitex, beach *Vitex rotundifolia*
vivax bamboo *Phyllostachys vivax*
Vogel's fig *Ficus lutea*
volcan, flor del *Solanum wendlandii*
volcanic onion *Allium cratericola*
voodoo lily *Sauromatum venosum*
Voss laburnum *Laburnum × watereri*
'Vossii'
vygie, orange *Lampranthus aureus*
vygie, pink *Lampranthus blandus*
vygie, red *Lampranthus coccineus*

W

Wagner sage *Salvia wagneriana*
wahoo *Euonymus americanus*
wahoo, eastern *Euonymus atropurpureus*
wahoo tree *Leucaena retusa*
wait-a-while *Acacia colletioides, Calamus muelleri*
wait-a-while creeper *Smilax australis*
wake robin *Trillium, T. ovatum*
wake robin, brook *Trillium rivale*
wake robin, dwarf *Trillium pusillum*
wake robin, furrowed *Trillium sulcatum*
wake robin, yellow *Trillium luteum*
walking iris *Neomarica northiana*
walking-stick, Chinese *Chimonobambusa tumidissinoda*
walking-stick, devil's *Aralia spinosa*
walking-stick, Harry Lauder's *Corylus avellana* 'Contorta'
walking-stick palm *Linospadix monostachya*
wall fern *Polypodium vulgare*
wall fumitory *Fumaria muralis*
wall germander *Teucrium chamaedrys*
wall pellitory *Parietaria judaica*
wall pepper *Sedum acre*
wall rocket *Diplotaxis muralis*
wall speedwell *Veronica arvensis*
wall toadflax *Cymbalaria muralis*
wallaby bush *Beyeria lasiocarpa*
wallaby bush, smooth *Beyeria opaca*
wallaby bush, sticky *Beyeria viscosa*
wallaby grass *Austrodanthonia, Notodanthonia*
wallaby grass, brown-back *Austrodanthonia duttoniana*
wallaby grass, hill *Austrodanthonia eriantha*
wallaby grass, lobed *Austrodanthonia auriculata*
wallaby grass, longleaf *Notodanthonia longifolia*
wallaby grass, red-anther *Joycea pallida*
wallaby grass, ringed *Austrodanthonia caespitosa*
wallaby grass, slender *Austrodanthonia penicillata*
wallaby grass, small-flowered *Austrodanthonia setacea*
wallaby grass, swamp *Amphibromus macrorhinus, A. neesii*
wallaby grass, velvet *Austrodanthonia pilosa*
wallaby weed *Olearia viscidula*
Wallangarra wattle *Acacia adunca*
Wallangarra white gum *Eucalyptus scoparia*
wallflower *Erysimum, E. cheiri*
wallflower, dwarf *Erysimum linariifolium*
wallflower, Moroccan *Erysimum mutabile*
wallflower orchid *Diuris longifolia*
wallflower, perennial *Erysimum mutabile*
Wallich's wood fern *Dryopteris wallichiana*
Wallis fescue *Festuca valesiaca*
wallowa *Acacia calamifolia*
wallum banksia *Banksia aemula*
wallum bottlebrush *Callistemon pachyphyllus*
wallum phebalium *Phebalium woombye*
wallum scribbly gum *Eucalyptus signata*
walnut *Juglans regia*
walnut, African *Schotia brachypetala*
walnut, American *Juglans nigra*
walnut, Arizona *Juglans major*

walnut, black *Endiandra globosa,*
Juglans nigra
walnut, butternut *Juglans cinerea*
walnut, California *Juglans californica*
walnut, Chinese *Juglans cathayensis*
walnut, common *Juglans regia*
walnut, English *Juglans regia*
walnut, Hinds' black *Juglans hindsii*
walnut, Japanese *Juglans ailanthifolia*
walnut, Manchurian *Juglans*
mandshurica
walnut, oak *Cryptocarya corrugata*
walnut, Persian *Juglans regia*
walnut, rose *Endiandra discolor*
walnut, Texan *Juglans microcarpa*
walnut, West Indian *Juglans*
jamaicensis
walnut, white *Juglans cinerea*
Walters viburnum *Viburnum*
obovatum
wampee *Pontederia, P. cordata*
wampee, Chinese *Clausena lansium*
wampi *Clausena lansium*
wand flower *Dierama, Ixia*
wandering daisy *Erigeron peregrinus*
wandering fleabane *Erigeron*
peregrinus
wandering heath *Erica vagans*
wandering Jew *Tradescantia albiflora,*
T. fluminensis
wandering speedwell *Veronica*
peregrina
wanderrie grass *Eriachne*
wandoo *Eucalyptus wandoo*
wands, fairy *Dierama pulcherrimum*
wanga palm *Pigafetta filaris*
wangrangkura *Eleutherococcus*
sessiliflorus
wao, mahoe *Melicytus lanceolatus*
waratah *Telopea, T. speciosissima*
waratah, Dorrigo *Alloxylon pinnatum*
waratah, Gibraltar Range *Telopea*
aspera

waratah, Gippsland *Telopea oreades*
waratah, Monga *Telopea mongaensis*
waratah, Tasmanian *Telopea*
truncata
waratah tree *Alloxylon flammeum*
waratah, white *Agastachys odorata*
Ward's weed *Carrichtera annua*
warilu *Eucalyptus gamophylla*
Warrego grass *Paspalidium*
jubiflorum
warrigal cabbage *Tetragonia*
tetragonioides
warrigal greens *Tetragonia*
tetragonioides
warrior, old *Artemisia pontica*
warrior-bush *Apophyllum anomalum*
wart leaf ceanothus *Ceanothus*
papillosus
warty peppercress *Lepidium*
papillosum
warty yate *Eucalyptus megacornuta*
wasabi *Wasabia japonica*
Washington hawthorn *Crataegus*
phaenopyrum
Washington thorn *Crataegus*
phaenopyrum
Washingtonia palm *Washingtonia*
filifera
watch-chain cypress *Crassula muscosa*
water apple *Syzygium aqueum*
water avens *Geum rivale*
water bent *Agrostis viridis*
water berry *Syzygium cordatum*
water betony *Scrophularia auriculata*
water birch *Betula fontinalis,*
B. occidentalis
water bush *Bossiaea aquifolium,*
Myoporum montanum
water buttercup, white *Ranunculus*
aquatilis
water buttons *Cotula coronopifolia*
water caltrops *Trapa natans*
water canna *Thalia dealbata*

water celery *Oenanthe javanica*
water chestnut *Eleocharis dulcis,*
 Trapa, T. natans
water chickweed *Callitriche stagnalis*
water chinquapin *Nelumbo lutea*
water clover *Marsilea, M. mutica*
water couch *Paspalum distichum*
water crowsfoot *Ranunculus aquatilis*
water dropwort *Oenanthe javanica*
water elm *Planera aquatica*
water fern *Azolla, Blechnum*
 ambiguum, B. camfieldii,
 Histiopteris incisa
water fern, alpine *Blechnum*
 pennamarina
water fern, black-stem *Blechnum*
 nudum
water fern, fishbone *Blechnum*
 nudum
water fern, hard *Blechnum wattsii*
water fern, New Zealand *Blechnum*
 discolor
water fern, soft *Blechnum minus*
water fern, strap *Blechnum patersonii*
water fern, swamp *Blechnum*
 indicum
water figwort *Scrophularia auriculata*
water foxtail *Alopecurus geniculatus*
water fuchsia *Impatiens*
water germander *Teucrium scordium*
water gladiolus *Butomus*
water gum *Tristaniopsis laurina*
water gum, dwarf *Tristania neriifolia*
water gum, giant *Syzygium francisii*
water gum, mountain *Tristaniopsis*
 collina
water gum, northern *Tristaniopsis*
 exiliflora
water hawthorn *Aponogeton distachyos*
water heath *Erica curviflora*
water hickory *Carya aquatica*
water horsetail *Equisetum fluviatile*
water hyacinth *Eichhornia crassipes*

water hyssop *Bacopa caroliniana*
water iris, Japanese *Iris ensata,*
 I. laevigata
water lettuce *Pistia stratiotes*
water locust *Gleditsia aquatica*
water milfoil *Myriophyllum*
water milfoil, Brazilian *Myriophyllum*
 aquaticum
water milfoil, red *Myriophyllum*
 verrucosum
water mint *Mentha aquatica*
water oak *Quercus nigra*
water panic, white *Panicum*
 obseptum
water pepper *Persicaria hydropiper*
water pimpernel *Samolus valerandi*
water plantain *Alisma plantago-*
 aquatica
water primrose *Ludwigia peploides*
water ribbons *Triglochin procerum*
water rose apple *Syzygium aqueum*
water speedwell *Veronica anagallis-*
 aquatica
water spinach *Ipomoea aquatica*
water tree *Hakea leucoptera*
water tupelo *Nyssa aquatica*
water vine *Cissus hypoglauca*
water vine, giant *Cissus hypoglauca*
water weed *Elodea canadensis,*
 Osteocarpum acropterum
water willow, Arizona *Justicia*
 candicans
water yam *Dioscorea alata*
watercress *Rorippa nasturtium-*
 aquaticum
watercress, common *Rorippa*
 nasturtium-aquaticus
watercress, marsh *Rorippa palustris*
waterlily *Nymphaea*
waterlily, Amazon *Victoria amazonica*
waterlily, Australian *Nymphaea*
 gigantea
waterlily, Cape *Nymphaea caerulea*

waterlily, Cape blue *Nymphaea caerulea*

waterlily, Egyptian *Nymphaea lotus*

waterlily, fragrant *Nymphaea odorata*

waterlily, giant *Victoria*

waterlily, giant blue *Nymphaea gigantea*

waterlily, prickly *Euryale ferox*

waterlily, pygmy *Nymphaea tetragona*

waterlily, royal *Victoria amazonica*

waterlily tulip *Tulipa kaufmanniana*

waterlily, woolly *Philydrum lanuginosum*

waterlily, yellow *Nuphar lutea, Nymphaea mexicana*

watermelon *Citrullus lanatus*

watermelon begonia *Peperomia argyreia*

watermelon peperomia *Peperomia argyreia*

watermelon pepper *Peperomia argyreia*

waterwheel plant *Aldrovanda vesiculosa*

waterwood, Pondo *Syzygium pondoense*

waterwort *Elatine gratioloides*

Watkins fig *Ficus watkinsiana*

watsonia, Beatrica *Watsonia pillansii*

wattle *Acacia*

wattle, alpine *Acacia alpina*

wattle, Australian golden *Acacia pycnantha*

wattle, Bancroft's *Acacia bancroftii*

wattle, Barrier Range *Acacia beckleri*

wattle, bent-leaf *Acacia flexifolia*

wattle, black *Acacia decurrens, Callicoma serratifolia*

wattle, bluebush *Acacia clunies-rossiae*

wattle, blunt *Acacia obtusata*

wattle, boomerang *Acacia amoena*

wattle, bramble *Acacia victoriae*

wattle, brown *Acacia brunioides*

wattle, brush ironbark *Acacia aulacocarpa*

wattle, Buchan blue *Acacia caerulescens*

wattle, Burrow's *Acacia burrowii*

wattle, Cape Leeuwin *Paraserianthes lophantha*

wattle, catkin *Acacia dallachiana*

wattle, cedar *Acacia elata*

wattle, Chinchilla *Acacia chinchillensis*

wattle, clay-bush *Acacia glaucoptera*

wattle, coastal *Acacia longifolia* subsp. *sophorae*

wattle, coil-pod *Acacia pravifolia*

wattle, Coonavittra *Acacia jennerae*

wattle, Cootamundra *Acacia baileyana*

wattle, corkwood *Acacia bidwillii*

wattle, creek *Acacia rivalis*

wattle, crested *Paraserianthes lophantha*

wattle, crowded-leaf *Acacia conferta*

wattle, curly-bark *Acacia curranii*

wattle, dagger *Acacia siculiformis*

wattle, dagger-leafed *Acacia rhigiophylla*

wattle, Deane's *Acacia deanei*

wattle, desert *Acacia victoriae*

wattle, Dorothy's *Acacia dorothea*

wattle, downy *Acacia pubescens*

wattle, drooping *Acacia difformis*

wattle, Drummond's *Acacia drummondii*

wattle, ear-pod *Acacia auriculiformis*

wattle, elephant ear *Acacia dunnii*

wattle, fan *Acacia amblygona*

wattle, fern-leaf *Acacia filicifolia*

wattle, flat-stemmed *Acacia complanata*

wattle, flax *Acacia linifolia*

wattle, Flinders *Acacia notabilis*

wattle, Flinders Range *Acacia iteaphylla*

wattle, fringed *Acacia fimbriata*
wattle, frosty *Acacia pruinosa*
wattle, Gittins's *Acacia gittinsii*
wattle, gold-dust *Acacia acinacea*
wattle, golden *Acacia pycnantha*
wattle, golden wreath *Acacia saligna*
wattle, Gosford *Acacia prominens*
wattle, granite *Acacia granitica*
wattle, green *Acacia deanei,*
   A. irrorata
wattle, hairy *Acacia lanigera*
wattle, Hamilton's *Acacia*
   hamiltoniana
wattle, harrow *Acacia acanthoclada*
wattle, Haviland's *Acacia*
   havilandiorum
wattle, hickory *Acacia implexa*
wattle, hop *Acacia stricta*
wattle, Howitt's *Acacia howittii*
wattle, jumping jack *Acacia*
   enterocarpa
wattle, knife-leaf *Acacia cultriformis*
wattle, Kybean *Acacia kybeanensis*
wattle, late black *Acacia mearnsii*
wattle, Mabel's *Acacia mabellae*
wattle, Maiden's *Acacia maidenii*
wattle, mallee *Acacia montana*
wattle, manna *Acacia microcarpa*
wattle mat-rush *Lomandra filiformis*
wattle, Mitchell's *Acacia mitchellii*
wattle, Mudgee *Acacia spectabilis*
wattle, Mueller's *Acacia muelleriana*
wattle, myrtle *Acacia myrtifolia*
wattle, narrow-leaf bower *Acacia*
   cognata
wattle, needle *Acacia carnei,*
   A. havilandiorum, A. rigens
wattle, northern silver *Acacia*
   leucoclada
wattle, oleander *Acacia neriifolia*
wattle, orange *Acacia saligna*
wattle, ovens *Acacia pravissima*
wattle, pinbush *Acacia burkittii*

wattle, ploughshare *Acacia*
   cultriformis, A. gunnii
wattle, poverty *Acacia dawsonii*
wattle, prickly *Acacia ulicifolia,*
   A. victoriae
wattle, Queensland *Acacia*
   podalyriifolia
wattle, red-stemmed *Acacia rubida*
wattle, Rice's *Acacia riceana*
wattle, rough *Acacia aspera*
wattle, round-leaf *Acacia uncinata*
wattle, rush-leaf *Acacia juncifolia*
wattle, sally *Acacia floribunda*
wattle, sandhill *Acacia acuminata*
   subsp. *burkittii, A. ligulata*
wattle, showy *Acacia decora*
wattle, sickle *Acacia falcata*
wattle, silver *Acacia dealbata,*
   A. neriifolia, A. retinodes
wattle, silver-stemmed *Acacia*
   parvipinnula
wattle, spike *Acacia oxycedrus*
wattle, spiky *Acacia maitlandii*
wattle, spreading *Acacia genistifolia*
wattle, spurwing *Acacia triptera*
wattle, sunshine *Acacia terminalis*
wattle, swamp *Acacia elongata,*
   A. retinodes
wattle, sweet *Acacia suaveolens*
wattle, Sydney golden *Acacia*
   longifolia
wattle, thorn *Acacia continua*
wattle, three-veined *Acacia trinervata*
wattle, varnish *Acacia verniciflua*
wattle, Wallangarra *Acacia adunca*
wattle, wavy-leaf *Acacia uncinata*
wattle, wedge-leafed *Acacia*
   pravissima
wattle, Western Australian golden
   Acacia saligna
wattle, western black *Acacia hakeoides*
wattle, western coastal *Acacia cyclops*
wattle, western golden *Acacia decora*

wattle, Wilhelm's *Acacia wilhelmiana*
wattle, woodypod *Acacia crassicarpa*
wattle, woolly *Acacia lanigera*
wattle, Wyalong *Acacia cardiophylla*
wavy hair grass *Deschampsia flexuosa*
wavy marshwort *Nymphoides crenata*
wavy-leaf ceanothus *Ceanothus foliosus*
wavy-leaf oak *Quercus undulata*
wavy-leaf wattle *Acacia uncinata*
wawa *Triplochiton scleroxylon*
wax flower *Eriostemon, Hoya, Jamesia americana, Philotheca*
wax flower, Bendigo *Philotheca verrucosa*
wax flower, box-leafed *Philotheca buxifolia*
wax flower, long-leaf *Philotheca myoporoides*
wax flower, narrow-leaf *Philotheca linearis*
wax flower, Philippine *Etlingera elatior*
wax flower, pink *Eriostemon australasius*
wax flower, prickly *Philotheca pungens*
wax flower, rough-leafed *Philotheca hispidula*
wax flower, small-leafed *Philotheca difformis*
wax flower, Tasmanian *Philotheca virgata*
wax, Geraldton *Chamelaucium uncinatum*
wax gourd *Benincasa hispida*
wax mallow *Malvaviscus arboreus*
wax myrtle *Myrica cerifera*
wax palm *Copernicia*
wax plant *Eriostemon australasius, Hoya carnosa, Philotheca*
wax tree *Toxicodendron succedaneum*
waxberry *Gaultheria hispida*

waxberry, green *Gaultheria appressa*
waxberry, lance-leaf *Myrica serrata*
waxberry, white *Gaultheria appressa*
waxleaf privet *Ligustrum lucidum*
wax-lip orchid *Glossodia major*
wax-lip orchid, small *Glossodia minor*
wax-myrtle *Myrica cerifera*
wax-myrtle, Madeira *Myrica faya*
waxwork *Celastrus scandens*
wayfaring tree *Viburnum lantana*
wayfaring tree, Chinese *Viburnum veitchii*
weather-glass, golden *Hypoxis hygrometrica*
wedding bush *Ricinocarpos pinifolius, R. tuberculatus*
wedding bush, northern *Ricinocarpos bowmannii*
wedding flower, Natal *Dombeya tiliacea*
wedding lily, Lord Howe *Dietes robinsoniana*
wedge pea *Gompholobium grandiflorum*
wedge pea, dainty *Gompholobium glabratum*
wedge pea, dwarf *Gompholobium minus*
wedge pea, pale *Gompholobium huegelii*
wedge pea, pinnate *Gompholobium pinnatum*
wedge pea, red *Gompholobium uncinatum*
wedge-fern, lacy *Lindsaea microphylla*
wedge-leafed wattle *Acacia pravissima*
wedge-leaflet fan palm *Licuala ramsayi*
Wee Jasper grevillea *Grevillea iaspicula*
weed, alligator *Alternanthera philoxeroides*
weed, ash *Aegopodium podagraria*

weed, bishop's *Aegopodium podagraria, Ammi majus*

weed, blue *Echium vulgare*

weed, Buchan *Hirschfeldia incana*

weed, butterfly *Asclepias curassavica, A. tuberosa*

weed, Cape *Arctotheca calendula*

weed, carrot *Daucus glochidiatus*

weed, caustic *Chamaesyce drummondii*

weed, Cretan *Hedypnois rhagadioloides* subsp. *cretica*

weed, Crofton *Ageratina adenophora*

weed, gall *Zygophyllum apiculatum*

weed, gomphrena *Gomphrena celosioides, G. flaccida*

weed, gypsy *Veronica officinalis*

weed, horny goat *Epimedium sagittatum*

weed, Indian *Sigesbeckia orientalis*

weed, Jamestown *Datura stramonium*

weed, jewel *Impatiens capensis*

weed, Jimson's *Datura stramonium*

weed, Joe Pye *Eupatorium purpureum*

weed, Lincoln *Diplotaxis tenuifolia*

weed, Mercury Bay *Dichondra repens*

weed, mitre *Mitrasacme polymorpha*

weed, onion *Asphodelus fistulosus, Nothoscordum gracile*

weed, pickerel *Pontederia, P. cordata*

weed, potato *Heliotropium europaeum*

weed, rosin *Grindelia*

weed, sage *Sida corrugata*

weed, Sargasso *Sargassum fusiforme*

weed, scorpion *Phacelia*

weed, silver *Potentilla anserina*

weed, skeleton *Chondrilla juncea*

weed, smart *Persicaria bistortoides*

weed, soap *Yucca elata*

weed, stagger *Dicentra eximia, Stachys arvensis*

weed, sticky *Parietaria judaica*

weed, tar *Grindelia*

weed, telegraph *Heterotheca grandiflora*

weed, toothpick *Ammi visnaga*

weed, trumpet *Eupatorium purpureum*

weed, tumble *Boophone disticha*

weed, turnip *Rapistrum rugosum*

weed, wallaby *Hamamelis vernalis*

weed, Ward's *Carrichtera annua*

weed, water *Osteocarpum acropterum*

weeooka *Eremophila oppositifolia*

weeping baeckea *Baeckea stenophylla*

weeping beech *Fagus sylvatica* 'Pendula'

weeping birch *Betula pendula* 'Youngii'

weeping boer-bean *Schotia brachypetala*

weeping boobialla *Myoporum floribundum*

weeping boree *Acacia vestita*

weeping bottlebrush *Callistemon viminalis, Melaleuca tamariscina*

weeping broom *Carmichaelia stevensonii*

weeping cabbage palm *Livistona decipiens*

weeping cherry *Prunus subhirtella* 'Pendula'

weeping cherry, Cheal's *Prunus* (Sato-zakura Group) 'Kiku-shidare Sakura'

weeping crabapple *Malus* 'Echtermeyer'

weeping cypress, Chinese *Cupressus funebris*

weeping elm *Ulmus glabra* 'Camperdownii'

weeping fig *Ficus benjamina*

weeping fig, Celebes *Ficus celebensis*

weeping fig, Hill's *Ficus microcarpa* var. *hillii*

weeping forsythia *Forsythia suspensa*

weeping grass *Microlaena stipoides*
weeping gum *Eucalyptus sepulcralis*
weeping lillypilly *Waterhousea floribunda*
weeping love grass *Eragrostis curvula*
weeping myall *Acacia pendula*
weeping paperbark *Melaleuca leucadendra*
weeping pine *Pinus patula*
weeping pinyon *Pinus pinceana*
weeping pittosporum *Pittosporum phylliraeoides*
weeping purple beech *Fagus sylvatica* 'Purpurea Pendula'
weeping sage *Buddleja auriculata*
weeping silver birch *Betula pendula* 'Dalecarlica'
weeping silver lime *Tilia* 'Petiolaris'
weeping silver linden *Tilia* 'Petiolaris'
weeping spleenwort *Asplenium flaccidum*
weeping spruce *Picea breweriana*
weeping spruce, Brewer's *Picea breweriana*
weeping sword fern *Nephrolepis falcata*
weeping willow *Salix babylonica*
weeping willow, Babylon *Salix babylonica*
weeping willow, golden *Salix × sepulcralis* 'Chrysocoma'
weeping willow, Wisconsin *Salix × pendulina*
weeping wych elm *Ulmus glabra* 'Pendula'
weeping Yoshino cherry *Prunus × yedoensis* 'Shidare-Yoshino'
weeping yucca *Yucca recurvifolia*
weigela *Weigela, W. florida*
weigela, old-fashioned *Weigela florida*
weld *Reseda luteola*
Wells' manzanita *Arctostaphylos wellsii*
Welsh onion *Allium fistulosum*

Welsh polypody *Polypodium cambricum*
Welsh poppy *Meconopsis cambrica*
West Asian wild fig *Ficus palmata*
West Himalayan fir *Abies pindrow*
West Himalayan spruce *Picea smithiana*
West Indian gherkin *Cucumis anguria*
West Indian holly *Leea coccinea*
West Indian laurel-cherry *Prunus myrtifolia*
West Indian mahogany *Swietenia mahogani*
West Indian tree fern *Cyathea arborea*
West Indian walnut *Juglans jamaicensis*
Western Australian blackbutt *Eucalyptus patens*
Western Australian Christmas tree *Nuytsia floribunda*
Western Australian golden wattle *Acacia saligna*
Western Australian grass tree *Xanthorrhoea preissii*
Western Australian pigface *Carpobrotus virescens*
Western Australian pitcher plant *Cephalotus follicularis*
western azalea *Rhododendron occidentale*
western birch *Betula occidentalis*
western black wattle *Acacia hakeoides*
western bloodwood *Corymbia terminalis*
western boobialla *Myoporum montanum*
western burning bush *Euonymus occidentalis*
western catalpa *Catalpa speciosa*
western coastal wattle *Acacia cyclops*
western columbine *Aquilegia formosa*

western coneflower *Rudbeckia occidentalis*
western cork tree *Hakea lorea*
western cottonwood *Populus fremontii*
western dog violet *Viola adunca*
western fescue *Festuca pratensis*
western golden wattle *Acacia decora*
western gray box *Eucalyptus microcarpa*
western hemlock *Tsuga heterophylla*
western hop tree *Ptelea angustifolia*
western hop-hornbeam *Ostrya knowltonii*
western juniper *Juniperus occidentalis*
western kapok bush *Cochlospermum fraseri*
western larch *Larix occidentalis*
western leatherwood *Dirca occidentalis*
western mugwort *Artemisia ludoviciana*
western myall *Acacia papyrocarpa*
western New Guinea kauri *Agathis labillardierei*
western poison oak *Toxicodendron diversilobum*
western poppy *Papaver californicum*
western prickly Moses *Acacia pulchella*
western red cedar *Thuja plicata*
western redbud *Cercis occidentalis*
western rosemary, slender *Westringia eremicola*
western rosemary, stiff *Westringia rigida*
western rosewood *Alectryon oleifolius*
western silver wattle *Acacia polybotrya*
western sky pilot *Polemonium pulcherrimum*
western soapberry *Sapindus drummondii*
western spiraea *Spiraea douglasii*

western sunray *Rhodanthe troedelii*
western sword fern *Polystichum munitum*
western sycamore *Platanus racemosa*
western trillium *Trillium ovatum*
western white pine *Pinus monticola*
western wild rose *Rosa woodsii*
western wild rye *Elymus canadensis*
western woody pear *Xylomelum occidentale*
western yellow pine *Pinus ponderosa*
westringia, short-leafed *Westringia brevifolia*
westringia, slender *Westringia eremicola*
westringia, violet *Westringia glabra*
wet-a-bed *Taraxacum officinale*
whalebone tree *Streblus brunonianus*
wharangi *Melicope ternata*
whau *Entelea arborescens*
wheat *Triticum*
wheat, bread *Triticum aestivum*
wheat, durum *Triticum turgidum* Durum Group
wheat, emmer *Triticum turgidum* Durum Group
wheat, Inca *Chenopodium quinoa*
wheatgrass *Elymus*
wheatgrass, blue *Elymus magellanicus*
wheatgrass, Magellan *Elymus magellanicus*
wheatgrass, rough *Elymus scaber*
Wheatley elm *Ulmus* 'Sarniensis'
wheel tree *Trochodendron aralioides*
wheki *Dicksonia squarrosa*
wheki-ponga *Dicksonia fibrosa*
whin *Ulex europaeus*
whin, petty *Genista anglica*
whip vine *Flagellaria indica*
whipcord hebe *Hebe cupressoides*
whipstick mallee ash *Eucalyptus multicaulis*

whiskers, cat's *Orthosiphon aristatus,*
O. stamineus
whiskers, old man's *Caustis flexuosa,*
Geum triflorum
whisky grass *Andropogon virginicus*
whistling tree *Acacia seyal*
white alder *Alnus rhombifolia,*
Clethra acuminata
white ash *Eucalyptus fraxinoides,*
Fraxinus americana
white aster *Aster engelmannii*
white baneberry *Actaea alba*
white Banks' rose, double *Rosa*
banksiae 'Alboplena'
white basswood *Tilia heterophylla*
white bat flower *Tacca integrifolia*
white bean *Ailanthus triphysa*
white beech *Gmelina leichardtii*
white birch *Betula pendula,*
B. papyrifera, Schizomeria ovata
white birch, European *Betula*
pendula
white birch, Japanese *Betula*
platyphylla var. *japonica*
white birch, Manchurian *Betula*
platyphylla var. *platyphylla*
white bloodwood *Corymbia*
trachyphloia
white bluebell *Hyacinthoides*
hispanica 'Alba'
white bolly gum *Neolitsea dealbata*
white booyong *Argyrodendron*
trifoliolatum
white bottlebrush *Callistemon*
salignus
white bouvardia *Bouvardia longiflora*
white box *Eucalyptus albens*
white breath of heaven *Coleonema*
album
white brittle gum *Eucalyptus*
mannifera
white broom *Retama monosperma,*
R. raetam

white butterbur *Petasites albus*
white butterfly bush *Bauhinia*
variegata 'Candida'
white caladenia *Caladenia alba*
white cat's whiskers *Clerodendrum*
glabrum
white cedar *Melia azederach, Thuja*
occidentalis
white cedar, Atlantic *Chamaecyparis*
thyoides
white cedar, coast *Chamaecyparis*
thyoides
white champaca *Michelia* × *alba*
white cheesewood *Alstonia scholaris*
white chervil *Cryptotaenia canadensis*
white Chinese wisteria *Wisteria*
sinensis 'Alba'
white cinnamon *Canella winteriana*
white cinquefoil *Potentilla alba*
white cloud tree *Melaleuca decora*
white clover *Trifolium repens*
white confetti bush *Coleonema*
album
white coralberry *Ardisia crenata*
'Alba'
white correa *Correa alba*
white cotton bush *Pimelea nivea*
white cushion daisy *Celmisia*
sessiliflora
white cypress *Chamaecyparis thyoides*
white cypress-pine *Callitris*
glaucophylla
white daisy, large *Brachycome*
campylocarpa
white dead-nettle *Lamium album*
white dipladenia *Mandevilla*
boliviensis
white dogtooth violet *Erythronium*
albidum
white dogwood *Ozothamnus*
diosmifolius
white elm *Ulmus americana*
white escallonia *Escallonia bifida*

white evening primrose *Oenothera caespitosa, O. speciosa*
white everlasting *Chrysocephalum baxteri*
white fairy lantern *Calochortus albus*
white false hellebore *Veratrum album*
white false indigo *Baptisia lactea*
white fir *Abies concolor*
white fir, Colorado *Abies concolor*
white fir, Pacific *Abies concolor* var. *lowiana*
white flowering quince *Chaenomeles speciosa* 'Nivalis'
white forsythia *Abeliophyllum distichum*
white foxtail *Ptilotus obovatus*
white frangipani *Plumeria obtusa*
white freesia *Freesia alba*
white ginger *Hedychium coronarium*
white globe lily *Calochortus albus*
white grevillea *Grevillea parallela*
white grub fern *Goniophlebium subauriculatum*
white gum *Eucalyptus alba, E. dalrympleana*
white gum, Bendemeer *Eucalyptus elliptica*
white gum, Dorrigo *Eucalyptus dorrigoensis*
white gum, Queensland *Eucalyptus argophloia*
white gum, Wallangarra *Eucalyptus scoparia*
white hairy wattle *Acacia centrinervia*
white hart hickory *Carya tomentosa*
white hibiscus, Hawaiian *Hibiscus arnottianus*
white horehound *Marrubium vulgare*
white ironwood *Vepris lanceolata*
white jasmine, common *Jasminum officinale*
white karee *Rhus viminalis*

white lace flower *Archidendron hendersonii*
white lily *Lilium candidum*
white lily, European *Nymphaea alba*
white lime, European *Tilia tomentosa*
white mahogany *Eucalyptus acmenoides*
white mahogany, bastard *Eucalyptus psammitica*
white mahogany, broad-leafed *Eucalyptus umbra*
white mahogany, narrow-leafed *Eucalyptus tenuipes*
white mallee *Eucalyptus dumosa*
white malletwood *Rhodamnia whiteana*
white mallow *Althaea officinalis*
white mangrove *Avicennia alba*
white maple *Acer saccharinum*
white Mexican rose *Echeveria elegans*
white mignonette *Reseda alba*
white milkwood *Sideroxylon inerme*
white mugwort *Artemisia lactiflora*
white mulberry *Morus alba*
white mule *Lophophora williamsii*
white musk mallow *Malva moschata* 'Alba'
white mustard *Sinapis alba*
white myrtle *Hypocalymma angustifolium, Rhodamnia argentea*
white narcissus, paper *Narcissus papyraceus*
white native iris *Diplarrena moraea*
white oak *Athertonia diversifolia, Lagunaria patersonia, Quercus alba*
white oak, American *Quercus alba*
white oak, California *Quercus lobata*
white oak, Oregon *Quercus garryana*
white oak, Rocky Mountain *Quercus gambelii*
white oak, swamp *Quercus bicolor*
white orchid tree *Bauhinia variegata* 'Candida'

white parsnip *Trachymene ochracea*

white passionfruit *Passiflora subpeltata*

white pear, South African *Apodytes dimidiata*

white perennial aster *Aster ericoides*

white petunia, large *Petunia axillaris*

white pine *Pinus strobus*

white pine, Chiapas *Pinus chiapensis*

white pine, Chinese *Pinus armandii*

white pine, eastern *Pinus strobus*

white pine, Japanese *Pinus parviflora*

white pine, Mexican *Pinus ayacahuite*

white pine, New Zealand *Dacrycarpus dacrydioides*

white pine, western *Pinus monticola*

white pineapple lily *Eucomis autumnalis*

white plumbago *Plumbago auriculata* 'Alba'

white plume grevillea *Grevillea leucopteris*

white popinac *Leucaena leucocephala*

white poplar *Populus alba*

white powderpuff *Calliandra portoricensis*

white purslane *Neopaxia australasica*

white quandong *Elaeocarpus kirtonii*

white rocket *Diplotaxis erucoides*

white rod *Viburnum cassinoides*

white rose of York *Rosa* × *alba*

white sage *Artemisia ludoviciana*

white sage, California *Salvia apiana*

white sails *Spathiphyllum wallisii*

white sally *Eucalyptus pauciflora*

white sandalwood *Santalum album*

white sapote *Casimiroa edulis*

white senna *Senna glutinosa*

white silky oak *Grevillea hilliana*

white siris *Ailanthus triphysa, Albizia lebbeck*

white snakeroot *Eupatorium rugosum*

white Spanish broom *Cytisus multiflorus*

white spruce *Picea glauca*

white spruce, dwarf Alberta *Picea glauca* var. *albertiana* 'Conica'

white star grass *Hypoxis capensis*

white stinkwood *Celtis africana*

white stringybark *Eucalyptus globoidea*

white stringybark, southern *Eucalyptus yangoura*

white sunray *Rhodanthe floribunda*

white sunray, small *Rhodanthe corymbiflora*

white supplejack *Ripogonum album*

white swamp azalea *Rhododendron viscosum*

white tamarind *Elattostachys xylocarpa*

white tassel flower *Calliandra portoricensis*

white thistle *Atriplex lentiformis*

white thorn *Acacia polyacantha, Crataegus laevigata*

white trumpet *Sarracenia leucophylla*

white velvet *Tradescantia sillamontana*

white violet, sweet *Viola blanda*

white violet, woodland *Viola blanda*

white walnut *Juglans cinerea*

white waratah *Agastachys odorata*

white water buttercup *Ranunculus aquatilis*

white water panic *Panicum obseptum*

white waxberry *Gaultheria appressa*

white willow *Salix alba*

white yam *Dioscorea alata*

white yiel-yiel *Grevillea hilliana*

whitebark *Betula utilis*

white-bark magnolia *Magnolia hypoleuca*

whitebark pine *Pinus albicaulis*

whitebeam *Sorbus aria*

whitebeam, dwarf *Sorbus chamaemespilus*

whitebeam, Himalayan *Sorbus vestita*
whitebeam, large-fruited *Sorbus megalocarpa*
whitebeam, Swedish *Sorbus intermedia*
whitebeard *Leucopogon setiger*
white-flowered currant *Ribes indecorum*
white-flowered gourd *Lagenaria siceraria*
white-flowered paulownia *Paulownia fortunei*
whiteroot *Pratia purpurascens*
white-spined prickly pear *Opuntia leucotricha*
white-stemmed gooseberry *Ribes inerme*
white-striped bamboo, dwarf *Pleioblastus variegatus*
whitethorn, coast *Ceanothus incanus*
white-tip nightshade *Solanum chenopodioides*
white-top *Austrodanthonia caespitosa*
white-topped box *Eucalyptus quadrangulata*
whitewood *Atalaya hemiglauca*
whiteywood *Acradenia frankliniae, Melicytus ramiflorus*
whitlow grass *Draba, Erophila verna*
whitlow wort, Chilean *Paronychia brasiliana*
whorled mint *Mentha* × *verticillata*
whorlflower *Morina longifolia*
whortleberry *Vaccinium myrtillus*
whortleberry, bog *Vaccinium uliginosum*
whortleberry, Madeira *Vaccinium padifolium*
whortleberry, red *Vaccinium parvifolium*
Wickham's grevillea *Grevillea wickhamii*
wicopy *Dirca palustris*

widow, black *Geranium phaeum*
widow iris *Hermodactylus tuberosus*
widow, mournful *Scabiosa atropurpurea*
widow's tears *Commelina*
wild almond, South African *Brabejum stellatifolium*
wild aster *Aster subulatus, Felicia filifolia*
wild banana *Musa balbisiana*
wild beet *Beta vulgaris* subsp. *maritima*
wild bleeding heart *Dicentra formosa*
wild buckwheat *Eriogonum*
wild buckwheat, shrubby *Eriogonum wrightii*
wild cabbage *Brassica oleracea*
wild Canterbury bell *Phacelia campanularia*
wild carrot *Daucus carota*
wild catmint *Nepeta cataria*
wild celery *Apium graveolens*
wild chamomile *Matricaria recutita*
wild cherry *Prunus avium*
wild China tree *Sapindus drummondii*
wild coffee *Psychotria capensis*
wild columbine, American *Aquilegia canadensis*
wild cotton, Australian *Gossypium australe*
wild crabapple *Malus sylvestris*
wild cranberry *Vaccinium oxycoccos*
wild currant *Rhus pyroides*
wild daffodil *Narcissus pseudonarcissus*
wild dagga *Leonotis leonurus*
wild date, African *Phoenix reclinata*
wild date, Indian *Phoenix sylvestris*
wild elder *Nuxia congesta*
wild fennel *Nigella*
wild fig, common *Ficus thonningii*
wild fig, West Asian *Ficus palmata*
wild flax *Linum marginale*

wild gardenia *Rothmannia capensis*
wild garlic *Allium cratericola,*
  Tulbaghia, T. violacea
wild geranium *Pelargonium australe*
wild ginger *Asarum*
wild gladiolus *Gladiolus undulatus*
wild goose plum *Prunus munsoniana*
wild gooseberry *Solanum ellipticum*
wild grape, California *Vitis californica*
wild hippo *Euphorbia corollata*
wild honeysuckle *Turraea floribunda*
wild hyacinth *Hyacinthoides non-*
  scripta, Lachenalia contaminata
wild hyssop *Pycnanthemum*
  virginianum
wild indigo *Baptisia*
wild indigo, Atlantic *Baptisia lactea*
wild ipecac *Euphorbia corollata*
wild iris *Dietes grandiflora*
wild Irishman *Discaria toumatou*
wild jasmine *Schrebera alata*
wild leek *Allium ampeloprasum*
wild lemon *Canthium latifolium,*
  C. oleifolium
wild lilac *Ceanothus sanguineus*
wild lupine *Lupinus perennis*
wild marigold *Baileya multiradiata*
wild marjoram *Origanum vulgare*
wild medlar *Vangueria infausta*
wild melon *Citrullus lanatus*
wild mignonette *Reseda lutea*
wild oats *Avena fatua, Uvularia*
  sessilifolia
wild oats, ludo *Avena ludoviciana*
wild onion *Allium cernuum, Bulbine*
  bulbosa
wild onion, pink *Allium acuminatum*
wild opium poppy *Papaver*
  somniferum subsp. *setigerum*
wild orange *Capparis canescens,*
  C. mitchellii, Prunus caroliniana
wild parsley *Hydrocotyle trachycarpa*
wild parsnip *Trachymene ochracea*

wild passionflower *Passiflora*
  incarnata
wild pea *Lathyrus*
wild peach, South African *Kiggelaria*
  africana
wild pear *Dombeya rotundifolia,*
  Pyrus pyraster
wild pear, pink *Dombeya burgessiae*
wild pear, South African *Dombeya*
  rotundifolia
wild pineapple *Ananas bracteatus*
wild plantain *Heliconia, Heliconia*
  bihai, H. caribaea
wild plum *Podocarpus drouynianus,*
  Pouteria australis, Prunus americana
wild plum, South African
  Harpephyllum caffrum
wild poppy *Papaver × hybridum*
wild radish *Raphanus raphanistrum*
wild raisin *Viburnum cassinoides,*
  V. lentago
wild raspberry *Rubus idaeus*
wild rhubarb *Rumex hymenosepalus*
wild rice *Zizania aquatica*
wild rose, western *Rosa woodsii*
wild rosemary *Eriocephalus africanus,*
  Ledum palustre
wild rye *Elymus*
wild rye, blue *Elymus canadensis,*
  E. glaucus
wild rye, Canada *Elymus canadensis*
wild rye, giant *Elymus condensatus*
wild rye, mountain *Elymus canadensis*
wild rye, western *Elymus canadensis*
wild sage *Salvia verbenaca*
wild sarsaparilla *Hardenbergia*
  comptoniana
wild senna *Senna hebecarpa*
wild service tree *Sorbus torminalis*
wild sesame *Perilla frutescens*
wild Spaniard *Aciphylla colensoi*
wild stock *Blennodia canescens*
wild strawberry *Fragaria vesca*

wild sweet William *Phlox divaricata,*
P. maculata
wild tepary bean *Phaseolus*
acutifolius
wild thyme *Thymus serpyllum*
wild tobacco *Solanum mauritianum*
wild turmeric *Curcuma aromatica*
wild wisteria vine *Hardenbergia*
comptoniana
wildepruim *Harpephyllum caffrum*
wildevy, gewone *Ficus thonningii*
wilga *Geijera parviflora*
wilga, brush *Geijera salicifolia*
Wilhelm's wattle *Acacia wilhelmiana*
wilkiea, veiny *Wilkiea huegeliana*
Willdenow violet *Viola blanda*
William, sweet *Dianthus barbatus*
Williamtown red gum *Eucalyptus*
parramattensis subsp. *decadens*
willow *Salix*
willow, Alaska blue *Salix purpurea*
willow, Arctic *Salix arctica, S. lanata,*
S. purpurea
willow, Arctic creeping *Salix reptans*
willow, Arctic gray *Salix glauca*
willow, Arizona *Salix irrorata*
willow, arroyo *Salix lasiolepis*
willow, Australian *Geijera parviflora*
willow, Babylon weeping *Salix*
babylonica
willow, balsam *Salix pyrifolia*
willow, basket *Salix purpurea*
willow, bay *Salix pentandra*
willow, beaked *Salix bebbiana*
willow, bearberry *Salix uva-ursi*
willow bell *Campanula persicifolia*
willow bellflower *Campanula*
persicifolia
willow, black *Salix nigra*
willow, brittle *Salix fragilis*
willow, Caspian *Salix acutifolia*
willow, common primrose *Ludwigia*
peruviana

willow, contorted *Salix babylonica*
'Tortuosa'
willow, coyote *Salix exigua*
willow, crack *Salix fragilis*
willow, creeping *Salix repens*
willow, dappled *Salix integra*
willow, dark-leafed *Salix nigricans*
willow, desert *Chilopsis linearis*
willow, flame *Salix* 'Flame'
willow, florist's *Salix caprea*
willow, French *Epilobium*
angustifolium
willow gentian *Gentiana asclepiadea*
willow, goat *Salix caprea*
willow, gold-twig *Salix alba* 'Aurea'
willow, gray *Salix cinerea*
willow hakea *Hakea salicifolia*
willow, halberd *Salix hastata*
willow, hemp *Salix viminalis*
willow herb *Epilobium*
willow, hoary *Salix elaeagnos*
willow, Indian *Polyalthia longifolia*
willow, Japanese *Salix integra*
willow, Java *Ficus virens*
willow, laurel *Salix pentandra*
willow, Mupin *Salix moupinensis*
willow, musk *Salix aegyptiaca*
willow myrtle *Agonis flexuosa*
willow, native *Acacia salicina,*
A. stenophylla, Callistachys lanceolata
willow, net-leaf *Salix reticulata*
willow oak *Quercus phellos*
willow, peach-leafed *Salix*
amygdaloides
willow, Peking *Salix babylonica*
willow, pencil *Salix humboldtiana*
willow, Peruvian primrose *Ludwigia*
peruviana
willow, pinkpussy *Salix caprea*
willow podocarp *Podocarpus salignus*
willow, polished *Salix laevigata*
willow, Port Jackson *Acacia saligna*
willow primrose *Ludwigia octovalvis*

willow, pussy *Salix caprea,*
S. *cinerea*
willow, red *Salix laevigata*
willow rhus *Rhus lancea*
willow, rosemary *Salix elaeagnos*
willow, sage *Salix candida*
willow, sandbar *Salix exigua,*
S. *interior*
willow, sharp-leafed *Salix acutifolia*
willow, shiny *Salix lucida*
willow, silky *Salix sericea*
willow, South American *Salix
humboldtiana*
willow, Swiss *Salix helvetica*
willow, thyme-leafed *Salix
serpyllifolia*
willow, violet *Salix daphnoides*
willow, Virginia *Itea virginica*
willow, weeping *Salix babylonica*
willow, white *Salix alba*
willow, Wisconsin weeping *Salix* ×
pendulina
willow, woolly *Salix lanata*
willow, yellow-twig *Salix alba*
'Chermesina'
willow-herb, smooth *Epilobium
billardierianum*
willow-leafed foxglove *Digitalis
obscura*
willow-leafed lettuce *Lactuca
saligna*
willow-leafed magnolia *Magnolia
salicifolia*
willow-leafed oak *Quercus phellos*
willow-leafed pear *Pyrus salicifolia*
willowmore cedar *Widdringtonia
schwarzii*
willow-myrtle *Agonis flexuosa*
Wilson barberry *Berberis wilsoniae*
Wilson's grevillea *Grevillea wilsonii*
Wilson's magnolia *Magnolia wilsonii*
Wilson's spruce *Picea wilsonii*
Wimmera ryegrass *Lolium rigidum*

wind grass, New Zealand *Stipa
arundinacea*
wind poppy *Anemone coronaria,
Stylomecon heterophyllus*
windflower *Anemone, A. coronaria,
A. nemorosa*
windflower, snowdrop *Anemone
sylvestris*
windmill grass *Chloris truncata*
windmill grass, curly *Enteropogon
acicularis*
windmill grass, tall *Chloris ventricosa*
windmill palm *Trachycarpus fortunei*
window bellflower *Campanula
fenestrellata*
window palm *Reinhardtia gracilis*
window plant *Fenestraria aurantiaca,
F. rhopalophylla*
windowleaf *Monstera*
windows, cathedral *Calathea
makoyana*
wine cups *Babiana rubrocyanea,
Callirhoe involucrata*
wine grape *Vitis vinifera*
wine palm *Pseudophoenix vinifera*
wine palm, Chilean *Jubaea chilensis*
wine palm, Hispaniolan
Pseudophoenix vinifera
wineberry *Aristotelia, A. serrata*
wineberry, mountain *Aristotelia
australasica*
winged broom *Genista sagittalis*
winged cassia *Cassia alata*
winged elm *Ulmus alata*
winged everlasting *Ammobium
alatum*
winged nepenthes *Nepenthes alata*
winged peppercress *Lepidium
monoplocoides*
winged sea lavender *Limonium
lobatum*
winged slender thistle *Carduus
tenuiflorus*

winged spindle tree *Euonymus alatus*
wing-leaf soapberry *Sapindus saponaria*
wingless fissure-weed *Maireana enchylaenoides*
wingnut, Caucasian *Pterocarya fraxinifolia*
wingnut, Japanese *Pterocarya rhoifolia*
wings, angel *Caladium bicolor*
wingwort *Ceratogyne obionoides*
winter aconite *Eranthis*
winter apple *Eremophila debilis*
winter buddleja *Buddleja salviifolia*
winter cherry *Physalis alkekengi, Solanum capsicastrum*
winter currant *Ribes sanguineum*
winter daphne *Daphne odora*
winter grape, sweet *Vitis cinerea*
winter grass *Poa annua*
winter heath *Erica carnea*
winter honeysuckle *Lonicera fragrantissima*
winter iris *Iris unguicularis*
winter jasmine *Jasminum nudiflorum*
winter marguerite *Coreopsis maritima*
winter mint *Mentha × villosa*
winter poker *Kniphofia ensifolia*
winter pumpkin *Cucurbita maxima*
winter purslane *Montia perfoliata*
winter rose *Helleborus*
winter savory *Satureja montana*
winter scouring-rush *Equisetum hyemale*
winter squash *Cucurbita moschata*
winterberry *Ilex decidua, I. verticillata*
winterberry, Japanese *Ilex serrata*
winterberry, mountain *Ilex montana*
winterberry, smooth *Ilex laevigata*
wintercreeper euonymus *Euonymus fortunei*
wintercress *Barbarea verna*
wintercress, Australian *Barbarea grayi*

winterfat *Krascheninnikovia lanata*
winterfat, Pamirian *Krascheninnikovia ceratoides*
wintergreen *Gaultheria, G. procumbens*
wintergreen barberry *Berberis julianae*
wintergreen, spotted *Chimaphila umbellata*
winter-hazel, buttercup *Corylopsis pauciflora*
winter-hazel, Chinese *Corylopsis sinensis*
winter-hazel, fragrant *Corylopsis glabrescens*
winter-hazel, spike *Corylopsis spicata*
Winter's bark *Drimys winteri*
wintersweet *Acokanthera oblongifolia, Chimonanthus praecox*
wintersweet, variegated *Acokanthera oblongifolia* 'Variegata'
wire lily, slender *Laxmannia gracilis*
wire vine *Muehlenbeckia complexa*
wiregrass *Aristida*
wiregrass, bunch *Aristida behriana*
wiregrass, dark *Aristida calycina*
wiregrass, Jericho *Aristida jerichoensis*
wiregrass, purple *Aristida ramosa*
wire-netting bush *Corokia cotoneaster*
wires-and-wool *Lemooria burkittii*
wireweed *Polygonum arenastrum, P. aviculare*
wirewood *Acacia coriacea*
wirilda *Acacia retinodes*
wiry panic *Entolasia stricta*
wiry rice-grass *Tetrarrhena juncea*
Wisconsin weeping willow *Salix × pendulina*
wishbone flower *Torenia fournieri*
wisteria, African tree *Bolusanthus speciosus*
wisteria, American *Wisteria frutescens*
wisteria, Australian *Millettia megasperma*

wisteria, Chinese *Wisteria sinensis*
wisteria, double Japanese *Wisteria floribunda* 'Violaceo-plena'
wisteria, Japanese *Wisteria floribunda*
wisteria, Kentucky *Wisteria macrostachya*
wisteria, native *Millettia megasperma*
wisteria shrub, orange *Sesbania punicea*
wisteria, silky *Wisteria brachybotrys*
wisteria, tree *Bolusanthus speciosus*
wisteria tree, scarlet *Sesbania grandiflora*
wisteria vine, wild *Hardenbergia comptoniana*
witch hazel *Hamamelis*
witch hazel, Chinese *Hamamelis mollis*
witch hazel, common *Hamamelis virginiana*
witch hazel, hybrid *Hamamelis × intermedia*
witch hazel, Japanese *Hamamelis japonica*
witch hazel, Ozark *Hamamelis vernalis*
witch hazel, Persian *Parrotia persica*
witch hazel, southern *Hamamelis macrophylla*
witch hazel, vernal *Hamamelis vernalis*
witch, Molly the *Paeonia mlokosewitschii*
witchgrass *Panicum capillare*
withe-rod *Viburnum cassinoides*
withe-rod, smooth *Viburnum nudum*
witloof *Cichorium intybus*
woad *Isatis*
woad, dyer's *Isatis tinctoria*
woadwaxen, common *Genista tinctoria*
woadwaxen, silky *Genista pilosa*
woadwaxen, silky leaf *Genista pilosa*

Woila gum *Eucalyptus olsenii*
wolfberry, pale *Lycium pallidum*
Wolgan snow gum *Eucalyptus gregsoniana*
Wollemi pine *Wollemia nobilis*
woman's tongue tree *Albizia lebbeck*
wombat berry *Eustrephus latifolius*
wonder tree *Idesia polycarpa*
wonga vine *Pandorea pandorana*
wonga wonga vine *Pandorea pandorana*
woo chu *Lactuca sativa* var. *augustana*
wood anemone *Anemone nemorosa*
wood apple, Indian *Limonia acidissima*
wood avens *Geum urbanum*
wood betony *Stachys officinalis*
wood bittercress *Cardamine flexuosa*
wood, Brazil *Caesalpinia echinata*
wood, carrot *Canarium australasicum*
wood, celery *Polyscias elegans*
wood, Chaka's *Strychnos decussata*
wood, cocus *Brya ebenus*
wood, deep yellow *Rhodosphaera rhodanthema*
wood fern *Dryopteris*
wood fern, crested *Dryopteris cristata*
wood fern, Japanese *Dryopteris sieboldii*
wood fern, leather *Dryopteris marginalis*
wood fern, marginal *Dryopteris marginalis*
wood fern, Wallich's *Dryopteris wallichiana*
wood forget-me-not *Myosotis sylvatica*
wood germander *Teucrium scorodonia*
wood grass *Sorghastrum nutans*
wood, holly *Auranticarpa rhombifolia*, *Heteromeles arbutifolia*
wood horsetail *Equisetum sylvaticum*
wood, kodo *Ehretia acuminata*

wood lily *Trillium*
wood merrybells *Uvularia perfoliata*
wood millet *Milium effusum*
wood oil tree, Japan *Aleurites cordata*
wood, Pernambuco *Caesalpinia echinata*
wood poppy *Stylophorum diphyllum*
wood, quassia *Picrasma excelsa*
wood rose *Rosa gymnocarpa*
wood rose, baby *Argyreia nervosa*
wood sage *Teucrium canadense, T. scorodonia*
wood, Shawnee *Catalpa speciosa*
wood, snake *Colubrina arborescens*
wood sorrel *Oxalis acetosella*
wood sorrel, red *Oxalis oregana*
wood spurge *Euphorbia amygdaloides*
wood trillium *Trillium luteum*
wood violet *Viola riviniana*
woodbine *Lonicera periclymenum*
woodland iris *Iris ensata*
woodland phlox *Phlox adsurgens*
woodland white violet *Viola blanda*
woodlouse cactus *Pelecyphora aselliformis*
wood-oil tree *Aleurites montana*
woodruff *Asperula, Galium, G. odoratum*
woodruff, blue *Asperula orientalis*
woodruff, mountain *Asperula gunnii*
woodruff, prickly *Asperula scoparia*
woodruff, sweet *Galium odoratum*
woodrush *Luzula flaccida*
woodrush, Canary Islands *Luzula canariensis*
woods, flame of the *Ixora coccinea*
wood-sage *Teucrium scorodonia*
woodsia, fragrant *Woodsia ilvensis*
woodsia, rusty *Woodsia ilvensis*
wood-sorrel *Oxalis articulata*
wood-sorrel, large-flowered *Oxalis purpurea*

wood-sorrel, yellow *Oxalis corniculata*
woody pear *Xylomelum pyriforme*
woody pear, sandplain *Xylomelum angustifolium*
woody pear, western *Xylomelum occidentale*
woodypod wattle *Acacia crassicarpa*
woolflower *Celosia*
woollsia *Woollsia pungens*
woolly banksia *Banksia baueri*
woolly betony *Stachys byzantina*
woolly blue curls *Trichostema lanatum*
woolly burr-medic, small *Medicago minima*
woolly buttons *Leptorhynchos panaetioides*
woolly cloak fern *Cheilanthes lasiophylla*
woolly clover *Trifolium tomentosum*
woolly copperburr *Sclerolaena lanicuspis*
woolly cycad *Encephalartos friderici-guilielmi*
woolly grevillea *Grevillea lanigera*
woolly lavender *Lavandula lanata*
woolly mantle *Eriochlamys behrii*
woolly manzanita *Arctostaphylos tomentosa*
woolly mint *Mentha suaveolens*
woolly mother-of-thyme *Thymus pseudolanuginosus*
woolly mullein *Verbascum thapsus*
woolly pear-fruit *Mischocarpus lachnocarpus*
woolly pomaderris *Pomaderris lanigera*
woolly rambutan *Alectryon tomentosus*
woolly rice flower *Pimelea octophylla*
woolly star-hair *Astrotricha floccosa*
woolly sundew *Drosera petiolaris*
woolly sunflower *Eriophyllum lanatum*

woolly sunray *Rhodanthe uniflora*
woolly tea-tree *Leptospermum grandifolium, L. lanigerum*
woolly thyme *Thymus pseudolanuginosus*
woolly tree fern *Cyathea woollsiana*
woolly waterlily *Philydrum lanuginosum*
woolly wattle *Acacia lanigera*
woolly willow *Salix lanata*
woollybush, Albany *Adenanthos cunninghamii, A. sericeus*
woollybush, coastal *Adenanthos sericeus*
woollybush, common *Adenanthos cygnorum*
woollybutt *Eucalyptus longifolia*
woollybutt, Camden *Eucalyptus macarthurii*
woollybutt, Darwin *Eucalyptus miniata*
woollybutt grass *Eragrostis eriopoda*
woollybutt, Tenterfield *Eucalyptus banksii*
woolly-fruit copperburr *Maireana sclerolaenoides*
woolly-head mat-rush *Lomandra leucocephala*
woolly-heads *Myriocephalus pluriflorus, M. rhizocephalus*
woolly-podded broom *Cytisus grandiflorus*
wormseed *Chenopodium ambrosioides*
wormwood *Artemisia absinthium*
wormwood, beach *Artemisia stelleriana*
wormwood, Canary Island *Artemisia canariensis*

wormwood, Chinese *Artemisia verlotiorum*
wormwood, common *Artemisia absinthium*
wormwood, Roman *Artemisia pontica*
wormwood, shrub *Artemisia arborescens*
wormwood, silver *Artemisia ludoviciana*
wormwood, silvery *Artemisia filifolia*
wort, bishop's *Stachys officinalis*
wort, Chinese St John's *Hypericum monogynum*
wort, St John's *Hypericum perforatum*
wort, swallow *Asclepias curassavica*
woundwort *Stachys*
woundwort, hedge *Stachys sylvatica*
wreath, bridal *Francoa, Spiraea, S. 'Arguta', S. × vanhouttei*
wreath leschenaultia *Leschenaultia macrantha*
wreath nasturtium *Tropaeolum polyphyllum*
wreath, purple *Petrea volubilis*
wreath, queen's *Petrea volubilis*
Wright's buckwheat *Eriogonum wrightii*
wrinkled giant hyssop *Agastache rugosa*
wrinklenut twig-rush *Baumea teretifolia*
wrinklewort, gray *Rutidosis helichrysoides*
wunu *Lepidozamia hopei*
Wyalong wattle *Acacia cardiophylla*
wych elm *Ulmus glabra*
wych elm, weeping *Ulmus glabra* 'Pendula'

Y

yabunikkei *Cinnamomum japonicum*
yacon *Polymnia sonchifolia*
yadbila grass *Panicum queenslandicum*
yam *Dioscorea*
yam, aerial *Dioscorea bulbifera*
yam bean *Pachyrhizus erosus,
    P. tuberosus*
yam, blue *Brunoniella australis*
yam, Chinese *Dioscorea batatas,
    D. esculenta, D. opposita*
yam daisy *Microseris lanceolata*
yam, elephant's foot *Amorphophallus
    paeoniifolius, Dioscorea elephantipes*
yam, greater *Dioscorea alata*
yam, lesser *Dioscorea esculenta*
yam, native *Dioscorea transversa*
yam, New Zealand *Oxalis tuberosa*
yam, Otaheite *Dioscorea bulbifera*
yam, potato *Dioscorea esculenta*
yam, water *Dioscorea alata*
yam, white *Dioscorea alata*
yanganbil *Austrostipa bigeniculata*
yang-tao *Actinidia arguta*
yanquapin *Nelumbo lutea*
yantao *Actinidia deliciosa*
yapunyah *Corymbia ochrophloia*
yapunyah, mountain *Eucalyptus
    thozetiana*
yard-long bean *Vigna unguiculata*
    subsp. *sesquipedalis*
yarey *Copernicia baileyana*
yarey hembra *Copernicia baileyana*
yarran *Acacia homalophylla*
yarreyon *Copernicia baileyana*
yarri *Eucalyptus patens*
yarrow *Achillea, A. millefolium*
yarrow, crimson *Achillea millefolium*
    'Cerise Queen'
yarrow, golden *Eriophyllum lanatum*

yatay palm *Butia yatay*
yate *Eucalyptus cornuta*
yate, bushy *Eucalyptus
    conferruminata, E. lehmannii*
yate, warty *Eucalyptus megacornuta*
yaupon *Ilex vomitoria*
yautia *Xanthosoma*
yayih *Euterpe edulis*
Yeddo euonymus *Euonymus
    hamiltonianus*
yellow adder's tongue *Erythronium
    americanum*
yellow alyssum *Aurinia saxatilis*
yellow archangel *Lamium
    galeobdolon*
yellow arum *Zantedeschia elliottiana*
yellow ash *Emmenosperma
    alphitonioides*
yellow asphodel *Asphodeline lutea*
yellow avens *Geum aleppicum*
yellow bachelor's buttons *Ranunculus
    acris* 'Flore Pleno'
yellow bamboo *Phyllostachys aurea*
yellow bark oak *Quercus velutina*
yellow bedstraw *Galium verum*
yellow bell bauhinia *Bauhinia
    tomentosa*
yellow bells *Tecoma stans*
yellow billy buttons *Calocephalus
    platycephalus*
yellow birch *Betula alleghaniensis,
    B. lutea*
yellow bloodwood *Corymbia eximia*
yellow box *Eucalyptus melliodora*
yellow buckeye *Aesculus flava*
yellow buckwheat *Eriogonum flavum*
yellow burr-daisy *Calotis
    cymbacantha, C. lappulacea*
yellow bush lupine *Lupinus arboreus*
yellow butterfly weed *Solidago
    confinis*
yellow buttons *Chrysocephalum
    apiculatum, C. semipapposum*

yellow calla *Zantedeschia elliottiana*
yellow catalpa *Catalpa ovata*
yellow chamomile *Anthemis tinctoria*
yellow chestnut oak *Quercus muehlenbergii*
yellow climbing bell *Littonia modesta*
yellow coneflower *Ratibida pinnata*
yellow cosmos *Cosmos sulphureus*
yellow cucumber tree *Magnolia cordata*
yellow day lily *Hemerocallis citrina*
yellow elder *Tecoma stans*
yellow fairy bells *Disporum uniflorum*
yellow flag *Iris pseudoacorus*
yellow flame grevillea *Grevillea eriostachya*
yellow flame tree *Peltophorum pterocarpum*
yellow flax bush *Reinwardtia indica*
yellow floating heart *Nymphoides peltata*
yellow forget-me-not *Amsinckia intermedia*
yellow foxglove, large *Digitalis grandiflora*
yellow garland lily *Calostemma luteum*
yellow ginger *Hedychium gardnerianum*
yellow granadilla *Passiflora laurifolia*
yellow groove bamboo *Phyllostachys aureosulcata*
yellow gum *Eucalyptus cypellocarpa, E. leucoxylon*
yellow gum, Tasmanian *Eucalyptus johnstonii*
yellow hakea *Hakea arborescens, H. nodosa*
yellow horned poppy *Glaucium flavum*
yellow ipomoea *Ochna natalitia*
yellow jasmine *Jasminum mesnyi*
yellow jessamine *Gelsemium sempervirens*

yellow jugflower *Adenanthos detmoldii*
yellow kangaroo paw *Anigozanthos flavidus*
yellow kapok *Cochlospermum fraseri*
yellow kowhai *Sophora tetraptera*
yellow kunzea *Kunzea muelleri*
yellow latan palm *Latania verschaffeltii*
yellow leek orchid *Prasophyllum flavum*
yellow mangosteen *Garcinia xanthochymus*
yellow mangrove *Ceriops australis*
yellow marguerite *Argyranthemum maderense*
yellow Mariposa tulip *Calochortus luteus*
yellow meadow-rue *Thalictrum flavum*
yellow mignonette *Reseda lutea*
yellow milk bush *Euphorbia mauritanica*
yellow monkey flower *Mimulus luteus*
yellow morning glory *Ipomoea ochracea*
yellow oak *Quercus muehlenbergii*
yellow oleander *Thevetia peruviana*
yellow oleander, large-flowered *Thevetia thevetioides*
yellow onion, small *Allium flavum*
yellow parilla *Menispermum canadense*
yellow pea *Senna clavigera*
yellow pear-fruit *Mischocarpus pyriformis*
yellow pine *Halocarpus biformis*
yellow pine, western *Pinus ponderosa*
yellow pittosporum *Pittosporum revolutum*
yellow plumwood *Pouteria myrsinoides*

yellow primrose, plains *Calylophus serrulatus*

yellow puccoon *Hydrastis canadensis*

yellow rattle pod *Crotalaria mitchellii*

yellow rocket *Leucospermum reflexum*

yellow rose, Afghan *Rosa primula*

yellow rush lily *Tricoryne elatior*

yellow satinheart *Acradenia euodiiformis*

yellow shellflower bush *Bowkeria citrina*

yellow silver pine *Lepidothamnus intermedius*

yellow skunk cabbage *Lysichiton americanus*

yellow star *Lindheimera texana*

yellow stars *Hypoxis villosa*

yellow stringybark *Eucalyptus muelleriana*

yellow suckling clover *Trifolium dubium*

yellow swamp orchid *Phaius barnaysii*

yellow tea-tree *Leptospermum polygalifolium*

yellow top *Calocephalus platycephalus*

yellow tree peony *Paeonia lutea*

yellow trumpet *Sarracenia flava*

yellow trumpet flower *Tecoma stans*

yellow trumpet tree *Tecoma stans*

yellow tulipwood *Drypetes australasica*

yellow twin-heads *Eclipta platyglossa*

yellow vine *Tribulus micrococcus*

yellow wake robin *Trillium luteum*

yellow waterlily *Nuphar lutea*

yellow wood, Chinese *Cladrastis sinensis*

yellow wood-sorrel *Oxalis corniculata*

yellow-berry bush *Maytenus cunninghamii*

yellowbush *Leucadendron comosum*

yellow-eye, slender *Xyris gracilis*

yellow-eye, tall *Xyris operculata*

yellow-eyed grass *Sisyrinchium palmifolium*

yellow-fruited thorn *Crataegus flava*

yellow-groove bamboo *Phyllostachys aureosulcata*

yellowjacket, large-fruited *Corymbia watsoniana*

yellowroot *Xanthorhiza simplicissima*

yellow-stemmed bamboo *Bambusa vulgaris, B. v.* 'Striata'

yellow-striped bamboo *Bambusa multiplex* 'Yellowstripe'

yellow-tails *Ptilotus nobilis*

yellow-top ash *Eucalyptus luehmanniana*

yellow-twig willow *Salix alba* 'Chermesina'

yellowwood *Cladrastis lutea, C. kentuckeana, Flindersia xanthoxyla, Podocarpus latifolius*

yellowwood, American *Cladrastris lutea*

yellowwood, bastard *Afrocarpus falcatus*

yellowwood, Breede River *Podocarpus elongatus*

yellowwood, Cape *Podocarpus elongatus*

yellowwood, deep *Rhodosphaera rhodanthema*

yellowwood, falcate *Podocarpus henkelii*

yellowwood, Japanese *Cladrastis platycarpa*

yellowwood, Outeniqua *Afrocarpus falcatus*

yellowwood, thorny *Zanthoxylum brachyacanthum*

yerba mansa *Anemopsis californica*

yerba maté *Ilex paraguariensis*

yerba santa *Eriodictyon californicum, Eryngium foetidum*

yertchuk *Eucalyptus consideniana*
yesterday, today and tomorrow
  Brunfelsia australis
yew *Taxus*
yew, Anglo-jap *Taxus × media*
yew, California nutmeg *Torreya*
  californica
yew, Canadian *Taxus canadensis*
yew, Chinese *Taxus chinensis*
yew, common *Taxus baccata*
yew, English *Taxus baccata*
yew, Florida *Taxus floridana*
yew, golden *Taxus baccata* 'Aurea'
yew, gold-tip *Taxus baccata*
  'Fastigiata Aureomarginata'
yew, Himalayan *Taxus wallichiana*
yew, hybrid *Taxus × media*
yew, Irish *Taxus baccata* 'Fastigiata'
yew, Japanese *Taxus cuspidata*
yew, Japanese nutmeg *Torreya*
  nucifera
yew, Japanese plum *Cephalotaxus*
  harringtonia
yew, Pacific *Taxus brevifolia*
yew, plum *Cephalotaxus*
yew, plum-fruited *Prumnopitys*
  andina
yew, Prince Albert's *Saxegothaea*
  conspicua
Yezo spruce *Picea jezoensis*
yiel-yiel, white *Grevillea hilliana*
yirrgi yirrgi *Carpentaria acuminata*
ylang-ylang, climbing *Artabotrys*
  hexapetalus
Yodogawa azalea *Rhododendron*
  yedoense
yohimbe *Pausinystalia yohimbe*
York, white rose of *Rosa × alba*
Yorkshire fog *Holcus lanatus*
yorrell *Eucalyptus gracilis*
Yoshino cherry *Prunus × yedoensis*

Yoshino cherry, weeping *Prunus ×*
  yedoensis 'Shidare-Yoshino'
Youman's stringybark *Eucalyptus*
  youmanii
youth and old age *Aichryson ×*
  domesticum
youth, fruits of *Paullinia cupana*
youth-on-age *Tolmiea menziesii*
yucca, alpine *Yucca baileyi*
yucca, banana *Yucca baccata*
yucca, beaked *Yucca rostrata*
yucca, blue *Yucca baccata, Y. rigida*
yucca, candle *Yucca gloriosa*
yucca, chaparral *Yucca whipplei*
yucca, false red *Hesperaloe parviflora*
yucca, giant *Yucca elephantipes*
yucca, Mohave *Yucca schidigera*
yucca, moundlily *Yucca gloriosa*
yucca, mountain *Yucca schottii*
yucca, narrow-leaf *Yucca*
  angustissima
yucca, Navajo *Yucca navajoa*
yucca, Schott's *Yucca schottii*
yucca, soaptree *Yucca elata*
yucca, soapweed *Yucca glauca*
yucca, spineless *Yucca elephantipes*
yucca, Torrey *Yucca torreyi*
yucca, weeping *Yucca recurvifolia*
yulan *Magnolia denudata*
yulan magnolia *Magnolia denudata*
Yunnan cypress *Cupressus*
  duclouxiana
Yunnan Douglas fir *Pseudotsuga*
  forrestii
Yunnan firethorn *Pyracantha*
  crenatoserrata
Yunnan lilac *Syringa yunnanensis*
Yunnan nutmeg yew *Torreya*
  yunnanense
Yunnan pine *Pinus yunnanensis*
Yunnan poplar *Populus yunnanensis*

Z

zambac *Jasminum sambac*
zamia palm *Cycas media,*
    Macrozamia moorei, M. riedlei
zamia, scaly *Lepidozamia peroffskyana*
zapirandi *Tabernaemontana*
    catharinensis
zapote injerto *Pouteria viridis*
zasa, kuma *Sasa veitchii*
zebra aloe *Aloe maculata*
zebra banana *Musa acuminata*
    'Zebrina'
zebra haworthia *Haworthia fasciata*
zebra plant *Aphelandra squarrosa,*
    Calathea zebrina, Tradescantia
    zebrina
zelkova, Caucasian *Zelkova*
    carpinifolia
zelkova, Chinese *Zelkova*
    schneideriana, Z. sinica
zelkova, Cretan *Zelkova abelicea*

zelkova, Japanese *Zelkova serrata*
zhi mu *Anemarrhena asphodeloides*
zieria, downy *Zieria cytisoides* ·
zieria, sandfly *Zieria smithii*
zigzag bamboo *Phyllostachys*
    flexuosa
zigzag bog-rush *Schoenus brevifolius*
zigzag goldenrod *Solidago flexicaulis*
zigzag, Solomon's *Smilacina racemosa*
zinnia, creeping *Sanvitalia*
    procumbens
zinnia, Mexican *Zinnia haageana*
zinnia, prairie *Zinnia grandiflora*
zoapatle *Montanoa tomentosa*
zombi palm *Zombia antillarum*
zonal geranium *Pelargonium* Zonal
    Hybrids
zorillo *Choisya mollis*
zornia *Zornia dyctiocarpa*
zoysia grass *Zoysia*
zucchini *Cucurbita, C. pepo*
Zulu fig *Ficus lutea*
zygadene *Zigadenus*
zygadene, star *Zigadenus fremontii*